TEACHERS FOR THE PRAIRIE

The University of Illinois and the Schools, 1868–1945

Henry C. Johnson, Jr.

Erwin V. Johanningmeier

TEACHERS FOR

THE PRAIRIE

*The University of Illinois
and the Schools,
1868-1945*

University of Illinois Press
URBANA CHICAGO LONDON

308.773
J63t
83804
July 1973

FOREWORD

As readers of this book will discover independently, Henry C. Johnson, Jr., and Erwin V. Johanningmeier are quite capable of speaking for themselves. Their basic concern is with how society employs ideas and institutions to transmit learning from one generation to another, a problem they treat both descriptively and normatively and with special reference to the University of Illinois. Their work rests on both careful research in archival sources and a firm grasp of the development of formal education in modern culture.

The authors are crystal clear about both their objective and method. At the outset they provide a bird's-eye view of the ground they intend to cover, and as they move over a large and varied terrain they demonstrate a nice capacity to deal with both the trees and the forest and to distinguish between the two. Near the journey's end they pause to pull loose ends together and reflect on the deeper significance of their material. Throughout their book the authors interpret rather than merely record the past. But since they understand that human nature is fallible in the academy as elsewhere, they are not unsympathetic critics. They have done their job thoroughly and well, and little remains to be said here.

Yet it may be worth emphasizing here that this volume takes two different and closely interrelated approaches to its subject. The authors readily admit that they have written an institutional history. They have produced a richly documented account of the development of teacher education at Urbana-Champaign. This penetrating essay on the problem of the University's relations to the practice of teaching and to the schools in the state of Illinois does not lack tension and drama. On the campus the rivalry between the older, established disciplines and the upstart known as pedagogy was keen long before events came to a climax in what the authors describe as "Runnymede." Throughout the state the University's relations with the public schools and its imperial attitude toward other public institutions of higher education created a host of difficulties. Basic to all of these developments was the hard question of how a university should organize itself to train teachers for the schools, and the authors suggest that the University of Illinois demonstrated an essentially conservative response to that challenge. My own researches in the University's history convince me that their judgment on such matters is basically sound.

In addition to institutional history Professors Johnson and Johanningmeier have also written intellectual history. An excellent conceptual grasp of the problem of education as integrally related to all of life informs this work, as the Preface and Epilogue make especially clear. Their entire volume may properly be regarded as a careful attempt to trace the practical realization of an idea in a given social environment. Thus while the authors have taken the history of education at Illinois on its own terms very seriously, they have also used it as a means of illuminating the larger problem of education in American culture. The book can profitably be read for its contribution to our understanding of both the particular and the general developments.

Winton U. Solberg

CONTENTS

FOREWORD   vii

PREFACE   xi

PART ONE : 1868–94

CHAPTER 1   *Prairie Teacher*   3

CHAPTER 2   *Capstone of the Educational Edifice*   19

CHAPTER 3   *False Dawn*   46

PART TWO : 1895–1918

CHAPTER 4   *The Boundless Prairie and the Infinite Sky*   87

CHAPTER 5   *The Modern Demand*   109

CHAPTER 6   *Confidence and Making Good*   154

CHAPTER 7   *Back to the Normal School*   188

PART THREE : 1919–45

CHAPTER 8   *Close to the Beaten Path*   219

CHAPTER 9   *New Foundations*   264

CHAPTER 10   *Itinerant Teachers and Scientists, New Style*   328

CHAPTER 11   *Runnymede*   389

EPILOGUE   *Pedagogy as a Problem*   447

BIBLIOGRAPHY   467

INDEX   485

PREFACE

     Institutional history is often a thankless task. Too frequently it counts for little, save as a starting point for a more rewarding career, a mere occasion for learning how to get one's footnotes straight or for exploring the mechanics of publication, with little concern for either depth or finish. Whether we have done more than that must be left to the judgment of the reader, of course, but, whatever our accomplishments, this popular image has unfortunate consequences. When the question is posed, "Why spend so much effort on the circumscribed themes which necessarily mark institutional history?" the answer is twofold: a great part of human history *is* institutional, and much of the contemporary cultural crisis is institutional as well. When institutional history is done casually or even shabbily (admittedly often the case), a certain kind of evidence which is of great significance and illuminating power eludes us. Unashamedly, then, we have written about *a* place at *a* certain point in time, in the belief that, if satisfactorily done and properly received, the task will be more widely appreciated than its apparently narrow circle of interest might suggest.

  Since history is inescapably an evaluative as well as an interpretative activity, some principle is necessarily present. In asking the central question, "What do schools or colleges of education do, and what ought they do?" we have been forced, obviously, to take an initially limited narrative to higher ground than a mere chronicle or description of men and events at Urbana or in central Illinois would have required. To ask how and why one institution dealt with the study of the schools and the preparation of teachers in a certain period, and to assess that action responsibly, may perhaps make some contribution to a theme about which we have all too little evidence, historical or otherwise. Thus the forming and answering of this interpretative question furnishes both the connecting framework of this book and an attack on a still vexing contemporary issue, for it would be difficult to establish that the question has yet been fully settled.

We believe, then, that the questions and answers implicit in doing this work have a significance beyond the institution which is the occasion for asking them. We have attempted, of course, only to answer them as they have been answered at the University of Illinois, yet in so doing we hope we have contributed a measure of concrete historical explanation—dare we say justification?—to the more fundamental question of whether there is a field of study called "education." As the reader will quickly gather, we do believe that there is such a study and that it can be defined and even be justified, though doubtless not by history alone. If our purpose was to offer a definition and justification for its own sake, it is obvious that we think it necessary to begin by saying that "professional" education can only be defined and ultimately justified by looking at education itself—i.e., at the teaching-learning process as it occurs in context, between learners and teachers in those quite concrete and historical institutions we call schools. That must be the focus, whatever else there is—and there is, of course, a great deal—which needs to be taken into account. That proposition may be controversial, but it is also central to this book, and the words which follow can be adequately understood and interpreted only in its light.

We have endeavored to answer this fundamental question by making certain particular inquiries. First, what moved the University consciously to take upon itself the function of teacher preparation? (It had, of course, been supplying teachers unconsciously—at least in terms of offering formal academic instruction.) The exploration of this question implies an examination of the social, educational, and the general cultural and intellectual movements of the time. Second, we have asked how the University would both relate itself to, and distinguish itself from, the normal school or teachers' college definition of the process of teacher preparation which had already become a paradigm. Here the exploration of the question requires an examination of the "new" university's attempt to develop its own peculiar identity and image. This question is important in its own right, we think, since the "new" university's attempt to define its mission had pervasive effects, both theoretical and practical, upon the new educational profession itself.

It is possible to merge these two questions into one, although their formal distinction is still necessary for purposes of clarity. That single question is, "Did the University approach the preparation of teachers as a 'professional school' task, or as the acceptance of responsibility for a set of phenomena legitimately to be investigated in its own right?" To put it another way, was the preparation of teachers a part of the "new" university's social and "vocational" responsibility, or was it part of the university's responsibility as a community of inquiry to investigate something called "education"? (If it was both, the question becomes one of how the two functions were to be related.) In this sense, the topic is, in effect, a study of how the professional education of teachers and the study of education for itself appeared to offer *conflicting* goals, ideals, and conceptions of the developing university's intellectual and social responsibility.

The examination of this question requires, then, two levels of inquiry. There is a "background" level which comprises the examination of the growth and development of the schools and their teachers during the formative period of both the new educational system and the University of Illinois (roughly 1850 through 1890). In addition, the growth of the American college and university in general must be examined, including some consideration of the traditional college, the "old" university and the "new" university, and the relevant political, social, and intellectual developments which shaped that growth. The prevailing mode of preparing teachers, both formal and informal—that is, by administrative structures and by the normal school and teachers' college—comprises still another background element which must be examined. Finally, the move toward professionalization in an initially amorphous teaching force, which touches on matters such as organization and certification, must be taken into account.

While this "background" material is both clearly relevant and worthy of more detailed study in itself, the primary areas of direct inquiry into this University's relation to education and teacher preparation will be focused by means of four subsidiary questions. First, we shall press our inquiry under the question of whether education was thought properly to be regarded as an "art" or a "science." The term "science" was used *both* in its old sense of a body of systematically interrelated knowledge and in the newer sense of an empirical and experimental study. The period of time with which this inquiry deals is characterized by a renewed examination of the nature of science and an attempt to resolve that confusing usage. Consequently, the issue was largely both unsettled and incapable of being satisfactorily settled. The term "art" was used largely as a residual category, partly because the term was so carelessly defined as to be practically speaking residual. Whether education was an art or a science formed a principal ground for the three more specific areas requiring investigation: we shall examine the changing place of the "laboratory," "practice," or "model" school; we shall inquire into the prescribed curriculum, both in terms of its "disciplinary" content (both the form and quantity it should take) and the "professional" studies thought requisite to adequate teacher preparation; finally, we shall analyze the prevailing educational philosophies and theories which both expressed and underlay all of these issues and movements.

The examination of these four principal issues, within the general historical development of the narrative, will illuminate certain ambiguities present in both the University and the field of pedagogy and will offer, we hope, a plausible interpretation of the peculiar difficulties which the field of education posed for the struggling new university. It may also shed some light upon the vexing question of whether, and in what sense, education is a legitimate "discipline."

Consequently, in Part One we attempt to tell about the teachers and schools in Illinois and about the University itself up to 1895—the date we consider the real beginning of pedagogical work at Illinois. We ourselves have debated what date if any can be stipulated as the pivotal moment, and the informed reader may wish to advance or retard the date we have chosen. There are sound reasons for either our choice or certain alternatives. In Chapter One, we examine the nineteenth-century Illinois schools and teachers in the person of Charles Shamel, using his diary. Besides being a fresh account not heretofore available, it is, we believe, strikingly representative in a concrete mode of the abstract, statistical, and generalized accounts upon which educational historians have tended to rely. We try to show how closely it manifests the more common description by giving something of that sort of picture as well.

The growth of the newly founded University of Illinois, itself the product of a distinct educational movement, follows in Chapter Two. This larger institution forms, of course, the immediate environment within which "education" arose. Both here and elsewhere we devote considerable attention to the style and vision of the University administration because, at least at the beginning, that immediate environment is in part a function of the administration. The American college and university in the nineteenth century was not yet a self-directing scholarly community. It dwelt under an imposed leadership, whether that leadership was a product of the Americanized "college" ideal and its socio-theological heritage or the later entrepreneurial model which frequently replaced it.

Chapter Three considers the first halting and necessarily confused attempts to introduce education to that essentially transitional university environment. The fact that these early efforts had little or no objective or administrative continuity with subsequent programs is less significant than their preparatory role and the fact that they display a field attempting to define itself not only at Illinois but elsewhere. It is also another look at the "Herbartianism" which moves from domination to counterforce in subsequent decades.

Parts Two and Three get down to the work in education in greater detail. Part Two takes us immediately to the present in a sense—to the time of the founding of the College of Education which presently exists. The chapters in these latter two parts have been organized around the men who either occupied the pedagogical chair or who were directors or deans of the School or College of Education. We plead no "great man" theory of history, but only the fact that the direction and shape of the work was in this case more often than not a reflection of the man and his interests and vision. This is particularly true of Arnold Tompkins, Edwin Grant Dexter, and William Chandler Bagley.

Chapter Four is an account of Arnold Tompkins's tenure at Illinois. He was the last of a type and the last of the nineteenth century. His presence serves as a foil for the examination of the twentieth century and the new pedagogical style and vision Edwin Grant Dexter was to introduce. Dexter's work, the arrival of President Edmund Janes James, and the formation of the School of Education (an event which was a halfway house in the founding of the College of Education) are examined in Chapter Five.

Chapters Six and Seven deal with Bagley's work at Illinois and the actual founding of the College. With Bagley the question, "What does a school of education do?" takes a new turn. For one thing, Bagley publicized the question. The reader may ask why we relied upon so many public sources in these two chapters as opposed to archival sources. Our answer is that, before Bagley, public sources did not exist. And their existence is itself significant. In part they reveal that during Bagley's tenure the central question takes explicit shape and becomes recognizable.

Chapter Eight begins with the organization of the College of Education about 1920 and introduces Part Three. Here we try to bring into still sharper focus the question, "What does a school of education do?" and trace the early development of the College at Illinois. Old academic skirmishes were revived—skirmishes for all their setting more akin to the disputes of the nineteenth century than the twentieth. Chapter Nine examines what is in effect the fashioning of a whole new orientation for the work in education, an orientation made necessary by changes in the schools and in the surrounding society. The examination necessarily takes place against the background of a University itself beginning to show signs of strain in spite of previous administrative attempts to maintain stability by enforcing rigidity. In Chapter Ten we analyze the gradual growth of this new orientation in terms of programs and activities which have a new focus and a new setting. In the concluding chapter we narrate the apparent collapse of the new thrust which reached a dramatic climax in the involuntary retirement of its chief architect, Dean Thomas Eliot Benner. The denouement took place in a University itself openly torn by the forces of change, and it furnished what was essentially a new beginning rather than a conclusion, in spite of appearances.

To those who may ask, "Why stop so abruptly at 1945?" we answer that to do anything more is to do what is too close to see. We would like to believe that we have shaped a chronicle of events into a history of the work in professional education at the University of Illinois. We are not sure that we or anyone can give any more than a chronicle of events since 1945. Many of those involved in and responsible for these events are only now bringing to a close their remarkable contribution. We could not yet give these people a history. We do not want merely to give them a past.

Perhaps the most serious shortcoming of this study is the fact that it is too much a study of the Dean's office, an administrative analysis —something of the sort of difficulty experienced with English history and its onetime preoccupation with "London history." Much of what is here is frankly "bureaucratic history," and only rarely (and sometimes by the most tenuous of inferences) is it possible to dig beneath the surface of "official statements" and (sometimes dangerously) rhetorical intentions, to anything resembling existential adequacy. But that is perhaps not wholly a misfortune. Whether we like it or not, American academic life has been bureaucratic; the lack of complementary evidence is both a reflection of that not unimportant fact and a function of a changed style in viewing oneself. That is, however, not intended as a confession of either impossibility or failure. Bureaucratic history is a form of history not without its own genuine importance. Nor does one need to adopt a totally pessimistic thesis that such administrative manifestations are mere "epiphenomena" drifting across the face of the "real history." Appropriate respect for possible dangers seems more to be indicated than naïve skepticism, and that respect we have tried to maintain.

It must also be borne in mind that these are narratives of particular events and actions; they are not complete histories of persons. The characters in this story may have other virtues (or other vices) of which no account is taken, simply because they do not appear to be decisive in these events. If it should be thought, nonetheless, that this volume tells tales best left untold if not unremembered, that is because we believe that history has a responsibility not only to the dead but to the living and the soon to live as well. History does press upon the present and even the future. Indeed, history and the present may be said to give each other meaning. Surely one of its functions is to illuminate the past in order to furnish alternatives for the present and the future; the examination of mistakes as well as successes is a vital element in fulfilling that task. As Samuel Johnson put it:

If the biographer writes from personal knowledge, and makes haste to gratify the public curiosity, there is danger lest his interest, his fear, his gratitude, or his tenderness, overpower his fidelity, and tempt him to conceal, if not to invent. There are many who think it an act of piety to hide faults or failings of their friends, even when they can no longer suffer by their detection; we therefore see whole ranks of characters adorned with uniform panegyrick, and not to be known from one another but by extrinsick and casual circumstances. "Let me remember, (says Hale,) when I find myself inclined to pity a criminal, that there is likewise a pity due to the country." If we owe regard to the memory of the dead, there is yet more respect to be paid to knowledge, to virtue, and to truth.[1]

Finally, in no sense does this work constitute a definitive history. A definitive history would demand a great deal more attention to certain aspects of the question at which we could only hint obliquely or to which we could only allude in passing. Some of the studies indicated, among others, are a thorough analysis of the demographic factors in the development of the schools and the university, an examination of the political, legislative, and financial matters integral to this study, and an inquiry into the role of the large and significant private and parochial educational system which is, in our estimation, a genuine but all too neglected part of "the schools." There are also many facets of the College's own development which merit finer description and analysis than we have been able to offer. For example, there is the work of the High School Conferences and the closely allied role of the High School Visitor; there is the development of the curricula in education, philosophy, and psychology, their interrelationship and ultimate divergence; there is the complex work of the Bureau of Educational Research, the "vocational" programs, and more. Finally, the theoretical analysis of the issues generated could be—and, it is hoped, will be—explicitly taken to deeper levels than we could achieve within the confines of space and narrative integrity. For our failure to accomplish all these we can only ask pardon and understanding in the demanding interests of bringing to light as powerfully as possible what we regard as the chief currents.

Much of the stuff of which history is made was patiently collected in one way or another by many over the past several years. We as authors have enjoyed the privilege of bringing to a certain kind of completion their several labors, as well as our own doctoral investigations. Among those whose work led them into the field covered by this book and shed light upon our inquiries, the following must be accorded special mention: Walter P. Krolikowski, John Swanson, Ronald M. Johnson, Jon McKenna, and Judith Hancock.

[1] Quoted in James Boswell, *The Life of Samuel Johnson L.L.D.* (New York: Modern Library, n.d.), p. 10.

Special reliance has been placed upon the work of Winton U. Solberg and the admirable history of the University which he has been preparing. If conversation is the seed bed of scholarship, his contribution far exceeds the location of names and dates. Professor Solberg has read and commented upon virtually all of the manuscript, and his wide knowledge and keen insights have provoked a richer appreciation of these events and movements on many occasions. Maynard Brichford, the University Archivist, has transmuted heaps of dust and paper into the matter of scholarship in superb fashion. His efficiency has been matched by his willingness and ability to see it used—a quality which, in our opinion, distinguishes archivists from curators. Rupert Evans, Dean of the College of Education, believed this attempt not only possible but valuable. From the first, he insisted that what was wanted was not a piece of promotion to be put into the hands of alumni and friends, but as much of a contribution to the important issue which forms its background as we could make it. Without his enthusiasm, encouragement, and support we might never have finished our undertaking. His successor and the present Dean of the College, J. Myron Atkin, has both continued that original intent and sustained it vigorously. Together with Professor David B. Tyack (now of Stanford University), Professor B. Othanel Smith (former chairman of the department of history and philosophy of education, now at the University of South Florida), and Professor William Oliver Stanley, these men have sponsored and sustained our efforts with patience, freedom, and integrity. Special grants from the Chicago Community Trust (thanks to the efforts of its executive director, James Brown, IV) and the Episcopal Church Foundation were indispensable in making possible the study and research of one of the authors. Professor Bozidar Muntyan, chairman of social foundations of education, and J. A. Battle, Dean of the University of South Florida's College of Education, protected the other author from all those petty annoyances that typically derail and delay completion of such undertakings.

And, in an important sense, the College and the University of Illinois in general require specific recognition. The very existence of this volume is a testimony to the growth of both. Not many decades ago, it would have been unlikely that a book such as this would be written with the support we have received. Almost certainly it would not have been published.

There are also those whose particular skills and patience were in their own way essential to its formal completion. Our relations with the University of Illinois Press, particularly with Richard Wentworth and Ann Lowry, have been both cordial and helpful. For constant help, and especially the preparation of what must have seemed an endless manuscript, we must express our gratitude to Betty Richards, Martha Baxter, and Ruth Gorrell, all of the College of Education. Barbara Bergan marshaled the resources of the institution and made them work, frequently at the cost of her private time and energy, and the contribution was enormous.

Our assistants, students, and colleagues at our present institutions also merit mention for keeping us thinking as well as working cheerfully beyond the call of their duties, humoring us, and filling in during our absences. At Illinois State University, Professor Dent Rhodes provoked, excused, and endured, and Sue Kleen and Elaine Palmer grew with the task until they became nearly indispensable. At the University of South Florida, Janice Hoover displayed unusual patience through typing and retyping and gave rare attention to tasks and details too numerous to catalogue. Virginia Maxfield and Patricia Cecil made countless trips to the library and filed and refiled notes with patience and good humor.

Finally, we turn to our families, and to the many other friends, colleagues, and fellow students who will go unmentioned but without whose sustaining patience and kindness nothing would have been possible. Whatever has been done is fully theirs as well as ours. Whatever has not been done, or is badly done, is ours alone.

PART I

1868–94

CHAPTER I

❧ *Prairie Teacher*

On Thursday, September 8, 1886, Charles H. Shamel left his father's prosperous farm near Stonington, Illinois, and made his way to the relatively new Illinois Industrial University at Urbana to begin the next phase of his education. Arriving in midafternoon, he went immediately to the University and consulted its leading practitioner of science, Professor Thomas J. Burrill, and then found a place to board. The following Monday, Shamel was successfully examined in algebra, philosophy, physiology, botany, and rhetoric. On Thursday, having paid the required fee of $22.50 and made an $8 deposit for laboratory expense, he began work in German, chemistry, geometry, and trigonometry, which last he found rather demanding. Friday evening brought his first meeting of the Philomathean Literary Society. Together with required chapel and military drill, these experiences introduced Charles Shamel to the heart of American higher learning as it was practiced in a land grant university toward the end of the nineteenth century.[1]

[1] Charles H. Shamel, "Diary," III, September 14, 1886, University of Illinois Archives, Charles H. Shamel Papers. Unless otherwise noted, all primary sources in this volume may be found in the University of Illinois Archives. See bibliographical listings for Record Series identification numbers to establish location. Record Series numbers will be supplied in the notes only for cases in which the location would be unusual and difficult to determine.

3

Our interest in this case lies in the fact that Charles Shamel was a teacher in the common schools. He had just received his "first-grade" certificate a few days before setting out toward Urbana. But he did not come to the University to increase his pedagogical competence. In fact, he did not intend to remain a teacher at all. Having learned to read from the family Bible at the age of four, Shamel had progressed rapidly through the *Youth's Companion*, dime novels, and Alden's reprints of great masterpieces until, still in adolescence, he fell upon one of the "truth-containing books" which changed his life, Spencer's *Education*.[2] That enormously influential work persuaded him beyond all doubt that science was the answer, and he thenceforward lived in that faith. It was the lure of science as a career which led him to the University. As with so many others in those years, he had turned to school-teaching as a means of getting ahead. Teaching in the common schools, like divinity study, was an available route for the ambitious youth who sought a way out of rural isolation. Fortunately, on his way Shamel left an extensive journal of his thoughts and activities, which illustrates in concrete fashion the general shape of the teaching "profession" and the American eductional system in the middle and late nineteenth century. More important for our purpose, it demonstrates the context of the peculiar relationship to professional pedagogy which characterized Illinois Industrial University in its early years.

Charles Shamel's "Diary" is very rough and uneven—he was fourteen years old when he began it—and the author has corrected or added spelling and punctuation. Corrections and additions are not indicated except where it might be useful. Note also that the University of Illinois was first called Illinois Industrial University.

[2] Charles H. Shamel, "Autobiography," I, 20, Shamel Papers. In contrast to the "Diary," the "Autobiography" was written very late in life and contradicts many of the events which he recorded in his youth. He paid no attention to his earlier interest in teaching, for example, and he magnified his commitment to science as consciously in opposition to religion. Part I is entitled "A Farm Boy's Solutions of the Riddles of His Universe." Although in fact raised in an atmosphere of punctilious if somewhat uninspired Protestant piety, Shamel later saw himself as having been a free-thinker from the beginning. (I, 16; III, IV, passim.) He described himself in the end as a "death defying materialist."

Shamel was an extremely interesting figure with a fascinating career. He ended up taking several degrees successfully and becoming one of the first, if not the first, attorneys specializing in patents. After taking his B.S. in chemistry at Illinois in 1890, Shamel went on to get an M.S. (Illinois, 1891), an LL.B. (Michigan, 1893), an A.M. (Columbia, 1905), and a Ph.D. (Columbia, 1907). He also played an interesting part, along with his brothers, in the University during his student days. See Winton U. Solberg, *The University of Illinois, 1867–94: An Intellectual and Cultural History* (Urbana, 1968), pp. 293, 320, 322, 324ff.

Conrad Shamel, Charles's father, had come directly from Bavaria and settled a short distance north of Springfield, where Charles was born in 1867.[3] Disenchantment with the local school, which Charles attended only briefly, in part led the Shamels to relocate near Stonington in Christian County in 1874. Charles's mother had inherited 120 acres in that neighborhood which, along with another eighty purchased, formed the basis of a frugally managed but constantly expanding investment which stood them all in good stead in later years.

That summer a small schoolhouse was erected eight miles east of the farm and Charles began his education afresh, with much greater profit. Taught by a husky young farm boy (and therefore singularly free of disciplinary problems, in spite of the mixed ages and nationalities represented) the sessions ran usually for six months, beginning September 1. (Frequently there were also two months of "spring school" for those too young to work at home.) Here the pupils began to master Ray's *Arithmetics* and such other delights as the state of the art (or the condition of their family coffers) permitted.[4] As he grew older and more able to help about the home place, Shamel attended school less and less, but he read more and more on his own. By the time he was fifteen, in 1882, Shamel frequently attended only half days and rarely got to the spring session at all. By 1884, having reached seventeen, his common school education was at an end. After some eleven years of sporadic but unrelenting study, he had exhausted the resources of the district schools.[5]

When only sixteen, Shamel had joined the Willey Literary Society, an association he maintained until he transferred his intellectual allegiance to the University. Through the debates, lectures, and discussions which marked the program of this tiny crossroads gathering, Charles kept his interests alive and growing. Together with an occasional neighborhood musicale, a visiting lecturer who described foreign lands or the wages of sin (especially intemperance, during these years) from the podium of a local church-schoolhouse, a revival or camp meeting, these literary sessions provided both relief from the grinding toil and refreshment for the mind and spirit. They comprised the "core curriculum" of a prairie education.[6]

[3] For this and what follows, see Shamel, "Autobiography," I, 1–12.

[4] Ibid., pp. 13–14. The precise schedule, or whether there was any school at all, was always dependent on whether any teacher was available.

[5] Shamel, "Diary," I, II, passim. See, for example, entries for February 28, April 17, October 2, 3, November 5, 1882; II, entries for January, 1884.

[6] Ibid., II, January 16, 1884; October 6, 1885; III, November 3, 1885; January 5,

Ever ready to advance himself, before he was through with the "common branches," Charles Shamel had taken the first steps toward becoming a teacher. At sixteen he began attending the teachers' institute at Stonington, and he ordered a catalog of books for teachers. He also began to explore his academic future, requesting bulletins from the University of Michigan, Illinois College (Jacksonville), Illinois Wesleyan (Bloomington), Northwestern, and DePauw (Greencastle, Indiana), among others.[7] The family savings, however, did not permit such rapid advancement. And so, after purchasing a suit and hat in Stonington, Shamel set out instead for Taylorville in the fall of 1884 to attend the high school and there prepare himself to be a teacher. At this well-regarded institution he commenced "algebra, higher arithmetic, history, physyology, & grammar" with gusto.[8]

In a scant academic year, Shamel and his fellow students made rapid (and, one would surmise, necessarily superficial) progress. They covered Edward's *Sixth Reader*, finished history and physiology, and then applied themselves to the Constitution, geography, natural philosophy, and English literature in the waning months.[9] In addition, with an eye on the future again, Shamel took on bookkeeping, offered at night by the high school's principal instructor. It was widely regarded as both useful and of disciplinary value, and Charles "threw up philosophy and English literature" so that he could devote more time to it.[10] In midyear, President Selim H. Peabody informed Shamel that he could enter the state university after the Christmas holidays, but family importunity still prevented this, and he returned to complete the course at Taylorville instead. By April 1, 1885, he had solved the last problems in Ray's *Higher Arithmetic*, and he soon packed up for home.[11]

Before March had arrived, Shamel already believed himself more than ready for the important teacher's examination. As was the curriculum that prepared him for it, if not in fact a good deal more so, the teacher's examination was rigid and bookish. On March 7, 1885, Shamel

1886; and passim. The importance of these meetings in Shamel's life may be surmised from the fact that the most extensive and careful entries are almost always those treating the sessions of the Literary Society.

[7] Ibid., II, February 20, 1884; June 23–August 21, 1884.
[8] Ibid., September 20, 22, 23, 1884.
[9] Most of the entries in the "Diary," II, from September 22, 1884, to April 4, 1885, deal with Shamel's experiences in Taylorville. He had "finished history" by December 15, less than three months after he began it.
[10] Ibid., January 16, February 19, 1885.
[11] Ibid., January 6, 1885.

and seventy or eighty others crowded into the office of the county superintendent, "Professor Boyd." Those who could found space at tables; others wrote the four-hour examination on books held on their knees. Shamel found the experience difficult and hurried in spite of his proficiency. The ordeal, which would entitle him to a "second-grade" certificate, consisted of stock answers to stock questions covering the common branches and (as a consequence of recent curricular reforms) some elementary science.[12] Preparation for it, as well as the more prestigious state certificate, which involved greater scope but essentially similar activity, comprised the factual mastery of standard authors. Ambitious teachers pored over these approved books in their spare time, often in small study groups, in the hope of advancing their status.

Shamel was informed in early April that he had passed. He noted later in life that without even completing the slim high school and normal school offerings—he had in fact completed less than the first year of work when he sat—he was regarded as competent to teach at the elementary level. At the time that must have been less than surprising, since his grades in one of the county examinations three years earlier had already entitled him to the "second-grade" certificate. That, he agreed later, was entirely too young; a fourteen-year-old boy ought not be in charge of a school room in which everything was taught, "from the primer to algebra."[13] But, at seventeen, armed with his certificate and a letter of recommendation from Taylorville's one-man faculty, Charles Shamel was ready to begin "another era" of his life. He began to look for a teaching position.

The end of April brought a local school election in his home district, and Shamel sought out the new board members to offer his services.[14] During the summer he apparently considered business college as an alternative, and he examined the current catalog of the state normal university. Had he intended to remain a teacher, he doubtless would have applied there, but he did not. By August his politicking appeared successful. The post was his, and the six-month contract at $40 per month was by no means an embarrassing one. In preparation he began to bone up on teachers' periodicals and search for Grant's *Memoirs*.[15]

---

[12] Ibid., March 7, 1885. Cf. Shamel, "Autobiography," I, 14; II, 1–14.
[13] Shamel, "Autobiography," I, 14.
[14] Shamel, "Diary," II, entries of April, 1885, passim.
[15] Ibid., August 6, 18, 31, 1885.

School opened Monday, August 31, with Charles Shamel as teacher and business manager, custodian, counsellor, nurse, and community social worker—a heavy responsibility for an eighteen-year-old. Attendance settled down to about twenty-three children. Official enrollment varied, and students entered and left virtually at will. At the end of the six-month period, however, there were seventeen boys and eight girls, ranging in age from six to sixteen and representing nine local families.[16] For purposes of instruction, Shamel had organized them into three advanced classes, A, B, and C, plus a primary class. Apparently these "classes" were not rigidly adhered to, and a student might perform at a different level in a particular subject on occasion. The higher classes worked in algebra, higher arithmetic, grammar, geography, reading, writing and spelling, and history. The younger students worked in the various primers. The method was almost entirely restricted to drill and formal recitation. The county superintendent paid one visit of less than half a day. He made no criticisms, but he did "give a plan of drilling the primary class in numbers." [17]

Shamel continued to improve himself professionally in every way open to a teacher in his position. In October he joined one of the popular "reading circles" which teachers frequently established for their mutual benefit. Admission was twenty-five cents and the cost of the books scheduled for review at the time—in this case Hewitt's *Pedagogy*, Barnes's *General History*, and any physiology text of the teachers' choice. In addition they worked over the Illinois school laws. Shamel found the biweekly meetings generally profitable, especially when they met in the county superintendent's office in order to seek his help in administrative matters.[18]

The turn of the year brought with it a high point, the annual meeting of the State Teachers' Association in Springfield.[19] This thirty-second annual meeting—the Association had begun in 1853—had a serious agenda and had not assembled merely for mutual inspiration, important as that might be. The education profession was beginning to

[16] Ibid., III, March 2, 1886.

[17] See ibid., esp. November 20, 1885.

[18] Ibid., II, October 24, November 7, December 19, 1885. The meetings were held in Taylorville. Hewett had been a prominent figure at the state normal university in its early days.

[19] For an interesting and detailed account of this meeting, held annually during the Christmas recess, see ibid., January 3 [1886]. The description in this and following paragraphs comes from this entry.

witness pervasive changes. The shape of these, shadowy though they were, could be glimpsed in the program itself. A committee reported on a method for nominating a state superintendent of public instruction. A paper on whether state normal schools were "An Essential Part of the Public School System" was discussed by the superintendent of the already influential Hyde Park High School and David Felmley, then principal of Carrolton but in a few years to be at the helm of the state normal university himself. Principal Homer Bevans of LaSalle asked "What Elements in Our Public Schools Train to Servile Dependence on Authority and What to Independence of Thought and Action"—doubtless an embarrassing inquiry at the time—and Mrs. A. F. Nightingale, teacher of elocution at the Central Music Hall in Chicago, gave advice on how to apply "The Delsarte Philosophy" to reading and physical culture. The teachers worried about the radically growing proportion of women in the profession. (Before the Civil War they had represented well below half the teaching force; at the end of it they were well over half. By 1885, they outnumbered men by very nearly two to one.) [20] "Hand and Eye Training in the Public Schools" was discussed by W. S. Mack of Moline. All in all, it was a bountiful three-day meeting, when the necessary business, elections, and an evening devoted to the examination of the reading circles were added in. The young schoolmaster went back to work impressed.

By July 5, after finishing the regular session and teaching a brief "spring school," Shamel was back at the normal department in Taylorville for a summer session.[21] Attended by some fifty students

[20] For the exact statistics, see State of Illinois, *Tenth Biennial Report of the Superintendent of Public Instruction of the State of Illinois, 1873–74* (n.p., n.d.), pp. 238–39. Also *Eighteenth Report . . .* (Springfield, 1891), p. XLIII. These *Biennial Reports* are invaluable sources for the study of education at all levels in the state of Illinois and will be relied upon heavily in this volume. The titles vary slightly and publication data is sometimes lacking in early issues. In most cases they were printed in the second year of the biennium indicated—unless the county superintendents were tardy in furnishing their local reports, apparently. Springfield was doubtless the place of publication, although the city is sometimes omitted. Since they will be used very frequently in the pages which follow, they will be referred to by an abbreviated form giving the number, the office, the second year of the biennium (whether the exact year of publication or not), and the page reference. For example, the references in this note would be rendered as follows: 10th SSPI (1874), pp. 238–39; 18th SSPI (1890), p. XLIII. Note that the system of pagination differs from volume to volume. Since the differences are of no significance, all Roman figures will be given in upper case, as in most of the *Reports*.

[21] "Diary," III, May 6, 10, July 5, 6, 12, 12/14, 15/16, 1886.

(who drifted in rather erratically), classes were formed in the common branches, the sciences, and bookkeeping. He first enrolled for the sciences and did some more work on the common branches. But later he joined special classes in elocution and physiology which required an additional fee of twenty-five cents each. These summer sessions lasted only a month, but they were followed immediately by the annual summer institute, which began on August 2 and lasted two additional weeks.[22] The first week was largely occupied with lectures delivered by four instructors to the some 120 participants. By the close of the first week, and all through the second, examinations for certification purposes were provided. In the first week, on Thursday, an opportunity was offered in arithmetic; Friday, in orthography; and Saturday, in the sciences—a special requirement for first-grade certificates. Shamel sat for the sciences.

As a consequence of his successful examinations, Shamel was awarded a first-grade certificate on August 28. That certificate vastly improved his status in the teaching profession. And it did more—it entitled him to preferential treatment at the state university. He would be admitted directly to university-level work. Although he had found teaching challenging and appears to have toyed momentarily with the notion of continuing in it, he saw his future elsewhere, and that was where the real value of the certificate lay. In this again, his attitude was characteristic of many—perhaps even the majority—of nineteenth-century schoolteachers even as late as the 1880's. The American educational enterprise was on the eve of a revolution, but that revolution had not yet occurred. Teaching school, while a legitimate and useful activity, was not yet a vocation to be sought for itself, let alone a profession, in the eyes of the majority.

The experiences, the attitudes, and the goals which we have examined through the eyes of Charles Shamel were not unusual; they were, indeed, strikingly typical. That this is so may be seen from much more conclusive evidence than the intriguing but limited entries in his youthful diary. His own career concretely illustrates the state of education at a given point, significantly the eve of the University of Illinois's first highly tentative steps toward accepting some responsibility for the field. The larger dimensions of the school problem need further sketching out, however. Illinois, like other states, came to ac-

[22] For this and what follows, see ibid., III, Aug. 2/3–14, 28, 1886.

cept the necessity of free public education only gradually. As the institution grew, the state and American culture in general were undergoing radical changes. Consequently, the burden placed upon the schools became daily more severe. Judged against the background of such rising responsibilities and expectations, the relative condition of the schools gradually and continuously worsened during the last half of the nineteenth century. This factor also shaped the entry of the state university into the field.

Created out of the old Northwest Territory in 1818, the state of Illinois had only achieved territorial status in its own right in 1809.[23] It was primarily settled by immigration from the largely rural neighboring territory to the southeast (a fact which was to have considerable educational importance), and its own increase in population was both gradual and almost exclusively rural. In 1800 the population of the area which would eventually become the state of Illinois, though it was then still part of the Indiana Territory, was about 2,500; by 1810 it had risen only to about 12,000. It was not until the years immediately preceding statehood that its growth was significant or inclusive of much of a professional class.[24] Even as late as 1840, fewer than 10,000 lived in what could be called cities, and the 1850 population of some 850,000 was still nine-tenths engaged in agricultural pursuits. By the mid-nineteenth century, however, the population was beginning to rise very rapidly. In 1860 it stood at 1,711,951, and the white "school-age" population (from six to twenty-one) alone was reckoned at nearly 550,000. Illinois's citizenry was still only one-fifth urban in 1870. In just twenty years, however, urbanization reached one-half.[25]

Public education in Illinois enjoyed a correspondingly inauspicious beginning. The ordinances of 1785 and 1787 governing the Northwest Territory had set aside some land for underwriting common school expense and encouraged education in general, but little or nothing came directly from these provisions. (Any educational activity in the area before this time was entirely informal.) By 1790, when St. Clair and Knox counties were formed, a semblance of communal

---

[23] For what follows on the early development of Illinois schools, I have relied principally upon John D. Pulliam, "A History of the Struggle for a Free Common School System in Illinois from 1818 to the Civil War" (Ph.D. dissertation, University of Illinois, 1965).

[24] Ibid., pp. 8–13.

[25] Carl Stephens, MS history, Stephens Papers. Record Series 26/1/21, Box 1, File, Ch. 1. 18th SSPI (1890), p. XLIII. Cf. Stephens, MS history, Ch. 3.

organization was beginning to develop, and what may be the first provision for an ostensibly public school was made at Cahokia in 1794. Kentucky developed much more rapidly than Illinois and, as has been noted, most of Illinois's population was drawn from her southern neighbor. These colonists were, however, largely accustomed to privately sponsored education—as, indeed, were most Americans at that time—and therefore did not move very strongly toward common schools. Education was almost exclusively peripatetic, clerical, tutorial, and largely restricted to private provisions made by prominent families. After 1812, more "settled" schools began to appear, formed about an increasing number of itinerant teachers who wrested a monthly tuition of from $1 to $2.50 from their pupils. Yet even Kaskaskia, the oldest of Illinois settlements, had no school at all as late as 1816.[26]

With the advent of statehood and a constitution, there was still no genuine progress, although the bill providing for statehood did specify some sources of revenue. It was at this time that a serious educational choice was made, largely by default. The state merely regulated the use of the potential school funds by acting as chartering agent and supervising the disposition of the legally sequestered lands. The originally specified township level of organization simply did not function in most cases. Schools thus grew up in areas of particular need by the creation of haphazard special districts designed for their local support and supervision rather than in congruence with statutory divisions and in accordance with a general plan.[27]

A liberal free school law was passed in 1825, well ahead of most states, but it was effectively emptied of its "free" provisions by the next legislature. Those to be taxed were to consent in writing, which of course rendered the likelihood of sufficient revenue rather small. The first specific free school plan was developed at Alton about 1830, but it was later rejected in the legislature. The growth of common school education on this quasi-public and private basis was sporadic and disorganized for the next twenty-five years. Not until the school law of 1855 did the common schools have an unquestioned right of taxation, and it is at that point that their real development begins.[28]

The staggering growth of genuinely public education can be most easily grasped by an examination of the table which follows.

26 Pulliam, "A History of the Struggle," pp. 8–13.
27 Ibid., Ch. 2, passim. See esp. pp. 26–28.
28 Ibid., pp. 38ff.

SCHOOL GROWTH IN ILLINOIS[29]

Year	State Population	School-age Population (6–21)	Total Number of Schools	Enrollment	Total Number of Teachers
1855	1,306,576	NA	4,454	173,531	5,684
1860	1,711,951	549,604 [a]	9,162	472,247	14,708
1870	2,539,801	862,624	11,011	652,715	28,081
1880	3,077,871	1,010,851	11,954	704,041	22,255
1890	3,826,351	1,163,440	12,259	778,319	23,164 [b]

[a] White only, at this date.
[b] There was a real decline previous to 1880. But the decline registered in 1883 (reflected in the small growth shown for 1890) was due to a change in the reporting basis.

The reader will note that the number of schools and teachers more than doubled between 1855 and 1860, and the teaching force nearly doubled again between 1860 and 1870. There was no possible way for this increase to be supplied out of adequately prepared personnel.

There was also an obvious and growing gap between enrollment and potential population. This was partly met by an enormous increase in private and parochial schools which paralleled that in the public sector. Yet, in spite of toothless provisions for compulsory attendance, in 1888 the superintendent of public instruction reported that more than 250,000 eligible children were in no school whatsoever. He was, even then, reluctant to press for punitive laws, preferring "moral suasion" and an adequate child labor restriction.[30]

By the 1880's, school organization (still substantially similar to that set up by the first law of 1855) had become confused and unwieldy. The major organizational unit below the state level was the township. Its supervisors were a body of trustees which formed the districts and appointed a treasurer to handle the school funds (both township and district). These trustees also managed the township high schools when there were any. Each school district had one or more schools. These districts were managed by three-member boards of directors who actually appointed the teachers, fixed their salaries, and determined courses and texts. The county superintendents had powers of visitation, and they distributed the state funds according to town-

[29] Figures in the table are drawn from 18th SSPI (1890), p. XLIII.
[30] 17th SSPI (1888), pp. cxciiff.

ships—but in this case the townships were the old congressionally specified units and not necessarily the operative political ones. The district directors could only appoint teachers certified by the county or state superintendents. Cities of 100,000 or more were exempt from these provisions, however, as were certain other cases. This fact eventually led to a drastic disintegration of educational strategy as the larger cities became in effect laws unto themselves. Futhermore, the state superintendent had, at best, a "moral" authority, though he could compel county superintendents to render reports on their systems and withhold the state funds where clear infractions of school law could be proven.[31]

School facilities remained rudimentary for a considerable period of time. Until well after the Civil War, since the population was still largely rural, the majority of school children went to the marginal, ungraded schools, many of which were physically unfit for habitation. (There were still nearly 800 log schoolhouses in 1874.) [32] Most were almost unequipped. Even in the mid-1880's there were almost no reference books in the school "libraries," usually a collection of cast-off volumes donated by neighboring families. Throughout Vermilion County, for example, in 218 schools, there were only seven unabridged dictionaries, five encyclopedias, and three gazetteers as late as the early 1880's. These schools were by no means unusual: Monroe County had "five or six" unabridged dictionaries and no other reference books of any kind.[33]

Virtually no unified or even vaguely standardized curriculum was possible.[34] By 1890, when something resembling one had been advanced, only about 8,000 of the more than 12,000 schools were even trying to use it, many of them admittedly "unsuccessfully." [35] The root cause of this was the nature of the teaching force. According to 1882 state reports, barely 50 percent of those teaching had managed to secure a secondary school education. Some 13 percent had attended a normal school for special pedagogical training. In fact, 6,847 (38.3 percent) had had neither secondary nor normal schooling. Some 1,500 teachers were still minors, often as young as fourteen or fifteen,

---

31 "The School System of the State of Illinois," ibid., pp. CLXXXIVff.
32 15th SSPI (1884), p. XVIII.
33 Ibid., pp. XI, 79–156 (esp. pp. 145, 130). In Henry County, seven of 260 schools had gazeteers; five had encyclopedias (p. 109). In Iroquois County, only 30 schools out of 236 even had unabridged dictionaries (p. 110).
34 Ibid., p. 111.
35 18th SSPI (1890), p. LXVI; cf. XCIII.

most of whom were in the ungraded schools.[36] The minimum age, even in 1894, was seventeen—an age which one county superintendent thought too young "as a rule." [37]

Every teacher was, at least theoretically, certified. The county superintendents had been empowered since 1865 to issue first-grade (two-year) or second-grade (one-year) certificates upon examination. The state office tried to get uniform questions for these examinations, but it had no power to compel their adoption.[38] Undemanding as the qualifications were, nearly one-fourth of the some 24,000 who attempted these examinations in 1877–78, for example, failed to pass them. Only 2,702 could qualify for the first grade.[39] There was also a "State Certificate" which had been adopted in 1861 to avoid the problem of constant renewal and the county circumscription. These coveted certificates, though based on an equally bookish and rigid conception of pedagogical proficiency, were very difficult to obtain.[40] Of the 108 who took the state examination in 1875, for example, only twenty passed.[41] Even the state certificates did not require professional training in pedagogy or educational history until the 1880's.[42] Only 513 of these lifelong certificates had been issued up to 1892. As State Superintendent Henry Raab said, the teachers were not yet professionally minded.[43]

[36] 15th SSPI (1884), pp. LXVI, LXXVI.

[37] 20th SSPI (1894), p. 83. As one writer put it, "girls and boys should not be placed in charge of schools" (p. 89).

[38] 6th SSPI (1866), pp. 133, 139.

[39] 12th SSPI (1878), p. 74.

[40] For example, 10th SSPI (1874), pp. 108–20. Preparation for the examination was stipulated strictly in terms of books to be mastered. In the sciences, for example, the examination covered not ideas but specified works, including "Hooker or Draper," "Quackenbos," and "Rolfe and Gillette (Handbook)." The last was a particularly recommended source since it covered sufficiently but not too extensively a number of the areas, apparently. (See esp. p. 113.) For an earlier examination, even more rote and bookish, see 6th SSPI (1866), pp. 133ff. At that time, the county superintendents could set any questions they liked—the effects of which policy one may well imagine. Superintendent Bateman, with only his "moral" authority to rely upon at that date, sent along some examples in hopes of furthering some standardization.

[41] 11th SSPI (1876), pp. 365.

[42] 15th SSPI (1884), p. XLVIII, which notes that pedagogy and history of education were now required as well. The breadth of the prospective teachers' learning had become a more serious consideration also.

[43] 19th SSPI (1892), p. L. In an unsigned editorial (possibly by George P. Brown), the *Illinois School Journal* complained that "the weakness of our school system, in country and city, is the ease with which ignorant young people can find a place as teachers." According to the *Journal*, they usually had graduated

As a consequence of all this, the educational experience of the average student was less than optimum in quality. It was also less than optimum in quantity. The school term was brief enough to begin with. (A 7.5-month average was not achieved until 1896.) [44] Even as late as 1892, although average daily attendance had increased by more than one-third since 1880, the typical ungraded pupil was in school only 83.9 days a year. His graded counterpart, by then slightly in the majority, attended for 132.[45] The situation became almost intolerable when coupled with instability of tenure on the part of the teaching force. In 1886, for example, 70 percent of the teachers were new to the particular schools in which they were teaching, and nearly half the schools needed more than one teacher to get through the brief academic year.[46]

By 1894, the educational situation in Illinois had become critical. There were now 11,619 districts and 239 high schools. Only fifty-four of the latter had separate buildings, and fifty-one schools still met in log houses. The 855,938 children who were enrolled for an average of about seven months were far below what the total should have been, but only a bit over half of that number were in the graded schools. The slack was in part taken up by the rapidly growing private schools which then numbered nearly 2,500 and enrolled more than 115,000 students. The period of 1892–94 had seen an increase of 1,464 private schools in Cook County alone (though this was probably in part the result of more careful reporting).[47]

There were 22,857 teachers, whose wages ranged from an average of $49.35 per month for women to $58.96 for men.[48] The low financial position of the teacher was both a cause and an indication of the key difficulty. Superintendent Raab raised the question of what factors were paramount in the employment of teachers in one of his reports: not capacity or training, he concluded, but the ability to "govern"—i.e., maintain strict discipline in the face of an unruly classroom—an

---

only from the country schools (elementary), and then received certificates by cramming for the easy, bookish questions on the examination. The editor's suggested remedy was, interestingly enough, neither the university nor the normal school, but more and better township high schools, from which common school teachers might be directly recruited. (*Illinois School Journal* 8 [April, 1889]: 351.)

[44] 21st SSPI (1896), pp. 17ff.
[45] 19th SSPI (1892), p. xxxviii.
[46] 16th SSPI (1886), p. xxxv.
[47] 20th SSPI (1894), pp. xix–xxix.
[48] Ibid.

acceptable wage demand, and personal contracts. Frequently, he confessed, the process of selecting a teacher was a process of auctioning off the post to the *lowest* bidder. The county superintendents agreed, and began a dreary recital of the facts. For example, several admitted that their "mendicancy" was the real cause for hiring many "teachers." Religious connections and local political influence were also important factors.[49] Even in the mid-1890's in Douglas County, for example, only fifty-six of 128 teachers had completed any work at all in a higher institution. There were but thirty-four who had even finished a regular high school curriculum. In White County, 79 percent of all beging teachers could be described as simply unprepared. Superintendent J. S. Cole in Logan County thought 30 percent of his teachers secured their appointment not on the basis of their qualifications but because of their willingness to accept less money. The chief consideration was "favoritism" along with meeting such criteria as "politics, religion, caste, etc." [50]

In short, it was a time when, as one state superintendent admitted, the schools were "continually under criticism." [51] The new attempts at curricular reform and standardization were being fought by "farmers and others," largely on economic grounds. There were charges of sectarianism on the one hand, godlessness on the other. Superintendent Richard Edwards spelled out specifically what he saw as the real dangers and difficulties of the schools in the mid-1890's. There were nine, most of which had long been present and would continue to be for some decades. (1) The vast scope of the enterprise, and all the money involved, posed constant dangers of administration and superivision. (2) The school systems often failed to take account of diversity. In the larger schools, the statistical norm was in danger of replacing concern for the individual, whose singular humanity education was charged to create. (3) In the numerically predominant rural schools, on the other hand, there was virtually no systematic instruc-

[49] Ibid., pp. 82–110, passim. See esp. pp. 86, 92. Cf. 21st SSPI (1896), pp. 219ff., 233, 237.

[50] 21st SSPI (1896), pp. 230, 245. Superintendent H. P. Coverly of Jo Daviess County put it succinctly: "Principal qualifications: a. Relationship. b. Religion. c. Experience and success. d. Cheapness" (p. 239).

[51] State Superintendent Richard Edwards assessed the problems in his essay, "The Dangers That Threaten Our Public Schools," with the particular intention of countering simultaneous charges of sectarianism and godlessness and (for perhaps the first time) issues of educational doctrine (18th SSPI [1890], pp. xciiiff.). The entire piece, like many writings from the hands of the state superintendents during this period, is interesting and instructive.

tion at all. (4) As size increased, teachers were abandoning their all-important moral function—although Edwards admitted that books which did not recognize God, or man's moral responsibility to Him, would not sell well in Illinois. (5) There was too much "cramming." Learning was still highly formal. (6) The teachers were on the whole very poorly educated in their subject-matter fields. Although they were, by 1890, beginning to devote attention to the problem of teaching as such, there was now a danger that teachers would neglect content "in the intensity with which they pursue special methods." (7) The public was disinterested. Due in part to its success, education was now taken for granted—like the sunshine, Edwards said. (8) There was a rising danger that the schools would be used for sectarian or partisan purposes. The superintendent believed that tendency should be resisted, since schools must aim at the truth and not "to impart an unreasoning bias." (9) Finally, and very important, the teachers lacked genuine professional training and did not view their teaching vocationally, as a lifelong work.[52]

The reports from the field, as we have seen, fully substantiated Edwards's analysis, particularly in regard to the state of the teaching profession. The preparation of teachers for the rapidly expanding educational enterprise would require radical broadening and deepening from its high shool and normal school base if headway was to be gained. Until that was possible, the outlook was bleak indeed. At the end of a report which showed that less than 20 percent of his teachers had "ever taken any full course of training for that work or any other," Champaign County Superintendent G. R. Shawan could only exclaim, "May God help the county superintendent." [53] It was no idle oath. At the close of the nineteenth century, at least in most of Illinois, there seemed nowhere else to turn.

[52] Ibid., pp. XCIV–C.
[53] Ibid., p. 68. A similar condition existed in many counties—for example, Madison and White counties. In the latter, 70 percent of beginning teachers were unprepared (pp. 79, 88). Superintendent Pittsford of Tazewell County principally blamed voter indifference in choosing school directors. Mr. Pittsford found his required duties so numerous, however, that he could devote no time to rousing the electorate to its obligations—perhaps something of an exaggeration. As a consequence, he believed, there was little hope for improvement. "As long as missionaries are sent to China to hunt heathen, and Bob Ingersoll's audiences are larger than the majority of congregations of our Christian churches, so long do we expect to see relatives and political friends chosen in preference to other applicants [for teaching positions]."

CHAPTER 2

Capstone of the Educational Edifice

When John Milton Gregory was elected the first Regent of Illinois Industrial University, an observer might well have concluded that the new University's development would be immediately and inextricably intertwined with the rapid growth of the common schools and the solution of their problems. Every indication seemed to favor such an expectation. As we have already seen, the schools were undergoing an enormous and trying expansion which began just previous to the University's foundation and reached a climax during its formative years. The perilous state of that expansion obviously warranted the seeking of help from any likely quarter, and the new state university surely qualified logically. And Gregory's own background might have been one of the major and perhaps the strongest of all indications. Baptist clergyman and late president of Kalamazoo College in Michigan, Regent Gregory had been in the forefront of common school development, not only in that state but to some extent in the nation at large.

Plausible as that expectation would have been, however, it was not fulfilled. Nothing of the sort occurred. The plausibility of the expectation could only have been based on an interpretation of the educational situation, and the relationship of the new University to it, which was in fact entirely lacking. The role of the new Industrial University vis-à-vis public education as a whole, and the personal mission of its Regent, would have to be defined from a distinctly different perspective which was only beginning to be worked out. The eventual entry of the University into a relationship with the schools and an active participation in the process of teacher education cannot be explained or understood apart from this stage of development.

When Abraham Lincoln signed the Morrill Act creating the land grant universities in 1862, among which was to be Illinois Industrial University, all but seven states had some publicly supported institution of higher learning.[1] However, the importance of these schools was (with a few notable exceptions) rather slight, and their distinctive role was not yet clear. Although their creation was largely the result of a growing disenchantment with the existing collegiate or university structure, shaped largely by such predominating institutions as Yale, Harvard, and Princeton, and a growing concern for broader educational opportunities as well, the character of the new universities was not set. The older colleges had been oriented around a social role which consisted largely of undergirding a Christian democracy—

[1] For what follows, we have relied particularly on the following works. For the development of American higher education and the land grant movement in particular, see John S. Brubacher and S. Willis Rudy, *Higher Education in Transition* (New York, 1958); Edward D. Eddy, Jr., *Colleges for Our Land and Time: The Land-Grant Idea in American Education* (New York, 1956); Richard Hofstadter and C. DeWitt Hardy, *The Development and Scope of Higher Education in the United States* (New York, 1952); Richard Hofstadter and Walter P. Metzger, *The Development of Academic Freedom in the United States* (New York, 1955); Frederick Rudolph, *The American College and University: A History* (Chicago, 1953); Laurence R. Veysey, *The Emergence of the American University* (Chicago, 1965); Rush Welter, *Popular Education and Democratic Thought in America* (New York, 1962). See also titles bearing on the subject in the Bibliography. The general interpretations are our own, however, unless otherwise indicated. For the development of the University of Illinois, there is only one book: Winton U. Solberg, *The University of Illinois, 1867–94: An Intellectual and Cultural History*. While we have explored the particular issues and events which will occupy our attention, Solberg's work will be referred to frequently and the reader is urged to consult it for a more thorough discussion of the context of this study. There are other works dealing with the University or allied matters, but they are seriously deficient in one or more respects. These titles may be found in the Bibliography. Of historic interest in the opening chapters, though not of general authority, are the following: Newton Bateman and Paul Selby, *An Historical Encyclopedia of Illinois*, 2 vols. (Chicago, 1905); John W. Cook, *Educational History of Illinois* (Chicago, 1912). See also William L. Pillsbury, "Historical Sketches of the State Normal Universities and the University of Illinois," in 17th SSPI (1888), pp. LXXVII–CXVI.

heavily Protestant and faintly aristocratic—an educational regimen which emphasized the interrelationship of character training and mental discipline. The growing chorus of criticism which surrounded the educational establishment found its unity in a complex theme. The critics crusaded for the elective principle, a mere device, in order to facilitate a shift to the broader interests and potential responsibilities present in the rapidly changing culture. The recurring melody was utility rather than virtue—though of course the utility had to be defended, at least at first, as really more virtuous than the heroic ornamentation it replaced. The grand theme was dressed with such embellishments as the manual-labor movement, a concern for an increased technological emphasis, and the need for an education in scientific agriculture.[2]

The slow response of Illinois was the result of many factors. Denominational reluctance, compounded about equally of devotion to principle and the need to protect vested interests, was obviously a major consideration. The state was already oversupplied with purportedly higher institutions. There was also a severe reluctance to face the financial implications.[3] The revenues previously provided had been mishandled and squandered. The remains of ill-timed and badly organized collegiate ventures littered the Illinois landscape, and the public was deeply suspicious of most such schemes. Futhermore, the state already had its university—a normal university. By its function, it had laid successful claim to the funds ambiguously earmarked for the general educational advancement of the state. It had done so with distinction, in fact, and it was not at all clear that an interloper on the educational scene was needed, nor of what species it should be when it appeared.

The land grant–university movement had many articulate spokesmen in Illinois, most notably Jonathan Baldwin Turner, but it is simplistic and essentially false to claim that it had its origin here.[4] The movement had deep and widespread roots in the past. As we have already suggested, there was a growing opinion that the older institutions were inadequate. The source of much of this disenchantment was a positive vision: full national development implied a general, scientifically oriented education, because science alone (via technology) could realize the material potential of the new land. The specific

[2] Solberg, *University of Illinois*, Ch. 1.
[3] Ibid., pp. 23ff.
[4] Ibid., Ch. 2, esp. pp. 22ff., 40–49, 62–64.

forms of this fervently held belief were many and varied. Some crusaded for older ideals in the name of the new emphasis, and there had been a consequent rebirth of interest in a national university. Others advanced various schemes for scientifically oriented industrial and agricultural institutions. Still others proposed a national scientific center. And there were schemes for combinations of such emphases. After a complicated distilling process, the nationally and purely scientifically oriented aspirations led to the creation of the Smithsonian Institution in 1846. The popular and utilitarian emphases were momentarily denied expression.

Growing pressure from enlightened agricultural interests in Illinois led to the epoch-making Putnam County Farmers' Convention at Granville in 1851, convoked to consider a progressive, scientifically oriented agricultural university for the state.[5] Jonathan Baldwin Turner gave the major address and provided the inspirational rhetoric which would shape practical efforts. Turner and others hoped to use the long-fallow educational funds of the state, but it became increasingly obvious that they would be devoted to another pressing need: creation of a state-sponsored institution for teacher preparation. As a consequence, the movement's leaders, and especially Turner, were required to think in national terms if their local objectives were to be obtained. The establishment of statewide free common schools in 1855 tipped the balance toward immediate action in the direction of preparing a teaching force and led to the founding of the state normal university at Normal in 1857. Turner sacrificed the purity of his vision and supported that movement eventually, though he at first hoped that the resultant institution would be a general, scientifically oriented university with a normal department as an integral part. In view of the enormous interest in and need for educational leadership at the lowest level, it is not surprising that only the normal function survived, though that fact was to have lasting consequences for both institutions in the future.

The agricultural and industrial interests joined forces and began to bring pressure to bear on Washington. Here they merged with others from around the nation who were beginning to do the same thing. In 1857 Congressman Justin Morrill of Vermont offered the "Agricultural College Act" which proposed to award lands to the states for the funding of colleges "where the leading object would be, *without ex-*

[5] Ibid., p. 43. Cf. Pillsbury, 17th SSPI (1888), pp. LXXVII–CXVI, for the normal school context.

cluding other scientific and classical studies, to teach such branches of learning as are related to agricultural and the mechanic arts . . . in order to promote the liberal and practical education of the industrial classes in the several pursuits and professions of life.[6] The proposal to use land as the basis of the funding, rather than actual capital, was probably the unique contribution of Turner. The bill as a whole, however, was a somewhat unwieldy and ambiguous amalgam which was not wholly satisfactory to any of the factions which had pushed for it. In spite of antifederalist opposition, the bill was passed in 1859, but Buchanan vetoed it on constitutional grounds. In 1861, Morrill reintroduced it, with slight modification, and it gained final passage in July, 1862.

Illinois accepted the act rapidly, even though its own delegates had not unanimously supported it.[7] As a result, the state was awarded 480,000 acres for income purposes. Immediately these potential funds created an intrastate scramble. Two private colleges, Knox and Shurtleff, hoped to get control of the money by creating northern and southern regional branches of a paper agricultural university in conjunction with their own campuses. They were unsuccessful. Governor Richard Yates eventually created a commission (which at first included no one representing the state's agricultural interests) to explore such major questions as what number of institutions ought to be proposed, possible sites, etc. Recommendations came from all sides, but little action resulted. As had been the case with the normal university, it was hoped that communities eager for the plum would make lucrative offers in order to gain it. The executive confusion resulted in a failure to clear any measure in 1865–66, and both public and private interests girded for an all-out effort in preparation for the 1867 legislature—though the private institutions soon withdrew from the battle for good. Attention centered on directly influencing the legislators, since it was apparent that nothing short of a legal debate on the floor of the capitol could settle so thorny an issue. Bloomington, Champaign-Urbana, Jacksonville, and Lincoln were the leading contenders for the location of the new university by virtue of their offers of financial support and their effective lobbying. The decision was made by the process of accepting or rejecting amendments specifying

[6] Solberg, *University of Illinois*, p. 54. For the Act, see *Congressional Globe*, 35 Cong., 1 Sess., 1697 (italics ours). The educational historian W. H. Cowley has appropriately called these italicized words the seven most influential words in the history of American higher education.

[7] For the following, see Solberg, *University of Illinois*, Ch. 3, passim.

sites which were attached to the funding bill and, on February 28, 1867, Governor Oglesby signed into law the version which gave the new institution to Champaign-Urbana.[8]

In short order a board was appointed and charged with the election of a regent, or president. Together they were to supervise the creation of Illinois Industrial University, a new model educational institution, neither the nature nor function of which was as yet clearly grasped. What definition there was, was negative: it was not to be a traditional college. As a consequence it was to offer no degrees or diplomas, have no old-style "president," and it was to work at the convenience of farmers during the six fall and winter months of the year. In positive effect, this negative definition meant that it would be the creation of its new Board and, most particularly, the regent they would elect.

The first Trustees met in March, 1867, and considered four nominees. Three were clergymen who had devoted themselves with distinction to the expansion of public education; the fourth was the superintendent of schools in Chicago—hardly a remarkable break with the style of the past! The lot fell upon John Milton Gregory.[9] Not particularly interested at first, Gregory finally accepted the post as a true "call." God perhaps had work for him to do in Champaign-Urbana. He immediately set about his first task, defining the new institution through the creation of a curriculum and faculty. In so doing he put into application an impressive background.

Gregory was born at Sand Lake, New York, in 1882.[10] As befit the times, his early schooling was sketchy and involved a good deal of family tutoring and self-instruction. He was able, however, to attend the common schools, and at fifteen he himself began to teach Latin and keep a school. In 1842, at the age of twenty, he went to Union College, then in the heyday of its prestige under its nationally

---

[8] Ibid., pp. 77, 79.
[9] Ibid., Ch. 4. The other clergymen were Daniel J. Pinckney of Mt. Morris (nominated by Matthias L. Dunlap), and Norman N. Wood of Jacksonville, former president of Shurtleff College (nominated by John C. Burroughs). J. L. Pickard was the superintendent (nominator not known). Gregory was nominated by Thomas Quick (pp. 85ff.).
[10] Ibid., pp. 87–90. For biographical material on Gregory, see also Harry A. Kersey, Jr., *John Milton Gregory and the University of Illinois* (Urbana, 1968). The original version was his "John Milton Gregory as a Midwestern Educator, 1852–1880" (Ph.D. dissertation, University of Illinois, 1965); Allene Gregory, *John Milton Gregory: A Biography* (Chicago, 1923) contains much material from Gregory's lost diaries which suggests his spiritual and philosophical bent.

known president, Eliphalet Nott. Gregory took the classical course, graduating Phi Beta Kappa in 1846. He then envisioned—or his family envisioned—a career in the law as the next step, but that was not to be.

As a child, Gregory was religiously precocious. Possessed of a deep, introspective (and sometimes perhaps oversensitive) piety, he finally decided he was instead called to the ministry in the Baptist church, although he had never had any formal theological training. He felt the stresses of the parish ministry (both physical and spiritual) very keenly, and his strength threatened to break. He then determined to abandon his settled pulpit and become an itinerant evangelist, but he finally accepted a steady pastorate again in Akron, Ohio. He grew increasingly doubtful of his ability to remain in parochial work, and, at the same time, like so many others in his situation, his thought turned gradually toward the growing public educational enterprise. That challenge seemed to him, as to others, to offer fulfillment of many of his ideals, along with relief from the demands which had made his parochial labors unbearable. His piety had always had a strongly social orientation anyway—he was a pronounced foe of slavery, as well as being antispiritualist and protemperance.[11] Again like many other educational leaders of his day, Gregory's dream for a future America was a profoundly religious one. The nation was, it was widely agreed, a religious community, and common school education was consequently a religious instrument for the achieving of the nation's true destiny. Thus, to be an educational leader could be the fulfillment of one's religious vocation. The only difference was perhaps an improvement (for those sharing Gregory's perspective): it was a nonsectarian role which freed one for fulfilling the widest possible mission.[12]

[11] Kersey, "John Milton Gregory . . . Educator," pp. 8, 38–43.
[12] Ibid., pp. 58–65. See also Gregory to J. B. Turner, February 4, 1871; Newton Bateman to Turner, February 16, 1874, in Turner manuscripts, Archives of the State of Illinois. It might be argued that much Protestant "ecumenism" had its origin in the nineteenth-century link between education and religion. Many clergy, tired of the internecine strife which had frequently characterized American church life for the preceding two centuries or more, turned to religiously motivated social or educational service as an expression of their vocation. They believed that education could be entirely religious and even Christian, albeit constitutionally forbidden to be "sectarian." ("Christian" did not in most cases include Catholicism, of course.) Thus educational institutions rapidly became early Protestant ecumenical experiments. Kersey's remark that Gregory found the University's

As a consequence the future Regent accepted an offer extended by his brother to join him in developing a commercial school in Detroit. His still-enormous energy drove him deeply into educational affairs of all kinds from the beginning. For six years, 1852–58, Gregory was a leader in the Michigan Teachers' Association, especially as its president and editor of its *Michigan Journal of Education*. In that influential vehicle, he continually passed on to the teaching force the best (as he saw it) of the new pedagogical ideas that were beginning to permeate the nation. In 1858 Gregory was elected superintendent of public instruction, the highest honor his peers and his constituency could bestow on him. He proved a vigorous officeholder, working tirelessly to improve programs and facilities for teacher preparation. He championed the free high school movement as well—a movement in which Michigan was to make signal contributions, not the least of which was the subsequent "Kalamazoo case" in which the legality of public secondary schools was clarified.[13]

Perhaps most important from our point of view, Gregory proposed in 1863 that the study of education be given a place at the already prestigious University of Michigan, as it was with the establishment of the first American chair of pedagogy in 1879.[14] This prescient recommendation may have been generated by his own experience in lecturing at the University for some three years, in connection with other courses, on the "practical problems of education." His efforts (perhaps the first at that level in the United States) were well received, though extremely limited: he covered the areas of history of education, philosophy of education, and "educational art and institutions" in five days. As fits with his later instruction at Illinois, the one auditor who has left a record noted that he moved rapidly into the subject of mental development and its curricular implications and concentrated on that aspect of the problem.

In 1864, Gregory accepted the presidency of Kalamazoo College, a struggling but active Baptist institution then in particularly desperate straits. The new president rapidly disentangled the twisted personal and financial difficulties which had been brought about by his predecessor

---

chapel a "substitute" for his forsaken pulpit (p. 66) misses the point entirely. University work was in all respects an acceptable *extension* of the ministerial calling, as the roles of faculty and administrators throughout the period amply demonstrate.

[13] Kersey, *John Milton Gregory and the University of Illinois*, pp. 24–29.
[14] Kersey, "John Milton Gregory . . . Educator," pp. 172ff., 441ff.

and initiated a vigorous rebuilding program. Like many other such colleges, Kalamazoo had a relatively flourishing normal department which offered pedagogical work. Gregory hoped to develop it and thus send forth an increased number of Christian teachers to meet the needs of the common schools. It would be a fitting climax for a man who had merited the title of Michigan's outstanding public-school reform leader during the previous decade.[15]

Gregory's general orientation in educational theory was a melding of several strains, without any well-defined partisan philosophy. He combined much of the old tradition with much that was new. As has been suggested, for him the nation was a religious community, "nonsectarian" but decidedly Christian—which meant, of course, Protestant. By direct implication, the schools were, as he called them, "noble nurseries of Christian freemen." Work was intrinsically ennobling, and the common, useful task a privilege. Learning was thus best justified not as an optional ornament but as a utilitarian necessity. "A life of beneficient, generous, efficient action," Gregory once remarked, "is the grand and holy aim of education." [16]

Gregory's lectures on pedagogy at Michigan, as well as those in mental science later at Illinois, reveal a surprisingly eclectic general philosophy coupled with a quasi-Kantian and Pestalozzian approach to educational questions. As did most of his contemporaries, he possessed a distinctly faculty-oriented psychology, which also served to define the proper divisions within all potential subject matter. There was, however, no deliberate obscurantism in him. He was more willing than most philosophers and pedagogues to make room for possible physically based accounts of cognitive activity and the potential contribution of evolutionary thought. And Gregory shared much of the popular optimism of his day which led him constantly to labor to bring all to science and science to all.[17]

The lack of any stable curriculum seemed the most serious difficulty facing the Michigan schools, and Gregory worked constantly to correct the situation. He thought a universal course of study was possible because, as we have noted, the various universally present intellectual faculties could be used to define it. The results of this mode of definition led to the usual sorts of content and method.

---

[15] Ibid., pp. 175ff., 204. Cf. Kersey, *John Milton Gregory and the University of Illinois*, pp. 42–46.

[16] Kersey, "John Milton Gregory . . . Educator," p. 93.

[17] Ibid., pp. 176ff. See below, notes 29, 40.

Gregory also placed a heavy emphasis on the moral content of education and on a good deal of crypto-theological content as well. He thought the best vehicles of achieving these moral objectives were history—as providing a nonsectarian basis—and the thoughtful study of the Bible. In toto the curriculum was to achieve the cultural growth of the free, morally responsible individual—*culture* meaning for Gregory, as for most if not all of his peers, *Christian* culture. As he reported to the state in 1859, "the true idea of education is that of a cultural growth—a trained development. Its chief end is the attainment of mental power and true character; its chief means the exercise of study and the enlarging influence of ideas." [18]

Gregory's convictions about teacher preparation were perhaps his most carefully worked out beliefs. It was, he thought, the foundation of all educational activity.[19] There were essentially three planks in his reform platform, all of great significance for his future work at Illinois.[20] First of all, a vigorous campaign was needed to extend and upgrade the competence of those already teaching by means of a strong institute program. As we have seen, the schools, created almost overnight, had been filled with "teachers" drawn from any and every source. That condition necessarily remained. Until better personnel could be prepared, those who were in fact carrying the load must be assisted.

Second, a *science* of education must be developed through extensive thought and research.[21] The locus of this crucial activity he stipulated quite precisely: *"in the normal schools."* [22] This specification, which he shared with most educational leaders throughout the nation at this time, meant that the by now obvious requirement of professionalization in the teaching force was to be focused primarily on the normal school. Fittingly, he advocated the establishment of "teachers' de-

[18] According to Gregory, schools were to be institutions in which "the soul might come to a full, rounded growth and ripeness, and the intelligence be furnished and fitted for a lifelong pursuit of knowledge." This and the quotation in the text are from his *23rd Annual Report of the Superintendent of Public Instruction of the State of Michigan . . . 1859* (Lansing, 1860), p. 48, quoted in Kersey, "John Milton Gregory . . . Educator," p. 140. See also ibid., pp. 150ff., on history and scripture.
[19] Ibid., p. 88.
[20] Ibid., pp. 164ff.
[21] The sources of "a true science of education" were "two parallel facts . . . —1st, a logical connection of sciences growing out of, or succeeding each other, in a certain natural order, and 2nd, a logical development of the mental powers, unfolding from each other in an established natural sequence" (ibid., p. 168).
[22] Ibid., p. 165 (italics ours).

partments" in the high schools or colleges of the state, a strategy becoming widespread throughout the nation.[23]

Aptly characterizing the normal institution as the "West Point of
our school system," Gregory saw its purpose as the *education* of
teachers, however. That is, the normal school was to take as its business the general education of teachers, not merely their practical
training. Here the teacher would study what he was to teach, but at
a deeper level, attempting to see the deepest logic of the particular subject matter and hence enabling himself to apply it flexibly. To this he
would join a thorough knowledge of the "mental faculties" appropriate to each branch of study. Finally, there would be advanced research
in education, pressing toward a true science of pedagogy, in terms of
which the student's performance could become in fact predictable.[24]

The third plank in Gregory's platform was the making of education into a fit subject for university study. He saw this as possible
precisely because it could be made a science and not remain merely
a practical art. As he said in his Michigan *Report* of 1863, "Why
should not the State University lend its aid and do *some part* of this
work, thus linking itself more closely to the mighty machinery of
public instruction, and stretching forth its helping hand to the grand
task of the universal education of the people?"[25] Indeed, why not?
Yet, when the new Regent set out the all-important first curriculum
for Illinois Industrial University, pedagogy was for all practical purposes entirely absent.

When he turned to developing the new University's offerings,
Gregory proposed at the outset six departments and some fifteen
courses, or programs of studies. The six departments were agriculture,
polytechnic, military, chemistry and natural science, trade and commerce, and general science and literature. Under the last, there were
seven areas of study which comprised the "University course," which
was necessary for regular standing and to which electives could be
added. These seven were mathematics, natural science and chemistry,
English, modern languages, ancient languages, history and social
science, and intellectual and moral philosophy. While education was

[23] Ibid., p. 170. For example, President Hill of Harvard had advocated this strategy at the National Teachers' Association meeting of 1864, the year in which
Gregory advocated the practice in his *Annual Report*.

[24] Ibid., p. 167, 169.

[25] The quotation is from Gregory's *27th Annual Report . . . 1863* (Lansing,
1864), p. 8 (italics ours). Cited in Kersey, "John Milton Gregory . . . Educator,"
p. 175.

specified as part of the material to be covered in intellectual and moral philosophy, as we shall see, it had nothing to do with the professional preparation of teachers.[26]

That Gregory's interest in teacher preparation had not been lost sight of with his move to Illinois was obvious. He immediately joined in the battle in this state, taking a leading role until the demands of his new University forced him to retire somewhat. The Regent joined the Illinois Teachers' Association, and was elected its president in 1867–68.[27] In that capacity, he took part in the struggle to establish a second normal school in the southern part of the state (now Southern Illinois University), and he pressed for legislation to create county normal schools and departments. He frequently addressed teachers' institutes, and he kept his ideas before a national audience by his constant writing and speaking. His continued and far-reaching leadership was finally recognized by his election to the presidency of the National Education Association in 1880.[28] The inescapable thrust of this evidence seems clear. It is quite accorded with Gregory's carefully worked out conception of teacher preparation. The problems of education were, as *practical* problems at least, to be solved elsewhere than the campus of Illinois Industrial University.

We have noted that the University's early *Catalogues* held out some promise of dealing with the subject of education. Their terse announcements are deceptively persuasive from our present vantage point and have frequently led to hasty opinions regarding the actual or intended role of the University in the field of pedagogy. The offerings for 1868–69, listed in the second catalogue issue, did include a course taught by Gregory in "mental and moral philosophy," and the second semester of this course is described as including the "Science of Education, or mental philosophy applied to Education." [29] That particular

[26] See Board of Trustees of Illinois Industrial University, *First Annual Report* (Springfield, 1868), pp. 47–64. The published reports of the Board will hereafter be cited by the volume number and year of publication—for example, this entry would read: 1st *Report* (1868). Cf. Solberg, *University of Illinois*, pp. 90–93.

[27] Kersey, "John Milton Gregory . . . Educator," p. 368.

[28] Carl Stephens, MS history, Stephens Papers, 2–35. Cf. John W. Cook, *Educational History of Illinois*, p. 230.

[29] The first *Circular and Catalogue of the Officers and Students of the Illinois Industrial University* [Champaign, 1869]—(these important documents will hereafter be cited simply as *Catalogue*, with the addition of the academic year covered)—listed the "Science of Education" under "Mental Philosophy," during the first term of the fourth year (p. 7). The second *Catalogue* (1868–69), from which the description is drawn, also shows it to involve two lectures each week (p. 12). See also State of Illinois, *Report of Committee on Courses of Study and Faculty*

title fits exactly the conceptions which the Regent held, as we have seen. The following year there is no entry, but the issue of 1870–71 includes a full year's course in philosophy and logic at the fourth-year level, including again "philosophy of education." [30] This announcement continues until 1889–90, virtually without alteration except for a growingly psychological description of the contents. In 1880–81 the course description was expanded to read "mental physiology or connection of body and mind, healthful conditions of thought, growth and decay of mental and moral powers," and it was in this context that "philosophy of education" was included. [31]

There is some other evidence which suggests a concern for education. The early descriptions of the aims of the "College of Science" include the preparation of "teachers in the higher institutions," and there are occasional references to an intention to prepare "teachers," "writers," and "professors," especially for "industrial schools." Such provocative hints, however, need to be viewed in the light of more concrete evidence. Any official mention of pedagogy was largely the result of the general utilitarian role in terms of which the new University justified itself. In 1871 Gregory, sympathetic to their scientific, utilitarian, and vocational emphasis, promised the horticulturists of the state that he would assist the introduction of what they were calling "the religion of agriculture" into the common schools by promoting popular interest in science through the University. The Regent argued that the common school curriculum required nothing less than to be turned upside down, so that the "practical business of life" might occupy the center of attention in place of the subjects which promised a bogus "rounded development." (Jonathan Baldwin Turner had quipped that that meant "round like a stove pipe and just as hollow.")

---

for the Illinois Industrial University (Springfield, 1867). This report discusses (pp. 9–11) the department of general science and literature but does not mention pedagogy. Its reliance on the authority of John Stuart Mill and William Hamilton is interesting to note and points up the curious conjunction of utilitarian and Scottish realist emphases which were a principal ingredient in Gregory's thought. At the beginning, Gregory apparently used the latter's writings as textual material in developing the course in mental science, and he was also very sympathetic to Reid and Stewart. He did not, however, share their belief in the intuitive certainty of many ideas, concepts, and moral principles.

[30] *Catalogue* (1869–70) does not show any offerings in mental or moral science at all. They do remain in the chart of the curriculum (p. 32) and still include the "Science of Education" in that place. (See *Catalogue* [1870–71], pp. 27, 35.)

[31] *Catalogue* (1880–81), p. 68. No instructor is listed, and there is little evidence that it was taught.

The horticulturists also hoped that both the needed scientifically and practically trained teachers and the requisite instructional materials might come out of the new Illinois Industrial University as well as out of the normal schools. But Gregory, for all his (doubtless genuine) sympathy, apparently went no further than establishing an informal extracurricular session for those he hoped would "fight and work for a reform in the Schools." This voluntary "teachers' class," and occasional exhortations delivered to the populace on the education of their children, seem to have made little if any sustained impression.[32]

The development of the library, which would have been essential for any serious program of formal instruction in education, suggests the same ambiguous picture. The first *Report* of the Board of Trustees (1867–68) notes that 1,092 volumes had been acquired for the library. But three or four of these are works dealing with pedagogy as such.[33] By 1869–70, of 3,480 bound volumes, 119 are classed as dealing with philosophy and education. However, only a handful are substantial works. The preponderance are official reports and documents, and much of the pamphlet literature catalogued dealt primarily with higher education.[34] Periodical holdings reflect the same picture. The first University *Catalogue* to list periodicals (1870–71) includes the *Michigan Teacher*, and various titles are added and dropped from that time onward for no discernible reason.[35] Except for the prestigious

[32] For the aims of the College of Science, see *Catalogue* (1871–72), p. 47, for example. Such notices continue without substantial change through the decade. Cf. the University's annual report in 11th SSPI (1876), which does not list pedagogy as an aim or field of study (pp. 237ff.), although teachers for "the higher institutions" are suggested as part of the province of the College of Literature and Science (p. 257). According to 9th *Report* (1878), p. 2, "the furnishing of teachers to the industrial schools of the country" was a purpose of the College of Literature and Science. Students in the School of Commerce were encouraged to assist with drill in bookkeeping in the Preparatory Department—not as a form of "practice teaching," however, but on the principle that "*the test of knowledge is the act of teaching*" (*Catalogue* [1878–79], p. 87). For Gregory's unofficial efforts, see *Transactions of the Illinois State Horticultural Society for 1871*, n.s., vol. 5 (Chicago, 1872), pp. 118–27, 205–15, but esp. pp. 118, 122–24; Gregory to Turner, March 15, 1872, in Powell Papers, Record Series 39/1/20, Box 9. State Superintendent Newton D. Bateman apparently shared the same hopes, and all hoped to work in a common effort. (See Turner to Bateman, January 8, 1872, in Bateman Manuscripts, Archives of the State of Illinois.)

[33] 1st *Report* (1868), pp. 209–15, esp. p. 213; cf. p. 124. It should be noted that there was already an extensive professional literature which would have been at hand if the function of teacher preparation had been taken seriously. The section labeled "Education" contained mostly textbooks and manuals.

[34] 3rd *Report* (1870), pp. 40–41, 127–63, esp. pp. 154–56.

[35] *Catalogue* (1870–71), p. 14.

American Journal of Education and *Education*, which were generally kept on hand, holdings in the field were varying and erratic, and there was a relative decrease rather than an increase as the years passed.[36] By the late 1880's, virtually no notice of the area is taken, although the professional literature had increased at an enormous rate, both in journals and in full-scale works dealing with educational history and theory.[37] In any institution of the time that took responsibility for the preparation of teachers seriously, these works were the foundation. Since no serious program of instruction in the area of pedagogy could have been built without much more careful attention to the rapidly expanding literature of the field, the inescapable conclusion is that no serious attempt was intended.

What, then, did the educational topics embedded in these courses signify? The original mental and moral philosophy course, before its retitling, was in fact the nearly universal finishing course of traditional nineteenth-century higher education. At the end of the student's academic career, he was given a final exposure to the patriarch of the college community, the president, who attempted to tie together all of the student's previous learning in terms of a heavily moral-theological interpretation of himself and the world of which he was a part. It was intended to be the climax of the traditional higher educational experience, as it had doubtless been for Gregory when he sat under Eliphalet Nott at Union College.[38] As a part of that final integration, thinking about education had a distinct and proper role. The future "Christian freemen" would have a responsibility for shaping the all-important educational engine which powered national progress. He must therefore have correct opinions about it, as well as about the other areas in which he had a duty as an enlightened citizen. Whether or not he was to be a teacher was irrelevant. Having an opinion about

[36] According to the 5th *Report* (1872), the library held some 8,000 volumes and was receiving a considerable number of periodicals. While twenty-one were "regularly" received in agriculture, education received only four (p. 21).

[37] The 13th *Report* (1886) makes no reference at all to pedagogical works (p. 87). What Lawrence Cremin has called the "extraordinary succession of seminal publications" was already beginning, but no serious effort was made to keep up. (See *The Transformation of the School, Progressivism in American Education, 1876–1957* [New York, 1961], p. 91.) John W. Cook at Illinois State Normal University also noted the "unprecedented multiplication" of pedagogical journals at the beginning of the educational revolution (20th SSPI [1894], p. LVIII).

[38] Andrew V. Raymond, *Union University: Its History, Influence, Characteristics, and Equipment*, 3 vols. (New York, 1907), vol. 1; and C. Van Santvoord and Taylor Lewis, *Memoirs of Eliphalet Nott, D.D., LL.D.* (New York, 1876).

education was part of being an educated man—as the frequent nineteenth-century books and articles dealing with education in a general way obviously demonstrate.[39] And it was closely related to the key dispute of the time—the question of the nature and status of man. It was in fact a concern for apologetic anthropology far more than for professional pedagogy that required the inclusion of educational questions in the curriculum of the time.

We have some limited evidence of what actually went on in the course in the form of student notes, papers, and examinations. The usual academic format during Gregory's time consisted of three fourteen-week terms. In the Regent's course the first embraced mental science, the second moral philosophy, and the third general philosophy. Education was involved only in the first term as a minor theme. In his lectures, Gregory primarily developed his elaborate philosophical psychology, although it was indeed in the area of education that he chose to demonstrate the crucial bearing of the nature of man and his reasoning powers.[40] A set of examination papers put on exhibition

[39] For example, *Forum*, which loudly advertised a series of articles to begin in January, 1888, dealing with critical issues in the public schools. These articles were to treat such problems as the "range of secular teaching," the scope and practicality of the curriculum, manual training, the quality of instruction, what sorts of education the generality of the populace ought to receive, and (heavily emphasized) the question of religion in the public schools and the growing force of parochial education. For example, *Forum* 5 (March-August, 1888), and its series on "What Shall the Public Schools Teach?" esp. pp. 47–56, 146–55, 289–98, 454–60, 574–83 (the last by Lester Frank Ward). There is also an article on "The Next American University" by Andrew D. White, pp. 371–82. Volume 2 (September 1886–February 1887) had already featured a series on "How I Was Educated," with contributions by such eminent figures as Timothy Dwight (pp. 250–61) and Andrew D. White (pp. 559–67). The "new" and the "old" in education, at all levels, were both roundly praised and condemned in its pages. The question of religion in the schools was but one aspect of a wider concern with religion itself, and religion in American social and political life. This is shown by the fact that articles on the schools are interspersed with articles on the papacy and another series, "Confessions of . . . ," done anonymously by members of various Protestant sects.

[40] For example, Ralph Allen Papers, passim, to which reference is made in this passage. (Most are from the academic year 1874–75.) Special attention should be given to the diagram—probably a course outline—of the "Representative Faculties," and the "Elaborative Faculties," an outline of the "General Properties of Matter as Known Through Perception," and the outline of "knowledge." There is also a signed "Logic Examination" which defines the subject as "the science which considers the laws of pure thinking" or the "elaborative" acts of mind. Logic is the study which is used, not for the discovery of, but "establishing and defending truth." It "gives mental discipline; for in its pursuance the student must exercise most careful and clear discrimination and tax to his utmost his reasoning faculties." Concept formation is a three-fold process of "simple apprehension,"

at the Philadelphia Centennial Exposition in 1876 make the content of the course quite clear. Each student had been assigned five questions to be answered and had then drawn five more from a possible fifty-four. The first of the required questions asked the student to state "the relative certainty and utility of mental and physical sciences." Since the answers correspond closely, apparently rigid reproductions of lecture material, they clearly demonstrate the content of the courses. In response to the first question, one student tells us that "mental science is valuable, inasmuch as it reveals the primary truths and first principles upon which are based all the sciences which relate to man: such as ethics, aesthetics, law, theology, political, and social science." As a consequence, mental science "must be the main support of the successful educator, or of him who would lay plans for the intellectual and social advancement of mankind." [41]

Gregory's official reports, both to the Trustees and to the superintendent of public instruction, show no professional interest in pedagogy. [42] The report of the initial committee to determine the course of study for the University, while discussing at length the aims and responsibilities of the new institution, makes no mention of education

---

"abstraction of essential attributes," and "generalization or union." As these definitions would in any case suggest, Aristotle and Hamilton are invoked as authorities for the position. There is also an examination paper dealing with "unconscious cerebration" which specifically develops a psycho-physical parallelism.

A brief, undated paper on "Education" defines it as "that which develops the faculties" and divides it into three "classes," moral, intellectual, and physical. Some of its more interesting assertions are the following: "2. Usual effects on an individual. Improve their morals, minds and bodies, besides making others respect them." "3. What are its effects on society—Enlarges it and leads to inventions." It suggests that an educated man should be compared to "a strong fleet ship with a good and intelligent captain" and instances "Ancient Grecians and Romans, Newton, Webster, Clay, Cawdry." Allen quotes Herbart and asserts that the way to get an education is to "think, study [and] act."

[41] Examination papers (1875–76), particularly the volumes from the mental philosophy class. The four remaining required questions are instructive (2) "What Are the Materialistic and Spiritualistic Theories of Perception?" (3) "Give the Psychical and Physiological Theories of Perception." (4) "Explain Unconscious Cerebration and Give Arguments For and Against." (5) "Give a Chart of the Presentative and the Representative Faculties." The group of elective questions dealt with such matters as perception, the properties of matter, Locke's and Descartes's theories of perception, and the classification of the sciences. The students' answers suggest that their instruction has been decidedly pro-"spiritual" and faintly idealist, in spite of the preoccupation with a moderate commonsense realism which was obvious in some of the other class notes.

[42] 9th *Report* (1878), pp. 6off.; 11th SSPI (1876), pp. 237ff.; 12th SSPI (1878), pp. 141ff., 163; 10th *Report* (1880), p. 184.

as a course of study, nor does it suggest that the new University will have any professional role in connection with the expanding state educational system.[43] Although Urbana was the site of the State Teachers' Association meeting in 1877 and the teachers were impressed with its development, there is not a hint that Illinois Industrial University had a part to play in the existing crisis in the common schools.[44]

Even if the "senior course" had had some professional intent, there could not have been many to take it. Just as in the high schools and the normal schools, the students who attended IIU quite frequently— in fact usually—could not complete their work. In his 1876 state report, Gregory noted that of the 1,098 who had matriculated in the previous eight years, only 116 had managed to graduate.[45] He had earlier noted that of the 406 actually enrolled in the new University, only thirty-one were at the fourth-year level.[46] Some graduates or partial attenders did end up teaching, of course, but they were relatively few. Of the alumni of the "classes" of 1872–76, thirty-three were actually teaching in 1876, but the evidence suggests that few of them took it seriously.[47] It was an acceptable post for a woman, and a man could scrape together a few dollars before pressing on to something more worthwhile. That was about it. The Regent from time to time exhorted the student body on the importance of education and the schools (usually in chapel), and the literary societies discussed pedagogical issues on occasion, but the interest was general, never professional.[48]

If, as was shown in the previous chapter, the schools were in a

[43] State of Illinois, *Report of Committee on Courses of Study and Faculty for the Illinois Industrial University* (Springfield, 1867), pp. 9–11.

[44] 9th *Report* (1878), p. 9. Cf. the Regent's own report (s.v. December 5, 1876, and pp. 60–61). The leading teachers' journal, the *Illinois Teacher*, offers no evidence that the meeting was held at Urbana because of any connection between the University and professional pedagogy.

[45] 8th *Report* (1877), p. 171. It should also be remembered that the University's student body was largely male.

[46] 6th *Report* (1874), p. 13. Attendance in mental philosophy (which included "education") was only nine, according to 5th *Report* (1873).

[47] 8th *Report* (1877), p. 22ff. The pages of the student newspaper, the *Student* and (later) the *Illini*, strongly—if admittedly only generally—suggest this interpretation.

[48] For example, notes on Gregory's chapel talk of December 16, 1877, in notebook, "December, 1877," Arthur N. Talbot Papers. The Regent's address dealt specifically with the topic, but apparently made no reference to teaching. Talbot, later a distinguished civil engineer and leading faculty member at the University, had himself been a school teacher before coming to Urbana, much as Shamel. Nonetheless, he had to enter the preparatory department.

critical situation during these years, why was there not the slightest suggestion that the University had any responsibilities or opportunities to be of service in solving the state's educational dilemma at the professional level? The answer is complex, of course, but a significant part of it is fairly obvious. In the first place, "education" meant the common schools (roughly, but by no means exactly, comparable to our elementary schools), not the elaborate, variegated enterprise we think of today. The high schools were not a significant factor until the late 1870's, at least, in the state of Illinois. In Chicago there was but one high school in 1868, although it enrolled the then enormous number of 495 students. The state reports did not even include high schools until 1870, when there were 108 (about one per county), most of which were special corporations and not closely linked to the general system. The number had climbed only to 128 by the report of 1877–78.[49] As a consequence, the content generally required for teaching proficiency was strictly that of the "common branches," or the most elementary subjects and skills, although we have seen that some rudimentary science (almost entirely bookish) was now beginning to be required. The teacher's role was still almost exclusively that of drill-master and disciplinarian, and the subject-matter preparation could be gained in any number of ways. (Frequently it was in fact gained by keeping one chapter ahead in the student's text!) Any reasonably bright individual, self-taught, could easily stand at the top of the "profession," especially if he availed himself of the by now widespread opportunities for on-the-job training via the reading circles, institutes, and other study groups.[50] Clearly there were no "university-level" implications in the "profession" itself at this point.

The question of educational method had been in practical effect largely ignored. Before universally available schooling and compulsory attendance laws, it was simply not necessary to cope with the recalcitrant or the unsuited student. Common school education had been inherently elitist, though not necessarily consciously so. Nor was it necessary to grapple with the question of the relationship between education and the common good, except (as had always been the

<hr>

[49] City of Chicago, Department of Public Instruction, *Fourteenth Annual Report of the Board of Education for the Year Ending July 3, 1868* (Chicago, 1868), pp. 120ff.; 8th SSPI (1870), pp. 2, 160; 12th SSPI (1878), p. 112.

[50] In his 16th *Report*, the state superintendent, noting a "restlessness in educational circles" which he thought indicative of a desire for reform, admitted that "our teachers are only one step ahead, if that." The examinations test scholarship, he said, but not *"fitness to teach"* (16th SSPI [1886], pp. ccxxx–ccxxxiii).

case) in the sense that a well-educated minority (coupled with an acceptably skilled majority) was required to provide direction in any cohesive society. Until the late eighteenth century, educational problems were almost wholly theoretical, and they could be solved by speculative philosophers and theologians. The child, as a miniature adult, should be taught the same logically ordered content which any mature human being ought to possess. Education had been so seen, with only rare and largely fruitless exceptions, for more than 2,500 years, and there was no serious need to change. With a select group, it worked—doubtless painfully, but at least for the most part.

When, in conjunction with the pervasive social and political changes of the eighteenth and nineteenth centuries, education began to be enormously expanded, at first in Europe but soon in the United States as well, a radical new reckoning was indicated. The philosophers (such as Rousseau and Herbart) were joined in the struggle to solve the problems of true "mass education" by those who actually taught (such as Pestalozzi and Froebel)—a shocking invasion into the ranks of educational theorists. The ideas of men such as these, though they had been around for some decades, were really only beginning to penetrate American educational thought by the mid-nineteenth century. And their point of entry was not the university but the "normal school"—an institution which was itself in part the product of the European educational revolution.[51] In a sense, the development of the normal schools had once been a "university movement." New York University had established a short-lived chair of educational philosophy as early as 1832. Francis Wayland had created a normal department at Brown, but it was also discontinued, in 1854. In the early

[51] In connection with this and subsequent remarks on the general development of the normal schools and the entry of pedagogy into the American university, see the following works: Merle L. Borrowman, ed., *Teacher Education in America: A Documentary History* (New York, 1965); Charles A. Harper, *A Century of Public Teacher Education, the Story of the State Teachers Colleges as They Evolved from the Normal Schools* (Washington, D.C., 1939); and *Development of the Teachers College in the United States, with Special Reference to the Illinois State Normal University* (Bloomington, 1935); G. W. A. Luckey, *The Professional Training of Secondary Teachers in the United States* (New York, 1903); Monroe, ed., *Cyclopedia of Education* (New York, 1911), esp. vol. 2, s.v. "Education, Academic Study of"; see also vol. 5 (New York, 1913), s.v. "Teachers, Training of," by George Drayton Strayer; Jessie M. Pangburn, *The Evolution of the American Teachers College* (Teachers College, Columbia University Contributions to Education, no. 500; New York, 1932); and James Richard Robarts, "The Rise of Educational Science in America" (Ph.D. dissertation, University of Illinois, 1963).

1850's, a number of normal departments sprang up in association with institutions of higher learning (including Iowa, Indiana, and Wisconsin), and there were several more in the next two decades. But none of these was significant, since all were part of the almost universally necessary preparatory apparatus of their host institutions and the level of instruction then offered was strictly secondary rather than collegiate—let alone of "university grade." [52]

In 1823, the Reverend Samuel Reed Hall, author of the now famous *Lectures on School-Keeping* which was the first "professional" text in education, founded a private three-year "seminary" devoted exclusively to the training of teachers at Concord, Vermont. It was the first such institution, and no comparable one was forthcoming for some time—at least, none that survived.[53] Experiments were tried in Massachusetts, still the educational center of the nation, but it was not until the late 1830's that the work of the Reverend Charles Brooks and (later) Horace Mann brought the efforts of that state's pioneer, James G. Carter, to fruition. In 1839, at Lexington, the first state-sponsored normal school opened its doors.[54] The movement had already spread widely, however. Backed by the example of the prestigious normal institutions of Prussia (the *Lehrer* Seminars) which the Reverend Calvin E. Stowe had popularized in his widely read "Report on Elementary Public Instruction in Europe," interest moved westward. Two private experiments had been tried as early as 1840 in Illinois (at Waverly and Springfield). It was this increasing ferment which formed the background of the movement to establish a state institution and which led to the creation of Illinois State Normal University by the Illinois legislature on February 18, 1857. Within a few years, the idea began to take hold very rapidly, and by the Civil War, New York, Pennsylvania, New Jersey, and Minnesota all had such institutions. By the end of the 1860's, Illinois enjoyed a second normal school, the famous Cook County Normal in which Colonel Francis W. Parker was to achieve his own revolution, and a third (the second sponsored by the state) was underway at Carbondale.[55]

[52] See esp. Luckey, *Profesional Training of Secondary Teachers*, pp. 63–85, 101.
[53] See esp. Robarts, "Rise of Educational Science," passim. Cf. Harper, *A Century of Public Teacher Education*, esp. Chs. 1, 2.
[54] Ibid.
[55] For the foregoing, see esp. Harper, *Development of the Teachers College*, esp. pp. 1–101; Eli G. Lentz, *Seventy-five Years in Retrospect, from Normal School to Teachers College to University, Southern Illinois University, 1874-1949* (Carbondale, 1955).

It was this rapidly developing normal school system which stood at the center of the trend toward professionalization of the teaching force, a trend only now becoming possible with the shift from the notion that teaching was an art and a science in the logical sense to the notion that teaching was in part a theoretical discipline with empirical as well as philosophical aspects.[56] Although the term "science" had wide and favorable currency throughout most of the nineteenth century, its usage was ambiguous. Few were certain of what it meant, especially as applied to education. At first it meant a systematic philosophical theory of man, mind, and the learning process—i.e., science in the traditional sense of an internally consistent, organized body of knowledge. It was in this sense that even Samuel Hall could plead for a science of education.[57] The teacher needed, on this view, two basic elements: a systematic philosophy, and practical experience. The normal schools devoted themselves to providing these crucial elements nowhere else to be found, and the Illinois normal schools were no exception. They were in fact very good at doing it. The prevailing normal school regimen thus consisted principally of some courses in theory and the mastery of the narrow areas of content required, in a practical setting. In deference to the problem of method, the prospective teacher learned what he was to teach as it was to be taught, thus

[56] For an interesting account of the struggle to develop teaching as a profession, see Dent M. Rhodes, "Professional Models for the American Teacher, 1815–1915" (Ph.D. dissertation, Ohio State University, 1965). A number of Illinois educators figured in the vigorous discussion of the problem which marked the entire period during which the University was attempting to find its way. Among them were E. E. Brown, George P. Brown, Burrill ("The Teacher's Profession," *Illinois Teacher*, 11 [December, 1865]: 363–69), Andrew Sloan Draper ("A Teaching Profession," *Ohio Educational Monthly* 42 [March, 1893]: 101–3), C. E. Hovey, and Edmund Janes James (all cited in Rhodes). The future President James and Charles DeGarmo on several occasions asked editorially, "Is Teachnig a Learned Profession," in their jointly founded and owned *Illinois School Journal*. After examining the question in respect to the United States, the editors concluded that it was not one in fact, but that it could be. Already a science (if unrecognized as such) rather than an art, and dedicated to the largest human interests, it lacked only the third criterion, sufficient economic inducement, to make it restrictive and competitive. In time that would be achieved. (See *Illinois School Journal* 1 [April, 1882]: 18ff.)

[57] Samuel R. Hall, *Lectures on School-Keeping* (Boston, 1829). Hall specified three elements necessary for the preparation of teachers: they must learn "the necessary branches of literature"; they must be "acquainted with the science of *teaching*"; and, finally, they required instruction in "the mode of *governing* a school with success" (p. iv). See also his introductory lecture dealing with the "*science of teaching*" (p. 13).

gaining a kind of teaching experience in the course of his own preparation.

The real normal school movement thus took its rise from a recognition of the fact (by now obvious, but then only partly glimpsed) that the form of what we already know and the form by means of which we *came to know* anything are not necessarily the same. The ground of this distinction was at first almost purely philosophical; only later did it become empirical as well. The American normal schools were capable of dealing with this distinction adequately in its earlier philosophical stage. But the fact that their curricula were shaped by the content the teacher was to impart narrowed radically their own development and rendered them nearly incapable of either enlarging their intellectual scope or deepening their level of operation.[58]

It is difficult if not patently absurd to fault them, however. In the middle years of the nineteenth century, it was not at all clear what an empirical science of education would look like anyway. It had, in part, to await such as that of Wundt in Germany in the late 1870's, and that of his American disciples, such as Titchener and Hall and others, in the 1880's and 1890's. Thus it was in fact impossible for professional education to move to Gregory's third stage of development (its implementation as a science at the university level) until there was agreement upon what it was, and until there were experimental scientific disciplines clearly related to its peculiar range of phenomena.[59] Furthermore, the fact of the matter was that this pro-

[58] For example, David Felmley, "The Development of the Course of Study," in Illinois State University [Faculty Committee], *Semi-Centennial History of the Illinois State Normal University, 1857–1907* ([Normal,] 1907), pp. 54–62. As William L. Pillsbury had put it, "It is not to be expected that a Normal school should afford a very complete course of study in the natural sciences; it should, however, teach the elements of [the] branches according to the true methods, so that its pupils may become qualified to teach others in turn." The normal was to teach its students *what* they were to teach, *in the manner* they were to teach it. That was the nub of the process. While this may have been true of the normals, it was already being disputed within them, as we shall see (17th SSPI [1888], p. CIV).

[59] Walter S. Monroe, *Teaching-Learning Theory and Teacher Education, 1890–1950* (Urbana, 1952). Some of the early laboratory psychologists (including Titchener) disapproved of the appropriation of their methods and studies by pedagogical interests. Hugo Munsterberg of Harvard dismissed their efforts as "cheap and vulgar." (See his "Psychology and Education," *Educational Review* 16 [September, 1898]: 116; and "The Dangers from Experimental Psychology," *Atlantic Monthly* 81 [February, 1898]: 165.) By 1909, however, Munsterberg had experienced a timely conversion. Suggesting that he had only opposed the *pre-*

cess of definition within pedagogy as a field of inquiry could not be terminated by a neat resolution. What the controlling empirical disciplines should be—whether psychology, sociology, or something else—what their relation to the traditional philosophical and historical inquiries was, and what "university level" study or research really meant, could not be specified cavalierly.[60] (Indeed, there is not yet a settlement in the middle of the twentieth century.) As a consequence, education at the university level began, and has remained, a dynamic, highly tentative pursuit, an attempt to fashion an ideal rather than the process of embodying one already accepted.

In sum, then, the substantive matter required for the preparation of common school teachers until nearly the close of the nineteenth century was inappropriate as a university responsibility both theoretically and practically and both in form and content. Until it increased in scope and sophistication, there was no need for the university to take a hand.[61] And, until any given university had attained

mature use of psychology, he found it possible to issue his own *Psychology and the Teacher* (New York, 1909). (See esp. p. viii.) William James likewise cautioned against generating the "art" of education from "the science of the mind's laws." ("Psychology and the Teaching Art," Ch. 1 of *Talks to Teachers on Psychology,* new ed. [New York, 1939], pp. 3–14.)

For the development of psychology, see Cremin, *Transformation,* pp. 100ff., and Edwin G. Boring, *A History of Experimental Psychology,* 2nd ed. (New York, 1950), esp. Chs. 14–16, 20.

[60] Comparing or contrasting pedagogical work between colleges and normal schools, or between institutions within those categories, before at least 1900, is extremely risky. It is in fact virtually impossible to generalize, since the categorizations and the schools themselves varied enormously. The word "college," and even "university," had little meaning until well into the twentieth century, as even a cursory examination of higher educational history will show. Noting the increasing incidence of "college" work in pedagogy at the beginning of the 1890's, the U.S. Commissioner of Education was also compelled to observe that any "intelligent graduate of a thoroughly taught high school" who had "attentively" read Compayre, Sully, and something on "methods and management" might very well "graduate immediately, and with honor, from the great majority of the normal departments or teachers courses of our colleges or universities." (*Report of the Commissioner of Education* [1889–90], p. 1020. Cf. citation and comment in Pangburn, *Evolution of the American Teachers College,* pp. 20ff.)

[61] There were two additional factors of considerable consequence. The constant shortage of teachers made it possible for less than thoroughly prepared teachers to secure employment at virtually any point in their educational careers. This was a continuous complaint of the normal schools, but see, for example, Pangburn, *Evolution of the American Teachers College,* p. 7. Second, the concept of the high school was itself in the process of formation. As long as it involved principally the traditional content, its personnel could be drawn from the colleges and neither they nor the universities needed to supply any professional ex-

sufficient development in the requisite areas of inquiry, which were themselves only in the process of birth, there was no possibility for it to do so. Illinois Industrial University, as a new and struggling institution, torn between the utilitarian currents of the times and its constituency and the theoretical ideals of its leaders, could and did cherish no such hope.

John Milton Gregory's task was quite properly first to build a "higher institution" of a new kind, and that meant defining it out of the matrix of conflicting hopes and expectations which characterized all American higher education throughout most of the nineteenth century. As a consequence, there was a paradoxical need on the one hand to distinguish the new University clearly from all other educational levels, and on the other hand to accept responsibility for public problems which were obviously in part related to the growth of the common schools. To be what it could be and to become the kind of place in which it could make a unique contribution to the resolution of educational problems, the University had to deepen itself and open itself to true science. There was no point in trying, as Jonathan Baldwin Turner had put it in reference to one of the earlier schemes, "to attach a normal canoe to their college vessel." Instead, the University had to become, as one observer put it, the "capstone of the educational edifice." [62]

---

pertise. Pedagogical theory was too generally restricted to the elementary grades to require incorporation at the college or university level. Strong arguments for university-level work in pedagogy appeared early, however. See National Education Association, *Addresses and Proceedings* (1872), pp. 28–38; (1875), pp. 138–47; (1877), pp. 139–49; (1880), p. 178–89.

[62] Regent's report in 10th *Report* (1880), p. 184. To distinguish the University from high schools, and place it at the top of the state system, would tend naturally to preclude its accepting the teacher-preparation function. As Gregory put it, "it is the aim of a University to lead well prepared students to the summits of learning, rather than to collect and conduct great numbers of immature minds along the lower and elementary paths. It should not encounter the rivalry of the high schools by . . . attempting to do their work, but should inspire these high schools with a noble impulse to do their highest and best, by opening above them a field of learning so large, so rich, so attractive and so useful, as to give the high school pupils a new motive. . . ." In short, it was to be a "fit crown for the vast and costly system of public education" (10th *Report* [1881], p. 79).

A faintly imperial tone had been struck from the start. The original *Report of Committee on Courses of Study and Faculty for the Illinois Industrial University* (1867), reflecting on the University's enabling legislation, remarked: "The reasonable construction of the Statute is that while the University shall not comprehend the ordinary common school studies, it shall so arrange its terms of admission that the public school may be able to meet them, and that there be left no

Nowhere were these puzzling, if not contradictory, demands upon the University more clearly revealed than in the program of school visitation and accreditation created early in its career. In view of later developments, the program appears deceptively professional in orientation. At this time it was nothing of the sort, although much later a quasi-pedagogical function came to be something of an intrinsic element. During its first twenty years, the University could not hope to distinguish itself from the lower schools as long as it was dependent upon the kind of students they were forced to turn out. Since most of its prospective attenders had only the common branches with some little work beyond, Illinois Industrial University required a preparatory department on its own campus. Only when it had enlarged and raised the slowly growing high school movement in the state could it hope to realize its own potential level of operation and restrict its efforts to true university interests. As a consequence, it deputated the Regent, or some other faculty member, to visit and accredit secondary schools, not so much to benefit them—though, of course, it did, and they hoped it would—as to protect its own position. The program was enormously time-consuming since the reports were considered individually by the faculty, and it was never really successful. It gained few students for the University, and it did little to influence the few high schools, particularly since the possibility of their educational elevation was dependent on more than exhortation.[63]

Thus, given the struggling and still ambiguous condition of the new University, the kinds of problems posed by the particular level of development which the common school system had reached, and the impossibility of specifying the direction in which education as a theoretical discipline should move, Illinois Industrial University could neither discern nor fulfill any clear responsibility. For all of John Milton Gregory's pedagogical experience and vision, the University could

---

unbridged chasm betwen the body of the State School System and the University at its head." For this *Report*, which was also published separately, see 1st *Report* (1868); also reprinted in Richard A. Hatch, comp., *Some Founding Papers of the University of Illinois* (Urbana, 1967), pp. 73-97. (In this source, the quotation is at p. 86.) As late as 1925, this passage was being cited as the charter for the University's authority over the high schools. See the University of Illinois, *Proceedings of the High School Conference of November 19, 20, and 21, 1925* ("University of Illinois Bulletin, Vol, XXIII, No. 27, Mar. 8, 1926"; Urbana, 1926), p. 11.

[63] This is clearly shown in the "Faculty Record," vol. I, esp. pp. 227-29, 239, 253, 275ff., 287, 291; III, 337. Cf. Stephens, MS history, 2-35.

at best define and prepare itself. The possibility of its achieving a distinctive role in advancing the public educational interests of the state was dependent upon certain crucial developments and factors which could be brought about only with the passage of time.

CHAPTER 3

❧ *False Dawn*

When the State Teachers' Association convened in 1889, the school problem and the apparatus designed for resolving it had become enormously more complex. Gone were the simple elements of the recent past: the scattering of tiny, isolated district schools, numbering in the thousands but nearly as various in quality; the thin sprinkling of academies and "high schools" (or "high school departments"), and the relatively numerous but struggling colleges. The base, the common schools, remained; but to this there had been added a new rapidly expanding secondary educational enterprise, a growing normal school system, and a state university about to come into its own.

Witness to this growing complexity was borne by the fact that the meeting of the Association, among its other accomplishments, included the establishment of a "college section." To signal this auspicious development Selim Hobart Peabody, second Regent of Illinois Industrial University, recently restyled the University of Illinois to preclude its all too prevalent confusion with a penal institution, was chosen to deliver an inaugural address. Regent Peabody saw that the new complexity which characterized educational development required careful ordering. The elements of a rapidly proliferating school system must be interwoven in terms of the tasks that faced it, and these tasks themselves were so bewilderingly complex and threatening that only a popular military metaphor could convey the urgency of the occasion. "We must," said Peabody, "organize our efforts as meticulously as we would organize an army."[1] The clear demand was for a "Grand Educational Army of the Republic" in which each division would bear its part. His address gave evidence that the University of Illinois was now ready to accept its responsibility for marshaling the educational troops. The University had come to accept this role only gradually, and its strategy—if indeed there was any—was still vague and sometimes even contradictory, but it was prepared to join battle. The events and factors which shaped its entry, principally the expansion of secondary education and the new place of science in the curriculum, and the entry itself, will be the concern of this chapter.

The growth of the American high school during the last third of the nineteenth century was extraordinary, and it affected every corner of the nation. There were 1,026 high schools in the entire United States in 1870, and they enrolled some 72,000 students. By the end of the century, the number of secondary schools had increased nearly sixfold, and their enrollment was nearly 520,000.[2]

The rapid expansion of secondary education during the last thirty years of the nineteenth century was a distinct national movement. In part, it represented a strong resurgence of the belief that public education—as quite consciously opposed to private or parochial education, a manifestation of the growing fear of Catholicism—was the answer to virtually every problem for virtually every man. On the one hand, a high school education was useful, perhaps even essential now, for the individual's advancement in an increasingly technological society. As one observer put it, the oxcart driver had been replaced by the locomotive engineer. But, on the other hand, education also had a clear political and social role. In its more extreme form this state-oriented function could even contradict American education's traditional parallel concern for the individual. Peabody, in sympathy with the general admiration for things German, remarked that the German educational system lay behind the German army and its ad-

---

[1] Speeches and Sermons (1889), Peabody Papers. Quotation is from "Inaugural," p. 2.
[2] John S. Brubacher and S. Willis Rudy, *Higher Education in Transition*, p. 164.

mirable efficiency.[3] C. H. Parkhurst, writing in *The Forum* in the late 1880's, maintained that the "public schools are an invention of the state, to be operated only in the interests of the state. The state has no proper concern for individuals except insofar as it judges their good to affect its own interests." [4]

In particular, the school system was seen as an essential tool for resolving certain crucial social problems now alarmingly evident. The problem of a growing urbanism was recognized, and that embraced the concomitant problem of assimilating the vast immigrant population. Parkhurst called the public schools the "digestive machinery, the stomach of the body politic." [5] Peabody himself, in a widely repeated speech, proclaimed that education in general and secondary education in particular served as "the great furnace of assimilation." [6] Extending his metaphor, one would presume that the purpose of American public education was to burn off the dross of "foreign" culture and recast the resulting amalgam into the true American mold. (Such an extension is not unlike many of Peabody's publicly expressed sentiments.) Furthermore, as Peabody told the State Teachers' Association in his 1889 address, the high schools were an essential ingredient in the equalitarian ideal ostensibly shared by all Americans. The secondary schools would, he thought, strike a fatal blow at the old educationally based class distinctions which still pervaded American social life by serving as colleges for the poor.[7]

The high school picture in Illinois mirrored the national development. In 1870 there were 108 public high schools, according to the first official reporting—a practice begun by the state of Illinois. State Superintendent Newton D. Bateman noted that most were special corporations, organized under local boards of education as their own projects, but "several" were now being developed under the provisions of the general school law.[8] By the 1877–78 biennium, the num-

---

[3] "The Duty of the State to Its University," p. 15, Peabody Papers. The exact quotation is interesting: "The organization of the German army has its roots in the German schools." Having argued that education is at its best where, as in Germany, it is "the foster child of the State" (p. 9), Peabody went on to illustrate the difficulties of education: "You cannot make a Gladstone as you erect a cathedral, or construct a Bismarck as you build or equip an ironclad" (p. 12).

[4] "What Shall the Public Schools Teach?" *Forum* 5 (March-August, 1888): 47.

[5] Ibid.

[6] "The Use of It," p. 22, Peabody Papers.

[7] "The Relation of the High Schools to the Colleges," esp. pp. 3, 9, 12, Peabody Papers.

[8] 8th SSPI (1870), p. 2.

ber had climbed only to 128, although enrollments were generally on the increase.[9] The relative instability of these institutions (and possibly the difficulties of collecting accurate data as well) are reflected in the fact that there were only 115 actually reported for 1881. But the new trend began to make itself evident by 1884, when the number of secondary institutions jumped to 164.[10]

In the mid-1880's there were attempts to take stock, and concerned citizens in many quarters began to ask both about the current state of the high schools and their future role. The 169 public high schools now enrolled (in 1886) 13,522 students, although only 1,517 were able to persevere through graduation. The secondary school teaching force then numbered 475 public servants who labored at monthly wages ranging from $45.75 to an unusually high $175 (paid to the two teachers at Macomb and Jerseyville). Their buildings and their tools were still little more than rudimentary. Most of these secondary schools were still only rooms annexed to the common schools of the principal, more flourishing towns. But there was by now a concerted effort to get libraries into them. "Libraries" far too often meant only random collections of cast-off books, but in some cases at least the number in these collections was impressive. Springfield High School had over 3,000 volumes, and the prominent Englewood High School nearly 1,500. But provisions such as these, as with everything else, were radically unequal. Nearly 25 percent of the some 41,000 volumes across the state were in just seven of the 169 schools. (The three Champaign-Urbana high schools shared only 1,100 volumes, for example.) [11]

The "typical" high school—dangerous as such a fiction is in the light of the extreme range of conditions—enrolled around eighty students. In any given year, only about 10 percent managed to graduate. Many high schools could offer but the first two years, although some also had a fifth year, customarily a "normal department." Usually there were two to perhaps as many as seven or eight teachers who covered all these grades, though a number of one-man operations persisted. The "average" library had less than 250 volumes.

There was, however, no doubt that the high school was here to stay. The general populace had come to regard it as a normal extension of the educational process, at least for those who could afford

9 12th SSPI (1878), p. 112.
10 14th SSPI (1882), p. IX; 15th (1884), p. XVIII.
11 16th SSPI (1886), pp. 194, 255, 260.

it. (Since most high schools were only in principal towns, the still largely rural population had to treat them virtually as boarding schools.) And businessmen were coming to find them useful to their interests, a clear sign that their provision would increase. Although the merchant classes of Adams County, for example, were pressing for a more utilitarian curriculum rather than the vestigial classicism which persisted in high schools everywhere, their interest meant that the schools were being taken seriously.[12] In 1888, State Superintendent Richard Edwards took a broad look at the Illinois school system and asked whether the public schools ought only teach the "rudiments" of knowledge. It was, he said, the state's "purpose in establishing the free school . . . so to improve the intelligence and the morals of the rising generation, that when that generation shall become the ruling power in the land, its rule shall be intelligent, virtuous and just." If that purpose was to be achieved, a further question needed to be posed: where should their education "stop"? Since both knowledge and the need for knowledge, at every level of life, were daily increasing, the high school had become not a desideratum but a necessity. It must not, he said, be "abolished"—which suggests that there were some still unconvinced.[13]

The best way to assure the future of the high school was to increase its quality, and the best way to improve that was to enlarge the basis of support. At the time the old school districts, especially in the predominately rural areas, were largely incapable of supporting any true secondary school. The best strategy seemed to be to move for a township-based high school. Educational leaders, including the University of Illinois, whose stake was considerable, applied themselves to this cause vigorously. The first township high school was Princeton, which had achieved that distinction by 1865. By 1886, there were only nine more, but the movement was underway.[14]

At the beginning of the 1890's, there were 208 high schools, of which over 100 had four-year programs. They enrolled nearly 18,000 students and graduated some 2,200 (of whom nearly three-quarters

[12] So reported the superintendent of Adams County. Having castigated parochial schools as "obstacles to progress," he conveyed the local businessmen's complaint that the public schools were not sufficiently "utilitarian." They were demanding changes (17th SSPI [1888], pp. 99ff.).

[13] "Ought the Public Schools to Teach Only the Rudiments of Knowledge?" in 17th SSPI (1888), p. cxcvii.

[14] Ibid., p. cxcviii. Cf. the emphasis on developing township high schools by Superintendent Henry Raab in 15th SSPI (1884), passim.

were women, it should be noted). Although Chicago's largest high school, West Division, had twenty-eight teachers, the total force of 612 averaged out to little more than three per school. And still only thirty had separate buildings.[15] By 1896, the total number of schools had risen nearly 50 percent (to 272) and the teaching force had nearly doubled. Forty-four enjoyed separate buildings. More than 30,000 were now enrolled, although still largely at the first- and second-year level. The following table is instructive.[16]

ILLINOIS HIGH SCHOOL ENROLLMENT — 1896[17]

	Year					
	First	Second	Third	Fourth	Fifth	Grads
Male	5,100[a]	3,100	2,000	1,000	145	1,100
Female	7,800	5,200	3,700	2,300	180	2,600
Total	12,900	8,300	5,700	3,300	325	3,700

a All figures have been rounded off for ease of comparison.

The "average" number of teachers was now a little over four, and the average enrollment was about 100. But averages now become rather dangerous, since the concentration in Cook County dominated the statistics. Only twenty-eight high schools had eight or more teachers, and almost exactly one-third of the force was employed by the twenty-four institutions lying within Cook County. Hyde Park High School alone had thirty-eight teachers. Without considering Cook County, which enrolled about 28 percent of the students, the average enrollment stood at about eighty-eight and the average teaching staff fell to 2.5 per high school.[18]

In any case, the need to supply some 1,100 competent secondary school teachers by the mid-1890's created a whole new dimension to the problem of teacher preparation in Illinois. The district school-teacher, who had usually received what little education he was likely to have at the high school, could not easily be promoted. Even his generally vigorous self-instruction would be inadequate, if quality was to be maintained. The total of the graduates of the normal schools —the majority of whom still destined themselves for the common

15 18th SSPI (1890), pp. 264, 269ff., xxix.
16 21st SSPI (1896), pp. 17ff., 28.
17 Ibid., pp. 420–34.
18 Ibid.

branches anyway—was pathetically inadequate. Expansion of the normal school system, both in quantity and quality, while feasible, was obviously time-consuming. The graduates of the colleges and better academies, while possibly suitably prepared in some respects, did not view secondary school teaching as an appealing future, in most cases. Thus it was to the growing state university that the attention of the educational world finally turned.

The need for an increase in the sheer number of teachers, however, was but one side of the problem. There was at the same time a radical change in emphasis in the secondary curriculum, as there was in the culture as a whole. That was the shift from a still classically oriented regimen to a new, scientific one. If the technological orientation which was coming to characterize American culture was to be deepened both individually and corporately, and if the parallel equalitarian trust of American society was to be realized, the shift was a necessity.

Science, both as a growingly prestigious academic discipline and as a cultural ideal, had long been influential in the United States. The scientific interests of the colonial period (especially in New England) and in the early national period were given slow but certain recognition even by the generally conservative academic establishment. William and Mary and Yale early extended curricular approbation, and the general educational and cultural ideals of Franklin, Jefferson, and such distinguished leaders as Thomas Cooper of South Carolina (among a considerable number of others) gained a wide influence.[19] The rhetoric of few public occasions failed to include a fervid apostrophe to science, along with religion and morality, as the hope of mankind. The link between science and the specific content and method of general education, however, was more strongly forged by Herbert Spencer than by any other single figure.[20] In four essays published in England between 1854 and 1859 and subsequently reissued as his volume on *Education*, Spencer dealt a death blow to the still rigidly classically oriented curriculum. Nor did these words come only to the ears of specialists. A great range of intelligent people were drawn to read him on account of his enormous general authority, and they fashioned their opinions by reference to his—as we saw, for example, in the case of Charles Shamel, in an obscure central Illinois community.

[19] Merle Curti, *The Growth of American Thought* (New York, 1951), pp. 123–77, 310–57; Cremin, *Transformation*, Ch. 4.
[20] Cf. Cremin, *Transformation*, p. 91.

Spencer argued that living, as a dynamic and interactive process, rather than learning, as an almost exclusively mental activity, was the chief aim of education. Given that principle, it was that which changed life that mattered, not that which "furnished" the mind, as the traditionalists were prone to say. Clearly, science dealt directly with the problems of life, and it consequently could and should be the very heart of the educative process. Spencer's convictions were taken up, applied, and reapplied by a succession of American cultural and educational leaders until a widespread movement that bore upon virtually every facet of American life resulted. The common schools, especially as they became truly public institutions and were forced to reckon with a national constituency, could not long remain untouched, and by the end of the Civil War they were already showing the effect of the new thrust.

The growth of science in the common school curriculum was gradual, and it began very early in the period. The "state certificate" or "diploma," created in 1861 to avoid the difficulties of the county examination system and as a recognition of the highest pedagogical competence, required the candidate to be examined in the "elementary principles" of anatomy, physiology, botany, zoology, and chemistry. These were "deemed essential to the highest success in some of the more recent and improved methods of primary instruction." [21] A casual glance at the examinations shows that such competence as was specified was rudimentary indeed, but it was the ideal. The requirements for demonstrating proficiency in this area, while still decidedly bookish, were materially strengthened in the changes inaugurated in the early 1870's to reform and update the certificate. The prospective examinee was advised to study the following in order to equip himself with the right answers. In anatomy, physiology, and hygiene, he should master Hooker or Draper, Youmans or Dalton; in botany, Gray's lessons; in zoology, Hooker or Tenney; in chemistry, Rolfe and Gillette's handbook, Cooley and Hooker; in natural philosophy, all the immediately preceding plus Quackenbos; and in astronomy, Rolfe and Gillette's handbook, Lockyer and Kiddle's short course. There was also an increased emphasis on mathematics, not merely as a disciplinary subject, but as a useful tool.[22]

[21] 7th SSPI (1868), pp. 87ff.
[22] 10th SSPI (1874), p. 113. As early as 1872, all those seeking certification as common school teachers were to be examined in the natural sciences. In 1874, this was amended to include only those who were seeking first-grade certificates.

The *Illinois School Master* for 1875 contained thirteen articles dealing with science. There were also numerous advertisements, notices, and reviews of works which dealt with methods for teaching the various sciences in the common schools or offered an increase of scientific knowledge to the teacher.[23] In one of the articles, E. A. Gastman discussed "The Natural Sciences in the Public Schools," pointing out that the recent provisions for science teaching had drawn widespread censure from the populace who feared that such frills would hamper "the efficiency of the instruction in what are generally considered the more fundamental and practical studies." [24] However, more science would result in better habits of observation, Gastman argued, which would then transfer to the student's literary inquiries, thus producing "more rapid progress in reading and spelling." The place for this work was at the elementary level. Since at that time few students could be expected to reach the high school level, only science in the common school would introduce the majority of the population to this essential area. The method, he thought, ought to be objective rather than bookish—"teach them to hunt for facts, but not in books"—and the interest aroused would confirm the validity of this procedure.[25] Yet books had their place. "What Cuvier, Agassiz, Darwin, Huxley, and scores of others have discovered, you nor your pupils can afford to be ignorant of." Even the school's moral aims would be advanced. In spite of the naturalism that might arise from such inquiries, it was easy to bring the pupil to the moral and theological lessons which could follow naturally from them. The laboratory, Gastman strongly affirmed, could be a place of worship.[26]

A decade later, Henry Raab, state superintendent of public instruction, asked, "What Can the Public Schools Do to Prepare Our Youth for the Work of Practical Life?" He found that a growingly technical society needed a competent labor force first of all, and that meant a new curriculum which would both convey the necessary knowledge and at the same time counteract the "rudeness, brutality, insubordination and frivolity—the disregard of all authority" which

---

But the requirements led to a marked rush for courses in the sciences (13th SSPI [1880], pp. 266–69).
[23] *Illinois Schoolmaster* 8 (1875): passim. The publication was owned and operated by two of Illinois State Normal's leading luminaries, John W. Cook and Edwin C. Hewett.
[24] Ibid., pp. 295ff.
[25] Ibid., p. 297.
[26] Ibid., p. 300.

he saw on the increase. For all of this, the school was now responsible. It must convey a whole new body of positive knowledge, Raab thought. Not only "the old three R's of primitive school culture" but natural history, natural philosophy (i.e., science), geography, and history. (It was the history which was to achieve the moral ends cited above.) Second, the school must advance a new "culture" which could achieve technical skill. And it must do this by equipping not just the teacher but the student with an appropriate grasp of method, and one which built upon his interest and self-activity.[27]

With very little fanfare, the revolution in the schools was in the making. People were beginning to discuss something called the "new education," and its leaders were waiting in the wings for the cues which would allow them to the limelight. In inquiring about what makes a good school, Henry Raab returned an answer in which pedagogical training was central, not peripheral. Why? If you ask a young prospective teacher what he intends to do, argued the superintendent, he will reply that he proposes to teach spelling, reading, writing and arithmetic. "Not one," all too unfortunately,

> will tell you that he intends to educate the children so that they may become intelligent and moral beings that may know what is right and wrong; that may do the former and shun the latter; that can help themselves and their fellow men; that will love their country and mankind. For this latter is what the common school must accomplish. Not how much arithmetic, grammar and geography is poured into the children's heads, but how good and strong men and women they have become! In this lies the difference between the old and the "new" education. The former took care of the branches to be taught, the latter considers the human being, the child, as the basis of its efforts. How to elevate the child to true manhood, to patriotism and good citizenship is the question today.

To view education differently, as centered in the child as the active principle, and as requiring social progress rather than private virtue as its criterion, meant a new approach to teacher preparation in which

[27] 16th SSPI (1886), p. cxxix. Raab noted that it was a new thing to hold the school responsible, but it was implicit in the school's new role. It need not, however, accept all the blame. There was a "general laxity of public morals" and also an increase of "socialistic, anarchistic and nihilistic doctrines." Essentially a conservative, the superintendent insisted that "repetitio est mater studiorium" and quoted Comenius, Plato, Goethe, and Benjamin Franklin (the last on the necessity of "polite and decorous conduct").

the sciences were not only a new element in the content, but instruments of teaching itself. What then, goes into *true* teacher preparation? Raab's answer was straightforward. Not only the subject matter but "the study of anthropology, of somatology and psychology in general, as well as ethics and sociology in particular." (He warned, however, against a "one-sided study of psychology," since man has also his "physiological" aspect—thus recording the largely mental emphasis the discipline then received.) [28]

By the mid-1890's the state examination for certification (relying in part upon the authority of the NEA's prestigious Committee of Ten) included up to eleven hours in the sciences, exclusive of mathematics. At the same time, English literature received only one and one-half hours, as did both general history and U.S. history. Clearly, the sciences were no longer mere counterweights in the curriculum; at least in the ideal, they were becoming a principal element.[29]

What was implicitly demanded, in this dual development of a whole new level of educational responsibility and a substantially new concept of what the curriculum should embrace, was a fundamentally different kind of teacher. In fact, it was becoming increasingly clear that the public educational system required two kinds of teachers, one for the elementary branches and another of a quite different sort for the high schools. There was, in the mid-1880's, no obvious source for this second kind of teacher, who required both professional educational expertise and specialized knowledge in the arts and sciences. In 1882, State Superintendent James P. Slade complained bitterly that the teaching force in the common schools was not only poor in quality but gravely deficient in quantity alone. He needed more than 4,000

[28] 15th SSPI (1884), pp. cxxivff. The first quotation is at cxxv, the second at cxxviii. Raab argues strongly here for more public normals, radically enlarged from their previous limitations.
Regent H. W. Everest of Southern Illinois State Normal University expressed strong reservations about the "New Education" (20th SSPI [1894], p. 21).
[29] 21st SSPI (1896), pp. 51ff. The examinations now call for discussion as well as for formal answers. The questions show a practical bent and stress the value of pedagogy. For example, in history the examinee is to "show the importance of Archaeology, Philology, and Ethnology in connection with History," discuss the Armada and show its relation to American history, give the history of the Homestead and Pullman strikes, and discuss the Monroe Doctrine—on the ground that it is now a matter of "agitation." He is still required to "recite" the career of the Duke of Alva in Holland, however. The candidate must also describe the qualifications of a good teacher of history, show how he would teach the Mexican War to seventh- and eighth-graders, and declare what professional organizations he had joined.

more teachers just to replace those who left, and they would have
to be provided by some state agency since there was no other source
equal to the problem. His proposed solution was to increase the number of normal schools.[30] Although the two then existing, Southern
Illinois Normal School and Illinois State Normal University, were
doing excellent work, at least two or three more were needed immediately. By 1886, Superintendent Raab proposed ten.[31] But for the
provision of the new kind of teacher, especially at the secondary
level, that solution was inadequate by itself.

While the normal schools and universities had done unparalleled
work in bringing about an interest in the sciences as a pedagogical
necessity and had valiantly attempted to furnish their graduates with
the necessary preparation, they were not as academic institutions capable of providing the requisite scientific knowledge. Their shape as
learning communities had been—and unfortunately would continue
to be for far too long—dictated by the structure of the common or
elementary branches and the pedagogical expertise appropriate to
them. They might, in their role of providing a general education for
prospective teachers, make available information about the sciences,
but they were not, by common definition, centers of scientific inquiry as such.

Superintendent Raab had placed a heavy burden on the normal
schools, existing or proposed, when he had so ably articulated the
new education as scientifically oriented (both in terms of content and
method). Having argued that both the "physical" and the "psychical"
factors of the child must be taken into account, he cautioned that "a
mere establishment of somatological and psychological principles is
not sufficient to form a basis for educational action and success; ethics
and sociology are to furnish a standard for the teachers work. The
aims of intellectual culture may be obtained by the application of
psychological principles, but the training of the will and moral cul-

[30] 14th SSPI (1882), pp. CI, CII. Admiration for the normal schools and their
graduates was, however, by no means universal. Superintendent Raab noted that,
contrary to European practice, non-normal school personnel were often preferred. He granted the pedantry which frequently resulted, and acknowledged
that normal school graduates were often bad teachers, but insisted that in principle they were the "salvation" of the schools. The untrained teacher's small stock
of content, loosely strung together, cannot "liberalize" the student, he argued, as
true education ought to do (20th SSPI [1894], pp. xcviff.). He also condemned
the current professional texts in education as mostly books of "tricks" (p. c).

[31] 16th SSPI (1886), p. ccxxxii. Note that he does not suggest the University as
a source.

ture must principally be governed by ethical and sociological principles.[32]

The good teacher, Raab insisted, will follow neither fad nor custom, but will base his efforts on a scientifically sound grasp of the situation. For example, "he will not attribute the failures of his pupils simply to their indolence and want of interest, but try to find whether they are not the consequences of his own lack of skill and other personal defects." He will *test* his work, and continue his own growth in understanding such matters. And the good normal school, from which he will come, will not just teach anthropology or psychology but will be itself based upon them in its own operation. Furthermore, such a school will be active in inquiry, exploring the mental disposition needed to learn, the child's development, the problems of perception, the differing effects upon children of their ages and situations in life, the psychological explanations of failure, and the problems of attention and interest! This was a new language, and doubtless an invitation to important progress in pedagogy, but it was indeed a burden too heavy for the existing normal structure to bear. It meant not only the sciences, but the scientific study of education itself. It was inconceivable that the creaking county normal departments could furnish such preparation. Even the premier institutions would require extensive strengthening to do so—if, indeed, they desired such a regimen. While many, perhaps even most, in the normal schools would have applauded Raab's intentions, there was little prospect (at least in Illinois) of their fulfillment.[33]

If science was, then, to become not merely something discussed but something done in the schools, and something which teachers not only knew about but used, they would require a wholly different kind of preparation. And that, we have suggested, implied a new locus for the giving of it. The teachers in the field perhaps saw this more clearly than anyone else. In December, 1885, the State Teachers' Association assembled at Springfield and petitioned for a new chair of pedagogy, not a new normal school. What was significant in their action was that they addressed their petition to the University, whose

[32] 15th SSPI (1884), p. cxxviii.
[33] Ibid., pp. cxxix. It is significant that Raab insisted also that this meant a new "model" school at the high school level for such exploration and training—something which the high school at Normal had not really fully achieved. (I.S.N.U. [Faculty Committee], *Semi-Centennial History*, pp. 48ff., 82–86. Cf. John W. Cook and James V. McHugh, *History of Illinois State Normal University* [Normal, 1882], pp. 219–22.)

Trustees (doubtless surprised) accepted it "cordially" and promised to consider the matter "at the earliest reasonable opportunity."[34] The University of Illinois had at last been drawn into a working relationship with the schools—a relationship which implied a presumed responsibility rather than an institutional interest.

Discerning an appropriate way of fulfilling that responsibility would not be an easy task, but it was at last on the agenda of the University's business. In reporting the teachers' petition to the Board of Trustees, Regent Peabody obliquely recognized what had brought it about. He emphasized that science for teachers was an especially important matter, requiring the strengthening of the College of Literature and Science. The College already offered a "peculiar training in scientific subjects as a foundation for teaching," he suggested. He noted further that "in this respect its field and scope is so different from those of the normal schools—invaluable as they are in the school system of the state. . . ." For this reason, Peabody thought, there could be no competition.[35] Unfortunately the state legislature did not see the matter so clearly, and, for the next biennium, the University's response to the Association's request was "frustrated by the action of legislative committees" which refused new funds. The University, still operating on a virtual shoestring, had no surplus to devote to the new enterprise, and so any concrete action was still some distance in the future.[36]

Under John Milton Gregory's patriarchal if not charismatic leadership, Illinois Industrial University had threaded its way through a

[34] 13th *Report* (1886), p. 97. (Full text provided.) It is interesting to note that just ten years previously (July 6-8, 1875) the "editors" and "proprietors" of the *Illinois Schoolmaster*, John W. Cook and Edwin C. Hewett, had visited Urbana: "We have been spending a couple of days under the shadow of 'The Industrial' in Champaign, and confess that we are 'full of it.'" They editorialized that Gregory was building a "broad and enduring work, and that "croakers must take back seats," now that he had shown what could be done. But the two distinguished leaders of schoolmen had seen no connection whatever between it and the schools whose problems concerned them. (*Illinois Schoolmaster* 8 [August, 1875]: 277.) The inside cover of that issue, however, advertises the *National Normal Reunion*, a journal which in fact strongly opposed "college methods" for preparing teachers. (See *National Normal Reunion* 21 [December, 1875].)

[35] 13th *Report* (1886), pp. 139ff. Peabody, while admitting the need to maintain science for teachers especially, really was more concerned with fostering literary study. He said that literature had played "Ishmael" to science's "Isaac." (Cf. 16th SSPI [1886], pp. 8ff.)

[36] 17th SSPI (1888), pp. 8ff.

confusing maze of issues. It had narrowly avoided an entirely utilitarian emphasis by dint of the Regent's crucial interpretation of the ambiguous provisions of the Land Grant Act, and hence had attempted, haltingly but relentlessly, to build up both pure science and literary studies as well as to meet the technical and agricultural needs of the state. It had weathered financial and political crises and gradually persuaded the legislature that the meager federal funds were not the end of the matter if a first-class university was in prospect. Its student body and faculty had also climbed gradually but steadily, although it attracted only a tiny percentage of the state's college-age population in its early years.[37]

Under the burden of so many difficulties and controversial issues, Gregory's effectiveness—his strength itself—diminished markedly by the end of the 1870's, and he finally resigned the regency in the spring of 1880. Less than two months later, on June 27, 1880, Selim Hobart Peabody, a former member of the faculty, was named to succeed him.[38] The new Regent's personality as well as his philosophy (an inviable mixture of the old and the new tradition, unfortunately articulated after the new was already achieving undeniable supremacy) did much to shape the University's slow and insensitive response to the challenge posed by the schools. Like Gregory, he had been a distinguished schoolman, and he was in addition a practicing scientist and popularizer of science. Yet he was, for all that, strangely removed from the educational situation and essentially less of the new age than Gregory. Born in Vermont in 1829, the son of a Baptist minister, he had attended Boston Latin School and the University of Vermont. He graduated from the latter in 1852, third in his class and with a distinguished record in mathematics and physics. He took up teaching for the next twenty-five years in Vermont, Pennsylvania, Wisconsin, Illinois, and Massachusetts, eventually becoming a high school principal and, in 1863, president of the Wisconsin State Teachers' Association. In 1878 he left his post as a physics teacher in Chicago's Central High School to accept the chair of mechanical engineering and physics at Illinois Industrial University, an appointment

---

[37] In 1870, for example, the University enrolled 388 students, but the college-age population of Illinois had already reached some 200,000. (Cf. Solberg, *University of Illinois*, p. 105.)

[38] For what follows, see Solberg, *University of Illinois*, pp. 215-22, and Katherine Peabody Girling, *Selim Hobart Peabody, a Biography* (Urbana, 1923), passim—although the latter is in some respects a case of special pleading.

he had declined at the institution's opening. He soon left, however, in 1880, to accept an editorial job in New York, from which he was called to become Regent.

At Illinois, Peabody set out to deemphasize the unstructured elective system which had characterized the course offerings during Gregory's tenure. His efforts in this direction gained him national prominence. He was named chairman of the Committee on Higher Education of the National Education Association, and in 1888 he issued a sharply critical report on that elective system. In spite of his scientific proficiency, his own educational philosophy was still distinctly oriented in disciplinary terms, and he openly preferred books to some of the newer pedagogical devices such as manual training courses and shop instruction.[39] Nonetheless, although enrollment and financial stability at Illinois generally declined during his administration—a fact by no means attributable to him alone, of course—he did use his knowledge and influence to improve the natural sciences. He raided Illinois State Normal University, bringing to Urbana its chief scientific inspiration, Professor Stephen Forbes, who brought along the state Natural History Laboratory over which he had presided from his chair at Normal. It was chiefly in this respect that Peabody was, though quite unconsciously, readying the University for its future work with the schools, even if it was at the expense of the state's overburdened normal institutions.

Peabody's platform for educational progress, like Gregory's, centered in the development of a network of state normal schools, the expansion of secondary education, and the provision of institutes for practicing teachers.[40] He also saw the state's educational system as reaching its apex in the state university, though there is little if any evidence that he discerned any unique pedagogical role for it. This lack of discernment, in spite of his long record as a schoolman, further illustrates Peabody's ambiguous—if not anachronistic—stance. As we saw in dealing with Gregory, pedagogy had long since made a bid to be included among the disciplines proper to a university and it was, by the late 1880's, already partly successful in pressing its claim in much of the nation. The University of Iowa had established a professorship in the philosophy of education in 1873, and Michigan gave

---

[39] Peabody's contributions to the National Education Association may be found in its *Proceedings* for 1886 through 1889. See esp. vol. 27 (1888): 268–75.
[40] Girling, *Peabody*, Ch. 6, esp. pp. 83–97.

concrete existence to Gregory's earlier dreams in 1879 when William H. Payne was appointed to the "Chair of the Science and Art of Teaching." The latter's *Calendar* for 1880–81 explained that Payne's appointment constituted "recognition of the truth that the art of education had its correlative science, and that the processes of the schoolroom can become rational only by developing and teaching the principles that underlie these processes." [41] Before 1890, several other prestigious institutions had followed the lead: Wisconsin (1881); Johns Hopkins, Missouri, and North Carolina (1884); Cornell and Indiana (1886); and Clark University (1889).[42] In part, of course, this was a by-product of the burgeoning German graduate study and research ideal which had received vastly augmented impetus with the founding of Johns Hopkins in 1876. Some academic giants, such as Eliot, had their reservations; others of equal stature, such as Barnard and Butler of Columbia, Hall and Harper of Clark and Chicago, did not share them.[43] They agreed, as Merle Borrowman has put it, that "if the study of education were scholarly, and if it yielded insights for a more rational direction of human affairs, it, too, could demand a place in the circle of liberal arts and sciences." [44]

The year 1890 was perhaps the key year. Walter Scott Monroe later called it the period of "small beginnings" (and such they were), but there was no doubt that in the 1890's the thrust of pedagogy was toward the college and university level.[45] The 1890 meeting of the NEA heard that twenty-one of the nation's 361 colleges and universities had a pedagogical chair—though doubtless often only a paper one—and the U.S. Commissioner of Education discovered 114 "teach-

[41] Ibid., Ch. 2; Pangburn, *Evolution of the American Teachers College*, p. 21; *Calendar* cited in Robarts, "Rise of Educational Science," p. 30.

[42] Newton Edwards and Herman G. Richey, *The School in the American Social Order*, 2nd ed. (Boston, 1963), p. 605. Cf. Pangburn, *Evolution of the American Teachers College*, pp. 22–28.

[43] Eliot reported that his faculty felt "but slight interest or confidence in what is ordinarily called pedagogy," but argued that "skillful teachers should be able to give some account of their methods." The quotation is from Pangburn, *Evolution of the American Teachers College*, p. 22. For the contrasting viewpoint, see Charles Kendall Adams, "The Teaching of Pedagogics in Colleges and Universities," *Academy* 3 (1888): 469–81; J. B. Sewall, "College Instruction in Pedagogy," *Academy* 4 (1889): 449–54; B. A. Hinsdale (who chiefly taught such courses at Michigan), "Pedagogical Chairs in Colleges and Universities," NEA *Proceedings* (1889): 559–68.

[44] Introductory essay in Borrowman, ed., *Teacher Education in America: A Documentary History*, p. 12.

[45] W. S. Monroe, *Teaching-Learning Theory*, Ch. 12. The quotation is from p. 308.

ers' courses" in 415 higher institutions.[46] Shortly after, there were thirty-one actual professorships of education and more than forty more in which pedagogy was linked to some other subject, usually philosophy but sometimes psychology.[47] Increasingly, important institutions (many located close to the University of Illinois) would begin such work: California in 1892, Minnesota in 1893, Nebraska in 1895, and Northwestern in 1898. New York University had offered graduate-level study in pedagogy in 1887–88, and it found the results so "salutary" that the first graduate school for pedagogy was promptly established in 1890.[48] By 1895, the subcommittee on the training of teachers of the enormously influential NEA Committee of Fifteen had made the issue quite clear: "Success in teaching depends upon conformity to principles, and these principles are not a part of the mental equipment of every educated person." Consequently, the college and university ought to provide instruction in "the science of teaching" and the "art of teaching." [49] Not only content but some grasp of method, and both at the university level, were indicated.

Those in power at the University of Illinois, however, showed only a modicum of awareness that any university, including Illinois, might have some responsibility for the building up of the common schools or the educational enterprise—as opposed to the regulation of them in the interests of the higher learning. When Peabody reported receiving the request of the State Teachers' Association, he lamely suggested that the University had always fulfilled something of that need. He remarked that "the subject has not been neglected, as much instruction is given in topics which would perhaps be transferred to such a teacher when one should be appointed." What did he mean by this? "The course of instruction in English and modern languages," he said, "with its line of theoretical and applied science, is especially

---

[46] Levi Seeley, "Pedagogical Training in Colleges Where There Is No Chair of Pedagogy," NEA *Proceedings* (1890): 673; U.S. Commissioner of Education, *Report* (1889–90), II, 1020.

[47] U.S. Commissioner of Education, *Report* (1891–92), II, 725ff. Eight others offered special lectures.

[48] Pangburn, *Evolution of the American Teachers College*, pp. 22–24; Willard S. Elsbree, *The American Teacher* (New York, 1939), p. 321. New York University's action was perhaps more a response to institutional needs than a case of professional leadership, however. The new school allowed the admission of women students at least in part to open up new financial avenues, and they needed something to study.

[49] "Report of Sub-Committee on the Training of Teachers," NEA *Proceedings* (1895): 238–59.

a teacher's course, and as such has been largely accepted especially by the ladies." [50] It could not, however, have been very "largely accepted," even by the ladies. In the institution's first twenty years, Peabody himself recorded, some 3,000 students had been served—i.e., had attended for one reason or another, including at the preparatory level. Of these, some 2,100 had actually matriculated and 485 had graduated. Yet Peabody could point to only sixty-one as actually teaching in any capacity.[51]

The "service" orientation which bulked so large in early apologies for the University did not extend in any serious way to the common schools. In addressing the State Teachers' Association, as late as 1885, on the purposes the University should serve, Peabody could offer no real encouragement in their obvious predicament. All education, he argued, ran in "two broad streams," both essential to bringing humanity to perfection. One was "exhuberant with youth," aiming toward power over nature by means of experiment and observation—the scientific and technical. The other—the "first"—was "venerable by age and glorious with the grand fruitage of many generations of scholars and thinkers, whose wisdom and culture have illuminated and sweetened the civilization of progessive centuries. Its objective purpose has been the growth of the intellectual and moral faculties of man and mankind, to appease the old hunger for the knowledge of good and evil, to build up the inner and spiritual life of man and thus by the noblest transfiguration to bring him nearest to that God in whose

[50] Regent's report, 16th SSPI (1886), p. 8. Ladies were, of course, relatively few in number in any case. Peabody was still making excuses rather than pointing to actions the following year. He gave passing recognition to the centrality of scientific competence as the causal factor when he reported (rather without foundation) that "very many of the graduates of the University become teachers, especially of the natural sciences, and for their benefit an enlarged course in pedagogy seems very desirable" (17th SSPI [1888], p. 9). The Regent's report in toto reveals clearly his essential conservatism in educational matters.

[51] 16th SSPI (1886), pp. 9–11. The *Catalogue* (1885–86) showed that thirty-three men and twenty-eight women had become teachers, but whether as a permanent vocation is, of course, not reported. (See pp. 99–111; the occupations are listed on p. 111.) Previous figures gave even less comfort: in 1882, fifty (of all graduates since the first full "class," in 1872) had been listed as teaching; but note that, whereas in 1876 thirty-three had been listed as then teaching, only eighteen of those were still doing so in 1882 (11th *Report* [1882], pp. 7–12). Peabody claimed that 20 percent of all graduates from 1872–85 were teaching, but the figure seems highly dubious. (See "The University of Illinois" [an address, significantly, to the Illinois State Teachers' Association, 1885], p. 24, Peabody Papers.) The *Illini* (June 8, 1881) notes that of the thirty-six men and ten women in the class of 1881, only three intended to teach.

image he was created." [52] That purpose, Peabody continued, would be accomplished not by science or technology but by "the humanities, of which thinking has been the central element," and "language as the vehicle of thought . . . mathematics and logic, inductive and deductive, as the methods of thought; philosophy, art, law, ethics, religion, the spiritual nature of man and of God as the highest and noblest objects of thought." [53] In a word, the schools' salvation lay in the classical curriculum. He made his loyalty unequivocally clear by insisting that the modern languages *could* never replace the old.[54] As was plain to all, he remarked on another occasion, it was this education which differentiated the cultured Englishman or Frenchman from the "rude savage who paddles his canoe on the Congo or Orinoco." It could even result in the creation of the newest and highest exemplar of all, a Bismarck, at least when freed from its narrowly ecclesiastical and individualistic past and properly linked to the state.[55] (Mirroring the nineteenth-century conflict between individualism and society, he severely castigated Thoreau for having "consorted with sparrows and blue jays" in violation of the iron law of "self-preservation" which required society.) [56]

The implications of all this for the high school were clear, according

[52] "The University of Illinois," an address to the Illinois State Teachers' Association (December 28, 1885), p. 5, Peabody Papers.

[53] Ibid.

[54] Peabody went on to stress science and service (see pp. 6, 25), but he also insisted that high school graduates needed Latin: "We care not a fig for what Caesar, or Cicero, or Virgil said, for itself, but we do want that the exact idea which the author had in his mind, and spoke in Latin, should be expressed in sharp, idiomatic English." The Regent allowed that in theory this might be achieved through modern language study, but, alas, he had "never known it so secured" (p. 26).

[55] "The Duty of the State to Higher Education," pp. 9, 10, 23, Peabody Papers. Peabody frequently criticized the South, as in this address, for its failure to unite education and the state more thoroughly and rapidly.

[56] Ibid., p. 2. If Peabody disliked antisocial individualism, its near relative, poverty, had at least one virtue—it compelled men to work hard, and those who worked hard became smart and rich, a very good thing indeed. He liked students who came from "the obscurity of humblest poverty." Eastern colleges once had "students of scanty means, but of large brains," he argued, but these institutions were now growing wealthy and (consequently) effete.

What state education does is to provide an opportunity for the poor to mix and rise. The Regent did note that rich men—the Drews, Vanderbilts, Vassars, Durants, Fields, and Leiters he instanced as examples—had a tendency to work at getting richer and to put off educational philanthropy to "the twilight of life's day." That was why public education had to intervene. The nation could ill afford the wait. The curious logic of his argument did not appear to bother Peabody (pp. 27–31).

to Peabody. The classical tradition of the humanities, divorced from certain of its dangerous tendencies, supplemented by the sciences, and joined to the service of the state, was the prescription for raising the populace to enlightenment and virtue by means of the high school. These secondary institutions needed more mathematics and more science *and* more classical authors as well. English literature, a subject "most inconsequential in its results," was worthless. With characteristic vigor, he once remarked that a bit of Latin work was better than "a hatful of Browning." In short, the high school had to replace the academy, yet extend its benefits to the "masses." The University's role was preeminently to stand for this ideal and force its accomplishment by its standard of admission.[57]

While Peabody agreed that Urbana ought to expand its professional schools, it is clear that it was already exercising its chief pedagogical function as he and (apparently) most of his colleagues saw it.[58] The preparation of teachers was essentially a secondary-level operation with only a thin line of professionalization—though the line was already growing far more rapidly than Peabody could discern—separating the normal school from the high school. Since preparing teachers was essentially high school work, and university work must be distinguished from high school work for the benefit of the secondary school itself, the University in principle had to eschew the business of teacher education. In fact, any essay would also be politically dangerous, conflicting with established interests and confusing the legislators and the University's constituency.

Torn by such contradictory principles and tactical beliefs, it is less than surprising that it took Peabody more than five years to give substance to his verbal acceptance of the teachers' petition for a chair of pedagogy. A faint but growing interest in pedagogy was in fact coming to the fore even on the Urbana campus, however, and so the interim was not without accomplishment. For example, L. S. Ross was assigned a "post-graduate" course in the College of Natural Science by the faculty in September, 1889. The significant thing is that the course included, for the first time as far as one can tell, "pedagogics." As was customary in the still-bookish educational regimen which characterized the University, the course was outlined by assigning certain author-

---

[57] The Relation of the High Schools to the Colleges," an address to the high school section of the Illinois State Teachers' Association (1889), pp. 16–24, Peabody Papers. (The quotation is from p. 23.)

[58] "The University of Illinois," passim, esp. pp. 25ff., Peabody Papers.

itative works. The principal element comprised standard texts in biology and zoology, but to these were joined Compayré's *History of Education,* Bain's *Education as a Science,* and Rosenkranz's *Philosophy of Education,* with miscellaneous matter assigned on special methods. Who was to superintend this "minor" area is not recorded, but there were many members of the faculty who had had such pedagogical training themselves. In any case, the course appears to be the first example of a specialist in what might now be called "science education" trained at the University.[59]

The problem of finances, which Peabody had cited as the chief obstruction to the University's entry into the pedagogical field, was relieved by the federal government. On August 30, 1890, Congress appropriated more land grant funds. At the September session of the Board of Trustees, Peabody brought four recommendations as to their deployment which he felt were in sympathy with the original intent of the Act, and a fifth which would augment "the *literary* side of the University." That was the significant context for proposing a chair of pedagogy, or "as [Peabody] should prefer to name it, a chair of psychology and pedagogy." The Board promptly agreed, and on September 23, 1890, authorized a professor of psychology. By early December, Peabody reported his mission accomplished. Charles De-Garmo, then occupying the chair of modern languages at Illinois State Normal University, had accepted appointment to the new post and would assume his duties on January 1, 1891. Pedagogy, or psychology (in fact both), had arrived on the campus.[60]

The move was widely noted and praised. The *Illini* hailed the establishment of the chair, and DeGarmo's former president, John W. Cook, expressed the pleasure of the profession in his annual report. "The state university," he remarked, "has honored the teaching fraternity

---

[59] "Faculty Record," III, Sept. 27, 1889. Cf. 16th *Report* (1892), p. 53. Burrill, like many others of the University faculty, had undoubtedly studied and used all of these pedagogical works during his days at Illinois State Normal University. Professor Forbes, another of the University's most distinguished scientists, had also had such experience at Normal.

[60] 16th *Report* (1892), pp. 16–22, 32, 37. (For quotation, see pp. 20ff. Italics ours.) Peabody cushioned the blow by reporting that he found DeGarmo "a gentleman of mature years and sound scholarship, widely and well known throughout the state." He had, the Regent assured the trustees, "made preparation in this speciality in a prolonged study in Berlin and Heidelberg." DeGarmo was, properly, professor of modern languages and reading. He also worked regularly in the Normal University's elementary school. But all of that was perhaps better left unsaid in University circles. (See 17th SSPI [1888], p. LXII.)

by the establishment of an advanced pedagogical course of study and by the selection of a man so closely identified with popular education to conduct it." Perhaps unaware of the educational sympathies of Peabody and the majority of the faculty at Urbana, Cook did not see, apparently, that his reasons for being encouraged ran almost directly counter to the University's own conception of its responsibility to the "fraternity." The merest acquaintance of either party with the other would have suggested the difficulties ahead.[61]

Charles DeGarmo was indeed "closely identified with popular education." Born at Mukwanago, Wisconsin, in 1849, he had graduated from the Illinois State Normal University in 1873. For a time he served as a principal of a grade school, but he returned to Normal to begin work in their model school as an assistant in the training department. In 1883, DeGarmo succumbed to the German fever and journeyed to Halle to work for the Ph.D. He returned in 1886 "saturated with German philosophy" to take the chair from which he was called to Illinois.[62] Perhaps more important than any formal duties, he participated in the founding of a Faculty Club at Normal for the discussion of pedagogical problems. From this club, and from the less formal but perhaps even more influential Philosophical Club founded by George P. Brown next door in Bloomington, more than anywhere else, there bubbled up the revolutionary ferment which was to make such a marked change in American education. The club members battered the administration and the Normal University Board with proposals for reform, centered around the dropping of Rosencrantz's *Pedagogics*, the doubling of the time in practice teaching and reading, and opposing every form of memoriter drill and other archaic formalisms. These proposals were seldom accepted in detail and they frequently were merely anachronistically absorbed into the older structure—Dewey's *Psychology* was added to Rosencranz, for example. But the tide had turned, and it began to flow ever more strongly thereafter, not only at Normal but throughout the nation. Here was the source of the "Herbartian" revolution which in a brief decade demolished the preeminence of both a tired Hegelianism and

---

[61] *Illini*, November 8, 1890. Cook's remarks on DeGarmo's acceptance of the "chair of psychology, logic, and philosophy" are in the ISNU report, 18th SSPI (1890), p. LVII.

[62] 18th SSPI (1890), p. LVII; 12th SSPI (1878), p. 182; Harper, *Development of the Teachers College*, Chs. 14–16. The Faculty Club was reorganized as the "Normal Pedagogical Club" in 1893.

a desiccated Pestalozzian classicism which was by now completely unrecognizable as the product of the great Swiss educational reformer.[63]

Entering in the middle of the academic year, DeGarmo was precluded from establishing any program before his arrival. Perhaps in anticipation of his coming, the faculty had approved an optional course in "theory of teaching" the previous December. The catalogue issue of 1890–91 bore the first full-scale treatment of education as a part of University curriculum, and for the first time it offered a two-year program "especially for those who intend to enter the profession of teaching." The area, styled "Philosophy and Pedagogy," included "Educational Psychology," "Science of Instruction," "Logic" (as a basis of curricular theory), "Special Methods" for the "common branches," "Mental Science," "School Supervision," "History of Education," and "Philosophy of Education." In addition, "Introduction to Philosophy" and "History of Philosophy" were listed—the latter concentrating on the "rise of the spiritual view of the world" and ending with Kant. The course descriptions are a curious blend of mild Herbartianism, and (contrary to the general practice) only the course in philosophy of education notes any texts. Those specified were Bain and a somewhat surprising inclusion, Rosencranz, which suggests that their selection may not have been wholly the work of DeGarmo.[64]

DeGarmo attended his first general faculty meeting on January 19, 1891, without memorable incident. A few days later the natural science faculty (to which he properly belonged) asked him to arrange two terms of work in sociology and the principles of science, thus filling

[63] [ISNU] *Semi-Centennial History*, pp. 42, 54–62. David Felmley, a colleague of DeGarmo's and later long-term president of the Normal University, analyzed "The Development of the Course of Study." He claimed that the ferment had begun at Normal about 1881, and was particularly stimulated by the article of John Quincy Adams, Jr., in the *North American Review* that year which described Colonel Francis W. Parker's work in the schools at Quincy, Massachusetts. This helped create a mood for theoretical revolution, Felmley claimed, and led to a conscious subordination of the traditional academic pedagogy to the activity in the training school. As time went by, the continued "philosophizing" led them to see not only the shortcomings of the schools, but those of the Normal regimen. As a result, Dewey's *Psychology* was introduced, etc. Felmley was a participant and not merely a distant observer, and the order of events as he describes them (philosophical activity leading to a dual movement toward new practical and scientific emphases) suggests the heart of the new strategy. (See esp. pp. 59–61; cf. pp. 82ff.)

[64] "Faculty Record," III, December 8, 1890; *Catalogue* (1890–91), pp. 65–68.

two embarrassing lacunae in the University's curriculum which were incontestably university-level in dignity.[65] In February, the Regent and the Vice-President were charged to make arrangements for the forthcoming meeting of the State Teachers' Association on the campus—without reference, apparently, to DeGarmo. In May, he was sent, in the safe company of the Regent, to discuss the possibility of extension work in Chicago—a type of work in which Illinois State Normal had had considerable experience. He attended a few of the scheduled faculty meetings, without contributing anything the secretary recorded.[66] His resignation, received on September 9, 1891, merited all the éclat which had heralded his coming: not only was the generally customary resolution of appreciation not voted, his departure was not even recorded in the "Faculty Record." The Trustees noted his departure with "regret." This was possibly mingled with pique, since they first insisted that he could not leave before December inasmuch as they had already approved his appointment for the coming year.[67] All in all, a curious send-off for the president-elect of Swarthmore and a future distinguished professor at Cornell, then at the prime of his educational reputation.

The causes of Professor DeGarmo's rapid departure from the University are virtually impossible to trace. The University itself was in turmoil. Peabody's anachronistic style, contradictory ideas, and his growing impatience had brought student unrest to its severest level in the history of the institution. The faculty meetings attended by DeGarmo were almost entirely preoccupied by disciplinary problems. This may have contributed to his decision.[68] As a con-

[65] Ibid., January 19, 1891; Natural Science Faculty "Record," January 21, 1891, p. 31.
[66] "Faculty Record," III, February 23, May 21, June 5, 1891. DeGarmo did not attend at least four regular meetings.
[67] 16th Report (1892), p. 151. The Trustees later approved John P. Gordy to fill the post in psychology, but it apparently fell through (p. 225).
[68] Solberg suggests the faculty's disciplinary preoccupation was the probable cause (University of Illinois, p. 272n). This seems unlikely. In the first place, DeGarmo was used to dealing intimately with students, although the atmosphere at Urbana was doubtless less encouraging than at Normal in what were its halcyon years. Nor would the apparent coolness of the faculty have put him off, at least as such. He knew very well what to expect, and he had the courage of his convictions. He inveighed against those who "sneer at their own conceptions of what the study of pedagogy is good for" (NEA Proceedings [1892], pp. 772–80). For more positive evidence, we may note that as soon as he arrived at Swarthmore, he proposed a program much more intimately connected with the general academic program than anything ever contemplated at Illinois. (See his "Scope and Character of Pedagogical Work in Universities," ibid.) If he had such de-

sequence of student protest, now active alumni pressure, and in all probability faculty disaffection as well, Peabody himself was in effect forced to resign in June, 1891. He was quickly replaced by Thomas J. Burrill, professor of botany and horticulture, who proceeded quietly to right the badly listing academic ship while the search for a permanent president was on. Another schoolman, Burrill had, like DeGarmo, graduated from the state normal in 1862. He joined the University's original faculty from the Urbana school system as professor of algebra, and he had maintained both insight and sympathy with the school situation and the University's potential contribution. But Burrill did not take control in time to save DeGarmo—if indeed anyone could have.[69]

Insofar as DeGarmo's reasons come positively to light, they were shared, in correspondence and conversations, with his former colleagues, who formed a tightly knit cadre of educational evangelists wherever they might happen to be. We shall see that there is some evidence from that quarter. Alternatively, the start of the difficulty may be deduced from DeGarmo's often-stated principles and their obvious conflict with the conceptions of pedagogy and teacher preparation which then prevailed at the University—a deduction confirmed by subsequent events and the small body of positive evidence available.

DeGarmo was a Herbartian. The Herbartians were disciples of Johann Friedrich Herbart, a German philosopher who went to Konigsberg in 1809 and began to lecture in pedagogics as well as in philosophy. He had established a pedagogical seminary and a practice school in close theoretical and practical conjunction with it. A student, Karl Volkmar Stoy, had carried Herbart's principles and methods to Jena, where Stoy's work was carried on by Professor Rein, under whom several of the Normal Herbartians had studied. Although DeGarmo chose Halle rather than Jena and actually specialized in languages, he also encountered the Herbartianism which had taken hold there, and he began to utilize that instructional method in his work.

Herbart's monumental philosophical system, and the pedagogical

---

signs at Urbana, his brief experience seems more likely to have convinced him that they were simply impossible.

[69] Solberg, *University of Illinois*, pp. 319–25, 328–30. The famous Congregationalist minister, Washington Gladden, was also considered. He rejected the possibility, however, perhaps finding little of the "hope that sends a shining ray/ Far down the future's broad'ning way" at Urbana.

system derived from it, included an extremely complex and heavily (although almost entirely speculatively) psychological analysis. Herbart was the first to develop a teaching method (with special emphasis on moral training) based upon a psychological description of the learning process. In his approach, content and method were systematically integrated in terms of general principles which could be taught, extended, and applied, creating the basis of a general pedagogical method. While subsequent Herbartians tended to focus upon and proliferate the intricate theoretical basis of the system, DeGarmo and his colleagues manifestly did not. They quickly separated Herbart's practical principles from their abstract theoretical foundations. As B. A. Hinsdale pointed out, in his review of DeGarmo's first important book, *Herbart and the Herbartians,* "Refusing from the first to hold a brief for the author of the system, Dr. DeGarmo keeps his eye steadily on educational applications and educational outcomes." Like his colleagues, DeGarmo saw in Herbart not an abstract solution to metaphysical problems but a practical system which could free the educational world from the rote memory work and the bookish recitations of the day.[70]

It may be that Peabody mistakenly assumed that DeGarmo was a doctrinaire Herbartian psychologist, driven by the prestigious germanic thirst for abstruse scholarship, and on that account worthy of a university seat. In any case, he was not. He proposed to prepare teachers, and for that Herbartian principles offered a workable, teachable method. Most important of all, teaching teachers meant having children for them to teach, as Herbart and all his subsequent expositors had agreed, because teaching was an action, learned by doing it—at least in part.[71] DeGarmo had, in fact, believed this long before going abroad. He had argued "The Importance of Model Schools to Normals" in 1883, and his opinions were subsequently given wide distribution in the influential journal, *Education.*[72] He had exhorted the NEA to consider "The Place and Function of the Model School," again achieving widespread notoriety. There was no doubt that a model school was central to his every notion about pedagogical train-

[70] *Educational Review* (February, 1895): 193.
[71] For the best discussion of this important point, see Harper, *Development of the Teachers College,* Chs. 14–16. Cf. E. V. Johanningmeier and Henry C. Johnson, "Charles DeGarmo, Where Are You—Now That We Need You?" *Philosophy of Education 1969: Proceedings of the Twenty-fifth Annual Meeting of the Philosophy of Education Society* (Carbondale, Ill., 1969), pp. 190–99.
[72] *Education* 4 (November, 1885): 173ff.

ing and research.[73] At the University of Illinois, however, there was no one to teach. There was a dwindling preparatory department, but it was strictly ancillary to the University's entrance requirements, still rigidly classical in spirit. In fact, many of the faculty did not even approve of the use of the University facilities by the prep boys. There would, there could, be no "Herbartian" revolution in pedagogy at Urbana, for it was denied one of its central elements. Doubtless it seemed pointless to a Charles DeGarmo to stay, since there was an educational world outside eager to accept his leadership. Had he wished to expound and discuss Herbart, he would perhaps have been welcomed. His mistake was that he wished to prepare teachers.

The next appointment was a good deal safer. After only a brief hiatus, William Otterbein Krohn was appointed assistant professor of psychology and pedagogy on September 14, 1892.[74] Krohn, born in Ohio in 1868, had earned a Ph.D. at Yale in 1889 and studied briefly in Europe. He then headed the department of philosophy, psychology, and ethics at Adelbert College and Cleveland College for Women at Western Reserve University from 1889 to 1891. Following that, he had accepted a year's fellowship at Clark University, from whence he was recommended to Illinois.

When Krohn arrived, the *Catalogue* still bore the untaught entries designed by or for DeGarmo, but by the next year, its pages fairly bristled with pedagogical studies of properly university grade, now under the aegis of the College of Literature. In "Philosophy," Krohn offered six courses. Included were "Psychology" (using William James's *Briefer Course*), "History of Philosophy" emphasizing the post-Kantians and Herbert Spencer, and "Experimental Psychology." All carried a heavily psychological orientation. In "Pedagogy," there were six courses: first, "Educational Psychology," in which the students were promised a glimpse of "the child's mind, with special reference to its contents on entering school," all with the aid of Sully's *Teachers Handbook of Psychology*. Next followed "School Hygiene," emphasizing the school setting, furniture, buildings, etc. Then came "Philosophy of Education," primarily concentrating on Bain, Spencer, and Rosenkranz. Ancient, modern, and comparative education were dealt with in "History of Education." Next was "School Supervision," a course primarily designed to treat all the administrative matters

---

[73] NEA *Proceedings* (1884), pp. 47–53.
[74] 17th *Report* (1894), p. 44. His salary was $1,800. The chair of pedagogy, as such, was established June 7, 1893. (See p. 122.)

likely to come before the superintendent. Finally, there was "Pedagogical Seminary," for advanced students, conducted "in a somewhat informal manner" and based on the current literature. These fulsome offerings were supplemented by visiting lectures by Charles F. Thwing of Cleveland and Albion W. Small of Chicago.[75] Whatever its limitations, the effect of this program was felt almost immediately. The commencement program of 1893 showed several theses with a pedagogical theme, and the number of those who went into teaching climbed noticeably.[76]

Krohn's activities were by no means restricted to the campus. He actively cultivated the school interests of the state. In particular, as befitted his close association with G. Stanley Hall at Clark, the new "child study movement" attracted his enthusiastic patronage. While at the University, Krohn founded the Illinois Society for Child Study and served as editor for the *Child Study Monthly*. His lectures along these lines were celebrated and took him to every corner of Illinois, as well as many places around the nation. Everywhere he went, groups of interested teachers formed to continue the scientific study of the child.[77]

By the early 1890's, interscholastic athletics, as well as other activities, had begun to reach something of the level of importance they are accorded today. Each year this drew a throng to the "Interscholastic Meet," and that throng included large numbers of school administrators and teachers. In the spring of 1893, the faculty for the first time conceived of the idea of entertaining the principals present for the May meet at a reception. Professors Brownlee, Barton, and Krohn, all men close to the schools, were chosen to make the necessary arrangements.[78] This was perhaps the shadowy antecedent of the important High School Conferences, which became annual events some years later and flourished for many years. The Conferences, while originally in the interests of the University, came to have significance for educational policy within the state, as we shall see.

It was clear that Krohn's chief interests lay in the field of psychology, and, doubtless at his suggestion, the Trustee's Committee on Instruction separated the chairs of pedagogy and psychology in June

---

[75] *Catalogue* (1892–93), pp. 117–20.
[76] Talbot Papers, file for 1892–94.
[77] Several county superintendents praise the profit garnered from Krohn's visits and his book. (See 21st SSPI [1896], pp. 219ff., e.g., p. 235.) Some (a very few) disliked his work. (Cf. p. 239.)
[78] "Faculty Record," III, April 17, May 20, 1893.

of 1893.[79] Henceforth, at least on paper, psychology and pedagogy were free to go their separate ways. (They were to come together again before long.) The *Catalogue* of 1893 still bracketed the courses in economics, pedagogy, philosophy, and psychology as "the Philosophical Group," and it would be well into the next century before the separation would be genuine.[80]

The division of the area immediately raised the problem of continuing the work in education as such, and a new appointment had to be sought. The lot fell upon Frank McMurry, another leading Herbartian and a close friend and colleague of Charles DeGarmo. He was appointed professor of pedagogics in July, 1893, and began his work that September, still as a member of the faculty of science.[81] McMurry, born in Crawfordsville, Indiana, in 1862, had prepared at the high school department of the Illinois State Normal University, finishing in 1879. He then attended the University of Michigan and went abroad, where he studied at both Halle and Jena, receiving his Ph.D. from the latter in 1889. He served on the faculty at Normal as professor of pedagogy and as a training teacher for two years and then returned to Europe for further study at Geneva and Paris. On his return he accepted the post at Illinois. Regarded as perhaps the greatest classroom teacher of the Herbartian cadre, McMurry was considered behind the others as a theoretical exponent of the movement. He was characterized by a contemporary as *"the teacher,"* a man who "knew all that ever had been learned about good teaching, or all that ever would be learned about good teaching"—an opinion in which Dean James Earl Russell of Columbia heartily concurred.[82]

McMurry lost no time in reshaping the curriculum. Krohn continued to develop the work in psychology, still closely related to pedagogy. It now embraced eight courses—including the "Psychology of Crime," "a special study of the criminal as a morbid individual," and a new offering in abnormal psychology. The program was also characterized by an increasingly experimental emphasis and could rely upon Krohn's own newly published text.[83] In pedagogy, McMurry stated his aims straightforwardly: "to offer as much work in the

[79] 17th *Report* (1894), p. 122.
[80] *Catalogue* (1893–94), pp. 62–65.
[81] 17th *Report* (1894), s.v. July 5, 1893; "Faculty Record," III, September 8, 1893.
[82] Harper, *Development of the Teachers College*, pp. 207–9, 300; Teachers College *Record* 27 (November, 1926): 295.
[83] *Catalogue* (1893–94), pp. 141ff. Cf. *Illini* (May 8 [June 8], 1893).

theory and practice of teaching as a specialist in that line can accomplish" in a two-year program. There were eight courses, including a new introductory course, a course in special method which involved observation and perhaps some practice teaching in the local schools, and last, the crucial element in the Normal Herbartian strategy, "Teaching in the Model School." [84]

It appeared from this that McMurry had achieved what DeGarmo had been unable to accomplish—viz., recognition of the Herbartians' cherished principle that pedagogics was primarily concerned with teaching, and that learning to teach properly involved actual experience in the classroom. He was able to announce that by "recent action of the trustees of the University a model school has been established as a part of this department so that students now enjoy an excellent opportunity for applying the conclusions reached in the classroom and for studying children closely. Any students may have the privilege of teaching in this school who are qualified according to the rules of the University, for the courses in pedagogy; all such instructions will be under the constant supervision of teachers regularly employed for that purpose." Furthermore, graduates of the state normal schools would now be admitted with sufficient standing to begin at once the two-year course for the "University certificate." [85]

McMurry's eager anticipation of victory was not without foundation, if it was overly optimistic. The Acting Regent, Thomas J. Burrill, had tendered the Board of Trustees a surprisingly enthusiastic recommendation of the proposed school, on an analogy with other laboratory and research facilities, in March, 1894. He cited privately and publicly expressed professional demands and concluded that "conditions are ripe for it now" at the University. The Committee on Instruction, which included two distinguished schoolmen, responded quickly and affirmatively, and the Board approved their action.[86] The *Illini* lost no time in trumpeting the news, noting the significant development in an editorial a few days later. It announced that "a model school has been established . . . as an addition to the department of pedagogy." "Training in teaching" would be the principal function, and it would

[84] Ibid., pp. 75, 133ff.

[85] Ibid., p. 75.

[86] 17th *Report* (1894), p. 219, 229. It would be, Burrill said, for "the investigation of practical problems, for the practical application of theory, and for the actual experience [of] pupil teachers. . . ." Some 40 pupils, six to ten years of age, were to be involved. (*Illini* [January 24, 1894].) McMurry had even proposed two individuals as teachers. (See *Report*, p. 252.)

"call here students . . . who might otherwise go to normal schools." [87]

The enthusiasm was ill timed. By June, Burrill was writing his newly elected successor, Andrew Sloan Draper (who had not yet left Albany, New York, where he had been superintendent of public instruction) that Professor McMurry was "liable to leave us." "Attempts," he reported, "have been made to establish a practice school," but since the space occupied by the engineers was not available, due to building delays, the outlook was dim. Burrill suggested "postponing" the venture. Draper agreed. Within days, Burrill reported McMurry's resignation. The new engineering building would not be ready before October 1, if then; the prospects for the model school were bleak. It was, in fact, a closed issue until the arrival of William Chandler Bagley more than a decade later.[88]

The *Catalogue* of 1893–94 also promised, and in this case delivered, the first real summer session at the University.[89] As early as 1879, the faculty had turned down a primitive summer session proposal designed among other things to supplement the meager disciplinary attainments of teachers. (Individual instructors had been permitted to, and did, offer work on a special basis, however.) Developed by McMurry and staffed by Krohn and his elder brother, Charles A. McMurry (then teaching at Normal), the new summer pedagogical curriculum featured three foundational courses: "Pedagogics," a general introduction to Herbartian educational theory and practice; "Psychology"; and "Child Study." The last, by Professor Krohn, explored the "order of development of mental powers, content of mind at six years of age, mental economy and waste in school room, adolescence in relation to study," etc.[90] While apparently meeting a widespread need and demand, actual enrollments were disappointingly low, suggesting to the Board of Trustees that one instructor would suffice. The cause, attributable to an outbreak of smallpox, was beyond remedy by the department of pedagogy, but the experiment did not last beyond the following year.[91]

---

[87] *Illini* (March 22, 1894).

[88] Burrill to Draper, June 26, 1894, and Burrill to F. M. McKay, July 11, 1894, "Regent's Letterbook, 1879–94," II, pp. 253–55, 289ff. McMurry was elected April 13, 1894, and arrived on the campus August 1.

[89] *Catalogue* (1893–94), p. 84.

[90] Ibid., p. 163. The expression "contents of the mind," or some variant, was the trademark of G. Stanley Hall and his disciples.

[91] 17th *Report* (1894), p. 272. In contrast to the University's still campus-

Besides being charged with the development of pedagogy, Mc-Murry had been saddled with the now onerous responsibility of school visitation for accreditation purposes. By the 1890's, it was a very time-consuming project, and there was no end in sight. (Indeed, not until after World War II did the University cease its special accreditation program.) The number of accredited schools had risen from some fifty in 1888 to more than 150 by the end of the century, and they demanded continuous reexamination. While various faculty members still participated, it was now expected that the major share of the load would fall upon the professor of pedagogy. In his brief year, McMurry had been forced to spend more than a month on the road, visiting twenty-one schools. (Later, President Draper actually thought that, in addition to his enormous teaching load, the pedagogical professor could spend eight to ten weeks at the business—possibly substituting an instructor from the model school to exercise his classroom responsibilities.)

Doubtless, McMurry chafed under these burdensome duties, especially since the visitation program had no real pedagogical value. But it was the failure of the school which moved him to withdraw. McMurry left to become principal of the Franklin School at Buffalo, New York, which he served for a year before a three-year stint as professor of pedagogics and dean of the teachers' college at the University of Buffalo. He then finished his distinguished career at Columbia. As soon as he had arrived at the Franklin School, McMurry developed a highly novel experimental program which attracted considerable attention.[92] John W. Cook, still president of Illinois State Normal University, put his finger on the whole matter when he wrote: "Isn't it a pity what you are doing at Buffalo could not have been done in Champaign? I extremely lament that you had to go to New York to work out your ideas." In the long run, what had been the chief difficulty for DeGarmo had been the same for McMurry.[93]

---

centered program, the normal school professors were taking their expertise out into the state. John W. Cook reported that in the summer of 1894 the Illinois State Normal faculty had probably reached 2,500 teachers throughout the state by means of lectures, institutes, etc. Many of these professors had devoted most of their vacations to such service activities. (20th SSPI [1894], p. LVII.)

[92] Harper, *Development of the Teachers' College*, p. 209.

[93] John W. Cook to Frank M. McMurry, Jan. 6, 1896. Cook Papers, Illinois State University Archives. For McMurry's visitation duties, see 17th *Report* (1894), pp. 219ff.

In contrast to the approach at Illinois, Francis W. Parker was reporting from Cook County Normal School that "the work of [his] school [was] *all* concen-

The choice of a successor to McMurry appeared to be a simple matter. It was to be his brother Charles, who had enormously impressed his hosts during the summer session. Burrill had cooled to Frank during the intervening weeks. He confessed to F. M. McKay, a Trustee, that he used to think Frank was the better man, but he now thought that incorrect. Charles was more "self-assertive" but at the same time "not so quick to act." Furthermore, he had "written two or three small works of late that [had] obtained a great reputation among pedagogical people."[94] President Cook at Normal regarded him highly, Burrill also reported, and might not give him up willingly, although it appeared that Charles was prepared to accept for $2,000. President Draper had also been looking, however, in company with J. E. Armstrong, another Trustee and a Chicago schoolman. Burrill wrote Armstrong, criticizing the instructional committee's failure to meet "through want of concerted action," and the poor "financial provisions" for the situation, and reporting that Cook was indeed unwilling to surrender Charles McMurry. As a consequence, he said, "it may be your man will be preferable."[95] "Your man" was William Julius Eckoff, who was nominated to the Board immediately after the acceptance of Frank McMurry's resignation, August 1, 1894.[96]

Eckoff, a forty-one-year-old native of Hamburg, Germany, had been educated both here and abroad (including earning two doctorates at Columbia and New York Universities) and had served in several school and university posts. A German who came to America to study, Eckoff was currently professor of philosophy and pedagogy at Colorado University. The new professor of pedagogics was also an Herbartian, but of a far different sort from his predecessors. His interests were much more narrowly focused on the theoretical sub-

---

trated in the practice work." His approach was based on "the pedagogical theory of concentration," he said, and would probably draw the fire of those "who believe in product and not process." He also stressed heavily the role of psychology. It is the purpose of the school "to introduce the latest outcome of psychological research, to make a special study of each pupil, and without regard to quantity teaching, adapt the subject matter to individual conditions" (20th SSPI [1894], pp. 279ff. Italics ours).

[94] Burrill to F. M. McKay, July 11, 1894; cf. Burrill to Nelson W. Graham, July 11, 1894; Burrill to McKay, July 13, 1894. "Regent's Letterbook, 1879–94," II, pp. 289ff., 287ff., 299ff. Cf. Burrill to H. J. Barton, July 3, 1894, "Official Letterbook" II, p. 269.

[95] Burrill to McKay, July 11, 1894; Burrill to Armstrong, July 19, 1894. "Regents Letterbook, 1879–94," II, pp. 289ff., 318. Draper, elected on April 13, did not take charge until August 1, 1894.

[96] 17th *Report* (1894), p. 268.

structure of the eminently practical principles which occupied the attention of the McMurrys and DeGarmo. He lectured on "the more difficult or critical parts of Herbert Spencer's philosophy" and on some minor works of Herbart not previously accessible in translation. He also fashioned a popular treatise on Herbart's doctrine of sense perception, among other less important writings.

His effect upon the curriculum at Illinois was rapid and obvious, clearly reflected in elaborate catalogue descriptions which betokened his rather pedantic rigidity. The two basic courses were restyled "Didactics" and "Systematics," and they were proclaimed in the *Catalogue* itself as true "pedagogy of university grade." He included a course in the pedagogy of the natural sciences, based upon Spencer and with special help from the library holdings of the zoology department. Another, in Latin pedagogy, was offered in cooperation with the Latin department and was an exploration of Quintilian—not, apparently, a course in language method.[97]

The new professor explained the pedagogical department to the students and the public in the pages of the *Illini*. Asserting confidently that its "importance to the educational interests of the state need not be emphasized," Eckoff stressed that the department would be better equipped than ever. The Board had authorized purchases which would more than double the pedagogical collection and had been especially generous in providing works from Germany, France, and England. But, most important was the new pedagogical apparatus, faultlessly Herbartian, which the engineering department was working up.

> The increased equipment in books and apparatus will enable the department to reduce the study of educational history to a study of the educational classics themselves, with connective talks by the professor. What is, perhaps, of even greater importance, the equipment enables this department to give for the first time in the history of American education a complete and authentic exposition of the Herbartian system from the original works of Herbart and with the instruments devised by Herbart himself.

In mathematics, for example, where Eckoff believed the problem was reasoning and not memorization, the "mathematical faculty" would be stimulated. By means of the Herbartian devices, cube roots would become as "real" concepts as those of inch or foot in the minds of

[97] *Catalogue* (1894–95), pp. 149ff. For Eckoff's obvious pedantry, see Draper to Henry Raab, October 5, 1894, "Official Letterbook" II, p. 457.

aspiring students. Their "mathematical power of imagination and apperception" would be strengthened—for the want of which many a student had failed because he couldn't "see" the theorems properly. All in all, the outlook for education was rosy indeed. All pedagogical problems had been solved and Urbana was to be the American Mecca of the new educational prophets, with a *Ka'ba* carefully constructed by the University's engineers.[98]

Eckoff had been warned in advance that there was no model school. The observation work in the Urbana schools, a primitive forerunner of external practice-teaching arrangements, had been founded on a personal arrangement with McMurry; hence it, too, was inoperative. The Urbana schools apparently did not wish to continue it with a "stranger." [99] While generally favorable to a school, Eckoff made no attempt to press for one. The revived summer session saw but two courses, solidly Herbartian, in pedagogics and psychology. These were supplemented by a series of public lectures, of which President Draper himself gave six on "educational topics." Professor David Kinley, then of the economics department, gave three on "Socialism and Social Reform." One (apparently enough) on "Why and How We Breathe" was delivered by Professor Summers in physiology.[100]

But somehow, for all of his intense preoccupation with true university work, Eckoff was not well received. Both he and Krohn had managed to draw the ire of David Kinley in 1895. Dean of the College of Literature and Arts, but eventually to be President, Kinley found Krohn's image as a University representative within the state decidedly unsatisfactory, although there is considerable evidence that his judgment was overly harsh if not capricious.[101] Eckoff was in

---

[98] *Illini*, October 25, 1894; March 7, 1895. In the latter place, Eckoff also complained that both the University and the secondary schools of the state were not using the best texts.

[99] Burrill to Eckoff, September 4, 1894. "Regents' Letterbook, 1879–94," II, p. 392. Cf. 17th *Report* (1894), p. 219; 18th *Report* (1896), p. 20.

[100] *Catalogue* (1894–95), pp. 176ff. Eckoff to Burrill, August 29, 1894, "Official Letterbook" II, p. 387, suggests that he favored a school and was somewhat surprised not to find one. But he did not make an issue of it.

[101] For examples of Krohn's reputation, see the *Illini*, which carried frequent articles suggesting that Krohn was very well received indeed. (See January 17, October 25, November 1, 1895.) The last reproduced part of a favorable article on him from the *New York Evening Post*. (See also January 1, April 3, September 25, 1896. The September article reported he had made more than 100 addresses during the summer.)

Kinley disapproved of Krohn's teaching, and in particular of one of his research projects. Draper, however, supported the psychologist and doubtless saved

Kinley's opinion "undesirable" because of his "irreconcilability to the existing order" in the University. He was also foreign to the school situation in Illinois and abrasive in the delicate role of school visitor. After having "thought long and earnestly on the matter," Kinley counseled Draper (who had reasons of his own) that "the interests of the college will be best promoted by their resignations." [102] Eckoff did indeed resign (another instance of the by now almost customary one-year tenure in pedagogy) in favor of the principalship of the Herbart Preparatory School in Suffern, New York.[103] He continued in such secondary school posts until his death in 1908, with much more success than he ever enjoyed in university work. Krohn, however, held on a bit longer, until 1897, though his labors became increasingly difficult.

With Eckoff's departure, a certain pivotal point was reached. He represented the end of a trial alliance between the University, the schools, and the pedagogical profession. The University had accepted the presence of some form of professional education at the undergraduate level, though its shape and role were obviously less than precisely delineated.[104] The University itself was just coming into its

him, although Krohn's personal difficulties were sometimes trying. (See Draper to Burroughs [sometimes Burrows] Brothers Co., Cleveland, Ohio, November 24, 1894, and Krohn to Draper, November 22, 1894, Draper Letterbook. Cf. T. C. Clendenon to Nelson W. Graham, March 9, 1895, copy in College of Education Papers.) Clendenon, President of the State Teachers' Association, protested rumors of Krohn's ill favor at Urbana.

[102] Kinley's untitled report on the College, under Kinley to Draper, March 6, 1895. Copy in College of Education Papers. See esp. p. 7. In connection with the work of visiting the schools, Draper faulted Eckoff for not digging deeper into the teaching quality at Champaign and Urbana (Draper to Eckoff, January 28, 1895, "Official Letterbook" III, p. 27). Draper, however, was embroiled in a bitter fight with the Urbana High School over his son's academic career—he was proving virtually unmanageable—and so the President's desire to see justice done was perhaps less than disinterested (Draper to Superintendent J. W. Hays, Urbana, October 20, 1894, "Official Letterbook" II, pp. 418–20).

[103] Draper was negotiating with possible successors before he informed Eckoff that it was against his interests and those of the University to remain. Eckoff promptly resigned the next day (Draper to Eckoff, May 28, 1895, Eckoff to Draper, May 29, 1895, in Draper Letterbook).

[104] *The Illini* carried some interesting evidence of this in the spring. Educational matters were much in the news, and the forthcoming graduation theses had a pronounced pedagogical (and Herbartian) ring: "The Dawn of Modern School Methods—or Pestalozzi, the Disciple of Rousseau and Forerunner of Herbart"; "The Educational Ideals of the Humanists and Realists: To What Extent Are They Reconciled in Pestalozzianism?" and "Experimental Determination of the Teaching Value of the Herbartian Horn-leaves, Triquetrum, and Spheicon, with

own. Under the gentle but thoroughly purposeful government of Burrill, the faculty improved radically in both scope and quality, embracing graduates from many of the nation's finest institutions. This growth was maintained by Draper, who also gave it substantial anchorage in the legislative halls of Springfield and the financial canyons of Chicago. The time had come for genuine university status, through acceptance of the larger university-level opportunities, not a merely feigned identity created by distinction from the lower schools. That meant, of course, a new emphasis on graduate-level research and instruction. Dean Kinley reported to Draper on the state of such study in the University in 1895. Not surprisingly, he found that it needed strengthening, and he urged that provision be made for three additional graduate fellows, one each for economics, history, and the romance languages. Although in April of that year Eckoff had requested a fellow in pedagogy, Kinley did not lend his weighty approbation to the proposal.[105] Draper was willing to see some relief for the visitation obligations of the pedagogical department, proposing a new post "primarily adapted to the visitation of the high schools seeking place upon our accredited list," and he suggested rescheduling the pedagogical offerings to make the visiting schedule of the instructors more efficient. (Their courses were not to interfere with their visitation work!) [106] But to the possibility of a kind of recognition of advanced work in pedagogy, Draper turned a deaf ear. He advised Eckoff that "no provision has been made for such a fellowship by the board of trustees, and it does not seem practicable to make such a provision in the department of pedagogy when the needs are so much greater in some other direction." [107] The tone of that response, so typical of Draper's Olympian style, would continue to echo in the years to come. Pressing pedagogy at the level of higher inquiry, the challenge inherited from Gregory, was still not a present possibility. It would be a work of the future.

---

a Volunteer Preparation Class in Trigonometry, on the Basis of Herbart's ABC of Intuition" (*The Illini*, April 25, 1895).

[105] Kinley's report, under Kinley to Draper, March 6, 1895. Copy in College of Education Papers. Kinley simply gave no consideration to the request or any other positive plans in the area of pedagogy.

[106] 18th *Report* (1896), pp. 71ff.

[107] Draper to Eckoff, April 11, 1895, Draper Letterbooks.

PART II ❧

1895-1918

CHAPTER 4

🌿 The Boundless Prairie and the Infinite Sky

In the 1890's the University of Illinois was suffering the pains of a transitional period. It had been nurtured along by its first two Regents and its Acting Regent, the wise and skillful professor of botany and horticulture, T. J. Burrill. Under the direction of Andrew Sloan Draper, its first modern president, and Dean David Kinley, the University was being readied for the era of perhaps its greatest development under Edmund Janes James. The University was granting degrees and diplomas (this had not been allowed by the state legislature until 1877); shedding its original name (in 1885); writing its first university yell (Rah! Hoo-rah! Zip, Boom, Ah!); listening to students complain about streetcar fares and bicycles on the sidewalks; charging admission to football games (ten cents); and in 1892 it started graduate studies. Under the aegis of James, it would come fully into the twentieth century and become a university in deed as well as in title.

As was the case in many other universities, the work in pedagogy at the University of Illinois had started around the bend toward modern times in the 1890's. However, that start toward modern times was only a start, and in retrospect, it was a false start. Though there had been a succession of distinguished professors stopping off at the campus between 1890 and 1895 to lecture on matters pedagogical, there is, as we saw in the last chapter, little evidence to suggest that the University was seriously interested in promoting the preparation of teachers, let alone the scientific study of education. These interests did not appear until after Arnold Tompkins came in 1895, as he himself put it, "to plant an idea." And then that idea was, for the most part, denied.[1]

In a letter to Henry W. Wilder of the Chicago Bridge and Iron Company in the spring of 1895, President Draper assessed the situation realistically. Agreeing that "one of the very best ways to promote University interests will be to secure more of our graduates in the positions of teachers in the high schools," he went on to admit that "it is also true that heretofore the work in the University has not been calculated to prepare teachers for the high schools." [2] If the work at Illinois had not been calculated to prepare teachers for the high schools, it certainly was not designed to promote the study of education as a discipline. In his 1895 report to President Draper about the state of graduate study in the University, Dean Kinley had shown that pedagogy was, at best, a stepsister in the circle of graduate studies at Illinois.

The significance of Dean Kinley's 1895 report lay not as much in what he said about pedagogy as in what he did not say. Kinley had reminded President Draper that the University, if it were serious about promoting graduate study, would have to free its "chief instructors . . . from the drudgery of elementary recitation work to have time for research and for the guidance of whatever students may be attracted to the university for advanced study." [3] He went on to add that the leading institutions of the country released their department heads from excessive teaching loads and then expected them "to extend the fame of their University by their original research." [4] To

[1] The writing of this chapter was inestimably facilitated by the work of Walter P. Krolikowski. See his "Arnold Tompkins: Midwest Philosopher and Educator" (Ph.D. dissertation, University of Illinois, 1965), esp. Ch. 7, "Tompkins at the University of Illinois," pp. 252–324.

[2] Andrew Sloan Draper to Henry W. Wilder, April 16, 1895, Draper Letterbooks.

[3] David Kinley to Draper, March 6, 1895, Draper Correspondence. Kinley's eight-page (typescript) report is not titled, but the first sentence announces it as "a statement of the condition of the College of Literature and Arts." (Quotation at p. 3.)

[4] Ibid.

strengthen graduate studies Kinley urged that provisions be made for three additional fellows in the University, in economics, history, and romance languages.

Apparently responding to the social and political ferment of the 1890's—the Pullman affair, the Haymarket riot, Coxey's march on Washington—as well as to what other universities were doing, Kinley wrote to Draper that "the great questions of the day are politic and social" and suggested that "in no way could the University . . . render a greater service to the State and country than by the establishment of a school of political science, economics, and history, similar to those which so distinguish Columbia College and the University of Michigan." [5] Pedagogy was not seen as having any relationship to either the political or the social developments of the day.

If Kinley did not perceive any relationships between the social and the political ferment of the day and education, he did present to Draper what was in essence a political problem. And Draper, as an educator, was familiar with the politics of education. Immediately before assuming his post at Illinois in August, 1894, Draper had been Commissioner of Education in the state of New York. During his tenure there, he saw the beginning of the attempts by Thomas Hunter, Nicholas Murray Butler, and other progressives to pull education out of politics. Draper himself had been the victim of a political dismissal, and he became a symbol of the progressives' success when he returned to New York as Commissioner of Education in 1905 under the newly established nonpolitical Board of Regents. Kinley's report was a reminder that the relationship between the University of Illinois and the state's high schools was a sensitive one, and needed constant and careful attention. It is perhaps significant that the new President saw the problem chiefly in these terms, and that his first efforts were principally directed toward alleviating it.

Upon his arrival, Draper found that the beginnings of a department of pedagogy had been laid. Perhaps the chief reason for continuing it—the external demand for a department was present but not yet forceful, and there was little pressure within the University for such a department—was the need for an effective system of visiting the various high schools throughout the state and approving or disapproving their courses of study. Draper had decided that the work of visiting high schools would be the responsibility of the department of pedagogy. Indeed, all other work of the department was

[5] Ibid., pp. 3–4.

nearly, if not completely, incidental to visitations. In March, 1895, Draper had recommended to the Board of Trustees that "a suitable person be employed who is primarily adapted to the examination of high schools seeking place upon our accredited list." Such a person would, said Draper, "spend as much of his time for that purpose as may be deemed necessary and the remainder of his time in the work at the University." [6] He further recommended that the courses assigned to the professor of pedagogy, the assistant professor of psychology, and the instructor in philosophy be arranged so as not to interfere with their visitation work. Illinois was not ready to invest its resources in the study of pedagogy.

In May, 1895, even before asking Eckoff for his resignation, Draper had negotiated with four men for Eckoff's position as professor of pedagogy. They were Francis Burke Branch of Philadelphia; James Kirk, Department of Public Instruction, Springfield, Illinois; H. E. Kratz, superintendent of schools, Sioux City, Iowa; and a promising Indiana schoolman and educator of teachers, Arnold Tompkins. On May 27, Draper asked Tompkins: "Could you come here to accept a position which would involve your taking charge of the pedagogical department, and examining high schools which desire a place on our accredited list?" [7] On the next day, May 28, Draper advised Eckoff: "The most careful consideration has brought me reluctantly to the conclusion that it is not to your interest or that of the University that you should remain in its service longer than the present year." [8] Within a few hours, Eckoff submitted his resignation.[9]

In his initial letter to Tompkins, Draper confided that he believed that there was a "grand opening" at Illinois for the "right kind of man." [10] To Draper, Tompkins was obviously that man. From the time of their first hurried interview in Chicago until Tompkins left Illinois to accept the presidency of the Illinois State Normal University in 1899, Draper thought very highly of him. In response to a circular on the department of pedagogy that Tompkins had written, Draper told him that "the only criticism I have to make is that you do not say enough in favor of yourself. . . ." [11] In time Draper came to recognize Tompkins's weak points, but they did not change his

[6] 18th *Report* (1896), s.v. March 12, 1895, esp. pp. 71–72.
[7] Draper to Tompkins (Chicago), May 27, 1895, Draper Letterbooks.
[8] Draper to Eckoff, May 28, 1895, Draper Letterbooks.
[9] Eckoff to Draper, May 29, 1895, Draper Correspondence.
[10] Draper to Tompkins, May 27, 1895, Draper Letterbooks.
[11] Draper to Tompkins, January 23, 1897, Draper Letterbooks.

opinion of the man. Tompkins's biographer, Walter P. Krolikowski, said that Draper wrote of Tompkins "like a proud but indulgent father." To Draper, Tompkins was "a prominent representative" of the University and a man who had "no superior." [12]

If Draper had decided to hire Tompkins before receiving testimonials about his ability and qualifications, the testimonials he did secure confirmed his initial impression. Lewis E. Jones, superintendent of instruction in Cleveland, wrote that (with the sole exception of William Torrey Harris) Tompkins was the clearest thinker in the profession. "The only objection I can see to having him take the position . . . in your institution," he warned Draper, "would be the danger that he would soon be the most popular professor in the institution, and that you would have to build a new building in which to house the students of his department." [13] George P. Brown, editor, treasurer, and business manager of the influential *Public School Journal*, wrote to one of the University's trustees that even though Tompkins was inclined to "wear a thin coat when it is more comfortable than a thick one," his inability to establish a department of pedagogy at the University of Illinois would "be pretty sure evidence that there is no demand for such a department in the University at present." [14] A. W. Moore of the University of Chicago, who was soon to become one of the nation's leading pragmatists along with John Dewey, James Rowland Angell, and George Herbert Mead, wrote that he believed that there was "no one in this country so well qualified in all respects and especially . . . professional capability, loyalty and social agreeableness—to take charge of a department of pedagogy in a university." Moore, who had been a student of Tompkins and who was presently his teacher, could "imagine no one better fitted to secure that close articulation so desirable between the department of pedagogy in a state university and the state school system at large." [15]

Tompkins not only knew the day-to-day world of the schools; he was also a philosopher. To Moore, Tompkins combined "rare philosophical insight with equally sane acquaintance with the details of the public school system." To William L. Bryan of Indiana University, Tompkins was "one of the two or three best products of the intense, rather narrow, Indiana State Normal Hegelism." As such, he had

---

[12] Krolikowski, "Arnold Tompkins," pp. 281–82.

[13] Lewis E. Jones to Draper, May 29, 1895, Draper Correspondence.

[14] George P. Brown to James E. Armstrong, May 29, 1895. Copy in College of Education Papers.

[15] A. W. Moore to Draper, June 3, 1895, Draper Correspondence.

"the defects and force characteristic of that school." Among the defects, claimed Bryan, was "the anti-scientific tendency to settle all questions 'from their idea,' using facts only as illustrations." Though Tompkins's students, like himself, became "strangers to scientific method,"
reported Bryan, his influence over them was "comparable to that of
Socrates." [16]

Tompkins was in the enviable position of neither looking for nor
needing work when Draper approached him. He was finishing a second year of study at the University of Chicago and was planning to
remain there for at least a third year. He was then forty-four years
old and had already put together a successful career in pedagogy.
He had graduated from the Indiana State Normal School and had
taken his master's degree from Indiana University. He had tended
school in the county and village schools near his farm home in Paris,
Illinois. He had held positions as a principal in the Hoosier towns of
Xenia and Worthington. After working as a school principal for
three years, he tried his hand at superintendency in Franklin, Indiana,
for three years. He then went on to take a professorship at De Pauw
University for five years, and in his last year at DePauw he was dean
of the normal school. His most recent year of full-time employment
was at the Indiana State Normal School, where he held the chair of
reading and English literature.

While at DePauw University, Tompkins had published *The Science
of Discourse*, and for nearly six years he had been editing the "pedagogical department" in the *Indiana School Journal*. During his year
at the Indiana State Normal School, he wrote *The Philosophy of
Teaching*. As superintendent at Franklin, he wrote a course of study
for the schools which had attracted much attention. It won him the
professorship at DePauw and was in use as a guide in many Indiana
schools.

Tompkins told Draper that he "was not seeking work at all." He had
all that he could do. At Chicago, he was pursuing his studies and writing. He had completed his *Philosophy of School Management* there
and was in the process of rewriting *The Science of Discourse*. He was,
as he told Draper, "making a fair salary by writing and lecturing." He
was free to pursue his studies at Chicago at what he termed his "pleasure" and decided that "nothing shall turn me from this general plan
and purpose." But Tompkins's plan and purpose contained an idea,
and he thought he could work out that idea at Illinois. He accepted

[16] William L, Bryan to Draper, June 1, 1895, Draper Correspondence.

Draper's invitation and undertook to carry out the work Draper had outlined for him, promising to come "in full determination to plant an idea." [17]

Draper presented Tompkins with a detailed outline of the work that was to be done at Illinois by that "right man." The first paragraph, beginning with the words "as to the pedagogical work in the University," was less than 100 words in length. The second paragraph, telling of the work to be done "outside the University," was nearly 350 words long.[18] Clearly, Draper was very eager to have Tompkins attend to the outside work—the good of the University demanded that.

It was Draper's desire "that the professor of pedagogy should attend the teacher's conventions and be active and prominent in them. . . ." Tompkins was to respond to any call which Draper might make upon him to deliver an address "at any teachers' gathering or at any public educational assembly." [19] Besides serving as a representative of the University's good will toward the schools' teachers, Tompkins was also to take charge of the high school visitation program.

As High School Visitor, Tompkins had to be "an excellent judge of what constitutes a high school, both as to the course of study and the teachers worthy a place in a school accredited to the University." He had to be "a man of tact who can get on with people generally and agreeably"; a man who "must make suggestions which can be acted upon." Draper wrote to Tompkins that he should be a man "who would be glad to talk to the students and, if the way opened, to stay overnight and give a public address to the people." "In a word," wrote Draper, "we desire to affiliate the whole high school system sharply and strongly with the University, and it will largely devolve upon you to do it. . . ." [20] Draper wanted Tompkins to improve the high schools of the state, especially those in the middle and southern parts. The University's growth was in large measure dependent upon the increasing numbers of students from the state's still underdeveloped high schools.

Tompkins's reply to Draper expressed his agreement with Draper's outline and ideas: ". . . I subscribe fully to your idea" and "I can

---

[17] Tompkins to Draper, May 28, 1895, Draper Correspondence.
[18] Draper to Tompkins, June 1, 1895, Draper Letterbooks.
[19] Ibid.
[20] Ibid.

accept fully the outline of work you present." [21] However, with the advantage of hindsight it appears that Draper and Tompkins were talking past each other. Draper wanted Tompkins to tend to his political problems with the schools, shape them into preparatory schools for the University, and conduct the pedagogical work on the campus. That pedagogical work was to be what the late nineteenth-century folk liked to call "work of a higher type." To Draper "the highest and best kind of pedagogical work" was work that began with students who had already conquered the work of the normal school. "We should not," he wrote, "trench upon the work of the normal school." [22] To specify "work of a high type" was, practically speaking, to specify that there would be neither a practice school nor a model school at Urbana.

In his first letter to Draper, Tompkins related that he had already designed a plan for the establishment of "a high type of school of pedagogy," a plan that had been "heartily approved by William T. Harris . . . and others of prominence." Tompkins's higher type of school was designed for "mature students of considerable culture and maturity." "Everywhere there are mature teachers—cultured and experienced—who have no place to pursue the high study of their profession." Tompkins's hope was to provide such a place. It was, he admitted, "a large hope and a large ambition." "But," he asked Draper, "what is not possible to a school bounded by the boundless prairie and over arched by the infinite sky?" [23]

The department that Tompkins had in mind would, he stated, have to be planted "firmly in the school sentiment of the state." The effort to establish it "would fall in perfectly with the general interests of the University, and the work of visiting high schools. . . ." [24] In his second letter, Tompkins wrote to Draper that he agreed that a practice school was not desirable. The practice school belonged to the normal school. The university, he wrote, "should not give the practice itself, but should present that philosophy which is potent in practice." The work of the university was to be "strictly philosophical," but it was also to lay "firm hold on the practical." [25] As practical and philosophical as his plan may have been, Tompkins's idea did not take hold at Illinois.

[21] Tompkins to Draper, June 3, 1895, Draper Correspondence.
[22] Draper to Tompkins, June 1, 1895, Draper Letterbooks.
[23] Tompkins to Draper, May 28, 1895, Draper Correspondence.
[24] Ibid.
[25] Tompkins to Draper, June 3, 1895, Draper Correspondence.

In the fall of 1895, Tompkins took up residence at 410 John Street in Champaign and threw himself into the work at the University. At the top of the assignment sheet was the high school work. He was appointed to Ira O. Baker's committee of faculty on admissions and accredited schools. Baker recommended that Tompkins assume the chairmanship of the committee, not only because Tompkins was the professor of pedagogy but also because he was easily the most qualified person to direct the committee's work. During his first year as chairman, the committee visited fifty-two schools. Tompkins himself visited nine.[26]

Before beginning the high school work, Tompkins had some doubts about the program's effectiveness and feasibility. In January, 1896, he told President Draper that he had spent much time considering his work so that he might perform it "with more efficiency." Tompkins did allow that the accrediting system was an efficient means of integrating the entire system of the state. There was no question that "professors of the University must know high schools, and high school men, and in a way to influence the high school men to urge their students to seek a higher education in the University." The accrediting system provided an avenue for influence, but it was also a source of ill will. The system told some high schools that their work was unsatisfactory and others that theirs was satisfactory. The difference between the best of the unsatisfactory schools and the poorest of the best was so subtle that it could not be objectively stated. The inability of the University's examiners to specify the difference caused them to appear arbitrary in their rulings, thereby creating unsatisfactory relations between the University and many of the public schools.[27]

Tompkins proposed that all schools and all students "be fully informed as to the preparation needed" to undertake study at the University and that the University accept the word of the schools as to the quality and the amount of work completed by the student. Poor preparation would be detected in the University classroom. Moreover, the accrediting system *notwithstanding*, "all students were virtually admitted on probation." Abolishing the lists of approved and nonapproved schools would enable the visitor to be more effective. What was once an inspector who could render an unfavorable verdict

---

[26] Krolikowski, "Arnold Tompkins," p. 262.
[27] According to Krolikowski: Tompkins to Draper, January 7, 1896, Draper Correspondence.

could now become a friendly visitor, informing the schools of University requirements and offering suggestions to help them meet these requirements.[28]

At Draper's request, T. J. Burrill responded to Tompkins's proposal. Burrill agreed that the program of school accreditation left much to be desired and even went on to question the usefulness of entrance examinations. However, he did question whether an unfavorable report from the University created "ill will." Often it gave to the superintendent and the teachers the occasion to press the school board or the community for increased financial resources and changes in schooling they had already recognized as necessary. Perhaps, as an answer to Tompkins's point that the difference between the best of the poorest and the poorest of the best could not be specified, Burrill recommended that the schools be accredited by subjects, thus allowing partial accreditation.[29]

The following May, Tompkins offered a second proposal.[30] In it he suggested that the high schools be required to prepare detailed descriptions of the work they offered, that the superintendents and the principals of the schools visit the University so they could become acquainted with the University work and the prior preparation it demanded, and that the faculties of the high schools determine the courses in which the students would receive credit. Neither of Tompkins's plans proved to be entirely satisfactory to the University faculty who wanted the students screened before coming to the campus.

Tompkins's efforts did have some consequence, however. His proposal to bring the high school people to the University did add impetus to the series of high school conferences which continued down to World War II.[31] Burrill's recommendation for partial accreditation was adopted. And the University did attempt to improve the accreditation system by creating a new post, the High School Visitor.

On June 9, 1896, President Draper told the University's trustees that "the time has come when it seems imperatively necessary that the University should employ a man whose special duty it shall be to visit high schools. . . ."[32] Such a specialist would, Draper confided, eliminate inconsistency in the application of standards and relieve the

[28] Ibid.

[29] According to Krolikowski: T. J. Burrill to Draper, January 10, 1896, Draper Correspondence.

[30] Tompkins to Draper, May 25, 1896, Draper Correspondence.

[31] Krolikowski, "Arnold Tompkins," p. 273.

[32] 18th *Report* (1896), p. 251.

faculty from annoying interruptions in their campus work. The Board agreed with Draper and appointed the principal of the Freeport, Illinois, high school, John Edward McGilvery, to the post. That was the beginning of a budget line which endured for over twenty-five years.

Visiting high schools and teaching were only part of Tompkins's assignment. He was also the University's representative to the school people of the state. It was a task for which he was well qualified. While at Chicago, he had been supporting himself as a free-lance lecturer at teachers' institutes and was very successful at it. During the summer before he came to Illinois, he spent seven weeks at teachers' institutes in Pennsylvania, three weeks in Indiana, and one week in Council Bluffs, Iowa. The following November (1895), he spent five days at an experimental, during-the-school-year county teachers' institute in Indiana.[33]

In March, 1896, he spoke in Chicago, addressed the Central Illinois Teachers' Association meeting in Danville, and the teachers' institute in Centralia, Illinois. During June, Tompkins delivered the annual address at the Michigan State Normal School, where his former teacher Richard Gause Boone was principal, and gave commencement addresses in the Illinois towns of Dixon and Wilmington.[34]

Tompkins's busiest year on the speaker's circuit was the 1896–97 academic year. While Tompkins undertook only a few engagements at county teachers' institutes in Indiana in that year, "he was," Krolikowski has recorded, "away from the University on every possible occasion from October through January." In April he presented major addresses to the Northern Indiana Teachers' Association at Elkhart and the Southern Indiana Teachers' Association at Franklin. During May and June, he journeyed about the state of Illinois, giving fourteen commencement addresses.[35] In the summer of 1897, he took part in a Chautauqua-like summer school at Bay View, Michigan, and participated in thirteen institutes. He also delivered five lectures on pedagogy in Salem, Massachusetts. In early September, he once again took the podium at Franklin, Indiana, and before arriving in Champaign for the fall semester he stopped off at Dwight, Illinois, to inspire still one more assembly of teachers.[36]

[33] Krolikowski, "Arnold Tompkins," p. 274.
[34] Ibid.
[35] Ibid.
[36] Ibid., p. 275.

Though the number of Tompkins's speaking engagements decreased sharply during the next two years, the range of audiences grew.[37] He spoke a few times in Illinois and took to the road to speak at county teachers' institutes in Pennsylvania, Massachusetts, and New Hampshire. In August, 1898, he addressed the American Institute of Instruction and gave what the *New England Journal of Education* called "one of the most brilliant addresses to which the Institute has ever listened." [38] Later in the year, he went to Iowa City, Iowa, and to Columbus, Ohio, where he is reported to have made "a very fine impression" at the National Superintendents' Convention.[39]

The schoolmen of the state were very pleased that Arnold Tompkins was available as a lecturer and speaker for their institutes, commencement exercises, and their club meetings. After a speaking engagement, Tompkins was frequently asked to return for a second and a third time.[40] Other institutions were seeking Tompkins's services and popularity as well. In 1897, he was offered the presidency of the Southern Illinois Normal School.[41] The following year he was one of the candidates for the principalship of the Eastern Illinois Normal School.[42] In 1899, when Colonel Francis Wayland Parker resigned as principal of the Chicago Normal School and John Williston Cook resigned from the presidency of the Illinois State Normal University, Draper was justifiably concerned about his ability to hold on to Arnold Tompkins.[43]

Though Tompkins did throw himself into the university work, teaching, visiting high schools, and lecturing about the country, his abiding concern remained the study of pedagogy at a "higher level." When, in 1895, he wrote to Draper that he had been harboring "a large ambition," he was writing of an ambition to which he had given considerable thought. He had laid out some of his own thoughts about teacher preparation and the study of pedagogy in 1891. On that occa-

37 Ibid.
38 Krolikowski, "Arnold Tompkins," p. 314*n*. He reports: "*The New England Journal of Education* says of the address: 'Dr. Arnold Tompkins of the Illinois State University [*sic*] gave one of the most brilliant addresses to which the Institute has ever listened.' " (Also quoted in the *Illinois School Journal* 43 [September, 1898]: 617.)
39 Krolikowski, "Arnold Tompkins," p. 275.
40 Ibid., p. 289.
41 Ibid., pp. 282–83.
42 Ibid., p. 283.
43 Ibid.

sion Tompkins took issue with the program which Nicholas Murray Butler had designed for the students of the New York College for the Training of Teachers (soon to become Teachers College) and which he had promoted in *Century* magazine in 1889.[44]

Butler believed that the program for the Teachers College was different from most other programs because it was designed for those students who had already completed a full high school course. Moreover, the program confined itself to strictly professional studies—the history and philosophy of education, a methods course, and practice-teaching. Tompkins noted that normal schools, unlike professional schools of theology, medicine, and law, were marked by a lack of similarity in every aspect except their purposes. Each was devoted to the professional preparation of teachers, but there were no similarities beyond this common aim. The curricula of the various schools differed significantly. Wherever common points were to be found, those points could be explained as the products of either chance or imitation. While most schools did offer courses in the history and philosophy of education and in the methods of instruction, there was, to the best of Tompkins's knowledge, no normal school that had organized its program around one central rational truth.

Tompkins agreed that there was no doubt that the program Butler described met the requirements of a teacher-training program. It called for adequate preparation before entrance, emphasized the necessity of specialized training for teaching by providing a special school for that purpose, and distinguished itself from other academic institutions by freeing itself from the responsibility for teaching the general cultural studies. Tompkins, however, was not persuaded by Butler's reasons for eliminating the cultural studies.[45]

"The law school," Butler claimed, "does not teach history, nor the medical school reading; neither should the training school give instruction in these branches." To Tompkins that was to say that "the normal school has never taught Kent's Commentaries, nor Flint's Practice of Medicine; therefore, the law school should not teach the one, nor the medical school the other." The fact of the matter was, Tompkins argued, that the law school did teach law and the medical

---

[44] According to Krolikowski, Tompkins did so in "The Normal School Problem," *Illinois School Journal* 36 (January, 1891): 15–24. See Krolikowski, "Arnold Tompkins," pp. 128*n*, 290, 321.
[45] Ibid.

school did teach medicine. The teacher-training school, therefore, had to teach reading and history and the other cultural studies because the teacher needed to know them to perform the teaching act. Butler had failed, according to Tompkins, to distinguish "the relation which these subjects bear to the teacher's profession and that which they bear to other professions." Tompkins would not exclude instruction from the curriculum on the grounds that it was either in the secondary schools or not in other professional schools. Teaching was not the same as administering justice or healing the sick. Moreover, Butler's program contained no one central rational truth.[46]

Tompkins was prepared to offer a rationale for teaching the cultural subjects in the teacher-training schools. The rationale he offered to Butler was in basic agreement with that presented by W. A. Jones some twenty years earlier and was the one Tompkins himself had offered in detail in his own work, *The Philosophy of Teaching*. "The nature of the teaching act," said Tompkins, "determines the necessary preparation of the teacher." And the act of teaching was in turn determined by "the mind process constituting the subject to be taught." The teacher had to know not only the subject he was teaching but how the learning mind learned the subject the teacher was teaching.[47]

Tompkins went on to observe that "nothing is a more common characteristic of the teacher than the fact that he has two professional lives, the one theoretical and the other practical, and the one having no relation to the other." Such teachers were the products of training that taught theory apart from "the actual educative process." These teachers were typically quite capable of giving "fair talk with absurd practice." The proper program, according to Tompkins, would see the teacher begin with "an actual experience of the educative process as each of the subjects is peculiarly adapted to produce it," and then proceed to a "full realization of the best which history and philosophy reveal." In good Hegelian fashion he explained that movement from the concrete to the theoretical would not produce "contradictions in the professional character of the teacher," but would resolve them.[48]

One year after Tompkins arrived in Champaign, Draper asked him

[46] Ibid.
[47] Ibid.
[48] Ibid.

to prepare a description of the department's work for the local news-paper. In that description, Tompkins once again repeated his position. Of the work Tompkins wrote: ". . . Besides the regular undergradu-ate work, there is a strong class of normal school and college gradu-ates—experienced teachers and superintendents—studying the philoso-phy of pedagogy. This work attempts to bring all phases of professional life into the unity of a great controlling principle. And with this the study is made concrete and practical. Universal laws are seen living in the minutest details of the teacher's labor." [49] Tompkins went on to explain that the work at Illinois was well suited not only for the classroom teacher, but also for "those who have undertaken the larger problem of management and of the supervision of instruc-tion." Illinois sought as students "those who have preparation and patient purpose to attain unto the higher phases of pedagogical think-ing." The department of pedagogy was devoted to "the continued and higher study of pedagogy." [50] As such, it was to be the crown of the state's system of normal schools.

Tompkins's plan may have been a worthy one, but it was not easily realized. There was an insufficient number of those who were "not contented with a merely passable preparation" and "anxious to gain a philosophic insight into the work they have undertaken." In Tomp-kins's second year at the University, the enrollment increased from forty-six to 120 students in the department of pedagogy.[51] However, after that one spurt, the enrollment remained stable. Moreover, the expectation that Tompkins would attract large numbers of graduate students was not met. In 1895–96, there was one first-year graduate student in pedagogy. There were seven the following year. In 1897–98, there were six graduate students; and the next year, there were again seven students studying pedagogy at a "higher level." [52]

Perhaps, as Krolikowski has suggested, the most plausible explana-tion for Tompkins's failure to attract a large number of students is that there were not enough college graduates in Illinois who were in-terested in earning an advanced degree in pedagogy.[53] The University had not been preparing people at the undergraduate level to pursue

[49] Ibid., p. 321*n*. This statement has as its heading, "Pedagogy in the University of Illinois," and is enclosed with a letter to Draper, November 4, 1896.
[50] Ibid.
[51] Ibid., p. 284.
[52] Ibid., p. 261.
[53] Ibid., p. 284.

the advanced study of pedagogy. That was the task and prerogative of the normal schools. In 1898, McGilvery, the High School Visitor, reported that of the 841 high school teachers in the state, only 464 were college and normal school graduates. Of these 464, only twenty-two were graduates of the University of Illinois.[54] Nor was advanced study needed to secure employment. The annual national demand for *new* elementary and secondary school teachers between 1890 and 1900 has been estimated to have been somewhere between ninety and one hundred thousand. That market demanded only a minimum of preparation and professional study.

Finally, Tompkins's idea was not a novel one. In essence he wanted (to use Harold Rugg's term) a school for the "teachers of teachers." In the fall of 1896, John Dewey, then chairman of the department of philosophy, psychology, and pedagogy at the University of Chicago, wrote that in addition to "schools whose function is to supply the great army of teachers with the weapons of their calling and direct them to their use, there must be those which direct their energies to the education, not of the rank and file, but of the leaders of our educational systems—teachers in normal and training schools, professors of pedagogy, superintendents, principals of schools in our large cities. . . ."[55] Dewey had founded such a school in January, 1896. Perhaps it drew students away from Champaign-Urbana. Chicago with its World's Columbian Exposition may have been more appealing than Champaign's boundless prairie and infinite sky.[56]

The lack of students in the regular sessions did not dampen Tompkins's desire to found a school of pedagogy devoted to the theoretical

[54] "Annual Report of the High School Visitor of the University of Illinois for the School Year Ending June 8, 1898, Submitted to the Committee on Accredited Schools, May 16, 1898," pp. 5–6. Copy of this ten-page (typescript) report in College of Education Papers.

[55] John Dewey, "Pedagogy as a University Discipline," *University of Chicago Record* 1 (September 18, 1896): 353.

[56] During these years, Chicago was perceived as a competing institution. For example, in 1896 Professor William O. Krohn wrote to Draper from Chicago to explain why he was there without Draper's prior consent. "I was called here to Chgo by wire to assist in framing program for State Tchrs Asscn which meets at Springfield [during] Christmas. I could not see you before leaving as I had to come on midnight train to reach Chgo in time for the committee meeting. My thought in coming, in addition to the urgency of the request was intensified by the belief that the State University should be represented on the program, that Chgo University should not have everything because of mere neglect or default on our part" (William O. Krohn to A. S. Draper, September 6, 1896, Draper Correspondence; cf. Solberg, *The University of Illinois*, pp. 337ff.).

and philosophical dimensions of pedagogy. It did, however, delay his attempts until the summer of 1899. As early as the spring of 1894, the faculty committees on instruction and on the summer school had recommended to the Trustees that instruction in "athletics, zoology, physiology, botany, chemistry, English literature, pedagogy, psychology, political economy and history" be offered in a novel four-week summer session. The committees did not expect a large enrollment and recommended that "different subjects be thrown together under one instructor whenever this is feasible." [57] The Board of Trustees, observing that those who would attend the session would be mainly teachers, recommended that "the subjects offered should consist chiefly of those which teachers are likely to demand." They added the proviso that the work offered had to be of university grade.[58] That summer thirty-eight students, twenty-five of whom were teachers, attended the University's first summer session.

The following December, the committee on administration of the summer school recommended that plans be made for another four-week session for the summer of 1895.[59] The next September, David Kinley, director of the summer session, reported that "the facts show that the session was a failure." [60] It had been advertised in two leading educational journals and fifteen to twenty thousand circulars had been distributed to the teachers throughout the state. Plans had been made for an enrollment of approximately 100 students. The actual enrollment turned out to be twenty-six, twelve less than the preceding year. Even though he was willing to attribute the failure to the "smallpox scare," Kinley expressed doubt "whether a large number can ever be gotten together here during the summer." [61] Except for work offered at the University's biological station on the Illinois River during the summer of 1896, further attempts at conducting a summer session were postponed until 1899.[62]

Both the failure of the summer sessions and the failure to attract students interested in the advanced study of pedagogy were great disappointments to Tompkins. But his commitment to his plan did not wane. His hopes were fired again in December, 1898, when the

[57] 17th *Report* (1894), pp. 234–35.
[58] Ibid., pp. 271–72.
[59] 18th *Report* (1896), pp. 49ff.
[60] Ibid., p. 165.
[61] Ibid.
[62] Krolikowski, "Arnold Tompkins," p. 294.

University faculty, after canvassing the state schoolmen about summer offerings, decided to conduct a summer session in 1899.[63] On December 6, 1898, the day after the faculty had voted to hold another summer session, Tompkins sent President Draper a statement on a School of Pedagogy under the guise of clarifying the summer school work. What Tompkins sent to Draper was much more than a summer program. It was a restatement of his general plan and hope to develop an advanced program in pedagogy.

Tompkins did not propose work for those whom Dewey was calling "the great army of teachers." Instead, reminding Draper once again that "normal schools put their emphasis on supplying the common schools with teachers," Tompkins insisted that "the University should put its emphasis on supplying special teachers and principals for high schools and superintendents of schools." He restated his belief that "the course should have for its basis a central philosophy of education which should be carried out and applied to all the details of work." [64] To carry out these principles, Tompkins was now willing to found a school of pedagogy as part of the summer school and forget about the program during the regular semesters. He all but explicitly proposed that the summer school simply be a school of pedagogy under his direction.

Tompkins proposed that all work in all departments of the University during the summer session be subordinated to the needs and rationale of the program in pedagogy. For example, he recommended that any student who was preparing to teach a given subject should earn six credits in that subject under the direction of a specialist and write a thesis on the pedagogy of his subject. Had this recommendation been adopted, it would have been necessary to offer courses in general cultural studies and, more important, to teach those courses from a special pedagogical point of view. The arts and sciences were not to be taught as they were ordinarily. The organization and method of teaching the course content were to give way to a new organization dictated by how the mind of a child learned the subject in question. Teachers and supervisors of teachers needed to know not only what was to be learned but also how it was learned.

As might have been expected, Tompkins's plan met resistance. The

[63] 20th *Report* (1900), pp. 52ff.
[64] Tompkins to Draper, December 6, 1898, and a two-page enclosure entitled "School of Pedagogy," Draper Correspondence.

professors of the arts and sciences did not want to teach courses in professional pedagogy. In the face of a worthy opposition, Tompkins had to back down and compromise. He told Draper that the differences between him and his opposition (the science people, Professor Meyer and Professor Forbes), issued from a misunderstanding. He claimed that he "desired to accept any special pedagogical work which they or any professor might in cooperation with me choose to do." He went on to add that he "had no thought of having anything to do with the regular courses offered in their own lines." [65]

Tompkins's claim that he had no intention of interfering with the other work in the University does not completely square with the actual situation. It was generally recognized that a summer session's success depended upon attracting many school teachers to Champaign-Urbana and the previous summer sessions were failures. That Tompkins had lost and was being forced into a compromise is indicated by a letter written to Draper by Professor Forbes, who was a principal source of resistance to Tompkins's attempt to subordinate all the summer work to the needs of pedagogy. In late February, Forbes told Draper that "in suggesting a correlation, amounting perhaps to a subordination, between pedagogy on the one hand and work in other departments on the other [Tompkins] clearly had in mind only such courses below university grade as should be offered because of their value to teachers as such—courses in algebra, in geometry, in preparatory Latin, and the like, for example." [66] Forbes went on to explain that Tompkins agreed that the nonpedagogical work of university grade offered during the summer should be offered from its ordinary point of view.

While there is no reason to doubt the accuracy of Forbes's report to Draper, there is little reason to believe that Tompkins really wanted the academic work for the teachers to be anything less than "university grade." Tompkins made it clear to Draper in December and even before that he was not planning work for "the great army of teachers." "The course offered in pedagogy," he consistently maintained, "should be on a higher philosophic plane than that offered by normal schools, since the students for whom it is intended have more maturity, scholarship, and experience than those supposed to attend normal schools, and since they are preparing to fill positions of higher

[65] Tompkins to Draper, February 10, 1899, Draper Correspondence.
[66] S. A. Forbes to Draper, February 20, 1899. Draper Correspondence.

responsibility." [67] To Tompkins, the leaders of education needed advanced study, not preparatory study.

Tompkins was not happy with the agreement he made with Forbes. It was inconsistent with his earlier positions and was not one he wanted to abide by. In early March, Tompkins sent a letter to Draper which, in effect, was a drawing of the battle lines and a lowering of the cannons. He was no longer willing to discuss the role of pedagogy and how it might be gotten underway. Now he wanted to know just what the University was planning to do. He explained that he had been eager to get the work underway at Illinois and that to do so he had declined other positions which would have paid him much higher salaries. He even agreed to work during the summer term at the expense of profitable institute work and what he called "a pleasant outing." "There is," he claimed, "not an interest in the University of more commanding influence for the good of the state and the University than that of the higher study of pedagogy." Despite this, other interests had been allowed to gain prominence and to control the work in pedagogy. It was a time for a change. He had made his decision: "I can not afford to bury my work in drilling on mere elements of the subject as an incident to other departments." [68] Tompkins would do pedagogy at Illinois or he would leave.

After T. J. Burrill, then Dean of the General Faculty and of the Graduate School, had spoken to Tompkins about the place of pedagogy in the University, the former Acting Regent confided to Draper that he thought Tompkins would be satisfied to have Draper suggest to the University's Trustees that the work in pedagogy needed development.[69] Tompkins had expected Burrill to intercede with Draper so he wrote another letter to the President, insisting that the formal establishment of the School of Pedagogy was all that was necessary to satisfy him. The working out of its details and the degrees the school would offer could all be handled at a future date. Tompkins was now willing to back away from the battle lines in return for a commitment. Tompkins was willing to settle for an expression of good faith and a token act. The actual shape the school would assume could, he said, "be determined as a matter of growth." [70]

The difficulties between Tompkins and the University were further

[67] Tompkins to Draper, December 6, 1898, and a two-page enclosure entitled "School of Pedagogy," Draper Correspondence.
[68] Tompkins to Draper, March 7, 1899, Draper Correspondence.
[69] T. J. Burrill to Draper, March 14, 1899, Draper Correspondence.
[70] Tompkins to Draper, March 14, 1899, Draper Correspondence.

complicated the following April, when George P. Brown, then editor of *School and Home Education*, reported the controversy between Tompkins and the University. Brown was clearly on the side of Tompkins and made no attempt to hide behind neutrality. "That Professor Tompkins is seeking to improve the breed of men rather than the breed of cattle, and to teach how to build character rather than bridges," the editor wrote, "does not seem to be a sufficient reason for doubting the value of his department." [71] From Brown's position, it appeared that the University was satisfied that a science of education was impossible and that the University believed the public was not yet pressing for advanced pedagogical study. Brown claimed the University did not hear the demand because it was listening to "those who are ignorant of the needs of such knowledge as an adequately supported department of education will reveal." [72] He allowed that a science of education was not yet established and that, at best, to establish it would indeed be difficult. But difficulty was not impossibility. He also reminded the University that its task was to lead the people rather than safely reflect their desires.

Brown's editorial was picked up by other journals, and Draper had to write denials to the Inland Publishing Company of Terre Haute, Indiana, and to Brown.[73] Brown did back down somewhat, but he continued to maintain that Illinois should have a school of pedagogy. Nor did the President's difficulties end when he had pacified Brown. They were soon complicated by Parker's resignation from the Chicago Normal School and Cook's resignation from the Illinois State Normal University. Draper knew that Tompkins was being considered for each of these vacant posts. In early June, he told Lucy Flower, chairman of the Board's Committee on Instruction, that he believed Tompkins would take the job left open by Parker were it offered to him. He did not know whether Tompkins would go to Normal.[74]

The issue Tompkins introduced finally came to a head when, on

[71] George P. Brown, "Pedagogy in the State University," *School and Home Education* 18 (April, 1899): 431–33. (*School and Home Education* had succeeded the *Public School Journal* in 1898.)

[72] Ibid.

[73] Krolikowski, "Arnold Tompkins," p. 303. Also see Draper to Inland Publishing Co. (Terre Haute, Ind.), April 17, 1899, Draper Letterbooks. Draper told the company that there was "no thought of abandoning our department of pedagogy" and further related that the department of pedagogy would be "strengthened."

[74] According to Krolikowski: Draper to Mrs. L. Flower, June 7, 1899, Draper Letterbooks.

June 13 at the Board of Trustee's meeting, Lucy Flower recommended "that there be established in the University a college for teachers" and "that Arnold Tompkins be elected dean of said college at a salary of $2,500 per annum." [75] The board discussed the Flower report, recessed, discussed, went to the Alumni Associations' banquet, and then returned to the Beardsley Hotel to take up the proposal again. Mr. Bullard introduced a substitute proposal, recommending that the "board give Professor Tompkins the assurance that he shall have every opportunity to make his department all that is necessary for the interests of the teachers of the State of Illinois, and that his salary be made $2,500 a year." [76] An attempt to postpone the question for a day failed, Bullard's resolution was defeated three to five, and Flower's report was rejected two to six. Tompkins had lost.

Before the month was over, Tompkins tendered his resignation to accept the presidency of the Illinois State Normal University. [77] By summer's end, his assistant, High School Visitor McGilvery, left for Ohio to take on the principalship of the Cleveland Normal School. [78] Efforts to replace Tompkins and McGilvery were not immediately successful. The last year of the century saw vacancy signs on the pedagogical shop at Illinois. A new beginning would be made in 1900.

[75] 20th *Report* (1900), p. 94. In 1895, Tompkins was hired at a salary of $1,800 (18th *Report* [1896], p. 102).

[76] 20th *Report* (1900), p. 101.

[77] Tompkins to Draper, June 21, 1899, Draper Correspondence.

[78] On July 24, 1899, T. J. Burrill wrote Draper, who was then in Paris, that ". . . Superintendent Jones of Cleveland is here conferring with Professor McGilvery as to the latter's appointment to the principalship of the Cleveland Normal School. I do not know what the result may be." (Also see Burrill to Lucy Flower, July 24, 1899, Draper Letterbooks.) McGilvery's resignation was accepted by the Board of Trustees on August 16, 1899 (20th *Report* [1900], p. 137).

CHAPTER 5

The Modern Demand

Tompkins's biographer, Krolikowski, has described Tompkins's acceptance of the presidency of the Illinois State Normal University as "a reluctant but definitive step back into the nineteenth century."[1] If it can be viewed as a trip back into the nineteenth century for Tompkins, it can also be interpreted as a sign that pedagogy was about to assume a new character at the University of Illinois. Almost as a signal of a new era, an announcement that a heavily Hegelian orientation had passed, the term "Education" replaced "Pedagogy" in the listing of courses and in the titles of appointees in the 1900–1901 *Catalogue*. Previously, the terms had been used interchangeably, but now the change was permanent. Soon the faculty would be complaining of insufficient stenographic service and petitioning for telephones, sometimes specifying "Bell."

It was not as easy to prepare for the new century and to put the pedagogical shop in order as it was to change a few words. Even though Draper was aware of the possibility of Tompkins's resignation, he had little time to prepare for the eventuality. And it may have been a possibility he did not want to entertain. Even as late as June 19, 1899, only two days before Tompkins submitted his letter of resignation, Draper was able to write: "It is not at all certain that Professor Tomp-

[1] Krolikowski, "Arnold Tompkins," p. 306.

109

kins is to leave us: Indeed, my belief is that he is not."[2] Once the
eventuality had occurred, Draper had no time to find a replacement
for Tompkins. He had made plans to spend the summer in Europe,
and, as he related to Chicago school reformer and Trustee Lucy
Flower, it was too late to change them.[3] Draper sailed for Europe and
left T. J. Burrill in charge of the University during the summer of
1899. As Draper's agent, Burrill had to find a man to occupy the chair
of pedagogy. Before the summer was over he also had to begin a
search for a new High School Visitor.

By early July, Burrill decided upon Louis H. Galbreath, who had
been recommended by Michael Vincent O'Shea, Frank M. McMurry,
and James Earl Russell.[4] He screened the candidate thoroughly and
methodically consulted all interested parties in the state.[5] However, his
efforts came to an unfortunate end when, in mid-August, Galbreath
died.[6] Pressed though he was, Burrill, as was his habit, refused to make
either a hasty or a weak appointment.[7]

Burrill did, however, manage to issue a clear statement of what
Draper demanded of the man in pedagogy. In a form letter—complete

[2] Draper to A. N. Raub, June 19, 1899. Also see Draper to George F. James,
June 19, 1899; Draper to M. V. O'Shea, June 19, 1899; Draper Letterbooks.

[3] Draper to Lucy Flower, June 21, 1899, and Draper to Lucy Flower, June 22,
1899, Draper Letterbooks.

[4] Burrill offered the position to Galbreath on July 10, 1899 (T. J. Burrill to
L. H. Galbreath, July 10, 1899, Draper Letterbooks). However, Galbreath was
contractually bound to begin work at the State Normal School at Charleston,
Illinois, in September, 1899. By deciding upon Galbreath, Burrill had to negotiate
his release from Charleston. (See Burrill to Flower, July 24, 1899, Draper Letterbooks. For Galbreath's recommendations, see M. V. O'Shea to Draper, June 19,
1899; Burrill to O'Shea, July 3, 1899; Burrill to Dean James E. Russell [Teachers
College, Columbia University], July 10, 1899; and Burrill to Russell, July 18,
1899, Draper Letterbooks.)

[5] On the same day that Burrill offered the post to Galbreath, he wrote to John
W. Cook, president of the Illinois State Normal University, to tell him that he
was "strongly inclined to recommend Professor Galbreath." He asked for Cook's
opinion and inquired whether he had a better suggestion. (Burrill to Cook, July
10, 1899. Also see Burrill to Cook, July 26, 1899.) Lucy Flower, chairman of the
Board's Committee on Instruction, was, of course, also consulted. (Burrill to
Alfred J. Bayliss, Superintendent of Public Instruction of the State of Illinois,
August 12, 1899. All in Draper Letterbooks.)

[6] F. M. McMurry, "Death of Louis H. Galbreath," School and Home Education
19 (September, 1899): 45–46.

[7] After Galbreath's death, Burrill told J. W. Cook: "We are letting the matter
of pedagogical appointments here rest for the time being. Really, I am quite at
sea concerning what should be done. I do not find anybody available who appears to me to come so near our requirements as did Mr. Galbreath" (Burrill to
Cook, August 25, 1899, Draper Letterbooks).

with "enclosed stamped return envelope"—sent out to William Torrey Harris, Nicholas Murray Butler, John Dewey, Charles DeGarmo, G. Stanley Hall, and others, Burrill let it be known that the University was seeking a replacement for Tompkins and that:

> To be considered one must have had the training of the best schools and must have acquired the reputation as a thinker and worker in the wide field of Education. He must not only be equipped for the discussion of Educational theories, but he must have had successful experience in educational practice. He will be expected to treat not only of the philosophy of education and of methods of teaching but to be able to speak with some weight of authority upon any phase of educational organization and administration, for it is the desire to make the department embrace more than pedagogy, even the whole field of public education. He will be expected to work in close and helpful relations with the Normal Schools of Illinois and to make the whole educational system of the state his laboratory. He must be a ready writer and speaker upon educational topics, capable of safely formulating and presenting the policy of the State University upon all manner of educational subjects.[8]

Clearly, the specifications for the job had not changed since 1894 when Draper outlined them for Tompkins. The salary for anyone brave enough to attempt these Herculean tasks of the pedagogical stable was to "depend largely upon the qualities of the individual."

When Draper returned from Europe, he found that the situation he had left was still there. He still had to staff the pedagogical department. That was not what he had expected. There were, he had written to Lucy Flower before leaving, "plenty of men who would like the position in pedagogy and I do not think it will be very difficult to find a man who is suited to it." [9] However, besides needing a replacement for Tompkins, Draper still had to find a High School Visitor and a psychologist. Psychology, he had reasoned, could wait until pedagogy had been settled. That would insure that the psychological work could be compatible with, if not subordinate to, the work in pedagogy.[10]

[8] Burrill to William Torrey Harris, U.S. Commissioner of Education, August 16, 1899, Draper Letterbooks. This same letter was also sent to teachers' agencies, superintendents, university presidents, and professors of pedagogy.
[9] Draper to Lucy Flower, June 22, 1899, Draper Letterbooks.
[10] Before leaving for Europe, Draper told Lucy Flower "not to worry about the position in psychology. It is," he related, "better to fill the other one [pedagogy] first and let that wait so that the man in psychology shall at least be in

The High School Visitor's position was filled in January, 1900, when with the aid of Alfred Bayliss, superintendent of public instruction for the state of Illinois, Draper managed to get Stratton D. Brooks, principal of one of Illinois's best high schools, released from his duties at the LaSalle Township High School.[11] Brooks's arrival for the spring term of 1900 allowed the University to meet what demand there was—it was not at all great—for pedagogical coursework.[12]

Draper himself published abroad that the University of Illinois maintained two filing cabinets with "comprehensive statements showing the ancestral and educational pedigrees of . . . promising and possibly available teachers."[13] At this juncture, the appropriate folder must have been empty, for in mid-September Draper found "it necessary . . . to go east in quest of a head of the department of pedagogy."[14] As usual, James Earl Russell's aid was sought and finally proved to be more than adequate. Russell had recommended Mr. Reeder, who was studying at Teachers College. Draper met him, "sized him up," decided he could do the job, and offered the position to him. Reeder, contrary to Russell's advice, refused "the call," claiming that he had already sacrificed too much in pursuit of his studies to have them end before completing the full course. After hearing of Reeder's refusal, Russell suggested that Draper look up Edwin

some accord with the man in pedagogy; and the man in pedagogy ought to exert some influence in filling the position in psychology" (Draper to Lucy Flower, June 22, 1899, Draper Leterbooks).

11 After Brooks accepted the position, he had to inform Draper that the La-Salle Board of Education felt "that the school has been built under such circumstances that it would be disastrous to change principals at this time, and at the meeting to-night unanimously and positively refused to release me" (S. D. Brooks to Draper, November 3, 1899; also see Alfred Bayliss, superintendent of public instruction of the state of Illinois, to Draper, November 11, 1899, Draper Correspondence). Bayliss had written "as strong a letter as [he] could" to the chairman of the LaSalle Board of Education, Mr. Mattheisen, urging that Brooks be released and that a Mr. Bridgman be hired as a suitable replacement.

12 The President wrote Lucy Flower, frequently his source of counsel in matters pedagogical, "We are not going to be embarrassed by the matter of a professor of pedagogy. There has been no considerable demand for the work. I suppose not more than half a dozen students have manifested any real anxiety for it. There is no reason why we should discontinue the work, but it will justify us in being deliberate in finding a first class man . . ." (Draper to Flower, September 25, 1899, Draper Letterbooks).

13 Andrew Sloan Draper, "The Ethics of Getting Teachers and of Getting Positions," Educational Review 20 (June, 1900): 41.

14 Draper to Burrill, September 13, 1899, Draper Letterbooks.

Grant Dexter, whom he had recommended earlier for the position in psychology at Illinois.[15] Draper saw little difference between psychology and pedagogy—at least he was not happy about each being represented by a separate department at Illinois—so he looked up Dexter.[16]

Dexter's credentials, though good, did not meet all the specifications that Burrill had set out earlier in the year. Burrill, in his form letter, wrote than any candidate "must have the training of the best schools" and, by implication, that the candidate would have to be thoroughly familiar with the state's public educational system, especially its high schools. Dexter had attended good schools and had had some experience in a high school and in a normal school. He was prepared for his work at Brown University, where he earned two degrees, and at the Worcester Academy in Massachusetts. After earning his master's degree in 1892, he went out to Colorado Springs where, for three years, he was the science master in the high school. From there he went to teach psychology for Z. X. Snyder at the Colorado State Normal School in Greeley. He took a year's leave of absence to complete the doctorate at Columbia University in 1899. When Draper got in touch with him, he was back at the Colorado State Normal School.

The specifications also called for the man in pedagogy to be a scholar, a leader, an administrator, and an ambassador of good will. He was to know the theory *and* practice of education. He was to be nothing less than a philosopher and master teacher rolled into one. Dexter's teaching, judging from the testimonials written in his behalf, was very good. However, he certainly was not a philosopher and had not earned the reputation of either a thinker or a scholar. His major work in education (*A History of Education in the United States*) and his major scientific study (*Weather Influences: An Empirical Study of the Mental Effects of Definite Meteorological Conditions*) did not appear until 1904.

Russell described Dexter's work as "methodical" and wrote that his "scholarship in education, unfortunately, is not as satisfactory as

[15] James E. Russell to Draper, November 9, 1899, Draper Correspondence.
[16] Draper had earlier told Flower that he had "always felt that it would have been just as well if the University had not established the three departments of pedagogy, philosophy, and psychology. It was done before I came here. I think two would have sufficed under our circumstances" (Draper to Lucy Flower, June 22, 1899, Draper Letterbooks).

it might be, inasmuch as he had done quite as much work in psychology and the natural sciences as in education per se."[17] James McKeen Cattell, apparently construing scholarship to mean method and approach to study as opposed to mastery, wrote that Dexter's scholarship was "excellent" and that he "had the advantage of a training in natural science as well as in education, psychology and philosophy." However, it was Cattell's opinion that Dexter had "not accomplished original work."[18] After Russell learned that Draper was corresponding with Dexter about the position, he wrote "I only wish he [Dexter] had a better scholastic equipment. . . ." Russell further suggested that Dexter, if hired by Illinois, be given the summer to prepare for the work he would have to undertake in the fall.[19]

There appeared to be no doubt that Dexter would be able "to work in close and helpful relations with the Normal Schools in Illinois." Cattell believed that Dexter would "be a good speaker in public, and would make a good impression at educational meetings."[20] Russell described him as a man who knew how to meet and how to lead people and reported that he was among the most popular men in Colorado, having "had unusual success in Colorado in his work with teachers throughout the state." He was a man of common sense who had "the New England culture and the western ability to get on with men."[21]

Acting on Russell's advice, Draper arranged to have a face-to-face meeting with Dexter to "size him up." On December 5, 1899, Draper and Dexter met and conferred in the office of the superintendent of schools in Omaha. The meeting proved to be a success. Before Christmas, Draper found a replacement for Tompkins, and Dexter had what amounted to a promotion. Soon Dexter would begin to turn out a steady stream of letters to Draper in anticipation of the work at Illinois. After taking the month of May out to lecture around the state of Colorado on "The Great Universities of the East" (complete with "70 lantern slides"), Dexter set out for Urbana to get the pedagogical work under way again.

Like Tompkins, Dexter was not looking for work when Draper contacted him. He had been "pleasantly situated" at the Colorado State

[17] Russell to Draper, November 9, 1899, Draper Correspondence.
[18] James McKeen Cattell to Draper, November 27, 1899, Draper Correspondence.
[19] Russell to Draper, November 24, 1899, Draper Correspondence.
[20] Cattell to Draper, November 27, 1899, Draper Correspondence.
[21] Russell to Draper, November 24, 1899, Draper Correspondence.

Normal School and had no desire to leave his post. Within the past year, he reported, he had "declined the offer of the chair of Pedagogy in the University of Nebraska and discouraged overtures which . . . might have led up to a similar offer from the Western Reserve University." He had also refused "other offers in Training Schools in the east." "In the matter of salary," he confided, "I should better myself very little by making the change." [22]

Though Dexter came to Illinois to take Tompkins's chair in pedagogy, he did not try to become a Tompkins. He was not a Tompkins. Nor was he a Kinley or a Draper. Kinley, Draper, and Tompkins were forceful men, men with powerful and, at times, imposing personalities. They were what their contemporaries in the nineteenth century liked to call "efficient men." Dexter, however, was not of the nineteenth century. More than anyone else who was involved with pedagogy at the University of Illinois, Dexter was of the twentieth century. His manner was different from those who hired him, supervised him, and preceded him.

While Tompkins was a bold, forceful person who was reported to have not a little charisma, Dexter, through his letters, strikes the impression of being a remarkably candid but diffident man. He had a sense of proportion; he saw that he was smaller than the world. He frankly admitted to Draper that he had "not had the experience with actual school problems that any of the men who have held the chair of pedagogy in your university have had." [23] He believed "Dr. Tompkins chair would be a difficult one for any man to fill," and was not sure he was "ready for it." [24] But Dexter was also sufficiently candid to admit that he was flattered by Draper's inquiry and expressed his willingness to tackle the job. He assured Draper that he would consider an offer from Illinois with favor. Such an offer, if tendered, would, Dexter claimed, be an expression of confidence in the success he had already achieved and "an appreciation of the fact that a man must, in a sense, grow in and to such a position as you have to offer." [25]

[22] Edwin Grant Dexter to Draper, November 15, 1899, Draper Correspondence.
[23] Dexter to Draper, November 21, 1899, Draper Correspondence.
[24] Dexter to Draper, November 15, 1899, Draper Correspondence. However, as communications with Draper continued, Dexter's confidence grew. Soon he was able to write Draper: "I am becoming more and more of the hope that when we have fully discussed the situation, it will seem evident that I am ready for it" (Dexter to Draper, November 27, 1899, Draper Correspondence).
[25] Dexter to Draper, November 15, 1899, Draper Correspondence.

With the clarity that distance now provides, we can see that Dexter's arrival was a signal that an old era had ended and a new one had begun. His approach to education was described very well by the editors of *School and Home Education* when they took notice of his selection in 1907 by President Theodore Roosevelt for the superintendency of schools of Puerto Rico. His appointment, the editors observed, "emphasizes again the modern demand for trained professional experts as the executive officers of our schools. This demand means that the people realize there are new problems in common school education to be solved, and that the tendency here as in other lines of work is to depend on men who have examined the known facts in a wide range of investigations, and possess a trained power of analysis of these facts for use as an aid in determining new policies." [26] Dexter's predecessor in Puerto Rico, Roland P. Falkner, was described as a statistician who was a "trusted adviser of government commissions because of his power to use statistics in a way to clear up problems of different kinds." Dexter was believed a capable successor to Falkner, for he possessed the same "power" with statistics. "This power," said the editors, "trained by the study of education itself, is apparent in all of Dr. Dexter's work as an author and as head of the department of education at the University of Illinois." In a short time, Dexter pulled pedagogical study from Tompkins's high philosophical plane to the empirical study of "new problems in common school education."

Dexter claimed to know the value of experience and the danger of what he called "a paucity of precedents." He also knew that "experience digs deep ruts." [27] He had not had either the years of experience (he was but thirty-two when he came to Illinois) or the intimate knowledge of the Illinois ways that came from day-to-day contact with the state's schools. He came with a new vision and, as we have noted, a new set of tools. He proceeded to draw a new furrow which was to mark off one era from another. He demonstrated that he had a vision of the work that needed to be done—a vision which was substantially different from that of either Tompkins or the University's spokesmen.

The differences between Tompkins and Dexter and their work are readily seen upon examination of the courses each offered and the aims each established for the department. In introducing his courses,

[26] "Dr. E. G. Dexter, Superintendent at Porto Rico," *School and Home Education* 27, no. 1 (September, 1907): 36.

[27] Dexter to Draper, November 21, 1899. Draper Correspondence.

Dexter put aside Tompkins's application of Hegel to pedagogy just as Tompkins set aside the doctrinaire Herbartianism of Eckoff when he came to settle down on the boundless prairie. The *Catalogue* for 1895–96 had included the courses Tompkins was to offer during his first year, but it had still carried the old description of the work of the department which told that "the point of view taken throughout is the highest known in the pedagogical field—the Herbartian." The year before Tompkins's arrival, Eckoff's "Didactics" (Pedagogy 1) had been based "on six of the minor works of Herbart" and his "Systematics" (Pedagogy 2) was "a full exposition of the system of Herbart on the two-fold basis of that thinker's General Pedagogy and Outlines of Pedagogic Lectures." Eckoff had also promised five other courses which, in addition to Spencer and Quintilian, included a course which dealt with practical matters: "School Law. How Not to Expel a Pupil. Teachers' Meetings and Conventions. Superintendents' Reports. The Teacher's Relation to the Public Press. Plotting an Attendance Curve."

Tompkins had introduced nine undergraduate courses [28] and three courses for graduates.[29] The nature of "organic elements," "organic unity," "universal aim," "subjective aspect," "objective aspect," "the

[28] The nine undergraduate courses were: "(1) The Psychology of the Teaching Process; (2) The Aim or Motive in Teaching; (3) The Universal Form of Method in Education; (4) The Universal Law and Problem of Thinking; (5) The Logical and the Psychological Factor in Educational Method; (6) Special Methods in the Common School Subjects; (7) Special Methods in High School Subjects; (8) Investigations;" and "(9) The School the Instrument of Education."
The *Catalogue* for 1897–98 promised only six courses: "(1) The Psychology of the Teaching Process; (2) The Universal Aim and Method of Education; (3) The Beautiful as a Factor in Education; (4) The Psychological Factor in Educational Method; (5) Special Methods in Subjects;" and (6) a continuation of the fifth course also called "Special Methods in Subjects."
During his final year at Illinois, 1898–99, Tompkins only offered four courses: "(1) The Psychology of the Teaching Process; (2) The Fundamental Aim and Process of Education; (3) The Logical Process Involved in Education;" and "(4) The Esthetic Aspect of Education."
[29] The graduate courses for 1895–96 included two courses in the philosophy of education and a course titled "School Management."
The *Catalogue* for 1897–98 announced six courses for graduate students: "(1) The Nature and Purpose of Education; (2) Universal Method in Education; (3) The Philosophy of Method; (4) The Philosophy of School Organization, Management, and Supervision; (5) Educational Ideals and Methods;" and "(6) School Systems."
On the eve of Dexter's arrival, 1898–99, there were only two courses for graduates: "The Philosophy of Education," and "The History of Philosophy and of Education."

logic, ethics, and esthetics of education," and "inherent law" were some of the terms Tompkins had used to show what work his under-graduates would tackle. His graduate courses were not so obviously marked by his application of Hegel to pedagogy. But the first graduate course in philosophy of education did treat the ethical, logical, and aesthetic aspects of education. Those were what Tompkins, like a good Hegelian, claimed to be "the fundamental categories of life and learning."

To the Herbartians pedagogy was "not only a professional, but a culture study." Accordingly, they broadened the work of the depart-ment "to meet the needs, not only of intending teachers, but of all University students." That is what they put into the Illinois *Cata-logue.*[30] Tompkins had designed the work for those students who de-sired "a more thorough and philosophic knowledge of the principles and practice of teaching than can be gained from the other means of professional preparation furnished by the state." Under Tompkins the work was further designed "to give a comprehensive insight into school education, its phases and problems; and thus to be of special service to those who are to hold commanding positions in school work."[31] Dexter explicitly stated that the department's aim was "to meet as fully as possible the needs of the secondary school teacher, and those of the city superintendent." He further modernized Tomp-kins's aim when he set aside Tompkins's phrase, "other means of professional preparation furnished by the state," in favor of the phrase, "normal schools of our state." He added that the normal schools were "well equipped for supplying the wants of the elementary schools."[32] Illinois was to train teachers for the high schools. Dexter did not list and describe courses for graduate students until the School of Edu-cation had been formed. He simply stated that advanced work in the history and in the philosophy of education "in which original sources are consulted and special periods critically studied" was available. And he added new features. "Experimental and statistical problems in edu-cation and child study" would be directed upon request. Those who presented themselves for advanced degrees in education would, Dex-ter announced, be expected "to present theses representing original work of merit, ready for publication."[33]

[30] *Catalogue* (1895–96), p. 59.
[31] *Catalogue* (1896–97), p. 53.
[32] *Catalogue* (1900–1901), p. 75.
[33] Ibid., p. 221.

In 1900–1901, under Dexter's direction, the education department offered nine undergraduate courses and one seminar.[34] The first course, "Principles of Education," examined "the basis for a scientific theory of education critically considered from the standpoint of the individual in his relation to the mass." It also studied "the developing powers of the child" as they related to what was becoming the aim, and sometimes the slogan of the day, "social efficiency." Other topics included "the more general problems of genetic psychology," "the making of a course of study," "method in teaching," "the recitation," "grading and promotion," and "examinations." The work started in this course was continued in four other courses: "Psychology Applied to the Art of Teaching" and three courses in methods.

The three methods courses included one called "General Methods," one devoted to science and mathematics, and one to language and history. By this time, Herbart was out and the Herbartians were in. DeGarmo's *Essentials of Method* and McMurray's *Method of the Recitation* were examined in the general methods course. The use of McMurry and DeGarmo, who were interested in practical school-keeping as much as in the philosophy of pedagogy, in place of the *ipse dixits* of the master, was a long way from Tompkins. His course in methods had spoken for itself: *"The Universal Form of Method in Education,* as determined by the nature of life. (a) In its subjective aspect. (b) In its objective aspect. (c) The three forms of the relation of 'a' and 'b.' Giving rise to the logic, ethics, and esthetics of education—the fundamental educational categories." [35] Under Dexter, the courses in special methods dealt instead with "special methods in English composition and rhetoric" and "English classics required for admission to the University," "use of laboratory manuals," "discussion and illustration of methods in algebra and geometry," and even "purchasing of apparatus." [36]

The promise to satisfy the needs of the city school superintendent was fulfilled in courses, seminars, and special lectures which examined

---

[34] The nine courses were: "(1) Principles of Education; (2) History of Education; (3) General Method; (4) Contemporary Educational Conditions and Movements in the United States; (5) Comparative Study of the Secondary Schools of France, Germany, England, and America; (6) High School Organization and Management; (7) Special Methods in Science and Mathematics; (8) Special Methods in Language and History;" and "(9) Psychology Applied to the Art of Teaching."

[35] *Catalogue* (1896–97), p. 183.

[36] *Catalogue* (1900–1901), pp. 220ff.

problems, not from a philosophical, but from an empirical point of view. The course in high school organization and management, usually taught by the High School Visitor, offered not only a "discussion of the essential elements of a good high school" but also a "consideration of the conditions existing in Illinois as determined by the work of high school visitation." Dexter's own course on contemporary educational conditions and movements in the United States included a careful study of "the school systems of our large cities and towns." [37]

The *Catalogue* of 1899–1900 announced that a seminar in education devoted to school supervision would be offered in 1900–1901. The seminar dealt with "the problems of the modern city superintendent from both the educational and business standpoints" and gave special attention "to the problems of school architecture and sanitation." This same seminar, according to the *Catalogue*, was a standard offering through the 1905–6 academic year. It was ordinarily conducted by Dexter and Brooks, but the students also had opportunities to learn from other experts. President Draper himself discussed "the subject of City Superintendents" with the students.[38] There were also special lectures for the students. For example, in the fall of 1901, the *Illini* announced that the department of education was sponsoring a series of lectures on high school organization and administration. The announced topics included "Problems of Administration in Large High Schools" by J. E. Armstrong, principal of Englewood High School; "State Aid to the High School" by Alfred Bayliss, state superintendent of public instruction; "Commercial Courses in the High School" by E. G. Cooley, superintendent of the Chicago schools; and "The Future of the Public High School" by J. Stanley Brown, principal of Joliet Township High School.[39]

Neither the presentation of practicing schoolmen to the campus nor the introduction of a new set of courses changed the past. Illinois had a past, a past that was inevitably pressing upon the future; and Dexter had to face that past. It was a past accustomed to hearing pedagogy defined in negative terms. Ever sensitive to the University's image, the spokesmen of the University had managed to do little more than

[37] Ibid., p. 220.

[38] On the morning of April 1, 1901, Dexter reminded Draper that the seminar met that afternoon and related that "the members of the seminar are promising themselves the pleasure of meeting you once more and hearing you discuss the subject of City School Superintendents" (Dexter to Draper, April 1, 1901, Draper Correspondence).

[39] *The Daily Illini*, September 24, 1901.

define the public relations aspect of the pedagogical department. All else they could say about pedagogy was cast into negative terms. It was very clear what pedagogy was not.

Perhaps the clearest statement of the University's negative definition of pedagogy is found in one of Burrill's letters. On August 8, 1899, Burrill had written to Louis H. Galbreath that there was a growing feeling against the organization of "a regularly organized school of pedagogy" on the campus.[40] Burrill allowed that there were schools for law, music, and library science at Illinois, but these were, he reported, essentially different from what a school of pedagogy would be. These schools had little or no connection with the other work offered in the University. A department of pedagogy would touch upon the subject matter of the other departments, and run the risk of doing work below "university grade."

Any work below "university grade" was, of course, the province of the high schools and the normal schools. There was a firm resolve against the founding of or the entering upon normal school work. Burrill reported: "Now it has been thoroughly well understood here that we do not want to make another normal school. We do not want to duplicate or imitate the work of the State Normal School. We do not want to make a department which will be specially open to those preparing themselves for ordinary teaching and who take only pedagogical work in the University." [41] Though no normal school work would be given, the University was willing, Burrill related, "to give our students who are well up in their literary and scientific branches a chance to learn how best to present these subjects in the school room." A teachers' bureau was founded in 1896 to help the few who wanted to find a place in the schools. And the University was also willing to engage in special work for teachers during the summers and even on Saturday mornings.

The position Burrill outlined may, in principle, have been defensible, but it certainly was not what the times called for. To use the military metaphor so popular in the nineteenth and early twentieth centuries, Illinois wanted to train leaders for the great army of teachers. The University wanted to train those who had already been equipped with the weapons of their calling and who already knew or had a good idea of how to fire those weapons. The plain fact of the matter was, however, that the army had not yet been out-

[40] Burrill to Galbreath, August 8, 1899, Draper Letterbooks.
[41] Ibid.

fitted. It was but a children's crusade. Those who had been to the University and were "well up in their literary and scientific branches" were not joining the great army.[42] In June, 1899, George R. Shawhan, the superintendent of Champaign County schools, told Dean Kinley that Saturday classes for teachers would be a profitable undertaking, for "in the sciences, few [teachers] know anything of Laboratory Methods, probably none of the use of the microscope."[43] In its concern about the capstone, the administration had lost sight of the foundation.

Dexter did not battle the negative definition. That was not his style. Moreover, battle really was not necessary, for the negative statement of the pedagogical work was as much the product of ignorance as prejudice (though prejudice would in time gain the upper hand). The character of the land, of American society, its schools, and even the university was changing during these years. Very often those who are closest to and even directing the changes are unable to see the direction of events. Illinois was no exception. While the pedagogical meetings and journals devoted considerable space and time to the discussion of the possibility of securing a corps of trained teachers and while other major universities, as we now know, were founding schools of education devoted to both the preparation of teachers and the advanced study of education as a discipline, Illinois was holding off. It did not see that these "small beginnings," as Walter Scott Monroe would later call them, were indeed beginnings. Rather, they appeared to be imitation normal schools.

Dexter knew the land was changing. He knew what the schools were trying to do, what they were doing, and what they needed. Strongly but quietly, he celebrated and attempted to accelerate these beginnings whenever and wherever he found them. Even before he arrived in Champaign, he showed that his task was to nourish them wherever they existed. In December, 1899, when Professor Forbes informed Dexter that "the Faculty of the College of Science have for some time entertained the purpose of tabulating suggested courses of study for the special benefit of prospective science teachers which should include not only the kind of science and scientific training which they need as a preparation, especially for high school work,

---

[42] In 1911, Lotus Coffman showed just what the state of the profession was. For some of his findings, see below, Ch. 6.

[43] Geo[rge] R. Shawhan to Kinley, June 6, 1899, College of Literature and Arts Correspondence.

but also the kind and amount of pedagogy which would help them to apply their scientific knowledge and methods intelligently in the public high school," Dexter wrote Draper that "the plan is one after my own heart." [44]

Forbes's letter gave Dexter the opportunity to voice his conviction that there was no reason why the University should not be "the recognized source of supply for the best fitted high school teachers in the market." It also gave Dexter the opportunity to make other observations. He explained that the market for teachers would not buy highly specialized teachers. What the schools needed were teachers who had specialized "on a group of naturally associated subjects." Dexter wanted "to see such groups specified in the proper place in the *Catalogue* and to see that those who took them made proper election from the courses [he had] outlined and also that there was a special course in methods adapted to each one of the groups." [45] What began with a proposal for prospective science teachers, at Dexter's hand, was implicitly a proposal for all prospective teachers whatever their fields of specialization. In a three-page letter, he responded to an idea and began to build the notion that the proper preparation for teaching demanded an organized sequence of course work.

In November, 1900, the faculty of the College of Science appointed Dexter to the chair of a committee charged with establishing and organizing a "pedagogical group." "The possibility of the immediate establishment of such a group leads me," he related to Draper, "to propose something at this time which I should otherwise have deferred until a later date." The proposal was, he wrote, "the establishment of a school of pedagogy, or better still I believe, a school of education." While he did not outline all features of a school of education, he did specify that it would grant degrees (A.B. or B.S.) and "fit [the students] to teach some special group of secondary school subjects." [46]

Dexter knew of no reason why a school of education should not be immediately established. "Such schools," he reminded Draper, "are being established quite generally in the larger universities." However, Dexter was not instructed to develop the plans for a school of education, even though he related that the conditions did seem "ripe for it"

---

[44] Dexter to Draper, December 31, 1899, Draper Correspondence.
[45] Ibid.
[46] Dexter to Draper, November 14, 1900, Draper Correspondence.

and specified that "it would not be in any sense a normal-school incubus to the University."[47] It was to take another four years and a new president of the University—Edmund Janes James—before the times were sufficiently ripe.

Dexter, unlike Tompkins, did not allow himself to become frustrated by less than perfect conditions and the absence of an official administrative arrangement to support the work in education. And conditions were less than perfect. When Dexter asked for stenographic help to aid him in his research, Dean Kinley advised Draper that he thought it "inadvisable to undertake to provide stenographic help for professors in their original research work," though six years earlier he told Draper that the department heads ought to be released from their routine recitation duties in order to give them time to extend the fame of the University by their publications. Dexter was a department head and was spending from eighteen to twenty-one hours per week in the classroom. Kinley also complained to Draper that Dexter did not transmit all correspondence through his own office and reported that he had doubts about "the scientific value of some of the work" Dexter proposed to do.[48] Kinley's doubts about education were never put to rest; indeed, they would persist through his own tenure as President of the University.[49] Yet Dexter did manage to start those activities which mark a full-fledged school of education.

One of Dexter's first projects was the establishment of a pedagogical library and museum. In September, 1900, he sent Draper a proposal urging the establishment of a museum. Thirteen months later he wrote that the museum was "only embryonic as yet, but is possible of full development if we push it."[50] Over 1,000 books and over "two thousand pamphlets and other objects of school interest" had already been acquired. The *Catalogue* for 1900–1901 described the "pedagogical library and museum" as a "unique feature" and related that its materials, "all of interest and value to the student of the theory and art of teaching," formed "a working pedagogical laboratory." By 1906–7, the *Catalogue* reported that in addition to an 8,000-volume

[47] Ibid.

[48] Kinley to Draper, October 25, 1901; March 6, 1895; October 10, 1901, Draper Correspondence. Cf. Dexter to Draper, October 11, 1901. Draper had apparently sent Dexter a note, asking him to comply with Kinley's wishes. See also Kinley to Draper, October 25, 1901, Draper Correspondence.

[49] See below, Chs. 7 and esp. 8 for an explicit account of the antipathy Kinley developed for professional education.

[50] Dexter to Draper, September 23, 1900, Draper Correspondence.

collection of textbooks, national, state, and city reports, courses of study, and "other educational documents of value," there was now "a considerable collection of photographs of school buildings, drawings, and constructive work by pupils in the public schools, and the nucleus of a representative collection of apparatus for the school laboratory." Also, "a card catalog of 9000 titles carefully classified, covering recent educational magazine literature" had been assembled. Materials for the study of pedagogy were being readied and made available.

Dexter, like many educationists before him and after him, believed there was a link between psychology and education. Like other young men of his era, he tried to reforge that link. When he noticed in the *Psychological Review* that T. L. Bolton, who had been offered the job in psychology at Illinois, had taken a position in the University of Nebraska, Dexter proposed to Draper that he himself "be put directly in charge of the work in both pedagogy and psychology." Dexter wrote that he believed "the two subjects cannot be even partially divorced" and predicted the "best results" would follow from uniting the two departments under one man. He explained that "certain problems in Genetic Psychology which I have in mind and which I believe will attract some attention could be much better carried on if the undisputed direction of the laboratory were mine." Dexter also had his own habits in mind in making the proposal. The proposed plan would give him a laboratory for his own work. "I hardly know," he confessed, "what I shall do without a laboratory or without problems in experimental investigation under way." The plan had the additional advantage of enabling Dexter to have "all the material for the two courses ready for the Catalogue at once." [51]

Dexter also knew just the man to get for the job in psychology if his plan were accepted by Draper. He recommended Stephen Sheldon Colvin, who had been a classmate of his both at the Worcester Academy and at Brown University. Colvin had a German doctorate from Strassbourg (1897), where he studied psychology and philosophy. Colvin had also served as an instructor at Brown University between 1892 and 1895 and at the time was teaching in the Worcester, Massachusetts, high school. He had also been taking some work at Clark University. Dexter described him as "a very bright man; almost a genius in some ways." He had not recommended him earlier because he knew that Colvin "had given so much time to the philosophical

[51] Dexter to Draper, March 13, 1900, Draper Correspondence.

side that I was not absolutely certain of his ability to direct the laboratory." [52] If Dexter were director of the laboratory, Colvin's emphasis on the philosophical side of psychology would present no difficulty.

Draper accepted Dexter's proposal to take charge of both fields as a solution to an immediately pressing problem. Psychology would be covered and the tight budget would be relieved of a bit of pressure. During the next year, Dexter's second suggestion was picked up. Colvin was hired as an assistant professor, beginning in the fall of 1901. When Colvin came, he helped with the work in education and Dexter continued to teach psychology. This arrangement lasted until 1904, when Draper recommended to the Trustees that Colvin be promoted to associate professor and that psychology be made a separate department with Colvin at its head. [53]

Dexter had help to solve an irksome administrative matter and had got himself a laboratory where he was able to show that his psychology was not an appendage to mental and moral philosophy. For Dexter, psychology was an empirical science which found its home in a laboratory where "experimentation" was conducted. Though it was a meager laboratory, it would soon take on some of the standard hallmarks of a psychological workshop. Early in the semester Dexter had to relate: "I very much need some work done in my psychological laboratory, both by a carpenter and an electrician." [54] He was planning to have shutters installed for darkening the room and electrical current for "running a motor and for light."

At the beginning of his second year at Illinois, Dexter sent Draper what he called a "somewhat lengthy communication," outlining the progress and plans of his department. [55] Besides reporting on the promising development of the pedagogical museum and the coursework which was, in Dexter's estimation, "going on with a good degree of success," Dexter told of "nine separate studies" which he had "every good reason to believe will prove sufficiently valuable to print." "A laboratory problem on the application of Weber's law to the temperature sense" was being investigated. With the aid of an assistant, Mr. Bonser (who by Dexter's calculation was being paid

---

[52] Ibid.
[53] 22nd *Report* (1904), p. 292.
[54] Dexter to Draper, n.d. (probably late September or early October 1900), Draper Correspondence.
[55] Dexter to Draper, October 1, 1901, Draper Correspondence.

twelve and a half cents an hour for his efforts), Dexter was "working on a statistical study of the high schools of Illinois, which," he claimed, "will be when completed, the most exhaustive study of the kind ever published for any system of schools." Mr. Bonser himself had in process "a study of fatigue in school children which will be," wrote Dexter, "one of the most worthy contributions of all." [56]

Professor Colvin was "nearing completion [of] a paper (40 or 50 pages) on the teaching of English," a 200-page bibliography of works on education was being assembled, and Dexter had begun "the tabulation of the 10,000 or so names in 'Who's Who' with respect to the education and other factors conducive to the 'Who's Who' kind of success." Dexter was also continuing his " 'science' study, for pupils of an adolescent age" and was planning "a careful study of pupils at the head and at the foot of the grades of the Champaign school system, to see how the two classes differ with respect to conditions mental, physical, hereditary and environmental." Allied to that study was what we would today call a study on the "dropout problem": Professor Brooks was studying "withdrawals from schools," and Dexter believed his work would "prove very valuable." [57]

In addition to the work that was already underway, Dexter was able to report that he had been asked to prepare "a 30 page article for the publications of the American Statistical Association" and that Scribner's wanted him to do a volume for their "Contemporary Science Series on The Psychology of Weather." These requests would have to wait, he explained, for his and his department's resources were already strained. He emphasized that his department was contributing to the "productiveness" of the general faculty and dared to point out to Draper that the productivity of that faculty was "none too great." He promised that his department would continue to do all that it could to extend the fame of the University and suggested that a part-time typist would be a considerable help in extending that fame.[58]

In January, 1902, just three months after telling Draper of the "nine studies," Dexter once again reminded Draper of his department's productivity and showed that he was aware of what other University departments of education were doing. He proposed the "establishment of an unpretentious series of 'University of Illinois Contributions to Education.' " The suggestion was not, Dexter emphasized, a request

[56] Dexter to Draper, January 25, 1901, Draper Correspondence.
[57] Dexter to Draper, October 1, 1901, Draper Correspondence.
[58] Ibid.

for the benefit of his own department.[59] His department did not need such an outlet for its work, for the education faculty—meager as it was—was having "no difficulty in publishing in well established journals anything ready for publication along education lines."[60]

Dexter was confident that his department could support such a series. "There are," he wrote, "in preparation in the department now studies of sufficient number and value to complete at least four quarterly issues of the 'Contributions,' and I am sure there is a sufficient number of producers in the department to continue such a series indefinitely with credit to all concerned." He informed Draper that other universities were beginning such publications and that were Illinois to do likewise, the University would be able "to present certain material which is being, and might in the future, be prepared."[61] And during his tenure as Acting Director of the School of Education, Colvin successfully initiated another series called the University of Illinois School of Education Bulletins.

If Dexter attempted to develop the University's relationships with the schools and to extend its fame through new channels, and particularly through the completion and publication of research, he did not neglect the old ways. Like his predecessors, he traveled to and spoke at various teachers meetings and maintained membership in the Illinois State Teachers' Association and the Illinois Schoolmaster's Club. However, he expanded these activities by participating in societies which embraced his professional interests at a national level.

In the spring of 1901, Dexter asked Draper to pay his expenses to the Child Study Conference which was to meet in Chicago. In making the request, he pointed out that during the past year, he had traveled to five teachers' meetings at his own expense and had spoken at all but one of the meetings. He also pointed out that "the Conference is doing a line of work which it seems to me the University should be identified with, and a line of work which is of especiall

[59] Dexter's claim that his department did not need an outlet for its work was certainly true of Dexter himself. In 1906, the Brown Alumni Monthly reported that, besides authoring two books, Dexter had published more than sixty papers in such magazines as Educational Review, School Review, Journal of Pedagogy, Pedagogical Seminary, Psychological Review, International Journal of Ethics, Education, Annals of the American Academy of Political and Social Science, Popular Science Monthly, Science, Scientific American, Worlds Work, and Harper's Weekly.

[60] Dexter to Draper, October 1, 1901, Draper Correspondence.

[61] Ibid.

interest to me." [62] While in Colorado, Dexter had served as president of the Child Study Section of the Colorado State Teachers' Association. His interest and activity in the child-study movement was soon to bring additional honor to him and publicity to the University. Before leaving Illinois he was to serve as president of the Child Study Section not only of the Illinois State Teachers' Association but also of the National Education Association.

In November, 1903, Dexter was able to report to Draper that Professor Michael Vincent O'Shea of the University of Wisconsin had asked him whether he would be able "to attend an executive committee meeting of The Society of College Teachers of Education if it were held in connection with the N.E.A. Superintendence Section meeting." [63] Earlier in the year, he reported that Professor Colvin had been invited to Brown University to serve as a visiting professor of philosophy. That invitation was, Dexter claimed, an honor bestowed upon Colvin "in which the University of Illinois would share," were Colvin granted a year's leave of absence.[64] Dexter also brought honor to himself and more publicity to the University when he was elected to serve as president of the National Society for the Scientific Study of Education in 1905.[65] In March, 1906, he was "asked to deliver a two weeks course of general lectures at the University of Kansas." [66] The invitation was no small honor. Paul Hanus of Harvard had been the guest lecturer in 1904, and O'Shea of the University of Wisconsin had delivered the 1905 series. Dexter was what, in another context, he would call a "drawing card."

Dexter also belonged to the American Geographic Society and was a fellow of both the American Association for the Advancement of Science and the American Geographical Association. He even carried the name of the University to Europe with his membership in the Société Jean-Jacques Rousseau and his service as collaborating editor of the journal sponsored by the Internationalen Societie für Schulhygiene.[67]

Besides pursuing his own research interests and running what was

[62] Dexter to Draper, April 20, 1901, Draper Correspondence.
[63] Dexter to Draper, November 10, 1903, Draper Correspondence.
[64] Dexter to Draper, March 25, 1903, Draper Correspondence.
[65] *The Illini,* March 5, 1905.
[66] Dexter to Edmund J. James, March 3, 1906, James Correspondence, Edmund Janes James Papers.
[67] *Brown [University] Monthly* 6, no. 6 (January, 1906): 134.

slowly becoming a department of education, Dexter was in charge of the summer session. In the fall of 1900, he began outlining plans for the 1901 session. His initial outlines and his subsequent work show that he addressed himself to the summer session with the same care, precision of planning, and success he carried to his other work. One of his first, though not sole, considerations was the development and projection of an attractive and favorable image of the session. He urged "that in the selection of men from outside the faculty, either for courses or special lectures, those of broad rather than local reputation be chosen." Such men would, he explained, be "drawing cards." He knew the summer session had to be sold to the teachers. Yet he was not trying to turn it into a Chautauqua. He urged that the chief officer of the session be called dean rather than director because "the title dean, at the bottom of an advertisement or printed statement would imply a more integral part of University work for the material presented, than would the term director." [68]

As one would expect, Dexter wanted to develop the work in education during the summer. At the risk of "unduly" pushing his own department, he proposed a special group of "three courses of two weeks each by outsiders." The first was to be on the German school system offered by Dean James Earl Russell of Teachers College; the second on the English school system offered by Professor Buchanan Ryley from England, who was "head of the Battersea Normal School for teachers and examiner of normal schools for teachers in the diocese of London and Rochester"; and the third on the American school system by Professor Nicholas Murray Butler of Columbia University, Superintendent Samuel P. Dutton, "or better still, President Draper." [69]

Two weeks later (November 11, 1900), Dexter added to his list of "drawing cards" when he suggested to Draper that "there would be no harm in writing" to Professors Hinsdale, Hanus, and O'Shea; Superintendents Maxwell, Balliet, Van Sickel, and Soldan. Dexter knew the abilities of the "drawing cards" were limited. They were, he said, "all general educators and not departmental specialists." However, these general educators could probably be secured "for their expenses or for a small charge." Specialists, he explained, "would most likely cost too much." [70]

[68] Dexter to Draper, October 29, 1900, Draper Correspondence.
[69] Ibid.
[70] Dexter to Draper, November 11, 1900, Draper Correspondence.

Using people "from the country at large" for the "special lectures" was not Dexter's only plan to attract students to the summer session. He asked permission to "cater to the attendance of the public school teacher by offering courses of a somewhat elementary nature." As a masquerade, the work which would be of an "elementary nature" could, he suggested, be offered under the department of pedagogy; that is, as courses in methods. Though these would be called courses in methods, "the content would have to receive much more attention than pedagogical application." [71]

Nor was Dexter trying to sell the teachers what they neither wanted nor needed. His desire to provide special courses for elementary teachers was "based almost entirely" on what the teachers had requested. He told that at the teachers' institute in Champaign during the summer of 1900, Professor Brooks had asked three questions of the teachers: "Do you expect to attend a summer school next summer? Is it at all probable? If you should, what subjects would you wish to take?" Dexter had the answers to these questions "in writing" and had made a "full tabulation of them." On the basis of this tabulation, he proposed "that Professor Howe be secured for physiology, physics and elementary science," for Howe's books "have given him something of a reputation among teachers and his name would be an attractive one." [72]

The *Announcement* of the 1901 summer session told that seven courses in pedagogy would be offered. The first three courses dealt with the American, German, and English school systems and were to be taught, as Dexter had proposed, by Draper, Russell, and Ryley. During the fifth period, (the first period after lunch) of the fourth week, President Draper lectured on the American school system. Besides explaining its "sources; beginnings; [and] evolution," he promised to treat the "necessity of taxing power and results; district, town, city, county and State organizations; the General Government and the educational system; the teaching force; legal rights and obligations of teachers; the school superintendent; the rise of high schools; agricultural and engineering institutions; State colleges and universities, and professional schools; education of defectives and wards; institutions on private foundation; completeness and flexibility of the educational system; adaptability to conditions; present tendencies;

[71] Dexter to Draper, October 29, 1900, Draper Correspondence.
[72] See three-page typescript, "Budget of Expense for the Summer Session 1901," under Dexter to Draper, November 24, 1900, Draper Correspondence.

[and] results." There is no record of Draper's having used lantern slides to illustrate his 225-minute journey through the American school.[73]

Russell, who had been allotted two weeks, was less ambitious than Draper. He only promised to treat subjects from a list which included "beginnings of German schools; the rise of Protestant Schools; the Prussian school system; student life in the higher schools; method of instruction in special subjects; the professional training of teachers; tendencies of school reform; and merits and defects of German secondary education." Ryley "intended to give the student a fair knowledge of the historical development and present conditions of the English schools." Had he been able to meet his promise to come to Urbana, he would have begun with the cathedral schools of the twelfth and thirteenth centuries, gone on to describe the current facilities of English schools, discussed Milton, Locke, Ascham, Bell, and other schoolmasters. "The great universities, Oxford and Cambridge, and the endowed public schools, Eton, Harrow, Rugby, Winchester, and others," he had promised, "will be discussed from the standpoint of personal acquaintance." He was to end with "descriptions of student life, discussions of recent educational acts, and the training of teachers." [74]

The special courses were supplemented by a series of special lectures. Chancellor E. B. Andrews of the University of Nebraska was to deliver four addressses "upon educational or historical subjects." Dexter's former superior, President Z. X. Snyder of the Colorado State Normal School, promised to "speak twice upon subjects of a general educational character." Superintendent James H. Van Sickel was to come from Baltimore to discuss "questions of interest to the superintendent and to the teacher." [75]

Dexter and Brooks both gave two courses each. Brooks offered a course on high school organization and management and one on special methods in science and mathematics. Each course would, Brooks related, make extensive use of the department's pedagogical library and museum. Dexter gave a course in "Principles of Pedagogy"

[73] *The University of Illinois Summer Term, 1901*, p. 16. Ryley was unable to meet his commitment. During the summer, Dexter wrote Draper: "We have saved about $250 on the budget o.k.d by you, by getting no one to fill Ryley's place, though Inspector Hughes lectures on his subject the last week of the term" (Dexter to Draper, July 31, [1901], Draper Correspondence).

[74] *The University of Illinois Summer Term, 1901*, p. 16.

[75] Ibid., p. 4.

(covering the standard topics for such a course) which would require the students to submit "two themes" and a course in educational psychology which was conducted in the psychological laboratory and promised to use the laboratory's "full equipment." [76]

Though the summer *Announcement* caught up with the *Catalogue* and substituted the designation "Education" for "Pedagogy," the 1902 summer session was much less spectacular than that of 1901. Dexter offered his principles course and once again required two themes of the students. Brooks presented a course in methods in secondary science, which appears to have been the same as his special methods course of the previous year. He also offered a course in high school organization and administration. The description of this course, compared to that of the course offered the previous summer in high school organization and management, indicates that the course had now been refashioned to cater to the supervisors of teachers rather than the teachers themselves. Brooks was also down for a course in the history of education which was to begin with primitive, Oriental, Greek, and Roman education, and end with modern education. Colvin offered a course on special methods in language and history for high schools.

Though the 1902 session had not been stacked with "drawing cards," a new feature was added. Besides telling the elementary teachers that there were many courses "suited to their needs," as it usually did, the *Announcement* pointed out that "the courses in *elementary science* which are being offered for the first time at this session, should prove especially valuable." [77] Dexter did not get Professor Howe, but he was allowed to "cater" to the elementary school teachers. Near the session's end (August 14, 1902), Dexter was able to report that the work had "gone along very successfully" and that besides Illinois, the summer scholars represented ten states and the "Indian Territory." Even Connecticut and West Virginia were represented, by one student each.[78] Subsequent sessions would introduce more "drawing cards" and make a greater effort to attract the teachers. Soon a more sympathetic president would arrive and offer summer scholarships to teachers from the state's schools.

Dexter's attempt to place both the preparation of secondary school

[76] Ibid., p. 17.
[77] *The University of Illinois Summer Term, 1902*, p. 7. (Italics ours.)
[78] "Summer Term Enrollments 1902," under Dexter to Draper, August 14, 1902, Draper Correspondence.

teachers and the pursuit of research into educational problems on a firm foundation within the University found a strong ally when, on August 23, 1904, the Trustees decided to ask Edmund Janes James, then president of Northwestern University, to take the presidency in Draper's room. That spring, Draper had been given and had taken the opportunity to return to the East as superintendent of public instruction for the state of New York. It was a fortunate occurrence, since Draper's effectiveness at Illinois was obviously coming to an end. He had been successful in impressing upon the state's lawmakers the fact of the University's existence and its need for increasing tax monies, but he was unable to cultivate research and scholarship of "university grade." While securing support for the University with the state's political and business leaders, Draper lost rapport with his faculty who had to resort to appointing a committee to reestablish it.[79]

James's previous experience and his concept of the proper role of a state university augured well for the state of Illinois, the University itself, and the work which Dexter had begun and was anxious to develop. The state university, he believed, more than the private university, should be sensitive to popular demands and willing to explore new ideas in the name of progress. James desired to exploit this sensitivity and will to create what today is called the "multiversity." Yet his notions were consonant with the ideals of the land grant college. The University was to be the "scientific arm of the state," conducting pure research after the fashion of the German university without abandoning the practical research the public demanded. The University, then, besides being a traditional university, was to commit itself to a popular ideal of the progressive era of which James was so much a part. That was "social service." And it was also to serve as a "civil service academy," supplying the state with all the trained and knowledgeable experts a complex industrialized society needed.[80]

If the University were to meet the challenge James set for it

[79] For a further discussion of James's career and philosophy, see the following extremely useful source: Richard Allen Swanson, "Edmund J. James, 1855–1925: A 'Conservative Progressive' in American Higher Education" (Ph.D. dissertation, University of Illinois, 1966). The reference for material in the paragraph is p. 154.

[80] Edmund J. James, "The Function of the State University," in [The University of Illinois], *Inaugural of Edmund Janes James Ph.D., LL.D., as President of the University of Illinois* (Urbana, 1905), Pt. 4, pp. 131–54 (441–64). (Reprinted in *Science*, n.s., 22, no. 568 [November 17, 1905].)

(James was ready to see that it did), it would have to disengage itself from preparatory or lower training and concentrate on the development of the graduate school and advanced training. The University was to be nothing less than the apex of the pyramid of public education. James's notion of disengagement was not, however, one of estrangement. While he wanted the University of Illinois to lead the state's schools, he did not want to compete with other schools. Where others were inclined to see competing interests, James, in the spirit of the progressive era, was inclined to see the chance for cooperation. Other educational institutions, both private and public, would not, he believed, be left to die in the awesome shadow of the University. The small colleges would be free to perform their proper function, to provide a liberal education for the state's youth as a preparation to advanced study. The private universities could only benefit from the interest in higher education Illinois would awaken throughout the state, just as Illinois had previously benefited from the founding and the dramatic growth of the University of Chicago. Moreover, as Richard A. Swanson has observed, James accurately foresaw "the day when all available colleges in the state would be insufficient to accommodate those seeking a higher education." [81]

James's desire to organize a school of education was, of course, an attempt to fulfill the expectations of his philosophy of higher education. But it was more than that. It was a desire prompted first of all by his belief that the quality of each level of education was dependent upon that of the next level. In his inaugural address he put it this way: "You cannot have good kindergartens unless you have good primary schools. . . . You cannot have good high schools unless you have good universities." [82] A corollary of this notion was that proper perparation for teaching at any given level in the state's school system was successful completion of the next level of the pyramid. Finally, James's desire to establish a school of education was a cogent reminder of his own education and of his early career. James, like many others who had come to construct the "great educational edifice" at Champaign-Urbana, came from the Illinois State Normal University.

In 1863 when James was a boy of seven, his mother, with him in tow, went to examine the model school at the Normal University,

81 Swanson, "Edmund J. James," p. 157.
82 James, "The Function of the State University," p. 149 (459).

approved of what she saw, and enrolled her son there. When he had finished the Normal's model school, grammar school, and the college preparatory course of its high school, he went to Harvard and then on to Germany. In 1877, the University of Halle awarded him the doctorate. The university officials there were so impressed with his thesis ("Studiern uber den Amerikanischen Zolltariffiseine Entwicke-lung und seine Einfluss auf die Volkswirthschaft") and his defense of it that they asked him to stay on at Halle as a *Privatdozent*. He declined the invitation, however, and returned to his homeland in August, 1877. In January, 1878, he began his sixteen-month tenure as principal of the village high school in Evanston, Illinois. In August, 1879, he went to Hoboken, New Jersey, to meet and marry his German sweetheart who kept alive his love of "things German." He took his bride to Normal where, in the fall of 1879, he accepted the principalship of the model high school.[83]

James's work as principal and as a teacher of Latin, Greek, and German earned him the title "the new Thomas Arnold" in the Normal community.[84] In later years, James was able to note that the historian James Harvey Robinson and U.S. Commissioner of Educa-tion Elmer Ellsworth Brown were among the students who attended the high school while it was under his charge and direction. More significantly, his stay at Normal also allowed him to develop friend-ships with his former teachers (John W. Cook, for example) and with other members of the staff, such as Charles DeGarmo.[85]

DeGarmo had been a student in the normal department of the Normal University while James was studying in the model high school. When James returned to take the principalship, DeGarmo was the principal of the university's grammar school. Each of the men was ambitious, and together they engaged in what may be called "educational entrepreneurship" when, in April, 1881, they bought the *Educational Newsgleaner*. They renamed the *Newsgleaner*, a local periodical without distinction, the *Illinois School Journal* and set out to remake what was an educational newsletter into a lively and opinionated journal.[86] The new owners immediately informed their readers that they had "definite and firm convictions on the

---

[83] Swanson, "Edmund J. James," passim.
[84] Illinois State Normal University [Faculty Committee], *Semi-Centennial History of the Illinois State Normal University, 1857-1907*, p. 112. (Cited in Swanson, "Edmund J. James," p. 30.)
[85] Swanson, "Edmund J. James," p. 30.
[86] Ibid., pp. 31-32.

various subjects" they would discuss and that they "intend[ed] to give them free expression." [87]

DeGarmo presented pieces on classroom techniques, while James, employing all the weight of his German training, frankly discussed local and national issues. While Congress was debating the merits of federal aid to education, James wrote a series of four articles, beginning in the winter of 1882, advocating federal aid to all public schools. It was James's first engagement with a national educational issue. As James learned and was to experience many times more, lawmakers have a way of not being influenced by schoolmen. But despite the demur of the nation's legislators, the series did meet with minor success. The *Chicago Tribune* followed his lead, and the Illinois State Teachers' Association, reportedly influenced by James's words, passed resolutions in favor of federal aid to all public schools.[88]

James resigned from his position at Normal at Christmas, 1882, and in the following March he sailed for Europe. During this period, DeGarmo decided to study pedagogy there. Upon James's advice he went to Jena. In time DeGarmo, of course, found his way to the University of Illinois, where his attempts to study teaching and to train teachers were frustrated, just as James's later attempts to provide facilities for the study of teaching and even the training of teachers would also be opposed. After a few months in Europe, James returned to take the new chair of public finance and administration at the Wharton School of Finance and Economy of the University of Pennsylvania. The *Journal* was sold to John W. Cook of the Normal University faculty and became a viable and influential publication. But James's interest in pedagogy had not been set aside permanently. At the beginning of his new career in Philadelphia, he let it be known that he believed that teacher training and the study of pedagogy belonged in the curriculum of the University as well as in the land's normal schools.[89]

James's attempt to establish a school of education at Illinois met opposition from several quarters. The Trustees were sometimes less than enthusiastic. His own faculty, already caught up in the methods-

[87] *Illinois School Journal* 1 (May, 1881): 16. (Cited in Swanson, "Edmund J. James," p. 32.)

[88] Swanson, "Edmund J. James," p. 33.

[89] James to M. J. Holmes, December 31, 1904, and James to George P. Brown, January 1, 1905. See also James, "Chairs of Pedagogics in Our Universities" (Philadelphia, 1885); "The Higher Education of Teachers at the University of Jena," *Journal of Education* 18 (December 6, 13, 1883): 365–66, 371–72.

versus-mastery-of-subject-matter treadmill, were hesitant about sanctioning the development of a new school over which it would have little or no control. And in time, President David Felmley of the Normal University (champion of the normal school interests) would raise his voice in protest against James's plan to make the University "a center from which all the latest and best methods of pedagogy should emanate with a view of uniformity in instruction." [90]

[90] *Chicago Tribune*, September 15, 1905. Quoted in Swanson, "Edmund J. James," p. 200. Also see ibid., pp. 202–3, for a brief account of Felmley's opposition.

For more complete treatment of the climax of the issue, see *Bloomington Pantagraph* during the period (e.g., December 19, 20, 21, 1910), in the pages of which Felmley customarily alerted his alumni and friends on educational issues. Felmley also put his complaint squarely to James, touched off by what he regarded as a railroaded resolution of support for the University's expansion plans at the recent High School Conference (and other such attempts). He said that the proposed $800,000 appropriation (about which amount he was mistaken) was more than the whole worth of Illinois State Normal. He cited support given to President Draper to enlarge Urbana, with the understanding that it would not attempt to rival the normals. Felmley had no opposition to a graduate department of education but only to an expanded teacher- and administrator-preparation program. He denied, and bitterly protested, the "historical" argument used to consign the normals to elementary teacher preparation, and insisted that the state normal system was the place to increase educational work. He forecasted the effects of such a move at Urbana: 1) the education faculty at Illinois, having little to do (in comparison to the heavy schedules of their normal school brethren) would dominate the professional meetings and organizations; 2) they would push for college-trained personnel in the schools, thus making it difficult for normal graduates to get work (a tendency already evident, Felmley said, due to the close cooperation between the University visitation program and that of the North Central Association); 3) high school students would be lured to Urbana by such teachers; 4) the University's program would soon prepare every kind of teacher and administrator, and not merely specialists. All in all, Felmley argued, "this proposal means the setting up of another ideal for the state, the ideal that all the intellectual and all the educational life of the state shall focus in the State University." "Do you believe," he asked James, "that the educational and intellectual interests of a state as large as Illinois are best servd [sic Felmley was a champion of spelling reform] by such concentration? Does it not mean a sort of educational trust? Is it not better to diffuse and distribute these nuclei of intellectual and educational endevor [sic]?" (Felmley to James, November 21, 1910.)

President James acknowledged, somewhat weakly, Felmley's charges, promising to study them but dismissing his fears as "surely groundless" (E. J. James to David Felmley, November 23, 1910). A further correspondence, in hopes of mitigating the difficulties and arranging a conference, was not very successful (Felmley to James, November 26, 1910; James to Felmley, Dec. 19, 21, 1910). In the last, James virtually apologized for whatever mistaken appearances there might have been—undermining the normal schools, he said, was "certainly as far from my mind and heart as anything I ever thought ["or felt," added by hand] about"—and he asked Felmley to move a resolution of support. Such a

On April 11, 1904, the Council Committee on the University Preparation of the Teachers for the Secondary Schools (S. A. Forbes, Thomas Arkle Clark, and E. G. Dexter) offered the University Senate a slate of generalities.[91] The Senate adopted them. There was official agreement "that the University may now do much more than it has hitherto done in the preparation of teachers for the secondary schools" and agreement that if the University did do more both the public schools and "the growth and reputation of the University" would be favorably influenced. Extension and systematization of the work offered for the few already preparing to become high school teachers, "more specific inducements and more important rewards," and "the preparation of a circular on the subject for wide distribution throughout the state, especially to graduating classes of high schools and normal schools" were all measures which would improve the situation. That is what the Senate believed. The Senate further agreed with the Committee that a set of requirements ought to be set down for those who desired to teach and that those who met those requirements should be given, upon graduation, "a certificate of competency to teach in the secondary schools" in addition to the "usual diploma." (It may be noteworthy that the requirements appear to be no different from those one would find in any college or university catalogue today.) The certificates were to specify what

resolution was, however, hard to agree on (James to Felmley, December 24, 1910; all these letters are in Illinois State University Archives).

It should be noted that Felmley was not an obscurantist or a rigid conservative; quite the reverse. Educated at Michigan (where he had the reputation of being perhaps the best student at the university, graduating in three years at the age of nineteen), he had been professor of mathematics at ISNU before taking the presidency. Strongly oriented toward science, he believed that it rather than the classics (including his own mathematics) should become the heart of the new education. Subjects like economics, which really do something to change the student's life, ought to be the real concern of the curriculum, Felmley thought. And he saw educational change as principally determined by social change. Politically and socially, Felmley had the reputation of being a radical—a radicalism which he attributed to religious grounds. A Granger, Free-Silver Democrat, single-tax and free-trade proponent, the Normal president was strongly committed to political action and very much concerned about academic freedom (Harper, *Development of the Teachers College*, Ch. 20. Cf. Ch. 19, esp. pp. 260–66).

[91] The material in this and the next several paragraphs which deal with the committee's report may be found in "Minutes of the University of Illinois Faculty Senate" 1, no. 83 (April 11, 1904). Cf. five-page (typescript) summary, "Copy of Actions Taken by the Senate of the University of Illinois in Connection with the School and College of Education from 1901 to 1914," in College of Education Papers.

subjects the graduate was, in the judgment of the University, qualified to teach.

Designing the requirements of such a certificate, or series of certificates, was no easy matter. It was recognized that "a general and
flexible system of requirements" was necessary because "of the diversity of high schools in Illinois." The flexibility, it turned out, would
allow the student to decide whether he wanted to teach "a three
years' or a four years' course in Latin, a year or two years in chemistry, a half-year's or a whole year's in botany. . . ." Choosing from
lists of approved courses supplied by the various departments, the
student would complete sixteen to twenty units of coursework in at
least one subject in order to qualify for a certificate of competency.
After qualifying in that first subject—today we call that the major
teaching field—he could earn certificates for other areas by completing eight to ten units of work. If constructed in the proper manner,
the certificates could be amended as the student earned additional
credits. Provision for amendment would, it was stated, "tend to hold
our teaching graduates in close and continuous relation to the University and indeed, to bring them back to us for professional and
graduate study." Of course, to be recommended for a certificate,
the student would have to "show a quality of work considerably
higher than that required for mere graduation." The most distinctive
feature of the entire scheme was that in time it could be turned over
to a team of bookkeepers for policing and administration. Today, we
call such bookkeepers certification officers.

Besides selecting courses from their departments in order to fashion
lists of courses appropriate for teachers, the various department heads
were "encouraged to offer brief fractional courses [that term was
not defined] in teaching methods special to their various subjects."
The methods courses were thought to be more important for the
sciences than for the literary subjects. The Committee put it this
way: "These special courses are particularly important where the
difference is great between high-school and college work in their
subjects, and where high-school methods have not been long established or generally agreed to,—more important, for example, in
physics than in Latin, in zoology than in mathematics."

There was also a suggestion for those who were to teach these
methods courses. The professors "responsible for the content and
management of these teachers' courses should be encouraged, and
indeed expected, to study the work of the best high schools in their

several departments." There was no indication that a rule for determining the best high schools had been found. Nor was there any
indication that the University might itself be responsible for determining what the best methods were.

The report also raised the issue of practice-teaching. It did not
join it. In fact, the term "practice teaching" itself was curiously
absent. There seems to have been general agreement that "professional training and experience are generally and correctly regarded as an important part of the preparation for secondary school
work. . . ." Two of the Committee (the dissenter was not identified)
believed that candidates for the certificate "should be given opportunity for the systematic observation, under supervision and criticism, of high-school work in the departments of teaching in which
they expect to engage." Perhaps the lack of facilities for observation
and practice allowed or even prompted the authors to be vague on
this point. However, in time the question of the facilities themselves
would become a central issue.

Finally, the Committee reported and the Senate concurred that
the improvement of the University's graduate work would help to
increase the University's "importance as a source of supply of teachers to the best grade of secondary schools." In a paragraph which
could easily have been written by Dexter, attention was drawn to
the fact that Illinois was "now sending out very few students com-
pentent to take charge of department work in first-class city schools."
In the good city schools a graduate degree was "virtually a condition
of employment." Until Illinois could place its graduates in such schools
just as other universities were, the University would be unable "to
reach a high and important part of [its] constituency." By adopting
the Committee's report, the Senate had recorded that it had an obligation to the schools.

The following October (1904), Dexter presented Dean Kinley
with another of his "somewhat lengthy" communications.[92] Dexter
was making "certain formal requests" which he trusted Kinley would
"lay before the proper legislative, or administrative, bodies of the
university." Prefatory to making his requests, Dexter presented a

[92] Dexter's proposals referred to in this and the two subsequent paragraphs
can be found in Dexter to David Kinley, October 27, 1904. Dexter compared
Illinois's number of high schools, high school instructors, and instructors in the
department of pedagogy to the number in the state universities in Indiana,
Michigan, Wisconsin, Minnesota, Iowa, Missouri, Nebraska, California, and Texas.

series of comparisons and ratios which were designed to show that, as Dexter wrote it, "my department is not receiving the support that conditions seem to warrant." He reminded Kinley that his department was a one-man department despite the growth of the University. When it was established in 1891, there had been only one man to do the pedagogical work. Between 1896, when a High School Visitor was appointed, and 1902 the Visitor devoted half his time to teaching on the campus. However, in 1902, when Professor Brooks resigned, the department once again became a one-man department. "Since that year," Dexter explained, "with the exception of one course for a single semester participated in by Professor Hollister, I have offered all the instruction of the department." He further explained that he could not expect any help from the Visitor, for his duties were likewise increasing.

Illinois, compared to other state universities, was doing very poorly by pedagogy. The University provided only one instructor of pedagogy for the state's 1,581 high schools, "while the average ratio for all the other states was 1 to 32." "The relative size of the instructional force in the department of Education at our University," Dexter wrote, "is so much the smallest of any of the [other] universities . . . being 1 to 399 while the average for all the rest is 1 to 42." Provision for the department had not kept pace with the general growth of the University. In 1891, the ratio of instructors in pedagogy to the general faculty was 1 to 36. In 1904 it was 1 to 399. This lack of support could not, Dexter claimed, be defended by the lack of interest in the pedagogical courses. "There are many more students within it," he related, "than have ever been before even when there were two instructors." There would be even more students if more work were offered. But Dexter himself could not offer more. He could do no more than teach the eight courses which were already on the books.

Further delay in the development of the department, in Dexter's opinion, was "likely to be disastrous" for the University. He offered four reasons to support his claim, each of which deserves some examination. The fourth was doubtless trivial: arrangements had been made for a special "departmental announcement," and any action ought to be taken before it was issued. The other three reasons were far more cogent, however. First, he stated: "We have in the University of Chicago a competitor which is fast gaining our field and will soon be recognized as the only higher institution in the state interested in the training of high school teachers if we do not soon act." This was not a specious claim. John Dewey had just ended his ten-year reign at the University of Chicago where he had been responsible for a staff of some one hundred persons and collective budgets of several hundred thousand dollars. Besides directing the combined departments of philosophy, psychology, and pedagogy which were responsible for graduate work in education, he presided over a newly formed School of Education made possible by the generosity of Colonel McCormick's daughter, Mrs. Emmons Blaine.[93] There was also a laboratory school—already worthy of notice by leading educators throughout the country—where prospective educational specialists could experiment and demonstrate, and the School of Education now included Colonel Parker's old Cook County Normal School. The assimilation of Parker's staff had allowed the school to train teachers, offer undergraduate courses in education, and operate a University Elementary School where demonstration and practice facilities were available to prospective teachers. There was also a separate University High School which in its design and operation had begun to approach the coming "American comprehensive high school." It had been fashioned from the South Side Academy and the Chicago Manual Training School. If anything, Dexter had understated his case.

Dexter's second reason was that the University's failure to act would encourage the normal schools to do what they ought not to do. "The normal schools of the State inspired by our evident apathy in the matter," he reported, "are turning their attention to our problems, in a way that will in the end prove disastrous not only to the preparation of the secondary but [also] of the primary force." [94] Dexter believed the normal schools were not even adequately equipped to train teachers for the elementary schools. Certainly they were not prepared to train secondary school teachers. The efforts and resources they would spend in behalf of secondary teachers would be spent at the expense of the state's elementary schools.

---

[93] For accounts of the organization of the University of Chicago's School of Education and Dewey's laboratory school, see Katherine Camp Mayhew and Anna Camp Edwards, *The Dewey School* (New York, 1936); Robert L. McCaul, "Dewey and the University of Chicago," *School and Society* (March 25, April 8, 25, 1961); Thomas Wakefield Goodspeed, *A History of the University of Chicago: The First Quarter-Century* (Chicago, 1916); and Arthur G. Wirth, *John Dewey as Educator: His Design for Work in Education (1894–1904)* (New York, 1966).

[94] Dexter to Kinley, October 27, 1904.

His third argument was that "school men throughout the state feel deeply that it is time for the state university to take up the problem [that is, the preparation of secondary school teachers] in an energetic way." Dexter fully recognized, he claimed, that the University was "not our whole machinery for the preparation of teachers," but he knew of no reason why Illinois should not begin to meet the expectations of the state's schoolmen.[95]

In light of his arguments, Dexter's request did not amount to much. He asked for only five thousand dollars. Yet that December, Dexter had to restate his design for spending the money (if it were appropriated) in connection with the President's request for a description of his department's needs. His report to James was more than a restatement, however. It also showed that there were differences between him and Kinley which were, perhaps, harbingers of what Kinley's attitude toward pedagogy would be when he filled James's room.[96]

When Dexter submitted his report to James, he attached his October letter to Kinley. Dexter had closed the October letter—a letter which neither in tone nor in substance showed any sign of cordiality—by telling Kinley that he would offer his resignation if the lack of support of his department were due "to any want of confidence" in him.[97] He began his December letter to James by recording that he had recently sent Kinley a letter, "expressing certain hopes which I entertain for the development of the Department of Education." Even though Dexter had requested Kinley to lay his October papers before the appropriate parties, he enclosed a copy of it with his letter to James noting that "that communication may, or may not, have been forwarded to you." Either Dexter did not trust Kinley (who, as we saw previously, insisted that all letters pass over his desk) to pass it on, or he wanted to express his sense of frustration at realizing what he believed to be a critical situation.

Kinley added his own letter to Dexter's December communication to James, calling "attention to the fact that [he] had already sent . . . [the] letter of October 27" and offering his appraisal of Dexter's recommendations.[98] Kinley claimed he was "heartily in favor of the development of Professor Dexter's department, both in the direction

95 Ibid.
96 Dexter to James, December 3, 1904, James Correspondence.
97 Dexter to Kinley, October 27, 1904.
98 Kinley to James, December 7, 1904, James Correspondence.

of more instructors and larger means." However, there were several points on which he felt "bound to comment." The first was "the organization of a School of Education." In his October letter, Dexter had *asked* "that steps be taken to organize and correlate all the various courses for teachers offered in the different departments in such a manner as to make them most useful." He had added: "My *suggestion* would be that such organization be in the form of a School of Education but *I would not urge* such organization." In his December letter, Dexter expressed somewhat more strongly his belief that the organization of a school of education was advisable. His main argument was that the efforts to prepare teachers needed to be coordinated. Some officer, he advised, was necessary for the sake of advising the students. "As it is [now]," he explained, "many students so arrange their preparation as not to fit the requirements of our high schools, through too narrow a specialization in some one department." He also believed "the best plan" would have "an officer who should be in some sense supervisory of all teachers' courses." [99] Kinley informed James that the organization of a School of Education had been discussed within the University "a few years ago" and that it was then decided "in the negative." When the "courses of Training for Business" were organized, "the same policy prevailed." [100] Wisdom had dictated that neither a school of education nor a school of commerce be established.

Kinley had three other objections to Dexter's proposals. He expressed his surprise at finding "a scheme for training teachers without a place in it for philosophy." [101] Though he did not elaborate on this point himself, it is worth noting that he had in this instance put his finger on *the* aspect which distinguished Dexter from Tompkins and which was to distinguish Dexter from his successor, William C. Bagley. Of the three men, Dexter was certainly the most empirically minded. His courses and his proposals show a very strong attachment and interest in day-to-day problems of the teachers and their superiors. His approach was, as we have seen, markedly different from that of Tompkins. To Kinley, who had strong reservations about the new psychology as well as a distinct fondness for philosophy, the omission probably was very striking. He had put his finger on a point which remains, to this day, a sensitive one.

[99] Dexter to James, December 3, 1904, James Correspondence.
[100] Kinley to James, December 7, 1904, James Correspondence.
[101] Ibid.

Dexter proposed a teaching force for the school which included, besides an instructor in psychology, seventeen instructors. These seventeen were not, however, to be full-time personnel in the school. Rather, Dexter's list was a recommendation that each "academic department . . . offer one or more teachers' courses—primarily in methods." This proposal was not, however, totally new. As Dexter explained, "some five or six" departments already offered such courses. He was urging that the other departments do likewise, especially the Departments of Manual Training (mechanical engineering) and Household Science. These two departments, Dexter recommended, ought to "be expected to do so as soon as possible, as teachers are in great demand in both these subjects, and we have the material equipment for their preparation as have few institutions in the country." [102]

Dexter's proposal at this point was in line with the report the Senate had adopted in April. Kinley objected, however. The objection Kinley offered was a weak appeal to an unspecified popular opinion. In comment upon Dexter's list of seventeen, he wrote: "I cannot help agreeing with those who think that discredit has been thrown on the whole subject of pedagogy by the apparent insistence of its professors that there are different methods, or principles, of instruction applicable to each subject, and that it is necessary, or desirable, for a person who is to teach the subject to take these courses in great detail." [103] Though Kinley did not offer any real reasons or explanations for his disagreement, there are some possible explanations. One is that were Dexter's point adopted, the very number of people involved would call for some administrative coordination. That would strengthen the case for the establishment of a school.

Another possible explanation is that Kinley was fighting for a threatened psychological doctrine. The famed Thorndike-Woodworth experiments which were widely hailed as the final blow to mental discipline and the transfer of training were then only three years old. Kinley, as we know from a letter he sent to Boyd H. Bode

[102] Dexter to James, December 3, 1904, James Correspondence. The seventeen areas in which Dexter wanted instructors were: elementary agriculture, art and design, botany, chemistry, French, geology and physical geography, German, history, household science, Latin, mathematics, manual training, music, physics, physiology, rhetoric, and zoology.

[103] Kinley to James, December 7, 1904, James Correspondence.

in 1919, held to the old doctrine.[104] If transfer of training took place (whatever that may be), general methods or one set of general principles would clearly have sufficed for all instructional tasks. However, the interpretation then generally given to the Thorndike-Woodworth work was that there was no such phenomenon, and that consequently a different body of subject matter or a different set of skills called for a different set of methods.

The issue of transfer of training could have real administrative consequences. Dexter did favor more than one organizational change and Kinley did resist them. Dexter proposed that a second High School Visitor be added to the staff and that each of the Visitors spend one semester visiting and one "at the University in instructional work, giving the students the advantage of his unusual experience in the field." At present, Dexter explained, the Visitor spent "little or no time" on the campus and "is handicapped from not being fully familiar with home conditions." Yet no one "who was out of touch with the schools" could be as valuable on the instructional force as a Visitor.[105] Finally, the Visitor's work as chairman of the Placement Committee would be rid of one of its difficulties. The Visitor would, under Dexter's plan, have the advantage of knowing both the prospective positions and the students.

The reasons Dexter gave for adding a Visitor and changing his duties were, according to Kinley, "specious." Kinley pointed out what Dexter had forgotten, or perhaps chose to forget—that the High School Visitor was "an entirely independent officer, responsible directly to the President." [106] From the University's viewpoint, the Visitor was a recruiter if not a public relations man. The Visitor's work was sensitive and his decisions often created resentments that took the prestige and diplomacy of the President to smoothe. On the other hand, if Kinley was more precise in stipulating the officially defined functions of school visitation, he entirely failed to join an

[104] Kinley to Boyd H. Bode, July 16, 1919, James Correspondence.
[105] Dexter to James, December 3, 1904, James Correspondence.
[106] Kinley to James, December 7, 1904, James Correspondence. Here Kinley has a point. Though he seems not to join in the pedagogical issue Dexter raises, he does present a reminder of constant public relations problem the University had difficulty escaping. And Dexter did not address himself to it. As was related in Ch. 4, the High School Visitor was a position that demanded Draper's attention and concern. James was in a similar situation. For a brief account of the public relations problems Hollister, as High School Visitor, presented to James, see Swanson, "Edmund J. James," p. 197.

issue which those before Dexter had raised and which Dexter was continuing to bring to the fore. Dexter was committed to the notion that there had to be a connection, and a strong one at that, between what was happening in the schools and the University's teacher training program.

In the October letter to Kinley, Dexter also urged "the appointment of an instructor whose duty it should be to have in charge observation and practice work which should and could be arranged for in the schools of Urbana or Champaign or the Academy, or all three." [107] Dexter did not press this point, for he knew, as he told James in December, that "heretofore the sentiment of the administration had been strongly against the use of the Academy in any way by any department." But he did not know what James's attitude was. Nonetheless, he did "strongly advocate some plan by which the preparatory school could be used legitimately for observation and practice by the students in my department." [108] The required observation and practice could easily be supervised by the principal of the Academy who, Dexter advised, should be appointed to his department (or school) and be given the position of assistant professor of education. Kinley, who in later years would not allow members of University High School any title which would suggest they were part of the University, did not offer a written comment on this proposal. However, it must be noted that Dexter was asking that a man who was in charge of work that was not of "university grade" be brought into the University.

By the following January, the matter was before the University Trustees. A resolution, introduced by Mrs. Abbott, directing that a three-man committee "be appointed to report to the Board upon the advisability of establishing a school of education with special reference to the preparation of teachers for secondary schools," was adopted. On February 20, 1905, the committee reported that, since the *University Bulletin* already stated that the department of education attempted to meet the needs of the prospective secondary school teacher and the city school superintendent, it construed its charge "to report upon the advisability of expanding what is now a department of the College of Literature and Arts into a separate school or college." The committee advised that it favored the expansion at the

107 Dexter to Kinley, October 27, 1904.
108 Dexter to James, December 3, 1904, James Correspondence.

"proper time" and asked James to give his recommendations at the June meeting of the Board.[109]

James then appointed a committee from the senate to investigate the formation of a school. The Senate committee did not approve of a full-fledged school of education. "It is the judgment of your committee," the report read, "that a school of education separate in administration from the existing colleges, and with a separate student registration is not advisable, because of the difficulty and friction which such a plan would introduce into our administration, and because all the educational purposes of such a school can well be accomplished without it." The committee did recommend that all instructors who taught courses for teachers be organized as a group "to be known as the 'faculty of the school of education.' " Though the members of the faculty of the school were to maintain their departmental affiliations, there was agreement that the faculty would need an administrative officer. He was to be called the school's "director" and "be charged with . . . promoting its interests in all ways possible." "All matters of educational policy initiated by the school" were to be "referred back to the several colleges . . . for approval." Once policies were established, the school of education was to "be responsible for the details of their administration." The committee further recommended that the department of education be allowed to add two or three instructors so that it could expand its work; that instructors be added to other departments so special courses for teachers could be given; and that the funds be provided to finance "advertising, lectures, and visits to high schools by the special department teachers." [110]

James presented the Senate's report to the Trustees on April 27, 1905, and the Trustees authorized him "to organize a school of education along the lines indicated" and asked him to "submit the details as to the particular chairs desired with the salaries of the same at a subsequent meeting of the Board." Before the end of the academic year, Dexter would have nearly all that he had requested in his October letter to Kinley.[111]

[109] 23rd *Report* (1906), pp. 40, 43, 44. The members of the committee were: Mr. Bayliss, Mrs. Abbott, and Mr. Nightingale.

[110] Ibid., pp. 62ff. The members were: S. A. Forbes, T. A. Clark, D. Kinley, E. Davenport, L. P. Breckinridge, A. H. Daniels, A. G. Hall, H. P. Carman, E. G. Dexter, H. A. Hollister, S. W. Parr, and H. J. Barton.

[111] Ibid.

At the end of the following May, the Senate committee judged it "desirable that the school of education should undertake the preparation of departmental teachers for high schools, including supervisors of manual training." The committee also endorsed what Dexter had been attempting since he arrived on the campus—"substantial preparation for the work of the school principalship and superintendency." The committee made no comment about the use of the Academy by the department of education, but it did believe it "desirable that an effort be made to establish such relations with the neighboring high schools as may be necessary to make such schools available for observation work by those of our students who are preparing to teach." And Dexter was advised by the committee to investigate "the feasibility of practice work by the students of the School of Education. . . ." [112]

Provision was also made for entry into the School. Graduates of the state's normal schools, provided they had also attended a University-approved high school, were to be given junior standing in the University, thus making them "eligible for enrollment in the School of Education." However, it was specified "that advanced University credits shall not be given to such students except for work judged to be the equivalent of the University courses for which such credit is given." Dean Kinley's motion specifying that the designation "junior standing" given to the normal school graduate did not excuse the student "from the prescriptions of the Colleges of Literature and of Science" was adopted. Finally, the Senate accepted the recommendation of the Committee on Certificates of Competency to Teach that all candidates for a certificate be required to complete "the following constant:" "Elementary Psychology" (3 credit hours); "Principles of Education" (5 hours); "High School Organization and Administration" (3 hours); "and 3 hours . . . in courses offered by the Department of Philosophy." Had the Senate required practice work of all candidates, it would have written what is still the typical pattern of requirements for a license to teach in the high school.[113]

On June 2, 1905, the Board approved the appointment of Dexter as Director of the School of Education for the 1905–6 year.[114] At the

112 For the report of the Committee on the Organization of the School of Education, see "Minutes of the University of Illinois Faculty Senate" 1, no. 118, (May 29, 1905). (Cf. n. 91 above.)
113 Ibid.
114 23rd Report (1906), p. 75.

same time Frank Hamsher, principal of the Academy, was appointed assistant professor [115] in the School, and James was authorized to nominate a man for a newly created "second assistant professorship in Education." Dexter, as director, was given a budget of $2,000 which was to be divided evenly between "special lectures" and "incidental expenses." In the fall, the *Daily Illini* was to write of what it called "an organization to prepare public school workers." This organization "includes," the paper reported, "thirty-one instructors of various academic ranks. Besides this, the five normal school presidents of the state, together with Hon. Alfred Bayliss, State Superintendent of Public Instruction, constitute a board of special lecturers, who, during the year, will discuss at the University topics of educational interest." [116]

The 1905–6 *Register* (1906–7 *Announcements*) was the first catalogue to tell of the newly formed "Faculty of the School of Education." It also told that the second assistant professorship had been filled. Besides listing Dexter and Hamsher as members of the department, it listed Edward Octavius Sisson. Before coming to Illinois, Sisson had been director of the Bradley Institute. In 1904, he left Bradley to finish his doctorate at Harvard. Upon completing his work at Harvard in 1905, he came to Illinois to help teach the expanded curriculum. His load for the year did not inspire laziness. Besides two graduate seminars (one on school hygiene and the other on the course of study), it included the old standby, "Herbartian Pedagogics." The new instructor was also responsible for a course in "Educational Classics" which treated not only Plato, Aristotle, and Quintilian, but Rabelais and Montaigne as well. He also chaired a novel offering called "Social Phases of Education" which promised the study of "the relation of education to vocation and crime." [117]

Assistant Professor Hamsher handled two courses: "Observation" and "Practice." In the observation course, the students, provided they were juniors or seniors, were to "observe regularly and systematically the instruction in particular classes in the academy and neighboring high schools" for four hours each week. In a fifth hour they were to confer with instructors. The claim for the practice course

[115] The following September, James asked for and received permission to appoint an additional instructor to the Academy to relieve Hamsher of teaching work there, thereby enabling rim to offer instruction in the University (24th *Report* [1908], pp. 4–5).
[116] *The Daily Illini*, September 28, 1905.
[117] *University of Illinois Announcements 1906–7; Register for 1905–6*, p. 258.

in the *Catalogue* was that the students were "assigned classes in available secondary schools for instruction under the supervision of the instructor or competent critic teachers." [118]

The 1905–6 academic year was, as events were to unfold, a turning point in the development of professional education at Illinois. At the end of the year, both Sisson and Hamsher resigned their posts. Hamsher left to take the principalship of Smith Academy in St. Louis. Sisson went to Seattle to become the chairman of the department of education in the University of Washington. Charles M. McConn, a faculty member of the Academy, was appointed "acting principal" of the Academy, but was not appointed to the School of Education faculty. Edwin Lee Norton, who had taught at the Ypsilanti Normal School and the University of Wisconsin after receiving his doctorate from Harvard in 1900, came to take Sisson's place. McConn and Norton were to remain on the faculty for the following few years, but the continuity, direction, and character of the work was about to be changed. In early April, 1905, James and Dexter had discussed the possibility of Dexter's becoming the U.S. Commissioner of Education in Puerto Rico.[119] It soon became a reality. On July 6, 1907, the Board of Trustees voted to grant Dexter "indefinite leave of absence without pay" to allow him to serve the federal government.[120]

Dexter's resignation can be taken as another benchmark in the development of the professional work at Illinois, much as Tompkins's resignation in 1899 had been the end of an era. Though the work in education had developed far beyond what it was in 1900 when Dexter arrived, there was still a long way to go before it would become what Dexter had envisioned, and, more important, what James wanted it to become. As president, James reported to the state superintendent of public instruction in 1906, that Illinois had taken only its first steps toward catching up with other major universities in the field of professional education:

Owing to the growing interest in the scientific study of education in all its different aspects, and to the growing demand on the part of the public for better trained teachers and superintendents, there has been a marked tendency of late years toward the creating of special schools and colleges of education, as an important part of university work. The Teacher's

118 Ibid.
119 Dexter to James, April 30, 1905, and April 16, 1906, James Correspondence.
120 24th *Report* (1908), p. 158.

College in connection with Columbia University in New York, and the College of Education in connection with the University of Chicago are perhaps the most ambitious attempts to satisfy this public demand. The schools of education organized in some of the state universities represent another form of organization intended, however, to accomplish the same result.[121]

Illinois had not, he explained, really established a school as other universities had. "The Board of Trustees," he related, "created a school of education, which was in some respects an enlargement of the existing department of education in the College of Literature and Arts and the College of Science, and in other respects a grouping together for purposes of administrative efficiency, the various courses . . . bearing more immediately and directly upon the future work of the teacher." Though he expressed his customary confidence in what had been begun, James concluded that the step taken was "inadequate." In 1908 James's appraisal of the work had apparently not changed. He submitted the same report, word for word, to the state superintendent.

The year following Dexter's resignation, Professor Colvin was appointed to act as Director of the School, and he and Norton handled all the courses. In 1908–9, Colvin continued as Acting Director, but a new faculty member was added to the staff. He was William Chandler Bagley. In spite of the fact that Bagley became the next permanent director of the School rather by elimination than choice, he not only picked up where Dexter had left off, but proceeded to develop the School more extensively than anyone would likely have envisioned. Under Bagley "the scientific study of education in all its different aspects" would reach a level not to be exceeded for more than a quarter of a century.

[121] 26th SSPI (1906), p. 392.

CHAPTER 6

❦ *Confidence and Making Good*

At the end of his first semester in the professorial ranks at the University of Illinois (January, 1909), William Chandler Bagley secured the approval of Professor Colvin, then Acting Director of the School of Education; Evarts B. Greene, Dean of Arts and Sciences; and President Edmund J. James to use the University Academy as a practice school.[1] The plan Bagley had submitted reflected a concern which had dominated much of his work prior to coming to Illinois. As a professor of education, as Director of the School of Education, as an untiring lecturer and editor, and as a rapidly rising national leader of educational affairs, Bagley was to wage a campaign on behalf of the professional training of teachers at the University of Illinois and throughout the country.

Within three years, Bagley had found a place among the top twenty-five educational leaders of the nation. In the early summer of 1912, Wood C. Straight of the *Brooklyn Daily Eagle* set out to determine which educators were shaping up and directing American

[1] Stephen S. Colvin, Acting Director of the School of Education, to William C. Bagley, January 19, 1909; Evarts B. Greene, Dean of Arts and Sciences, to President Edmund J. James, January 22, 1909; and James to Greene, January 22, 1909, all in James Correspondence.

educational thought and practice.[2] Straight began by establishing an "electoral college," consisting of nearly twenty-five professors of education in universities and normal schools; fifteen representatives from boards of education, such as Jane Addams, John Martin, and Egerton L. Winthrop, Jr.; some forty prominent leaders of educational thought, such as Butler, Draper, Jordan, Claxton, and Hall; and a dozen leading editors, sociologists, and writers, such as Lyman Abbott, Walter Page, and Charles Zeublin. After Straight counted the college's ballots and determined who the twenty-five leading educators were, he found Bagley to be twenty-first on the list. Others elected ahead of Bagley included Charles W. Eliot, G. Stanley Hall, Nicholas Murray Butler, John Dewey, Booker T. Washington, and James B. Angell.

Bagley had brought himself attention and the University publicity of a favorable sort. He had also won the support of the friends of the schools. Straight reported that "the rank and file of good solid, confident and unassuming supporters of the schools have elected Bagley as one of their official answers" to the muckrackers who were asking, "Are the Public Schools a Failure?" Wherever Bagley went, Straight related, he left behind him "a memory of enthusiasm, confidence, and making good." Wherever and whenever he talked to teachers, he emphasized "skill, knowhow, and craftsmanship." Straight could have added that Bagley was convinced that "skill, know-how, and craftsmanship" in teaching could be learned only by studying teaching in a model school. He could also have added that Bagley was keenly aware of how unprepared most teachers were to assume their obligations, and that he took every opportunity to tell about it.

Bagley's discussions of the preparation and status of teachers not only reveal the status of the profession halfway into the "progressive era" but also show that he was a friend of nearly every educational interest in Illinois. While he supported the scientific study of education and co-founded and co-edited the *Journal of Educational Psychology* (1911),[3] he talked to the state's teachers [4] and to the parents and teachers as a contributor and eventual editor of Illinois's *School*

2 Wood C. Straight, "An Election of Eminent Educators, VII-Bagley," *Brooklyn Daily Eagle*, June 3, 1912. Also see George A. Brown, "An Election of Eminent Educators," *School and Home Education* 32, no. 1 (September, 1912): 4.
3 J. Carleton Bell, C. E. Seashore, and Guy Montrose Whipple were his co-editors and co-founders.
4 Bagley was a frequent speaker at conventions of Illinois teachers and those of teachers in other states. In 1908, 1909, and 1910 he delivered such timely lectures

and Home Education.[5] While he fought for the establishment of practice facilities for teachers on the campus of the University, he complained about competition among educational institutions and praised the work of the normal schools. He argued that the nation did have a real interest in education and an obligation to tend to that interest with dollars from the federal coffers, and that was an argument not inconsistent with President James's own desire to see the founding of a national university.

In March, 1910, William Carl Ruediger and George Drayton Strayer published the results of their investigation into "the qualities of merit in teachers" in the *Journal of Educational Psychology.* It is very likely that, as an editor of the journal, Bagley had read the article before its publication. If he had not, he certainly had read it by the following October when he devoted a six-column editorial review to it in *School and Home Education.* Though Bagley recommended that their investigations "be repeated with a larger number of schools in order to make certain that the results are entirely trustworthy," he had no serious reservations about the findings of the two investigators. The results were, he wrote, "thoroughly in harmony with the experience and convictions of the public-school men."[6] Ruediger and Strayer had couched in statistical form the experience and convictions of Bagley and many other practicing schoolmen.

In undertaking to determine what qualities constituted "general merit" in teachers, Ruediger and Strayer had isolated eight specific qualities. They found that the two most important qualities were (1) the ability to maintain order in the classroom, and (2) the ability to impart instruction. To Bagley it was "especially significant . . . that the two specific qualities found to be most important . . . are capable of development, either through the formal training that is

---

to the Illinois teachers as "Recent Results and Tendencies in Child Study," "The Possibility of Training Children How to Study," and "The Preparation of Teachers with Reference to Moral Ideals, Aims and Prejudices." (See *Proceedings* of the Illinois State Teachers' Association for these years.)

[5] From the time of his arrival to his departure, Bagley was a continuous contributor to *School and Home Education.* In 1912 he assumed its editorship. This journal, while designed for professionals more than for parents, was not aimed at other university professors of education. It was written for those who were working in the schools and those whose immediate interest was the common school.

[6] William C. Bagley, "Some Implications of the Ruediger-Strayer Survey," *School and Home Education* 30, no. 2 (October, 1910): 45.

offered by a teachers' training school or through the self-discipline that comes with experience." [7]

To Bagley there was no doubt that Ruediger and Strayer had shown that good teaching was dependent upon both experience and formal training. From their data the two investigators concluded that it took five years of experience for the elementary school teacher to reach what they termed "first class efficiency." [8] They found that no teacher who had less than five years experience ranked in either the first or the second rank of "general merit." They further related that while 28 percent of all the normal school graduates of their sample ranked in either the first or the second rank of "general merit," only 17 percent of the college graduates were in either of the upper two ranks. In the lower two ranks of "general merit" there were to be found only 16 percent of the normal school products and 44 percent of the college graduates. No teacher "who was merely a high school graduate" was to be found in either of the upper two ranks.[9]

In Bagley's opinion, the Ruediger-Strayer survey underscored two clear needs. First, there was an obvious need for more facilities for the training of teachers. Second, it was necessary to find the means to retain teachers in the profession "just as they are about to enter upon a period of real efficiency." [10] The public, said Bagley, was failing to differentiate between good and poor teachers and also failing to provide the proper rewards for good teaching.

By pointing out that more facilities were needed for the training of teachers, the investigators were providing the educationists with data for making a case with the public. By showing that normal school graduates were more efficient than were college and univer-

[7] William C. Bagley, "The Qualities of Merit in Teachers," ibid., p. 44.
[8] William C. Bagley, "Experience and Teaching Efficiency," ibid., p. 45. Ruediger and Strayer had investigated the "qualities of merit" for only elementary school teachers. In April, 1912, Bagley reported that the principal of the Hittle, Illinois, township high school, A. C. Boyce, had undertaken an investigation similar to that of Ruediger and Strayer to determine the qualities of merit of high school teachers. Boyce found that it took only three years for high school teachers to reach maximum efficiency and that the ability to impart instruction was more important than disciplinary ability for high school teachers. Comparing the two studies, Bagley concluded that "the importance of professional preparation is clearly indicated by both studies" (William C. Bagley, "Qualities of Merit in High School Teachers," *School and Home Education* 31, no. 8 [April 1912]: 319–20).
[9] Bagley, "Experience and Teaching Efficiency," p. 85.
[10] Bagley, "Some Implications of the Ruediger-Strayer Survey," pp. 45–46.

sity graduates, they had, in Bagley's judgment, shown not only that normal schools must be better supported, but that colleges and universities "should also provide facilities for practical training in the technique of teaching as the normal schools offer." [11]

In 1911, one year after Ruediger and Strayer published their survey, Lotus D. Coffman, who had just been appointed lecturer in the School of Education at Illinois, published his study of the American teacher: *The Social Composition of the Teaching Population.* Bagley was even more impressed with its findings than he had been by those of the Ruediger-Strayer survey. Like his predecessors, Coffman provided quantitative descriptions of teachers. But his findings were not as well known to the schoolmen as those of Ruediger and Strayer. Bagley confessed that he found Coffman's findings "unbelievable." However, it was a disbelief of horror and chagrin. Bagley was forced to believe because, as he said, "the internal evidence of the statistics shows a very high degree of probability that they are [true.]." [12]

The incredible characteristics of the teaching population which Coffman revealed were the general immaturity of the teachers, their inadequate or total lack of professional training, the brief time most teachers spent in the service of the schools, the poor status and even poorer salaries offered teachers, and the dreadful condition of the normal schools. Coffman had shown that the nation's schools were staffed by teachers who were, in large measure, inexperienced and either untrained or ill-trained for teaching. The profession of education needed 125,000 new teachers each year just to fill the places of those who were leaving the profession. The average length of service was but four years. The normal schools, training schools, and teachers' colleges were graduating only about 19,000 trained teachers each year. That rate was not quite sufficient to fill new vacancies created by the increase of specialization of teaching fields and the growth of the school population.

Coffman had demonstrated, Bagley wrote, that the greater proportion of the new teachers entering the profession each year (excluding the 19,000 who were specially trained) came from families of not less than six children each (at the time the average American family had four children); "that the greater proportion of them come from

11 Ibid., p. 46.
12 William C. Bagley, "Dr. Coffman's Study of the Teaching Population," *School and Home Education* 31, no. 3 (November, 1911): 92.

families the average income of which is less than eight hundred dollard a year; and that most of them enter the work of teaching with no intention of making a life career but merely because it offers opportunity to obtain a little badly needed money without involving the expenditure of much time in preparing themselves for the work." [13] For women, teaching was a stepping-stone to marriage; for men, it was a stepping-stone to administrative positions in and out of education. Coffman had shown that at best the teachers were as good and as prepared for their tasks as Charles Shamel was. To Bagley, Coffman had turned in an indictment—an indictment not against the teachers but against the public conscience.

There was, Bagley reported, an easy and obvious remedy to what Coffman had found and described. Many were proposing that certification requirements be strengthened and that teachers' salaries be raised to attract better candidates. Bagley was not opposed to either of the recommendations, but he was opposed to what would be required to effect them. To adopt them, he explained, would be to put "boys and girls" out of work. Bagley had no desire to turn the children's army on to the streets. Nor did he want them in the classrooms as teachers. To keep them in the schools was an expensive act of charity. "Our sympathy goes out to these young people," he confessed, but there is no earthly reason why this form of charity (and in effect this is what it is) should be given at the expense of millions of children." [14]

Bagley went on to explain that if certification standards and salaries were gradually raised as many had proposed, the sociological base of the profession would gradually shift to those families who could afford to send their children to the training schools. Bagley voiced his objection to this in the form of rhetorical questions: "Should we not leave the profession of teaching open to any youth of the land irrespective of his parents' economic status, provided only that he himself shows capacity for the work? Otherwise are we not in effect making class distinctions in the very calling that must be depended upon to keep alive our ideals of democracy and equal opportunity?" [15]

Bagley argued that if it is admitted "that public school service is at least as important and fundamental to social welfare as military

[13] William C. Bagley, "The Injustice of Low Standards," ibid.
[14] Ibid.
[15] William C. Bagley, "The Remedy: Normal School Training at Public Expense," ibid., p. 93.

and naval service," then the way out of the dilemma he had described was for the normal schools to pay their students just as the naval and military academies at Annapolis and West Point paid their cadets. Bagley believed this proposal would have the advantage of allowing all who were able to teach the opportunity to do so, and, at the same time, insure that all teachers would be prepared for their tasks. The "teacher cadets" were to be paid a living wage "on the pledge that they will enter the service and remain for at least five years after graduation." [16] Apparently Bagley assumed that after five years of service the teachers would volunteer to make the "service" a career.

Bagley anticipated a number of possible objections to his plan. Some, he claimed, would object on the grounds that his plan "would give the state normal schools a tremendous advantage over other educational institutions." [17] To that objection he answered that "schools are fighting against one another when they should stand shoulder to shoulder in the common fight against ignorance, superstition, the decadence of respect for law, and a thousand other ills that constantly threaten to tear away the pillars on which civilized society rests." [18] Schooling was too great and too important a "public service" to allow "senseless competition" to determine its course and success.

Bagley's commitment to public education had begun in the 1890's —in that decade of American history which historians of American society as well as of American education have singled out as a great dividing line, separating one era from another. In 1895, Bagley was graduated from the Michigan Agricultural College and was set to begin a career in scientific agriculture. However, he found that the Panic of 1893 had introduced a measure of sobriety to the Gay 90's. There were few jobs. For Bagley there was none. So, not unlike Shamel, he turned to teaching as a way of earning money while waiting for something better.

Bagley accepted a post in a one-room school in the village of Garth, Delta County, in the Upper Peninsula of Michigan—a community which has since been reclaimed by the wilderness. Except

[16] William C. Bagley, "A Further Advantage of Paying Salaries to Normal School Cadets," p. 94.
[17] William C. Bagley, "Some Objections Considered," ibid.
[18] Ibid.

for the summer of 1902 when he worked as an inspector of orchards and nurseries under the Illinois state entomologist, Bagley never again practiced his agricultural expertise professionally. Unlike Shamel, he found a life's career in the service of the schools. The task of teaching, I. L. Kandel has written, "inspired him with an ambition to find out more about the principles of education and to inquire whether such principles could not be discovered and established by scientific methods." [19]

In order to learn about the new science of the mind, Bagley spent his summer vacation of 1896 at the University of Chicago, where he studied psychology and, under Jacques Loeb, the physiology of the nervous system. In September, he returned to the sawmill village of Garth for his second and final year. The next year Bagley went to the University of Wisconsin, where he received the master of science degree in 1898. There he studied under Joseph Jastrow, Michael Vincent O'Shea, and John William Stearns. From Stearns, Bagley took courses in the history of education, school supervision, modern educational systems, the Herbartian pedagogy, and the philosophy of modern science. The work he took from O'Shea included child study, hygiene of mental development, and the methods of teaching. Besides enrolling in Jastrow's courses in the psychology of the nervous system, experimental psychology, and abnormal psychology, Bagley wrote his master's thesis, "On the Correlation of Mental and Motor Ability in School Children," under the direction of the Polish psychologist.

From Madison, Bagley went to Cornell University to study psychology and education. The beginnings of Bagley's studies at Ithaca in 1898 coincided with the beginning of Charles DeGarmo's tenure at Cornell University. He undoubtedly continued his study of the Herbartian pedagogy under DeGarmo. Formally, he enrolled in DeGarmo's courses in the psychologic foundations of education, the science and art of teaching, and philosophy of education. In addition to his work in education and psychology under Isaac Madison Bently and Edward Bradford Titchener, Bagley also studied neurology and invertebrate zoology at Cornell. In 1900 he completed, under the sponsorship of Titchener, his doctoral dissertation, "The Appercep-tion of the Spoken Sentence: A Study in the Psychology of Lan-

19 I. L. Kandel, *William Chandler Bagley: Stalwart Educator* (New York, 1961), p. 6.

guage," and received the eighth of the fifty-four doctorates licensed by the czar of the Cornell psychological laboratory.[20]

Upon receipt of his doctorate, Bagley found himself standing at the edge of a new era in both education and in psychology. In a year Thorndike and Woodworth would publish their work on "transfer of training." Departments and schools of education were being defined and founded. It was clear that the separation of psychology from philosophy was to be a permanent one and, as Edwin G. Boring observed, the basic characteristics of American psychology were already shaped: "American psychology was to deal with mind in use."[21] At the same time, a small cadre of new scholars, schooled in psychology and in education, were trying to unite the two and push education into the circle of university respectability.

Bagley was prepared to take part in the study and in the debates which were being generated by those devoted to the development of this new university discipline—pedagogy. He had studied education with O'Shea and DeGarmo and had studied psychology in what was becoming one of the most important centers for psychological study in America, Titchener's laboratory at Cornell. However, he chose not to enter the battlefield populated by James, Dewey, Munsterberg, Titchener and others.[22] He chose instead to work at the level of day-to-day practice where the actual teaching-learning process took place. He wanted to work in the public school.

While the universities and the guardians of the established disciplines were having doubts about this new phenomenon, education, the public schools were not always willing or able to accept the new model educator. Upon completing his study at Cornell, Bagley remained there to work in Titchener's laboratory until January, 1901. He was not able to find immediate employment in what he termed the "public-school service." Later, he learned that he would have had more luck "if he had not mentioned the fact he was a doctor

[20] Edwin G. Boring, "Edward Bradford Titchener," *American Journal of Psychology* 37, no. 4 (October, 1927): 506.

[21] Edwin G. Boring, *History of Experimental Psychology*, 2nd ed. (New York, 1950), p. 506.

[22] For an account of the debate about the possibility of applying psychological principles to education and Bagley's participation (or nonparticipation) in it, see E. V. Johanningmeier, "William Chandler Bagley's Changing Views on the Relationship between Psychology and Education," *History of Education Quarterly* 9, no. 1 (Spring, 1969).

of philosophy." [23] After spending a semester working in the laboratory and inquiring about jobs in the public schools, he secured a principalship of an elementary school in the system that William Torrey Harris had fashioned.

In 1902, Bagley left St. Louis where he learned the "ABC of schoolcraft" for the Montana State Normal College in Dillon, Montana. He began his work at Dillon as director of the school's training department and professor of psychology and pedagogy. In 1904, he was appointed vice-president of the college. From 1903 to 1906, when he left Dillon to become the superintendent of the practice school at Oswego, New York, he served as superintendent of the Dillon public schools.

In a history of the normal school at Dillon, Edward F. Spiegle has reported that as professor of psychology and pedagogy, Bagley taught the "then infant subject of psychology as applied to education." [24] In his courses at Dillon, Bagley appears to have emphasized "individual differences" and "how to deal with the exceptional child." As director of the school, Spiegle has written, Bagley "modernized" it and "established the system at the training school that is largely still in effect today [1952]." [25]

When Bagley began teaching at Dillon, there were no special facilities provided for the training of student teachers; so he set out to use the classrooms of the public schools for this purpose. Initially, reported Spiegle, "the townspeople greatly resented this 'foreigner' coming into their town and using their children for 'guinea pigs.'" However, within a few months Bagley had convinced the "whole town that it was a privilege to expose their children to these new methods of education." [26] From Spiegle's account, it seems that "new methods" included the use of maps, sand-tables, globes, aquariums, and "other devices."

By 1908, when he arrived at Illinois, Bagley was equipped to take charge of the education department and the School of Education. To turn to an overworked phrase, he knew both the theory and the practice of education. He had the proper credentials for work of

---

[23] William C. Bagley, *A Century of the Universal School* (New York, 1937), p. viii.

[24] Edward F. Spiegle, "Historical Study of the Formation and Early Growth of Western Montana College of Education" (Master's thesis, Western Montana College of Education, 1952), Ch. 6.

[25] Ibid.

[26] Ibid.

"university grade." He had spent the summer of 1908 at Teachers College, Columbia University, teaching genetic psychology and grammar school methods. He had also worked in and supervised public schools. And he had worked in and developed "a practice school." He saw no conflict in his position. His interest was in the professional preparation of teachers. Whatever it took to accomplish that task was, for Bagley, a legitimate enterprise. His first two books (*The Educative Process* [1905] and *Classroom Management* [1907]) reflect that position.[27]

The plan Bagley had submitted for using the University Academy as a practice school did not raise a new issue at Illinois. The need for practice and observation facilities was apparent to the faculty (at least the claim had been voiced) and to President James before Bagley introduced his proposal. As was recorded in the previous chapter, Dexter had asked James for his opinion on using the Academy as a practice school. In January, 1907, James had communicated to the University Trustees a resolution passed by the Illinois State Teachers' Association, requesting the University "to consider the question of the establishment of a practice school as an important factor in the preparation of . . . teachers."[28] The following June, the Faculty Senate recommended "that practice work be established as it best may be under our conditions,"[29] though it did not mention the Academy.

While Bagley was using the Academy for a practice school, its purpose, function, and its relation to the University were being investigated by the Carnegie Foundation. The Carnegie investigation, in turn, prompted a series of discussions about the Academy's relationship to the University and to the School of Education among Charles W. McConn, then principal of the Academy, President James, and the Faculty Senate. A report to James from McConn dated November 10, 1909, revealed that the Carnegie Foundation inspectors had visited the campus and the Academy the previous spring and had disapproved of the Academy's close relationship to the University. McConn believed that the Foundation could not completely oppose Illinois's having an Academy, for fourteen of the fifty-five institutions approved by the Foundation maintained academies.[30]

[27] Each of these books is discussed briefly in Ch. 7.

[28] 24th *Report* (1908), pp. 69–70.

[29] Ibid., p. 134.

[30] McConn to James, November 10, 1909, James Correspondence. This is a four-page letter; the last page is a list of the colleges and academies which were

Specifically, the Foundation disapproved of the following: (1) that the Academy was on the same campus as the University itself; (2) that the students of the Academy could enroll in University courses; (3) that "double" entrance credits were given for Academy courses; and (4) that the Academy course did not always take a full four years to complete. McConn showed both that the Foundation had approved of academies with similar features and that steps were being taken to correct what had met with disapproval. However, there was one exception. There could be no separate building for the Academy until the question of a building for the School of Education had been resolved.

On November 24, 1909, two weeks after he sent James his report on the Academy's standing with the Carnegie Foundation, McConn submitted "a statement in regard to the present functions of the Academy." His statement was a careful and informative review of the status of academies in both local and national terms. He began by once again reviewing the Foundation's objections. The first one is of particular note. The only reply that was necessary to the objection that the school was "on the same campus," in McConn's estimation, was "merely to point out that such a location is an essential feature of the plan for using the Academy as a department of the School of Education—just as much so here as at Columbia, Chicago, Minnesota, and other universities where a secondary school is maintained for practice, experimental, and model purposes." [31] He went on to add the important fact that "the plan for utilizing the Academy *in this way* was emphatically approved by the representative of the Foundation who was here."

In a document he prepared for the occasion, entitled "The Function of the Academy," McConn presented a clear and precise account of what is today commonly called a laboratory school. He maintained that "the present and possible usefulness of the secondary school of the University [was] four-fold." The Academy could serve as (1) a

---

approved by the Carnegie Foundation and which maintained academies, or preparatory schools. The letter has a cover page which reads: "Report of Mr. C. M. McConn, Principal Academy in Re Academies in Institutions Admitted to The Carnegie Foundation, November 10, 1909."

[31] McConn to James, November 24, 1909. This was a six-page letter to which was appended a thirteen-page document entitled "The Function of the Academy." To that McConn added a three-page appendix, showing what institutions maintained academy-like schools in conjunction with their schools, or departments, of education. All in James Correspondence.

preparatory school; (2) a practice school; (3) an experimental school; and (4) a model school (McConn's terms). What distinguished his report was his description of how the Academy could be used. Each use was carefully marked off from the others. He did not confuse the various functions—practice, experimental, and model—with each other; each was distinct.

Under the heading "As a Preparatory School," McConn complained that it had "been pointed out *ad nauseam* that the other large state universities . . . have long since discontinued their academies, and . . . that, therefore, Illinois should do likewise." [32] What these "pointers out" failed to see, McConn argued, was that educational conditions in Illinois were different from those in other states. A large part of Illinois, he related, "lies entirely south of the terminal moraines and is consequently a comparatively barren and backward region." Besides, this southern region had been populated "by immigrants drawn from an unprogressive class of Southern whites." These "historical conditions" resulted in slow and uneven development of public education, "and in particular of the public high school," in Illinois. There were still four counties—Calhoun, Hardin, Polk, and Putnam—without high schools. "And in the other ninety-seven counties of the state exclusive of Cook County 'the average high school area per county is about 24 square miles, or two-thirds of one township.' " [33]

While other state universities were experiencing declines in their Academy attendance, the attendance was growing at Illinois. It was presently 45 percent higher than it was in 1904–5, and McConn expected it to continue to grow. There would be a need for the Academy, he claimed, "for several decades to come." To heed the argument of the "pointers out," he concluded, was to settle a question of educational policy "in accordance with fashion rather than conditions." [34]

Use of the Academy as a preparatory school was a "traditional function" and as such was, McConn argued, "only the beginning of its usefullness under present conditions." There was a peculiar irony in Illinois's backward and uneven educational conditions and in the continued existence of its Academy, which McConn said some would consider "a vestigial organ." At a recent meeting (February, 1909) of the

[32] McConn, "The Function of the Academy," p. 1.
[33] Ibid. Here McConn was quoting from H. A. Hollister, "Present State of the High School in Illinois," *School and Home Education* 25, no. 7 (March, 1906): 271–78. Hollister was, it will be recalled, the University's High School Visitor.
[34] McConn, "The Function of the Academy," p. 2.

National Society of College Teachers of Education, McConn wrote, it was officially recorded that practice teaching was "an essential part of any adequate preparation of high school teachers as well as of elementary teachers." The same meeting had also concluded that "the only really satisfactory plan for providing such practice will be for each institution . . . to have its own practice school." The public school was not deemed an appropriate place for student teachers to practice, for the supervisor from the university was hampered by having no control of either the teaching force or the curriculum. Besides, use of the public school introduced the additional burden of "responsibility to a public school board." [35]

The desirability of having a practice school, as the National Society of College Teachers of Education advocated, was also shown by the schools who established them. "No less than seven state universities, several of which had formerly discontinued academies, have within the last five years established or reestablished secondary schools for the express purpose of providing practice teaching." [36] However, McConn noted that these schools were doing so "with much difficulty and in most cases with only partial success." At the February meeting of the NSCTE, Illinois and Missouri were the only state institutions recognized as having "secondary schools 'fully organized and offering complete opportunities for practice.'" The University of Mississippi tried but failed to found a practice school. Four schools "of prominence"— Cornell University, Ohio State University, the University of Wisconsin, and the University of California—had been trying to establish schools. "But the great difficulties in the way of building up a new secondary school," McConn claimed, "where the field is already occupied, and the almost equal obstacles to be overcome in taking over an independent school have so far thwarted their efforts."

Illinois had precisely what other schools were trying to establish, a completely equipped school. "Here we have a large secondary school (enrolling over 300), thoroughly organized, firmly established, adequately equipped for present purposes, offering a full course and numerous electives (including such subjects as Bookkeeping, Domestic

[35] Ibid., pp. 2–3. According to McConn, the question is from F. E. Farrington, "Practice Work in University Departments of Education," *Observation and Practice Teaching*, Yearbook of the National Society of College Teachers of Education, 1909, p. 34.

[36] McConn, "The Function of the Academy," p. 3. The seven universities were: Minnesota, Missouri, Nebraska, South Dakota, Arkansas, North Dakota, and Wyoming.

Science, and Agriculture). Its location in the same building with the School of Education makes it available to the fullest intent for the purposes of that School." [37] The survival of Illinois's Academy which was "due to unfortunate conditions in the state," McConn urged, "may surely be looked upon as a most happy chance." The maintenance of the Academy would provide "a unique opportunity to do a new work of the utmost importance for the high schools of the State."

Besides the "academic considerations" which he had just presented, there was the demand from the state's public schoolmen. McConn reminded James that in both the administrative section and the general meeting of the last High School Conference (November 18–20, 1909) there had been unanimous approval of the resolutions urging the University to require "proficiency in observation and practice teaching" of all candidates for the teacher's certificate and to outfit and house the Academy so "that it shall become a model State High School which shall exist primarily . . . for observation and practice teaching in the training of high-school or secondary teachers." The administrative section of the Conference also urged the principals and superintendents to notify the "heads of departments in this University that preference will be given in the future to candidates for high school positions who have some experience in practice teaching in the subject or subjects which such candidate desires to teach." [38]

[37] Ibid., pp. 4–5.

[38] McConn, "The Function of the Academy," pp. 6–7, where he reproduced for the President's benefit the two resolutions which follow (spelling corrected):

"RESOLUTION endorsing practice teaching in the University of Illinois; offered by Superintendents W. L. Steele of Galesburg, P. R. Walker of Rockford, and H. B. Wilson of Decatur, in the Administrative Section of the High School Conference of the University of Illinois, at Urbana, November 19, 1909. Passed unanimously.

"WHEREAS the need for more high-school teachers is growing rapidly and the need for greater skill in teaching is paramount in our high schools, be it resolved by the Administrative Section of the High School Conference of the University of Illinois:

"First: that we heartily endorse the present plan of the School of Education of the University of Illinois in providing practice teaching training in the University Academy in the training of high-school teachers.

"Second: that it is the sense of this section that the University of Illinois should, as soon as possible, require of all intending teachers who wish to be recommended for teaching in the high schools of the State, proficiency in observation and practice teaching.

"Third: that it is the sense of this section that the University of Illinois should, as speedily as possible, so house and equip its Academy as that it shall become a model State High School which shall exist primarily as a training school under

To support his case that the Academy could serve as "an experimental school," McConn cited the opinions of Charles H. Judd, director of the School of Education at the University of Chicago, Professor Strayer of Columbia University, and Illinois's own William C. Bagley. He explained that the Europeans had long recognized "that Education must check and test [its] results by experimental methods, just as other sciences do, if these results are to be received as equally valid with those of other subjects." "Last Saturday" (November 20, 1909), Mc-Conn reported, Professor Judd at a meeting of teachers on the campus of the University of Chicago urged, "as the inevitable first step in the creation of [a Science of Education] and in the solution of even the simplest problems of the secondary school, the development and dissemination, as rapid as possible, of a technique of gathering, sifting, and recording educational data by the experimental method of parallel sections." [39] At the February meeting of the NSCTE, Professor Strayer made much the same claim, calling for experimental schools where curriculum changes could be tried, where new teaching methods could be tested, and where psychological experiments on child development could be conducted.

According to Strayer, an experimental school was "large," had "more than one class of the same grade," had a "non-selected group

---

the direction of the School of Education for observation and practice teaching in the training of high-school or secondary teachers.
> Signed by Committee
> W. L. Steele, Galesburg, Illinois
> P. R. Walker, Rockford, Illinois
> H. B. Wilson, Decatur, Illinois

"RESOLUTION endorsing practice teaching in the University of Illinois; offered by Superintendent J. G. Moore of Lexington in the General Section of the High School Conference of the University of Illinois, at Urbana, November 20, 1909. Passed unanimously.

"WHEREAS the Administrative Section has unanimously and enthusiastically endorsed the present plans for practice teaching now in operation by the School of Education of the State University, and had pledged its support to the extension of this movement.

"*Resolved*, that this general Conference approves this action of the Administrative Section, and in order to further the efficiency of this endorsement respectfully urges all superintendents and principals in favor of this movement to inform heads of departments in this University that preference will be given in the future to candidates for high school positions who have some experience in practice teaching in the subject or subjects which such candidate desires to teach."

[39] McConn, "The Function of the Academy," p. 8. This is McConn's quotation of Judd for which he supplies no reference.

of children," and was staffed with "competent teachers." [40] McConn submitted "that in the case of every point desiderated the Academy of this university answers to the description." McConn's contention that "no other state institution in the country has so remarkable an opportunity waiting to be utilized" may have been true. However, his claim that the University Academy met the specifications set out by Strayer was less than accurate. The Academy was not, as Colvin had pointed out, and as the University *Catalogue* described it, a typical high school.

While serving as Acting Director of the School of Education, Colvin advised James that he was investigating a plan for practice teaching that Walter B. Jacobs had developed at Brown University. That plan was designed to bring "the students in education in touch with the high schools of Providence." [41] Colvin believed Illinois would be "forced" to rely on the local schools surrounding the University for practice facilities and that the University would "ultimately" have to work out an agreement with the schools. The Academy, he maintained, could not be used "to any great extent for the development of our observation and practice work, unless we *radically reorganize the academy* and make it *into a typical* secondary school." [42] Colvin had his doubts about the "desirability" of reorganizing the Academy. He did not state why he had doubts, but they may have been part of his belief that Illinois should not establish "anything that would resemble a normal college." He did advise against unduly emphasizing "the narrowly pedagogical features which have been justly criticized in many institutions of higher learning" and advocated that the School's "fundamental characteristics . . . be broadly philosophical and scientific." [43]

Whatever the precise reasons for Colvin's doubts, his insistence that the Academy was not a "typical" secondary school was a legitimate one. The *Announcements* for 1906–7 specified that "the special ambition of the school [the Academy] is to give its students that thorough

[40] Ibid., p. 9. This is McConn's quotation of Strayer. He gives the following citation: "Strayer, G. D.: Observation in Connection with Coll. and Univ. Schs. or Depts. of Ed., in Observation and Practice Teaching, pub. by the Nat. Soc. of Coll. Teachers of Ed., 1909, pp. 65–66."

[41] Colvin to James, October 24, 1907, James Correspondence.

[42] Ibid. Italics ours.

[43] This is taken from what Colvin described in his letter to James (October 24, 1907) as "some thoughts which I have put together in regard to the organization of the School of Education." These thoughts are attached to the October 24 letter to James.

preparatory training which is so essential to success in the later work of the college." [44] In language reminiscent of the Committee of Ten, the *Catalogue* stated: "While the Academy aims primarily to be an efficient preparatory school, its course of study is such that it offers to young men and women who do not intend to enter college an excellent training of high school grade." [45] Of the eleven faculty members, four had master's degrees, two had bachelor's degrees (one A.B. and one B.S.), two had Ph.D.'s, and only three were listed as having no degree. Students were, it was related, allowed to avail themselves of the many facilities of the University. And, as was shown above, the student was allowed to complete the course at an accelerated rate and enroll in University classes. The Academy was what its successor, the University High School, would become—a prep school. Neither the students who attended the Academy because they seemed too old for the high schools in their own towns ("those who have been delayed in their education") nor those who had the resources to pay for the journey to Urbana as well as the room and board at the Academy were "typical" students.

In quoting Bagley to add weight to his case, McConn struck a chord that must have been familiar to James. Bagley, like James, believed that "the University [was] definitely committed to the scientific investigation of problems confronting the people of the State." The schools did offer problems.[46] Some school problems could be solved outside a school. "Others, perhaps, even more numerous and more pressing, require a properly equipped laboratory school for effective treatment." The graduate students in the department, McConn explained, were already conducting research which required a laboratory school. (This development will be discussed in the next chapter.) The Academy offered an opportunity which had already been seized. McConn did not want to surrender it.

Finally, the Academy could be used as a "model school." The function of a model school was "allied" to that of an "experimental school" but was, McConn stated, also "to be differentiated from it." [47] The model school could serve the state's schools by showing what should be taught and how it should be taught. The Academy was beginning

[44] *University of Illinois Announcements, 1906–7*, and *Register for 1905–6*, pp. 360–61.
[45] Ibid., p. 361.
[46] Quoted in McConn, "The Function of the Academy," p. 9. McConn does not give a reference.
[47] Ibid., p. 12.

to demonstrate three courses—bookkeeping, domestic science, and agriculture—which were "but partially established in the high schools." At present, however, these new courses were "imperfectly organized, injudiciously equipped, [and] vaguely taught." The Academy was attempting "to demonstrate . . . what a 'unit' in each of these subjects should mean—what content is desirable in each case, what minimum of equipment is necessary and how it may be economically installed, and what the method of presentation should be." Superintendents and principals who were planning to introduce these new courses as well as teachers who had already started them had already shown "much interest" in what the Academy had to demonstrate. The University departments most directly concerned with this new work, McConn reported, believed "that this interest will increase as the courses become more widely known."

Through a model school the University could help introduce new subjects into the curriculum of the public schools and "accomplish a great deal . . . toward raising the standard of the work in them throughout the state." Illinois's "model school," McConn emphasized, was particularly effective. Model schools had "to keep each detail within the limits of high school conditions." The model could not be beyond the reach of the public school. The "unfavorable" location and condition of the University's school were actually advantages. Visitors from the public schools were "compelled to say, 'They accomplish this in those ground-floor rooms in the Academy. We can certainly do as much.' " [48] There were no "special circumstances" to dissuade the state's schoolmen of the practicality of the Academy's demonstrations.

In January, 1910, McConn prepared still another report on the Academy. In a letter to James, he stated that it was prepared "for the use of the committee which is considering the relations of the Academy to the University." [49] As its title—"Data Concerning the Discontinuance and Re-establishment of Secondary Schools in Eighteen of the Principal Western State Universities"—indicates, the report told of these universities' plans and policies on preparatory schools. The trend was, he reported, to cease maintenance of the academy "as a preparatory department pure and simple." Academies were being closed for four reasons: (1) "a falling off in attendance"; (2) "to stimulate the high schools"; (3) "to raise the institution to full colle-

48 Ibid., p. 13.
49 McConn to James, January 6, 1910, James Correspondence.

giate rank by relieving the university faculty of secondary instruction";
and (4) "for economy." [50]

None of the reasons applied to Illinois in McConn's judgment. At
Illinois, "the registration up to November 1 of this year (1909) was the
largest for that date in the history of the school." The second point
was not even an issue. In the 1870's and 1880's, some schools closed
their academies as a way of forcing the state to develop secondary
schools. At present, he explained, Illinois had 225 "accredited high
schools" and 537 "smaller high schools." One Academy of 300 students
would not constitute competition that the public schools could not
meet. To the contrary, closing the Academy would, McConn told the
Senate, displease the state's high school men. He pointed out that the
Committee of Seventeen (1907), the National Association of State
Universities, and the National Society of College Teachers of Education all agreed that practice teaching was a necessary part of teacher
preparation. And he once again noted that the High School Conference had endorsed practice teaching and had asked the University
to require it of all "intending teachers." [51]

Because the Academy staff had been "entirely distinct" from that
of the University for several years, the third reason also failed to
apply. The fourth reason—economy—was subject to interpretation.
Until 1907 the income from the Academy was greater than its expenditures. In the last two years expenditures had been increased to bring
it "to a rather high degree of efficiency." However, even after the
increase, the Academy's deficit was "only about $2500." McConn con-
ceded that if the question were one of maintaining a preparatory
school, the question of economy would eventually prevail. But he was
not willing to concede that point. In fact, he argued, the $2,500 was
a bargain. Universities which were attempting to establish schools for
practice had to spend more than $2,500 from university funds. "At
California, for example, President Wheeler recommended (in his Biennial Report of December, 1906, pp. 21, 22) an appropriation of $10,000
a year for the maintenance of the proposed training school for high
school teachers." [52] At the University of Minnesota, the expenses for
the training school were borne by the university. In 1908–9, the Uni-

[50] C. M. McConn, "Data Concerning the Discontinuance and Re-establishment
of Secondary Schools in Eighteen of the Principal Western State Universities,"
p. 4. This is a sixteen-page typescript appended to his January 6 letter to James
described above.
[51] Ibid., pp. 6–7.
[52] Ibid., p. 10.

versity of Nebraska received $527 in fees from the students of its Temple High School, while Illinois had collected $12,479 during the same period.

McConn concluded his report to James with a warning that Illinois would be "throwing away an exceptional opportunity to perform a distinct and important educational service for the whole State if the Academy should be discontinued." In his report to the Senate, he emphasized that "the only conclusion that we can draw from considerations of economy would seem to be that we should seize the opportunity." [53] McConn's conclusion was based on the assumption that a training school was a desirable thing, and on what he thought was an obvious point, i.e., that Illinois had "an unusual opportunity to provide one that will be nearly self-supporting." However, his assumptions were not accepted, and his conclusions did not prevail.

The minutes of the Trustees indicate that the Academy was discussed on April 12, 1910, but the details of the discussion were not recorded.[54] The following September, James presented the Trustees with a set of recommendations the Faculty Senate had adopted on April 18, and asked "that the resolution of the Senate . . . be referred to a special committee . . . with a request for an early report." [55] The Senate's report contained eight recommendations. The first two urged: "1. That the Academy be discontinued after June, 1912. 2. That in place of the Academy there be established a training, experimental and observational school of secondary grade, which shall serve as a laboratory for the School of Education under the control and direction of the Department of Education." [56] The remaining six recommendations constituted a set of guide lines for the operation of the "experimental and observational school."

The special committee agreed that the Senate's report had been "admirably drawn and . . . endorsed in general the views therein expressed." After a discussion of the recommendations which included the recognition that there were no funds available to effect the recommendations of the Senate, the special committee recommended that the Board of Trustees adopt the following resolutions: "*First:* That the University Academy be discontinued at the close of the present aca-

53 Ibid.
54 25th *Report* (1910), p. 531.
55 26th *Report* (1912), p. 25.
56 Ibid.

demic year, 1910–11. *Second:* That the trustees of the University ask the next legislature for the sum of two hundred fifty thousand dollars ($250,000.00) for the erection of a separate building for the School of Education, which shall also contain provision for the model high school recommended by the Senate and endorsed by the committee." [57] On October 5, the Trustees voted to adopt the first recommendation but postponed action on the second.

The Trustees' decision to close the Academy forced Bagley to discontinue his courses in both observation of teaching and practice teaching. This dissolution of an institution seemed to call for the creation of a new one. According to Bagley, "it was primarily because of this fact that the campaign for a training school was undertaken." [58] The campaign was for a School of Education building which James and Bagley wanted to use primarily for a practice school similar to the model high school James had supervised at Normal. The campaign, engineered by James and Bagley, began before the Academy closed.

On October 15, 1910, James told the Trustees that the teachers of the State were "much interested" in his request for funds for a new building. To show that they were, he presented a set of resolutions adopted by the Eastern Illinois Teachers' Association at their Charleston meeting on October 14 and 15. The teachers' statement read:

WHEREAS, The more progressive universities of this country have established or are establishing schools of education or teachers' colleges, which shall adequately represent in the university organization the needs and ideals of the teaching profession; and,

WHEREAS, The present facilities at the University of Illinois for the training of special teachers of agriculture, manual training, domestic science, and other branches, and for the training of supervisory and administrative officers, are inadequate to the demands that the schools of the State are making upon the University for trained workers in these fields; and,

WHEREAS, The investigation of general educational problems, which is so important in view of the many changes that the system of public education is constantly undergoing, cannot be adequately undertaken by the

[57] Ibid., pp. 34–35.
[58] William C. Bagley, "History of the Department and School of Education [of the University of Illinois]," p. 13. This history was prepared by Bagley for President James in February, 1916, and remains unpublished. The twenty-page typescript is to be found in the Illinois Historical Survey, University of Illinois.

University of Illinois because of the lack of proper buildings and equipment; therefore be it

Resolved, That we do hereby request the trustees of the University of Illinois to give to the School of Education of that University the support that is needed for its development to the point where it may adequately serve the needs of the State; and be it further

Resolved, That we petition the General Assembly of the State of Illinois at its coming session to appropriate out of the funds of the State not less than two hundred fifty thousand dollars ($250,000.00) for the erection and equipment of a building for the School of Education at the University of Illinois; and be it further

Resolved, That the secretary of the association be instructed to send a copy of these resolutions in the form of a petition to the Governor of the State, to the president of the Board of Trustees of the University, and to both houses of the General Assembly; and be it further

Resolved, That we pledge ourselves individually and collectively to do whatever we properly can to assist in obtaining such appropriation.[59]

The teachers' resolution has been quoted in full because it shows the work of James and Bagley. It was no coincidence that James advised the Board of the teachers' action just a few days after their decision to close the Academy. On October 10, Bagley sent a memo to James to "remind" him to "write to President [Alfred] Bayliss of Macomb regarding the resolutions for the School of Education." [60] That same day James wrote to Bayliss pointing out the work he had done previously for the School and told him "we are getting round now to see if we can't make this [School of Education] a more effective enterprise." [61] He wanted Bayliss to present to the Military Tract Teachers' Association the resolution that the Eastern Illinois Teachers' Association was to adopt.

After receiving James's report concerning the resolutions of the teachers, the Board noted that there was no quorum and adjourned.[62] The adjournment failed to stop what Bagley later called the "campaign." In November, James learned that President Felmley of the Illinois State Normal University opposed Illinois's plan to train high school teachers, superintendents, principals, and special teachers of

[59] 26th *Report* (1912), pp. 41–42.
[60] Bagley to James, October 10, 1910, James Correspondence.
[61] James to President Alfred Bayliss, Macomb Normal School, October 10, 1910, James Correspondence.
[62] 26th *Report* (1912), p. 43.

mechanical arts and agriculture.[63] Felmley's opposition was serious, but James decided to meet it.

On December 20, 1910, the President wrote to A. F. Nightingale, Cook County superintendent of schools, to ask his support for the resolution which was to be presented at the meeting of State Teachers' Association in Chicago. James reminded Nightingale that he and Bayliss "were on the committee which recommended to the board of trustees the establishment of this school of education." As far as James knew, Felmley was "the only normal school man opposed" to Illinois's plans and requests. Yet James told Nightingale: "I think it is very necessary to make an active campaign for this resolution." [64]

The resolutions of the state and the district teachers' associations were not all that James needed. As Bagley reported, "the item in the budget which carried an appropriation for the building was not approved by the Legislature of 1911." [65] Felmley's opposition, which he made public in a letter to his students in the *Bloomington Pantagraph*, proved to be more influential than the resolutions, the direct petitions to the legislature by school districts and teachers' associations, and even the willingness of the schoolmen to testify in Springfield.[66]

As member of the department of education and as the Director of the School of Education, Bagley had an interest in the development of the School and its facilities. His position and interest also demanded that he enlist support for the enterprise. On November 19, 1910, Bagley expressed his ideas about a School of Education and its functions before the High School Conference of the University of Illinois. The next month these ideas were reproduced in *School and Home Education*.

[63] A copy of the original letter, Felmley to James, November 21, 1910, may be found in the archives of Illinois State University, together with further correspondence of considerable interest. In a letter to Bagley, dated November 23, 1910, James requested that it be circulated to Hollister, Greene, and Kinley so there could be a "confab about it." In a letter to Bagley (dated November 29, 1910), James wrote that "his [Felmley's] idea . . . that the University should not train 'high school teachers, superintendents, and principals and special teachers of agriculture and mechanic arts . . .' allowed for no common ground at all." For an index as to what Felmley wrote see Hollister's reply to Felmley, December 5, 1910. For a nine-page letter explaining the University of Illinois's defense of its College of Education and teacher training, see Bagley to Felmley, Nov. 28, 1910, President's Papers, 1909–11 (D–F). (David Felmley file.)
[64] James to A. F. Nightingale, December 20, 1910, James Correspondence.
[65] Bagley, "History of the Department and School of Education," p. 13.
[66] Ibid., pp. 13–14. Also see [University of Illinois] *Alumni Quarterly* (January, 1911): 29–30.

The campaign had begun. Bagley, of course, was immediately interested in finding a way to provide facilities so the program in practice teaching could continue. His attempts to convince his listeners and readers of the wisdom of his position show that Bagley was beginning to clarify what had been ambiguous in his work and thought. He stood for both the professional preparation of teachers and the ideals of the university—scholarship and scientific inquiry. He himself had tried to apply the "pure" sciences to the practical task of instruction in the public school. Now his concern was with the practical. He spoke about the preparation of teachers and virtually ignored the possibility of using the school he was trying to establish as a laboratory school. Now he wanted a reorganization of the School of Education— a reorganization which would give it greater independence from the total university.

Bagley told the participants at the High School Conference that the School of Education at the University of Illinois was little more than a name. The School was, he related, supposed to comprise all those members and departments of the university that were interested in the preparation of teachers. This organization gave neither directive nor supervisory power to the Director of the School. Its "loose organization" did not allow the School to have its own student body. And, without its own student body, Bagley explained, the pedagogues were "seriously handicapped in equipping our graduates who go into public-school service with an adequate body of professional ideals . . . [which] must come not primarily from direct instruction, but from the *esprit de corps* which is developed in a community of work, interest and purpose." [67]

Bagley went on to explain that during the two and a half years that he had been associated with the School of Education he had undertaken to develop "the type of work that seemed to offer the greatest possibilities of service under existing conditions." That was, he stated, "the work of practice teaching as applied to the training of high school teachers." [68] He had made provisions whereby seniors and graduate students could secure actual practice teaching. Each practice teacher was allowed to assume the responsibility for a class five hours each week under the systematic supervision of specialists in the teaching of

[67] William C. Bagley, "Some Possible Functions of a School of Education," *School and Home Education* 30, no. 4 (December 1910): 136.
[68] Ibid.

the specified subject, the principal of the Academy, and the education department.

In Bagley's estimation the work had been successful. Practice teaching was a requirement neither of the University nor the education department. University policy regarding the recommendation of teachers required neither practice teaching nor any other professional work as a prerequisite for recommendation for a teaching position. "And yet," Bagley reported, "the applicants for this practice-teaching are very much more numerous than our present facilities will accommodate." [69] Approximately thirty students enrolled in the practice teaching course during the 1909–10 academic year. The expenditure of an additional thousand dollars, Bagley estimated, would provide facilities for nearly sixty students for the following year.

However, instead of spending another thousand dollars, the Trustees had voted to discontinue the Academy. That move meant, Bagley related, not only that there would be no practice teaching offered at the University of Illinois for at least two years but that the trained supervisors of the Academy, the pupils, and other facilities would be dispersed and have to be taken up from scratch again. Such a situation, according to Bagley, called for immediate redress. He told the teachers that a course for the preparation of teachers which did not include practice teaching under the supervision of specialists who knew not only their subject matter but also how to adapt that subject matter to adolescents was "like Hamlet with Hamlet left out." [70]

The practice school was "the most important part of the School of Education in so far as the professional training of candidates for high school teaching is concerned." [71] While the training of the candidates for teaching positions was the primary function of a School of Education, there were other functions that it could fulfill. The School was to meet the demands of the state for all kinds of teachers. "Whenever there is a legitimate demand for teachers of any of the subjects in which the university gives adequate academic instruction," Bagley maintained, "the School of Education must, on its side, provide professional equipment for candidates for such teacherships." [72] There was, Bagley reported, a need for teachers of music, art, agriculture, domestic

[69] Ibid., p. 137.
[70] Ibid.
[71] Ibid., p. 138.
[72] Ibid.

science, and manual training. To prepare such teachers adequately, a school of education needed not only the shops of the engineering school and the agriculture school but also "the typical secondary school equipment and some measure of practice teaching under supervision." [73]

A third type of teacher that the school of education ought to train was what Bagley described as "the special teacher for backward children." [74] He pointed out that the University of Iowa was planning to found "a colony for backward children" where the university's psychologists would be able to make diagnoses and where the appropriate special teachers could be trained. Besides Iowa's plans, the University of Pennsylvania and certain foreign cities had such colonies, and it was Bagley's conviction that Illinois should have such a "colony" too. "Indeed," said Bagley, "I think it is the function of the university in cooperation with the public school men and representatives of the state schools for backward children to take the initiative in this matter." [75]

To borrow a phrase from Dewey's discussions of the various functions of schools of education in the mid-1890's, Bagley's judgment was that the primary function of a school of education was "to supply the great army of teachers with the weapons of their calling and direct them to their use." [76] To accomplish this end, a school of education needed a firing range which would duplicate the facilities of the public schools. At least at this point, Bagley was not calling for a laboratory where new weapons could be developed.

Besides outfitting the foot soldiers, a school of education was to train the officers of the pedagogical army, that is, it was to provide facilities for the preparation of superintendents, principals, and supervisors of music, manual training, drawing, agriculture, and domestic science. To train these officers, Bagley reported, "a broadening of our facilities for graduate work in education and allied subjects" was needed.[77] "Broadening of facilities" seems to have meant, in part at least, changing the residence requirements of the graduate school.

Bagley wanted the Graduate School of the University of Illinois to change its residence requirements and expand its course offerings during the summer session so that principals and supervisors could com-

[73] Ibid., pp. 137–38.
[74] Ibid., p. 139.
[75] Ibid.
[76] John Dewey, "Pedagogy as a University Discipline," *University of Chicago Record* 1 (September 18 and 25, 1896): 353–55, 361–63.
[77] Bagley, "Some Possible Functions of a School of Education," p. 139.

plete their course work toward a master's degree by attending three summer sessions. He further wanted the Graduate School to allow the last quarter of work, the thesis, to be done in absentia. He wanted to allow these graduate students to work out the problems they were dealing with on a day-to-day basis and to present their solutions as master's theses. Bagley did not consider this recommendation to entail a lowering of standards. These problems were, he insisted, "very frequently much more involved than those which are represented by the average master's thesis." [78] Moreover, his proposals could be defended on the grounds of "social service." Both the student and the public schools would benefit from such an arrangement. The student would secure the expert direction of professors who could help apply the scientific method to the solution of these problems; the public schools would benefit both directly and indirectly. The problems of some schools would be solved, and the solutions of these problems would be available to all the schools through the publication of the theses.

The course Bagley wanted to start for the University of Illinois was markedly different from that which Dewey had laid out for the University of Chicago. At Chicago there was an experimental, or laboratory, school where the graduate student could undertake pedagogical experimentation, the results of which might or might not be capable of immediate adoption for the public schools.[79] Bagley wanted to allow the student to complete the distinctive feature of graduate study—the thesis—away from the University. To Bagley, "almost every school system might well become a laboratory." [80] He wanted a system that would be of immediate service to the state's schools. His ideal was not pure research; it was "social service."

Bagley did not believe that the function of "social service" was in-

---

[78] Ibid.

[79] Dewey, "Pedagogy as a University Discipline," pp. 362–63.

[80] Bagley, "Some Possible Functions of a School of Education," p. 139. By claiming that the public school was to be, and could be, the School of Education's laboratory, Bagley was echoing what had been voiced much earlier at Illinois. For example, Andrew Sloan Draper, President of the University, wrote to Lucy L. Flower of the Board of Trustees: "I do not believe the University will ever be disposed to maintain practice schools in connection with this department. The public school system is the laboratory of the department [of Education]" (Draper to Flower, June 22, 1899). The following September, in a letter to Professor Howard Sandison of the State Normal School at Terre Haute, Ind., Draper wrote that the man who took Tompkins's place "should make the public school system his laboratory. . . . It is not our purpose to organize practice schools" (Draper to Sandison, September 18, 1899; all in Draper Letterbooks).

consistent with the ideal of the University—an ideal identified as "the discovery and dissemination of truth." [81] Indeed, Bagley was willing to extend the function of the University and the School of Education "to meet the needs of the State in so far as these needs are for skill, knowledge, ideas, and ideals." [82] These needs could be met through what Bagley identified as a "bureau of Correspondence" and "extension work." [83] Extension work consisted of giving off-campus courses to teachers, lecturing at teachers' institutes, and addressing teachers' organizations.[84] Bagley explained that "while this extension work is not the primary function of the School of Education, it is certainly one function of this school to do extension work in connection with public school needs." [85]

Bagley maintained that many schoolmen around the state frequently wrote to him, "asking for specific information on educational matters." [86] He further related that he tried to answer these letters and that he assumed he was thereby rendering a useful service to the public school people. However, he suggested that his services would be even more helpful were there a Bureau of Correspondence to which the school people could address their questions. The function of the bureau would be "to seek out desired information if it can be found, and call the attention of the research departments to the need if the information cannot be found." [87]

Bagley's outline for a School of Education contained little discussion of the need for educational research, where that research was to be conducted, and who was to do it. But in an editorial dated January, 1911, summarizing the arguments for extending the School of Educa-

[81] Bagley, "Some Possible Functions of a School of Education," p. 140.
[82] Ibid.
[83] As Director of the School of Education, Bagley inaugurated extension work in education at the University of Illinois in 1912–13 in the form of off-campus courses. During 1912–13, Professor Lotus D. Coffman offered a course in educational sociology for approximately twenty teachers in the Urbana schools. The following year, he conducted a course in educational measurements for the teachers of Decatur, and Bagley gave a course in educational psychology in Springfield (Bagley, "History of the Department and School of Education," p. 16).
[84] Bagley himself participated in all forms of extension work. Between October 1, 1910, and May 10, 1911, he had delivered "forty-two lectures outside the University." He had given these not only throughout Illinois but in Kansas, Indiana, New York, Alabama, and at the University of Missouri (Bagley to James, May 10, 1911, James Correspondence).
[85] Bagley, "Some Possible Functions of a School of Education," p. 140.
[86] Ibid.
[87] Ibid.

tion at Illinois, Bagley did note that provisions for educational research were needed: "There is a pressing need in education today for the scientific investigation of educational problems. Such investigation should be undertaken by the State Universities in the field of education as in other fields. This cannot be done with maximum efficiency, however, without a laboratory in the form of a model and training school." [88] Though Bagley did state in that editorial that a laboratory was needed for research, it does not seem appropriate to construe that statement to mean that he viewed the practice school as a laboratory school. He rarely spoke of the school as a laboratory school, and most often spoke of its training (practice) and observational functions. Though he did write, in his original proposal, of "the desirability of furnishing the School of Education with a practice department in which the essential features of the *laboratory method*, which has been found so effective in other technical courses, can be applied to the study of educational theory," [89] he did not speak of using the practice school as a center for educational research. By "laboratory method" he seems to have meant that students could observe what they had been told in their "theory" classes. The school was to be a place where the students were to see the theory of education demonstrated just as students of physics watched their professor explode balloons in bell jars. The other points that Bagley emphasized in his original proposal also suggest that by "laboratory method" he meant observation and practice. He had stressed that the establishment of practice work would allow superintendents to assess the qualifications of the candidates while watching them teach. He had also noted that work on the training of supervisors of teachers could be undertaken were the Academy used as a practice school. But the establishment of that work did not entail any experimentation with either pupils or practice teachers.

McConn had specified four possible functions for the "school." In the mid-1890's at the University of Chicago, Dewey had founded a laboratory school (which had been the subject of national interest) and sharply differentiated the research and service (training) functions. Bagley had determined to advocate the practice function. Why he did not advocate other functions as well cannot be precisely

[88] William C. Bagley, "A Summary of Arguments for a School of Education," *School and Home Education* 30, no. 5 (January, 1911): 178.

[89] The plan—eight typed pages—is attached to a letter from Stephen S. Colvin to William C. Bagley, January 19, 1909.

answered, but remains a disturbing and puzzling position. As an active participant and leader in educational affairs, and as a professor at Illinois, he did encourage research. McConn's 1909 statement on the "Function of the Academy" reported that the graduate students in the department were conducting investigations which required an experimental school. Bagley's position did, however, demonstrate his commitment to the notion that effective teacher preparation had to include practice work. It also showed that the teachers of the state had a strong spokesman in the University. Bagley knew the needs of the teacher and never failed to lose sight of them.

Even in 1915—after a site had been purchased for the school— Bagley emphasized the practice function. Though he did not deny the possibility of using the practice school for some experimentation, he emphasized that the school was to be primarily a school for the training of teachers. In 1915, in a letter to James he clearly stated:

> The primary purpose of the school should be definitely understood by all connected with it to be the provision of facilities for observation and practice teaching. While it is desirable to utilize the school for certain other purposes (for example, the testing of new methods and devices of teaching and administration), these should always be looked upon as subordinate to the primary purpose and should at no time and in no way interfere unduly with the fulfillment of this primary purpose.[90]

In September, 1916, when the *Daily Illini* announced the approval of the architectural plans of the School of Education's high school, Bagley was quoted as saying that "the high school will be primarily for practice teaching purposes." [91]

By insisting that the school was to be primarily a practice and model school, Bagley was not, as was stated above, denying either the need for educational research or the possibility of using the school for research and experimentation. However, he was limiting the kinds of experimentation that could be undertaken there. By insisting that its primary purpose was to train teachers, Bagley was demanding that the school be operated in concert with the best of public school practice. To use Dewey's terms, Bagley agreed that the function of the school was "to provide better teachers according to present standards."

This commitment to present standards also entailed a commitment to a particular structuring of the educative process. Bagley was as-

---

[90] The letter is reproduced in 28th *Report* (1916), p. 768.
[91] *The Daily Illini*, September 24, 1916.

suming that the ingredients of the educative process consisted of a teacher, an optimum number of pupils, a body of subject matter, and a series of skills and attitudes that the teacher was to convey somehow to the pupils. By commiting himself and the school to "present standards," Bagley was disallowing the right of pedagogues to work in the school as chemists and biologists worked in their laboratories. The pedagogues in Bagley's school would not attempt "to create new standards and ideals."

How Bagley would have used the school is, of course, a moot question. The building was not even ready for occupancy until 1919, two years after his departure from Illinois, and even then it was not used. The process of securing the approval and the funds for the bricks and mortar was a long one, marked by repeated delays. The first sign of success in the campaign came in 1913. At that time, the University's resources were somewhat improved in that its appropriation was made for the first time out of revenues from the mill tax. The Universitity's budget as submitted by the Trustees included a line of $125,000 for a building for the School of Education.[92] The University Register for 1914–15 announced that the "Board of Trustees has approved plans for a building to be used as a laboratory for the School of Education and to include quarters for a training school of secondary grade and has purchased a site upon which the first wing of this building will be erected." [93]

In February, 1916, Bagley wrote to James: "It is hoped that a building for the training school will be ready for occupancy in September, 1917." [94] When Bagley expressed his hope, the architectural plans for the building had not yet been approved. Plans prepared by the supervising architect, Professor J. M. White, had been submitted to the state architect, James R. Dibelka, but they did not meet with his approval. The facing of the building was modified, but the Trustees were in turn dissatisfied with the new edifice. It was not until July 11, 1914, that the Trustees approved "the general design of the building" which was described as "an adaptation of the English collegiate gothic." [95] But their approval proved to be temporary. On June 15, 1915, Mr. Hoit of the Trustees successfully moved that the approval be reconsidered, and Dibelka's revised design "for the Educa-

[92] Bagley, "History of the Department and School of Education," p. 14.
[93] *University of Illinois Annual Register 1914–15* (Urbana, 1915), p. 201.
[94] Bagley, "History of the Department and School of Education," pp. 14–15.
[95] 28th *Report* (1916), pp. 41–42.

tion Building in the collegiate gothic style of architecture" was thrown out. The University's supervising architect was accordingly directed to prepare new plans and all bids for the new building were rejected.[96] After examining and discussing six designs and three complete sets of plans, the Trustees, on May 27, 1916, approved "the design of the exterior prepared by Holabird and Roche" and "the Supervising Architect was instructed to proceed to the construction of the first wing of the building." [97]

The following September, the *Daily Illini* reported that the University was "to have a new $600,000 School of Education." There had been $200,000 appropriated for the west wing, which was scheduled to house "the department of the practice high school." [98] The entire building was planned as an H-shaped building which was to house the high school in one wing, a junior high school in a second wing, and an auditorium, classrooms, offices, and laboratory facilities in the center section. Though the first wing of the building was completed in 1918, the University High School (the successor of the Academy) was not allowed to occupy it until 1921. Under wartime exigencies, rather than furnish the building, an attempt was made to find other purposes for it. In the fall of 1918, the Trustees considered but did not act upon "a plan for converting the Education Building into a general hospital for the Students' Army Training Corps and the School of Military Aeronautics and the other students of the University." [99]

Bagley did not remain at Illinois to see the completion of even the first wing of the building. On May 1, 1917, the Trustees accepted his resignation, effective August 31. If he had remained at Illinois to the end of his professional career (1946), he would still not have seen the completion of the H-shaped building. Nor would he have had the cooperation of the University administration. When the school moved into the building in 1921, David Kinley was then President of the University. Kinley's attitude toward the school and toward professional education was the very antithesis of James's. On his orders, the students of University High School, unlike those of the Academy, were not allowed to use any other University facility. Even at com-

---

[96] Ibid., p. 301.
[97] Ibid., p. 937.
[98] *The Daily Illini*, September 24, 1916.
[99] *Transactions of the Board of Trustees* [of the University of Illinois], *July 17, 1918, to June 15, 1920*, p. 152.

mencement time, University High School had to rent a hall to conduct its exercises.[100]

The closing of the Academy and the delays in the completion of the new building, besides causing Bagley to discontinue his practice teaching program, also caused a delay in correcting what Bagley had called a "loose organization" in 1910. In February, 1916, he told James that "the organization of the School of Education, in so far as it involves the establishment of relationships between the Department of Education and the remaining departments of the University, has awaited the organization of the training school."[101]

Reorganization of the School was not effected until nearly a year after Bagley resigned when, on May 27, 1918, the University Senate voted "to recommend the establishment of a College of Education with the customary administrative organization." Five days later, the Board of Trustees authorized the President to undertake what the Senate had approved.[102]

[100] From p. 1 of a three-page mimeographed document headed "Appendix A: History of Efforts at Illinois to Secure Laboratory School" and dated December, 1947; College of Education Papers.

[101] Bagley, "History of the Department and School of Education," p. 15.

[102] *Transactions of the Board of Trustees* [of the University of Illinois], *July 17, 1918, to June 15, 1920*, p. 75.

CHAPTER 7

 Back to the Normal School

Bagley's departure from Illinois in 1917, like Arnold Tompkins's resignation in 1899, can be viewed as a sign that one era had ended and that another was to begin. More precisely, for Bagley, it was a return to normal school work, a return which may have begun in 1914 when Elliot W. Major, governor of Missouri, invited the Carnegie Foundation to examine and evaluate the supply and the training of teachers in his state. Bagley was among those whom William S. Learned, director of the survey, asked to assist in preparing what is now known as the Missouri survey.[1] Between 1914 and 1917 Bagley was granted leaves of absence and reductions in his work load to enable him to assist Learned.[2] And when, in 1917, Bagley accepted James Earl Russell's invitation to join the faculty of Teachers College, Columbia University, he was granted an immediate year's leave of absence to continue work on the Missouri survey. Finally, in the fall of 1918, Bagley went to New York to organize the newly created department of teacher education at Teachers College.

Bagley's participation in the Missouri survey brought him back into

[1] William C. Bagley, William J. Learned, et al., *The Professional Preparation of Teachers for American Public Schools* (New York: Carnegie Foundation Bulletin no. 14, 1920), p. xv.
[2] Bagley to James, April 27, 1915, James Correspondence; 28th *Report* (1916), pp. 247, 884.

firsthand contact with the normal school after six years of university work. His new position at Teachers College also took him back to the normal school. The new department which he was to organize was to be "concerned with the work of the normal schools and teachers' training classes . . . and the organization, management, and curriculum of schools for the training of teachers." [3] His acceptance of Russell's invitation may have been an attempt to clarify an ambiguity in his own professional life.

Bagley's career and the positions he took on various issues project an ambiguous image. If Tompkins typified the nineteenth century, and if Dexter was the representative of the twentieth, Bagley stood for both. As was noted earlier, he was among the first to attempt to apply the new science, psychology, to the educative process. At the same time, like DeGarmo and the McMurry brothers, he tried not to lose sight of the public school classroom, its teachers, and their needs and problems. His first two books are illustrative of the attention he paid to the pressing empirical exigencies of the classroom as well as to the theoretical dimensions of these problems.

In his first book, *The Educative Process* (1905), Bagley promised the reader no less than "a systematic and comprehensive view of the task that is to be accomplished by the school." [4] The "basal principles of the educative process" which he presented were based only on that data from psychology and biology that had been "vouched for by modern authorities in those fields." In his review of *The Educative Process* Edwin Grant Dexter remarked that biology, psychology, and sociology had "slowly, but surely, compelled a new formulation of educational theory." In his judgment, Bagley had presented "a new statement of the general theory of education" from the viewpoint of the modern sciences. It was not, he wrote, "a review of what others have said." [5]

[3] Quoted in Kandel, *William Chandler Bagley: Stalwart Educator*, p. 14. Kandel does not give the source of the quotation. In July, 1917, Bagley wrote to his former teacher at the University of Wisconsin, Michael Vincent O'Shea, that he had accepted his new position at Columbia University because it would allow him to concentrate upon the work he was "anxious to do"—that is, "the training of normal school specialists." (See Bagley to Michael Vincent O'Shea, July 10, 1917, in Michael Vincent O'Shea Papers, State Historical Society of Wisconsin, Madison, Wisconsin. For Bagley at Columbia, see Lawrence A. Cremin, David A. Shannon, and Mary Evelyn Townsend, *A History of Teachers College, Columbia University* [New York, 1954], esp. pp. 48ff.)
[4] Bagley, *The Educative Process* (New York, 1905), p. 5.
[5] Edwin G. Dexter, "Review of *The Educative Process*," *The School Review* 14, no. 6 (June, 1906): 418.

Guy Montrose Whipple judged Bagley's second work, *Classroom Management* (1907), to be a "distinct advance" over other works of its kind because it dealt "not with 'chicken-feed' trivialities, but with a system of fundamental principles in their concrete applications." [6] Though it may have been a "distinct advance," it was still in the genre begun by Hall, Abbott, and Page. It was a practical book for teachers. In it Bagley told the neophytes and the aspirants to teaching how to have the students hang their wraps, how to distribute papers and pencils, how to use the chalkboard, and how to secure the course of study were it not already in the teacher's desk drawer. It was an "advance" in that Bagley presented not only the practical tips but also psychological explanations of them.

During his years at Illinois, Bagley's conception of the relationship between psychology and education was suffering a change.[7] He was moving away from many of his original positions and apparently felt the need to revise much of his work. In the spring of 1915 he wrote to James: "I wish to rewrite the two books that I first published." [8] Although revisions of neither ever appeared, after this date Bagley did not write any books in educational theory or practice based on and supported by psychological doctrines or studies. While his views toward the relationship between psychology and education were changing, his ideas about teacher preparation were crystallizing. From the time of Coffman's study (1911), Bagley, as a contributer and later as an editor (beginning in 1914) of *School and Home Education*, frequently noted that there were insufficient numbers of trained teachers and celebrated the development and strengthening of normal schools, especially the founding of practice facilities.

Bagley's detailed prescriptions for teacher training appeared in 1920 in the section of the report of the Carnegie survey dealing with the curriculum of the normal school.[9] In 1918, the same year that the Senate and Trustees authorized the organization of a College of Education at Illinois, Bagley gave a preview of what he would say in the

[6] Guy Montrose Whipple, "Review of *Classroom Management,*" *Educational Review* 35 (May, 1908): 520.

[7] For a fuller account of Bagley's changing conceptions of the relationship between education and psychology, see E. V. Johanningmeier, "William Chandler Bagley's Changing Views on the Relationship between Psychology and Education," *History of Education Quarterly* 9, no. 1 (Spring, 1969).

[8] Bagley to James, April 27, 1915, James Correspondence.

[9] William C. Bagley, "Curricula of the Normal Schools," in Bagley, Learned, et al., *Preparation of Teachers.*

Carnegie report in two addresses delivered before the NEA. He told the NEA that he had "in mind . . . a fundamental reorganization of all our work with the professional end constantly in view." [10] He criticized the typical programs of both the liberal arts college and the normal schools. These programs either neglected the professional courses or the subject matter courses or simply tacked the professional courses on to a typical liberal arts curriculum. Bagley's judgment was that "everything that goes into the teacher-training curriculum should be admitted solely upon the basis of its relation to the equipment of the successful teacher." [11] Bagley was articulating what had been at issue at Illinois and elsewhere, but not clearly articulated, from the time of DeGarmo. His notion was simple. Preparation for teaching required a specialized training. If the university were to provide that training, it would have to recognize that it was unlike anything else it was doing. As Bagley put it, the program for teacher preparation "must include scholarship of a high order, but a unique quality of scholarship." [12] By "scholarship of a high order," Bagley meant work of "collegiate grade." In the Carnegie report he wrote that graduation from a four-year high school should be the prerequisite for entrance into either the normal school or the teachers' college, whether one desired to become either a teacher in the common school or in the secondary school. But the University and its guardians who feared that the work in education would not be of university grade were hesitant to admit education even when it attempted to disguise itself in psychological garb.

The plan the Illinois Faculty Senate approved in 1918 failed to recognize that education was different from the traditional disciplines, that the focus of professional education was the preparation of teachers. The Senate specified that the instructors of "courses in special educational theory and practice (such as agricultural education and the teaching of English) . . . shall be members of both the Faculty of the college of education and the other colleges concerned, and shall have such quality of scholarship and teaching ability as to permit of their offering courses in both colleges." [13] The University

---

[10] William C. Bagley, "The Distinction between Academic and Professional Subjects," NEA *Proceedings* (1918), p. 230.
[11] Ibid.
[12] Ibid.
[13] *Transactions of the Board of Trustees* [of the University of Illinois] *July 21, 1916 to June 11, 1918*, p. 758.

was not prepared to recognize that the faculty of the College of Education was, in principle, interested in a "unique" set of problems. The pedagogues could obtain status and legitimacy as long as they did not appear to be what they were. The guardians of the university disciplines apparently feared that the teachers' courses, left in the hands of the pedagogues, would, to use one of Bagley's phrases, "be limited to the rudimentary content that the prospective teacher is to pass on to his future pupils." [14]

Bagley, then, like his predecessors Tompkins and Dexter, was not able to develop and organize the work as he would have done in the best of all possible worlds. Like his predecessors, he questioned the support his colleagues in the University were willing to give him. But he himself had their support. His success must be attributed to his abilities and manner. But part of his success may have been due to his ambiguity. Dean Evarts B. Greene, for example, saw him as both a respectable member of the academic community and as a successful schoolman.

In a letter to James in April, 1909, discussing possible candidates for the directorship of the School of Education, Greene expressed both his respect for Bagley and the suspicions many had about the "new model educator." Greene told James that his mind turned "more and more toward Professor Bagley's appointment as director." None of the other three men he had mentioned to James were, he said, "Professor Bagley's equal." He noted, as his first reason for suggesting Bagley, that Bagley "had at Cornell University a sound training in the fundamental subjects of philosophy and psychology, which is rather rare among those who have gained prominence in educational work." [15] Yet Bagley had taken only two philosophical courses as part of his graduate training: one in philosophy of modern science from John William Stearns at Wisconsin, and one in philosophy of education from DeGarmo at Cornell.

Second, Greene reported that Bagley, in less than a year, had shown himself to be "an unusually effective teacher" who aroused "considerable enthusiasm" among those who took his "formal courses in education." As far as Greene could determine, Bagley had also "managed effectively . . . the practice and observation work . . . in connection with the Academy." Finally, Bagley was popular with the

[14] Bagley, "Distinction between Academic and Professional Subjects," p. 231.
[15] Greene to James, April 12, 1909, James Correspondence.

state's schoolmen. That was, Greene reported, an opinion in which "Professor Hollister, who [was] in a position to learn the opinions of school men," concurred. Greene finished his appraisal of Bagley's qualifications in this way: "I believe that in the difficult work of developing our plans for the school of education he will know how to work harmoniously with the men who are primarily interested in scientific and literary scholarship." That was the opinion of an historian.

At a later date, Greene, in response to Bagley's apparently having spoken "of the existence of some prejudice against the department of education on the part of members of the faculty," advised Bagley of "the two general questions which are most commonly raised regarding departments of education in the United States." The first question was, Greene confided, whether departments of education "set a sufficiently high estimate on general scholarship and specific training as compared to technical pedagogical training." It was also often asked, he related, "whether the department of education is not by tradition rather more aggressive than other departments in its efforts to secure various forms of special recognition which will tend to turn students in this particular direction."[16] Greene went on to assure Bagley that no one in the Department of Education had ever been as "successful in gaining the confidence of his colleagues" as he had been. However, there were points, as Greene advised, at which Bagley had to be on his guard.

Greene's estimation of Bagley was shared by others. For example, in his Annual Report for 1911–12, A. H. Daniels, then acting dean of the College of Literature and Arts, wrote: "We are fortunate in having a man of Professor Bagley's ability and professional attainments." Bagley was, he reported, "widely and favorably known by his writings."[17] He had also grown in favor with his colleagues on account of his sound training and agreeable personality.

In July, 1912, Daniels told James that Bagley had just declined a $5,000 post at the Milwaukee normal school and had previously declined the presidency of the normal school at Macomb, Illinois.

---

[16] Greene to Bagley, November 10, 1910. This letter was originally in the Stephens Papers but now can be found in the College of Liberal Arts and Sciences Papers, 1910–11, File A-K.

[17] A. H. Daniels, "College of Literature and Arts, Annual Report for the Year 1911–12 [and] Recommended Budget for the Year 1912–13" (a thirty-four page typescript submitted June 22, 1912), p. 24, James Correspondence.

Daniels feared that Bagley, who had not been given an increase for the coming year, would say nothing but would quietly withdraw at the end of the year. Salary was important to Bagley, he related; but, he continued, Bagley "is more concerned with the attitude of the administration toward his work." According to Daniels, Bagley was not "entirely certain as to what [the attitude] really is." Daniels wrote because he was "convinced that Professor Bagley [was] too valuable a man" to lose.[18]

The following year, Daniels again had nothing but praise for Bagley in his annual report of the College of Literature and Arts. Once more he drew attention to Bagley's "reputation as a writer" and the "esteem" his colleagues had for him. "To one familiar with the history of the Department of Education in this University," he wrote, "its development under Professor Bagley as director is exceedingly gratifying." To Daniels, the future of Education was a promising one. "With the promise of the building for the training school for teachers," he assured James, "I am confident we shall have a Department that in its personnel and equipment will measure up with the best in the country." [19]

Though there were doubts about the legitimacy of his enterprise, Bagley's administration of the work in education was not a total failure. More than his predecessors, he was able to promote "the scientific study of education in all its different aspects" even when he had his own doubts about the conclusions of the new science. While trying to forge a link between psychology and education, he was able to challenge its findings and interest Illinois's first recipient of a doctorate in education to pursue his reply to Thorndike. A noteworthy example is his response to the now famous Thorndike-Woodworth experiments of 1901 which were widely interpreted as the death knell of formal discipline and transfer of training. Bagley found an alternative to both the new and the old positions. He agreed that Thorndike and Woodworth had valid conclusions and that the old arguments could not stand against the new science. But, he argued, there was a dimension that lay outside the scope of the new investigations. He claimed that "ideals" could be taught and that if "ideas were con-

18 Daniels to James, July 23, 1912, James Correspondence.
19 A. H. Daniels, "College of Literature and Arts, Annual Report for the Year 1912–13 [and] Recommended Budget for the Year [1913–1914]" (a thirty-five page typescript submitted June 30, 1913), pp. 25–26. See also Daniels to James, July 23, 1912. Both in James Correspondence.

sciously learned they would, in effect, apply in a variety of situations." [20] He never offered experimental evidence to support his position (which was tantamount to supporting the old position), but Rugg's doctoral dissertation, the first in education at Illinois, did support it. On April 26, 1915, Harold Ordway Rugg's dissertation, "Descriptive Geometry and Mental Discipline," which was supervised by Bagley, was approved and accepted. Rugg concluded that a "disciplinary outcome" from a scientific school subject could be established, and that this "outcome" did, in effect, serve as an agent for the transfer of training.

The following May, Charles Elmer Holly's dissertation, supervised by Lotus D. Coffman, was approved and accepted. Holly's work, like Rugg's, reflected an interest of his supervisor. He studied "The Relationship between Persistence in School and Home Conditions" in several Illinois communities. Rugg and Holly were awarded the first Ph.D. degrees in Education at the University of Illinois in June. Holly went on to teach education and psychology at Ohio Wesleyan University and served in the Psychological Service of the U.S. Army. Rugg was appointed to the faculty at the University of Chicago and turned his attention to standardized testing. Eventually he became famous for his efforts devoted to the promotion of aesthetic education and his development of a series of social studies texts. The latter field represented a long-standing interest which had also marked Rugg's career at the University of Illinois. He and Bagley had undertaken a pioneering study of seventh- and eighth-grade history texts (appropriately empirical by virtue of random selection and an incredibly laborious word-count made with the help of graduate students) covering the period from 1865 to 1915. The instructional topics were recorded according to their relative depth and frequency, and changes

[20] For Bagley's first discussion of Thorndike-Woodworth, see "Ideals versus Generalized Habits," *School and Home Education* 24, no. 3 (November, 1904). He also presented this position in Ch. 13 of *The Educative Process* (New York, 1905) and Ch. 12 of *Educational Values* (New York: 1911).
Thorndike pressed the all-encompassing claims of psychology in his opening essay to the new *Journal of Educational Psychology:* "Psychology is the science of the intellects, characters and behavior of animals including man. Human education is concerned with certain changes in the intellects, characters and behavior of men, its problems being roughly included under these four topics: aims, materials, means and methods. Psychology contributes to a better understanding of the aims of education by defining them, making them clearer; by limiting them, showing us what can be done and what can not; and by suggesting new features that should be made parts of them" (*Journal of Educational Psychology* 1, no. 1 [January, 1910]: 5).

in their content were carefully analyzed; the results were finally published in 1916.[21]

As the presence of graduate students indicates, a faculty capable of supporting doctoral work had been assembled in the Department of Education. In 1908, when Bagley was appointed to the Department, Lewis Flint Anderson, who had earned his doctorate at Clark University, was appointed assistant professor of education. During his five-year stay at Illinois, Anderson was given complete charge of the work in the history of education. Upon his recommendation the University purchased the Aron library, a collection of 10,000 printed books, manuscripts, and engravings dealing with the history of education in Europe from the sixteenth to the mid-nineteenth century. The collection had been assembled over a forty-year period by Henry Aron, whom Anderson described as "a member of the Gesellschaft fur deutsches erziehungs-und Schulgeschicte, a specialist in the history of education and one of the most successful collectors on that subject." [22] The Aron collection included works by and about "great German educational leaders and reformers, such as Luther, Melanchthon, Ratke, Comenius, Francke, Hecker, Basedow, Pestalozzi, Herbart and Froebel." Its "set of Pestalozziana" was reported to be among the most complete (if not *the* most complete) set known. Among the manuscripts was a set of the educational writings of Weigel, who had been "an influential educational reformer of the 17th century and the instructor in mathematics and mechanics of Leibnitz and Semler at the University of Jena." [23]

When Anderson resigned in 1914 to take a post at Ohio State University, Kinley deplored the resignation as the loss of "a type altogether too unusual in departments of education nowadays." Kinley approved of Anderson because he did scholarship rather than "field work." [24] Bagley, after looking for a successor for Anderson, wrote that his original belief had "been abundantly confirmed; the belief, namely, that there are only two or three men in the country whom we could rank with Professor Anderson as a leader in the field of educational history." Unfortunately, those men were "not available

---

[21] W. C. Bagley and H. O. Rugg, "The Content of American History as Taught in the Seventh and Eighth Grades," *University of Illinois Bulletin* 13, no. 51 (Urbana, 1916).

[22] L. F. Anderson, "A Brief Statement Concerning the Aron Library," attached to Anderson to James, August 19, 1913, James Correspondence.

[23] Ibid.

[24] Kinley to James, April 28, 1914, James Correspondence.

for present appointment." [25] There would be no professor to guide the students through the Aron collection.

Lotus Delta Coffman joined the Illinois faculty in the fall of 1911 as a part-time member, spending two days of each week in Urbana and four in Charleston, where he was the superintendent of the training department in the Eastern Illinois State Normal School. Coffman began full-time service at Illinois in the fall of 1912 as professor of education, taking charge of the work in school administration and supervision. Before he left in 1915 to take the deanship of the College of Education at the University of Minnesota (where he eventually became president), Coffman was appointed to the directorship of the Illinois School Survey upon the recommendation of Chicago's influential Ella Flagg Young.[26]

The dean of the School of Education at the University of Kansas, Charles Hughes Johnston, accepted a professorship in secondary education at Illinois in 1913. Before taking the deanship at Kansas, Johnston had been a professor of secondary education at Dartmouth College and the University of Michigan. Throughout his brief career he wrote and talked of the need to broaden the concept of the high school. At the University of Michigan Johnston conducted a seminar on curriculum in which the students were directed to inquire into the history, the current status, and the specific values of each of the high school subjects.[27] At Illinois he directed his students to investigate the social organization of the high school. His own notion of the "socialized high school" found expression in two well-edited books: *High School Education* (1912) and *The Modern High School* (1914). Besides writing on the high school and trying to clarify the various discussions of the new "junior high school," [28] Johnston was interested in comparative education and the actual practice of educational administration.

Had Johnston not met an untimely death in an automobile accident in September, 1917, he would have been the first Dean of the College of Education. Even before he was appointed, Bagley thought him a

[25] Bagley to James, May 12, 1914, James Correspondence.
[26] Bagley to James, February 18, 1914, in 27th *Report*, (1914), p. 722.
[27] *University of Michigan Catalogue, 1909–10*, p. 162, according to citation in Leigh G. Hubbell, *The Development of University Departments of Education in Six States of the Middle West with Special Reference to Their Contributions to Secondary-School Progress* (published Ph.D. dissertation, Catholic University of America, 1924), p. 79.
[28] Charles Hughes Johnston, "The Junior High School," *Journal of Educational Administration and Supervision* (1916): 413–24.

suitable replacement for himself. When he was being considered for his post at Illinois, Bagley wrote James that it was "probable that we shall find him [Johnston] well adapted to the duties of the directorship of the School of Education." [29] At the time of his death he had become acting director of the School.

In May, 1914, Bagley wrote James to call to his "attention the unusually favorable opportunity of securing at the present time one of the leaders in the field of educational psychology in the person of Professor G[uy] M[ontrose] Whipple, of Cornell University." [30] Whipple, who was then thirty-eight, had earned his A.B. from Brown University in 1897 and, like Bagley, completed his doctorate in 1900 at Cornell in Titchener's psychological laboratory. Also like Bagley, he studied neurology and education as minor subjects in pursuit of his doctorate.

Except for one year (1907–8) during which he served as "supply professor" in the University of Missouri, Whipple had spent his entire career at Cornell. From 1898 to 1902 he was an assistant in Titchener's laboratory. In 1902, he had become a lecturer in education and he was appointed to an assistant professorship in 1904. His "special interest" was the then infant field of "mental tests." His "Manual of Physical and Mental Tests," first published in 1910, was, Bagley reported, "recognized as the standard work on the subject." [31] It had just been revised and had been translated into German and Russian. He had also completed a "number of important monographic studies," such as "A Guide to High School Observation," "Questions on School Hygiene," and a translation of Offner's "Mental Fatigue." And, like Bagley, he was one of the four co-founders and editors of the *Journal of Educational Psychology*.

Whipple's availability was an opportunity which Bagley wanted to seize. He admitted that "a first-class man in vocational education" was needed, but none who "would be a valuable addition to our corps" was available. Whipple's addition would give the department new stature and allow the University to develop new lines of work. Bagley explained it in this way:

[29] Bagley to James, March 14, 1913. Also see James to Kinley, May 28, 1912, both in James Correspondence. James wrote Kinley that Johnston struck him "as one of the best and most helpful men to consider in connection with the position here." He then added, "Bagley wishes to be let out of his administrative work."
[30] Bagley to James, May 18, 1914, James Correspondence.
[31] Ibid.

Dr. Whipple would admirably round out the Department of Education giving us a recognized authority (second, I should say, only to Thorndike and possibly Meumann) in the field of educational and clinical psychology and school hygiene; a research man of proved ability; and an excellent teacher, especially of advance students. He would command the respect of his colleagues in other departments, and would give the Department prestige with the men who are working in auxiliary education and in the field of mental hygiene both in the state institutions and in Chicago and other large cities. We already have calls for courses in clinical psychology and in mental tests, and we should also be in a position to cooperate with the state institutions, the juvenile courts, and other agencies that are dealing with clinical cases. The development of the work in school hygiene and sanitation is, of course, equally important. . . . Clinical psychology, educational psychology, and school hygiene are related topics which would naturally fall to the same individual. This phase of our work I have long felt needs development. In view of the importance of the field and of Dr. Whipple's availability, I am convinced that an appointment of this type would form the best step that we could take at the present time.[32]

Bagley reported that he discussed Whipple's qualifications with Professor Bentley of the psychology department (Bentley was on the staff at Cornell while Bagley and Whipple were students there), and Bentley agreed that Whipple "would make an excellent addition to our present corps." Professors Coffman and Johnston added notes to Bagley's letter, stating that they concurred in Bagley's judgment and recommendation. Bagley's recommendation prevailed, and James agreed to hire Whipple. In time history confirmed Bagley's appraisal of Whipple's work and abilities. By 1929, the historian of experimental psychology, Edwin G. Boring, had listed Whipple as among those who "have already become prominent in the history of American psychology."[33]

When Whipple arrived, he took over the courses in educational psychology, health administration, and school hygiene. His main interest was, however, "mental tests." His "Manual of Mental and Physical Tests" came to be regarded as having "summarized the field as Washburn's book [*The Animal Mind* (1908)] had done for animal

[32] Ibid.
[33] Edwin G. Boring, *A History of Experimental Psychology*, (New York, 1929), pp. 412–13.

psychology and Titchener's *Manuals* for experimental psychology." [34] Illinois was not, however, able to hold on to Whipple. During the first semester of the 1918–19 academic year, Whipple was granted a leave of absence to allow him, as the Board of Trustees recorded, "to carry on certain important investigations at Pittsburgh in connection with the development of psychological tests." In Pittsburgh, Whipple worked as the director of the Bureau of Salesmanship Research in the Carnegie Institute of Technology. In March, 1917, the Board of Trustees received a letter from Bagley "endorsing a communication from Professor Whipple regarding the establishment . . . of a Bureau of Educational Service." [35] The Board's minutes only note that "no action was taken on this recommendation." [36] In June, 1918, the Board authorized the organization of a Bureau of Educational Research. But before it actually began, Kinley, who was soon to take James's chair as president, complained of its cost and damned it with faint praise. Whipple did not return to Illinois but went to the University of Michigan where he became the director of its newly founded Bureau of Tests and Measurements. (By 1922 it had become the Bureau of Educational Reference and Research).[37]

Both Whipple's arrival and departure from Illinois can be viewed as minor signs that the work in education had suffered new changes. The budget line that Whipple filled was the one opened by Anderson's resignation. Anderson, the historian, the literary scholar, to use Kinley's characterization, was replaced by an empiricist. That left the Department of Education with neither a historian nor a philosopher, though Boyd H. Bode, who was a member of the philosophy department (and who had also received his doctorate from Cornell University in 1900), did join Bagley in the teaching of seminars on educational values and the philosophical bases of educational theory.

Whipple's arrival is an instance of what Michael B. Katz has identified as the move from theory to survey in the study of education between 1902 and 1920 at the University of Chicago and elsewhere. By the 1920's, Katz records, "the earlier emphasis on history and philosophy was replaced by a stress of psychology, measurement and

[34] Ibid., p. 645.
[35] *Transactions of the Board of Trustees of the University of Illinois, July 21, 1916, to June 11, 1918*, p. 267.
[36] Ibid.
[37] *University of Michigan Catalogue*, 1922–23, p. 578. (Cited in Hubbell, *Development of University Departments of Education*, p. 88.)

administration." [38] While Dewey directed the work in education at Chicago, he and his colleagues were attempting to forge a theory of the educative process. To Dewey and others of this era, history and philosophy, and even sociology, were as crucial as psychology and the other empirical fields of investigation. By 1920, under the direction of Charles H. Judd, Chicago, like other universities, was attempting to develop "a discipline through surveying the field of education as it existed in the real world and then breaking down its subdivisions as minutely as possible." [39] An institutional manifestation of this transition in the study of education was the increase in specialized course offerings. For example, Katz points out that at Chicago William S. Gray noted in his 1920-21 report that "in place of general courses in public school administration, courses are now given in school finance, the administrative management of pupils, and the organization and supervision of the teaching staff." [40]

Illinois also witnessed what some would now call proliferation and what Bagley described in 1910 as placing "the chief emphasis . . . upon the advanced undergraduate and graduate courses." The *University Register* for 1908-9—the first to include Bagley—shows that the Department then offered fourteen courses. Of these, two were designated to be "introductory courses"; six were "intermediate courses"; five were for "advanced undergraduates and graduates." There was also one seminar in the philosophy and history of education for graduate students. None of the eleven advanced courses was devoted exclusively to educational psychology. They were the "General Method" course, the course in "Observation and Practice," and Education 1— "Principles of Education." However, in some quarters the "principles" course was thought to be a philosophy of education course. Typically, such "principles" courses dealt not only with how education did occur, but also with how it ought to be conducted. Three of the courses—"High School Organization and Management," "School Law," and "School Hygiene"—dealt with the school as an institution. Two of the courses were what would now be called "school and society courses"—"Social Phases of Education" and "Contemporary Educational Conditions and Movements in the United States." Five

38 Michael B. Katz, "From Theory to Survey in Graduate Schools of Education," *Journal of Higher Education* 37, no. 6 (June, 1966): 328.

39 Ibid., p. 327.

40 "The College of Education," in University of Chicago, *The President's Report* (Chicago, 1922), pp. 19-20. (Quoted and cited in Katz, p. 327.)

of the remaining six courses included the history of education, educational classics, the comparative study of various educational systems, and Herbart. And there was a course in the "Principles of Aesthetic, Moral, and Religious Education."

The *Register* for 1909–10 bore the stamp of Bagley's interest in the educative process as it occurred in the school. It described a two-semester course in "observation and practice teaching" which included:

> (a) the systematic observation of classroom work in the Academy of the University and in neighboring high schools; (b) weekly conference for the discussion of observations; (c) one lecture each week upon the technique of teaching; (d) the preparation by students of plans illustrating the various types of school exercises discussed in the lectures; (e) the reading and summarizing by each student of the standard text on the teaching of the subject elected; and (f) a review of the subject matter that the student proposes to teach.[41]

During the last five weeks of the semester, the student was allowed to teach "a review-class of secondary grade." In the "Practice Teaching" course the student was allowed to teach "a class of secondary grade during the entire semester" under the direction and supervision of both the department of education and the Academy's instructors.

There are, unfortunately, no accounts to tell either what a semester, or a week, or even a day, in the observation and practice course demanded from the student or how it impressed him. When the trustees closed the Academy, Bagley directed Frances Morehouse, who had been a supervisor of practice teaching in history, to set down the principles of supervision that had been formulated by the supervisory staff. The object of her paper was to record and preserve those procedures that had been adopted. In effect, she provided an elaboration of the *Catalogue* description of the course.[42]

But direct observation of the educative process was not limited to those who enrolled in the practice and observation course. T. E.

[41] *University of Illinois Register, 1909–1910*, p. 298.

[42] Frances Morehouse, *Practice Teaching in the School of Education, University of Illinois 1893–1911* (University of Illinois School of Education Bulletin no. 7, University of Illinois Bulletins, vol. 10, no. 8, October 21, 1912). While Morehouse does tell what principles and rules the staff created and used, her historical account of practice teaching at Illinois is not completely accurate in every detail. For example, Morehouse records that Professor F. M. McMurry introduced practice teaching at Illinois in 1893–94. These plans were made but Draper did not allow them to be executed, as we have seen.

Musselman, who was graduated from the University in 1910, enrolled in one of Bagley's introductory education courses.[43] Sixty years after the course, he set down his impressions of that experience.[44] He recalled that Bagley "could instill interest in his teaching problems that reacted in general constructive discussions among his students." "His classes," Musselman wrote, "were always informative." Musselman also told how Bagley kindled this interest:

> As an illustration, I remember being directed to a large basement room in Old Main Hall. We were asked to take notebooks, and enter quietly, to take notes, and in no way to interfere with the progress of instruction being carried on. He requested absolute silence.
>
> In this larger classroom was an alert woman teacher with a mixed class of negro and white children from 6 to 8 years of age. She was clever and had a number of play problems which she presented to her young companions. To them it was play, not schooling. Yet we were making an analysis of the speed with which the children accepted suggestions, and the depth of their reaction—black—white—male—female.
>
> Days later we enjoyed another similar experiment, the children being 10 to 12 years old. . . .

After the visits, Bagley "beautifully analyzed and discussed" the suggestions and recommedations the visitors had offered in their reports. The "entire experiment," Musselman has related, "inspired all of us older students to a more gracious outlook on the possibilities of the teaching profession."

As we have already noted, the Academy was closed in 1911 and the practice courses were discontinued. Bagley and the other members of the faculty thus lost their opportunity to study the educative process on the campus. The state's high schools were there, but they were not used by the educationists (most probably because they were not available). Even the contact the faculty had with the schools through the visitation system came to an end as the Visitor's office came to be a separate function under control of the President's office rather than the Department of Education.

By 1919 both the Faculty Senate and the University Trustees had approved the organization of a College of Education, and the work in

---

[43] James H. Kelley, ed., *Alumni Record of the University of Illinois* (Urbana, 1913), p. 538.
[44] Musselman to E. V. Johanningmeier, September 23, 1966. A xerographic copy of this two-page typed letter is now in the University of Illinois Archives.

education was, for the first time, being offered by the newly formed College. Almost as a preparation for the new administrative arrangement, the number and nature of the courses changed just as they were changing in other universities. The faculty did not lose sight of the public schools, but the scope of its sight increased to include national as well as state and local problems and issues. As it dealt with the issues, it reduced them to their constituent parts. And, in the process, the classroom where the teaching-learning process actually occurs fell from the center of focus.

The *Register* for 1916–17 reveals that the Department of Education by then offered nearly thirty courses. There were no significant changes in the two introductory courses, though the "principles" course was now called "Introduction to Education." It was a required course in that the student who wanted "the official indorsement of the Appointments Committee for teaching positions in secondary schools" had to complete the course successfully. By 1919 it appears to have become, unfortunately, a rather typical introductory course. It was then being taught by M. J. Stormzand, who had not yet finished his doctorate and who felt that he was stuck with using Bagley's *The Educative Process.* Stormzand wrote O'Shea of the University of Wisconsin that he had "two large sections, 175 students altogether, of Bagley's old 'Education 1.' " He related that he had adopted O'Shea's teaching technique for himself. That was, he wrote, "the free give and take form of class discussions." He used to test the students on the required reading with "the various types of psychological and schools tests." [45] These practices were providing him with materials which he felt would be useful for a study on teaching methods. Besides Bagley's book, Judd's *Introduction* was used. However, he planned to drop Bagley and make Judd's work the text for the course.

At the intermediate level, the course in "General Method" was replaced by "Technics of Teaching," a course which was also required by the Appointments Committee. This new course promised a more practical fare than did old methods courses. In methods the student was supposedly taught how to apply "the principles of education, psychology, and logic to the art of teaching." In "technics," which was taught not by any of the professors, but by the graduate assistants, the student was told about "types of classroom exercises and preparation of teach-

[45] Stormzand to O'Shea, December 3, 1919, in Michael Vincent O'Shea Papers, State Historical Society of Wisconsin, Madison, Wisconsin.

ing plans" and was required to observe teaching in "neighboring high schools." With Whipple's arrival, an introductory course in educational psychology at the intermediate level was begun. Like his mentor, E. B. Titchener, Whipple promised both lectures and demonstrations. "Social Education" which replaced "Social Phases of Education" was now listed as an intermediate course, but was not offered in 1916–17.

The greatest expansion of courses took place at the advanced level. While the department offered five courses for "advanced undergraduates and graduates" in 1908–9, it presented thirteen offerings in this category in 1916–17. Some of the expansion at this level was the result of moving from one category to another (e.g., "School Hygiene" had been moved from the intermediate category). Some of the expansion was the product of splitting courses. In 1908–9, there was an intermediate course in high school organization and management which promised "a discussion of the essential elements of a good high school, together with a consideration of the conditions existing in Illinois; proposed solution of the many problems of secondary education; desired lines of progress; building up of an accredited high school; equipment; courses of study; electives; [and] discipline." In place of this course, three courses at the "advanced" level were introduced: "Problems of Educational Administration," "Principles of High-School Education," and "High-School Curriculums." The work in "Educational Classics" which had been a one-semester course was now a two-semester course.

There were also new courses. Johnston began to offer a course in the new field of "Vocational Education." Whipple, besides teaching the intermediate course in educational psychology, offered work in "Problems in Educational Psychology," "Mental Tests," and "Auxiliary Education." The latter course studied "institutions and methods for training defectives and delinquents; Binet-Simon tests and other methods of mental diagnosis; educational treatment of morons and moral delinquents; sensory defectives (the blind and deaf); public institutions of auxiliary education and their administration."

Herbartian pedagogics, like the work in aesthetic, moral, and religious education, was dropped. However, separate courses in German and French "educational literature" which required only "moderate facility" in the language were added to the offerings. Finally, as a sign of the new era, a new course treating "method in educational research," in which the student studied how to apply statistical methods in educational investigations, was introduced. According to the catalogue, the course was "ordinarily required of all candidates for advanced degrees." [46]

All graduate students were required to attend the "Departmental Conference" which was conducted by the departmental staff "every alternate Monday from 7 to 9 p.m." Graduate courses in "Principles of Education" and the "Elementary Curriculum," as well as new seminars, dealt with secondary education, educational psychology, and educational theory. The last examined "the philosophical bases of educational theory," and was jointly taught by Bagley and Boyd H. Bode.[47]

While the number and range of courses the faculty taught expanded, the faculty's off-campus activities increased. And it is likely that the off-campus work was done at the expense of the campus work. For example, Bagley reported to James that between October, 1910, and May, 1911, he had given forty-two lectures outside the University. These lectures were presented not only to the schoolmen of Illinois, but also to audiences in Kansas, Indiana, New York, Alabama, and Missouri. They took him away from sixty-two of his own campus lectures—more than the equivalent of a three-credit course—an absence which his colleagues necessarily had to fill.[48]

Besides lecturing in and out of the state, Bagley produced a steady stream of editorials on educational matters in *School and Home Education* and the *Journal of Educational Psychology*. In 1912, he was asked to become the managing editor of *School and Home Education*. In asking James for his approval, he related that his disposition to accept was influenced not only by the advantages that would accrue to the University but also by his own "personal taste for editorial work and for writing." [49] James inquired how it would affect his teaching. Bagley replied that it would not affect it, adding that his editorials were drawn from the material he prepared and presented in his classes. But by 1916, Bagley had as a consequence virtually lost touch with undergraduates who were preparing themselves for work in the schools. In February, 1916, the Board of Trustees authorized President James to grant Bagley "a readjustment of his work and

[46] *University of Illinois Annual Register*, 1916–17, p. 303.
[47] Ibid., p. 304.
[48] Bagley to James, May 10, 1911, James Correspondence.
[49] Bagley to James, April 10, 1912; also see Bagley to James, April 16, 1912, both in James Correspondence.

salary during the second semester of the present academic year, similar to the arrangement . . . made last year, whereby he may be released from the undergraduate work and some of the routine details of the office, but may continue as head of the Department of Education, directing its policy and carrying on his regular work with graduate students. . . ." [50]

Johnston, like Bagley and Coffman, also served his profession as an editor. He was the managing editor of the *Journal of Educational Administration and Supervision.* Johnston also served as a member of the reviewing committee of the National Commission on the Reorganization of Secondary Education, the commission that produced the famed "cardinal principles" document twenty-five years after the Committee of Ten presented its report. Whipple served on the National Research Council's Commission on the Mental Examination of Recruits. And Bagley was a member of the Committee on Psychological and Pedagogical Aspects of Military Discipline and the NEA's Commission on Emergency and Readjustment. He had also been collaborating with Charles A. Beard on American history texts for the elementary school. Through their publications Bagley, Whipple, Coffman, and Johnston had achieved national recognition during their years at Illinois.

Though the faculty had become involved in national organizations and issues, their attention to the schools of their own state was not lessened. Indeed, the faculty continued to tend to the the relationship between the University and the schools, but also to grow further away from the public school classroom. The summer school remained an important link between the two, and a new link—extension work— was begun "in a tentative and experimental way" in 1912. As Bagley explained in 1912, the two—extension work and the summer school— were not unrelated. He pointed out to James that he and Coffman had been asked to offer extension work. Besides these specific requests, there was, he reported, a demand for it throughout the state as demonstrated both by requests and the success of the extension work already undertaken by the Macomb normal school. Many of the students who enrolled in the extension courses offered by Macomb also attended Macomb's summer school. That was a point Bagley urged James to consider.[51]

In proposing extension work, Bagley may have been considering

[50] 28th *Report* (1916), p. 884.
[51] Bagley to James, September 16, 1912, James Correspondence.

much more than merely carrying established courses to off-campus teachers during the regular school term. To be sure, he was doing that and the teachers did want such work. However, even the teachers wanted more. During the summer of 1912, the teachers adopted a resolution asking "the University officials to make it possible for the Director of the School of Education to extend training to the teachers in service, as follows: first, a high grade course in correspondence; second, lecture courses to be given by experts in educational matters; third, a systematic series of bulletins dealing with new and vital findings in the frontier field of education." [52] In the spring of 1912, Bagley gave his "hearty approval" to "A Plan for the Organization of Educational Extension in Illinois" which called for the establishment of "centers of experimentation on educational problems." [53] The plan suggested that schools representing "typical environments" could be selected to study "the teaching of agriculture," "the economical administration of education in small centers, such as villages and small towns," and the "problems of city administration" in cities such as Chicago, Peoria, and East St. Louis. It was also proposed that the University could aid in the "development of the township and union district high school as a means of providing a free high school for all."

The author of this plan wanted to tie this extension work to existing activities of the University: the High School Conference and high school inspection. The various problems were to be studied by teachers and principals "under university direction." The results of the studies would, according to the plan, be published as educational bulletins. The High School Conference could, it was related, serve as a clearing house and organizer of the work. The schoolmen who were studying these educational problems were also to become part-time high school inspectors, allowing not only a more detailed inspection of high schools but also "a wider opportunity for the study of school problems by local principals of the stronger high schools."

The plan was, in effect, a proposal to establish an expanded form of what Bagley had previously proposed and identified as a "Bureau of

[52] Hollister to James, n.d. From location in the James Correspondence it would appear to be July, 1912. The text of the resolution itself shows that it definitely was the summer of 1912.

[53] This plan had neither author nor date. However, its position in the Hollister file suggests February or March, 1912. It is a two-page typescript. The bottom of p. 2 had the following notation: "This general plan meets with my hearty approval [signed] W. C. Bagley, Director School of Education."

Correspondence." [54] At this point, however, it was proposed that all these activities plus the offering of "special lecture courses" be centered in a "department of school administration." The establishment of such a bureau or department was, as we have seen, nearly six years away. But a small beginning was made. In 1912–13, Coffman offered an extension course in educational sociology for some twenty teachers in the Urbana schools. The following year Coffman gave a course in educational measurement at Decatur and Bagley offered educational psychology at Springfield. Though these courses were well attended, they were not continued, Bagley reported in 1916, because "there seemed to be little demand for extension courses that would carry University credit." [55] However, the faculty continued "to lecture at teachers' institutes and to address teachers' organizations."

The summer school still remained a matter of concern, though its status was not as critical as it was in the age of Tompkins. In September, 1912, Bagley, as director of the summer session, reported that there had been a marked decline in the 1911 enrollment and offered a series of explanations, criticisms, and recommendations. Some factors which accounted for the decline the University could not control: the heat of 1911 had taken its toll on most midwestern enrollments, and the holding of the NEA convention in Chicago had prompted teachers to enroll at the University of Chicago's summer session. Yet it could not be denied that there were "certain conditions in our policy that would in any case have impeded the growth of the session." [56] The University had reduced the credit that could be earned in one session from nine to eight hours and had dropped the six-week courses. Chicago and Wisconsin had six-week courses (and, it might be added, were much closer to lakes).

Bagley observed that the teachers were seeking out the better equipped and financed programs. The Illinois budget was $23.25 per capita of attendance, while it was $53.87 at Chicago and $40.07 at Michigan.[57] "*The attitude of the university community toward the summer session*" was another impeding factor.[58] The better faculty,

[54] William C. Bagley, "Some Possible Functions of a School of Education," *School of Education* 30, no. 4 (December, 1910). Also see Ch. 6 above.

[55] William C. Bagley, "History of the Department and School of Education of the University of Illinois," p. 16.

[56] Bagley to James, September 17, 1912, p. 2, James Correspondence. This letter, including its five tables, constitutes a fifteen-page typed report.

[57] Ibid., p. 3.

[58] Ibid.

Bagley claimed, will not or "cannot" stay on the stipend the University has paid. While the general feeling of the faculty at Illinois was one of opposition to being involved in the summer program, at other universities the summer session work was recognized as equal to that of the other sessions. He offered a proposal whereby "men of professional rank" would be invited to teach during the summer at no pay with the understanding that two such summers would entitle them to one semester's leave at full pay.

Finally, the University had ignored some students and failed to provide adequate programs for others it had sought to serve. It had sought "the more mature and better educated class of public school teachers" and had neglected " 'the rank and file.' " [59] The effect of this policy was to turn the elementary school teachers to the normal school. For the "more mature" teacher, the University had offered a standard fare of introductory courses. Bagley wanted an organization of the work laid out for several years so students could plan and complete an entire program.

As an administrator, Bagley was aware of another area of importance, the politics of education. He saw that the teachers needed help in securing the legislation they desired and was willing to assist them. In December, 1913, Bagley noted that the legislative committee of the Illinois State Teachers' Association was considering bills dealing with a sanitation code for constructing school buildings, new administrative units, pensions, tenure, and the source and extent of funds for public education. He recommended that the School of Education add an additional man to its staff to aid the State Teachers' Association in the collection of data and the writing of legislative proposals.[60] James expressed interest in Bagley's proposal to aid the teachers, but he feared the possible conflicts of interest "with other state departments which are engaged in this same work." [61]

However, the following year, 1914, provided the School of Education with an occasion to aid the Association. At the Association's request, the Illinois School Survey was organized in 1914. Superintendent of Public Instruction Francis Blair appointed a commission to plan the survey. At the suggestion of Ella Flagg Young, who was a member of the commission's executive committee, Lotus Coffman was appointed

[59] Ibid., p. 4.
[60] Bagley to James, December 5, 1913, James Correspondence.
[61] James to Bagley, December 8, 1913, James Correspondence.

director of the survey.[62] In all, three of Illinois's faculty took charge of separate phases of the work: besides directing the survey, Coffman was responsible for the "Teaching Population"; Johnston for "Vocational Education"; and Bagley for the "Program of Studies." Coffman was also appointed secretary of the State Teachers' Association and editor of its journal, *The Illinois Teacher*, at this time.[63]

Perhaps the most important tie between the University and the schools was the one effected by the High School Visitor. When Stratton D. Brooks resigned from the post in 1902 to become assistant superintendent of schools in Boston, he was replaced by Horace Adelbert Hollister. Unlike many of his predecessors, Hollister came to the University to finish his career rather than begin it. When he arrived in 1902, he was forty-five years old and already had twenty years of experience in public school administration and supervision in Iowa, Kansas, Missouri, and Illinois. When asked to come to the University, he was the superintendent of schools in Sterling, Illinois. Remaining at Illinois for over a quarter century, he rendered yeoman service to the University, the state secondary schools, and in the development of the new and difficult field of accrediting associations. He became one of the "two men who were the most influential in setting up and directing the early machinery for the accrediting of Schools." [64] With Allen S. Whitney, who held a like position at the University of Michigan, Hollister got the North Central Association of Colleges and Secondary Schools organized and established.

Among Hollister's tasks and achievements was the High School Conference. In his annual report for 1903 he had recommended that the University organize a meeting of the state's high school teachers for the sake of obtaining uniform standards in the high schools.[65] No immediate action was taken, but on September 27, 1904, Vice-President T. J. Burrill reported that a committee of the Council of Administration was considering the status of the teaching of English language and literature and of the sciences in the high schools. "The schools," he related, "generally will gladly welcome any assistance in

[62] 27th *Report* (1914), p. 722.
[63] Bagley, "History of School and Education," pp. 16–17.
[64] Calvin Olin Davis, *A History of the North Central Association of Colleges and Secondary Schools, 1895–1945* (Ann Arbor, 1945), p. 30.
[65] Our source for this is Hubbell, *Development of University Departments of Education*, p. 105. He apparently used *Proceedings of the High School Conference, 1910*, which gives a brief history of the Conference.

this and it is believed the University may be able to render some real service in the matter. . . ." He requested and received an appropriation of $200 to allow him to begin plans for a conference with "20 selected superintendents or teachers and a committee from the University faculty." [66] That appropriation provided for a three-day conference in 1905. The meeting of approximately seventy-five teachers was divided into three sections, and the high school work in English, biology, and physical science was discussed. These subjects were chosen because they presented "the most urgent need of action in order to unify the work." [67]

By 1910 the Conference had become an annual affair which met on the Thursday, Friday, and Saturday of the week before Thanksgiving. According to Hollister, the conferences "were becoming among the most important educational meetings of the state, if not, indeed, of the central west." [68] In 1913 he was able to relate to James that "some of the members of the University of Chicago faculty [had] confided to [him] that [the 1913 Conference] was far and away the best Conference held in the state." [69] That was a considerable compliment, for Chicago had its own meetings for the high school teachers.

The growth and success of these annual meetings were, in Hollister's opinion, due to two factors. First, they were an open invitation from the University to the high schools "to come and participate with the University in the adjustment of all matters . . . [i.e.,] questions of accrediting and admission requirements; the training and scholarship of high school teachers; and the nature and amount of work which high schools should undertake to do." The organization of the Conference itself was the second factor. It consisted of several "sectional meetings for intensive work along lines of interest to special departments of high school work. . . ." [70] The general meetings which usually dealt with administrative matters were, Hollister explained, "minimized." Hollister urged that the success of the meeting could only be insured if members of the appropriate University departments gave special attention to the problems of the schools and dealt with them in the section meetings. The way to counter the "rather

[66] 23rd *Report* (1906), p. 5.
[67] Hubbell (pp. 106–7) quoting *Proceedings of the High School Conference, 1910*, p. 5.
[68] Hollister to James, June 9, 1910, James Correspondence.
[69] Hollister to James, November 24, 1913, James Correspondence.
[70] Hollister to James, June 9, 1910, James Correspondence.

prevalent spirit of antagonism among the high schools toward the universities," according to Hollister, was to meet the high schools "with a frank, open policy of sincere good will, and by a recognition of the importance as well as the difficulties of the work they are doing." [71] The rational self-interest of the University, he seemed to say, demanded a frank relationship between the University and the schools.

Hollister was successful at keeping the Conference going and in enlisting the aid of the faculty. In 1911, the *Alumni Quarterly* told that the last Conference "was an unusually successful one." Nearly 800 teachers and superintendents had enrolled. That was "a large increase over the enrollment last year, and ten times as large as the first meeting of the Conference." [72] In subsequent years the Conference would have to compete with the usually simultaneous "Homecoming" —another Illinois creation—for quarters for its participants. "The housing facilities of Champaign and Urbana," Hollister wrote, "are entirely inadequate for such a combination of probable visitors to the University." [73] Each had become too large to live with the other. Moreover, the festivities of the Homecoming celebration sometimes distracted the teachers, especially those who had been Illini.

In 1913, the Conference counted registration by sections which represented the interest of the enrollee. There were fifteen sections and 982 enrollees.[74] The "administrative" section was the largest, but it did not constitute a majority. After the 1915 Conference, it was reported that its "attendance and the general spirit . . . were on the highest level ever yet attained." Among the special features of this Conference were Hollister's "discussion of the Junior High School problem," "an exhibit of aids and accessories for high school library work, procured and arranged by Miss Mary E. Hall, of Brooklyn," and "the emphasis put upon the direct method of teaching Latin, through the presence of Miss Theodora E. Wye, of Columbia University, who gave a model recitation before the Classics Section." Harold

[71] Ibid.
[72] "High School Conference," *Alumni Quarterly of the University of Illinois* 5 (January, 1911): 29.
[73] Hollister to James, October 7, 1913, James Correspondence.
[74] The sections and their enrollments were: administrative, 203; agricultural, 35; biology, 56; classics, 103; commercial, 32; county superintendents and village principals, 26; domestic science, 52; English, 144; geography, 18; manual arts, 11; mathematics, 84; modern language, 51; music, 41; physical science, 54; social science, 45; and there were 27 who professed no sectional interest. From a one-page document entitled "Statistics on the High School Conference of 1913."

Rugg, now at the School of Education, University of Chicago, presented a paper on the "experimental Determination of Standards in First Year Algebra." [75] In 1916 Hollister predicted that it might be necessary to house the teachers in the YMCA and in the churches, for the Conference seemed "destined to reach an attendance of at least two thousand." [76]

Hollister was to remain at Illinois and to continue to work with the schools. Indeed, he was the one prominent figure who would remain through the general dissolution of the faculty which marked the end of an era. When the 1917–18 academic year began, Werrett Wallace Charters had just arrived from the University of Missouri where he had been professor of the theory of teaching and Dean of the Faculty of Education. He was immediately appointed Acting Director of the School of Education, even though the Board of Trustees had authorized his faculty appointment only that spring (March 13, 1917), less than two months before Bagley submitted his own resignation. There was, however, no one else. Whipple had been given a leave of absence; Johnston met with his fatal automobile accident; Coffman was already at Minnesota. When the College of Education and the new Bureau of Educational Research were finally authorized, only Charters was left to take the helm.

The College did not begin to function as a college until the 1919–20 academic year. During the months between its authorization and its actual beginning, it fell to Charters to inaugurate at Illinois what was becoming a new era in American education. It was his task to begin the organization of teacher training programs in "Home Economics, Trades and Industries, and Agriculture" and to coordinate these efforts with the State Board of Vocational Education so the University could comply with the Smith-Hughes Act. He continued as caretaker until the arrival of Charles E. Chadsey in 1920, but departed shortly thereafter himself.

The new College did not prove to be stable under the pressure of the changes which were occurring both in and outside of it. This was partly because it was a paper college grown from a paper school, and partly because the faculty who had developed the work had been drawn away.

[75] From a five-page (typescript) document entitled "The 1915 Conference," Hollister File, James Correspondence (1915–16).

[76] *Transactions of the Board of Trustees of the University of Illinois, July 21, 1916, to June 11, 1918*, p. 183.

In 1916 James had written in his "Biennial Report" to the state superintendent of public instruction that the quality of the work of the Illinois high schools was "rapidly improving" and that "the demand for trained teachers is a rapidly rising one." [77] The School of Education had attempted to meet that demand in the past, he continued, and "during the last biennium it has done much more to help along this work by the further development of its facilities." [78] James was then hopeful that Illinois would soon have a College of Education comparable to those at Columbia (New York) and Chicago. Yet it was a hope, he seemed to know, that had to be realized in steps. Earlier, in his "Biennial Report" of 1906, he had written that the organization of the School was "inadequate" in light of the state's needs, but was a step "destined to be of far reaching influence and beneficence." [79]

While James did want the College, he had not been so sanguine as to believe that authorization of the College was the final step. He expressed this when on June 27, 1917, he wrote Dean Babcock of his reluctance to give up the plan:

> I should be very reluctant, after all the discussion and deliberation which we gave to the subject of the organization of the School of Education to have it all go for naught, by letting everything sink into innocuous desuetude.
>
> I think it's often times worth a good deal to have a title, even if we haven't got much behind it, back of the front of which, so to speak, we can erect our structure.[80]

As the next chapter will show, the structure "back of the front" was neither quickly nor easily built. The next decade was to be marked by a lack of development rather than a continuation of it. The next decade was not a fitting tribute either to James or to the faculty which had given character and élan to the work in education.

[77] Edmund J. James, "Biennial Report on the University of Illinois," in 31st SSPI (1916), p. 400.
[78] Ibid.
[79] Edmund J. James, "University of Illinois," in 26th SSPI (1906), p. 392.
[80] James to Babcock, June 27, 1917, James Correspondence.

PART III ❧

1919–45

CHAPTER 8

Close to the Beaten Path

The prospects of a continued enlargement of the role of education as a university discipline required radical revision with David Kinley's accession to the presidency of the University of Illinois in the room of Edmund Janes James. Spurred on by the boundless energy and large vision of William Chandler Bagley, education had attained a condition of steady development under James. Although these achievements were well rooted in the period of Dexter's leadership, with Bagley they came to an obvious fruition. The work enjoyed a measure of self-determination, a privilege given academic expression in the creation of the new College. The course offerings in pedagogy were deepened and expanded, culminating in the first Ph.D. program. The long-awaited model school, while not even yet in operation, was at last a certainty. The faculty had grown in stature and, of course, greatly in number. The field of education was no longer wholly dependent upon the personality or the ability of a single individual nor could it be entirely restricted by the vision of any one man. Relations with the common schools were wider and stronger, as well, under the able direction of Hollister. In short, Illinois's School of Education had caught up with the national movement within the field, and at least in some respects was sharing in the leadership of that field. Pedagogy, it appeared, had come of age.

While on the surface education enjoyed a strikingly large and frequently genuine measure of success, a curious ambiguity still lurked beneath. In certain respects this ambiguity was part of Bagley himself. He had managed to advance both the education of teachers as a university function and the extension of pedagogy as a subject for full-scale, university-level inquiry. But, as we have seen, Bagley was still struggling to grasp clearly and decisively the proper relationship of these two elements both in theory and in practice. Although President James had never been embarrassed by the business of preparing teachers, David Kinley, then dean of the graduate faculty, as well as many of his colleagues, frequently vacillated between approval and skepticism. It was doubtless Bagley's productivity at the higher levels of scholarship together with his unquestionable administrative statesmanship which had undergirded the academic settlement achieved. But, with the virtually simultaneous removal of Bagley and James, it was not surprising that the grounds of this settlement were eroded, and that matters took a very different turn. Since the fundamental difficulty, a difficulty closely linked to the ambiguity we have observed, proved decisive for this next period (and for the future), it will be useful to pay some attention to it in its own right.

Essentially, the problem was this: education as a field of study and inquiry could be viewed from two distinct perspectives. It could, more obviously, be seen as principally a matter of teacher preparation. Viewed from this vantage point, it seemed to imply a certain required body of "content," largely shaped by the actual state of the secondary school and its developing curriculum. (The College was at this time almost exclusively oriented toward the high school.) Along with this relatively fixed substantive matter there were, in addition, certain "professional" considerations: a somewhat vaguely defined need for "method"—which virtually all were by now willing to admit was useful—was perhaps the first. This method, as we have seen, was largely although not exclusively philosophically derived even at this date. But there was clearly defined agreement on the propriety of some more general psychological foundations for the prospective teacher as well, and such a smattering of educational history and philosophy as might be required to develop an awareness of the significance of the educational enterprise as a whole within the context of western culture.

From the other perspective, the field of education could be regarded as an area or subject of inquiry which, like other university areas of inquiry, was justifiable in and of itself without necessary regard to its immediate employment. Far from being itself clearly defined as yet, and much less prevalent, this point of view subsumed at least two further alternative interpretations. On the one hand, education could be regarded as a "science," meaning in this case an organized inquiry focused upon certain constituent disciplines which by now were validated by stable academic tradition. These disciplines were specified by being ranged around a distinct institution, the public school, with peculiar demands of its own, a definable history, and so on. On this view, higher inquiry in education implied the investigation of these constituent disciplines and the theoretical and historical analysis of the institution. Hence, the foundations lay in such areas as general philosophy, psychology, and social and educational history. From research in these, educational theory and practice could supposedly be derived (in fact logically deduced). It could then be formulated, put into practice, tested, and ultimately given to teachers as the vital element in the process of tooling up the practical enterprise of schooling.

On the other interpretation, advanced inquiry in education—and, it should be noted, teacher preparation as well—appeared quite different. From this vantage point education was essentially an empirical inquiry. (The difference between this and the previously described "science" of education is obviously rooted in a distinction in the philosophy of science itself. Although a discussion or judgment upon this distinction can have no place here, it was—and still is—of the utmost significance.) In this case, primary pedagogical research of university grade would focus not on constituent or concomitant disciplines but directly upon the act of teaching and learning within its various actual settings. To this inquiry, philosophy, psychology, and the other traditional disciplines are of primary significance—but, practically speaking, they are ancillary. Instead of being in themselves the focal point of educational activity or inquiry, they could provide points of view or departure, distinguish principles of interpretation and evaluation, and generate new possibilities for insight into the objective process being investigated—the process of schooling. But they could not take its place.

To define more precisely the difficulty which faced the College, the problem for the discipline of education, both at the University of Illinois and throughout the field, was that educationists themselves were not clear as to which of these aspects or interpretations (alone or in combination) ought to prevail. Nor were they clear on how they might be related, in theory or in practice, on a university campus. This has already been apparent in the uneasy and erratic development which the work in pedagogy experienced at Illinois.

In contrast to this confusion, the academic "establishment"—for such there was, in the sense of a particular aggregation of prestige disciplines, administrative systems, etc.—knew very clearly (at least on their own view) that any proper university subject had to meet at least two crucial criteria. First, it must address a precisely definable phenomenon or interrrelated set of phenomena as the focal point of its investigation. This was true of all the traditional disciplines then basking in the sun of university approval—even if the consequent warmth had made them somewhat forgetful of their checkered rise to respectability. Although their claims did not always go undisputed, there could be no doubt that Latinists, historians, chemists—or even economists—knew what they were investigating. Second, it was expected that there would be a describable and easily manageable procedure by means of which the specific phenomena could be investigated. The customary forms of description, categorization, and measurement were on the whole satisfactory. Both these procedures and their correlative phenomena had already been defined by a stable intellectual tradition in most cases and there would be no "task" or "mission" definition of university activity possible for perhaps two generations.

In consequence, the educationists faced a strategic dilemma. If education at the advanced level accepted the first of the alternative viewpoints of itself as a science, and therefore undertook clearly defined "basic research" in such established fields as psychology, philosophy, sociology, or even in history, it would at least partly satisfy the criteria sacred to the academic establishment. It would look orthodox; it might even gain acceptance. But, at the same time, it would also experience an entirely new difficulty, a difficulty in identifying itself or justifying its separate existence, since these traditional activities were also at least apparent duplications of existing enterprises. The mere fact of their orientation to a vague thing called "education" or the schools rarely permitted their independent prosecution by educationists, at least without considerable demurrage on the part of apparently more legitimate practitioners. If, on the other hand, education proposed to follow the second alternative and see itself as properly concerned with teaching and learning in the schools as an activity in itself, the phenomenon purportedly under investigation slipped from view. It simply could not be glimpsed through the rigidly prismatic vision of the academic-administrative establishment. The titled exponents of the prestige disciplines simply could not recognize the analysis of schooling, of the act of teaching and learning wherever and under whatever educational circumstances it might occur, as a respectable academic concern. In sum, the dilemma was posed by the fact that on either view, given the traditional academic orientation, education could be faulted, either substantively, or methodologically, or both.

The heart of the program Bagley had bequeathed was reasonably orthodox. Its first component, the provision of a superior grade of "content" for secondary teachers, was now universally acceptable, and Illinois was no exception. It was even desirable, especially in light of the continuing failure of the normal schools to break their curricular (i.e., their financial) bonds. Together with a minimum of theory and practice, such a program could be a university function, though not on a strictly university level—i.e., it would not operate at the level of original research. It would perforce exist only at the undergraduate base of the university. Higher research might also prove acceptable. It could, failing all else, be seen as a "service" function, and therefore in accord with Illinois's peculiar character as a land grant institution. But, Kinley was skeptical even of that, not only for educationists but for others as well, as we shall also see. Consequently, the attempt of Bagley's successor to cloak the peculiar research of educators under the monographic forms acceptable to the establishment would not ultimately succeed.

The University's future president was an academic traditionalist, at least in those respects most relevant to the question of whether or not to regard education as a legitimate university discipline. The ambiguity of Bagley (revealed, for example, in his distrust of impaling educational theory upon the already established eminence of Thorndike and Woodworth's stimulus-response psychology of learning) and his traditional mode of analyzing education made him personally capable of being accepted. He had inaugurated the highest level of graduate research in education yet obtained at Illinois, but at the same time he had worked directly with educators in the field. He had encouraged historians and theoreticians, yet he had also brought forth a school in which one might observe and experiment. Consequently, Bagley was acceptable to Kinley and other bona fide members of the University faculty, even though what he had built was also inescapably "modern." The educationist, as Bagley saw him, did not shy away from contemporary issues or problems; he did not delimit pedagogical activity by harnessing its efforts exclusively to the traditional academic disciplines. The Bureau of Educational Research, the particular content of his Ph.D. programs, the new practice school—all these testified to the fact that Bagley was also of his age, and that could give cause for alarm. The settlement had been personal; it was not yet safely theoretical or public.

Shortly before offering his own resignation, Bagley's interim successor, W. W. Charters, counseled President James (in reference to the question of speeding the opening of University High School) that "this is the time to advance." Educational progress was in the air, Charters thought, "stimulated by the war." By June of that year (1919), however, James's health was failing so markedly that he was forced to request a year's leave following commencement. It proved terminal, and by the fall of 1920 David Kinley had assumed permanent possession of the president's office. If there was to be an "advance," it would be at the hands of an entirely new leadership both in the University and in the recently born College of Education.[1]

As one of his last official acts, James had been authorized by the Board of Trustees, as of June 10, 1919, to offer the College deanship to Charles Ernest Chadsey.[2] The president had written Chadsey that his acceptance was the "unanimous and earnest desire" of all who had met him on the campus, and that in spite of the post's comparatively modest salary—the $6,000 was in fact the highest salary paid any dean—it offered a "really great opportunity." James felt the University was, in his words, "destined to move steadily forward as one of the

[1] W. W. Charters to James, February 4, 1919, James Correspondence. Charters also wrote Kinley suggesting that the new Education Building (University High School) be named for James. (See his letter of July 22, 1919, James Correspondence. See also 33rd SSPI [1920], p. 437, 439, and *Catalogue* [1920–21], p. 51.) Kinley set the prevailing tone of the new administration at the outset. In reviewing his first year, he exulted over the fact that "no deficits had been incurred and that he had kept the University's work in a "high state of efficiency" (*The President's Report, 1922–23* ["University of Illinois Bulletins" 21, no. 23, Urbana; Feb. 4, 1924 (?)], pp. 5–6). Note this particular series of University "Bulletins" was specially printed during Kinley's regime as a series of Presidential Reports. They will hereinafter be cited as *President's Report*, with the appropriate date following. The entire series is of great value in understanding Kinley and this period at Illinois.

[2] 30th *Report* (1920), p. 398.

great educational institutions of the country and the world." Impressed, Chadsey accepted quickly and cheerfully. He was, he said, confident that he would never regret his decision.[3]

Born in Nebraska in 1870, Chadsey had been educated at Stanford University (taking both bachelor's and master's degrees there) and at Columbia (where he had taken a second master's and the Ph.D., awarded in 1897). He had held a principalship and superintendencies in western school systems before becoming superintendent of schools in Detroit, a position he occupied with some distinction for seven years. In fact, his reputation was such that Charters considered him the "premier superintendent of the United States."[4] He did indeed enjoy national prominence, lecturing frequently on the problems of school administration and serving as president of the prestigious department of superintendence of the NEA in 1911–12.

Just before coming, in March of 1919, Chadsey had been elected superintendent of the Chicago public schools in the midst of a vicious political contest—a fact which may have caused some hesitancy about his appointment.[5] Chadsey had been elected superintendent on March 12, 1919, by the Board of Education. The mayor, however, on May 19 appointed sufficient new members to control the Board, and they proceeded to elect Peter A. Mortenson as superintendent on May 26. Chadsey, in the interests of freeing the Chicago schools from the political domination which had throttled them for years, took the case to court and obtained a ruling in his own favor. He pressed the matter primarily to prove that the school board was a "state board of unquestioned independent powers and responsibilities," as he put it in his statement before the court. Mortenson, however, appealed the decision and he furthermore refused to be guided in the interim by the prior court's judgment. Although legally ousted, with the assistance of city police officers he denied Chadsey access to the offices and records. Ultimately, he even caused the Board to rewrite Chadsey's proper

[3] James to Chadsey, June 10, 1919; Chadsey to James, June 16, 1919, James Correspondence. James had added the note about the dean's relative salary in a manuscript "P.S.," pointing out also that the vice-president got but $7,000.

[4] For biographical data, see Charters to James, June 11, 1919, James Correspondence; the "Morgue" of the University Archives; and *Who Was Who in America*. Charters also informed James that Chadsey had been offered a post at Chicago, but that "he and his wife are fond of a small town" and plan to buy a home and become "permanent."

[5] Charters warned the President to "consider the political situation" before deciding (Charters to James, May 29, 1919, James Correspondence).

duties into nonexistence, usurping his powers under the guise of establishing an "associate" superintendency. Chadsey won the second test also and thereupon resigned, but the dispute was another chapter in the long estrangement between the Universiy and the Chicago schools. This separation continued for many years and effectively removed the College of Education from any real educational involvement with one of the nation's most important urban areas.[6]

It may have been true, as James and Charters prophesied, that the postwar years were ripe for "advance" in the area of professional education. It may also have been true that Charles E. Chadsey was the man to lead that advance. His reputation and his attainments, while significantly different from Bagley's, were nonetheless both timely and imposing and he had, as the Chicago school board could attest, a proven quality of independence. But the fact of the matter is that his tenure produced virtually nothing of positive significance. It was an almost disastrous hiatus in the "progress" which was so eagerly anticipated. So negative was it that it is not possible to trace any definable movement, except in the most trivial statistical terms. The 1920's became a territory marked not by roads which traversed it but by a round of circular skirmishes—mere remnants of a battle once thought concluded.

More than anywhere else, the source of this debilitating suspension of positive activity lay in two decisive factors. The first was Chadsey's seeming lack of both strategy and theoretical interest. The second was David Kinley's intransigent antagonism toward what he was compelled to see as the academic pretentions of professional educationists. Kinley, for all his diminutive but pugnacious stature, stood stolidly astride the potential course of educational advance like a colossus. With his feet planted on the firm ground of social and academic conservatism, he deflected the college from continued advance along the high road of exploration into the rut of tradition. It was his aim, he suggested, to keep the University "close to the beaten path," and (among other disciplines) education would be no exception to that policy. Even though Chadsey's listless program was essentially a retrenchment, at best a lackluster routinization of a few of the vigorous sorties which

[6] The description of Chadsey's difficulties with the Chicago school board is taken from a published pamphlet, *The Summary of the Show Cause Proceedings, People of Ilinois* vs. *Peter A. Mortensen and Charles E. Chadsey, in the Matter of People of Illinois* vs. *Albert H. Severinghaus, et al., No. B-53, 706* (n.p., n.d.), pp. 20, 27, passim. A copy is in the University of Illinois Library. Also see George S. Counts, *School and Society in Chicago* (New York, 1928), esp. Ch. 12.

had characterized the Bagley period, it still could not escape the steady and frequently open opposition of Kinley.[7]

Born in Dundee, Scotland, in 1861, Kinley had come to the United States in 1872. His undergraduate work had been completed at Yale, after which he served for some six years as a teacher and principal at the high school in North Andover, Massachusetts. He forsook school-keeping for Johns Hopkins, where he spent two years, and finally completed his doctorate in economics at Wisconsin in 1893. Hired at the University of Illinois as an assistant professor of economics the same year, Kinley rose rapidly to full professorial status and became Dean of the College of Literature and Arts, serving in that capacity until 1906. He then took the reins of the new Graduate School, assuming the University vice-presidency along the way.[8]

By the time he reached the presidency, Kinley had developed a well-defined philosophy of education. He also possessed a strong sense of mission, the principles of which he enunciated clearly while translating them neatly and easily into tactical decisions and directives. Inaugurating a series of annual *President's Reports* in 1922, he spelled out these official beliefs, put the University under their judgment, and when he thought it necessary publicly chastised those who failed to measure up to his criteria or pursued contrary interests. As did everything else, the College of Education fell under their jurisdiction.

At the end of his career, Kinley insisted he had always seen the 1920's as a crucial point in history. The decade after a war, he thought, was always characterized by a lack of "fixity of purpose and [a] breaking away from old moorings in conduct." Consequently, it was a time to strengthen and focus, rather than to expand and broaden, one's interests and powers. To this general duty, in academic terms, he dedicated himself from the start. Always the classical, family-purse economist, Kinley demanded punctilious observance of budgetary provisions and strict financial accountability to the people of the state, who owned (in every sense) the University with whose stewardship he was entrusted. The purpose of that University was, he believed, the provision of sound leadership for the good of society.

[7] *President's Report* (1929–30), where Kinley summarized the "aims and ideals" of his "plans and policies" during his administration, esp. pp. 7–8. The quotation was actually from Harold DeWolf Fuller.

[8] Biographical data from University "Morgue," *Who's Who in America* and *Who's Who in American Education*. Kinley also wrote a brief autobiography which sheds considerable light on both his policies and his personality (*The Autobiography of David Kinley* [Urbana, 1949], esp. Chs. 1–3, 17–19).

Admitting the impossibility of a literal cost accounting in terms of this peculiar product, he nonetheless felt morally obliged to justify financially the whole enterprise to those virtual investors who dwelt outside the campus.[9]

His intellectual stewardship, Kinley realized, was far more complex and elusive. The aim, we have said, was to be "leadership." The old classical curriculum had in fact provided it—though he appreciated the fact that leadership was perhaps more a human response to opportunity than a manufacture.[10] The newer educational regimen now in fashion might accomplish this task also, but only if it faced the crucial challenge which threatened the entire enterprise. This crucial challenge Kinley described variously as vocationalism, professionalization, or undisciplined election; it came down, ultimately, to the conflict between the fixed, general studies which integrated men and societies and the proliferating specialties which tore them asunder. He believed that the university's peculiar and thankless task in the early twentieth century was to advance the prolific particularity of the modern intellect without losing the integrating generalizations embedded in the wisdom of the past. The growing complexity of the university, endlessly splitting into new departments and courses, manifested the potential conflict embedded in these contrasting principles. The tendency toward fragmentation was, he thought, the result of introducing purportedly new subjects and new applications (or "attempted applications") of the old disciplines, such as "agricultural economics," for instance.[11]

Kinley believed these novelties frequently stemmed from the "self-interest" of the faculty and other special interest groups or—and this was perhaps the chief enemy, in his view—"some of the psychological theories that have become temporarily popular in the past twenty years." By the latter he meant the notion that there was no "general talent," no general intellectual ability or power which individuals could perfect. That egregious error had led in turn to the dangerous practical maxim of educational modernists that all learning must be

[9] *President's Report* (1929–30), p. 7; (1922–23), pp. 5–6, 23, passim. For an interesting and earlier example of Kinley's general conservatism, see the report of his remarks to the Conference on the High School in 1899. He argued that the high schools should not expand, since their role was general rather than professional, and since the populace would not be able to afford such an expansion (*The Illini* [May 26, 1899], p. 530).

[10] *President's Report* (1922–23), pp. 8–10.

[11] Ibid., p. 11; (1924–25), pp. 7–11.

in particular areas. "We have been told," he said, "that it is foolish to think of getting mental training by what has been described as the mental gymnastics of studying mathematics, the languages, and sundry other subjects that do not have obvious utility or reference to specific callings or specific adaptation to the character and purposes of the particular student." At least tentatively, Kinley was convinced that this educational theory rested on "what is called the doctrine of interest and liberty." This nefarious doctrine stemmed chiefly from the new behavioral "scientists." All the psychologists were not to blame, he admitted, but most seemed unwilling to accept the fact that "the evidence is heavily on the side of belief in both general talent and general mental training as being possible on the side of so-called non-utilitarian subjects." [12] Unfortunately even the humanities had succumbed to the fever, so that one could no longer study "history" or "literature," but only the "Pre-Revolutionary Period" or "English Literature from 1688 to 1789." Without integration, and the knowledge of relations, the courses in the traditional regimen had become themselves educationally dangerous, as the art of medicine would if it were allowed to degenerate into a mere compound of courses.[13]

While not infrequently convinced that he needed to apply the birch rod to the entire University, Kinley's chief whipping boys were agriculture, the developing "social sciences," and professional education. Agriculture had produced so many hybrid courses such as agricultural economics that he soon expected, he said, to see "agricultural athletics" appear. It was overspecification of this sort which drew his chief ire, although he had just accepted with alacrity Senator W. B. McKinley's endowment of a chair in the "Economics of Public Utilities"! [14] In respect to the social sciences, Kinley noted in his final *Report* that he had protected the students, as their parents would

<hr>

[12] *President's Report* (1923–24), p. 13–14. Kinley had told Boyd H. Bode some years before that he found an article by the latter ("Reinterpretation of Transfer Training") "interestingly" done but unacceptable in its thesis: "I confess . . . that I have not been able to fall in line with a good deal of the recent educational theory that thinks it has sent to the scrap heap some of the old beliefs" (Kinley to Bode, July 16, 1919, James Correspondence).

[13] *President's Report* (1923–24), pp. 16–17. Cf. pp. 14, 15, where Kinley argues that specialization fosters "the movement towards class consciousness," and accuses the humanities of having "made efficiency and service their aim and standard instead of wisdom, character, and leadership"—a curious charge to come from his pen.

[14] *President's Report* (1923–24), p. 14, passim, esp. report on developments in commerce.

wish, from certain kinds of research, and especially psychological research. Besides being possibly "more indicative of prurience of thought than of a spirit of scientific inquiry," such research, as was frequently the case in all the social sciences, was methodologically dubious as well. Although he had sat at the feet of Sumner and breathed the electric air of Johns Hopkins, Kinley had remained strangely unmoved by the new intellectual currents. He was inalterably persuaded that the wise observer must accept the findings of such inquiries with great care. In this field as perhaps no other, he said, "conservative judgment is very necessary." And, while the demands of inquiry by itself might carry one into dangerously disturbed waters, the vocation to educate he thought analogous to the ministry. It carried a high responsibility to guard the cultural deposit of faith and to suppress dangerous novelties.[15]

As befitted his convictions about the social sciences, Kinley's attitude toward education as a particular area of study was a curious blend of reluctant acceptance and obvious disaffection. Although his posture was clearly and publicly expressed, the reasons for it were not so apparent. He could accept personally a Bagley, and perhaps a Dexter, at least in part, but the newer thrusts in pedagogy still bothered him deeply. It seems likely that the growing movement toward grounding educational theory in psychological principles was unacceptable to him. Attacking the nascent discipline at what was admittedly perhaps its weakest point, Kinley put the whole matter very squarely in view in his 1923–24 *Report*, noting:

> There have been certain fields pushed into public attention, the substantiality of which is an open question in the minds of some thoughtful people. Consider, for example, the field of education, technically so called. We all have our colleges and schools of education. We once thought that our colleges and universities were themselves colleges and schools of education. When one reads the literature of this field he is tempted, as he is when he reads some of the literature of sociology and psychology, to wonder whether after all the so-called field of study did not emerge into public attention largely because its devotees invented a terminology and then thought they had a science.[16]

[15] *President's Report* (1929–30), pp. 9, 13. Cf. p. 20 on research in the social sciences. He stressed once again that he had "not yet seen the advantage of replacing the experience and wisdom of an older generation with the unlimited choice and purposeless election of the untrained student" (p. 11).

[16] *President's Report* (1923–24), p. 15. Kinley found it unfortunate that other departments had offered only "passive resistance towards the introduction of these

Yet Kinley could also admit, even if his actions usually belied his claimed beliefs, that there might be a middle ground. Acknowledging, late in his tenure, the "rapid spread of the demand for courses in 'education,' technically so-called," he tried to make his position clear once again. Education, he said, "meant courses in teaching methods, the psychology of teaching, etc." While school boards were showing a dubious tendency to require increasing amounts of this sort of thing as a condition of certification and employment, there were also "some who insist that anyone who knows his subject is able to teach it and can see nothing in the idea that from psychology and the history of education we can learn much about proper methods of teaching." Perhaps with his own teaching experience still in view, Kinley would accept neither pole. "The truth, in my opinion, lies between these two extreme views." He agreed that "an inspection of the courses offered under the head of Education in almost any institution is likely to give the disinterested observer the impression that many of them are superficial," indicating his continued doubt that a new terminology represented a new field of inquiry. He claimed—though one is inclined to question the allegation, for which, incidentally, he offered no evidence—that there were "still people who ask for courses in methods of teaching subjects although confessing that they have never studied the subjects." It was "bad," he thought, "to insist that 'methods' of teaching learned from psychology data and pedagogical experiment are all that is necessary for a person to teach successfully zoology, history, or what not, without reference to the logical, objec-

---

subjects." (Cf. Kinley to Boyd H. Bode, July 16, 1919, James Correspondence.) Kinley's own resistance was by no means passive. For example, in the fall of 1925, an "Educational Inquiry" was set up to examine the University's programs and policies. The President's correspondence in connection with the matter offers ample evidence of his deep-seated hostility to educationists. He took counsel with Dean Guy S. Ford (of the University of Minnesota), conveying his concern for "avoiding the word survey. I want also to avoid the kind of people who make 'surveys.' Most of them have been made I think (just between you and me) by people who are primarily schoolmasters. They have had the pedagogical slant." The President closed by asking Ford to "think about it, regard as confidential my comments on the schoolmaster, and talk with our friend [Lotus] Coffman . . ." —whom he was apparently willing to forgive for having been both a school-master and a master of schoolmasters. (See Kinley to Ford, December 5, 1925.) Ford replied that no one from Minneapolis could accept, admitting that he shared "something of [Kinley's] feeling about such educational experts as view a university as a sublimated high school." (See Ford to Kinley, December 15, 1925. For all of this and other material of interest, see Educational Inquiry File, Kinley Correspondence, Record Series 2/6/1, no. 128.)

tive unfolding of these subjects." Yet he granted that it was equally bad to have only this logical grasp, and "still worse to insist that one who 'knows his subject' can therefore teach it, even if he is unable to present it logically and knows nothing about psychology and teaching methods." Such men, Kinley thought, might do well to sit at the feet of "the proponents of educational psychology and philosophy." [17]

Another aspect of Kinley's attitude toward education, and one which would have large practical force in his decisions, was his firm belief that it should avoid governmental supervision, especially anything suggestive of national control. His inauguration had been celebrated by a conference on the matter, and he continued jealously to ward off "any further extension of this so-called Federal-State cooperation in Education" in whatever guise it might appear. He was dead set against any national department of education, and he resisted programs in which he thought such thinking was implicit. In this he was strongly supported not only by many of his faculty colleagues but by Chadsey and the state superintendent of public instruction, Francis G. Blair, as well.[18] Doubtless, much of this was a logical extension of his antediluvian social and economic convictions. Education needed to remain free to serve the "public good," but the public

[17] *President's Report* (1926-27), pp. 11ff. Curiously, however, when Kinley suggested that the University faculty might examine their teaching, even possibly in consultation with the College, Chadsey himself backed timidly away: "I do not think, under normal conditions, we in the College of Education are in a position to give systematic assistance to other departments in the University. The reasons for this are obvious. We do not have the mastery of the content taught in other lines of work, and, therefore, could not command the type of consideration from even inexperienced men in those subjects that would be desirable." The department heads, or those who have "greater skill in this particular kind of work," should do it. The Dean's response was a wholesale capitulation on the issue of whether the educationist had any valid or useful contribution to make. (See duplicated letter, Kinley to Department Heads, December 23, 1929. For Chadsey's response, see Chadsey to Kinley, January 1, 1930, both in College of Education Papers.)

[18] *Catalogue* (1920-21). The formal inaugural was December 1, 1921. Chadsey to Kinley, July 27, 1920, concerned a proposed national program for preparing physical education teachers and is the source of the quotation. In the same location there is an untitled synopsis of "40-odd" current congressional bills dealing with education, or having educational significance, which Chadsey prepared for the President. He "heartily disapprove[d]" of S.B. 3006 (a kind of World War I "G.I. Bill" sponsored by Senator Lenroot), for example. For further evidence of Chadsey's attitude, see Chadsey to Kinley, April 5, 1929. All in Kinley Correspondence. For Blair's convictions on federal "control" as a dangerous development which began with Smith-Hughes legislation, see 33rd SSPI (1920), p. 16.

good was effortlessly if unconsciously translated by Kinley as that of the business community or the entrepreneurial class. As befit his stance, he had only scorn for a Veblen, with whom he had been casually acquainted. He found him, for all his admitted ability, an entirely dangerous man.[19] Although fittingly lauded on his retirement for his democratic faith, as manifested in his attempt to keep higher educational opportunity open to the citizens of the state, Kinley's was the classical, individualistic democratic faith; it had little reference to the concern for the social and economic aspects of democratic thought, which was springing up all around him.[20]

Much of Kinley's concern and many of his criticisms both of higher education in general and the field of education in particular were beyond question apropos. His arguments were frequently incisive, his epithets generally telling. Had his convictions always issued in straightforward administrative behavior, a constructive dialogue might have ensued. In any case, his vision shaped ineluctably the range and depth of development open to the College of Education. Thus, from the start, the College's program and the events of the decade bore the dual imprint of the President's beliefs and the particular ability and experience of the College's dean. The program which had flourished under Bagley, and remained substantially unchanged under Charters's tutelage, with few exceptions grew quiescent under Chadsey. The candidate for graduation from the College of Education

[19] Kinley to the Rev. W. G. Poor [an old acquaintance], September 16, 1926, Kinley Correspondence. Kinley had met Veblen through Poor some years before, but he now had "little use for him, as the saying goes. He [Veblen] has become ultraradical, embittered, and like most of those people, in my opinion, unfair." The President did, however, own that the famous economist was "intellectually" one of the "keenest" writers of recent times.

In 1895, Kinley had addressed the University Club on the "Wages System," drawing attention (according to an *Illini* reporter) to the fact that, although the federal government was regulating industry, "as moral education increases," there would be "less need of state interference." He also noted that "the leaders in the world are the capitalists, and if there is any nobleness in them the system will be improved" (*The Illini* [April 18, 1895], pp. 441ff.).

[20] The teaching profession was a particular instance of this change, especially during the late 1920's and 1930's. The teachers, long ignored by the status quo both in the Illinois legislature and in academic circles, were beginning to see politics as necessarily linked to their own economic improvement, as well as to that of their less fortunate students. See, for example, the volumes of the *Illinois Teacher* during the period. This development is clearly evident in vols. 17 and 18, which cover the period from 1928–30. They also show that the University and its College took no lead in such matters, if they acknowledged their importance at all.

(who would get a diploma toward state certification without additional examination) was admitted to the College at the beginning of his junior year. Exceptions to this were the full four-year programs in athletic coaching, physical education, and industrial education. These programs, plus the standard sequence for secondary school teaching and/or administration and the special Smith-Hughes curricula in agricultural education and home economics education, comprised the four basic curricula of the College as such. (A program in public school music education and one for specialists in educational research were added later.) The two-year sequences normally required seventy academic hours chosen from the general offerings, but grouped about a twenty-hour core in education. These twenty hours included a required sequence of three-hour courses in educational psychology, technic of teaching (a general methods course), principles of secondary education, and a special methods course in the area of disciplinary specialization (which area required at least twenty "academic" hours). Finally, there was a three- to five-hour course in observation and practice teaching. History of education was usually included, but it was definitely made optional later.[21] By the end of the period the specifications were made more precise—due in part to more precise definition by the state—and there developed the possibility of a "two-track system," whereby the student could either reside in the College of Education and complete its curriculum or pursue his specialization outside the College and include sufficient education courses to prepare for, or cover, certification examinations. The College program came to include, by 1928, substantially the above-noted courses and hours (without history, except for those treating education as a major) and a required specialization in two common high school subjects (of at least twenty and sixteen "academic" hours). The alternative University program required eight hours of English; twelve hours of education, including at least educational psychology and the technic course (although the North Central Association called for fifteen hours); three majors of sixteen hours and three minors of not less than eight hours in high school subjects; and the necessary electives.[22]

The programs and courses reflected the situation in the high schools of the state. At the turn of the century there had been something

[21] *Catalogue* (1919–20), pp. 185–89; Kinley to Chadsey (and reply), November 28, 1922, Kinley Correspondence; *President's Report* (1922–23), pp. 81–83; and 31st *Report* (1922), p. 286.

[22] *Catalogue* (1928–29), pp. 140–47, esp. p. 147. For "liberal arts" track, see also p. 247.

over 300 secondary institutions, enrolling less than 50,000 students. By 1920 the state's population stood at nearly 6.5 million, and the high schools enrolled over 127,000 students. The schools in which they studied were still, however, a mixed lot. There were now well over 800 high schools, but nearly 300 did not yet have a full four-year program. Their size can be judged from the fact that they were staffed by some 6,000 teachers, or a little more than seven each on the "average." (Still a dangerous average, due to the enormous disparity between the metropolitan and rural schools.) Nor were these teachers yet sufficiently prepared. Nearly two-thirds were now normal school and/or college graduates, but even at this date over 400 had only finished high school and six had not even managed that. (At the elementary level, it was even worse: some 3,500 schools still had fifteen or less students, nearly 10,000 teachers had not gone beyond the high school graduation, and nearly 3,000 had not even achieved their diplomas.) [23]

Legislative efforts to insist upon at least high school graduation for teachers had been bottled up in committee on the grounds that they would empty the schools—as indeed they would have—and the increasing population continually worsened the problem. The need for radically enlarged numbers of adequately prepared secondary school teachers was obvious.[24]

The University reported that its programs were developed directly to meet this need for "graduates to fill satisfactorily positions as high school teachers, or as principals, supervisors or school superintendents." [25] But to accomplish this was growing increasingly difficult. Given the condition of the high schools, it was not possible to turn out narrowly (and therefore proficiently) prepared specialists, unless its graduates would restrict themselves to a few urban high schools, and thus also turn their backs on the bulk of the educational task faced by the state. At the same time, expectations for these smaller schools were expanding radically. They were supposed to offer as full curricula as possible, as well as supplementary programs, and that meant that members of the teaching staff were required, whatever their scholarly hopes or pretentions, to be academic jacks-of-all-trades. As Superintendent Blair appropriately observed, the schools had be-

---

[23] *President's Report* (1922–23), p. 14; 33rd SSPI (1920), Appendix B, esp. pp. 1–11. Note that of over 3,200 who tried to gain a second-grade elementary certificate by examination, less than 1,500 were successful (p. 121).
[24] 33rd SSPI (1920), pp. 30, 442.
[25] Ibid., p. 441.

come the new "Noah's Ark," loaded to the gunwales with difficult and often competing demands.[26]

The course offerings designed to meet the situation and its complex demands were extensive but relatively uninspired, and they showed unmistakeably the bent of Chadsey's own interests. The dean offered work in administration, primarily, although he also offered a popular "problems" course—described as "nonprofessional." Robert Francis Seybolt, newly arrived from Wisconsin, singlehandedly maintained strong but limited offerings in educational history at both the undergraduate and graduate levels, and he made fresh contributions to the field at the same time. Secondary education, general methods, and supervision were in the hands of Paul Everett Belting, late of Eastern Illinois at Charleston, until he left midway in the decade. His work was then parceled out to J. A. Clement, A. W. Nolan, and others who taught these courses in addition to other responsibilities. Throughout the period Edward Herbert Cameron handled the numerous and heavily patronized offerings in the area of educational psychology, again at both levels. He also developed a course, originally titled "Auxiliary Education," which led into the field of special education (although President Kinley resisted its becoming a program). Walter Scott Monroe, assisted later by Odell, offered extensive work in the various research areas such as statistics and measurement, and advanced work in methods, as well as directing the Bureau of Educational Research. A. B. Mays carried responsibility for the area of industrial and vocational education, including a number of special programs to which we will turn shortly. Mrs. Charles Hughes Johnston had remained following her husband's untimely death, and she came to fill an important role in the College also. She continued Chadsey's popular "problems" course and took over the comparative education course from Seybolt—all at a ridiculously low compensation justified by her lack of formal credentials.[27]

As Chadsey reported, midway in the decade, the courses were "well organized," and, although this applied equally to the undergraduate level, they could be seen at the increasingly important graduate level

[26] 34th SSPI (1922), p. 24–25.
[27] *Catalogues* for the period; also blue sheets (authorizing faculty changes) for the period, usually in President's correspondence files under title of the Dean of the College of Education. For example, for Seybolt and Belting, see blue sheets in James Correspondence, Record Series 2/5/3, no. 174, Charters File. See also enrollment study, dated March 1, 1920, in Chadsey File, Kinley Correspondence.

as centering "around problems of high school administration, high school supervision, high school curricula, and the problems of general education administration." Notably absent from these administratively and psychologically oriented programs was the field of educational philosophy. At the beginning of the period, Boyd H. Bode, on regular loan from the philosophy department, had taught a course in "Educational Theory" at the graduate level only (and reduced to a half unit). This offering claimed to explore the "philosophical basis" of education. However, Bode left to begin his distinguished career at Ohio State in 1921, and he was not replaced. Professor Cameron, the psychologist, picked up the course in his stead and continued to offer it thereafter. There was, perhaps, no important distinction between the fields—or at least so one might have been led to conclude. It is not insignificant that when a thousand turned out to hear John Dewey lecture in the 1927–28 academic year, he was sponsored by the Liberal Arts College and addressed himself to problems of general philosophy.[28] There is little evidence of much interest in him in the College of Education.

As has been suggested, graduate work increased dramatically in importance and extent during the period. Particularly in conjunction with the growing summer sessions, the upper-level courses continued to attract larger and larger numbers of teachers, and even more administrators, who journeyed to the campus to increase their competence (and their pay scale) now that institutional advancement was everywhere becoming tied to academic credentials.[29] While 1924 saw only sixteen master's degrees awarded, just four years later there were forty-three. (Ph.D.'s, however, were much less popular and showed no really significant change during the period.) This onrush gave the Graduate College of the University a considerable boost (enrollments of education were second only to chemistry), especially during the summers. But it soon began to worry A. H. Daniels, the Graduate dean, when he sensed—quite properly—that many were enrolling just as a continuation of (or even as a replacement for) undergraduate-level instruction. Later, under a less kindly and hospitable administration, relations with the Graduate College would become critical.[30] On the other hand, graduate scholarships and fellowships for really

[28] *President's Report* (1925–26), pp. 81, 79; *Catalogue* (1921–22); *President's Report* (1927–28), p. 39.
[29] *Catalogue* (1922–23), p. 251; (1923–24), p. 263; (1925–26), pp. 265–66.
[30] *Catalogue* (1924–25), esp. p. 11; (1928–29), p. 140–47; *President's Report* (1922–23), pp. 114ff., esp. p. 117; (1923–24), pp. 83, 102.

advanced work in education during the regular academic year remained very difficult to procure.[31]

Two special features of the College's activity demand particular notice—the Smith-Hughes programs and the development of the University High School. The Smith-Hughes Act had been passed in February, 1917, just two months before the United States entered World War I. Its provisions established a federal board for vocational education, which distributed funds to the states in accordance with the plans they developed. Although the act met with considerable criticism from well-known schoolmen, more than 1.8 million dollars were parceled out during the program's first year. Enthusiasm for it was a result of a long utilitarian tradition in education, of course, and the law was a symbol of a long-awaited practical orientation on the part of the schools. But even educational philosophers with as slight inclinations to elitism as Dewey were alarmed lest (among other difficulties) it create a parallel educational process and a dual system of control.[32]

During the 1920's the courses connected with the Smith-Hughes legislation were an important aspect of the College's work. The work had been expanded in 1918. A plan was developed for training industrial teachers, as well as those in agricultural and home economics education, on the less than sufficient grounds that if the University failed to act, the cities—and Chicago in particular—would take over the function. The plan obtained approval under James and in October, 1918, a Chicago center was authorized, with "departmental" offices to be located in the Continental and Commercial Bank. Other centers were established in Rockford, Urbana, and Champaign, and the work appeared off to a good start, in spite of initial reluctance.[33] By the

---

[31] 31st *Report* (1922), p. 195. Cf. *President's Report* (1923–24), p. 83. The production of Ph.D.'s in education had reached enormous proportions nationally during the decade. For example, between 1918 and 1927, Harvard had produced 77; New York University, 80; Iowa, 69; George Peabody, 51; California, 42; Ohio State, 35; Pennsylvania, 28; Chicago, 59; Catholic University, 28; Wisconsin, 26; Stanford, 31; Yale, 24. Teachers College, Columbia, in a league by itself, had produced 306; the University of Illinois, 13. (See Bureau of Educational Research, College of Education, *Bulletin No. 42* [Urbana, 1928], pp. 350–61.)

[32] Edward A. Krug, *The Shaping of the American High School* (New York, 1964). Ch. 10 treats the development of vocational education; see also pp. 414ff.

[33] W. W. Charters to E. J. James, June 29, 1818, James Correspondence, and proposal dated July 3, 1918, same location. See also Charters to James, October

time of Chadsey's arrival and Kinley's ascendancy, however, some of the issues involved were subjected to a review by a specially appointed committee. Kinley was none too hospitable, due to his general reluctance to accept the admittedly vague "service function" of the University implied in the original proposal and his considerable opposition to the untidy academic and financial arrangements associated with it. The work, however, was reapproved and Arthur B. Mays was authorized to "head" it in 1921. Mays, born and first educated in Texas, had studied at Bradley Institute and Columbia and eventually taken a master's in the field at George Peabody. He had taught industrial arts in Texas and Alabama before directing vocational education for the U.S. Army, from which post he had come to Illinois for what proved to be a long and distinguished career.[34]

The Chicago extramural work did not survive. Threatened from the beginning by unstable financing, the office was closed in 1920. Not only was its fiscal support shaky, there seemed no need for its services —there was considerable competition, and the Chicago schools did not care to employ its specially trained "mechanics." Not only in Chicago but elsewhere, superintendents were simply not willing to insist on academically trained specialists when staffing the vocational curricula in their schools. Finally withdrawn to what was substantially the Urbana area, however, the work took hold and maintained a modest but steady enrollment throughout the decade. Chadsey hoped—and to some extent that hope was fulfilled—that industrial education might make a satisfactory correlative study for those in the enormously successful physical education programs. The financial difficulties which plagued the industrial courses largely stemmed from problems of reimbursement by the federal government and the state, and Kinley bickered constantly about the travel expenses necessarily involved in the supervision of the extramural work.[35]

10, 25, November 22, December 10, 26, 1918. Also Lloyd Morey to James, November 2, 1918, and miscellaneous descriptive items under or near these letters. All in James Correspondence.

[34] Chadsey to Kinley, October 20, 1919; February 22, March 29, 1920; Kinley Correspondence. There was apparently a dispute over whether A. W. Nolan (in agricultural education) would head it, or whether there was to be any "head" at all—since the Smith-Hughes work was not, strictly speaking, a department. (See also 31st *Report* [1922], p. 192.)

[35] Chadsey to Kinley, October 18, 1920; Kinley to Chadsey, October 20, 1920. The Knights of Columbus were running a program which offered competition

The programs in home economics education and agricultural education fared about the same and raised similar problems. However, in one
respect they broke fresh ground. Particularly in agricultural education, the practice requirements stipulated by the federal programs
outstripped the capabilities of the University High School. (There
were not many farmers in attendance at the official practice school.)
This eventually led to locating some of the practice work outside
the confines of the University. In the beginning, recourse was to the
Champaign and Urbana high schools, but before long, in 1927–28, it
was necessary to move the agricultural work farther afield to the
town of St. Joseph as well. First these arrangements provided only
for home economics and agricultural education, but they soon included public school music as well.[36]

The University High School posed a particular problem for the
development of practice-teaching experience; but, as we have seen,
its nature and function had been a general problem from the beginning.
Although the footings had been laid and the dedicatory rhetoric composed as early as the fall of 1916, the high school did not open its
doors for five more years, in spite of the growing and obvious need.[37]
Finally ready for use in 1919, it simply sat there in its curious Gothic
splendor. Acting Dean W. W. Charters had reluctantly suggested deferring the school's opening in the spring of that year, on account of
momentary financial difficulties. The immediate postwar years had
brought a rather severe budgetary crisis upon the University. Almost
upon arrival, Kinley solemnly informed Chadsey that "general expenses should be cut to the bone" even if it meant that the University
would have to "put up, temporarily, with inferior service." This
straightened condition prevailed for some time, and Chadsey, cooperative as usual, informed Kinley the next year that he was "in
common with all of the deans of the University . . . keenly aware
of the financial difficulties which confront the University at the

also. On the closing, see Chadsey to Kinley, September 17, 1920; *President's Report* (1922–23), p. 81. On financial problems, see Chadsey to Kinley, September
26, 1923; June 9, 1925. All letters in Kinley Correspondence.

36 W. W. Charters to James, March 8, 1919, James Correspondence. The
"Chadsey File" in Kinley Correspondence (1922–23), Record Series 2/6/1, no.
76, contains much information on the problems of Smith-Hughes teachers, esp.
during July, 1923. (*President's Reports* [1922–23], pp. 81–83; [1926–27], College of
Education Report, passim; [1927–28], p. 48.)

37 James to Bagley, October 25, 1916; Bagley to James, September 5, 1916, in
James Correspondence. Chadsey to Kinley, October 24, 1919, Kinley Correspondence.

present time." He therefore suggested still another year's postpone-
ment, which would save an estimated $97,000, although he pointed
out the dire consequences of failing to meet the practice-teaching
requirements which were to be scheduled into the school's opening.
Kinley, of course, agreed, doubtless delighted as much to delay the
proliferation of educationists as to exercise his financial stewardship.[38]
However, the high school was scheduled definitely to open September 12, 1921, and it did so under the principalship of Lewis W. Williams.[39]

A student body of ninety regular pupils had been recruited, at a
tuition charge of twenty-five dollars per semester. There were also
some thirty-five University students technically enrolled in secondary
school courses to remedy their deficiencies, although Kinley was
strongly "averse" to such an arrangement on the grounds that it might
lower the maturity of the college-level students.[40] The school provided
training opportunities for fifteen senior education students at the beginning, and by the following year twenty were able to participate in
handling the student body of 112. Admitting the enrollment was not
large, Chadsey still thought it "adequate to take care of the needs of
the College of Education." [41]

What the "needs" were, however, did not seem clear to anyone—
except perhaps to Kinley, in a negative fashion—either then or later.
The question of the definition of the school's nature and function
had remained unresolved virtually from the beginning, and even Bagley's intellectual precision had allowed the issue to go unfocused, as
we have seen. In part this fuzziness was the consequence of rhetoric:

[38] Charters to James, February 4, April 17, James Correspondence. Charters regarded the delay in opening the high school as a "serious mistake" (Chadsey to
Kinley, October 24, 1919; February 27, 1920; Kinley to Chadsey, December 22,
1919; February 28, 1920, Kinley Correspondence). For further evidence of Kinley's rigid and overly scrupulous approach to minor expenditures (which must have
absorbed a large proportion of his time and energy throughout his presidency),
see Chadsey to Kinley and reply, November 6, 1919; Kinley to Chadsey, December 22, 1919. Kinley Correspondence. The President worried particularly about
travel expenses, a mark of the "new" University which he never accepted and
which was especially harmful to his attitude toward the College of Education.
[39] Chadsey to Kinley, August 3, 1921, and esp. Chadsey's "Memo" to McConn,
August 11, 1921, Kinley Correspondence.
[40] 34th SSPI (1922), p. 523; and "Memo", Chadsey to McConn, August 11,
1921; Chadsey to Kinley, October 10, 1921; Kinley to Chadsey, October 11, 1921;
all in Kinley Correspondence. According to Chadsey to Kinley, April 4, 1923,
Kinley Correspondence, the age distribution for that year ran from twelve years
to over twenty-one.
[41] 34th SSPI (1922), p. 523.

the school had to be "sold" to various constituencies, and the grounds for obtaining their potential support varied to the point of contradiction. Chadsey himself defended it on widely disparate bases. Most frequently he portrayed it as a "practice" school, essential to meeting the now growing demand (although as yet only outside Illinois) for practice teaching as a certification requirement.[42] "Observation" or "visiting" were usually linked to this use, although they sometimes were listed as the school's primary functions, especially later when its slow growth in fact precluded using it to meet the demand for "training."[43] He also called it a "laboratory" school on occasion, but he sometimes went on to define that as nothing more than an opportunity to offer experience to students.[44] He seldom if ever saw it as an opportunity for research and experimentation. It was, of course, a decided benefit to the faculty, who might send their children there— and hence create, if without intent, a subsidized preparatory school which would neither acquaint students with the conditions generally prevalent in education nor permit realistic experimentation.[45]

Kinley saw the school as an administrative anomaly. It necessarily involved mixed levels of operation, since it was in, but not of, the University, so to speak. For him it was the question of legitimizing the school's appropriations which required a decision as to its purpose. Since that was, at bottom, a fiscal issue, he consulted his chief financial aide, E. J. Townsend, rather than the College's dean or the school's principal. Thompson drew the clear conclusion that its purpose was primarily for "training high school instructors" and secondarily to serve as "an educational experiment station to test out important educational theories." Any other purposes (including, apparently, student benefit) could "at best be regarded as desirable" and therefore "no really good reason" could be found for making appropriations to such

---

[42] For example, Chadsey to A. J. Janata, November 1, 1924, Kinley Correspondence. Here the practice function is listed first in terms of "the value of our University High School to the University as a whole." Chadsey argues that practice teaching is "coming to be a requirement for the teacher's certificate in many states" (though it was not yet so in Illinois). He also suggests the potential benefit to faculty children. (See also *President's Report* [1923–24], p. 63; 33rd SSPI [1920], p. 442; 34th SSPI [1922], p. 523.)

[43] For example, see *President's Reports* (1924–25), p. 51; (1925–26), p. 80.

[44] *Catalogue* (1921–22), p. 178. The observaton and teaching function is also cited here.

[45] *President's Report* (1927–28), College of Education Report, passim, but esp. p. 48; *Catalogue* (1928–29), p. 146; Chadsey to A. J. Janata, November 1, 1924, Kinley Correspondence.

ends. Kinley agreed, and apparently felt that it was he rather than anyone else who could best serve as the judge of what activities fit his financially determined categories. On grounds such as these, the President decreed that there could be no provisions for band instruments, and no general physical exams, even if admittedly "the better high schools of the state" had already accepted such practices.[46] An auditorium and a gymnasium also proved hard to come by, even though Kinley disliked holding school functions in University facilities. They tended, he thought, to confuse the public. Using University buildings suggested that the school's programs were true University actitvities, which in Kinley's view they manifestly were not.[47]

Throughout the period, the cloak for critical academic judgments touching both the University High School and the College was money. Kinley constantly fought to hold down salaries, often by appeals to altruism on the part of the recipients coupled with deep and legalistic

[46] Chadsey to Kinley, November 14, 1923 (and various other letters at the same location). Kinley's response is sometimes rendered in interesting marginalia. The financial arrangements were constantly questioned, even (as in this case) when there were unexpended funds for "equipment." On this occasion, Kinley complained that "The Superintendent of Business Operations" had reported to him that the instrument requisition had borne a penciled notation " 'Try to get this through' or some such phraseology." That angered him enormously. "I do not know," he said ". . . who did this. But if I am correctly informed about it I think it is something we should all warn our subordinates against" (Kinley to Chadsey, December 1, 1923). For the ruling, see E. J. Townsend to Kinley, December 6, 1923. For physical examinations, see Chadsey to Kinley, September 24, 1926. The President abruptly refused these, after considerable delay, in Kinley to Chadsey, October 9, 1926. All in Kinley Correspondence.

[47] Several letters under Kinley to Chadsey, May 27, 1929. Chadsey wanted to move the High School's commencement from Wesley Methodist Church to Smith Auditorium. Kinley refused, insisting "it would be a mistake to put, by any action we might take, the exercises of the high school on a par in the public mind with the exercises of the University." The previous spring, Chadsey had appealed for funds—understandably, in the light of the extensive building program Kinley had mounted—to complete the school, and especially to provide a gymnasium and auditorium. (See Chadsey to Kinley, March 23, 30, 1928. The letters give an interesting picture of the College's general situation.) The President also objected to such titles as "Instructor" or "Assistant" at the High School. Its personnel were to be known as "Teachers," doubtless lest they be confused with their superiors (Kinley to Chadsey, July 16, 1928). He also worried about distinguishing the University academically from the growing junior colleges, in one case denying credit transfer on the grounds that "advanced students should be confined to courses of greater intellectual resistance, so to speak." (See Kinley to William J. Bartholf [Principal of Crane Junior College], July 13, 1928, and also Kinley to Chadsey, July 19, 1928, where the President decries the general prevalence of such low-"resistance" courses in college programs. All in Kinley Correspondence.)

suspicions on his own part.[48] He feared at one point, for example, that summer session faculty might in fact be collecting "double" salaries. Against Chadsey's judgment, he insisted on charging for the new teacher-placement service. He frequently detected deviousness in the requests for financial approval which crossed his desk. And he found it necessary, in the midst of a generally rising economy and a University now growing prosperous again, to drop temporarily the commercial subjects from the high school curriculum.[49]

The high school was also an anomaly to Kinley in respect to its academic constitution. In the College's program, the special "methods" courses gave credit toward graduation, but they were all located either in the College of Liberal Arts and Sciences (primarily) or in the School of Music. (They were thus beyond the direct control of the College of Education.) The practice work connected with these special courses, however, required supervision. This supervision was furnished by High School faculty members, who were technically on the payroll of the College of Education. Kinley early feared the potential thrust of such a mixing of academic levels, as he saw it. It might confuse work of high school and university grade. Consequently, he decreed that no one who taught in the High School was also to teach at the university level. And when he encountered an instance of mixing—or one which he thought might qualify—he peremptorily challenged it.[50]

After years of acquiescing in Kinley's supervening policies and their dubious economic justifications, Chadsey finally came to the conclusion that no debilitating financial condition existed. "I think,"

[48] For example, Kinley to Chadsey, July 4 [!], 1921, Kinley Correspondence, regarding the salary of L. J. McHarry. As usual, Kinley argues that Illinois's salaries aren't so bad, that money isn't everything, and that the staff needs more "spirit." He had just refused to allow a lower-echelon secretary (Miss Ida Luther) to "resign" even to work on the new University Stadium drive. Since she had agreed to work, Kinley insisted, she could only quit—with all the moral condemnation that implied. (See Chadsey appointment file, Record Series 2/6/1, no. 30, esp. the correspondence ca. May, 1921.) When M. E. Herriott resigned his College faculty post, partly because the President would make no counter-offers, Kinley made it all clear: "I am unwilling to commit myself in too many cases for the next year. It seems to me that our younger people must learn to take their chances with us to a greater extent than they seem willing to do now" (Kinley to Chadsey and reply, January 2, 1929; all in Kinley Correspondence).

[49] Chadsey to Kinley, October 22, 1921; November 5, 1924; July 3, 1925. See also the Dean's protest to Kinley's proposal to eliminate summer session scholarships, in Chadsey to Kinley, June 25, 1929. All in Kinley Correspondence.

[50] Catalogue (1923–24), p. 261; Kinley to Chadsey, May 19, 1922; May 23, 1927; Chadsey to Kinley, May 31, 1927. All in Kinley Correspondence.

he said in 1928, "that I am able to sense the general needs of the University and I am very sincere in my belief that the time has come when the needs of the College of Education are greater than those of any other organization on the Campus." It was as close as the Dean ever came to an outright challenge of Kinley's policies. He had reference to the still incomplete state of the High School, the inadequate provision of offices for the College, and something much more important. It had now become apparent that the students in education could not find even the prerequisite high school–level teaching experience within the confines of the University's operation. Furthermore, as Chadsey pointed out, there was now a growing junior high school movement— a movement in which Charles Hughes Johnston of the University's own faculty had provided leadership. And there was an elementary educational level which the University had never really touched at all. It was time, he thought, to face the necessity of doing something about the whole range of education, lest the University be unable to "hold its own" in the field. Chadsey then proposed to establish a junior high school. The proposal, which he had actually cherished for some time, was backed by a petition of thirty-eight "citizens of Urbana" who expressed their desire to see such work incorporated with that of the University High School. He believed that to accede to this request would both expand the potential range of the College's work and provide the needed increase of practical opportunities for teaching experience.[51]

Junior high school work, however, let alone elementary education, would also comprise a crossing of a mysterious and now traditional borderline. That line was the shadowy demarcation between the province of the University and that of the normal schools. Growingly circumscribed by their original conception and hedged in by anachronistic legislative provisions, the Illinois normal schools were at the nadir of their existence in the early 1920's. The very financial success of the University, in part, had led to their virtual impoverishment in terms both of faculty and equipment. As David Felmly, the patriarch of Illinois State Normal, exploded in his annual report to the state superintendent in 1920, "the older members of our faculties have been caught like rats in a trap." Superintendent Francis Blair agreed that the schools, the "pedagogical cantonments, navy stations and aviation fields" of the state, were being neglected, and he called

[51] Chadsey to Kinley, March 30, 1928, Kinley Correspondence; 33rd *Report* (1926), p. 635. Cf. *President's Report* (1925–26), p. 80.

for action.[52] A somewhat more dispassionate analysis of the situation, by Normal's Dean O. L. Manchester, appropriately entitled *The Normal School Crisis*, had shown that the normal school professors were getting less in 1920 than they had in 1914. In many cases they earned less than their least-experienced students could command immediately upon graduation. The injustice and the unreasonableness of the situation finally gained widespread attention, and a successful attempt to repair their fabric and their prestige was made. By the mid-1920's all of the normal schools were freed to give four-year degrees, their programs began to expand, general accreditation was achieved, and their physical plants were augmented.[53]

There was, however, still little official rapport between them and the University. The normal institutions, now denominated teachers' colleges, were often suspicious and narrowly defensive, the University frequently maddeningly condescending. Their new four-year programs meant that the teachers' colleges might reenter the high school field—although Superintendent Blair felt certain they would not—and a move to expand the University's program such as Chadsey proposed might comprise a further threat to usurp their one distinctive function.[54]

The time for expansion was not yet propitious, for these and other reasons, and so in reporting the Urbana citizens' petition to the Board of Trustees, Kinley made a decisive recommendation uncluttered by explanations of the obvious: "I recommend that the petitioners be informed that the Board does not see its way clear to comply with their request." The Trustees concurred. The University High School and its parent College of Education, like the student body, would once again be restrained from forsaking the beaten path.[55]

Bland and unimaginative as it was, Chadsey's program simply could not allay the President's dormant anxieties even when it evaded

[52] 33rd SSPI (1920), p. 493; 34th SSPI (1922), p. 12.

[53] Manchester's appeal was published by the office of the state superintendent of public instruction, together with a letter from Francis Blair (Springfield, 1921). See p. 30 for the quotation. For the normal school legislation, see 36th SSPI (1926), p. 32.

[54] For clear evidence of the University's attitude, see Kinley to Chadsey, October 7, 1921, and reply, October 27, 1921, Kinley Correspondence. Chadsey consistently supported the position that the normal schools were to be in effect nothing more than the College's farm clubs, although he admitted that this "would not be received in the best spirit by some of [their] executives." (See also 36th SSPI [1926], p. 32.)

[55] 33rd *Report* (1926), p. 635.

his direct ire. An academic terrier, Kinley nipped constantly at the heels of all of his faculty, not merely the educationists. Although Kinley was careful to address his fellow Masons cheerfully as "Brother," his letters and directives to his associates and (especially) his subordinates bristled with pique and suspicion. He constantly questioned or bargained over appointments and recommended abrupt dismissals. He wrote Chadsey in connection with one prospective addition to the staff in 1921 that he was "unable to escape the feeling that many of our appointments in education are weaker than appointments in corresponding places in other departments. If it were not for my complete confidence in your good judgment, I would hesitate more often than I do." (Obviously the compliment was ill devised to bring encouragement, and the carbon was marked "destroy.") [56] General charges such as the above were often contained under specific, and frequently petty, issues. He constantly picked at the competence of minor employees, and he was a stickler for red tape, the latter frequently coupled with appeals to duty and faithfulness. Judgments regarding small expenditures, especially for travel, escaped his accountant's eye no more easily than substantive financial issues. And they constantly mirrored ill humor and suspicion—as, for example, when he accused an outside organization which had requested a specific number of delegates from the University of attempting to dictate its policy! [57]

If Kinley's hostility was raised by the general thrust of the College's program, as well as by the actions of its personnel, he regarded certain features of it as particularly dangerous. Preeminent among these cases was the work of the Bureau of Educational Research. The Bureau had arisen from a proposal of Guy Montrose Whipple to Bagley in 1917. Whipple suggesteed that the new "measurement techniques" which were being developed could be used in education, to evaluate

[56] Kinley to Chadsey, August 5, 1919, Kinley Correspondence. In this case, the President had found out that Yale was not going to advance Professor Cameron for a time, so he could be bargained with for less than originally suggested. For typical dismissals, see Kinley to H. A. Hollister, July 2, 1919. This quotation is from Kinley to Chadsey, July 11, 1921. (There is considerable evidence that many letters were deliberately removed from the files during Kinley's administration.) See also a letter from the Provost to Chadsey, August 19, 1926 (copy in Chadsey File, Record Series 2/6/1, no. 125): "Would not such an appointment as this [in agricultural education] weaken a department which is already none too strong and increase rather than diminish, the existing suspicion as to its standards?"

[57] For evidence, see Kinley to Chadsey, July 1, 1929, Kinley Correspondence; 31st *Report* (1922), pp. 84–85; Eugene Davenport to Kinley, June 13, 1921; Chadsey to Kinley, June 24, 1921; Kinley to Chadsey, March 25, 1926 (and supporting letters). All in Kinley Correspondence.

"mental abilities and traits" and to determine the effectiveness of "school products." This kind of work, which had already been investigated to some extent by faculty at the University, ought to be formally incorporated under a special bureau, he believed, as had already been done at several other western state universities, most notably Wisconsin, Nebraska, Kansas, and Indiana. The question was inevitably raised whether it would conflict with the province of the normal schools and whether—curiously—it would be "a form of university extension work and hence a type of activity foreign to the general policy of the University of Illinois." [58] Agreement was reached nonetheless, and Bagley requested a "Bureau of Educational Service" with a rather broad design. The proposal was approved and Burdette Ross Buckingham, a measurement specialist of reputation from Teachers College, Columbia, then chief statistician for the Wisconsin board of education, came on to head its operation in 1918. Shortly afterward he was joined by Walter Scott Monroe, a Kansan with a Chicago doctorate who had just been appointed at Indiana.[59]

The program developed by Buckingham and his promising colleague was a broad and vigorous one. It sought to draw together the problems of schoolmen from all about the state and to begin work on them. This orientation alone had brought an enthusiastic response from some 250 educational leaders throughout the state—one which quite swamped the Bureau's facilities, in fact. Typically, the problems involved techniques of quantification and measurement (particularly the problem of isolating the "supernormal" and the "subnormal"), but they also reached heavily into administration, supervision, curriculum development, and vocational education. The things the Bureau proposed to do were taken from, and clearly went to the heart of, the actual work of the schools. Additional research of a more strictly theoretical sort would be generated within the Bureau, however, and the results of all such work would be broadcast by means of quarterly bulletins and periodic circulars.[60]

[58] Whipple to Bagley, March 3, 1917, James Correspondence. For an example, see 1916 standardized algebra test developed by Harold Rugg, et al., in Hollister File, Record Series 2/5/3, no. 88.

[59] For the request, see Bagley to James, March 5, 1917. Cf. Charters to James, June 5, 1918—where it is styled the "Bureau of Cooperative Research." For staffing, see Charters File, Record Series 2/5/3, no. 174. All in James Correspondence. Cf. 31st *Report* (1922), p. 129.

[60] For the original program see eleven-page letter, Buckingham to Charters, December 16, 1918, plus attachment, under Charters to James, December 20, 1918, James Correspondence. It treats every aspect of the proposal most thoroughly

The Bureau's report for 1918–19, when Kinley took the reins, shows that these objectives were not only well on the way to achievement but had even become considerably enlarged in the process. The small staff had assembled a very large amount of information relative to what was being done in the schools, not only from throughout the state but from all parts of the nation. This information was being cross-indexed so that the Bureau could act as a kind of clearinghouse on regular programs, research projects, thesis work, biblography, and so on. Requests to do intensive surveys at such places as Evanston and Crawford County were declined, but the staff had attempted to cooperate with research work being done in Chicago. Perhaps most prescient of later developments was their program to analyze teaching activity in the schools. An attempt to devise a "scientifically defensible method of teaching reading" was underway. They had initiated experimental programs to examine the testing process as it was related to promotion policy at Danville, Springfield, and Decatur.

Most important of all, from the point of view of their future, Bureau personnel had worked on the development of standardized tests in arithmetic, geography, history, and grammar. Over 75,000 of these tests in various content areas had in fact been sold, and the Bureau anticipated the need to print a million in the year ahead. They had also given particular attention to programs of general intelligence testing, as "bases of action" in the schools. Besides evaluating existing tests, the Bureau administered some 16,000 in various local schools and even ran the famous Army alpha tests on a select group of faculty and students in the University. In every case their criterion for including a project or an activity was clear. As Buckingham said, "We cannot avoid asking ourselves, 'How does the experimental work of the Bureau match up with the subjects in which the school people are interested?' " The Bureau had ample evidence to show that they were interested.[61] Just after his arrival, Chadsey wrote Kinley an enthusiastic commendation of the Bureau's work, which he saw

---

and conveys extensive evidence of its eager reception by schoolmen. There is a slightly sharp tone to Buckingham's report, which suggests that even then, in the Bureau's first few months of operation, its director feared for its future.

[61] The foregoing material is taken from a thirty-page (typescript) "Memorandum on the Work of the Bureau of Educational Research" for the year ending June 30, 1919 (with additional prefactory material and exhibits), doubtless prepared under Buckingham's supervision. (See Buckingham File, Record Series 2/6/1, no. 4, Kinley Correspondence. For this paragraph, see esp. pp. 3, 12, 17, 18, 23, 25, 27–29.)

"reaching out into the public school system of Illinois in a very effective way." By 1920, the new Dean reported, they were sending out nearly 3,000,000 tests annually—excellent "publicity," in his opinion.[62]

In January, 1921, the famous Winnetka superintendent of schools, Carleton W. Washburne, wrote Kinley that he believed the Bureau to be "in advance of . . . any similar department in any state of the Union." It was, Washburne thought, bringing to reality the great hope of schoolmen, that of placing education "on a scientific footing." Education had unfortunately "been based rather upon philosophic theories and psychological notions" instead of "scientific research." He appreciated Kinley's "support" of the Bureau.[63] Washburne's words were an egregious, and deliberate, falsification of the situation: the purpose of his letter was actually to save Buckingham and the Bureau from the effects of Kinley's very active disinterest. Indeed, "distrust" would be a more appropriate description, since, as Kinley later said, he regarded psychological testing and the predictions based thereon, as "divinations." [64] But Kinley had already found safe grounds for achieving the ends dictated by his prior theoretical commitments. The marketing of tests by the University was a clear violation of the rights of the business community. They represented unfair competition on the part of a public institution. Furthermore, since authors' royalties were involved, there was a potential conflict of interest as well.

Kinley had mounted an extensive investigation of the issue, beginning in 1920 with an attempt to regularize the Bureau's business procedures.[65] The fact was that commercial publishers had watched from afar the development of the tests (both at Illinois and elsewhere, although the University was the most prominent institution in the enterprise) and, noting the rapid growth in their use, had only lately entered the field. The commercial houses were now paying royalties, and it became obvious that the University could not compete without

[62] Chadsey to Kinley, January 8, 1920, Kinley Correspondence. (A report on the tests by W. S. Monroe can be found at the same location.)

[63] C. W. Washburne to Kinley, January 6, 1921, Kinley Correspondence.

[64] Kinley actually used this term in his *President's Report* (1924–25), p. 15.

[65] Chadsey to Kinley, January 8, 1920; Lloyd Morey to Kinley, June 18, 1920 (including two-page financial summary, and marginalia with Kinley's initials which suggest that one of his purposes was to control personally the funds involved); Charles McConn to Morey, June 21, 1920; and Buckingham to Morey, June 1, 1920 (a defense of the Bureau's procedures). All in Kinley Correspondence.

following suit.[66] However, the President's administrative assistant, C. M. McConn, informed Buckingham that Kinley felt "a good deal of doubt as to the justifiability of the University's conducting any publishing business in competition with commercial publishers," and suggested that he confer about the matter.[67] Buckingham returned the argument that testing was still in its infancy and that it needed the University to guide its development. To put it into the hands of commercial enterprises might destroy its quality, as well as place its benefits beyond the financial reach of the schools in many instances.[68]

In any case, the issue needed resolution by the late summer of 1920 or the work could not be continued. Investigating the matter for the President, agriculturalist Eugene Davenport backed Buckingham's position entirely as to the facts, and he proposed that faculty developing tests assign the copyrights to the University and then receive half of the royalties paid for the tests by the Bureau.[69] Chadsey agreed and began to take action on that basis, although Kinley was still on vacation and had not yet made any recommendation.[70] The President was apparently not satisfied, however, and the matter was reopened during the fall. By then even the Bureau regarded the volume of tests as "embarrassingly large," and they agreed that the printing and marketing of the tests should be put out commercially but remain under the University's "supervision" via the Bureau. Kinley found even this unacceptable. He insisted that "the University should not be doing the great volume of commercial business that has built itself up around the work of the Bureau of Educational Research." He was also unalterably opposed to any payment of royalties for "*the so-called educational tests*," and he felt the University had, and could have, no prerogative of supervising commercial publishers.[71]

Chadsey acquiesced. The tests were turned over to the Public

---

[66] Buckingham to Kinley, July 1, 1920, pp. 4–5, Kinley Correspondence.

[67] McConn to Buckingham, August 11, 1920, Kinley Correspondence.

[68] Buckingham's second extensive defense of the Bureau is a nine-page signed "Memorandum as to the Policy of the Test Business, Bureau of Educational Research," dated (by Eugene Davenport, who apparently transmitted it) August 19, 1920. All in Kinley Correspondence. For this contention, see pp. 1–3.

[69] Eugene Davenport to Chadsey, August 23, 1920; Buckingham to McConn, August 12, 1920; Kinley Correspondence.

[70] Chadsey to Kinley, September 10, 1920, Kinley Correspondence. A list of the tests at issue is also furnished at this location.

[71] Chadsey to Kinley, October 4, 1920, and attached "Memorandum"; Kinley to Chadsey, October 19, 1920; all in Kinley Correspondence. Italics ours.

School Publishing Company in Bloomington. Even Monroe himself (who had authored a test of which well over a million copies had been distributed) surrendered any claim to royalties, in spite of the fact that (like others) much of his work in developing the test had originally had no connection with the University.[72] In a kind but ineffectual gesture, Chadsey thought the Trustees might consider favorably a modest raise instead—say, $500—in return for his services. The matter was closed. The University would not compete with, not dictate to, the business community, nor would faculty again personally profit from their works.[73] Severe budget problems soon ensued, of course, since much of the Bureau's expanding work had been financed from the profits, and during the following year the Bureau was reorganized. It would henceforth issue only such reports and bulletins as posed no threat. And, amidst a flood of protest which Kinley deviously side-stepped by pleading ignorance, B. R. Buckingham went off to the Ohio State University to develop his ideas.[74]

There were other programs housed under the College of Education which drew a markedly more enthusiastic response from the President, however. Chief among these was the enormously successful program in athletic coaching. The program, developed by George Huff, had its origin in a number of factors.[75] The rapid rise of collegiate ath-

[72] Chadsey to Kinley, October 20, 1920, Kinley Correspondence.

[73] Ibid. Kinley's philosophy was evident on other occasions also: see McConn to Chadsey, February 3, 1921 (over honoraria); Kinley to Chadsey, May 6, 1926 (on outside work); Chadsey to Kinley, February 3, 1921 (on royalties for Rugg and Bagley); and President's Report (1929–30), p. 21 (where Kinley states he had reinvestigated the "interference" of University agricultural products with "local business"). All letters in Kinley Correspondence.

[74] Chadsey to McConn, February 1, 1921; Chadsey to Kinley, July 12, 1921; Kinley Correspondence. The President's Report (1925–26), p. 79, records that "the work of the Bureau of Educational Research, which began its work in 1918, has not changed materially in its aims during the last three or four years." (!) But cf. 25th SSPI (1924), and its four-line notice on the Bureau's work, p. 481. For the protests, see the Buckingham File, Record Series 2/6/1, no. 29, passim, but esp. H. B. Fisher (superintendent at Streator, who submitted a resolution honoring Buckingham for his work) to Kinley, January 10, 1921; Fisher to Kinley, June 8, 1921; and letters from other prominent schoolmen. In what appears to be deliberate chicanery, Kinley consistently answered that he had never heard of the possibility of Buckingham's departure until receipt of the particular letter he was answering!

[75] For evidence, see Huff Files in Record Series 2/5/3, nos. 88, 181, passim. See esp. a preliminary outline of the proposed athletic coaching program and budget (in no. 88); an N.C.A.A. letter on college athletics by Huff, dated December 5,

letics, the somewhat later but definite trend toward interscholastic competition in high schools, and the general interest in improved physical education standards generated in the aftermath of World War I all contributed. The success of the program was built upon the widely accepted reputation of two men, principally Huff and his colleague, Robert Carl Zuppke. Huff, a Champaign boy and alumnus, had directed physical training and athletics at the University since 1895 and had shaped the program from its earlier exercise and recreational function to its introduction as a subject for study and, ultimately, the formal training of teachers and coaches. German-born, Zuppke had attended the State Normal School at Milwaukee and later received a bachelor's degree at Wisconsin. After coaching in Muskegon, Michigan, and Oak Park, Illinois, he had joined the University in 1913 to begin a tenure as head coach which would last until 1941. His indisputable success in producing strong athletic contenders and attracting students guaranteed him warm—if not, indeed, preferential—treatment not only by the administration but by the Trustees and an ever widening circle of the public as well. Zuppke, Huff, and others of the enlarging staff ranged throughout the United States, carrying their advice and encouragement (and the University's name) to athletic leaders and sports fans everywhere, largely through the medium of popular addresses on such topics as "Health as a Business Asset," "Leaky Buckets" (on physical defects), and "A Man's Man." [76]

1918; Huff's defense of the proposals, dated March 11, 1919; and W. W. Charters to Kinley, May 8, 1919, on the establishment of the department (all in no. 181). President Draper was credited with the original increase in emphasis on athletics (Kelley, *The Alumni Record*, p. 25).

[76] For the treatment of Zuppke and others of the staff, see, for example, 34th *Report* (1927–28), p. 186. Chadsey recommended and Kinley concurred that "Zuppke be given a leave of absence on *full pay* from December 11 to February 8, to enable him to go to California to be with his mother who is seriously ill. Professor Zuppke has *no class work* until the second semester and no football practice until the beginning of the second semester" (italics ours). Granted that such kind treatment ought to be accorded anyone, including a coach, it must also be noted that at that time few got leave without pay, almost no one with pay, and most were carrying enormous teaching loads year 'round. When the request was first made to Chadsey, Professor (and Chairman) Lundgren argued that Zuppke had "no particular duties until the second semester, in order that he may rest up after the strenuous football season" (Lundgren to Chadsey, December 8, 1926, Kinley Correspondence). In spite of what we have seen to be his policy and practice, there is no indication whatever that the President caviled even slightly at this expenditure.

For the oratorical efforts of the staff (Huff termed it "public service work"), see three-page list of addresses (more than eighty in 1924–25 alone) delivered

Though such work was from the beginning essentially distinct from the College of Education, a regular four-year course in coaching was developed for 1919–20 and placed under the aegis of the new College as a special department.[77] It met the growing demand, and the numbers on the staff and in the courses skyrocketed. By 1924, 130 prospective coaches were graduated; requests for even more had come in from forty-two states, accelerated by the fact that the alumni of the program not only compiled exceedingly good won-lost records but maintained "the highest standards of clean play and sportsmanship" as well. Within six years enrollment in the program jumped from 67 to 368, and nearly 500 active coaches were signing up for the equally successful summer offerings—an expression of interest not hindered by the fact that the University had won or tied for championships in seven sports during one of those years. Soon the program accounted for more than half of the burgeoning College enrollment, a condition which prevailed for most of the decade. Budget and staff climbed accordingly, supplemented by the income available from record-smashing gate receipts handled through the University-directed Athletic Association.[78] By 1926, athletic coaching required twenty-one staff members. For comparison, fifteen handled all the general course work in education and twenty-three operated the entire High School and the supervision program. While on the regular accounting sheets the financial share allotted to the coaching program appeared modest, the facts were otherwise. Its salaries and expenditures in 1928–29, for example, were not to be covered by the some $35,000 budgeted through the College proper. They required over $115,000, nearly four times more than any other single activity of the College, and an amount nearly equal to three-quarters of its total budget for all other purposes combined. The balance was drawn from the seemingly inexhaustible coffers of the Association.[79]

The program's success, however, was not without problems. Its faculty achieved rank and tenure far in excess of any formal academic

in locations as geographically various as New York City and Topeka, Kansas, in Chadsey File, Record Series 2/6/1, no. 113, under report on Physical Education, Huff to Chadsey, May 6, 1925.

[77] Charters to Kinley, May 8, 1919, Kinley Correspondence.

[78] President's Report (1923–24), pp. 61, 139; (1924–25), pp. 48, 88; Huff to James, November 9, 1917, James Correspondence. For comparison, the work was about ten times the size of that in all Smith-Hughes areas combined.

[79] Trustees Reports for the period, passim, but esp. 34th Report (1928), pp. 46–49, 695–97.

qualifications—leading even Kinley to demur quietly, for a time.[80] Their salaries completely outstripped those of tenured faculty of corresponding academic status, and they were sometimes put on tenure immediately on arrival.[81] In 1928–29, for example, Huff and Zuppke were drawing salaries of $8,000, identical with Chadsey's—a rate made possible by $11,000 of supplemental income from the Association. Lesser lights, including one instructor who had only the rank of "associate," were drawing $6,000. On the other hand, an associate in education was fortunate to receive half of that amount. E. W. Dolch got $2,600, Mrs. Charles Hughes Johnston $2,400, and the High School teachers as low as $1,500. Full professors in Education proper, such as Nolan and Mays, were at the $4,000 level. The next year, Huff and Zuppke were raised to $10,400 and $10,000 respectively.[82] And to bear as much as its modest share in this enterprise, the College had to cut corners elsewhere—as, for example, in the curriculum of the High School. Even Chadsey eventually felt required to resist such "unduly large or rapid increases," but his protests were virtually ignored.[83]

[80] For example, Huff had recommended Gill, Jones, Zuppke, and Schuettner for assistant professorships (along with Griffith), on the ground that "the work would be dignified somewhat if these titles were granted." See Huff to James [it was actually handled by Kinley], June 11, 1919, James Correspondence. The Acting President hesitated, except for Zuppke, who was the only one with any degree at all (Kinley to Huff, July 10, 1919, James Correspondence). All were later advanced, however. For further examples, see the case of Lundgren in Chadsey to Kinley, June 28, 1920, and Chadsey to Kinley, March 19, 1924, both in Kinley Correspondence. In the latter case, the individual in dispute was teaching University courses without "background"—i.e., no "general education" at all—and, incidentally, entirely paid by the Athletic Association.

[81] Huff to Chadsey (three-page letter and attached exhibits), May 6, 1925, Kinley Correspondence. The customary defense, as here, was the keen competition for these men. In his letter, Lundgren (whose initial professorial appointment caused some hesitation—see previous notes) was already being recommended for a full professorship. Note also that, as again was common, the *actual* budgets included A. A. supplements, but they were frequently unmentioned when comparisons were made with other departments. For instant tenure, see 34th *Report* (1928), p. 2.

[82] For the 1928–29 budget, see 34th *Report* (1928), pp. 695–97. (Cf. 1926–27 figures, pp. 46–49.) In 1929, athletic coaching had a staff of 40; education, 13; the High School, 21. In 1929, the true coaching department budget totalled $123,050, with $35,400 charged to general physical education, $34,850 charged to athletic coaching, and $52,800 supplied by the A. A. In 1930, the total budget was increased to $126,500 (more than three times that of education). The College athletic coaching budget had been reduced, but the Association increased its supplement to $57,500 (35th *Report* [1930], pp. 297–99, 647–49).

[83] Chadsey to Kinley, July 3, 1925, Kinley Correspondence. Chadsey had made College budget cuts of $3,300, even more than Kinley had requested. How? "As between the work in Athletic Coaching and Supervision and High School In-

President Kinley, on the whole, stood firmly behind not only the program in athletic coaching but the general prominence of athletics in the University. Nor was his approval merely tacit. In his very first presidential *Report*, he had cast an optimistic eye over the whole scene. Noting that the drive to erect the new Memorial Stadium was going well, he paused to reflect on the criticisms of athletics now growing considerably stronger. "Whatever evils athletics may have brought us," the President opined, "they must be credited to some measure with the advantage of having replaced worse things." Kinley thought that the increasing pace of social life on the campus, and the automobile, posed far greater dangers to getting an education.[84] A few years later, the criticism of "big-time" college athletics had mounted to a loud and angry protest over much of the nation. But the President was still not "impressed" with the critics' "vague charges" (such as the supposed over-excitement of the students). Nor could he see this enterprise as a case of "commercialism." The mere fact that the gate receipts were large was not, ipso facto, an evil, he assured the public, although the drinking that took place in and around those gates might be. And he had a consoling word for a bewildered faculty, whose jealousy had already been kindled by budgets such as we have just examined. Coaches' salaries, he admitted, were doubtless larger than those of others, but that enlargement was based not on discrimination but on the law of "supply and demand"—a very sacred canon

---

struction, I have decided to eliminate [equipment, and a teacher in the commercial subjects now much in demand] from the latter. While I think some of the increase in Athletic Coaching might have been reduced [the saving in supervision and high school instruction would be] to better advantage." Although not "altogether happy" about it, the Dean could excuse his efforts "on the general theory that it is better to refrain from extension rather than cripple the departments already in existence. . . ." For Chadsey's later protest, see Chadsey to Kinley, April 5, 1928, Kinley Correspondence. In this letter, Chadsey noted that one proposed raise, for Coleman R. Griffith, was in spite of the fact that his salary was already "much larger than that of anyone in psychology excepting Professor Bentley [its head] and that Mr. Olander's salary is twice, if not more than twice, as large as that which he would receive were he teaching in the general department of Education. . . ." Pleading for "temperance," Kinley's only objection was that the whole proposal shifted some more financial weight from the Association to the University. Association salaries are, he said, higher "on account of market conditions," and the University should not pay its share by the Association's scale, but by its own (Kinley to Chadsey, May 16, 1928, Kinley Correspondence).

[84] *President's Report* (1922–23), pp. 47, 49. See also a duplicated memorandum, addressed to the alumni by Kinley, advertising a rally "in interest of the stadium" and soliciting pledges; in Chadsey File, Record Series 2/6/1, no. 30.

indeed for President Kinley.[85] Noting that a high proportion of the athletic coaching students were from out of state, the President did, however, suggest to Chadsey that both standards and fees might be raised; and at the end he was inclined toward dropping the final week of the football season, since "the physical strain on the varsity team" seemed excessive. But it was, all in all, a very successful enterprise.[86]

As Chadsey approached what was to be the end of his deanship, he grew increasingly restive. His own reports demonstrated inescapably that the College of Education had simply marked time, if indeed it had even held its ground. He had reported for the year 1926 that it was "difficult to point to any outstanding incident in any of the work of the College," and that description fitted the whole of his administration as well as its parts.[87] Even the occasional bright spots were disappointingly dim. The high school visitation work, although ably handled by Hollister, grew increasingly difficult to manage.[88] The relationship between the University and the schools which it implied had always been a problematical one, fraught with perils to both parties. Frequently the systems or particular schools visited were embroiled in local disputes, and the Visitor's judgments were apt to be interpreted in the light of them. While not entirely unproductive, the relationship was still not a positive one, since its chief concern had necessarily to be the University's interests and not those of the schools. The Trustees, with a candor probably unintended, even lumped the Visitor's budget appropriations under "public relations" in 1922.[89]

[85] *President's Report* (1926–27), pp. 35–37. Two pages later, he decries the prevailing "pessimism" about the University, alleging that its failures stem from the decline of the general curriculum and a consequent lessening of "thinking."

[86] Kinley to Chadsey, January 15, 1926, Kinley Correspondence; *President's Report* (1928–29), pp. 41–42.

[87] *President's Report* (1925–26), p. 77.

[88] H. A. Hollister to Kinley, July 7, 1919, Kinley Correspondence. Hollister, besides describing the problems for the new President, immediately protested Kinley's proposed economics. The Visitor, doubtless at times something of a martinet himself, did not hesitate to accuse Kinley of making a "hurried survey" of the situation and to bemoan the fact that "the extent of this work has never seemed to be comprehended by the President's Office." He also maintained that the salaries now being paid were less than those offered for "the merest crossroads principalship."

[89] See esp. the Hollister File in Record Series 2/5/3, no. 181, for evidence on the Visitor's problems as they were revealed in connection with hiring A. W. Clevenger. Cf. Kinley to Chadsey, March 10, 1925, Kinley Correspondence: "Our experience has shown us that it is dangerous *for the University* to get into local educational quarrels and on the whole we have refrained from

As a consequence the office of Visitor itself stood farther and farther apart from the concerns of the College.[90] The activity in which it came closest to fulfilling a truly positive educational function was its continued sponsorship of the High School Conferences, the annual meetings of teachers and administrators from about the state with college and university people. In these meetings school problems, curricular development (through special interest groups in each area), and administrative policy were subject to review and guidance from campus authorities as well as visiting educational leaders. From about 3,000 at the beginning of the decade, the Conference drew an "aggregate" attendance of well over 5,000 by its end.[91]

Perhaps the central issue facing the visitation program during the period was that of its relationship to other efforts at evaluation. Whether the visitation and accreditation of Illinois high schools should be a general state or a University function had been debated as early as 1915. The problem had always been further complicated by the similar work of the North Central Association, with which the Uni-

---

making such inspections" (italics ours). In 32nd *Report* (1924) there is a thorough discussion of the problems of "inspection," pp. 104ff. The entire description supports the interpretation that the procedure was a prudential one, principally designed to protect the University.

[90] Kinley to Chadsey (and reply), January 18, February 13, 1926, Kinley Correspondence. Chadsey calls Hollister a "titular member of the [College's] staff."

[91] For attendance, see *President's Report* (1929–30), p. 51. It is difficult to escape the notion that the Conferences were primarily *occasions* for school men to meet; they were not programs designed to offer leadership to the schools. The University's contribution was largely in terms of supplementary content, the sort of "keeping up with the field" which had been the mark of the old teachers' institutes. For a brief history of their beginning, see *Proceedings of the High School Conference of November 17, 18, and 19, 1910* (University of Illinois School of Education Bulletin no. 4, Urbana, n.d.), pp. 5–7. (The list of claimed accomplishments recorded on p. 7 supports the view suggested above.) The other teacher-preparation institutions came to play a smaller role (as did other colleges and universities, with the exception of a few such as Chicago and Northwestern); thus they did not advance this much needed objective either (ibid., p. 72; cf. *Proceedings . . . 1917* [University of Illinois School of Education Bulletin no. 19, Urbana, 1918], p. 8). By 1925 even Hollister candidly admitted almost total "failure." The Conferences had become "mere programs of papers and speeches" and not the "study of problems." The cooperation sought between the University and the schools ("most urgently to be desired") had not materialized; and the University "rank and file" had not always been sympathetic. See his opening address, "Inter-relationship of High Schools and University," in *Proceedings . . . 1925* (University of Illinois Bulletin, vol. 23, no. 27, March 8, 1926; Urbana, 1926), pp. 11–15, but esp. pp. 12, 13, 14. (There was a virtually imperial tone to his opening words, however—an unnoticed negative factor, perhaps, in spite of his undoubtedly good intentions.)

versity was also involved, and the growing regional factionalism in the state.[92] Superintendent Blair admonished the Trustees in 1921 to open the institution's doors to graduates of any Illinois high school "recognized" by the state office equally with those on their own list. He also criticized the waste involved in the overlapping programs and threatened to make it a matter for the legislature. The Trustees decided there was indeed an issue, and they ordered both Blair and President Kinley to present the criteria that were being used in their respective programs. After lengthy discussions, an agreement was reached in the spring of 1923. By its provisions, each body could inspect for the other if so requested by the school involved, and there was to be a rotating geographical division of labor along a north-south axis. The proposal was experimental, subject to cancellation by either party if it felt its interests were not properly safeguarded, yet the University was still somewhat chary in accepting it. Hollister was retained past the normal age of retirement to see the arrangement through, an unusual exception to University policy, and it finally prevailed as established procedure.[93]

As we have noted, College enrollments climbed rapidly, from 87 in 1919–20 to 1,031 in 1929–30, and the staff grew from 22 to 74 (reaching a high of 77) in the same period. The increase in students was, as we have also suggested, heavily influenced by the athletic coaching program, and the same was true in respect to growth in the staff. Athletic coaching and University High School personnel accounted for some two-thirds of the faculty during much of the time. The same situation prevailed in the summer sessions, where the considerable growth was again largely attributable to programs for coaches and school administrators.[94] There was a genuine advancement in the development of extramural work, and further foundations were laid for later programs in special education. The Bureau of Educational Research had accepted its diminished role and, while it issued some

[92] Hollister to James, December 3, 1915; Hollister to [Dean] Thomas Arkle Clark, January 1, 1916 (which discusses the development of a "Chicago bloc"); James to Hollister, May 15, 1916; and Hollister to James, September 4, 1916. There is also a typical budget (for 1916–17) at the same location, Record Series 2/5/3, no. 88.

[93] 34th SSPI (1922), p. 14; 31st *Report* (1922), pp. 83, 226; 35th SSPI (1924), pp. 318–19; 32nd *Report* (1924), pp. 104ff., 197; *President's Report* (1923–24), p. 24; 33rd *Report* (1926), pp. 635–36.

[94] *Catalogue* (1923–24), p. 263; (1929–30), passim; *President's Reports* for the period, esp. (1922–23), p. 69; (1924–25), p. 48; (1929–30), p. 67; 35th *Report* (1930), pp. 297–99. Cf. 34th *Report* (1928), pp. 26–27.

worthwhile studies, Chadsey himself admitted that its circulars made "no pretense at being strictly original work." They were designed to make more readily available research mostly done elsewhere, and they made no great stir even at that.[95]

All in all, the problems the College faced bulked larger at the end than at the beginning. The practice-teaching problem had grown critical, yet there was no suggestion that it would be faced.[96] The high schools of the state had made enormous strides in the decade, enrolling more than 300,000 students by 1930, less than 8,000 of whom were now in other than four-year programs. The secondary school teaching force had been improved radically as well. More than three-quarters had now finished a college or a four-year teachers' course; less than 200 had only finished high school. (The situation in the lower grades was, however, still quite drastic.) Certification requirements had been both raised and more broadly applied.[97] The programs to meet these requirements, however, were still none too strong, even at the University. Many were essentially formless, only specifying a certain number of hours in a given area. For example, the original athletic coaching curriculum had (with some exceptions) only required blocks of time in education and in physical education or coaching subjects. Out of 136 hours, the student might spend as little as thirty hours in "general education" courses. He could round out the balance of his program with such popular offerings as "Campcraft," "Scoutcraft," "Single-line Marching and Gymnastic Dancing," or such cognate studies as "Oral Expression" ("Public Speaking I"), "Sports Writing," and "The Newspaper" (the latter courses specially offered by the journalism department), rather than the more solid work which was available. Mostly, of course, he tended to delve ever deeper into football, basketball, and baseball, approaching each from a number of different standpoints—each with its own course. While the music and home economics curricula were certainly no better, and probably even worse (not as subjects, of course, but as examples of a purportedly

---

[95] *Catalogue* (1927–28), p. 542; *President's Reports* (1923–24), p. 62; (1925–26), p. 79 (for examples of studies); *President's Report* (1924–25), pp. 49–50, the source of the quotation. For work of the Bureau, see, for example, Bureau of Educational Research, College of Education, *Bulletin* nos. 41–50 (Urbana, 1928–30), esp. *Bulletin* no. 42, which summarizes ten years of work (1918–27) and lists publications.

[96] *President's Report* (1928–29), pp. 56–58, for an extensive analysis and plea regarding practice teaching; but cf. (1929–30), following p. 67, where no response has occurred.

[97] 38th SSPI (1930), pp. 2, 9, 11–12.

educational regimen), it was the athletic coaching course which was put under examination first. The examination led to its being recast in a somewhat more liberal direction, but the real significance of this action was that it began a long look at *all* the teaching curricula which would preoccupy the University for some years to come.[98]

The most distressing problem in the formidable array of difficulties which the College faced was, however, a general one. Except for helping to prepare the individual teacher, the College had virtually no rapport with the schools of the state, at least in any distinctive leadership capacity. Years before, in 1916, Hollister had told President James that the high schools of the state were looking to the University to lead them in bringing themselves to perfection. But for good reason, they had, by the end of the 1920's, simply ceased to do so.[99] The issues that practicing educators faced were clear—as even a cursory examination of their professional literature will document. The problem of the small rural school, the crucial question of adequate distribution of financial aid, the relation of the schools to rapid social changes, the need for the teacher to become an intelligent practitioner of the politics which decisively shaped the institution he served—these were their major concerns. The College of Education did little or nothing about any of them. For example, it dropped its course on the rural school before the decade was half over, although there were still more than 10,000 one-room schoolhouses by the advent of the 1930's.[100] The

[98] *President's Report* (1926–27), pp. 64–65; *Catalogues* (1919–20), pp. 188–89; (1923–24), p. 265; (1926–27), p. 267; (1928–29), pp. 144–45. See also Huff to Chadsey, June 7, 1929, College of Education Papers, for the director's frank admission of "the need for a more definite listing of graduation requirements."

[99] Hollister to James, May 12, 1916, James Correspondence. Cf. Francis G. Blair, "Fifty Years of Education in Illinois" in 33rd SSPI (1920), pp. 97ff., which mentions little recent contribution by the University.

[100] For example, the *Illinois Teacher*, esp. for the period 1928–30. In 1922, 166 school districts enrolled less than five pupils, 2,243 enrolled between eleven and fifteen, and in 1,581 districts average daily attendance was less than nine pupils. Illinois had ranked forty-third in the nation in terms of increases for school expenditures in the decade 1910–20; it was twenty-third in percentage of income devoted to the schools, and twenty-fifth in per capita expenditures—although ninth in per capita income (35th SSPI [1924], pp. 31–34). The issuance of free text books had been tried since 1917, but it was being debated and the Superintendent himself was dubious (p. 18). Later Superintendent Blair wrote an article ("The School Teacher as a Social Factor") in which he said this new social view was the product of only the previous decade (36th SSPI [1926], p. 34). In that volume, the College reported only "years of normal development"— almost a bad pun—in its sparse and lackluster description of its work, but "the football season of 1925–26 was the most prosperous in the history of our organi-

technological revolution in teaching, just beginning to be apparent, was met with indifference. When Will Hays wrote Kinley about the potential effect of the "talkies on pedagogy," Chadsey could manage only guarded optimism when asked for his counsel. (He had been much more enthusiastic about a proposal for observing Comenius' birthday.) [101] The faculty were not abroad at the meetings of the profession, nor were they addressing themselves to the teachers in print. The schools of Illinois openly and necessarily looked to the reviving state teachers' colleges and universities, to the University of Chicago, and to Columbia for leadership.[102]

It may have been that Chadsey's health was declining. There can be no doubt that his spirits were, especially as he saw that his policy of passively accepting the dictates of the administration had borne no fruit. His final reports suggest a curious blend of impatience and quiet desperation. On April 9, 1930, after a two-day illness not at first thought serious, Charles Ernest Chadsey died. His widow was awarded the maximum death benefit ($3,000), and the President's office sent flowers and expressions of sympathy.[103] But on the whole neither Chadsey's death nor Kinley's own retirement a few weeks later drew much notice, at least from school people. In a sense, the reason for it was simple: the College of Education at the University of Illinois had largely faded from view both in the state and in the nation. Whatever vision Charles Ernest Chadsey had once had for it, withdrawal was virtually its policy. The reason for this curious sterility after the

zation. . . ." Combined home and away attendance reached 363,398 (ibid., pp. 484, 505-8). See also circular on "Inequalities in Educational Opportunities in Illinois," ibid., pp. 52-90, esp. the section on one-room school districts, p. 65.

[101] Will Hays (Motion Picture Producers and Distributors of America) to Kinley, September 25, 1929; Chadsey to Kinley, October 3, 1929; Chadsey to Kinley, March 11, 1921; and cf. Kinley to Chadsey, May 19, 1923 (and other letters and items at the same location, regarding the development of "visual aid"). All in Kinley Correspondence.

[102] For example, Superintendent Blair's praise of Teachers College, Columbia, in 36th SSPI (1926), p. 31, as well as the teachers' journals and meeting programs for the period.

[103] Chadsey to Kinley, May 5, 31, 1928, and esp. March 30, 1928; Mrs. C. E. Chadsey to Kinley, April 24, 1930; all in Kinley Correspondence. Cf. 35th Report (1930), p. 558. Chadsey was only fifty-nine. The state superintendent's annual report, customarily a vehicle for eulogizing departed educational leaders, appeared to take no notice, except to record that Acting Dean Monroe had issued the College's contribution which, of course, noted the Dean's passing (38th SSPI [1930]). Obituaries for Chadsey and notices of Kinley's retirement in the school journals were almost embarrassingly (but perhaps necessarily) modest, in contrast to the traditional panegyrics.

budding promise of the previous decade was not hard to account for. Except possibly during a few brief months, Charles Chadsey had never been the Dean. His promised vision and talents had been rigidly contained within the conception of the College and the deanship held by the University administration. He might have been a man peculiarly fitted to offer the schools the kind of practical leadership which—rightly or wrongly—they were seeking. But it was Kinley, not Chadsey, who had charted the path.

CHAPTER 9

ᘓᘓ New Foundations

On "Black Friday," October 29, 1929, the American economy fell into the most severe and frightening depression in its history. With its fall, the old order in American life began to collapse. A few months later, Charles Ernest Chadsey was dead and David Kinley ready to retire from the lonely eminence he had fashioned for himself as President. The conjunction of these events meant that, after a brief interregnum, there would be a new dean, a new president, and a wholly new set of conditions which would affect not only the College and the University, but society and education in general. Although retrospect may sharpen such turning points overmuch, there is no doubt that the events of the year 1929–30 represented a pivotal moment in the College and the world outside. Therefore, our first concern in this chapter will be to describe and illustrate the pervasive effect of this revolution as it touched the College, the University, and the schools. Then we shall examine the philosophy which Chadsey's successor brought to his work and begin to inspect the program with which he hoped to make that philosophy operative.

When Chadsey unexpectedly died in the opening days of April, 1930, there was clearly only one member of the faculty who possessed the requisite personality and commanded sufficiently universal respect to keep the demoralized College alive. That man was Walter

Scott Monroe, professor of education and director of the Bureau of Educational Research. President Kinley, quickly conferring with his successor-elect, President Harry Woodburn Chase of the University of North Carolina, temporarily appointed Monroe to finish Chadsey's term. In the fall, the Board of Trustees increased his monthly salary by $75, since he continued to bear all his previous responsibilities as well, and gave him regular appointment as Acting Dean.[1]

Whether Dean Monroe had any well-defined plans to restore the vigor of the College is difficult to determine. In any case, the times were obviously not propitious for enlargement, nor did his interim status encourage it. Reviewing his first year of administration as a whole, Monroe felt compelled to characterize it as "uneventful," except for the choice of the "successor of Dean C. E. Chadsey"—which suggests that even he did not think of his own term as a deanship. Whether recognized or not, however, important changes were taking place which would become major themes in the next College administration. Most obviously, the schools and their teachers were reeling under the social and financial effects of the Depression, by now in full swing.[2]

In 1930 the common schools of Illinois had in most respects begun to look like the institutions we know today. At the secondary level, there were now nearly 1,000 high schools. Over two-thirds of them were full four-year institutions enrolling all but a very small fraction of the more than 300,000 secondary pupils. The state now had a population of over 7.6 million and of all those eligible for schooling, public schools were enrolling about 68 percent and the private schools another 14 percent, a total of some 82 percent—a significant increase even over the recent past. Most of the gap, of course, existed at the higher secondary level: while there were over 136,000 students in the ninth grade, only something more than 40,000 had reached the twelfth.[3] Here the Depression came to play a decisive and curiously positive role. Lacking opportunity for the once necessary or desired employment,

[1] Kinley to Chase, April 9, 1930, and accompanying correspondence, in Chase Correspondence. Chase accepted responsibility for the necessary appointments, but Kinley handled matters for some time. See also 35th *Report* (1930), pp. 558, 580. Monroe was first appointed May 9.
[2] College of Education "Annual Report" (1930–31), p. 1, College of Education Papers. Even the report on Monroe's own Bureau of Educational Research sounded tired: the Acting Dean reported its efforts diminished due to use of its personnel for instructional purposes, but at least it had produced "about the same number of pages" as before!
[3] 38th SSPI (1930), pp. 1, 11ff., passim.

students simply tended to stay in school, and enrollments began to soar. While only 50 percent of high school-age young people were actually enrolled in 1929–30, by 1935 the figure had reached 70 percent. At the same time, however, fewer and fewer could easily go on to the expensive education necessary to become teachers, and less and less money was available to operate the schools themselves. In short, the schools witnessed the greatest demand in their history; yet they were financially among the hardest hit of all public institutions, for reasons which we shall see more carefully in a moment.[4]

At the elementary level, while the state had made enormous strides in its cities and towns, the relative disparity of rural schools was still actually increasing. More than 10,000 one-room schools survived—in fact, forty-nine new ones had just been built—of which only a little over two-thirds met minimum state standards. More than 3,700 of these tiny schools enrolled fifteen pupils or less. In this respect Illinois was, especially relative to its population and wealth, one of the most backward states in the nation educationally.[5]

School revenues fell precipitously with the Depression, of course, but their decline was exacerbated by the peculiar source of the schools' income. The common schools, then as now, were almost entirely dependent upon personal property and real estate taxes. And it was primarily these taxes which were in default. As a consequence, the school systems were often going completely broke. Tied to a

[4] Thomas E. Benner's "Social Changes Require a Changed Curriculum" (prepared about 1935 and later reprinted in the *Illinois Teacher*) and "Education and the New Deal as Reflected in the Cleveland Meetings of the National Education Association" (an address for Phi Delta Kappa meeting, April 10, 1934), both in Benner Papers. Note that the interpretations of these developments in the schools and the teaching "profession"—a term which needs qualification wherever it is used in this volume, since it represented more of a hope than a reality—are principally those of Dean Benner. The evidence suggests the picture of the schools as he saw it and on the basis of which he developed his strategy. See also Edward F. Potthoff, "Some Factors Which Should Guide the University of Illinois in the Education of Teachers for Illinois High Schools." This fourteen-page mimeographed summary "for purposes of discussion," dated July 28, 1936, may be found in Record Series 2/9/1, no. 18, under Benner to Willard, September 30, 1936. The study, which had been underway for some four years and had enjoyed the patronage of the North Central Association, is more important both as describing conditions and as formative in College and University strategy. The results were produced and published in many different forms emphasizing various aspects. See, for example, twenty-two-page version under H. B. Johnston to M. T. McClure, February 11, 1938, in Record Series 2/9/1, no. 26. Wider use of the Potthoff study can also be found in 42nd SSPI (1938), pp. 78ff.

[5] 38th SSPI (1930), pp. 9, 10.

rigid property-evaluation system which adequately reflected neither general prosperity nor general decline, the school systems were almost totally denied funds, especially in rural areas. Where their demands were honored, the distasteful consequence was foreclosure on an impoverished populace—an atmosphere less than conducive to educational progress, obviously. Many, including future Dean Thomas Eliot Benner, were advocating state and even federal sales taxes directly on behalf of the schools to break the double swath cut by the sword of financial distress. Such a tax would, they believed, both reduce foreclosures and still keep the schools alive.[6]

The teaching force had made remarkable progress at all levels in the previous decade. In terms of academic credentials they were far more proficient than their predecessors. At the elementary level, of the nearly 48,000 teachers, more than 27,000 were graduates of colleges, teachers' colleges, or at least two-year normal school programs. Of the remainder, almost 20,000 had at least some preparation beyond the secondary level. A bare thousand had completed less than a full high school program, and almost no one was now entering the profession directly after high school graduation. Of the more than 11,000 secondary teachers, in excess of 9,000 were now graduates of colleges, universities, or four-year teachers' colleges. Only 198 had finished high school alone, and only five had failed even to complete that. Two-year normal school graduates, once common at every level, now comprised less than 10 percent of the secondary teaching force.[7]

But in spite of apparent quantitative improvements, the quality of

[6] Discussion of Michigan tax situation and similar conditions in Illinois under Benner to Chase, October 18, 1932, Chase Correspondence. The whole presents an interesting picture of conditions in the schools during the Depression. For more on the Illinois problem, see *Illinois Teacher* 23 (September, 1934): 3. The state, legally responsible for distributing some $10.5 million to elementary schools annually, had not met that figure since 1929. In fact, it was now (1934) $9.5 million in arrears, and the distributive school fund was $7 million in arrears for the year 1934 alone. See also H. M. Thrasher, "Illinois High Schools in Crisis," ibid. (November, 1934): 83ff., 90. Assessed valuation of Illinois property had dropped from $8.7 billion to $6.4 billion between 1927 and 1933. A further problem was the glaring inequity from district to district: some counties had assessed valuations six times larger than others, some districts 128 times as large as others. One district had an assessed valuation per pupil in attendance 428 times as large as another, and some poor districts were actually able to fund at less than $20 per pupil. See editorial "Be Ready to Answer" (by Robert C. Moore, Secretary of the Illinois State Teachers' Association), ibid. (January, 1935): 139.
[7] Ibid., pp. 2, 3, 9, 12. There were also now 2,751 teachers of "special subjects" such as music, drawing, etc.

academic and professional preparation of these teachers was still far from satisfactory. It had perhaps grown even worse, at least relative to the new conditions. If the high school was to become in fact what it had long been in rhetoric, the "people's college" which offered a liberalizing general education to the majority of citizens, it was abundantly evident that the high school teacher of the day was neither giving nor probably capable of giving that liberal education. The reason for this was twofold. In part it was due to the inadequacy of the high school itself. But the reason which particularly rankled the College's future dean, and which he found the "stumbling block" of reform, was that most high school teachers had themselves reached nothing which "could be called a truly liberal education." The empirical evidence was at hand, turned up through an exhaustive study carried on by one of the College's own faculty, Professor Edward F. Potthoff. (Other investigations, on a regional and national basis, confirmed the belief that Illinois was no glaring exception.) [8]

The picture these surveys painted was dismal indeed. In general, most arts teachers had no science, most science teachers had no adequate background in the arts, and the prevailing lack of any general education requirements for certification legalized their shortcomings. Furthermore, and of crucial importance, high school teachers taught general areas, not carefully restricted specialties. They were required to be "science" teachers, not even "botanists"—much less the paleobotanists or vertebrate zoologists which the colleges and universities were graduating. And in Illinois, Potthoff showed, a heavy percentage of teachers were teaching not only several courses but courses in three or more departmental areas, often with little or no preparation at all. Consequently students preparing to teach spread even their specialized preparation as thinly as possible over a maximum number of "areas" in order to gain economic viability in the job market. Finally, not only

---

[8] For this and the following paragraph, see Potthoff Report, (both 1936 and 1938 summaries—for location see note 4); William S. Gray, ed., *The Academic and Professional Preparation of Secondary Teachers* (vol. 7, "Proceedings of the Institute for Administrative Officers of Higher Institutions, 1935," Chicago, 1935), esp. Gray's summary, pp. 229–33, and Dean Benner's contribution, pp. 22–30. Cf. vol. *6, General Education, Its Nature, Scope, and Essential Elements* (1934). See also Benner's address, "What Subject Matter Preparation Is Desirable for Secondary School Teachers," delivered to the North Central Association, April 12, [1935?], in Benner Papers. The last contains a general review of national programs assessing the situation. The quotations are from Benner to Henry Suzzallo (then with the Carnegie Foundation), May 4, 1933, Chase Correspondence. For other inquiries into the schools and the preparation of the teachers during the 1930's, (studies which were also very influential), see Bibliography.

was their special preparation frequently superficial, and their general education almost entirely lacking as a result of trying to squeeze out as many marketable specialties as possible; training within their specialties was also outrageously narrow. For example, in Iowa (where, as elsewhere, most "science teachers" had to teach more than one science course), 91 percent of the physics teachers had never had any biology. Even in California, where standards were relatively strict, one-fourth of the biology teachers had never had any other science at all.

As we have already mentioned, part of the difficulty in providing adequate general education at the secondary level lay in the stage of development of the high schools themselves. Although they were now present in virtually every area in Illinois, many were still pitifully small—the average enrollment nationally was barely over 100—and the move toward consolidation had still borne little fruit. The result again was the schools' demand for pedagogical jacks-of-all-trades. The studies of Potthoff and Gray had brought this problem sharply into view. The principal thrust of the Gray report was that the whole shape and content of teacher preparation was dangerously inadequate. Potthoff's study, which ran from 1933 to 1936 and eventually came under the auspices of the prestigious North Central Association, investigated a particular facet of this problem. It primarily focused on the relationship of actual teaching demands to the program of preparation. Potthoff found that more than 80 percent of all teachers (except for those in the "special" subjects) were actually offering instruction outside their major field. In Illinois in 1931–32, for instance, the 3,490 teachers who staffed the high schools of twenty teachers or less were teaching 716 different combinations of subjects. To put it another way, only about five teachers were teaching any one combination. In fact 96 percent of all combinations were taught by less than twenty teachers. The implications for academic content preparation were obvious.[9]

Furthermore, the high school curriculum was itself changing radically, moving away from the disciplinary orientation which had been

[9] Benner's "What Subject Matter Preparation Is Desirable for Secondary School Teachers," esp. pp. 3, 7; and his "Education in Illinois," both in Benner Papers. In the latter, Benner noted that there were more than 12,000 separate school districts in the nation, and that Illinois had more "one-room districts" than any other state. The Dean's figures for Illinois were drawn from the Potthoff study. (See note 4.) In the mid-1930's, Illinois still had 7 percent of all one-room schools in the nation, and 2,656 of its schools still enrolled less than ten pupils (41st SSPI [1936], p. 14).

appropriate when it was designed primarily as preparation for the traditional colleges and universities. Curricular study had been forced on the high school by the chaotic social and economic situation. When widespread unemployment had finally ended child-labor practices and the high schools were bulging, the "selective character" of high school education had to give way to a general function, based upon the demands of a new and broader constituency.[10]

The curriculum was tending more and more toward "explicit social functionalism," becoming more "democratic" and more "American" in its emphasis. By now, two-thirds of those in the high schools were not interested in or able to consider college, and the provision of exclusively college-bound "tracks" was simply unrealistic. When the College of Education came to accept this new educational logic, its leaders were not, of course, arguing for vocationalism or cultural barbarism—quite the reverse. Their point, in concert with many others, was that this terminal position implied an increased, broad general education task, not a reduced one—and one that could not be left to the colleges. Furthermore, as Dewey and his disciples had been pointing out for some time, it was no longer possible to convey the *whole body* of cultural knowledge to anyone, let alone to the random secondary student. As a consequence, a definite thrust toward a more general and methodologically oriented course of study was indicated. But that ran counter to the rapidly increasing specialism in the colleges and heightened the fears of the disciplinary aficionados under whom prospective teachers were trained.[11]

The teaching force in Illinois was making these new needs perfectly clear. The teaching profession, though often stricken with abject poverty, faced with such radically increased demands, responded with an act of faith in its own essential function: the answer was more education. Except for those very badly prepared teachers who felt

[10] According to the federal census data, Benner reported, children (aged 10–15) who were gainfully employed had increased both in percentage and in raw numbers until 1910, when a peak of 18.4 percent was reached. By 1930 this had fallen to 4.7 percent and was expected to be less than 1 percent by 1934. High schools had enrolled about 0.5 million in 1900; by 1930 they were at 4.5 million, with another million in growth expected by 1934. (See "Education and the New Deal . . ." in Benner Papers.)

According to Charles H. Judd, in 1870 the total of all high school subjects taught in the nation was nine; by 1930, 250 were offered. See William S. Gray, ed., *The Training of College Teachers* (vol. 2, "Proceedings of the Institute for Administrative Officers of Higher Institutions, 1930" [Chicago, 1930]), p. 97.

[11] 1938 summary of Potthoff Report, in Record Series 2/9/1, no. 26, esp. pp. 6, 13. The Deweyan motif is very strong throughout.

compelled to support a system which permitted them to spread themselves as thin as their knowledge, most wanted more education, more
reeducation, and more stringent certification requirements. They
wanted extension courses to guide their halting attempts at curricular
reform, and they wanted courses set in terms of their new educational problems, not rigidly structured by traditional disciplinary
precedents.[12] New philosophical issues were also presenting themselves. The move toward curriculum reconstruction had raised the
issue, still unsettled in American educational history, of precisely who
was the repository of teaching authority, the teacher or the community. (It was now becoming popular to call teachers whose hopes
for curricular reconstruction were too unusual, "Reds.") [13] By the
waning years of the decade, the teachers' demands had been partially
answered at the certification level. The new limited state high school
certificate provided for no acknowledgment of studies of less than
sixteen hours, allowing either three "majors" or one single and one
double major. This was hardly satisfactory, of course, but it was bet-

[12] Ibid., pp. 1ff., 6–12. See J. W. Carrington, "Meeting the New Demands on
Education—*A Plea for a Concerted Attack upon the Problems Facing the Public
Schools*" in *Illinois Teacher* 23 (January, 1935): 131ff., 149.
   Just how poor many teachers were, especially in the southern half of the
state, is difficult to imagine. The *Illinois Teacher* was dotted with large advertisements (sometimes full-page) throughout the Depression period which offered
discreet loans to school personnel, keyed with pictures of anxious teachers
puzzling over their financial problems and saying, "I just had to have some
money." Household Finance Corporation advertised its special "Household
Teachers Loan," for which "only your teaching contract is needed as a reference." But conditions need not be inferred from the apparent market: a teacher
had written to the journal in April, 1936, and the editor used her case for his
editorial pleading for federal help. She had collected eleven unpaid "orders"
for back wages from 1931–33, totaling nearly $1,200, and the school coffers were
empty. Although going on and off relief, she had refused to give up teaching.
"Hundreds" of teachers were in similar straits, the editor maintained. (See
Illinois Teacher 24 [May, 1936]: 289.) For especially bad conditions around the
state (with particular emphasis on the southern districts), see L. R. Grimm,
"Is There an Emergency," *Illinois Teacher* (November, 1936): 68–70; cf.
(October, 1936): 37ff., 57; and Walter Crosby Eells, "An Illinois Argument for
Federal Aid" (September, 1936): 23. The teachers were especially disheartened by
the fact that state revenues (and the general economic level) had risen, yet their
position was still growing worse. They noted that some teachers were making
only $400 a year and doubted that at least two members of the Illinois Educa-
tional Commission (President Robert Wood of Sears-Roebuck and M. J. Spiegel)
who had annual salaries of $85,000 and $59,000 respectively could share their
sense of urgency. (See *Illinois Teacher* 23 [May, 1935]: 286.)
[13] Milo L. Whittaker, "Who Shall Be Master of the School Masters," in *Illinois
Teacher* 23 (April, 1935): 240ff., 264. See also State Superintendent Blair's discussion of the new "loyalty oath" for teachers, in 48th SSPI (1934), p. 27.

ter than what had previously prevailed. And Illinois's inveterate preference for small, locally controlled high schools made grander visions overly sanguine.[14]

Unlike their professional predecessors in the mid-nineteenth century, and in spite of the University's general lack of enthusiasm, the teachers now thought of Urbana as the place to go with their problems and those of their schools. There were no more high school normal programs by 1930, and the old country teachers' institute programs (which had died entirely in some states) were creaking badly. While the development of normal schools into four-year teachers' colleges meant that they could at least theoretically supply the required liberal dimension to teacher preparation at the elementary level, even there it would necessitate a fight against their own tradition. The University believed that, even if successful in their bid for increased breadth, the teachers' colleges could not and should not attempt to satisfy the requirements for preparing secondary teachers or offer graduate work to specialists and administrators.[15] (As we shall see, the interests and

[14] Correspondence under A. J. Janata to C. H. Engle (secretary of the Illinois State Examining Board), January 17, 1938, Willard Correspondence. Positions for teachers were at a premium. Nationally, only 25 percent of graduating teachers could find any employment in 1931, and less than 50 percent in 1934. See Lewis W. Williams, "Opportunities in the Teaching Profession," *Illinois Teacher* 24 (December, 1936): 113, 127. With such conditions, of course, only the best prepared could hope for any employment, and then only if they were willing to accept the pitifully small wages.

By 1940, the schools of Illinois demonstrated further changes, many of them effected by the Depression. Enrolling nearly 1,250,000 pupils (of whom some 380,000 were in high school), they employed nearly 50,000 elementary teachers and almost 14,000 at the secondary level. Although less than 2,500 of these teachers were now merely high school graduates, and 6,200 had their master's degrees (there were now 129 with doctorates), over 41 percent had taught less than two years and less than 1 percent more than twenty. While only 21 percent of those who enrolled in the high schools completed their work in 1930, by 1939, 38 percent did. On the other hand, there were still 3,620 one-room schools (in fact, twenty-seven had just been constructed!) and 654 schools still enrolled five pupils or less. Although operating and capital outlays had increased to more than $65,000,000, for high schools alone, the average annual salary for teachers from 1929–39 was $1503.06, and in seventy-two counties their wages had decreased overall during the period (43rd SSPI [1940], pp. 252–267, 273ff.).

[15] 38th SSPI (1930), pp. 11, 12. The new Dean set forth his views in one of his most important addresses, "Teacher Training and the Liberal College." Benner gave this address at the "Conference on Teacher Training" held on the occasion of the dedication of the new Graduate Education Building at the University of Chicago, March 14, 1932. It was repeated at a meeting of the National Association of High School Inspectors and Supervisors in Washington, D.C., and eventually published in *School and Society* 35 (April 31, 1932). (MS in Benner

intentions of the teachers went largely unheeded by the University, however. Teachers at all levels then turned to these teachers' colleges for the help they wanted, and the teachers' colleges began to respond.) The teachers turned to the University to be prepared and particularly to have their preparation expanded. They pressed for evening courses in the spring of 1932, and for Saturday graduate work that summer. They thronged the special "extra-mural" centers in unprecedented numbers. Under the aegis of the Progressive Education Association, the teachers explored the socioeconomic roots of their situation and tested the validity of their programs in the famous "Eight-Year Study." The State Teachers' Association bristled with activity. Research, analysis, and reappraisal were everywhere, and leadership was needed. But the University to which they turned was itself in dire straits and was forced, quite as they were, to wrestle with changing times.[16]

A suddenly impoverished state and an impoverished population could afford to send neither funds nor students: budgets and general enrollments at Urbana plummeted. University enrollments slipped only slowly to 11,255 (2,961 attended the summer session) in 1931, but they fell rapidly to 9,926 (2,802) and 9,465 (2,294) in the following two years, not to begin climbing again until after the midpoint of the decade. The University voluntarily cut its asking from $5.6 to $3.9 million during 1931 and 1932, and salaries were reduced by 10 percent across the board. Already submarginal, the University's budget of 1933 was saved from further radical diminution by stringent limitations on its requests, and it held fairly steady for the next few years.[17]

Papers. See esp. pp. 6–8, 12ff.) If the teachers' colleges succeeded—which he seems to suggest they wouldn't—Benner believed they might become "the outstanding institutions of liberal education in the United States" (p. 13).

[16] For the teachers' requests, see Chase to Benner, March 16, 1932; R. W. Hyndman to Benner, June 13, 1932; in Chase Correspondence. According to Director Robert B. Browne, of the some 3,700 students attending the summer session in 1936–37, almost half were teachers in public and private schools, and a "considerable proportion were preparing to teach" (42nd SSPI [1938], p. 114). For the teachers' attempts to cope with their new situation through the work of the Progressive Education Association, see files of that title in Record Series 2/9/1, nos. 5, 13. By the end of the 1930's, the college and university route to teaching was virtually completely established. During the 1938–40 biennium, 7,627 teachers were given certificates by academic credentials, and only 411 (including 350 at the elementary level) by examination (43rd SSPI [1940], pp. 54ff.).

[17] For the general financial situation at the University, see 36th *Report* (1932), pp. 502, 510, 512, 526, 560, 601, 606—a series of special reports designed to acquaint the Trustees with the University's financial condition. For salary cuts, see pp. 55off., and 37th *Report* (1934), p. 183. Cutting and (more important)

The lack of money was by no means the University's only difficulty —perhaps not even its chief one. The time had also come for a thorough reexamination of its nature and operation as an institution of higher learning. In its new President, the University had found the man to recognize the importance of that challenge and one with the courage to meet it. Harry Woodburn Chase, born in Groveland, Massachusetts, in 1883, had received his bachelor's and master's degrees at Dartmouth College (1904 and 1908). His Ph.D. (1910) had been earned at Clark University, however, in the relatively new field of psychology. While pursuing his doctorate, Chase had directed a clinic for subnormal children at Clark, and upon completion of his work he accepted a post in psychology at the University of North Carolina. Both popular and effective, Chase was made Acting Dean of the College of Liberal Arts in 1918 and advanced to the presidency in 1919, a position he held until called to Illinois.

As gregarious, urbane, and gentle as Kinley was distant, intensive, and pugnacious, Chase moved easily not only in academic circles but in a wide range of civic and cultural areas. His enormous list of affiliations and honors both at home and abroad demonstrated both his academic and his social competence. His uncompromising belief in public education was evidenced by continued leadership in the field and later won him the gold medal of the New York Academy of Public Education (1948). Unlike Kinley, Chase appeared to bring no preconceived notions about the nature or value of a college of education when he arrived on campus. He viewed his entire faculty as colleagues worthy of being entrusted with increased responsibility, rather than seeing himself as a taskmaster charged with curbing their dangerous tendencies. His interpretation of a faculty may have been, prac-

---

holding the budget level as high as possible involved intricate political maneuvers in Springfield too complex to be treated adequately here. For extensive evidence, see, for example, the [Governor] Horner File, Record Series 2/7/1, no. 53; cf. under Benner to Janata, May 5, 1933; Benner's May, 1933, correspondence, esp. with Mrs. Laura Hughes Lundy (of the Illinois League of Women Voters); Janata to Benner, April 12, 1933; H. B. Johnston to Benner, June 8, 1933; all in Chase Correspondence. As this evidence suggests, the College's new Dean took an active part in the "educational" campaign to persuade the populace and its legislature that schools and colleges should not be cut short. However, it was George Huff, the popular athletic director, who seems to have been one of the University's chief "lobbyists" in Springfield. For evidence, see Huff File in Record Series 2/7/1, no. 10 (esp. Huff to Chase, September 22, 1930) and no. 53 (esp. Chase to Huff, March 24, 1933). For enrollment changes, see statistical tabulations in *Catalogue* (1931–32), (1932–33), (1933–34), (1934–35).

tically speaking, optimistic. Given the nineteenth-century character of administration perpetuated by his predecessor, the University was not, as a whole, prepared to accept that optimistic interpretation, but it did open up new possibilities.

Under Kinley the University had tended to return to the heavily centralized, downward-oriented concept of leadership which had characterized the campus before establishment of the Faculty Senate in 1901. Kinley was inclined to deal with a limited group of administrative personnel rather than with the faculty as a whole, and he rigidly respected existing departmental power structures. Within a few weeks of his arrival, President Chase attempted a frontal assault on the status quo. He saw that size alone now made any such concentration of leadership inadequate, and he realized fully the social and educational implication which had accompanied that style of leadership.[18] On November 19, 1930, the President encouraged the University Senate to repossess its emasculated powers by charging its members to undertake "a comprehensive study of the general educational organization and administration of the University. . . ." On December 1, the Senate responded by ordering the creation of the famous "Committee of Nine" to fulfill the assigned task. Under the chairmanship of A. J. Harno, and including E. H. Cameron from the College of Education, the Committee set to work, broadening its efforts and representation by establishing a number of subcommittees with particular responsibilities. In spite of the extension in its personnel, however, the study still tended heavily to reflect the seniority-preoccupied Senate (which was essentially limited to full professors). But change was in the air, and the younger men on the campus formed their own informal committee; many of their resolutions made more interesting reading than those of their elders.[19]

[18] This trend was also specifically recognized by the survey commission of the American Council on Education which examined the University's progress in 1943. See their *University of Illinois Survey Report* (n.p. [Washington, D.C.], 1943), pp. 25–27.

[19] For development of the self-study, see Chase to University Senate, November 19, 1930, and other matter in Self-Survey File, Record Series 2/7/1, no. 60. For the Senate's establishment of the "Committee of Nine," see Senate Minutes, Record Series 2/7/1, no. 19 (esp. G. P. Tuttle to Chase, December 2, 1930). Note that early suggestions for personnel included Griffith and Seybolt, as well as Cameron. The Committee finally included (besides Harno and Cameron) E. L. Bogart, H. F. Fletcher, M. T. McClure, H. F. Moore, W. A. Oldfather, H. P. Rusk, and P. L. Windsor. H. E. Cunningham was secretary (Senate File, Record Series 2/7/1, no. 19). For the "informal" committee, see Chase to H. N. Hillebrand (who acted as their secretary), June 15, 1931, in Self-Survey

By February, 1932, the Committee had done its work and asked to be discharged. In spite of more than a hint of stuffiness (confirmed by a rapid tendency to fall back into the old ways when the work was done), the University's eldest statesmen had ranged widely and deeply. They proposed a number of important reforms in the areas of organization and tenure, and a revision of the statutes, among other things.[20] Although on the whole Education was little affected directly, there were two matters of tangential significance to the College: upon recommendation of the subcommittee which investigated "Health Service, Sanitation of Buildings and Grounds; the Athletic Association; the Department of Physical Welfare; and the Scholastic Subsidy of Athletes"—a bewildering set of inquiries indeed!—the Committee of Nine proposed integration of all the health and physical education work and its removal from the College of Education. The Senate accepted the proposal, but held it up pending examination of a similar experiment at the University of Pennsylvania. The results apparently favorable, a new "School of Physical Education" was carefully detailed and approved by the Board of Trustees on June 11, 1932, and the College of Education was free to go its own way.[21]

The second (and in the long run far more significant) matter was the creation of a new unit for "self study." The survey had produced so much data and raised so many issues that Chase thought it "ought to be continued and its materials kept up to date." Accordingly, in the summer of 1933 a "Bureau of Institutional Research" was established to work up budgetary advice for the President's office. The Bureau was put under the direction of Coleman Roberts Griffith, who had recently joined the staff of the College of Education, and Arthur H. Winakor of the Bureau of Business Research.[22] Griffith, who

File, Record Series 2/7/1, no. 60. One of their suggestions was that the University take "complete control" of athletics.

[20] Senate minutes (February 1, 1932) in Record Series 2/7/1, no. 40. For results, see previous location and also Senate File in Record Series 2/7/1, no. 9; Self-Survey File in 2/7/1, no. 60, esp. mimeographed "Final Statement."

[21] For action regarding the School of Physical Education, see Senate minutes (October 19, 1931, June 6, 1932) in Record Series 2/7/1, no. 40; G. P. Tuttle to Chase, in Senate File, Record Series 2/7/1, no. 40. The change was suggested on the grounds that the split authority in athletic matters was confusing, that professional curricula needed integrating, and that it would cost little or nothing. There is no evidence that the move was sponsored by the College of Education—in fact, it lost a profitable operation—and no College personnel were on the subcommittee.

[22] Chase to A. H. Daniels, July 5, 1933, in Self-Survey File, Record Series

rapidly assumed leadership of the Bureau and fashioned almost single-handedly its function in both College and University affairs, thereby became a leading figure in the subsequent development of the College of Education. Born in Guthrie Center, Iowa, in 1893, Griffith had taken his bachelor's degree at Greenville (Illinois) College and come up to Urbana to do graduate work in psychology, achieving a Ph.D. in 1920. Except for a brief stint at the University of Berlin on a Guggenheim fellowship, Griffith spent his entire career at Urbana. As his dissertation suggested ("The Organic and Mental Effects of Repeated Bodily Rotations"), he became a specialist in the psychological aspects of physical education and athletics, in connection with which he conducted considerable research and amassed a sizable volume of publications. Under Griffith's guidance the Bureau of Institutional Research soon crossed the line between data-gathering and program analysis and evaluation. It assumed a unique policy-making role which will be of primary importance in connection with later events.

The zeal for self-examination and reorganization was not restricted to Illinois. Especially since just after the turn of the century, American higher education in general had been a highly self-critical institution. In spite of periods and pockets of conservatism, the American university, spurred on by critics and prophets within and without, had looked almost continuously into the dark nooks and crannies of its organization and program. While Kinley had resisted much of this tendency, Chase let it loose, not grudgingly but enthusiastically. Not only large, formal inquiries were encouraged; many others of a smaller and more private nature went on as well. Together with the pressing burden imposed by social and financial crisis (which had of course added considerably to the desire for reappraisal), the constant atmosphere of inquiry and evaluation doubtless kept both faculty and administration somewhat at nerve ends during much of the 1930's, and even into the 1940's.[23]

2/7/1, no. 40. See also Griffith's memoranda explaining and justifying his work, same location.

[23] By 1932, the Senate issued a "warning" of possible action against "bureaus and surveys," which it thought were beginning to threaten the University's "main" function. (See Janata to Monroe, April 29, 1932, Chase Correspondence. See also special committee to study "measures of economy and efficiency," which reported confidentially to the Council of Administration on March 28, 1933; see Self-Survey File in Record Series 2/7/1, no. 41.) The committee found, inter alia, that "reorganization seems to be indicated" in many of the professional curricula. (Other and larger-scale inquiries will be noted later as they bear on the narrative.)

Chase's predilection for inquiry and reform were not the only habits which did not serve to make his life (or that of the institution) easier. While attractive from our vantage point, his style and personality developed into issues themselves. Chase was among those presidents of the University who attempted to relate themselves not exclusively to the legislature or the Board of Trustees, or even to the internal administrative structure, but to rank and file faculty members and even to ordinary students. He was perceptive and sympathetic in considering the difficulties of undergraduates as they struggled to pursue academic careers in the throes of social and financial upheaval. His sensitivity extended even to the students at University High School— students whom another high university administrator, still in the Kinley vein, could refer to as "laboratory specimens." [24] And the new President also mounted a frontal assault on the straight-laced mores and folkways which encumbered the institution, a campaign in which his attractive and gracious wife set a new (and likewise controversial) standard of female style. For example, he was the first to breach the long-standing rule on smoking; she was among the first women to do it at all—at least publicly. Since a change in the written code would have been unthinkable even at this late date and would only have occasioned acrimonious debate, Chase simply encouraged faculty members to smoke in their offices if they wished (after due precaution had been taken). But such cavalier disregard of sound morals did not go unnoticed.[25]

It was an exciting and refreshing administration, one might presume to judge, but also and perhaps necessarily a brief one. It seems likely that Chase must have himself seen that, given the recent past, anyone's presidency could have been at most only a brief and liberating inter-

[24] For Chase's attitude toward students, see Chase to Harno, March 7, 1931, in Self-Survey File, Record Series 2/7/1, no. 60. Regarding High School students, see Chase to Huff, December 11, 1931, and Harno to Chase, December 11, 1931 (the source of the epithet), both in Huff File, Record Series 2/7/1, no. 32. President Chase even reported the deaths of laborers on the physical plant staff in his annual report. (See 39th SSPI [1932], pp. 269ff.)

Dean Benner had come to have strong opinions about the Kinley period and hoped that Chase's successor would not bring about a return to old habits. He filed these hopes with the selection committee for a new president in 1934. See his "Memorandum," under A. C. Willard to Benner, July 31, 1934, Benner Papers. In the memorandum, Benner also claimed that, for all the surveys, the University had remained a "conspicuous exception" to the growing self-criticism characteristic of American universities.

[25] Benner to Chase, December 13, 1931 (in reference to Chase's directive of December 9), Chase Correspondence.

regnum. In any case, and for whatever cause, when he was offered the chancellorship of New York University in the spring of 1933, Chase accepted it, yielding his chair to Arthur H. Daniels, an interim appointment. Chase had let in considerable light and fresh air. The openness which he attempted to bring was not universally welcomed, however, and the University and its Board of Trustees took steps to provide a successor less likely to raise fundamental issues or tread on the toes of established leaders. They could make this virtually certain by choosing one of their own number, a president who had a long history in their own house and betrayed no inclination to social or academic iconoclasm. This they did by electing, after a desultory search, Arthur Cutts Willard, a distinguished professor of heating and ventilation and Acting Dean of the College of Engineering.[26]

Arthur Cutts Willard had been born in 1878 in Washington, D.C. After taking his bachelor's degree in Chemical Engineering at the Massachusetts Institute of Technology in 1904, Willard had taught briefly in California and at George Washington University and had served in the Quartermaster's Corps as an engineer. He came to the University of Illinois in 1913, where he rose to head of the department of mechanical engineering by 1920. Along the way he authored or coauthored several texts and other contributions to his field, and he served as consultant to many federal and civic projects. Among the latter, his work on the Holland and Lincoln Tunnels in New York, and the proposed Chicago subway had gained him a widespread reputation. A quiet man who sometimes appeared bewildered by the rush of conflicting events and opinions, Willard took as his first task the "cooling down" of the system. While tending to return to a centralization of the University in the President's office (and the old administrative network spun off from it), the office itself slipped into many hands. Unlike Kinley, who had managed everything he could for himself, under Willard this academic and administrative bureaucracy proliferated and amassed increased power at home as the President devoted much of his personal attention to the legislature (where he enjoyed conspicuous success) and the University's wealthy industrial alumni and constituency. Never a schoolman, Willard betrayed little interest in, and less knowledge of, the state's dangerously trembling public

[26] The selection committee included Willard himself, along with Roger Adams, A. B. Coble, H. W. Mumford, and a representative from the Chicago Medical Campus. See Senate minutes (April 3, 1933) misfiled with 1931–32 minutes, in Record Series 2/7/1, no. 40. See also 37th *Report* (1934), passim.

educational system. And so, all in all, neither the mood nor the condition of the University (or its administration) could offer much to promise the needed revivification of the moribund College of Education toward which the teachers were addressing their hopes. But it is to that College that we must now turn our particular attention. Whether it should have or not, everything had awaited the coming of a new dean. Since the manner of his selection in itself sheds considerable light on the condition of the College, we shall examine it in some detail.

"Adaptability," President Kinley had proclaimed in charging the nominating committee, should be the final and prime requisite in a new Dean for the College of Education. Unlikely though it may seem, Chadsey had apparently been too obstreperous to suit. There was a vast array of necessary qualities of which Kinley thought the committee ought to be cognizant in its search: a candidate ought to possess high professional standing (as evidenced by publication and stability in his present position), personality, wide acquaintance and the ability to make "contacts," and administrative skills, to note the chief. Little wonder then that the search for such a Hyperion of pedagogical virtue occupied many months and required the canvassing of a veritable army of candidates. The committee itself was a curious assemblage, and it appeared to betray Kinley's lingering distrust of the educational fraternity. Appointed on April 23, 1930, under the chairmanship of A. H. Daniels, it numbered no one from the College of Education. The President excused this on the somewhat shaky ground that the Education faculty itself ought to be under consideration, though the record does not support that possibility as either real or desirable. (President Chase corrected the matter by adding Monroe and E. H. Cameron on July 31.) [27]

Under philosopher-dean Daniel's vigorous leadership, the committee was in action within a few days. In mid-May, Monroe, betraying evident fatigue and disenchantment, submitted a few names of his own for consideration, a list remarkable primarily for the fact that it cor-

[27] Kinley to A. H. Daniels, et al., April 23, 1930, Kinley Correspondence. The nominating committee included (besides Daniels) K. C. Babcock, R. D. Carmichael, Herbert Woodrow, and A. W. Clevenger (the Visitor and perhaps the only man in touch with the schools). See also Chase to Daniels, July 31, 1930. Most material on the process of selection can be found in two locations, the Education Deanship, Alphabetical File (where Chase's letter will be found), and Education Deanship, General File, both in Record Series 2/7/1, no. 28.

responded with none of the others. It was quickly evident that both College and University faculty opinion would polarize around Monroe and educational psychologist Cameron themselves. Robert F. Seybolt, although one of the most respected scholars on the staff, was barely mentioned. Unpopular with his own colleagues, he himself supported Cameron most enthusiastically. The committee perhaps wisely (though possibly without intention) virtually disregarded either candidate. Since almost no faculty members entertained both men as possibilities, to have nominated either would likely have split the College irreparably. Instead, their first report, issued on June 13, 1930, unanimously recommended Leonard V. Koos of the University of Chicago, with George A. Works of the same university a distant second choice.[28]

The committee had considered fifty-seven men in its first round alone. Perhaps due to the times, there was no shortage of candidates. Many were figures in educational as well as general academic circles—men such as George F. Zook, W. C. Reavis (the Chicago influence was obvious), Alfred Hall-Quest, and Edward S. Evenden. Others formed a curious lot which reflected the current instability of the academic world and the educational profession. Many were self-entered, especially the superintendents of impoverished school systems and the presidents of shaky colleges and normal schools. Some were obviously notorious characters, such as the president (and, of course, founder) of a "Research University" in Washington, D.C., who boldly announced that he had "made a great discovery in the psychology and pedagogy of thinking that would be of great value to the State of Illinois. . . ." A few were the center of dark and controversial rumors.[29]

By mid-June, when Kinley chose to bring Chase into the picture, the further exploration of prime candidate Leonard V. Koos was under-

---

[28] For Monroe's contribution, see Monroe to Daniels, May 14, 1930, Chase Correspondence. Cameron showed the greater strength locally and was also backed by Charles H. Judd of Chicago. Monroe had some off-campus support as well. A few former faculty members also received recommendations, including L. D. Coffman, B. H. Bode, and W. W. Charters. Secondary Professor Clement suggested George Counts. For all, see Education Deanship, Alphabetical and General Files in Record Series 2/7/1, no. 28. For Seybolt's reputation for unpopularity, see Monroe to Chase, March 16, 1931, Chase Correspondence. For his recommendation, see Seybolt to Daniels, May 17, 1930. For Committee report, see Daniels, et al., to Chase, June 13, 1930, in General File.

[29] For all candidates, see location in previous note. For "Research University," see L. W. Rapeer to Chase, June 24, 1930, Alphabetical File, location above.

taken under the refreshingly benign eye of the President-to-be. Chase immediately sought the confidence of President Coffman of Minnesota and Dean Arps of Ohio State's School of Education. Neither was particularly enthusiastic about Koos, preferring to press for someone who would be more likely to break fresh ground in education. In fact, Arps appears to have given Koos the coup de grace by suggesting that he might be unable to "meet the humanists on their grounds" and by criticizing him as too rigid and unimaginative. In any case, Koos withdrew on his own, and the field was open again. The entire process of selecting the next candidates proceeded under the influence of the President-elect, and the difference in style from the Kinley administration was immediately apparent. It reflected Chase's radically different philosophy and background, a difference that would have significant effect on both dean and College.[30]

The selection committee labored all through the summer and fall of 1930, issuing a report of their activities on December 2. They had drawn up two lists from the welter of names under consideration. The "First List" comprised Edward Samuel Evenden (of Teachers College), George C. Kyte (in elementary education at the University of Michigan) John Cayce Morrison (assistant commissioner of elementary education in New York) and George Frederick Zook (president of the University of Akron). The "Second List" included Francis Leonard Bacon (superintendent of schools in Evanston, Illinois), Julian Edward Butterworth (professor of rural education at Cornell University), F. J. Kelly (president of the University of Idaho), and William C. Reavis (of the University of Chicago). The committee recommended both Kyte and Morrison equally. Since they proposed approaching Morrison first, he was immediately offered an interview, which he promptly declined. At about the same time, Chase submitted (or, perhaps better, conveyed) four names for the committee to consider *if* it cared to do so. They were Bancroft Beatley (a Harvard educational psychologist), Thomas Eliot Benner, Clarence E. Partch (dean of the College of Education at Rutgers), and T. C. McCracken

---

[30] Kinley to Chase, June 14, 1930, in General File (location in n. 28). See L. D. Coffman to Chase, June 24, 1930, in Alphabetical File (location above). Coffman recommended F. J. Kelly (see below) and John K. Norton, research director of the NEA. See also Chase to Arps, June 18, 1930, and connected correspondence, all in Alphabetical File (location above). Arps (who had been at Illinois) preferred H. T. Moore (president of Skidmore College) and George S. Counts to any others. And their exchange of letters is very interesting on the problems the College faced.

(dean of the College of Education at Ohio University). McCracken had already been considered and dismissed (in spite of William C. Bagley's recommendation) on account of his advanced age.[31]

For some reason Kyte was not pursued further, and attention shifted to Kelley. His candidacy, while unsuccessful, demonstrated so perfectly the intrinsic difficulties the new dean would face that it is worth noting. The committee (which, it will be recalled, now included Monroe and Cameron) was actually lukewarm toward him, although the President found him "far more distinguished" than anyone else under consideration. Accordingly, Kelly was brought to the campus to lecture and be on view in early March. Following that appearance, Chase asked every member of the College faculty (as well as others) to record his opinion by letter. The responses were highly significant; they ranged from the highest of praise to virtual vilification, finding in Kelly such disparate qualities as to suggest that two different men had appeared. Again, the most prestigious members of the College faculty took polar positions: Monroe (and those associated with him) found Kelly highly desirable; Seybolt condemned him unreservedly, as did Cameron (somewhat less vituperatively). In general, those in the "academic" fields found him less attractive, but not all. A sizable number of answers, however, revealed that Monroe's own candidacy was still very much alive, since Kelly was frequently compared with him and many thought Monroe at least Kelly's equal if not his superior. Obviously, the College faculty still had no common mind, and the atmosphere was clearly so tense as to bode little good for the future. Chase thanked those who had expressed their opinions and—with, one might suppose, a sigh of relief—reported that Kelly had accepted a post in Washington anyway.[32]

[31] For committee report, see Daniels to Chase, December 2, 1930, and "First List" and "Second List," all in Education Deanship, General File, Record Series 2/7/1, no. 28. See also Chase to J. C. Morrison, December 5, 1930, reply December 10, both in Alphabetical File, same location. For Chase's suggestions (which he made plain were not his candidates as such), see Chase to Daniels, December 15, 1930, Alphabetical File. (Chase had, however, mentioned Benner before; see Chase to Daniels, November 11, 1930, in General File). McCracken was in his mid-fifties.

[32] For committee response, see Daniels to Chase, December 24, 1930; the President's evaluation is in Chase to Daniels, December 26, 1930; both in Alphabetical File, location above. It is sometimes suggested that Benner was Chase's own candidate, but obviously not until later. Chase was very warm toward Kelly, who also enjoyed considerable outside support—see, for example, George A. Works to Daniels, December 22, 1930, same location. For some thirty local reactions to Kelly, see the Alphabetical File (location above). It is possible that

While Morrison and Kelly were still under scrutiny, Benner (although not then a serious candidate) had been invited to participate in the College's regular lecture series on educational issues. He was to appear on the campus on April 6 to discuss education in Mexico. Meanwhile, William C. Bagley had espoused Benner's cause and, once it became evident that none of the other candidates would be both satisfactory and acceptable, attention began to focus on him. Benner's appearance was an almost unqualified success, drawing enthusiastic praise not only from the faculty of the College but throughout the University as well. Within the month, he was offered the post, which he accepted by wire on May 5, 1931. Chase immediately replied that he was "delighted" with Benner's decision. The choice had been made.[33]

Exiled in lurid Latin fashion from the chancellorship of the University of Puerto Rico in 1929 for refusing academic preferment to the *inamorata* of a high government figure, Thomas Eliot Benner was currently a visiting professor in higher educational administration at Teachers College, whence he was quietly seeking a permanent position. Born in Danvers, Massachusetts, February 11, 1894, the new dean had received all of his higher education at Harvard, completing an A.B. in 1914, an A.M. in 1916, an Ed.M. in 1923, and an Ed.D in 1924. Rather widely experienced as a schoolman, Benner taught English at the Merston University School in Baltimore, and had served a high school principalship and several superintendencies in Maine and Massachusetts by 1919. He then moved south to become a statistician and editor for the Alabama state department of education and served briefly as acting dean of the School of Education at Alabama Polytechnic Institute before accepting the appointment to Puerto Rico in 1924. Despite the appearance of his hasty exit, Benner's work at the university there was long and widely praised, and he was welcomed

---

Monroe had originally suggested Kelly (see Monroe to Daniels, June 6, 1930, same location). By this time Monroe's "candidacy" was much stronger than Cameron's. For conclusion, see Chase's letter of appreciation to all contributors, March 17, 1931, same location. By this time the interregnum was itself already proving troublesome; see A. B. Mays to Chase, March 9, 1931, same location.

[33] Daniels to Chase, March 14, 1931, in Benner File, Record Series 2/7/1, no. 3, and accompanying correspondence—including Bagley's recommendation, with its dark reference to "the Illinois situation." See telegrams, Benner to Chase and Chase to Benner, May 11, 1931, both in Education Deanship Alphabetical File, Record Series 2/7/1, no. 28. For appointment, see 36th *Report* (1932), p. 218.

back to it many years later, after the conclusion of his deanship at Illinois, to aid the university's growth and expansion. Governor Theodore Roosevelt, Jr., had endorsed his work enthusiastically and in 1930 proposed him for the presidency of Rutgers. He was seriously considered for the presidency at several other entirely respectable colleges and universities during his tenure at Urbana; Harvard's prestigious Paul Hanus, having heard of Chase's imminent resignation, even thought Benner might be a worthy successor to head Illinois. Frequently called upon for advice in higher educational matters throughout the nation, in the post–World War II years he rendered distinguished service in rebuilding higher education in Austria and Korea. The new Dean was, then, an unusual combination of youth and vigor, with widespread experience beyond that common for a man of his years and in precisely those areas most needed for success at Urbana.[34]

When Benner moved to Urbana to prepare to pick up the reins in the fall of 1931, the prospect could not have been encouraging. Closer inspection and early experience only confirmed the rumors of institutional malaise which had already reverberated in the distant halls of academia. Men of respected strength and judgment would have been understood had they declined the whole business. Benner looked long and hard and warmed to his task.[35]

The College of Education at the University of Illinois in the early 1930's was a place in which those interested in education could expect only to be "bottled up or buried," as a consequence of the deliberate aims of "entrenched and powerful antagonists who determined University policy and attitudes." So spoke one of the nation's most influential educational leaders, Dean Arthur J. Klein of the Ohio State University's School of Education. Although his opinion was delivered in retrospect, Dean Klein claimed much more than personal judgment in support for it, and there is no lack of evidence that he conveyed, albeit sharply, a general belief of the times. Benner quickly discovered a surprising "coolness" toward the College nationally when he accepted the post—an attitude which apparently stemmed principally from the College's "aloofness" from the schools of the state on the one hand and the many national programs (especially those involving

---

[34] Theodore Roosevelt to Benner, November 10, 1930; Paul Hanus to Benner, February 15, June 8, 1933; both in Benner Papers.
[35] For Illinois's reputation, see note 33 above, and following paragraph.

the federal government) on the other.[36] For more than ten years the College had received "but lukewarm support," and as a consequence a once distinguished faculty had been "dissipated," Benner believed. An admitted national leader at the end of World War I, by the early 1930's the College was no longer in sight in the judgment of no less an authority than the American Council on Education. The 1920's had been a time of unprecedented growth for most American colleges of education, but not for Illinois. Other midwestern institutions had nearly doubled their faculties; Illinois's increased by a bare quarter, which now put it only at about half the level of the others in size and power. The same was true of facilities. The campus building boom which Kinley had sparked saw a bare $25,000 devoted to the College of Education.[37]

If the College's reputation was dubious as the 1930's began, its immediate situation was desperate. The Chase administration did not lack conviction about the College's needs; it simply lacked cash. The College's 1931–32 budget, already wholly inadequate to the needs, was slashed still further in the next biennium, and even the original, marginal budget level was not regained until the 1937–38 appropriation.[38] The case of Principal Lewis Williams of University High School illustrated just how marginal it was. He was recommended for salary increase (because of achieving the doctorate) in spite of the budget restrictions of 1932–33, and it was noted he had enjoyed only a $250 raise since 1921. Travel funds necessary for a peripatetic faculty were relentlessly cut, and it was even proposed to "convert

[36] Copy of A. J. Klein to Coleman Griffith, July 10, 1945, Benner Papers. For the significance of this letter, see Ch. 9 below. See also Benner to Willard, June 18, 1935, Willard Correspondence.

[37] College of Education "Annual Reports" (1935–46), p. 1 (the source of the quotations), and (1944–45), pp. 1–3; both in College of Education Papers. These were both prepared by Benner and are especially significant, since he claims that the 1935–36 "Report" was a special faculty project and the 1944–45 "Report" was his extensive review of the College's development under his administration.

[38] The budget (exclusive of the athletic coaching program and other peripheral responsibilities) dropped from $162,475 in 1931–32 to $125,925 in 1933–34. There was no marked improvement until 1937–38 (when it reached $168,067, but included some new responsibilities), and it did not climb significantly above the level which it had obtained at the beginning of the Depression until 1939–40 ($199,915). (See 36th *Report* [1932], pp. 320–22; 37th *Report* [1934], pp. 310–12; 39th *Report* [1938], pp. 398–401; 40th *Report* [1940], pp. 418–22. See also College of Education "Annual Reports" [1935–36], p. 1; [1944–45], pp. 1–3; College of Education Papers.) Note also that Benner had to go to work on possible economy moves within days of his arrival (Benner to Chase, October 7, 1931, Chase Correspondence).

summer session salaries into leaves of absence," a particularly severe penalty for the College of Education due to its heavy involvement in summer programs.[39] University enrollment slipped increasingly from 1931 to 1933, as we have shown, until it leveled off, to begin climbing again only after the midpoint of the decade. The Education enrollment declined more dramatically. From an enrollment of 1,046 (including the athletic coaching program) in 1931, the College bottomed at just over 500 students in 1933 (now without the program) before it slowly began to climb back along with the general University trend. While, as we have said, teachers and prospective teachers wanted to get and improve their educations, they could not very well do so at Urbana, at least without help—help which, as we shall see, the University was singularly reluctant to understand or give.[40]

Salaries were not reduced at once, but heavy general cuts were made in the 1933–34 budget and additional, smaller ones the next year. Benner's own salary was dropped to $7,600 from $9,000, for example, and Cameron's from $7,000 to just over $5,000. Faculty of lesser status were reduced to the $2,500 to $3,000 bracket; instructors and high school personnel got less than that, of course. No one was hired except in extreme necessity, and attrition was eagerly anticipated rather than feared, since it meant added funds to hold the line. By 1935–36, Benner was beginning to "restore" salaries with tiny increments. (He continued to decline them entirely for himself until the first significant general raises in 1937–38, and he never again received his original salary.) Ordinary teachers in the high school were still making from $1,400 to $1,900, and even by 1939–40 most of them were still only in the $1,700–$2,200 range. Clerical workers were receiving something between $100 and $116 per month.[41]

The students were in correspondingly desperate condition. The

[39] Chase to [Deans and Directors], March 6, 1933, College of Education Papers. See also College of Education budget proposal, under Monroe to Chase, May 4, 1931, Chase Correspondence (includes material on Williams). Regarding the summer session proposal, see E. H. Cameron to Chase, April 20, 1933 (and accompanying correspondence), College of Education Papers.

[40] *Catalogues* (1931–32), (1932–33), (1933–34), and (1934–35).

[41] The material in this paragraph is drawn from a general analysis of Board of Trustees' *Reports* and College budget papers and records throughout the period. See esp. 37th *Report* (1934), pp. 310–12; 38th *Report* (1936), pp. 297–300; 39th *Report* (1938), pp. 398–401; 40th *Report* (1940), pp. 418–22; College of Education "Annual Report" (1931–32), p. 1, and accompanying budget charts and economy proposals.

University was forced to establish a "soup kitchen" for those who had almost literally nothing to live on but still refused to give up. With some difficulty, Benner persuaded the Board to allow superintendents, principals, and teachers of school systems cooperating with the University's programs to attend at the same rate that University appointees enjoyed. (Surprisingly, they had previously been required to render full tuition even if they took only a single course.) The Trustees also agreed to accept Chicago Board of Education scrip—but no one else's—for tuition payment, on one condition: those offering it had also to present a promissory note "endorsed by some *responsible* person" and to agree to pay 6 percent interest until they could replace it with "hard cash." That was a hard bargain indeed, and Benner constantly had to fight against the entrepreneurial notion that the students (and especially teachers) should be looked upon as a source of income. He continually argued that a Depression was instead a time for increased service to all the students they could get, and that anything which limited access to the University would bear ill fruit in the future. Neither the Trustees nor the legislature seemed to share this belief, nor (at least as far as common schoolteachers were concerned) did the new University administration.[42]

In spite of such difficulties, however, the College was doing what it could to meet the demands of the schools and their teachers. There were, for example, now more education majors enrolled in graduate work than came from any other area of the University, and the College staff was beginning to be hard pressed. Their students were heavily concentrated in the summer sessions and were largely drawn from a hundred-mile radius of Urbana. Mostly they were in pursuit of the master's degree, now coming to define the upper echelons of professional leadership. As a consequence, Saturday morning work for commuters was expanded. More significantly, for the first time, requests were received for moving the graduate courses to off-campus

[42] For meals for "indigent students," see 37th *Report* (1934), p. 381. For tuition cuts, see 36th *Report* (1932), p. 610; cf. College of Education "Annual Report" (1944-45), p. 3, in College of Education Papers. Note that the University had earlier refused to reduce fees for local schoolteachers doing graduate work: Janata to Monroe, February 19, 1931, Chase Correspondence. For Board attitude on "scrip," see 36th *Report* (1932), p. 445 (italics ours). As we have shown previously, many teachers had received virtually nothing but scrip for their efforts. It seems difficult to justify refusing to accept this paper when they were in fact civil servants who were sacrificing their very livelihood in order to keep the schools open. And, the equation of "responsibility" with solvency was ill considered, to say the least.

centers where they would be within reach of the teaching force. (The peculiar quality and intentions of these students, and the obtaining of a graduate faculty appropriate to their requirements, would, however, pose some considerable difficulties.) [43] The College lent all the weight it could to curricular reform programs. Even President Willard welcomed one such conference on the campus, appealing with characteristic blandness to "citizenship" as the preeminent need and exhorting the assembled educators to "see . . . clearly" in order to "proceed wisely." [44] The College tried to stretch its already overtaut budgets to include increased extension work. It put interns into school systems and attempted to do something about getting its better-trained personnel into the schools—both of which were "expensive" and drew Comptroller Lloyd Morey's ghostly ire. Such unusual assays betrayed, he thought, a tendency to allow programs to rush ahead where funding had not yet tread. [45]

Whatever the appearance of these palliatives, the new Dean had not come to Urbana merely to cut budgets or to steer a comfortable course through the shoals of economic depression. He had in mind a plan which promised a fundamental reconstruction of the process of teacher preparation and a whole new definition of the College's relationship to the schools. That was the real need as he saw it. Both his analysis and his plan were founded upon a very strongly held philosophy, a philosophy which took account of both the social conditions in which the University and the College found themselves and the difficulties inherent in American higher education. Unlike the egregiously distorted popular image of the "progressive educator," Benner did not believe that reforming the teacher (particularly, but not exclusively, at the secondary level) meant refurbishing his methodology, revamping his content in terms of atomistic life situations,

[43] (Monroe's) College of Education "Annual Report" (1930–31), pp. 1–3, College of Education Papers. For more on extramural graduate instruction, see 42nd SSPI (1938), p. 79. By 1937–38, 200 graduate students were in such courses (ibid., p. 130).

[44] "Greetings from President A. C. Willard," under Willard to R. T. Gregg, April 1, 1936, Willard Correspondence. See also College of Education "Annual Report" (1935–36), pp. 4–5, College of Education Papers; and Benner to Willard, January 8, 1936; Harno to Benner, January 27, 1936; both in Willard Correspondence.

[45] Benner to Willard, June 24, 1937; Lloyd Morey to Willard, June 26, 1937; Benner to Willard, July 3, 1937 (a good outline of College programs); all in Willard Correspondence. See also College of Education "Annual Reports" (1936–37), pp. 3, 4, 6, and (1937–38), pp. 6, 8, College of Education Papers.

or revising his archaic social theory. Principally it meant the revitalization of his "general education."

There were two principal strains in Benner's concept of education as he approached this task.[46] First of all, he was strongly convinced that our institutions of higher learning had developed in ways unsuited to the temper of contemporary life and unresponsive to American social and political requirements. The only hope for the nation, in the midst of so severe a crisis, was the enlightened sense of purpose and direction which a *truly liberal* general education could bestow. But the university, Benner thought, had tended to emphasize exclusively the formation of the private intellect, primarily in terms of science.[47] This preeminence of science had come at the expense of "philosophy." By philosophy, Benner meant development of fundamental and intellectually integrative beliefs which could free the educated man from a selfish individualism and provide him with the ability to view his life in broadly social terms. More science in the curriculum could not accomplish this, Benner thought. What was required was the "guiding hand" of a sort of socially oriented moral philosophy. This philosophy ought to be stressed not only in the institutions of higher learning but also in the high school, where we transmute the essentially individual morality inculcated by the home by giving students the needed social character "traits." [48] The unfortunate tendency of the traditional college and university curricula (and the high schools which initiated them) was to provide individual expertise and promote private virtue, and that made them institutionally elitist in character.[49] The true "common good" was no longer the university's

[46] For what follows on Benner's general philosophy of education, we have relied for purposes of quotation principally upon his many addresses and articles, particularly those early in his career at the University. The Dean was, however, very consistent in the way he viewed education and its problems throughout this period; this basic philosophical structure is revealed in all of his work and especially in his "Annual Reports." These addresses are all to be found in the Benner Papers.

[47] "Thoughts about Education for Character," esp. pp. 1–2, 6, Benner Papers.

[48] Ibid., pp. 6, 8. The Dean was, at this point, very much concerned with the Glueck's pioneering work on juvenile "delinquent" behavior, which he saw as confirming his thesis. (See esp. p. 4.) At bottom, Benner saw most of these problems in psychological rather than philosophical terms.

[49] Throughout his career, Benner was concerned with the students at the University, particularly those who had been washed out and needed a "second chance." See, e.g., Willard to Educational Policy Committee, July 21, 1936, copy in College of Education Papers. (The University rejected some of his proposals, however. See Benner to Willard, December 15, 1936, same location.) He was also concerned with developing the "political" awareness of students, which he

principle of discrimination; thus it foundered continually on either a narrowly intellectual research expertise for the few, or a crassly materialistic vocationalism for the many. Both emphases—and narrowly based scholarly inquiry was simply another version of vocationalism —led to the disintegration of early college-level education by specifying its goal as the attempt to refine out and intensively develop particular skills and abilities. The disintegration could be counteracted only by a stiff program of general education.

The scientific monopoly in education (which Benner was even willing to say had in fact *caused* the "social turmoil") and the preoccupation with individual scholarship were the unfortunate fruits of our acceptance of the German university deal. With a candor and perceptiveness somewhat unusual for the times, Benner offered as proof of this criticism the silence of the great continental centers of learning in the rapidly developing European political situation. He hotly disputed Flexner's view of the University as something which could live apart from such problems, and he exalted the "service" concept which was so significant a strain in the land grant tradition—although we must guard against even that becoming a form of "legislation" over others, he thought.[50] (There is, it might be wise to point out, no evidence whatever that Benner was in the slightest degree either antiscientific or antiliterary in spirit. His originally warm acceptance on the campus was, on the contrary, partly a result of his thorough educational background and his entirely literate demeanor.) [51]

The relationship of his general educational philosophy to the particular social demands of the 1930's was crystal clear to Dean Benner, and he did not hesitate to bring the point. Arguing amusingly (though not without force) that nations have cultural depressions just as they have economic ones, he was even prepared to suggest that a cultural depression may have brought on the nation's recent financial collapse. The essence of the cultural depression which had taken place in America was the confusion of "rugged" individual-

---

thought was at a seriously low ebb. (See Benner to Willard, April 2, 1937, College of Education Papers—in which he also pleaded that the newly proposed student "union" should be planned by behavioral scientists to make it more effective in improving student life.)

[50] "Thoughts about Education for Character," esp. p. 6; and his "Remarks" to a dinner for city superintendents (Urbana, November 18, 1931).

[51] For example, he was put on the Senate's important Academic Policy Committee. See Senate minutes (October 19, 1931) in Record Series 2/7/1, no. 40.

ism with "ruthless" individualism. The latter had perverted our beliefs into an affirmation of a kind of "numerical" progress, defined in terms of material changes alone—a perversion which Benner found concretely manifested in the Chicago World's Fair.[52] The educational parallel of this perversion of values was the belief, widespread before the Depression, that "equality of educational opportunity" meant nothing "more than an open road to wealth and power for the individual." [53]

If Benner's convictions about the social crisis were strong, however, neither his political nor his educational responses were doctrinaire. Quite the contrary. He could dismiss the New Deal with damningly faint praise: "In its essence, the so-called new deal is a belated effort to secure recognition of some of the problems which have been created by industrial, economic, and political change, and a belated effort to find solutions for them." [54] Educationally, it followed consistently that "it would be most undesirable if public education in the United States were to determine its program in terms of the New Deal. That program, if it is to be sound, must go back of the New Deal to fundamental values." [55] Yet Benner was in no way a defender of the nation's dangerously overblown commercial interests. Here he found himself in agreement with no less a figure than Boston merchant prince Edward A. Filene. Filene had confessed that education had to grow during this period, if only to wrest the function of value inculcation from the industrial forces which were attacking the schools in order to effect false economies. The Dean was convinced that neither the home (which was no longer self-sufficient and therefore not so educative as it had been) nor the church (which, as Walter Lippmann had persuaded him, was rapidly declining) could any longer meet the challenge. The school alone stood between the populace and the threatened social and cultural disaster.[56]

[52] "Radio and the Cultural Depression," Benner Papers (1934 lecture).
[53] "Revising Educational Opportunity," Benner Papers, [1934?].
[54] From "Education and the New Deal as Reflected in the Cleveland Meetings of the National Education Association," p. 2, Benner Papers.
[55] Opening words of "What Have the Schools Done to Meet the Demands of the New Deal in Education?" (an address to the Illinois City Superintendents Association and the Illinois State School Boards Association, November 22, 1934).
[56] "Education and the New Deal . . . ," pp. 2, 3; "Social Changes Require a Changed Curriculum," pp. 2, 3; cf. "Education and the Social Sciences." All in Benner Papers.

Benner still shared the traditional American distrust of federal government as an instrument. He believed, like many of his fellow educators, that the power to execute policy too easily became the power to make policy. One can imagine his relish when he uncovered what he took to be a case of educational dictatorship inimical to democratic principles in the instructional program of the C.C.C. And, looking back over the potentially dangerous Smith-Hughes program, with their threatening federal tentacles, the Dean rejoiced that Illinois had been "more successful than most state universities in maintaining its independence with regard to federally subsidized educational programs"—a posture which he thought the University "should maintain as completely as possible." [57]

As a consistent extension of his position, Benner never waxed enthusiastic over the Progressive Education Association. Although later called a "moderate progressive," he disagreed sharply with many in their camp (if not with the organization as such) and never tried to make Illinois a center of influence in the movement. Indeed, he found the belief that "teachers could or should determine the nature of the 'new social order'" nothing more than a "silly notion." [58] A group of these folk had been active at the influential "Cleveland Conference" of educators, but they were, he affirmed, a "minority." The "overwhelming majority" had strongly resisted their attempts to "define the nature of the ideal social order and work directly to bring about its establishment." Sensible leaders found such reconstructionism both "impossible and ridiculous" and preferred (well, Benner thought) to seek the "old truths and old ideals," with an appropriately humble acknowledgment of their previous lack of success. A platform stressing the centrality of social change as benignly as this, he argued, although doubtless threatening enough to hard-core conservatives, was acceptable to groups as diverse as President Hoover's commissioners and the American Historical Association. Nor did Benner see this consciously moderate position as removing him from the broader progressive movement in education. The progressive movement was, as he told President Willard, a roomy affair, embracing everything

---

[57] A mildly liberal bulletin, "'You and Machines,'" had been withheld from distribution at C.C.C. camps by the national director. (See Benner to A. J. Janata [and enclosure], January 17, 1935.) The quotation is from Benner to Willard, October 20, 1941. Both in Willard Correspondence.

[58] "What Have the Schools Done to Meet the Demands of the New Deal in Education?" p. 2, Benner Papers.

from "extreme conservatism to the lunatic fringe." Thomas Eliot Benner clearly belonged to neither.[59]

If neither Benner's educational philosophy nor his social and economic convictions would have alienated him from any but the most unregenerate on the Urbana campus, the same could not be said for the conception of teacher preparation which he drew from it. As he informed Henry Suzzallo in 1933, his past experience had given Benner certain convictions about teacher education which had "driven" him "continuously for the past two or three years." The argument behind them was simple and straightforward, and he used every available opportunity to make it public.[60]

The Dean believed the high schools were still the "people's colleges" upon whose health the health of the society depended. They were also the University's particular responsibility, as an institution for teacher preparation distinct from the normal schools or teachers' colleges. If the high schools were to keep the nation healthy, they must give all a truly liberal education—i.e., one such as we have just described, comprised of socially relevant content undergirded by a broadly philosophical and social value orientation. That liberal education would in turn require a truly liberally educated teacher. Now, if the essential requirement of a teacher was that he be liberally educated, and not merely pedagogically competent, the crucial locus of teacher education was in the College of Liberal Arts and Sciences. The College of Education could not really assume the responsibility for it. The educationist's contribution was important and useful, Benner believed—although he was quite willing to see its share of time considerably reduced, especially at the undergraduate level—but it was not and could not be the central focus.[61]

[59] "Education and the New Deal . . . ," esp. p. 3; "Social Changes Require a Changed Curriculum," p. 1. The remarks on the Progressive movement are from Benner to A. J. Janata, October 13, 1936, Willard Correspondence or College of Education Papers. Willard had been asked to discuss "Progressive Education" at a meeting of the National Association of State Universities and appealed to Benner for help in defining what it was. The dean's brief response conveys little enthusiasm or sympathy for it, and defines the movement as a movement of educators "interested in improving the curriculum and procedures of the schools, laying special emphasis upon the problems of the students and some of the newer understandings of individual and social needs."

[60] Benner to Suzzallo, May 4, 1933, copy in Willard Correspondence.

[61] The best source for this is "Teacher Training and the Liberal College," an address given on more than one occasion and eventually published in *School and Society* 25 (April 30, 1932). But see also Suzzallo letter (in previous note) and Benner's later "The Status of Education as a Department of the Graduate

Consistent with his point of view, the new Dean was thoroughly convinced that, no matter the appearances, the common schools' first problem was by no means wholly, or even principally, financial. The socioeconomic situation had merely cast into bold relief the long-present necessity of fundamental educational change. The fall had exposed the intellectual and spiritual poverty of the old education. Pedagogical reform meant, then, for Benner, the recasting of the model teacher in a form materially distinct from the academically aristocratic mold of the past. That possibility in turn rested upon the development of a sound "new" concept for the institutions which prepared teachers and which ought to continue to shape them professionally. Thus the first step was, quite literally, to reform the College and the University. But the tide of American college and university curricular development was then running ever faster against such purposes; and the change in University administration from Chase to Willard meant that this project at Illinois would be more difficult. (While Chase had been entirely open to radical reform in the College of Education, as well as elsewhere, Willard clearly was reluctant if not unable to envision it.) [62]

The fragmentation characteristic of available college courses was the major barrier to well-rounded high school instruction. The colleges virtually had no general education to give prospective teachers, only congeries of special offerings. According to a national study of fifty-seven colleges and universities, in the entire area of English, only two courses were taken by more than 20 percent of those studying in the area: 91 percent took a composition course, and about two-thirds took a general course in English literature. The next most widely taken course, American literature, was taken by only 17.5 percent. The rest of the students' time was spent in highly specialized studies arranged

School" (discussed fully below, Ch. 11). In the last, Benner assails the prevalent but mistaken belief that "the chief purpose of research and teaching in education is the development and inculcation of teaching methods," primarily in disciplinary terms (p. 3).

[62] For Chase's attitude, see, for example, correspondence in connection with a proposal of E. O. May (Robinson Township High School) in Education File, Record Series 2/7/1, no. 28. Willard seems always to have prided himself on being a "realist," disciplining the enthusiasms of those inclined to more radical reform. See, for example, his remarks to those attending the High School Conference, "Looking Ahead in Education," reprinted in *Illinois Teacher* 23 (June, 1935): 332, 339ff. While paying rather uninspired homage to some of the problems teachers were grappling with, Willard could not help cautioning that they were in a "very real and imperfect world"—a counsel they little needed (and perhaps found less than consoling) at the bottom of the Depression.

in a bewildering confusion of patterns. It was no wonder, Benner thought, that one midwestern university had found that high school students outscored its senior history majors on high school history examinations. The university students had covered very little ground. There was little likelihood, Benner concluded, that students with preparations such as these would ever bring any breadth to their specialties, let alone radically improve the general educational background of the nation's secondary schools.[63]

If the College of Liberal Arts and Sciences was really responsible for preparing secondary teachers—as it was and always had been, Benner insisted—and if it had not met its responsibilities, the reason was easy to find. Since general education was the fundamental requirement for a good secondary education, Benner argued, the American high school was in effect "being choked out of existence as a result of the complete domination of the liberal arts college by the graduate levels of instruction."[64] The colleges had sold their humane English souls to the teutonic technicians of the graduate school. Specialization and the attendant fragmentation of areas of inquiry, the hallmark of graduate-level scholarship, had seeped down to the arts colleges and virtually destroyed any possibility of a general educational program. The rapid growth of this tendency during the late nineteenth century, when the German influence was strongest, was obvious. At Wisconsin, for example, undergraduate English electives had increased from two to forty-six in the twenty years following 1885, chemistry from two to thirty-two, and history from two to twenty-eight. Economics, nonexistent at the beginning of the period, offered thirty-three courses by 1905.[65] And due to their own exposure to the graduate school in the course of their training, the liberal arts faculties who taught such courses were both incapable of, and inhospitable to, giving them a general education orientation. The only hope was the provision of some sort of "general culture" faculty, whose curricular criteria and conception of good teaching would be drawn neither from the narrowly commercial nor the technical in-

[63] "Teacher Training and the Liberal College," pp. 8, 9. When another major university had analyzed the programs of its history majors, it found that only four courses were taken by as many as 50 percent of the group: introduction to American history, introduction to European history, English history to 1700, and the teaching of history. The programs of one sample group of ten history majors aggregated forty different courses.

[64] Ibid., p. 1; "Remarks" to High School Conference, November 20, 1931, p. 1—the source of the quotation. Both in Benner Papers.

[65] "Radio and the Cultural Depression," p. 7.

terests of the graduate-level specialists, but from broadly humane concerns. In short, said the Dean, the University's liberal arts college had to be "liberated" from the Graduate School. And for Benner that was no rhetorical commonplace; it was a specific target upon which he set his sights at once, although he did not succeed in setting off the implicit explosion until much later.[66]

With such a philosophy in mind, Dean Benner wasted little time in beginning what fundamental reforms he could. Little more than a year after his coming, the new Dean notified President Chase that, after some "informal discussion" with individual faculty members within the College of Education, he was ready for some "policy" changes. His platform was clear: the proper preparation of secondary school teachers involved first the development of their "general culture," and "socializing of the student." Second, there was the requisite specialization or, as the Dean liked to call it (borrowing a pedagogical barbarism from Glenn Frank), the " 'scholarizing' " of the student. Third, and a distant last in importance, was the provision of the students' professional expertise. Only the last was the province of the College of Education. Since the accomplishment of the first two objectives required a change of heart and an acceptance of responsibility on the part of a domain not under his control (the University's College of Liberal Arts and Sciences and, by implication, the Graduate School), he proclaimed at once that teacher preparation had to become an all-University program. That would take time and a change of disposition; all Benner could do for the moment was to encourage research such as Potthoff's and hope that these dismal observations would move the other colleges and departments to rethink their of-

---

[66] "Teacher Training and the Liberal College," esp. pp. 8, 12. The erstwhile liberal colleges resisted, Benner believed, his equation of "liberal" with "socializing," partly because it would provide less discrimination among students and less justification for flunking out the ordinary ones and preserving the traditional elite corps. (See p. 8.)

It is worth noting that much of this is very similar to Dewey's approach (as, for example, in *Democracy and Education*), although it lacks Dewey's radically scientific orientation. Virtually never, however, did Benner appeal for support to Dewey or to *any* of his leading disciples. In fact, as far as the public posture of the College was concerned (and really from the time of his rise to prominence around the turn of the century), Dewey might as well not have existed. (Dewey did lecture once on education, during Dexter's days, in 1907.) That is not, of course, to suggest that Benner was necessarily either uninformed or antagonistic regarding Dewey's general position. He was later faulted by Coleman Griffith for bringing too many Columbia people in, especially in psychology, but that is about as obvious as any allegiance got.

ferings. We shall examine his efforts to achieve this goal more carefully a few pages on.[67]

In attempting to promote change within his own College, Benner's strategy was to make some small modifications in the undergraduate programs (to bring them more closely into relation with the rapidly changing high school) and then to look ahead to the College's chief task, the development of adequate graduate work along more stringently professional lines. Under the constant pressure to maintain or actually diminish his budget even though state and University revenues were in fact already increasing, Benner scrupulously avoided any attempt to restructure radically the existing courses or programs or to proliferate the offerings. He preferred to alter quietly their spirit and content. As a result, there is little change apparent in the 1930's, either in staff or in courses.

In general, his strategy would involve a gradual shift (as the opportunities presented themselves) from the previous preoccupation with psychology and methods to the problems of curriculum development. That subject was, as Robert Browne said, "the topic of the hour in educational circles" in the 1930's, just as tests and measurements had been in the 1920's. To this modest program Benner added a gentle but insistent attempt to expand the integrating role of philosophically based educational theory, one cast in unmistakably social terms. In so doing he revived at Illinois an area of professional study which had gone virtually unpracticed since the days of Bagley and Bode.[68]

On the eve of the Benner period the *Catalogue* had betrayed obvious sympathies. Of the forty-two courses listed to be offered in a typical

[67] Benner to Chase, October 21, 1932, Chase Correspondence. His first address to the College faculty emphasized the necessity of developing the undergraduate preparation of teachers on an all-University basis. Benner also announced his concern for the teacher's general education and his intention to press for improvements in the programs offered in the other departments and colleges in 41st SSPI (1936), p. 154. He appears to have taken inspiration from, and to have modeled some of his proposals on, reforms being undertaken at Ohio State. (See Benner to Chase, November 16, 1932, Chase Correspondence.) It is interesting to note that these reforms were of considerable reputation and were partly the work of two former College faculty members, W. W. Charters and Boyd Bode. (See William S. Gray, ed., *The Training of College Teachers*, vol. 2, "Proceedings of the Institute for Administrative Officers of Higher Institutions" [Chicago, 1930], esp. pp. 229–32). The Dean seems to have remained loyal to this policy until the 1940's, when he reluctantly came to the conclusion that the other colleges were simply incapable of, or uninterested in, doing anything about it.

[68] For example, Benner to Willard, March 15, April 4, 1935, College of Education Papers. See also *Illinois Teacher* 23 (April, 1935): 246, 255, 262; *Illinois Teacher* 24 (January, 1936): 152 (the source of Browne's remark).

winter term (exclusive of the twenty-two special methods courses actually housed in the College of Liberal Arts and Sciences and the School of Music), a large proportion were concerned with administration and supervision, and eleven were clearly oriented toward educational psychology of a distinctly disciplinary bent. For example, Coleman Griffith offered "Ed. 49 The Principles of Intellectual Development—the facts of animal, folk, and child psychology." The course required two prerequisites in psychology as well as the consent of the instructor. Historical or philosophical foundations were represented only weakly. History of education was required for graduation in the College program and certification, but it was entirely in the academically conservative if competent hands of Robert Francis Seybolt, who maintained a virtually identical format to his course work until he had to abandon his teaching. Some increased breadth was given to the area by bringing in men such as Thomas Woody and Charles F. Arrowood during the summers, or by moving someone of a different persuasion over during Seybolt's frequent absences. Educational philosophy was not required for undergraduates; in fact, it was unavailable. The graduate course in "Educational Theory" was still taught by Cameron, a psychologist, even after 1933 when it was restyled "Philosophy of Education" with no change in description. By the mid-1930's an undergraduate course in "Modern Theories in Education" was added, and by the mid-1940's a new introductory course, "The American Public School," was required by law as an orientation course. The faculty who offered it clearly show that it was an attempt to introduce a particular broadly social-philosophical bent in prospective teachers.[69]

[69] *Catalogue* (1929–30), pp. 251–53. For changes, see *Catalogue* (1932–33), pp. 251ff., and p. 137 (where the following significant statement occurs: "As the aim of these curricula is to prepare students for professional work in the educational system, the College is considered a professional school."). Cf. (1937–38), p. 278; (1938–39), p. 236; (1944–45), p. 275.
According to the 1932–33 *Catalogue*, the College was offering B.S. degrees in education, agricultural education, home economics education, and industrial education. If the student took the B.S. in education, he entered the College in his junior year (otherwise earlier). To graduate, he required 120 hours, including twenty in education (three in educational psychology, two in technic, two or three in special methods, three in principles of secondary education, and three to five in educational practice). Each student was to specialize in two subjects, at least twenty hours in the "first" major and sixteen hours in the "second"—except that agricultural education required forty-nine hours, home economics education thirty-six, and industrial education twenty-five. Those who did not register in the College could prepare for teaching by "electing" College courses while resident

The confusion over what the "foundations" of education were which was strongly evident at Illinois was not exceptional. Educational theory had generally been philosophically derived previous to the turn of the century—even when it was heavily oriented toward speculative psychology—and it had usually possessed a broad social context. During the first quarter of the twentieth century, however, science (and particularly laboratory psychology, with a distinctly disciplinary and narrowly professional cast) had nearly preempted the field. By the 1930's, national events and the intrinsically social orientation of the "progressives" had brought the need for a more general educational theory into the academic limelight once again. The new theories, while much more concerned with political, economic, and social philosophy, still preserved a strong affinity for the social and behavioral sciences, in the best Deweyan fashion.

The difficulty at Illinois was that much of the work in the key areas in psychology and foundations was still in the hands of very strong figures—men such as Seybolt, Cameron, and Griffith—who were essentially men of the 'teens and 1920's. Too old to be likely to change and too young to retire very soon, they were also both legally and popularly beyond ouster. Financial restrictions made outweighing them impossible. The consequence was a growing cleavage which threatened to destroy Benner's entire program. In practice, the Dean chose to pour new content into the old course structures. When able, by the later 1930's, to hire promising junior faculty, Benner got in men whose principal interests and genius lay in broadly philosophical theory to teach both psychology and the "practical" courses. The psychol-

---

in other colleges or schools. There were twenty-eight areas of specialization proposed: agriculture, art, biology, botany, chemistry, civics, commercial subjects, economics, English, general science, geography, German, history, home economics, industrial arts, journalism, Latin, law, library, mathematics, music, physics, physiology, physical education (men's or women's), Spanish, speech, and zoology.

The "Limited State High School [grades 7-12] Certificate," valid for four years, could be had without examination by successful graduates who had six hours in English, fifteen in education (including educational psychology and principles of teaching), and specializations in three subjects (of ten, twelve, and sixteen hours, respectively)—although the College warned that it did "not usually recommend candidates whose preparation does not go beyond these minimum requirements." After four years of successful teaching, and one more year of study, these certificates could be exchanged for "life" certificates. The North Central Association was then requiring (for teachers in schools which it approved) fifteen hours in English, fifteen in education (minimum), fifteen in any foreign language *taught*, fifteen in science (including *at least* five in any science taught), and fifteen in social studies. (See *Catalogue* [1932–33], pp. 137–39.)

ogists he brought subtly but pointedly shaped the thrust of that area into a concern with children, the classroom, and the act of teaching and learning, rather than continuing to emphasize the advance of a traditional laboratory-oriented discipline.[70]

One of Dean Benner's most important reforms, a part of his opening platform for reorganization which he began to set in operation in 1936, dealt with the general methods course, Education 10 or "Technic of Teaching." The teaching of the various sections of this course was gradually transferred to the heads of departments in the University High School and students were registered in sections related to their prospective fields. Thus the laboratory school faculty began to play a much more important role in the undergraduate program, and the College began to give instruction in the teaching of particular subjects on its own, apart from the specialized courses offered in the academic departments. A further consequence was the close integration of practice teaching with methodological instruction.[71]

There were many other changes. Much of the work in supervision and administration was moved to the graduate level, especially during Benner's first five years. The growing emphasis on curriculum was mirrored in new and revised courses which tended to emphasize specific rather than general curriculum problems. Vocational education, both industrial and agricultural, tended to receive increased emphasis at the graduate professional level, while the preparation of teachers at the undergraduate level in these areas lagged. (Home economics began to withdraw from its relationship with the College.) Unfortunately, curricular interest in the rural schools tended to wane in conjunction with the flagging undergraduate agricultural program, in spite of the pressing needs of the schools.

By the fall of 1939, the College of Education felt ready to rewrite substantially its statement of purpose and make public the change of orientation that had taken place within it. The new *Catalogue* stated, somewhat optimistically, that the College was

concerned with learning as a process, the principles and methods of teaching, and the organization of schools as agencies of culture. The courses of study, which are centered on the development of the individ-

[70] For example, *Catalogue* (1940–41), p. 241, where T. V. Smith was brought in to do philosophy of education. Cf. College of Education "Annual Report" (1937–38), esp. pp. 1–3, College of Education Papers.
[71] Benner to Willard, September 16, 1936, Willard Correspondence. Cf. College of Education "Annual Report" (1933–34), p. 3, College of Education Papers.

ual as a social unit, fall into groups dealing with the philosophy, principles, and history of education, the psychology and technology of teaching, the management of school systems, the methods of extension and research, the planning of programs for group instruction and individual activities, the development of attitudes and habits necessary for success in complex environments. These groups have in common the aim of anticipating the needs of students as explorers and cultivators of the fields of learning in which they will become teachers.[72]

The proclamation was premature, more an expression of hope than a description of the actual state of affairs. New Foundations had been laid and the new edifice sketched out; but many of the elements necessary for its completion were not yet ready to be incorporated.

We have already noted that one of the Dean's fundamental goals was the modification of the "academic" content bequeathed to prospective teachers. But the problem of logically and practically integrating and reorganizing teacher preparation in the academic fields required intra-institutional cooperation, and it lagged interminably. In spite of the clear thrust of Potthoff's evidence, virtually no advances were made on the initiative of the departments. Although Dean Benner's frequent homilies on the need for "all-university" assessment were perhaps less specific than they might have been—a failure for which he was to be grievously faulted later—there is little or no evidence to indicate that anyone else even felt much urgency until the 1940's.

Given the University's traditional and centralized methods of control, the first problem was that of providing for the possibility of general curricular change in some more flexible but responsible manner. During this decade, teacher preparation curricula, just as all others, were submitted directly to the all-powerful Senate. There they immediately bore the brunt of the political and philosophical bifurcations and squabbles which characterized the University as a whole. Benner early decided that some intermediary body, where discussion could take place and in which the College could exercise its proper role, was a necessity. The control of academic content, both general and special, lay with the other colleges; as we have noted, Brenner had no quarrel with this arrangement per se. The problem was to secure some regular, operative process for building the various curricula where critical evaluation not only of subject-matter demands but of general education

[72] *Catalogue* (1939–40), p. 159.

and the professional requirements of the schools would have liberty to function.

As early as 1936 the College proposed the creation of a new University body, later to become the "University Committee on Teacher Education," to achieve this objective. This Committee, composed of representatives from all the departments or areas of study in which teachers were to be prepared and open to what Benner saw as the integrative and professional influence of the College, would send on recommendations free of the bias and power ambitions of single departments. By such a procedure, a typical example of the optimistic and somewhat uncritical democratic faith which characterized Benner's actions both within the College and in the wider University, the mortmain of the academic establishment could be broken.[73]

When the logic of a solution seemed clear, Benner believed not only that action should follow immediately but that it would. The establishment, however, from the presidency downward, was in no hurry to accede either to the logic or the practical necessity. An all-University committee, on which Monroe sat as chairman, seconded the College's general concerns in 1939. In spite of reluctance on the part of the Graduate School, Willard appointed an intercollege body during 1941 to explore the problem of teacher education and develop curricula (hopefully in concert with other institutions as well as intramurally), but neither a sizeable group of proposals nor a workable structure would be ready before the mid-1940's.[74]

[73] College of Education "Annual Report" (1935–36), p. 3, College of Education Papers. The committee had its genesis in discussions of the Potthoff Report (which we have examined) and was much influenced by the national interest in improving general education.

[74] "Report of the Survey of Courses and Curricula of the University of Illinois at Champaign-Urbana," issued May, 1939, in Willard Correspondence. The aim of the committee was to investigate the number and relation of courses and their "economy." Regarding the College of Education, the survey remarked that "until the current year there has been no curriculum committee or other formal provision for appraising the listed offerings and the indicated programs of study or for planning more coordinated and effective courses" (p. 33). It also noted that the College of Liberal Arts and Sciences was working on a curriculum for secondary school teachers. (See L.A.S. Report, p. 7.) The document is located in Senate, Publications of the Committee on Educational Policy File Record Series 4/2/0/14, no. 1. See also College of Education "Annual Reports" (1940–41); (1944–45), esp. p. 15; *Catalogue* (1945–46), p. 468. There are also the original minutes and records of the committee in College of Education Papers, but the early material is unfortunately sketchy. The committee did not begin to function formally until the fall of 1943, under the chairmanship of A. J. Harno and with Charles W. Sanford as its "coordinator."

More was going on than an apparently unsuccessful attempt to reorganize teacher-preparation curricula. While, as President Chase himself had noted, Dean Benner in theory placed "heavy reliance on the liberal arts college" in his general approach, that college felt the pressure implied in the Dean's suggestions beginning to mount, and it did not wax enthusiastic over the proposed *détente*. The roots of some of the difficulty had preceded Benner's arrival. Walter Monroe, acting as Dean in 1931, had requested that the special methods courses in other schools and colleges be cross-listed in Education, as a 1918 Trustees' definition of the College's function had clearly recommended, so that their administration could be regularized and students could get proper credit. Provost Kendrick Babcock had agreed (as had President Chase), noting that in fact some departments were not extending any credit for them toward their own requirements anyway. But the College of Liberal Arts and Sciences went even further and announced in the *Catalogue* that no credit would be offered for any course in Education which was also listed not only under educational practice, but under agricultural education, athletic coaching, home economics education, or industrial education, as well. Benner protested this unilateral action to Chase, who promptly suggested that the Dean get the college to rescind its action. It had been taken, the President candidly remarked, in order to remove from that college's midst anyone who might in any way be " 'tainted.' " Benner requested removal of the notice, but no action was promised. He renewed his request, pointing the obvious need of closer cooperation between their respective colleges. Chase supported him warmly, commending Benner's good intentions. The only response, however, was a tart reply by the assistant dean, who resented "Benner and his x x letters," and accused him of not knowing the facts. The "no credit" entry was not removed from the *Catalogue* until the 1936–37 issue.[75]

From time to time Benner made other suggestions which implied a closer relationship with the College of Liberal Arts and Sciences, but they were generally discouraged either by the college or the administration. Neither the College of Liberal Arts and Sciences nor the Willard administration warmed to change: a 1939 inquiry found the college's general curriculum "practically unchanged" since its in-

[75] Chase to H. F. Fletcher, May 5, 1932; W. S. Monroe to Chase (and enclosure), April 20, 1931; K. C. Babcock to Chase, April 30, 1931; Benner to Chase, March 9, 1932; Benner to Fletcher, April 27, 1932; Fletcher to Chase, May 5, 1932; all in Chase Correspondence.

ception some twenty-five years before, and it singled out English and mathematics (two areas especially in demand for prospective teachers) as particularly recalcitrant. The investigating committee, although entirely free of large-scale influence from the College of Education, found on the other hand that conditions in that College were relatively good. The committee seconded most of its proposals and spoke in language remarkably similar to the kinds of things Benner had been saying for some ten years.[76]

At the bottom of the growing hostility was the presence of a "two track" system of teacher preparation in which the prospective teacher could remain registered either in the College of Education or some other school or college and still gain certification—in the latter case by using the College's education offerings as service courses under the elective rubric. This threw a heavy and unpredictable demand on the College of Education, which (for example) enrolled scarcely a third of those in the class of 1940 actually preparing to teach. Nearly 20 percent were enrolled in the Arts College, which promised them the required practice teaching—although the College of Education had no certain method of planning for them. The College vigorously opposed this situation, not only because of the difficulties of staffing and scheduling which it created but also because many of the programs which had arisen under it had become almost ludicrously unbalanced and extended. "General education" had become a mere contrivance for the extension of specialized studies, and the provision of elective time for broadly educative study had nearly disappeared.[77]

By 1940 the College of Liberal Arts and Sciences had come almost to developing its own college of education, perhaps on the now reversed conviction that the best retaliatory strategy would be to absorb the pedagogical responsibility itself. It even began to generate courses which had professional educational functions, without prior consultation with Benner or anyone else—except possibly the administration's rapidly rising *eminence gris*, Coleman Griffith, who

[76] For example, Benner to A. J. Harno, February 14, 1935; Harno to Benner, February 19, 1935 (in which the Provost expressed his fear lest the University be "caught on the far swing of the pendulum in initiating changes"); both in Willard Correspondence. For Arts College criticism, see L.A.S. Report, p. 7, under "Report of the Survey of Courses and Curricula of the University of Illinois at Champaign-Urbana," in Senate, Committee on Educational Policy Publications, File, Record Series 4/2/0/14, no. 1. Cf. note 74 above.

[77] College of Education "Annual Report" (1940-41), Appendix II, esp. pp. 1-3; (1938-39), pp. 6ff. See also *Catalogue* (1939-40), p. 159.

while technically a member of the Education faculty had witnessed
his conversion by publicly debating whether education had any professional content at all. In general, and in spite of Benner's intentions,
then, the actual development of relations between the Arts College
and the educationists during the 1930's and early 1940's boded no
good either for the Dean personally or for his special projects. It also
increased the potential for administrative friction when the long-
awaited all-university program for teacher education actually lumbered
into operation in 1943–44.[78]

One of the things Benner hoped to accomplish, at least in part,
through the creation of a teacher-education council was the achievement of a more "professional" attitude in prospective teachers. He
also hoped to effect a more careful screening of candidates. In his
first annual report, the Dean had signaled his intention "to bring about
closer relationships with the several professional organizations of
teachers and school administrators throughout the state and to establish closer contacts with local school systems." Remorselessly driven
by economic pressures, in the 1930's the teaching force turned more
and more toward their professional organizations as a rallying point
in their battle for survival. The concepts of organization and professionalization had much clearer meaning as the school systems fought
off the growingly popular tax-reduction drives and as the competition
for the relatively diminishing number of teaching posts became intense. Curiously enough, the state of Illinois, once a leading supplier
of professional school personnel, was not now producing enough
competent practitioners even for its own use, and the key posts (especially in administration) were going to "foreigners" from other states
whose credentials were superior. By 1937 the situation was so bad
that a bill was introduced (unsuccessfully) to require a one-year residence in the state prior to employment as a teacher or administrator.[79]

---

[78] Benner to A. J. Harno, December 16, 1940. See also the President's entirely
noncommital acknowledgment, Willard to Benner, December 18, 1940; both in
Willard Correspondence. For the all-University program, see College of Education "Annual Report" (1943–44), p. 6; 45th SSPI (1944), p. 43.

[79] College of Education "Annual Report" (1931–32), p. 2; (1932–33), p. 1,
College of Education Papers. For more on the need for professional growth and
its link to teacher organization, see "Growing Professionally," in 39th SSPI
(1932), pp. 49ff. For continued lack of professionalism, see 44th SSPI (1942), p.
93. See also Illinois Teacher 22–25, passim; "Annual Report" (1933–34), p. 2.
For bill, see Janata to Benner, May 19, 1937, Willard Correspondence. Benner
also crusaded for an appointed superintendent of public instruction in order to
remove that office from political machinations and increase a professional spirit.

At the undergraduate level, two chief problems were present. One was the selective admission of candidates for teaching degrees, the other their professional guidance during their preparation. Since no students (except for those in the four-year vocational programs) enrolled in the College until their junior year, and many never did (following the Arts College path to certification), it was difficult even to identify the candidates for professional education. Their programs tended to be unrealistic and decidedly "unprofessional" both in spirit and content. And the University's experience at employment time had, Benner thought, "long indicated a need for increased supervision of the programs of prospective teachers" to improve their qualifications. But there was no such agency; and there would not be until the all-university program got into operation.[80]

The selection problem was posed by the obvious tendency of some of those who "couldn't do" in other fields to enter teaching. Noting that education students tended to be distributed according to the "dumbbell pattern"—one portion of the prospective teachers falling markedly above the University academic average and another just slightly below it—the College began very early to press for admission reforms and to study the problem intensively. The Board of Trustees approved a C-or-better requirement in at least three-quarters of their previous undergraduate work (at Illinois or elsewhere) for all who sought College registration in 1934, and this was forced up to a 3.5 general grade-point average as an "experiment" in 1940. (In order to control the quality of candidates registered elsewhere in the University, these restrictions were attached to practice teaching, by then a certification requirement, rather than to College admittance alone.) [81]

But the problem was deeper than mere arrangements or screening procedures. What Benner wanted was a thorough professionalization of the content of all the programs. Formally, they remained for the most part unaltered at the undergraduate level all during the 1930's, centered

He found opposition not only from the state's powerful agricultural interests but even from educational organizations, where the county superintendents and many other administrators feared such professional development.

[80] 37th *Report* (1934), pp. 158ff.; Benner to Chase, October 8, 1931, Chase Correspondence; College of Education "Annual Report" (1931–32), p. 2, College of Education Papers.

[81] College of Education "Annual Report" (1932–33), p. 1; (1936–37), p. 5, College of Education Papers; 37th *Report* (1934), pp. 158ff.; 40th *Report* (1940), p. 971. Under Willard to Benner, April 14, 1938, there is evidence that both Sanford and the Bureau of Institutional Research had made studies of the problem, but neither has come to light.

in the sequence of Education 25 (educational psychology), education 10 (technic of teaching, or general secondary method, later specialized as we have noted), Education 6 (principles of secondary education), and the practice work. These courses and programs, long in the hands of pedagogical conservatives, could only gradually be emptied of their disciplinary orientation and placed on the broader, social foundation to which Benner was committed. Made possible only by the development of new leadership in the College faculty, the initial transition was particularly the work of three new men, Bunnie Othanel Smith, Charles Wilson Sanford, and Edwin Hewitt Reeder.

Smith, the first major faculty appointment since the Depression, and Sanford (whose perceptive leadership at University High School and subsequent work on the University teacher-education program we shall examine more carefully in the next chapter) studied the programs carefully during the middle and late 1930's "with the expectation that it [would] be possible to agree upon an improved program of professional courses which could be tested experimentally." They were to be in operation by the beginning of the 1940's.[82]

Although the undergraduate courses and programs received considerable attention in the attempt to reconstruct their content and orientation, it was the graduate work which actually had priority. This was in keeping with Benner's own convictions about the role of the College and the level at which professional education ought to operate. It was also in keeping with the march of events—the powerful North Central Association had recently ruled that the principals of approved high schools must now have at least master's degrees, and the general trend toward higher degree work had widespread support in the field.[83]

The general development of the graduate work embraced three principal emphases which we shall examine. The first was the development of five-year programs for teachers. While this movement was supposed to be simply an expansion of undergraduate requirements and was never really successful, its importance to the story at Illinois

---

[82] College of Education "Annual Reports" (1937-38), p. 2—the source of the quotation; and (1938-39), p. 5. See also Sanford's University High School Report, p. 6, at location of College's "Annual Report" (1939-40), all in College of Education Papers.

[83] College of Education "Annual Report" (1933-34), p. 1, College of Education Papers, See also J. W. Carrington, "Meeting the New Demands on Education—*A Plea for a Concerted Attack upon the Problems Facing the Public Schools*," in *Illinois Teacher* 23 (January, 1935): 131ff., 149.

is crucial. The second was the provision of graduate specialization in the vocational fields, a movement not enormously important to the profession but again a vital element in the growing conflict within the University over the nature, scope, and autonomy of pedagogical work. The third was the development of entirely new advanced-degree programs which would break decisively with the past. We shall examine each of these in turn and then note how each of them, together with the Dean's other projects and intentions, helped set the stage for the major intra-university conflict over the College which erupted in the next decade.

The origin of the five-year programs may be traced back as far as the Potthoff investigations of the early 1930's. As we have noted, these studies were concerned both with the ill-formed subject-matter preparation of prospective teachers and (of particular concern to Benner) with their dwindling general education qualifications. Various attempts to construct more adequate curricula within the academic departments during the subsequent years had shown conclusively that the three requisite elements in teacher preparation—adequate specialized academic content, especially when two or three fields were still needed to achieve "employability"; general education; and professional expertise—simply could not be gained in four years by any ordinary candidate. The state teachers' colleges had also grown increasingly aware of this problem during the decade and had moved to expand their curricula into a potential fifth year in certain areas. Both Benner and the University administration were alarmed by this development, although in somewhat different ways. The University administration feared it presaged entry into the field of graduate work on the part of the colleges; Benner had additional reservations about what would happen if the graduate-school attitude prevailed. The Dean urged Willard in 1935 to "take a more aggressive attitude (by which I do not imply institutional or personal hostilities) toward the seriously threatening interest of the Teachers Colleges in offering graduate work." Failure to do so, he thought, would place "the future development of this University . . . in very real danger." Finally a meeting was called at Normal in early 1940 at which the University and the colleges discussed the problem and their respective interests. Several joint meetings followed, resulting in a final settlement adopted at Macomb in May, 1941. The University wanted the programs that were approved in these consultations described as "five-year" programs in order to make clear that when they were offered at the teachers' colleges they were making no claim to traditional graduate competence. It was a vain hope, as it turned out, since few were inclined to spend an extra year for the same degree (a fact which caused their failure elsewhere) and since the colleges had no intentions of limiting themselves to please Urbana's long-cherished notions of educational supremacy.[84]

The University administration appointed an all-university committee in 1941 to make its own five-year proposals as a result of the statewide cooperative study on teacher preparation that had issued from the general turmoil. Some proposals were constructed, and the whole effort was later concentrated locally in the University Committee on Teacher Education when it became operative. In the meantime, the University and the state colleges continued to confer. They commissioned William S. Gray of the University of Chicago (whose negative assessment of the situation had helped spark interest in 1934) to investigate again. In 1942 he reported and again declared the problems unsolved, particularly in the area of "special subjects," those not in the traditional academic curriculum. In regard to the latter, he showed that neither the colleges nor the University were meeting the needs of the schools. (Further attempts to meet these needs turned out to be, as we shall see, the occasion for a radical redefinition of the teachers' colleges' relation to the University at Urbana and a source of growing friction between the College and the University administration.) [85]

[84] There were three particularly significant attempts to formulate new curricula —those by the English department, the French department, and a cooperative one on social studies. For a more extensive treatment of the statewide conferences, see College of Education "Annual Report" (1940–41), esp. its two appendices, "Conference with Teachers" and "The Problem of the Education of Teachers at the University of Illinois." For Benner's attitude, see Benner to Willard, June 8, 1935, in Carmichael Papers, Record Series 7/1/2, no. 4. Graduate Dean E. J. Moulton of Northwestern was also worried about the movement toward graduate studies, especially at I.S.N.U. He proposed that Chicago, Northwestern, and Illinois combine forces to oppose what could become an "intolerable" situation, although he admits that he knows little about the Normal institution. See E. J. Moulton to R. D. Carmichael, April 17, 1934, same location. See also "Memorandum of Conference with Dean T. E. Benner," dated March 19, 1936 (same location) which, with its enlightening marginalia, clearly suggests that the Dean intended to use the threat of graduate work in the state colleges as a stick to pry things loose at Urbana.

[85] This cooperative study was called "Conference of the Six State-Supported Institutions of Higher Education in Illinois." The material in this paragraph is based upon the records and papers of the University Council on Teacher Education. Many of these records and papers have, unfortunately, been lost, destroyed, or disturbed in their arrangement since they were annotated. Some of

Whatever their intentions, the explorations of five-year programs had one genuine effect: they gave added impetus to the growing demand for graduate-level work in education. According to College figures, regular graduate instruction (still primarily at the master's level) jumped 220 percent between 1937–38 and 1940–41. Summer graduate work, which had previously bulked so large, increased by only 78 percent during the same period. (It had, however, shown an increase of 169 percent over the ten-year span since Benner's arrival.) Master's degrees in education in 1930–31 had represented but 14 percent of all master's, but by 1941 they comprised 35 percent of the total.[86]

The general scope and nature of the increasing graduate offerings were slowly shaped in terms of developments in the schools and in the wider field of education during Benner's first ten years. We shall explore some of these elements in more detail subsequently, but the thrust is clear. In the area of administration and supervision, the older courses were condensed and streamlined, while new courses were added. They included courses on more specific levels of administration and supervision, including such fields as higher education and public relations, and a course in school law. The offerings in the administration of vocational education were considerably expanded. The methods courses moved from their previous concern with transmitting theoretical classroom techniques to a concentration on the scientific analysis of learning strategy and its attendant difficulties—along with a parallel emphasis on establishing diagnostic and remedial programs in the schools.[87]

In response to the same interest we have noted in the undergraduate offerings, the graduate field of curriculum more than doubled in the number of courses available and became more analytical and specialized. In psychology, the same change marked its development on the graduate level as on the undergraduate. Increasing emphasis was placed on

---

the remaining minutes and record summaries offer support, however. See College of Education Papers.

[86] Figures are from College of Education "Annual Report" (1944–45), pp. 15, 16, College of Education Papers. It should be noted again that this report was Benner's final summation and was designed to demonstrate the progress he believed he had achieved. The figures have not been exhaustively checked, but they appear to be accurate, and their general thrust is doubtless correct.

[87] For the "new" law course, see Benner to Harno, July 8, 1932; Harno to Benner, July 12, 1932; both in Chase Correspondence. Although they thought the course a novel departure, a similar course had been offered during Bagley's regime.

the practical psychological problems of the classroom. The work in psychology was not yet a major factor in its own right, however, perhaps for reasons which we shall examine later. (Except for the work of Dolch and the recently arrived Glenn Meyers Blair, the expansion of educational psychology to a position of national prominence would have to await the arrival of Benner's successor, Willard B. Spalding.) Adult education was an emphasis new during this period, as well as the radical expansion of vocational and technical work. Home economics education gradually became separated from the College, but commercial education was added to its interests. The summer offerings became in general more practically oriented. There was a decided increase of emphasis at the graduate level (due in part to the declining number of non–degree holders in the field who had previously come back merely to catch up) and particular attention was paid to the areas of administration and supervision.

The change in core requirements at the graduate level betrayed the philosophical shift which had gradually occurred since Benner's arrival. The graduate programs required the undergraduate core (educational psychology, the technic of teaching, and the principles of secondary education) as a prerequisite, and they added two other stipulations. All students were required to complete educational statistics (usually taught by Odell), educational research (Monroe), and advanced educational psychology (Cameron). In addition, those who had not had history of education as undergraduates were required to take either ancient and medieval education or the history of American education. (Both were taught by Seybolt, and the latter course required either the former or the general survey course in educational history as a prerequisite.) The College immediately dropped the statistics and research courses as requirements in the first group, keeping only educational psychology, the history requirement, and the undergraduate prerequisites. In 1932–35, the technic course was no longer prerequisite, and "equivalents" could be offered for the others. The obvious rejection of the previously strong research orientation (at least as practiced by Monroe) did not escape notice, nor did it improve internal relations, as we shall see. But the pattern remained substantially unaltered otherwise, except for some modifications in the writing requirements, through the end of the decade.[88]

By 1939, however, Benner announced that he had plans for a com-

[88] *Catalogue* (1930–31), p. 267; (1931–32), p. 302; (1932–33), p. 252. The *Catalogue* (1934–35) spelled out the graduate procedures more carefully. Slight

plete reworking of graduate study both for teachers and educational specialists. He at first proposed that the University consider his ideas through a committee. After a conference with Dean R. D. Carmichael of the Graduate School, the Dean decided it was wiser to withdraw his proposal until a "better foundation" had been laid for "introducing the question of professional education for public school service to the executive faculty." (The "Executive Faculty" served as the governing body of the Graduate School.) Carmichael's enthusiasm for the project was not marked.[89]

While its contemplated totally new graduate programs remained in temporary abeyance, the College did not remain idle. The work in graduate "commercial education" was initiated in 1937, and (of much greater significance) the touchy question of the elementary fields was raised and gently answered. As far back as 1934, Benner had noted that the College was not equipped to work in this area. While the preparation of elementary teachers had remained, by a sort of gentlemen's agreement, the province of the teachers' colleges, the training of elementary supervisors and administrators was technically closed to them, since it presupposed graduate-level offerings. Benner had early pointed out that the University's weakness in the latter area was a tempting invitation to the teachers' colleges to enter the graduate ring. If the University had no facilities or programs at the elementary teacher preparation level—its part of the informal bargain—it could not adequately develop specialists and administrators for the elementary level. Reeder had been brought on to work with candidates in advanced elementary work, but by 1941 the College was quietly offering Education 6a and 10a, elementary-level sections of the two purportedly secondary-level courses in "Principles" and "Technic." In addition, there had been practice teaching at the elementary level for some time, not by intent so much as by necessity. Many who came up via the non-College route to certification simply intended to work at the elementary level, and the College could in fact do little to change their demands.[90]

---

modifications in the writing requirements were made in (1935–36), but they will be discussed later since they had a considerable significance.

[89] Benner to R. D. Carmichael, December 8, 1939; and Carmichael to Willard, December 12, 1939; both in Willard Correspondence. For Carmichael's attitude both at the beginning and later, see Carmichael Papers, Record Series 7/1/2, no. 4. Benner had discussed his intended actions informally with the Graduate dean in March, 1939.

[90] Benner to Willard, July 10, 1937; and Benner to Bell, August 7, 1937; Willard

By 1940, the College thought it safe to make the philosophy behind its graduate programs plainer. After that June, graduate students still had to complete the undergraduate core requirements and the advanced educational psychology, but they now could choose either the history of education options or Education 101, "Philosophy of Education." The latter course (usually taught either by Robert Bell Browne or William O. Stanley) tended to emphasize the new broadly social orientation which Benner had been gradually introducing. There was also a new course in the sociology of education, crosslisted from the sociology department, which increased the opportunities to imbibe the new spirit which was blowing rather strongly over the campus.[91]

The most significant move of all, however, was the decision to renew the demand for the totally new graduate program option immediately. On October 1, 1940, the University Committee on Educational Policy submitted to the Senate, with a "pass" recommendation, the College's proposal for an unprecedented Master of Education and Doctor of Education degree. (Although Benner had held them back supposedly to lay a "better foundation," the programs still enjoyed only reluctant approval from the Graduate School.) The Senate Committee was, it said, "satisfied that there [was] a need for the kind of post graduate work . . . described in the field of public school administration" and that comparable programs were being offered elsewhere. The Senate and the Board of Trustees concurred, and the programs and courses were first offered in the 1940–41 *Catalogue* as available for the summer session of 1941.[92]

Correspondence. For elementary work, see College of Education "Annual Report" (1933–34), p. 2, College of Education Papers, and *Catalogue* (1941–42), p. 253.

[91] *Catalogues* (1941–42), p. 254; (1940–41), p. 245. The *Catalogue* (1938–39) also listed an extension course, "Social Trends in Education," given by O. F. Weber at East St. Louis (p. 239).

[92] For the new degree provisions and their original interpretation, see H. N. Hillebrand, chairman, et al., to the University Senate (and accompanying "Graduate Study in Education—Admission and Degree Requirements"), October 1, 1940, Willard Correspondence. For Carmichael's attitude, see Carmichael to Willard, October 7, 1940, in Graduate School Dean's Office Administrative Correspondence, Record Series 7/1/2, no. 1. See also *Catalogue* (1940–41), p. 245, for the degree program as it appeared. Note that the proposal before the Senate stressed that "the program leading to the degree of Ph.D. will be continued for those graduate students who wish to prepare themselves primarily for research and college teaching. The new degrees are intended to meet the needs of those school *employees* who have no responsibility and little opportunity for research but who should have broad, fundamental, and practical preparation and the ability to utilize professionally the contributions of research *and of philos-*

The heart of Benner's labors over the previous decade and the fullest exemplification of both his philosophy and his strategy, the programs were a radical departure from previous Illinois practice. Each was to be a strictly professional degree. Ostensibly designed to supplement the existing master's and doctoral programs, they were in fact developed to provide immediate ways around them—if not to replace them entirely. Based upon an already completed M.A. or M.S., and requiring at least two years of subsequent satisfactory experience *in the schools*, their whole orientation was different. The disciplinary research component in the traditional degrees was replaced by a field-research requirement and an emphasis on the development of the skills necessary for research *utilization*. Furthermore, a specific philosophical emphasis was quite clearly built in. While this philosophical emphasis was intended to characterize every aspect of the programs, it was particularly evident in two key, newly developed courses: one was Education 200, "Education and the Individual," taught by a team primarily composed of educational psychologists but much more practical and developmental in spirit than had previously been the case. The second, Education 201, was a two-semester course entitled "School and Society," open only to the new professional degree students or (unlike Education 200) Ph.D. students who had "special permission." As the former conveyed the new orientation to research and psychology, the latter conveyed the new social-philosophical orientation.[93]

The proposed programs were enormously long and demanding. The directing committee had the power to review and require supplementation of both the candidate's general education and his professional education, even if he had the A.M. or M.S. degree. A minimum of eight units of graduate work, carefully planned, was required for the

---

ophy. The latter group includes the majority of public school *employees*" (italics ours). The inclusion of philosophy was, of course, both unusual and significant, and the use of the term "employees" to characterize schoolmen perhaps inadvertently betrayed the University's sympathies.

The powerful Griffith had early believed that "professional" work for educationists should consist of work for school administrators or strictly graduate-level studies, and wherever possible no "content" should be in the hands of the College of Education. See Bureau of Institutional Research, "Memorandum No. 67," dated November 14, 1935. Copy in Carmichael Papers, Record Series 7/1/2, no. 4. This general attitude was widely shared.

[93] For sources, see previous note. If the Ph.D. was retained for "teachers," the anticipated number was obviously limited, since Benner clearly thought a college of education a professional school, and most of its work would require specialization of this sort rather than the traditional variety. For the new courses, see *Catalogue* (1941–42), p. 256.

Ed.M. The Ed.D. candidate, in addition to satisfying the master's requirements, had to pass a preliminary examination (which was in the hands of the Graduate School, but could not be attempted by the candidate without a previous review of his preparation by the College) and three additional examinations conducted exclusively by the College. These were to cover (1) his ability to think critically in the area of his professional competence; (2) the general field of education; and (3) any other areas thought necessary by his own committee. Once admitted as a candidate, he would begin immediately to develop and conduct a field study, the whole to have not less than three summers' and two regular academic years' duration. His course work would consist exclusively of continuous and concurrent enrollment in a special seminar and an intensive reading program to equip him for his study, although auditing of other courses might be recommended. If he already held the Ph.D., he was exempt from the master's level course work, except for the core courses. After completion of his study, the candidate was again to be examined by a committee appointed by the Graduate School (and authorized to cover more than the study, it was noted). Furthermore, the student was liable for examination by any other department in which he had worked; he had to stand all the final examinations continuously "even though this might require several sessions." The reporting of his study, finally, had to meet all the traditional Ph.D. requirements as to form.

The problem of recruiting students for such an academic marathon beggars the imagination, but the College had high hopes. The program was outrageously heavy and cumbersome because it had two essential functions: the first was to provide a different, professionally oriented field of study for educationists; the second was to meet every conceivable demand which the Graduate School could generate. In spite of the latter objective, however, the Graduate School was not happy with it, and there were difficult days ahead. Before examining these difficulties, however, it will be necessary to describe the third major area of development which marked the College's growth during the Benner years, that of vocational and technical education. The growth of this particular area also puzzled the Graduate College and contributed to the creation of the ugly confrontation to come.[94]

---

[94] College of Education "Annual Report" (1940–41), p. 3, College of Education Papers. According to the Report, seventy-nine students (all with M.A., M.S., or equivalent) applied and were examined in April, 1941. Thirty-eight were admitted to work on the M.Ed. in the summer session of 1941. According to a

As we have already shown, the Smith-Hughes programs had held at a limited but stable level of operation for some time. The principal source of their modest vitality was not in work on the campus but in the varying extramural locations which had brought the work to all parts of the state. For example, during 1931–32, eight courses in six basic vocational subjects were being offered in Cicero, Harvey, Joliet, Mattoon, Spring Valley, Springfield, and LaSalle. The crash did not affect the work immediately, but in 1933–34, as the results of economic collapse began to be felt everywhere, enrollments fell drastically. They dropped by some 50 percent in the vital extramural locations. By 1935 the University was reexamining the relatively heavy financial commitments necessary to retain instructional work at extramural locations. The facilities at Urbana were ancient and increasingly inadequate as well, both in terms of equipment and personnel. Arthur B. Mays and Benner, however, hoped not only to maintain but to improve the vocational programs. They argued that worsening social conditions and the changing role of the high school only made action the more imperative, in spite of the obvious difficulties and a general lack of sympathy for the area.[95]

Relief appeared in the form of the George-Deen Act, which President Roosevelt signed into law on June 8, 1936. The act set aside federal funds (required, as with the previous Smith-Hughes monies, to be matched by the several states) for the training of teachers and administrators in agriculture, trade, industry, and home economics. If properly made, proposals could be subsidized beginning the following fall. During the summer, Benner and Herbert W. Mumford, dean of the College of Agriculture, agreed upon general policies and submitted them to the University as the basis for requesting appropriation of the required state funds. They pointed out that the crucial need was

---

later report, the new professional degree program had enrolled sixty-six second-year students and fourteen third-year students during its first three years, and its enrollees had been successful in obtaining better jobs (45th SSPI [1944], p. 43).
[95] College of Education "Annual Report" (1931–32), p. 1, and accompanying documents, esp. A. B. Mays to J. W. Thompson, May 23, 1932; "Annual Report" (1933–34), p. 1; College of Education Papers. See also Benner to Chase, June 28, 1933; Chase Correspondence. There is an interesting exchange (covering some three years) in and around A. J. Janata to Benner, October 3, 1935, in College of Education File, Record Series 2/9/1, no. 26. The material was originally drawn together for consideration of the need for increased shop facilities. It shows also the rising policy role of Coleman Griffith and the Bureau of Institutional Research—see esp. its Memorandum no. 67—and an early hint of the College's feeling of frustration in the face of it.

at the graduate level: there had been no graduate vocational work until that summer, when a minimal program in industrial education had been inaugurated. The consequence for the University had been that opportunity for leadership in the field (as opposed to training a few teachers) had gone by default to other schools such as Iowa State, Ohio State, Minnesota, and Wisconsin. The Board agreed and approved some new appointments (now including commercial education) in August, 1937, in anticipation of the new state and federal funds.[96]

As a result of the financial transfusion, the programs at Urbana took an immediate upswing, as they also did at the other state colleges. The extramural work flourished again, particularly in Chicago, where the greatest emphasis was put; there appeared to be a growing interest in graduate work, especially in industrial education. Continuing success bred increased needs, however. In anticipation of further expanding interest, H. M. Hamlin was brought on in agricultural education (1938) and his work was so rapid and so effective that by June, 1940, almost 25 percent of the graduates who intended to teach were in agriculture. Benner pressed for more budget allocations, on the argument that all graduate vocational education "should be centered upon this campus." But as conditions in Europe rapidly worsened and the nation prepared at least to supply its "allies," the vocational-technical work met with new problems. Under the pressure of rising employment and burgeoning wages, industrial education fell off dramatically. The same "war conditions," on the other hand, actually increased the demand for skilled agricultural workers, even while agriculture teachers were being drawn away from the field.[97]

As a consequence of these developments, in the spring of 1941, final approval was granted to a new undergraduate program in vocational agriculture. The joint work of the Division of Agricultural Education in the College, the College of Agriculture, and the Federal Vocational Education Board, the four-year curriculum claimed to include

[96] Benner to Willard, July 20, 1936, College of Education Papers. For Benner and Mumford's work, see Benner to Willard, July 27, 1936, Willard Correspondence; see also 39th *Report* (1938), pp. 427ff.

[97] A. B. Mays to Benner, May 27, 1938, in support of College of Education "Annual Report" (1937–38); "Annual Report" (1938–39), pp. 1, 2, 9 (the source of the quotation), 10. On changes induced by the war, see "Annual Report" (1940–41), pp. 6, 7; and Appendix II, p. 1 (the source of the graduation figures). Note that, according to these figures, of the June class of 1,882 graduates, 661 were preparing to teach, of whom only 36.4 percent were actually enrolled in the College. Cf. the effect of the increasing demands in vocational education on the University's relationship with the teachers colleges, Ch. 10 below.

"a broad base of fundamental science and other general training believed to be essential for prospective high school teachers." In fact it accomplished no such thing. Rather, it mirrored the whole problem attendant upon "specialized" education, not only from the University's perspective but in terms of Benner's previously stated policy as well. The program required 130 hours for graduation (which alone made it very tight). Of these hours, fifty-two were filled by required courses in agriculture and twenty-seven to twenty-nine by required courses in science (most of which were vocationally oriented, the only possible exception being general psychology). Eighteen hours were required in education, but twelve of these were in strictly agricultural education. Consequently, in four years of work there were only seventeen hours of "general courses"—two hours of hygiene, six hours of physical education and military science, six hours of "Rhetoric," and (about the only course even faintly approaching a general education ideal) three hours of economics. There was no language, no literature, no history, no mathematics (as such); and the fourteen to sixteen unspecified hours were both glaringly inadequate to the task of providing breadth and tantalizingly open to usurpation for vocational purposes.[98]

As we showed earlier in this chapter, Dean Benner's philosophy of education and his proposals for the preparation of teachers laid heavy emphasis on two factors: the centrality of a general education as defined by contemporary social relevance, and the development of a new professional orientation. Each, he had argued, was threatened by the mesmerizing graduate-school image then fashionable in the United States. Purportedly educational curricula such as we have just examined—there were others of similar rigidity and illiberality, of course—scarcely accorded with Benner's own most cherished convictions; they were equally inhospitable to traditionalists in the academic establishment, though for somewhat different reasons. Faced with curricula it found bewildering, and graduate programs it could only view as hostile to its interests, the University's still dominant academic and administrative power structure began to marshal its forces.

There is no doubt that the Graduate School deliberately dragged its feet on the new professional degree programs. The School's most influential leaders regarded them as "radical and almost revolutionary," possessed of "elements of grave danger" which would have to be "off-

[98] For this paragraph, see description in 41st *Report* (1942), p. 259.

set by careful administrative procedure and control from the graduate school office." Consequently Dean Carmichael informed Benner in early December, 1941, that "the philosophy of education underlying the tentative proposals [for administering the graduate degree] which you transmitted to me with your letter of November 8, 1941, appears to be unsound. It departs in a rather fundamental way from some basic ideals which have underlain and still underlie the graduate work in every major institution with which I am or have been acquainted." The proposals, he insisted, now made explicit certain long-growing tendencies which show "we have already gone rather too far" in the new direction. More than a year before, Carmichael had quietly and prudently informed President Willard of his lack of interest in the programs, suggesting that his concern was financial. He thought they should not be initiated and then withdrawn for lack of funds, since that would be unfair to the "limited number of students" who might possibly want them—thus demonstrating that, as Pope accused Addison, he could "damn with faint praise and assent with civil leer." [99]

The absence of communication—as it would now be termed—was in itself indicative. Carmichael had made little attempt to work with Benner, and Benner had usually merely assumed either the worst or the best. Carmichael preferred to form his policies by tightly guarded conversation with his personally selected advisors, and he always had the ear of the administration. His was the position of power, and it needed no formal structure since no one had ever thought of calling it to account. Benner, as was not seldom the case, was puzzled by the treatment accorded his graduate proposals. Their logic was right, and there was both practical and academic justification: The teaching force had come actively to distrust the Ph.D.-holder, the Dean believed, with some justification. And men such as the entirely respectable Charles Sanford, soon to direct the new all-university committee on teacher preparation, had remarked on the need for a new style of professional training in education for some time. Perhaps even more compelling a reason, Benner himself was the product of just such a degree program

[99] For Carmichael's remarks, see Carmichael to Benner, December 1, 1941, in College of Education Papers; Carmichael to Willard, October 7, 1940, in Graduate School Dean's Office Administrative Correspondence, Record Series 7/1/2, no. 1. See also Education, 1941, File, 7/1/2, no. 4. The conservatism of the Graduate School had long since been revealed in its attitude toward the reform of graduate education for prospective college teachers which marked the early 1930's. See A. H. Daniels's report on Illinois (in which the problem is virtually denied) in W. S. Gray, ed., *The Training of College Teachers*, pp. 222ff.

at no less an institution than Harvard, the mother of all American universities. But, of course, that was not the issue.[100]

If the professional degrees were somewhat frightening to academic traditionalists, the expansion of vocational education was, as we have suggested, simply not understood. Even though programs in the area had enjoyed considerable success, they had never been large and they were relatively expensive, if only because of their extramural location. But it was what they were *about* that tended to befuddle many from faculty members to Trustees. An interesting illustration of this fact had been provided in 1940. The Graduate School's powerful research board had denied sabbatical leave to Arthur F. Dodge in industrial education, mostly because they could not see that his work as a teacher lay not on the campus but within the industrial structure outside the institution. (He had proposed a tour of industries as his projected study.) The obvious ire in Benner's protest of their denial might have been stimulated by the fact that less than two years previously Coleman Griffith had been cheerfully extended leave to organize some athletic research for P. K. Wrigley's Chicago Cubs! [101]

The Graduate School had its reasons, however, particularly for its antipathy toward the professional degree programs. Their method of administration did represent a serious challenge to its authority, one which had been building for some time. Benner's convictions about the graduate education model had led him to try to replace the old-style master's thesis (and its implicit "pure" research orientation) with a couple of long papers back in the mid-1930's. He then quietly dropped requiring these—a ploy which Carmichael maintained he did not discover until 1940. The executive faculty did approve dropping the thesis, after the College agreed to replace the papers with two units of graduate work outside their professional fields, where it

---

[100] For Benner's attitude, see notes on interview with Thomas E. Benner by Walter Krolikowski, July 26, 1962, p. 2. For Sanford's position, see p. 6 of his University High School Report, in support of College of Education "Annual Report" (1939–40), both in College of Education Papers.

[101] College of Education "Annual Report" (1938–39), pp. 1, 2; Willard to Benner, October 15, 1941; Benner to Willard, October 20, 1941; cf. Benner to Willard, February 16, 1940. For the Dodge case, see Benner to Willard, January 20, 1940. All in College of Education Papers. For Griffith's leave, see Griffith to Willard, January 10, 1938, Willard Correspondence; 39th *Report* (1938), pp. 594ff.

The executive faculty of the Graduate School seems probably (and Dean Carmichael certainly) to have regarded any "vocational" area as improper matter for graduate-level study. See the handling of issues such as audio-visual materials and industrial education in Record Series 7/1/2, no. 4.

could appropriately be had, but Carmichael's colleagues regarded all such subtle moves as somehow replete with "deviousness" and perhaps even "subterfuge" or "fraud." Exchanges such as these—although the College was hardly innocent—continued to exemplify for Benner the Graduate School's unshakeable disciplinary preoccupation (and, from his point of view, its own unrecognized brand of professionalism). These events gradually persuaded the College that it must move outside the whole traditional degree framework. And the School's continued tendency to control the College's programs after the setting up of the new degrees confirmed that necessity in the minds of the Dean and many of his faculty.[102]

The arrangements for the new degrees proposed by the College necessitated an assault on a critical area: personnel. The Graduate School had been reluctant to admit College faculty to full standing, particularly those in the vocational areas. What the Dean proposed (and what inflamed Carmichael) would in effect allow the College to provide a front for nonapproved faculty to direct the research programs carried on under the new degree umbrellas. Benner had pointed out (and statistics confirmed) that students rarely wanted to work under the old guard who had been approved, and no one was allowed to work under those who were popular. Something had to give. The College's decision was to build the new degree programs in which the new personnel would be put beyond the graduate school's reach by a novel set of arrangements. The new "committee" structure for directing the candidates could be viewed as an attempt on the part of the College of Education to create its own graduate college under the "dictatorial" control of Benner rather than the purportedly liberating influence of the University Graduate School, which would have only the role of final approval. On this point Carmichael was adamant: graduate study meant one student under one faculty member, whose jurisdiction was granted by the one graduate faculty.

[102] Carmichael to Benner, September 11, 1940; January 30, 1941; Carmichael to Benner, December 20, 1940; Benner to Carmichael, December 26, 1940; all in College of Education Papers. Benner had what he regarded as other examples: the Graduate School had attempted to restrict the amount of credit summer session students could earn. (See Benner to Carmichael, March 31, 1942, and accompanying correspondence.) It had also asserted its control over all programs beyond the fourth year in agricultural education, even when (as in the "five-year" programs, which were officially defined as nongraduate) the College regarded them as only supplementary. (See Benner to Carmichael, April 21, 1943. All in College of Education Papers. See also Carmichael Papers, Record Series 7/1/2, no. 4, esp. Education, 1941, File. Cf. Notes, 89, 92, 99, 101).

Without this provision, A. H. Coble believed it would be impossible to protect the "independence" of the "few sound scholars" still left in the College. When a considerable number of students turned up to enter the program, Benner felt encouraged; he did not appear to notice that Carmichael's correspondence had turned icy cold.[103] The frosty tone which had come over the conversation was not entirely without reason, of course. As we have suggested, the College's actions could appear to contradict Benner's own words about educational breadth. But the problem was that "education" meant two different things to the two parties, hence each could appeal to the "same" principle and fault the other for denying it. Many whose judgment contributed to the policy dispute were like Coleman Griffith. He had previously given some support—although very little—to the College's programs and aspirations, and then only when they coincided with his widely shared educational philosophy. But at least as far as teachers were concerned, Griffith was still convinced that there were only two respectable components in their preparation: the legitimate subject-matter fields, and certain special fields of inquiry relevant to them, e.g., school administration, pure psychology, and child development. The hybrids which tended to appear in pedagogical programs were obviously sterile, if existent at all.[104] Other faculty members, like Provost Albert J. Harno, were personally more open. They were, however, scarcely less puzzled as they faced the competing demands of a growing range of "professional" programs of which Education's was only one instance.

Harno, who had generally been reasonable and usually even friendly

[103] Various notes and memoranda by Carmichael, A. J. Harno, A. H. Coble, H. M. Gray, and others in Education, 1941, File, Carmichael Papers, Record Series 7/1/2, no. 4. See also College of Education "Regulations and Procedures Relating to Advanced Graduate Study in Education," College of Education Papers. According to the *Catalogues*, from 1920-21 through 1930-31, there were sixteen Ph.D.'s awarded in Education. From 1931-32 through 1940-41, there were eighteen, but twelve of those had been awarded through 1934-35. The last five years had averaged only one each year. The statistics were, as statistics, ambiguous, of course. They could be read a number of ways: as suggesting that the old College faculty had lost even its modest drawing power, or that the new faculty were themselves inferior, or that there was simply a decline in the traditional programs and an unwillingness to work with the approved members. The evidence does, however, seem to favor the last interpretation. For the student response to the new programs, see note 94 above. Note also that even though the new M.Ed. was extremely demanding, twelve were awarded from 1942-43 through 1945-46.

[104] Griffith's "Memorandum" no. 203, in 40th *Report* (1940), pp. 119ff. (quotation at p. 119). Cf. note 92 above.

to the College, raised the crucial issue with Benner as they debated the departmental location of a "personnel" course in 1941.[105] The difficulty was to resolve with distributive justice "the vexing problems of the organization of knowledge, the natural preferences of departments, the pride of administrative officers, and the budget of the university." Harno perceptively saw that the problem of "overlapping" courses was in reality no mere administrative wrangle. It was a fundamental change which demonstrated the increasing interpenetration of the traditional disciplines as the coming *new* university addressed itself to problems rather than tending its traditional cultural gardens. The difficulty was—and perhaps still is—to find *any* principle of discrimination which could take the place of the old disciplinary boundaries. The quandary was genuine. By 1941, it seemed that Kinley's fears (which were, it might have been noticed, not entirely dissimilar to Benner's) had indeed been confirmed. Chaos, born of sheer individual interest and need and without obvious theoretical delineation, was about to occur. The agriculturalist, Harno suggested as an example, used to concern himself with "pigs, cattle, corn and plows"—a happily concrete and circumscribed set of phenomena. Suddenly, however, he was becoming concerned with *all of life,* and he appeared bent on organizing and studying that somewhat diffuse and abstract phenomenon only from his own viewpoint—which meant that no other courses would do. He could no longer entrust any instruction to other departments, let alone another college. He must fashion his own version of most if not all of the traditional disciplines. With the pragmatic wisdom of the lawyer he was, Harno had tried to make his decisions, he said, on the basis of (1) actual social need; (2) whether such needs were satisfied by other courses; (3) the presence of a particular emphasis (i.e., scientific, academic, or applied); and (4) the hard reality of a finite budget.

Yet, for all of this perceptive analysis, even Harno could not quite bring himself to accept the change. In the case before him, he held to his belief that psychology was a science and education an "art"— an art in which psychology was applied. Professional education con-

[105] The material in this and the following paragraph is drawn from the Provost's extensive and candid discussion of his problems in Harno to Benner, January 23, 1941, in College of Education Papers. The whole is still well worth reading. A typical example of the other approach, as held by Benner, was the Dean's insistence that all the College's faculty should have had school experience: "Otherwise their discussion of [for example] educational psychology or the principles of secondary education becomes purely theoretical and remote" (Benner to Willard, March 21, 1938, Willard Correspondence).

sequently involved, he said, "the practical application of data [presumably derived from "pure" inquiry] to an art like education." He could see that sometimes the demands of the recipient really did influence the data applied, but the Provost's approach implied a fundamental bifurcation which was unacceptable to professional educationists and countervailing to their quest for autonomy in the University. The object they studied did not give their programs decisive shape, his argument implied; that shape stemmed from the root inquiries which had customarily been made in the disciplines. There were for Harno, as for many others, still only two constituents of academic reality: true sciences and practical arts.

Under the weight of what he came to interpret as mere academic and administrative intransigence, Benner visibly hardened. His implied prophecies fulfilled, the Dean's intensity and passion turned somewhat sour, particularly as he could not really count on total support even within the College. (The split between the old guard and the new breed had neither disappeared nor been healed.) He became increasingly irritated by what he saw as the administration's insensitive refusal to treat seriously the growth of the College, both actual and potential. And he found one man increasingly in the center of the opposition. Coleman R. Griffith came more and more to stand in Benner's eyes for the whole mass of academic and social conservatism which seemed to block realization of the College's hope. The new foundations he was attempting to lay simply could not be put down very deep.[106]

In roughly the first ten years of Thomas Eliot Benner's tenure as Dean, then, the College of Education had executed a radical about-face in terms of both its general policy and its practical thrust. It was in virtually no sense the same institution which had passively gone to wrack, overwhelmed by the Kinley administration. In the first place

[106] Benner argued that the College's graduate load had increased 442 percent in the five years from 1934–35 to 1939–40 (College of Education "Annual Report" [1940–41], p. 1). Cf. (1938–39), where he had argued that a graduate increase of 247 percent had been met with only a 96 percent increase in faculty (p. 1). As the College's faculty polarized, Benner came to govern more and more informally —he was accused of relying upon a de facto, if unintended, "kitchen cabinet"— rather than discussing policies in regular fashion, and this antagonized those who felt themselves thereby disenfranchised. It is perhaps worth noting here that the growing lack of sympathy with the University status quo was by no means limited to the College of Education, as we shall see in connection with later events.

it had developed a characteristic and relatively conscious philosophy, which was also father to a reasonably clear conception of teacher preparation. That in turn had issued in a relatively consistent (if unpopular) administrative strategy. While allegiance to this philosophy was in no sense enforced within the College—given the relatively static faculty which the Depression created, it could not have been even if so intended—it was in fact widely shared. Unfortunately perhaps, but unavoidably, that philosophy tended to separate the new faculty from the old, who found it socially, educationally, and pedagogically unsound and dangerous. (The influential Griffith was reported to have dismissed the new professional "School and Society" seminars—the apotheosis of the new approach—as mere "propaganda courses.") [107]

The new philosophy resulted in a pronounced shift from a purely disciplinary orientation in the curriculum to a much more broadly practical and professional one. The formulation of courses and programs in such terms, however, raised once again for conservatives the spectre of academic and cultural disintegration against which President Kinley had so assiduously crusaded. Nor was their antipathy without force or hard to understand. Whether the University was to become the utilitarian instrumentality by means of which the general welfare was to be directly and immediately advanced, or whether it was to remain the pristine temple of the arts and sciences, had not yet been decided. (Indeed, well over one hundred years after the birth of the new university movement, it is perhaps still not clear precisely where the path of wisdom lies.) The disciplines were the gods of our academic forefathers, and jealous gods. To talk of humane study, when humane was instrumentally and socially defined, merely cloaked the idol which had been erected within the sacred grove. Like any other abomination, it required to be destroyed lest it corrupt the community.

There were two very practical results of the College's new posture and its accompanying bid for leadership which we shall examine further in subsequent chapters. In a curious if not contradictory denial of its own philosophy, the College chose to argue for its own revivification on the ground that it alone, as a College in the state's preeminent University, could fulfill the educational and pedagogical ideals it had defined. An interesting brand of academic imperialism thus resulted from Benner's tendency to argue that the College ought to be enlarged in order to prevent the old normal schools–now teachers' college from enlarging themselves. Here the logic of in-

[107] Benner to Russell D. Gregg, August 1, 1944, Benner Papers.

stitutional development nullified the logic of school development. There was no reason to believe that the dormant College could become adequate to the needs of the state schools in the requisite amount of time, and no logic demanded that it should. Rather, the need was to develop all the state's educational resources as rapidly as possible, in order to raise it from its near bottom rank vis-à-vis public schooling.

Finally, the College's new designs implicitly quarreled with the powerful College of Liberal Arts and Sciences and explicitly challenged the authority of the Graduate School. The College's words and actions were in fact a judgment upon the Arts College, since they implied that it was not doing its job. The Graduate School, as Benner had made abundantly clear, was the generic cause, not only of its own difficulties but of the malaise in the humanities and liberal sciences. Its acquiescence in what Benner had called the "graduate-college mentality" had succeeded in doing precisely what it had faulted educationists for doing: disintegrating knowledge and proliferating courses beyond human relevance. Failing in his attempt to provoke it to the needed self-examination, Benner then assaulted the Graduate College administratively, throwing the ideological dispute into an intra-institutional power struggle.

All of this flew in the face of what was still an essentially conservative University as well. If the College was changing, the University had on the whole remained the same, which heightened the pressures building up to a potential rift. (It should not be assumed that this restiveness was restricted to educationists; it was far more widespread.) Had Chase remained as president, matters might have gone very differently. But as it was, his administration represented only a brief hiatus, the influence of which largely ended with his departure. The policies of Kinley were deeply embedded in the seniority-defined institution, and when Chase's successor was drawn from the same ranks, it was obvious that more than superficial change anywhere in the University would have to await new leadership—as the stormy career of the next president, George D. Stoddard, demonstrated.

The further development and final disposition of the College's programs, the origin, philosophy, and setting of which we have examined here, will occupy our attention in succeeding chapters.

CHAPTER 10

Itinerant Teachers and Scientists, New Style

During the 1920's, the field of education within the state of Illinois had been dominated by the University of Chicago and Northwestern, although the burdensome task of educating the rank and file of the profession was largely left to the impoverished normals. Strong outside influence had been provided by the State University of Iowa, Iowa State College, Ohio State University, and to some extent the University of Minnesota, whose president, Lotus D. Coffman, had not forgotten his heritage as a schoolman and was remembered as an Illini. A broader but much less immediate influence emanated from the Teachers College on the Manhattan Mount Zion of American education. If the University of Illinois wished to achieve a position of leadership once again, two things were obviously necessary: it must get out into the state with vital programs, and, if it was to do that, it needed to return to the problems of the schools and education and not concern itself exclusively with the logical or experimental antecedents of them. In laying new foundations, Benner consciously provided a platform for such an attempt, as we have seen. But certain key factors in this outward movement and the revolution which it implied within the College, noticed only in passing in the previous chapter, are worthy of examination in their own right. Accordingly, we shall now look more carefully at the changing concept of educational research and the closely related question of University High School, the problem of developing relations with the schools, and the expansion of Illinois higher education and the developing teachers' colleges.

The opportunity to do more research, as measured by increased funds, facilities, and personnel, was a constant request of the College of Education in the decade following Benner's arrival in 1931. In the beginning, the petition was usually made on general principles, although during the later years such proposals were increasingly justified on the grounds that the state's teachers' colleges couldn't perform this function, shouldn't do so, and wouldn't if the University made itself adequate to the task. Why did the undertaking of research pose such a problem for the College of Education? It would have seemed virtually axiomatic, given the prevailing notion of a university's business. In fact, however, the problematical state of educational research had deep roots both inside and outside the College. We also noted that the University was still plagued by the problem of defining research, particularly in light of the growing dichotomy between pure and applied science, and finding appropriate academic homes for it. The administration of the University, and probably the general faculty, shared the notion that education was at bottom a practical art to which science might be applied. Consequently, its true research ought to be "pure," housed with the pure researchers. (The one possible exception lay where its research verged on the general service function now somewhat more cheerfully accepted as part of the University's responsibility—as in school surveys and curriculum analysis, for example.) [1]

Taking stock in mid-decade, and discontented with their traditional banishment, the College faculty pleaded for more graduate research assistantships. They noted realistically that funds for their graduate research would have to be specifically appropriated. Since they taught almost no lower-division courses, they could not disguise research appropriations under budget lines for instruction, "as is done in departments where the greater part of the budget for freshman instruc-

[1] The College announced its renewed service emphasis in 40th SSPI (1934), p. 446. See also "Annual Report" (1939–40), pp. 9–12; (1940–41), p. 5 and Appendix I on the "Conference with the Teachers' Colleges;" A. J. Harno to Benner, January 23, 1941 (and previous exchanges, December 16, 1940, January 10, 1941). All in College of Education Papers, the last in File "Provost, 1936–44."

tion constitutes, in effect, a subsidy for research." They needed money to bring in good *schoolmen*, they said—perhaps not realizing fully that, in the eyes of academic solons, dusty, down-at-the-heels pedagogical fieldmen did not sufficiently resemble true researchers, the bright young postgraduates fresh from the pristine laboratories of pure inquiry.[2]

The problem appears even more curious against the fact that the College had at least the remains of a program of research of its own, largely embodied in the once-robust Bureau of Educational Research. Increasingly, it puzzled the administration (and perhaps antagonized it as well) that the new Dean, virtually from the moment of his arrival, appeared determined to unseat that program and replace it with another. When forced drastically to curtail the College's budget, Benner had chosen to effect the stipulated immediate economies "almost entirely in administration . . . and the Bureau of Educational Research." His recommended budget for 1932–33 slashed the Bureau program (which was even then less than half as large as the expensive and educationally dubious Athletic Coaching operation) by more than 50 percent, a cut more than four times larger than any other. Its work was virtually abandoned, except for some projects awaiting completion and one or two modest inquiries, and the Bureau was physically transferred to the Administration Building, where it could be housed more economically and be under closer scrutiny by the College.[3] Moves such as these, coupled with the dropping of the research courses which its personnel had offered in the professional sequence, did nothing to improve relationships. By 1935 the Bureau had declined to little more than Walter Scott Monroe and a stenographer, and it was with an almost audible sense of relief on both sides that he undertook the editorship of the American Council on Education's *Encyclopedia of Educational Research*. For the next five years, Monroe met his remaining courses, but he devoted the major share of his talent and effort to the *Encyclopedia* and his still considerable role in general University affairs.[4]

[2] See "Annual Report" (1935–36), p. 7, 8. The 1934 survey of the University by the American Council on Education confirmed the problem of research personnel.

[3] See "Annual Report" (1931–32), p. 1 (the source of the quotation), in College of Education Papers; Benner to Chase, June 3, 1931; Benner to Chase, April 4, 1932 (and accompanying budget for 1932–33); Benner to Chase, July 6, 1932, all in Chase Correspondence.

[4] Benner to Willard, March 14, 1935. Cf. Willard to Benner, February 12, 1935; Monroe to Willard, January 17, 1936 (and accompanying exchange); all

Why would Dean Benner involve himself in such a controversial move, predictably inhospitable not only to Monroe and his staff but to the larger University and its administration? The answer appears to be twofold. The first problem was one of institutional power. The Bureau had *been* the research program of the College, not merely one of its projects. From his position as its director, the popular Monroe had controlled not only its own research but in effect all of the College's research, since the University's general research funds were always directly funneled through it. That meant, as Benner clearly saw, that if the wider work of the College was to have any research aspect, the hold of the Bureau would have to be broken. Furthermore, by virtue of his financial control, Monroe also exercised a considerable—if unintentional—control over the concept of research which was to prevail. Benner objected to this in principle, and he also disagreed with the particular philosophy which had become established. The only answer, as he saw it, was to gain for the College as a whole (via himself and an all-College committee, of which Monroe would be a member, but nothing more) the administration of funds and the function of approval.[5]

During the late 1920's and 1930's, research in the area of child growth and development came back into the popular and academic limelight which (in a somewhat different form, of course) it had occupied several decades before. As it did so, it provided a clear illustration of the conflicts engendered by competing conceptions of research and inquiry, especially when related to education. The scientific study of the developing child, and the dissemination of this knowledge to his puzzled parents, seemed to be the answer to all the problems of the school (and the home as well), at least in the popular view. By the mid-1930's, enlightened groups such as the Illinois Federation of Women's Clubs and the American Association of University Women were pressing for increased work in child development and the provision of classes for "parent education." The College

---

in Willard Correspondence. See also notes on personal interview with T. E. Benner, July 26, 1962, by W. K. Krolikowski, copy in College of Education Papers. For activities of the Bureau, see "Annual Reports" of the College, (1937–38), p. 7; (1938–39), pp. 12, 13; (1939–40), p. 12; (1940–41), p. 5.

5 See Benner to Willard, July 18, 1935, and March 3, 1937, in College of Education Papers. Monroe, as we have seen, had been a strong local contender for the deanship with support both inside the University and outside it. See Education Deanship Files ("General" and "Alphabetical") in Record Series 2/7/1, no. 28 (1931–32). Cf. interview cited in note 4.

of Education had been, as we have noted, beginning to emphasize child development for some time, and by 1937 it was proposing to offer parent education courses as well. In the summer session of 1938, a "Demonstration School" including the nursery level had been set up, and the Trustees were considering the Bureau of Institutional Research's recommendation that they create "at an early date . . . a preschool clinic for the training of teachers, for research purposes in child development and to provide observational material for students in Home Economics." [6]

The difficulties appeared at once. How was such inquiry to be provided for administratively? There were at least three interested parties: the Education people, the psychologists, and the home economics department; each had different intentions and divergent modes of research. Benner, not surprisingly, believed the principal need was for a *school* at the nursery and early elementary level. Convinced that locating the research in a school could easily serve the others' needs as well, he welcomed their participation and proposed they share its governance. But if the College should become the statewide center for advancing these new interests, adequate "laboratory" facilities were implied. These should, however, take the form not of a pure psychological laboratory, or a pedagogically vague preschool "nursury" of the popular sort, but the form of an educationally structured program which would provide for all these research possibilities and allow projects running from the early years through the high-school level. (In short, he advocated the sorts of programs and facilities that had already been in operation at places such as Chicago, Iowa, Minnesota, Michigan, Ohio State, Missouri, and Wisconsin, and which had given these institutions a commanding lead over Illinois.) [7]

The "Psycho-educational Clinic" which Blair and Dolch were operating with the aid of their few graduate students brought in cases of pronounced learning difficulties which were encountered in the schools. This was a step in the right direction, but Benner believed their program needed expansion in itself. The greater need was for positive investigation and experimentation, not just diagnostic and

[6] College of Education "Annual Report" (1935–36), p. 6, College of Education Papers. See also 40th *Report* (1940), pp. 548–49, 119–20 (the source of the quotation), which referred to the University's "obligation to the secondary schools of the state which cannot any longer be evaded" and admitted that even the proposed appropriations would not be adequate.

[7] College of Education "Annual Report" (1938–39), p. 4; (1939–40), pp. 7, 8, College of Education Papers.

remedial work, and that could be achieved only through a full-scale educational system. Underlying all this was, of course, the conviction that the educator was concerned with the process of teaching as it occurs in schools, not merely with the physical mechanism of learning or its narrowly functional aberrations.[8]

If Benner's implicit argument was understood, it was at least never accepted. An early proposal for a more distinctly laboratory-oriented program in cooperation with the psychology department was suspended by the Graduate School early in 1938, on the grounds of budget deficiencies and (more significantly) pending an evaluation of the research program of one of the participating psychologists.[9] The criteria for that "evaluation" were bound to be those of "pure" research and, however valid some of the objections might have been in the particular individual's case, bound to be inimical in the long run. But pressure for such work increased, and about a year later a full-scale investigation of the issue was conducted by the Graduate School. In February, 1939, the "Committee on a Program of Training and Research in Child Development" issued a detailed report. That Committee, composed of H. H. Anderson, Lita Bane, E. H. Reeder (of the College of Education), and Herbert Woodrow, and headed by Coleman Griffith, recommended the establishment of a "pre-school, experimental laboratory." The "laboratory" was to have some fifty children by 1939 and 100 by 1940. Second, an elementary school was to be established for the first three grades by the fall of 1939 (enrolling about seventy-five children) and extended upward "as soon as conditions [would] allow." The report implied that the College of Education was not really concerned with high-level, exclusively theoretical research, and it mirrored Dean Carmichael's lack of enthusiasm for the proposed project.[10]

Proposals, recommendations, and expressions of informed opinion from several committees and interested persons dotted the academic landscape. But very little happened. The question of how such a

[8] College of Education "Annual Report" (1939–40), pp. 9–10; (1940–41), p. 5. For more on the psycho-educational clinic and its relation to the schools and the building program, see 43rd SSPI (1940), p. 117.

[9] A. J. Harno to Benner, February 3, 1938, College of Education Papers.

[10] See twenty-one-page report of "Committee on a Program of Training and Research in Child Development," under Griffith to R. D. Carmichael, February 14, 1939, esp. pp. 20, 21, in File Child Development Program 39–40, Graduate College Administrative Correspondence, Record Series 7/1/2, no. 3. The marginalia suggest the attitude of Carmichael and others toward the College's role. See esp. p. 21.

program should be housed was put to successful practitioners in the field, and the responses proved ambiguous. The people at Berkeley (among others) said it must not be an "appendage"; those at Minnesota warned sharply against detaching it! The crux of the problem at Illinois seemed always to lie at one point: who would head it? Initially, the hope was to find some stellar academic figure who could steer a course between all the interests. He would in fact be asked to develop the plans from a distance (as part of the evidence that he ought to be hired) and thus unlock the political and ideological straightjacket which had kept the project at a standstill.[11]

In the spring of 1939 it looked very much like that stellar figure would be Kurt Lewin. Lewin was then fashioning a program at Iowa City, after recently departing Harvard, but he appeared ready to move if the welcome was generous enough. The educationists and the psychologists seemed to agree on him warmly and genuinely. Carmichael, however, was hardly enthusiastic—he was in fact extremely guarded. When one of the preliminary proposals was submitted later that year, the dean of the Graduate School found himself "unable to see any element of vision in it." He regarded it as immature in plan and judgment and insufficiently integrated. In short, it left him "quite unconvinced." [12] And Lewin's reputation could not save it, either—if, indeed, he had any. Carmichael, admitting a growing suspicion that Lewin wasn't all his backers thought him to be, was doubtless delighted to get hold of some reviews critical of Lewin's work (particularly his novel "topological" approach to psychology) which were conveniently supplied him by the home economics forces through their parent College of Agriculture. His candidacy collapsed, and with it the whole project. Carmichael found attractive the home economists' suggestion that the full-scale project be held up to await better planning, especially in its organiza-

[11] See Roger G. Barker to Carmichael, May 17, 1939, and attached documents, in location cited above. See also File Teacher-Training and Research in the Field of Child Development, 1939, esp. Kurt Lewin to R. D. Carmichael, May 1, 2, 1939, and reply, May 3, 1939; Director Harold E. Jones (University of California) to Carmichael, April 15, 1939, and Carmichael to Jones, April 20, 1939. For the Minnesota reaction, see also File Committee to Present a Program of Research in Child Development-Report, 1939, and esp. the report itself, dated August 10, 1939.

[12] Carmichael's notes on the report of the "Committee to Present a Program of Research in Child Development," Graduate College Correspondence, Record Series 7/1/2, no. 3. See also Roger G. Baker to Carmichael, May 17, 1939, and attachments in File Child Development Program, 1939, same location.

tional aspects—though there was no evidence to suggest that the proposal was in theory any less attractive than the successfully operating schemes against which it was compared. The home economists were then encouraged to go ahead with their own modest "preschool laboratory" immediately. Their strategy, which was in fact based on a supposed "prior claim" on the area, thus prevailed, and it specifically excluded any role for the College of Education. Consequently, the College never gained access to any broad child development programs, nor could it establish work at the level of early schooling at any time during Benner's tenure—or thereafter.[13]

In all of this, the Bureau of Institutional Research again exercised a powerful influence. While Benner and Griffith had been able to agree in general principle on the desirability of some project, and in particular on Lewin's candidacy for its direction, relations were growing more strained.[14] The Bureau issued one of its ostensibly factual but inescapably political memoranda (Number 223) during the thick of the struggle in May, 1939. Benner, noting that the Bureau had been in part his own creation and stressing his desire to avoid even "the *appearance* of controversy" with it, nonetheless felt compelled to reply. Ignoring the Bureau's attack on the "faculty distinction" of the College, the Dean felt the whole problem of "new programs" was the central issue. The Bureau had suggested that financial aid to all new programs could be deferred, except possibly some help for the "Child Research Laboratory" scheme which was to be funneled through the Graduate School Research Board. Benner objected that the so-called "expansion" of College programs—as, for example, in connection with increasing practice-teaching requirements and extramural work—was normal growth, dictated by conditions within the College's proper constituency (the schools). It was not ambitious to develop new programs. Yet budget requests were being lopped off without so much as a conference. The Dean was, he said, willing to give priority to the "Child Research" proposal even over

13 See Files, "Committee to Present a Program of Research in Child Development," and esp. "Child Development Laboratory Correspondence and Blueprints 1938–40," all in Graduate College Correspondence, Record Series 7/2/1, no. 3. In the latter location see letters under Carmichael to H. P. Rusk, January 22, 1940, and esp. Lita Bain to H. P. Rusk, January 15, 1940.

14 Griffith to Carmichael, April 4, 1939, in File Committee on Teacher Training and Research in the Field of Child Development, 1939, Graduate College Correspondence, Record Series 7/2/1, no. 3. The letter betrays a hint of anti-Semitism.

the increasing routine needs of the College, but not willing to see neither need met—which had been, he felt, the case.[15]

Finally, although the University took no further serious action, the outside pressures continued. Schoolmen and other interested groups relentlessly badgered the College for increased research and educational programs at the nursery and elementary level. Those pressures appeared to the Trustees to come ultimately from Benner, because his previous proposals had been frustrated. There is no reason to suppose that they would have had to, and no very strong evidence to indicate that any of them did (except insofar as he expressed his customarily saguine hopes for action when he went out on the hustings). The Board, however, summoned the Dean to explain the situation in the spring of 1941—an "opportunity" which Benner thought would be entirely helpful. But, for all his hopes, nothing he said in his defense and nothing from the outside groups contributed in evidence ever significantly influenced the University administration in any positive direction. In fact, subsequent events indicate quite the reverse.[16]

As might be obvious already, the child development project was but one facet, albeit a major one, of the whole question of the nature and role of the "laboratory school" in a college of education. At the University of Illinois, deprived as it was of anything except a secondary school (and a perpetually shakey one at that), the question was merely what to do with the University High School. Although other (and usually confused) apologies had not been lacking, it had been most readily and understandably justified as a "practice school." When numbers were small, and practice teaching a kind of luxury, it had emerged as the principal instrument for taking account of that aspect of teacher preparation. However, when practice work became required for certification and the College began to enroll hundreds rather than dozens, practice teaching itself had to be radically revised.

Practice teaching had for some time been a program requirement and had usually been provided. With the growth of the College, however, it soon came to exceed the customary provisions for it at Uni-

[15] See Benner's seven-page "Analysis of Memorandum No. 223," dated June 3, 1939, esp. pp. 1, 2, 3; and Benner to Willard, May 17, 1939; both in College of of Education Papers. In the latter, Benner apologized to the President, the Provost, and the Bureau of Institutional Research for an error in his remarks on the budgets.

[16] 41st Report (1942), p. 283. The date of Benner's appearance was May 15, 1941.

versity High School. At first only the vocational subjects posed a problem—it was difficult to maintain a vocational agriculture program at a sophisticated prep school—but by 1933 the registration in academic subjects had exceeded the school's limitations also, and the work was expanded to other schools in Champaign-Urbana.[17]

The neighboring high school instructors who provided supervision for the students in their practice teaching were called "cooperating teachers." Although their work was both important and demanding if done thoroughly, they were not at first paid anything for their efforts. They were, however, given a vague, quasi "appointment" to the University staff, under rigid prohibitions, and eventually received some benefits (as, for example, in the case of tuitions). By 1939 they were regarded as having a form of rank in the University High School.[18]

The arrangement seemed always to be a problem. The participants were difficult to supervise, the administration never seemed quite clear about the intent or demands of the program, and the difficulty of forecasting which and how many students would be involved was notorious.[19] When practice teaching became a state requirement in 1938, these problems increased. Benner pleaded for more University facilities as the ultimate answer, but only his immediate proposal to pay those who were appointed to supervise the work was accepted by the Trustees. This initiated a continuing budgetary wrangle. In 1938 an additional item of $8,500–$9,500 was not happily received, even though it meant that the teachers were only receiving $10 per semester. (This figure, as Benner had proposed from the beginning, was later raised to $25.) Even Willard agreed that a $5 assessment of the students to cover the cost would be less than fair, since their economic outlook as teachers was dim enough anyway. Furthermore (and perhaps more persuasive), the state teachers' colleges were making no such charges, and the University's position in respect to them might be even more unfavorable if it did so "unilaterally."[20] Yet, as the net-

---

[17] Benner to Chase, June 28, 1933, Chase Correspondence.
[18] Benner to Willard, October 13, 1934; 38th *Report* (1936), pp. 21, 67ff., 141–42; Willard to Benner, September 17, 1934. Both letters in Willard Correspondence.
[19] Benner to Willard, April 6, 1937; Benner to Nell B. Johnston, April 30, 1938 (and attached correspondence); Willard Correspondence.
[20] Benner to Willard, May 24, 1937, and attachments, College of Education Papers. Also see Benner to Willard (and attached suggested letter), May 24, 1937 (the suggested letter was sent as Willard to A. J. Harno, et al., May 26, 1937);

work of cooperating schools and teachers grew rapidly, so did the costs. Practice-teaching enrollment increased by 62 percent in four years, until it reached 628 in 1939 (an increase of 101 in one year). And by that fall, the program stretched from Belleville to the suburbs of Chicago and from Quincy to Robinson.[21]

Since the University High School was no longer even the principal instrument for extending facilities for practice teaching, its whole role had to be reexamined. What did it contribute and what should it contribute? Without a practical justification any longer, it finally had to develop a theoretical one. Was it, *could* it be, a *"laboratory"*? In what sense? The development of an answer to these queries and the no less vexing problem of communicating that answer to the larger University and its administration will now occupy our attention.

When Benner had arrived at Urbana, the University High School, never more than a pallid, almost monstrous image of the ideas which had been its conception, was not in good health. Suppressed, as we have seen, for ten years under Kinley, its faculty morale low, its students ill-housed and even badly taught (at least by the criteria then coming to prevail even in the larger market towns), the school seemed to have little to offer. Principal Lewis Ward Williams had struggled manfully to maintain it from its inception, but shortly after the new

and Benner to Willard, April 23, 1937, and attached "Report on the Problem of Providing Practice Teaching to Prospective Teachers," dated April 23, 1937, and signed by Benner; all in Willard Correspondence. Cf. 40th *Report* (1940), p. 798; and Willard to Sanford, October 3, 1940, Willard Correspondence.

[21] College of Education "Annual Report" (1938–39), p. 5, College of Education Papers; 40th *Report* (1940), pp. 667, 953–55.

Two interesting sidelights were revealed when the first cooperating teacher appointments were announced in 1935. There was, and there continued to be, provision for elementary school practice work, even though the University was not supposed to be in that, the field of the teachers' colleges. There were also Roman Catholic religious authorized as cooperating teachers, and practice work took place in their schools. Beginning with Sister Clotilde, principal of nearby St. Mary's School, the number in fact grew rapidly until the war years. At that time, the number was gradually reduced (for some reason which still remains mysterious); there were no further appointments of parochial school personnel after 1943. They may have been dropped due to declining need during the war but not reestablished later as a matter of policy. Although the McCollum case did not reach a Supreme Court verdict until 1948, it is conceivable that the general atmosphere of concern over church-state issues which surrounded it may have been of influence. For elementary work, see 38th *Report* (1936), pp. 141ff. See also 41st *Report* (1942), pp. 707ff., 818ff., 856–58. For the McCollum case, see *McCollum* v. *Champaign Board of Education*, 333 U.S. 203 (1948).

Dean's arrival he resigned to work with the rapidly expanding Appointments Committee which he had also nursed along for some years. He was succeeded in 1932 by a locally prepared Ph.D. who had occasionally taught educational history and who had a firm grasp on both the theoretical views and the practical problems he faced. That man was Charles Wilson Sanford.[22]

The problems which Sanford faced had, as we have seen, a considerable history. Following Senate recommendations in 1910 for "a training, experimental and observation school of secondary grade," the Trustees had requested $250,000 for an *education* building which would include a "model high school." (The relationship between High School and College facilities had been a question from the beginning.) It was some five years later before the school site had even been secured, and the building—a small part of the proposed complex—was not used for school purposes until the fall of 1921. In spite of the enormous building boom under Kinley, no further work was done until 1930. (In fact, the plans themselves disappeared under what Benner interpreted as suspicious circumstances.) In 1930 an unexpended budget item of $26,000 had been used to throw up a hastily conceived cinder block "gymnasium" which had been designed without consultation with either the College or the High School faculties and had been "so located as to preclude completion of the original plan."[23] A modest and underpaid staff had kept the school functioning during the 1920's against considerable odds, but, as Monroe reported when he assumed temporary control in 1930–31, the enrollment was decidedly anemic.[24] When Benner arrived, the 150 tuition-paying students—some of whom, curiously enough, were apparently still University students using the school to erase their deficiencies, as they had in the old preparatory department—were served by a staff of nineteen, including the librarian. Almost immediately, and largely in response to Sanford's leadership, staff and students began to climb. By 1937–38, student enrollment had increased by 70 percent and staff by 50 percent, although even then the nearly

[22] *Catalogue* (1932–33), p. 11; (1934–35), s.v. Education, passim.
[23] File "Laboratory School," Benner Papers, esp. "History of Efforts at Illinois to Secure Laboratory School." See also Benner's final "Annual Report" (1944–45), pp. 1–3, same location.
[24] College of Education "Annual Report" (1930–31), submitted by Monroe to Chase, and Chase's reply to Monroe. Both were originally in Chase Correspondence, but now appear to have been misplaced.

250 students and twenty-eight full-time faculty and staff were by no means an optimal number.[25]

Beginning with President Chase's regime, the students had been more hospitably received, and the faculty were now frequently doing graduate work in the University. At the request of schoolmen who were summer students in the College, the High School had kept its doors open during the summer of 1933, with the equivalent of some sixty-five full-time pupils on a special fee basis. The schoolmen thought it necessary "as a means of exemplifying the theory presented in summer session courses in education," and it seemed to serve a need for some local high school pupils. Since that first experiment was successful, the financially beleaguered Trustees approved it as a permanent arrangement, provided it continued to be self-supporting.[26]

Obviously, the general climate had improved somewhat. But if there was some progress, the school was still physically inadequate—in fact, very badly inadequate—as Benner soon noted. Completion of the truncated plant was of dubious possibility, and the location itself, far removed from the other work of the College, was a negative factor. Routine constructive maintenance, let alone improvements, had been almost nonexistent, even in the palmy 1920's. In the Depression, virtually nothing could be done beyond the development of a new cafeteria service. In fact, the condition of the plant was so bad that in 1936 the University's own High School Visitor condemned it unreservedly. Far from being the "model school" it had been designed to be, the physical features were less attractive than those of all but the worst. Its fourth floor "auditorium" really nothing but an "unfinished attic" (and a potentially disastrous fire trap); with bare, concrete floors in its classrooms, bereft of the facilities now virtually required for extracurricular activities, University High School, at the close of the Depression, did not seem worth saving. It is understandable that both the Dean and the energetic new principal proposed that it be redone entirely, not as a high school alone but as part of a total educational complex.[27]

[25] College of Education "Annual Report" (1932–33), p. 1; (1933–34), passim; C. W. Sanford to Benner, June 6, 1934; "Annual Report" (1937–38), p. 9; all in College of Education Papers. See also Benner to Chase, June 28, 1933, Chase Correspondence; and 37th *Report* (1934), pp. 102ff.

[26] Chase to George Huff, December 11, 1931; A. J. Janata to Benner, February 25, 1933; both in Chase Correspondence. See also 37th *Report* (1934), p. 188 (the source of the quotation) and p. 433.

[27] College of Education "Annual Report" (1933–34), p. 2; Benner to Willard, October 4, 1934, Willard Correspondence; "Annual Report" (1935–36), pp. 4–6.

But the real problem, and the necessary presupposition of any physical rebuilding, was a clear conception of its nature and purpose. It appeared obvious that only if such a philosophy could be articulated, and then communicated to the wider University and the legislature itself, could any real change take place. Both Benner and Sanford devoted themselves wholeheartedly to the task. The *Catalogue* of 1932–33 had proclaimed that "the laboratory of the College of Education centers around the work of University High School," but went on to define that "laboratory" work as essentially educational practice, observation, and participation in educational "activities." That this was an inadequate concept and one made increasingly dubious by the expansion of practice teaching, both Benner and Sanford were quick to see. When, by the mid-1930's, increasing state and university budgets made educational expansion feasible, both pressed convincingly for a whole new orientation defined in terms of service and research. The High School faculty were encouraged to take leadership in the statewide curricular reforms that were the topic of the hour (a task in which Sanford contributed a great deal personally). And, particularly from 1937 to 1940, the principal perceptively analyzed the research problem and laid out well-conceived practical proposals for the school.[28]

Sanford pointed out that the University High School was advertising its priorities when it stated as its objectives: (1) superior instruction for pupils of high school grade; (2) opportunities for observation and practice; (3) the provision of "a laboratory for the College of Education"; (4) the provision of assistance to the teachers of the state "in the solution of their educational problems." Admiting that the first was now being accomplished "with a considerable degree of effectiveness," the principal did not suggest that it might be antithetical to the others, and that the criteria for "superior" which were actually operative might be extremely dubious. He argued that the second objective, particularly in respect to practice, was clearly becoming irrelevant and impeding rather than advancing progress. Primarily he fastened on the third, the "laboratory" objective. It was, he said, "seldom" achieved since the *College* staff rarely used the school, practice-teaching requirements tied up classes, the teachers were overburdened by instructional work,

---

"Annual Reports" in College of Education Papers. Note that the complaints are registered by the University's own High School Visitor.

28 *Catalogue* (1932–33), p. 138; College of Education "Annual Report" (1935–36), pp. 4–6; (1936–37), pp. 4ff.; both in College of Education Papers.

and (perhaps most significantly) they had not been chosen for their ability to do experimental work. This "failure to utilize the high school as a laboratory," he said, was "one of the most serious deficiencies of our entire set up. . . ." It tended to "confine the college staff to theories not exemplified in practice" (a constant concern). As a further consequence, it deprived the staff of stimulation and tended "to atrophy the inquiring attitude of mind which is the virile quality of an institution." [29]

Instead of being preempted for less vital functions, Sanford argued, the High School ought to press inquiry into at least four "problems of significance." The first was the improvement of instruction in "written expression" by bringing to bear the "psychological point of view." The second, which gave witness to the new pragmatic curricular winds which were blowing through the College, was the finding of appropriate "experiences in reflective thinking" which would be utilized at the various grade levels. Criticizing the continued prevalence of mere memory work in all schools, and the failure of most teachers to understand what was actually "involved in thinking," the principal sought improvement particularly through the social and natural sciences. The third, which again conveyed a pragmatic flavor, was "the problem of making history functional" instead of "formal and academic," an objective to be accomplished by discovering the ways in which "the past is immanent in the present." Fourth was the notorious "problem of evaluating achievement," which he properly saw as a necessary concomitant of any work in the others.[30]

Sanford proposed "conjoint activities"—a near paraphrase of Dewey —between College and High School as the basis for research which would serve the needs of the schools, noting that conditions in the schools would provide the criteria for significance. These activities should form the experimental basis for a thorough revision of the professional courses in the College and a new set of objectives for the High School. Observation should be practiced in conjunction with theory-building and in advance of any practice teaching. The whole College–High School operation, the principal argued, should deal with

[29] *Catalogue* (1938–39), pp. 155ff. For Sanford's reflections, see Sanford to Benner, May 24, 1938 (under "Annual Report" [1937–38]), College of Education Papers.

[30] Sanford to Benner, May 24, 1938, esp. pp. 4–7 (under "Annual Report" [1937–38]), College of Education Papers. The entire report is excellent and still worth reading for itself.

public school problems, not merely its own interests. The increasingly heterogeneous student population of the 1930's and the demands of "democratization of the schools" compelled this, he thought. The previous preoccupation with theory by itself had led to effective criticism but no positive, constructive leadership—anywhere in the state. To increase the potential for leadership, the practice teachers should be moved into the public schools, and the teachers brought in to the University High School.[31]

Benner, obviously impressed, passed Sanford's recommendations on with enthusiasm in the Annual Reports of the College. In particular, he made them the foundation of his appeal for a new, unified school facility, combined with offices and more academic laboratory facilities. But there was one crucial obstruction: the High School had been reduced, beyond doubt, to a private preparatory school. Sanford formulated, and Benner accepted, a kind of simple, threefold platform for the needed rennaisance: a broader program, which was in turn dependent upon the elimination of tuition and the recruiting of a truly representative student body. No educational research of any value to the ordinary schoolteacher would ever likely come from its highly selective constituency. In submitting his contribution to the College's 1937–38 "Annual Report," Sanford vigorously pressed a recommendation that "the University High School be made a typical school." [32]

The phrase "typical school" became almost a technical term, standing for "typical of the schools the University High School and the College were designed to serve." Since its "instructional aim" was almost exclusively college preparatory, its students highly selective, and its classes "as a rule" entirely too small to be comparable, the High School simply could not serve them. Experience at the High School, whether for teachers, College students, or research faculty, simply did not generate more than a few of the problems actually facing the common schools. The only remedy would be to abolish the tuition so dear to the University and "set up criteria for obtaining typical pupils." The tuition had been dropped for the 1938 summer session demonstration classes, and immediately almost twice as many applicants presented

[31] Ibid., esp. p. 8.
[32] Ibid., p. 7, 8 (the source of Sanford's remarks). Cf. College of Education "Annual Report" (1938–39), pp. 11–13; (1939–40), pp. 7, 8, and attached Building Program Report. For more on Sanford's position see his (?) six-page report in conjunction with the College's "Annual Report" for 1938–39. All in College of Education Papers.

themselves as there were places, allowing "a more typical pupil group" to be obtained. However, no permanent reforms were effected, in spite of Sanford's (and Benner's) renewed pleas.[33]

Although research plans had been "tentatively formulated" as early as 1935, virtually nothing occurred. Except for some almost trivial studies of nutrition, there was—because there could be—almost no institutionally organized and funded research or experimental activity at any time during the Benner period. Unfortunately, the school was a "success" as it was. In 1941 Harvard University placed it at the top of its list of college-preparatory institutions for the period 1934–40 —a fact which Benner ought to have reported with mixed emotions. At preparing the sons and daughters of faculty and local sophisticates for academic careers it was doing exceedingly well. In the face of achievements such as that, it was of little importance that the institution glaringly failed to meet the needs for which it had been constructed, those of the College and the state.[34]

The development of a useful research program depended, in Benner's view, not only upon a revised concept of the school but also upon its extension to wider levels of operation. The schoolteachers of the state, still largely working at the nursery to eighth-grade level, could not look to a secondary school program for the answers to most of their questions. Secondary educators, on the other hand, could not explore the roots of their problem. Benner had pressed early for an extension downward toward the junior high school level, and some attempts had been made to work them in as "sub-freshmen or special group freshman classes," but nothing really came of it. Every research or expansion proposal, like almost every other College program, was drawn up short by the hopeless inadequacy of the physical facilities.[35]

[33] College of Education "Annual Report" (1938–39), pp. 11, 12; and Sanford's University High School Report under the College's "Annual Report" (1939–40), pp. 1–3 (in which he asks, inter alia, for "facilities for football"). For summer session classes, see Sanford to Benner, May 24, 1938 (under "Annual Report" [1937–38]), p. 2. All in College of Education Papers.

[34] Benner to Willard, April 4, 1935, College of Education Papers. See 37th Report (1937–38), p. 10, where Benner remarks that these research plans gave "promise of leading to improved practice in the public schools of the state." All in the College of Education Papers. For the "Harvard" judgment, see Benner to Willard, February 8, 1941, Willard Papers. It might be worth noting, in this connection, that the High School's constituency was heavily populated with the children of those who opposed ferociously the College's plans and principles.

[35] Benner to Willard, April 4, 1935, College of Education Papers; 37th Report (1934), p. 593; College of Education "Annual Report" (1939–40), and attached Building Program, in College of Education Papers.

In March, 1935, Governor Henry Horner requested a large appropriation of PWA funds for constructing University buildings. When the news was made public, Benner protested to President Willard that no mention of any facilities for Education was made. He also drew attention to the fact that he had read in the newspapers of the preceding January 20 that the Trustees had already had a meeting in which advocates of various campus building projects had appeared to plead their cases. The College, so far as he knew, had not been invited, nor had it (consequently) been included in the list of projects reported out to the state planning commission that February. Pointing out that at least one project had been "agitated" off campus (and suggesting that the College could do so, if that was the recommended strategy— which of course it supposedly was not) he reinforced his long-standing claim that the need for a complex of educational buildings was "critical" in bringing the College of Education "to anything approaching a state of health." Benner followed this the next month (April) with an extensive and careful plea to the Administration for "resuming" the interrupted building program by constructing a U-shaped complex which would add elementary, office, and laboratory facilities. He pointed out very clearly the relationship of this proposal to graduate work, to other departments, and to the growing question of the research role of the University vis-à-vis the state colleges. He laid out a proposed population of 850 students (nursery through high school) and attempted to show how this broader system would both aid the University in taking a position of leadership in the burgeoning curricular-reform movement and also aid in resolving the practice-teaching problem.[36]

Although the Dean renewed the request at the end of the following month as well, there is no evidence to suggest that the administration greeted his proposals with any serious concern, let alone any enthusiasm. When the University Council discussed the long-awaited resumption of building that December, it accorded *no part* of the College's proposals higher than a *third-class* priority—which was the academic equivalent of dead storage. Nor did the Trustees evidence any particular anxiety over the future of the College. About the only

[36] Benner to Willard, March 19, 1935, College of Education Papers. The building he referred to was apparently the proposed Journalism building, strongly advocated by the Illinois Press Association (Report of the University Council, December 4, 1935, Willard Correspondence). For Benner's proposals, see Benner to Willard, April 4, 1935, College of Education Papers.

action they took beyond the routine was the munificent gift of a plaque commemorating Bagley's founding of Kappa Delta Pi (presented with proper trumpeting of educational interest on February 20, the Society's twenty-fifth anniversary) and a September joust with a peculiarly knotty problem, the provision of clean towels for University High School.[37]

The following biennium's complement of Trustees took a more generous view of the matter, however. At the end of January, 1937, a "Composite List of Requests and Proposals for New Buildings and Land Acquisitions," prepared by a specially appointed committee, was reported through the President. More extensive in its scope, but probably little more than a survey of the University's hopes, the list included a "first unit" for the College (in ninth place) and assigned it to the 1941–43 biennium. This unit was intended largely for office and instructional space. Item thirty-five proposed to extend Main Street through Illinois Field and the subsequent "construction of new College of Education practice schools [note the plural], moving from its present location University High School to this site and adding school facilities down below the kindergarten age." The new complex would also enjoy the use of the University's old gymnasium facilities and, upon completion, the present school building was to be remodeled for engineering or journalism. The most optimistic guess anticipated this might occur sometime during the 1945–47 biennium, or about ten years later. But apparently Dean Benner was neither optimistic about the future nor pleased with present progress. A few weeks later he again put the College's building needs extremely bluntly—if not quite rudely—to Hiram T. Scovill, thus breaking what had been at least an official calm. Logical defensibility was not, the Dean might have learned, the equivalent of practical acceptance by the power structure.[38]

The administration's meticulously scheduled inaction of 1937 was answered by a College committee proposal for the establishment of three elementary grades and a nursery and kindergarten, drawn up in November, 1938. To be housed in two existing structures on West Springfield, this operation reached the blueprint and cost-estimate stage, but funds were again denied. The following spring witnessed

---

[37] Benner to Willard, May 30, 1935, College of Education Papers; "Report of the Actions of the University Council of December 4, 1935" (dated December 17, 1935), copy in College of Education Papers. For Trustees' action, see 38th *Report* (1936), pp. 566ff., 39th *Report* (1938), p. 34.

[38] 39th *Report* (1938), pp. 155ff. Benner to Scovill, March 6, 1937, Willard Correspondence.

the final collapse of the ill-starred cooperative program in child development, which had also made school building promises favorable to the College. But the very next spring, in March, 1940, apparently now convinced it might as well be refused a whole loaf as a half, the "Committee on a Building Program of the College of Education" brought forward plans for a nursery to high school complex, including a psycho-educational clinic, which was estimated to cost $1,500,000. Perhaps designed to sell by contrast, an alternative immediate plan was also submitted. This plan called for a temporary fifty-pupil kindergarten, a six-grade elementary school for 150 children, and a very modest psycho-educational clinic. This was to be operated in four old structures on West Springfield Avenue and one block away on West Stoughton. Neither the master plan nor the inexpensive alternative was thought feasible, however. Several further appeals for the same plans, or variants of them, were submitted during 1943, 1944, and 1945. All were argued on the need for research and service, and the immediate threat of losing theoretical leadership in education to surrounding universities and the growing state teachers' colleges. Most had conscious and increasing extra-university support, which by now had been shown to be obviously profitable. As late as mid-1945, although matters appeared somewhat more hopeful by then, the President was still promising only a high (and elusively future) priority to the school buildings. The College's committee deliberations suggest that they believed their extensive work during this period was important. Examination of the records of the Trustees and the University and state planning committees, however, gives not the slightest evidence that the matter was ever taken seriously on their part.[39]

The instructional and administrative space requirements of the College were met somewhat better, though hardly with ample provision. When the ancient University Hall was badly damaged by a storm and had to be abandoned, an appropriation was secured in 1938 for a new classroom building, later to be known as Gregory Hall. The College,

[39] "History of Efforts at Illinois to Secure Laboratory School" and attached correspondence and documents in File "Laboratory School," College of Education Papers. According to College records, specific proposals or recommendations were made in November, 1938, February, 1939, March, 1940, May, 1943, and August, 1944. For the original child development proposal, see College of Education "Annual Report" (1936-37), p. 5, College of Education Papers. A thorough search of the records in which the University building considerations were developed shows nothing to support either the College's hopes or the administration's ocasional rhetorical promises to the College and schoolmen. The marginal notations, as well as the "silence," speak very clearly.

which already enjoyed 6,890 square feet of space, was designed in at 9,906—something less than a vast improvement. The Psychology Department was allotted 13,000 and Journalism 15,000 square feet.[40]

The College's facilities remained, then, for all practical purposes, precisely where they had been on Benner's arrival. As proposal after proposal languished in committees and bureaus, so did the research and service plans which were inescapably bound up with them. When the state school inspector visited William Chandler Bagley's "model school" twenty years after its opening, he found its restricted programs generally praiseworthy but its facilities entitled only to the severest condemnation. The physical education program was the case in point. The High School's "locker, shower and toilet rooms are grossly inadequate," he said, and the whole operation needed to be brought "up to and beyond what [was] expected in the high schools of the state." Housed in a temporary, dysfunctional gymnasium, the physical education staff could offer but three recent improvements as evidence of progress: thermostats, automatic flush toilets, and soap dishes in the showers.[41]

In terms reminiscent of the revolutionary attempts to retrain the teaching force in the field fifty years before, Dean Benner reported to the President in 1936 that the teachers of the state wanted the University to take the lead in programs for "itinerant teacher training." The teachers saw a need for a new revolution in their work, and, if financial distress prevented their return to the campus for the new philosophy and methodology, they believed the University ought once more to come to them.[42] As we have noted, Benner was extremely conscious of the need to get the College out into the schools and to get the schools into the College. Its virtual withdrawal during the

[40] 39th *Report* (1938), p. 833; Willard to Benner, May 15, 1941, Willard Correspondence. The letter shows something of the problems of personality which were developing, and the difficulties of communication.

[41] Benner to Willard, March 21, 1941, and supporting correspondence, College of Education Papers.

[42] Herbert W. Mumford (Agriculture) and Benner to Willard, July 20, 1936, College of Education Papers. The quotation is on p. 2. For an example of the teachers' concerns, see J. W. Carrington (Director of Training Schools at Illinois State Normal University), "Meeting the New Demands on Education—*A Plea for a Concerted Attack upon the Problems Facing the Public Schools*," in *Illinois Teacher* 23 (January, 1935): 131ff., 149. For the administration's lack of insight, see Willard's statement of the University's concern, along with his subtle chastisement of special interest groups and their demands, *Illinois Teacher* 23 (February, 1935): 165.

previous decade had destroyed its role as a leader in the common schools of Illinois and nearly eliminated it as a contributor of importance. The new Dean had immediately encouraged the College staff to bend its efforts in helping the schools face the alarming financial crisis, and the faculty also had worked strenuously to provide leadership in the influential curriculum-study movements which were afoot.[43] By the mid-1930's Benner pleaded for a curriculum specialist who would have a "joint appointment" with the Chicago school system and the College. Although unsuccessful, he saw this arrangement as not only an opportunity for service but as an opportunity for research in the state's major educational system, one which had lain essentially untouched by the College since its formation.[44]

The College moved to become more accessible by establishing professional correspondence courses in 1934–35. The following year it offered its first professional (as opposed to vocational) education courses on an extramural basis. These courses, offered at key locations throughout the state, came to comprise a large part of the College's teaching load. In 1936 a graduate "internship" program was proposed and initiated. Graduate students in both professional areas and in academic specializations were employed half-time to three-quarters-time as teachers (under special supervision) or as administrators while they did regular or Saturday classwork. Through the program, teachers and administrators were aided in improving their competence, but they were still able to support themselves, and closer ties with key school systems were developed. Flourishing for a time, the plan proved difficult to administer and faded in importance; but it did set a pattern for graduate study which has continued to the present day.[45]

[43] College of Education "Annual Reports" (1931–32), p. 2; (1932–1933), p. 1; (1933–34), p. 2; (1937–38), pp. 6, 8. Even University High School publications were circulated to bring about closer contact. See, for example, *Science Club Bulletin*, under Janata to Benner, December 23, 1935, Willard Correspondence.

[44] Benner to Willard, March 15, 1935; cf. Benner to A. J. Janata, April 8, 1935, both in College of Education Papers. Benner pointed out that other school systems were doing this; Des Moines had just hired a Harvard man as its special advisor. To some, however, even curriculum was an illegitimate field for inquiry. See, for example, Benner to W. H. Rodebush (Chemistry), May 22, 1941, copy in Carmichael Papers, Record Series 7/1/2, no. 4.

[45] *Catalogue* (1934–35), pp. 341ff. The correspondence courses, under Robert Bell Browne, were "Principles of Secondary Education," the "Technic" course, "Educational Psychology," and "Recent Developments in the Teaching of Arithmetic." For extramural courses, see *Catalogue* (1936–37), pp. 351ff. Graduate courses were first offered at Carbondale, Normal, and Charleston (as part of the move to meet the need for graduate work at the state teachers' colleges) and an

During the mid-1930's, Benner and O. F. Weber of the College faculty were called upon by the Illinois Educational Commission to play a prominent role in a statewide study of school problems. Perhaps the commission's most important recommendation was for a state "Board of Education." Benner backed the idea vigorously and also proposed an appointed state superintendent, in the hope of removing the schools from their long-standing connections with party politics and improving their professional efficiency. Although the measure failed—due, Benner believed, to the very political interference the bill was designed to thwart—he saw as an "important by-product" of the study its "contribution towards the restoration of the University to leadership in Illinois." [46] As the decade moved into its closing years, the Dean believed that his efforts were paying the needed dividends. The University was placing increasing numbers of administrators in high posts in the more important school systems.[47]

The movement out into the schools was not, however, without its difficulties. Leadership in changing times, when the debate between the old and the new often became acrimonious and dangerous, required a willingness to face controversial situations and act in them. Benner never lacked this willingness, and neither did a number of his colleagues. Nor did they escape the penalties. The potential pitfalls were

undergraduate course was offered at Effingham. For the internship program (first used at Decatur), see A. J. Janata to Benner, May 27, 1936 (and attachments), Willard Correspondence; College of Education "Annual Reports" (1935-36), p. 9; (1936-37), p. 3; (1937-38), p. 9; College of Education Papers. For a general review of these projects and the financial fears which they aroused in the administration, see Benner to Willard, July 3, 1967 (which credits Sanford with developing the internship program); cf. Lloyd Morey to Willard, June 26, 1937; Benner to Willard, June 24, 1937; all in Willard Correspondence.

[46] College of Education "Annual Report" (1935-36), pp. 9, 10 (the source of the quotation); Benner to Willard, July 10, 1937 (where Benner accounts for the proposed School Board's failure); both in College of Education Papers. See also Willard to Benner, July 12, 1937 (and accompanying "confidential" report by Mrs. Laura Hughes of the Illinois League of Women Voters); Willard to Benner, June 16, 1938; all in Willard Correspondence. Significant progress toward these goals was not made until the adoption of a new Illinois constitution in 1970.

[47] College of Education "Annual Report" (1937-38), p. 6, College of Education Papers. The "Appointment" or "Placement" Service (as it was variously called) was somewhat ambiguously related to the College, and at times Benner seems to have wanted it out, replaced by a strictly teacher-placement office (possibly run by the High School Visitor). See Benner to Willard, May 28, 1935; A. J. Janata to Benner, February 1, 1937 (and attached correspondence); Benner to Willard, February 15, 1937; Willard to Benner, April 6, 1938 (and accompanying correspondence). Cf. Benner to Willard, June 24, July 3, 1937. All in Willard Correspondence.

especially widespread in the program for high school visitation and accreditation and its related activities. The visitation and accreditation (or "inspection") programs had been headed since 1928 by Arthur W. Clevenger, the former assistant who had been brought back from the University of Michigan to take the place of the venerable Horace A. Hollister, the virtually life-long governor of these matters.[48]

As we have noted previously, the Visitor's work, although related in a very delicate way with it, was not in fact under the supervision of the College of Education. Responsibility for the work was not clear. In 1915 the Board of Trustees had officially adopted the Senate's policies in the matter—the historical source of the University's accrediting and admitting standards. It had, however, never officially empowered the standing "Committee on Admissions from Secondary Schools," which the Senate had created in 1931. Furthermore, by this time the onerous task of continually inspecting the schools to enforce standards was shared with the state superintendent and closely duplicated by the North Central Association. Benner recognized very early the ambiguity and confusion implicit in these arrangements, and he expressed the hope that the College and the Visitor's office might collaborate more closely.[49]

In 1935, the Trustees moved to regularize the Senate Admissions Committee, establishing officially its membership and duties and placing the Visitor as its ex officio secretary. The Committee was authorized to supervise all accrediting activity, determining (on approval by the Senate) conditions and criteria for judgment. The Trustees suggested also that one of its functions was to "encourage and promote the development of sound educational policies pertaining to secondary education in the State of Illinois," and that it should publish information bearing on that function. The difficulty, a historic one as we have seen, was of course that "sound" could in the long run mean only "to the University's advantage," since the fundamental aim of the program was the protection of its interests. The Committee's personnel were in most cases not schoolmen, and their conception of a good high school was generated by the relationship of secondary education to higher education. Their powers of inspection were a de facto (though not necessarily intentional) threat to the schools. Benner had recognized this for some time and drawn attention to it. He even proposed

[48] 31st *Report* (1922), p. 27; 34th *Report* (1928), p. 543.
[49] 38th *Report* (1936), p. 190; Benner to Chase, May 17, 1933, Chase Correspondence.

that a completely new agency, if necessary outside the College, be established to develop more positive relations with the high schools.[50]

Although there was practically no evidence that accrediting high school systems provided grounds for valid or consistent prediction in individual cases—indeed, what evidence there was strongly suggested otherwise—alternatives were not easy to devise. Nell Johnston, one of the College's most popular faculty figures, brought back from her leave in England a considerable interest in entrance examinations as the hoped-for solution. Earlier in favor of some statewide testing programs for high school students as educational devices, Benner was not (and had not been) enthusiastic about using them as admissions or school-evaluation procedures. He feared that the content of the tests would likely be dominated by the same academic concepts as prevailed in the inspection programs. He also argued that the evidence was as strongly against tests as predictors of academic achievement as it was against accredited systems. In fact, he believed that all such "accrediting" by the University should be dropped—especially since other agencies would continue it in any case. The University might, he suggested, routinely test students from the bottom 50 percent of all high schools instead. The enormous saving of money could then be devoted to some form of positive leadership for the schools.[51]

As a consequence of the inspectorial function, College and University representatives were frequently called upon for school "surveys." These surveys were usually conducted in anticipation of curricular or other reform proposals in school systems, at least ostensibly. They frequently demonstrated, however, not only the difficulty of providing educational leadership when the University had its own interest to serve, but the potentially explosive situation school development generated. Surveys were often called for at times of local

[50] 38th *Report* (1936), p. 190 (the source of the quotation); Benner to Willard, November 19, 1934, and accompanying correspondence, College of Education Papers. Benner hoped that the state office itself would come to offer more genuine guidance, including even an attempt to elevate the "moral" tone of the communities in which the schools were located.

[51] Benner to Willard, March 26, 1938 (and other correspondence at same location), College of Education Papers; "State-wide Testing in High Schools and Its Bearing on Admission to College" (address to the Federation of Illinois Colleges, February 18, 1935—repeated in substance on several occasions) and Benner's six-page mimeogaphed "Notes on State-wide Testing in the High Schools, with Special Reference to Illinois," in Benner Papers. See also Benner to Chase, April 26, 1932, in Chase Corespondence; Benner to Willard, November 16, 1939; Willard to Benner, November 21, 1939; Ball to Benner, March 16, 1940; "Memorandum" of A. J. Janata, May 3, 1940; all in Willard Correspondence.

crisis in the schools, and the "evidence" provided by the evaluations and suggestions of the survey teams was turned into political ammunition of the most volatile sort. For a College and University which ultimately depended for its very existence upon a public legislature and a delicate balance of informal interests, the possible results were less than delectable. During the 1930's there were two cases (among many) which demonstrated with utter clarity all the difficulties which had marked the relations between the University, the College, and the schools. These were the Galesburg school survey and the problem of establishing relations with the Chicago public schools.

Dean Benner, John A. Clement, Edwin H. Reeder, and Oscar F. Weber conducted a survey at the request of the Galesburg public schools in 1938. Their investigative actions were routine, and their conclusions, filed in an extensive report, were no more unusual or threatening than those of many other inquiries into a specific educational system. The situation, however, turned out to be otherwise. Although the invitation had appeared entirely innocent on the surface, it was ultimately connected with local political dynamics. School board elections had just preceded issuance of their report, and it became obvious that the information and judgments which it contained were desired for use against certain individuals in the hotly contested race. President Willard, upon learning of this situation, pointedly queried Dean Benner about the advisability of the whole practice. Alarmed at the prospect of University involvement in a nasty squabble within a community of some size and potential influence, he raised the question of whether the College should thereafter accept such requests without official permission of the University. The Dean admitted that the investigators had in some sense been taken in by the whole business. He did not think the answer to the problem lay so much in gaining permission for such sorties as it suggested a wholesale review of policy. He reiterated his long-standing belief that the University's relationship with the schools had to be founded on something entirely more positive to avoid the situations.[52] But if the Galesburg case had given the President pause, other events were already brewing which made it appear pale and innocuous in comparison.

[52] Willard to Benner (and reply), April 5, 1938, Willard Correspondence. For the report at issue, see File "G," re: Galesburg Public Schools, Record Series 2/9/1, no. 27. It is interesting to note that a Willard memo on the "Benner Case" may be found at the location of the correspondence, suggesting rather temptingly that the administration considered using the ill-fated episode against Benner later. It did not do so, however.

Shortly before the Galesburg case came to a head, on March 8, 1938, the Dean of the College of Education reported to the President that on the previous afternoon, at half past four, the superintendent of schools of the city of Chicago had warned him by telephone that he would "take legal action" by means of the Board of Education's staff of attorneys, if the Dean "persisted in making speeches against him and his administration." [53] As if this threat were not disconcerting enough, Benner reported, Superintendent William H. Johnson then proceeded to challenge him to meet " 'man to man.' " Obviously, something of a nadir in positive relations between the University, the College, and the state's most important (and politically influential) school system had been reached. The situation did not, of course, reflect a momentary fit of pique; behind this challenge to fisticuffs there lay a long history of decline in the Chicago schools and inaction on the part of the College and University.

Relations with the Chicago public schools, the nation's second-largest urban system, have not occupied a large part in our narrative. The reason is that there had been virtually none. In part this was not the fault of either the University or the College, since the city and its environing Cook County had largely been a law unto themselves both politically and educationally. It was, by the 1930's, beginning to be obvious—though the issue is not settled even at this writing—that the educational bifurcation of Illinois was no more defensible than its political split into "downstate" and "upstate." The issue, however, is of such importance that some of the considerable historical background required for it to be fully understood must be sketched in.

Chicago was America's most rapidly growing metropolis, raw-boned and full of contradictory elements introduced by foreign and domestic migrations and sharpened by the radical restructuring of American life which paralleled its rapid and undisciplined growth.[54]

---

[53] For this and what follows, see esp. the following (along with other materials too numerous to mention, at the same location): Benner to Willard, March 8, 1938; signed "Memoranda" to accompany that letter, March 8, 1938; copies of Benner to W. H. Johnson, March 8, 1938, and Almer M. Pennewell et al. (under name of the Chicago Church Federation) to "Brother Pastors," February 5, 1938. There is also an interesting handwritten note accusing the Dean of inconsistency in his handling of the affair—a charge which has some grounds. See also File "Chicago Public Schools," in Record Series 2/9/1, no. 25, passim.

[54] For what follows here and on subsequent pages for general background, we have relied chiefly on four accounts: George S. Counts, *School and Society in Chicago* (New York, 1928); National Commission for the Defense of Democracy through Education of the NEA of the U.S., *Certain Personnel Practices in the*

The first school had been established in 1816 when the city was but the location of a small army post. Incorporated only in 1837, Chicago had achieved a population of over 100,000 at the beginning of the Civil War. Even this phenomenal increase was paled by its growth to over 1,000,000 by 1890, which in turn had tripled to over 3,000,000 by the mid-1920's. Its school growth kept pace, of course, multiplied by the simultaneous increase in school attendance which accompanied the astronomical rise in population. In 1841, Chicago's schools enrolled some 410 children. By 1860, with the advent of common school laws, there were more than 14,000. By 1880, enrollments had quadrupled to nearly 60,000; and barely twenty years later, at the turn of the century, the figures passed the quarter-million mark. By the mid-1920's, more than half a million were attending the schools.[55]

By this time, education had also become the city's biggest public business, with an annual budget of over $70,000,000. The first superintendency had been created in 1853, but by 1926 there were five assistant superintendents, fourteen district superintendents, fifteen supervisors and directors of special subjects. There were 317 elementary and secondary principals who exercised administrative responsibility over the 12,000 teachers who staffed its 310 public elementary schools, twenty-five high schools, and its own normal college. All told, the Board of Education employed more than 15,000 of the city's slightly more than 36,000 employees.[56]

Although there were exceptions, it cannot be said that the "city on the make" had ever taken its educational problems too seriously. Chicago's political and social life had been as raucous and sprawling

---

Chicago Public Schools (Washington, 1945); Bessie Louise Pierce, *A History of Chicago*, 3 vols. (Chicago, 1937, 1940, 1957)—esp. vol. 3, *1871–1893;* John T. McManis, *Ella Flagg Young and a Half-Century of the Chicago Public Schools* (Chicago, 1916).

There is as yet no adequate history of the Chicago public schools. Other sources were examined along with the general periodical literature and are noted in the Bibliography, but they are mostly of little or no value. Counts's book, for all his notorious reputation, stands up the best and is remarkably free of unnecessary philosophizing. The Pierce history treats educational developments most inadequately. (See her Ch. 11, "The Increase of Knowledge," in vol. 3, which covers the public schools only very thinly—for example, Colonel Francis W. Parker is mentioned only as an *author* of books on education!) The school board's own records are, as the narrative will explain, virtually worthless, since they are official cover-ups of the real story; its "historical" summaries of "progress" were mere public relations puffs.

[55] Counts, *School and Society in Chicago*, pp. 19, 28–32, 60ff.
[56] Ibid., pp. 28–32.

as its growth, and the schools mirrored all the stresses, strains, and temptations which could be expected to afflict such a community. The growing educational enterprise offered ideal opportunities for graft, defalcation, and political chicanery. By the 1890's, the Chicago school system had become an obvious disaster, and the now growing body of "solid citizens" began to turn their attention to what was to prove a long task, making up for their previous shortcomings while radically new demands were multiplying their difficulties. Financial and political scandals of one sort or another succeeded each other with increasing rapidity and caused notorious battles. For example, the *"Tribune* Property Case," which had begun in 1895 over some highly dubious uses of school land transactions for personal and corporate profiteering, dragged on until 1910, while fresh incidents continued to arise.[57]

Many thought the roots of the difficulties lay in the city's antiquated school laws. These laws were, as we have noted, exempt from much of the conformity in school practice exacted from other cities and counties throughout the state. The city's early, almost skeletal school organization required expansion, it was thought. In 1891, the state had permitted the city a new twenty-one–member Board of Education, to be appointed by the mayor—and thus, it was rather optimistically hoped, free from political-party generation—on the advice and consent of the City Council. In 1893 the Board was given power to manage its property, levy taxes, and appoint its own superintendent.[58]

These improvements, however, did not work well from the start. Freedom from political interference was of course a sheer myth, and the scandalous conduct continued unabated. In deference to public outcry, in 1897 Mayor Carter H. Harrison, one of the city's better governors, appointed a commission to investigate the situation and make recommendations. The commission, under the chairmanship of one of Chicago's brightest new intellectual stars, William Rainey Harper, made its report a year later. Admitting the city's checkered educational history and alleging serious charges against the new Board, the commission recommended, inter alia, streamlining the Board to eleven members, radically increasing the power and independence of the general superintendent, and encouraging a rapid organization and professionalization of the teaching staff so that they could assist in shaping policy. Partly because these proposals cut sharply into vested interests, nearly two decades elapsed before many of the Harper

57 Ibid., pp. 56–60.
58 Ibid., pp. 28–43.

Commission's reforms were taken seriously—in fact, some of them never were, even though the problems still exist.

While the recommendations sat, political interference reached new heights and the supply of questionable deals and issues remained constant. The mayor removed, quite arbitrarily, wholesale numbers of Board members in 1907—when one-third were summarily discharged —and again in 1913. The one significant improvement was the teachers' successful struggle to gain increased autonomy and professional responsibility. This movement was largely the work of Chicago's two greatest educational figures, Ella Flagg Young (later a Trustee of the University) and Margaret Haley. Both were typical of the best "reforming women" of their day. Beginning as an elementary teacher in 1877, Mrs. Young had risen through the ranks of the elementary principalship and assistant superintendency to become the first woman superintendent from 1909–15. In her climb she amassed a long and distinguished list of liberal accomplishments which spurred the professional development of the teachers. During a momentary period of disenchantment, she had taken a doctorate at Chicago, where she fell under the considerable influence of its new social philosophy, as well as drinking in new educational doctrines from men like Dewey and Parker. Her dissertation, "Isolation in the Schools," became the pocket guide to later reform movements, particularly the attempts at professional organization under Haley. She provided the genesis of the controversial "Teachers Councils," through which teachers were to participate in decision-making.[59]

During the late nineteenth and early twentieth centuries, in the face of the frightening situation we have described the teachers of Chicago —and the various administrators as well—rapidly accepted the necessity of organization. High-sounding (and usually powerless) "professional" groups arose, very self-conscious and largely occupied with discussion. Even these were not encouraged by either the city or the Board, since they were at least potentially dangerous. But the authorities reserved their real ire for the new union-modeled organizations, particularly Margaret Haley's "Chicago Teachers Federation." In the unassuming role of "Business Agent," Miss Haley created the Federation in 1897 out of the teachers' need to confront the authorities corporately over the question of pensions and salaries. In 1902, the Federation actually affiliated with the Chicago Federation of Labor, thus in effect proclaiming itself a "union." All went well until

[59] Ibid., pp. 9–12; Ch. 12, "The Heritage of City Hall Domination"; pp. 52, 62ff.

1915 and the passage of the malodorous "Loeb Rule," named for Jacob Loeb, a prominent Board member and later its president. The "Loeb Rule" forbade teachers to be members of teachers' unions, organizations of teachers affiliated with any union, or even—and this was particularly aimed at Margaret Haley—any organization which had officers or employees not active members of the teaching force. When, under the aegis of Chicago's new political power, Mayor William Hale ("Big Bill") Thompson, teachers were actually dismissed for membership in the Federation, the fight was on. Turning apparent defeat into victory, Margaret Haley and the Federation lost the suits they brought against the Board but wrested a form of tenure for their teachers and secured their right to create and belong to whatever organizations they chose, as long as they were not *directly* connected with unions. (That dubious proviso has itself long since lapsed, of course.) [60]

Thompson's first election, in 1915, signaled the virtual thirty-year war over the schools in which the University came to be involved. In 1917, the "Otis Law" was enacted to effect (highly selected) reforms. Loosely based on the Harper Commission's recommendations, the law reduced the Board to eleven members, but their appointive basis was retained. The Board in turn now appointed three equal officials, a superintendent, a business manager, and an attorney. Each had his province. The superintendent exercised *control* of academic matters, texts, apparatus, and so on; but their *provision* and maintenance fell to the business manager. The superintendent's recommendations (or a two-thirds vote) was required for all major decisions, such as appointments or building proposals.[61]

All of this was supposed to guarantee peace in the schools, but nothing of the sort occurred. Immediately a dispute arose over the act of reducing the Board's membership. During 1917–18 there was a kind of Avignon papacy, in which two Boards fought for the legitimate title. This dispute, occasioned by Thompson's attempt to use the new law to serve his interests, had led to former Dean Chadsey's difficulties, since he had been elected by the legal twenty-one member Board, while his adversary had been put up by Thompson's packed replacement. Other scandals multiplied as well. Spurred on by still another real-estate windfall in connection with the location of Wendell Phillips High School, a grand jury investigation took place in 1922.

[60] Ibid., pp. 53ff., 94–97, 102, 250ff.
[61] Ibid., pp. 32–43.

The first or "July" grand jury found widespread evidence of wrong-doing but failed to indict anyone! The "August" grand jury was, however, constrained to continue the investigation, and it was further extended by a special "September" one. The latter two actually began to indict, in the face of almost unbelievable evidence showing graft, slush funds, financial cover-ups, and constant political malfeasance. For example, the Board was carrying an unitemized entry of nearly $9,000,000 described merely as "incidentals." The latest pedagogical devices had been dearly bought: phonographs worth $40 at the extreme had been billed and paid at $187 each. Strange new "companies" had arisen to supply the schools with goods and services, the emoluments going to well-known political figures and Board cronies. The waves of indignation swept "Big Bill" and his superintendent out in 1923, in favor of an exemplary but unfortunately weak Democratic reform candidate, Mayor William E. Dever, who brought along a reform superintendent, William McAndrew, in 1924.[62]

McAndrew was the man to use the leverage of the new, "strong" superintendency. He went to work at once, but his strategies, far from alleviating the disputes, actually heightened controversy to a fever pitch, exposing all of the inherent contradictions in both the city and its sadly captive schools. The new superintendent moved to crush the teachers' councils and their organizations, introduce the junior high school, and establish the "platoon system." Although scrupulously honest and conscientious personally, McAndrew's strong-arm policies cost him widespread support among the teaching force almost at once. His proposals also revealed very clearly the curious alignment of forces in the city. The working classes, headed by the unions, vigorously opposed both the junior high school and the platoon system as inherently elitist programs. This curious attitude stemmed from a previous attempt of Superintendent Edwin G. Cooley who, in 1911, following a tour of European city schools, hoped to introduce a "two track" system for vocational and general education. The labor interests had seen this as an attempt to fob off a second-class educational system upon the workers of the city—proven, they thought, by the fact that the commercial and industrial leaders who backed it so vigorously did not enroll their sons, even though they touted it as the gate of opportunity to the business and manufacturing world. Subsequent vocational education efforts in the city were severely hampered, and the junior high school and (more understandably) the platoon

62 Ibid., pp. 9, 250ff., 260ff.

system were interpreted as later installments of the same anti-labor plot.[63]

The religious organizations had also begun to shed something less than light in Chicago. The city's Roman Catholic population, already large in the mid-nineteenth century, had risen to some 45 percent by the late 1920's, almost exactly balanced by the Protestants. Its parochial school system enrolled nearly 160,000 students in 329 elementary and thirty-five secondary schools. Frightening as was their growth alone, in the days when every rectory could be viewed as a pillbox of the papacy, an even more inflammatory—and even less credible— rumor suddenly appeared: Mayor Dever was allegedly stacking the Board of Education with Catholics, and teachers of that persuasion were deliberately infiltrating the public school ranks and attempting to gain control of the city's normal school. Proof of this was supposedly vouchsafed by the fact that a move to increase religious and moral instruction in the public schools (blatantly Protestant and of doubtful constitutionality) had been coolly received by the superintendent and others. Although a practicing Unitarian and a Mason, McAndrew was even suspected of being an agent of the hierarchy, so intense were the popular suspicions. Analyzing the scene, George S. Counts deftly wielded his sociologically ground version of Occam's razor to cut through such rumors. It was not, he argued, necessary to predicate a "Papist plot" to explain the increasing presence of Roman Catholics; ordinary social and economic forces would be "sufficient." [64]

Conflicting loyalties to their teachers, their various faiths, and their differing conceptions of the public good led the confused populace to effect a dramatic return of "Big Bill" Thompson. Thompson promised to rid the city of McAndrew, a move which drew support from widely disparate quarters. His campaign rhetoric, now famous, stressed "America First" and vowed to oust the Dever-Merriam-McAndrew "tories," whom he accused of slanting the children's educational experience in a pro-British and anti-American fashion. Obviously a Scotsman, McAndrew was accused of being one of the "pro-British rats" who favored feeding "Schlesinger his-

[63] Ibid., pp. 81ff., 137–87. The labor interests also vigorously opposed intelligence testing as an elitist move.

[64] Ibid., pp. 230–40. Counts remarks: "That Catholic girls in increasing numbers are turning their attention to teaching may be true, but the explanation of such a tendency does not require the hypothesis of a Papist plot. The operation of ordinary social and economic forces would seem sufficient" (p. 240).

tory" to Chicago's teachers who were going to school down on the Midway. From a distance one would be compelled to believe that no one took Thompson's oratory seriously. But the situation was otherwise. Some thought Thompson's rhetoric metaphorical, suggesting that his widely heralded threats against "King George" were really crypto-Protestant war cries directed against George Mundelein, the less than popular German cardinal who reigned over a rather actively anti-German constituency. Although such interpretations hardly merit attention, the fact was that just about everybody had some reasons, real or imagined, for wanting McAndrew out and Thompson back in. Both desires were achieved in 1927, after the one brief term of "reform." [65]

With conditions such as these, and particularly under a man with Chadsey's experience, it is understandable (if not wholly creditable) that the University did not press its attention on the Chicago schools. The High School Visitor and his state counterpart slipped in and out, remaining essentially silent if not actually whitewashing the unbelievable situations which developed time after time. Under the combined weight of his own incredible maladministration, his by now obvious connection with the mobsters, and the Democratic landslide which was beginning to develop, Thompson was finally ushered out, to be replaced by the ill-fated Anton J. Cermak. Cermak was no radical reformer, but he was an improvement. He was followed by the Kelly-Nash "machine" which, although it became a byword in American metropolitan political history, gave the city its best government in at least twenty years.

While the city may have improved administratively, educationally the decline continued, if anything more rapidly than ever. The "Thompson" Board of Education, which had in effect hung and then "tried" McAndrew, remained in power and, particularly under the presidency of James B. McCahey, continued to milk the school system. William J. Bogan, who replaced McAndrew as superintendent, was an honest and devoted public servant who did his best to restore teacher morale and educational quality, but it was a losing battle. In 1933, under banner headlines which proclaimed Wiley Post's solitary

---

[65] Ibid., pp. 269–83. Counts, with characteristic vigor, called Thompson's Americanism a "smoke screen," employing "flamboyant flapdoodle" to cover up the fight to control a "rich satrapy" (p. 337). Cf. an interesting, though largely anecdotal, account of the whole affair in Edward Wagenknecht, *Chicago* (Norman, Okla., 1964), pp. 68ff.

crossing of the Pacific and the winning path of Repeal, a "Save Our Schools" rally anticipating an attendance of 30,000 was scheduled for the Stadium. Billed as "Chicago's answer to attempts of a handful of political appointees to wreck the city's school system," the meeting was called to protest McCahey's summary reduction of kindergarten provisions, physical education programs, junior high school programs, band and orchestra, lunch services, and his threat to close Crane Junior College. All of this, done at a stroke over Superintendent Bogan's protest, was accomplished under the cover of Depression economy demands and with but one dissenting vote on the Board. Thomas Benner, now the new Dean at Urbana, did enter the dispute at this point and was given front-page (but not very prominent) coverage for his condemnation of the Board and its "destructive proposals." But the weight was carried by the University of Chicago, Northwestern University, and a multitude of religious and civic groups. Chicago's Robert Hutchins, the city's academic *enfant terrible*, blasted the Board's decision as "political jobbery," and his professor of educational administration, Nelson B. Henry, termed the Board's program the "most contemptuous act [of expert opinion and public rights] of any public body, in history." [66]

Little came of the campaign, however, and matters continued to worsen, difficult though that is to imagine. Superintendent Bogan fatally collapsed in the traces in 1936, exhausted from pulling against the combined weight of Depression decline and the incredible school authority. That threw open the superintendency, and the Board, still in McCahey's iron grip, determined to find a more tractable candidate than Bogan or his predecessor. The lot fell rather easily upon William H. Johnson. A Chicagoan by birth in 1895, Johnson had held several teaching and administrative posts in the city and suburbs from 1917 to 1935, when he had been forced on Bogan as an assistant

[66] Although given wide coverage, see the interesting accounts in *Chicago Herald and Examiner*, July 21, 1933 ("Special" edition). Speakers included Charles H. Judd of the University of Chicago, John H. Fitzpatrick (a labor leader), and several prominent clergymen. Another rally, to be held on the South Side, was to feature Clarence Darrow. The paper ran "Save our Schools" as column filler (seven times on the front page alone). Trustee McJunkin had reported a deficit of $10,000,000 as grounds for the action, but the Board had preferred its own economies to those recommended by an outside survey under George D. Strayer of Columbia. Hutchins's blast appeared in the "Final" edition, also the source of the Henry quotation. Additional weight was supplied by T. V. Smith, Walter Dill Scott (president of Northwestern), Charles E. Merriam, and Kenneth (later "Tug") Wilson, the popular athletic director at Northwestern.

superintendent. One month after the superintendent's death, in March of the next year, Johnson was made superintendent.

The new administrator lost no time in arranging affairs to suit himself. That fall over 700 candidates sat for the principals' examination. The results proved remarkable: of the 155 who were successful, 122 had prepared for the examination either by taking the administration course which Johnson had taught at Loyola University, or by obtaining his private tuition. The superintendent soon introduced a new make-weight "oral exam" by means of which (allegedly on previous orders from the superintendent's office) deficient candidates who were acceptable could be padded sufficiently to pull them through, and competent candidates who were not wanted could be pushed down below the acceptable overall mark and dismissed. And there was much more. Teachers believed the system was being infiltrated with deliberately planted spies: their sabbaticals were canceled, they were transferred on a few hours notice, and more.[67]

Once again there was a great public outcry. A "Chicago Schools Committee" appeared, with Thomas E. Benner's name displayed on the letterhead. In February, 1938, Benner wrote Willard of his interest in the "scandalous" condition of the Chicago schools, arguing that the University was compromising itself by accepting them without protest. He told the President that he himself was "undoubtedly" largely responsible for the great public ferment which was then building up—a remarkable claim in the light of his later denials of any interest or machinations whatever! The anomalous situation moved Benner to suggest once again the creation of a whole new accreditation procedure which would radically change the High School Visitor's office. It was time, he thought, that a system of evaluation which applied (*mutatis mutandis*, one would assume) equally to both Tolono and Chicago be developed, perhaps by the Bureau of Institutional Research.[68]

[67] National Commission for the Defense of Democracy through Education of the NEA of the U.S., *Certain Personnel Practices in the Chicago Public Schools* (Washington, 1945), esp. pp. 19ff., 48–50, 57ff.

[68] Willard to Simpson, November 23, 1937, and other correspondence in File Chicago Public Schools, Record Series 2/9/1, no. 25. Benner's name appears on this letter. See also the very important letter, Benner to Willard, February 16, 1938, in Willard Correspondence. For evidence of how desperate the situation was, see *Chicago's Schools*, "official organ of the Citizens Schools Committee," some copies of which have been preserved in the Benner Papers. Benner's name was on the "Advisory Board" list, but his remarks were relatively mild. See esp. vol. 4, nos. 5–6 (March–April, 1938), vol. 2, no. 10 (June, 1936), and vol. 3, no. 4

Although all that we have described formed the context, the curious matter which lay directly behind Johnson's telephone challenge to Benner a few days later was the fact that, at least apparently, the superintendent had gotten possession of the Dean's memo to the President. Only Willard and Clevenger had received copies, so far as the Dean knew. It seemed logical to Benner that it must have been Clevenger, whose loyalty and integrity he had never previously questioned. Benner was also puzzled by the fact that, on the same day, the *Tribune* (which was supporting both Mayor Kelly and Superintendent Johnson at this juncture) carried a report of an address by the Visitor: "North Central Head Lauds High School System." Startled, the Dean immediately refused to make a previously arranged address to the regional conference of the AAUP, fearing it would now carry political overtones. He also wrote Johnson, denying that he had either made speeches or written letters attacking the superintendent "either by name or by title," and proposing what amounted to a mutual apology for the incident. (The daily papers suggested that Benner's refusal to speak had been forced, although he denied it convincingly in public.) [69]

The whole school matter continued to fester. Later that month, the *Chicago Daily News* editorialized it as a pedagogical dispute between the progressives and the conservatives—hardly the case. Benner and the University quickly pulled in their horns. When the AAUP became concerned over the canceled speech, Benner informed the national organization of the situation in detail. He admitted refusing

---

(June, 1937). A key issue was McCahey himself, who had cut instructional appropriations even while bureaucratic expenses were mounting, among other flagrant examples of mismanagement. Prof. Ernest O. Melby of Northwestern had made some very strong criticisms, particularly compared to those emanating from Urbana. The Unitarian Fellowship for Social Justice, in a pamphlet, *An Appeal for Civic Action*, reprinted the public records which gave substance to the charges and labeled Johnson "ethically unfit" to head the schools. It is perhaps worth noting that in his letter to Willard, Benner refers to the visitation and evaluating of schools as "protecting its entrance requirements."

[69] Benner to Willard, March 8, 25, 26, 1938, and accompanying "Memorandum" in Willard Correspondence; *Chicago Daily Times* (March 14, 1938), inter alia. There had been some previous difficulties with local political dynamics, sometimes denominated the "Morrison Hotel" issue—state employees, including Clevenger, had shown an interesting tendency to restrict their residence to that hotel, which was in the hands of a prominent public figure. (See the File "High School Visitor," Record Series 2/9/1, no. 27.) Benner to Willard, March 8, 1938, suggests that Benner and Clevenger were some distance apart on various matters. The Dean's address was to be "The Administrator and Academic Freedom"—a theme easily enough applied to the situation, whatever Benner's intent.

the invitation because of Johnson's threat and for fear of hurting the University. He made the point that the University's fortunes hung upon the attitude of the new reform Democrat administration of Governor Henry Horner, which had not been friendly, and they dared not risk increasing hostility in Springfield by losing the support of the Kelly-Nash regime in Chicago. There were simply too many conflicting interests to allow either an effective, positive program of school visitation or a forthright leadership role in one of the most serious school crises ever to mark a major American school system.[70]

Although the University henceforth took no part, the Chicago school situation grew even worse. Johnson was accused of controlling textbook patronage, and even of making himself a shadow "co-author" of approved texts in order to collect royalties. He arbitrarily ordered philosophy of education—quite definitely progressive and social—eliminated from the curriculum at the city's normal school. He fought the Teachers' Federation vigorously, if not indeed brutally. The Board itself was investigated by the state's attorney's office in 1939, and it turned out evidence of bribes, contract deals (especially with relatives of school officials), political kick-backs, low-bid refusals, substitution of materials, and definite contract relations with "racketeers." These results, however, were curiously suppressed, and the administration held on. Finally, in 1944, at the request once again of numerous civic and educational groups, the NEA was called in to conduct an examination. In a period of less than ninety days, more than 600 teachers had been transferred, apparently capriciously and as a means of intimidation. The Board and the superintendent, with the exception of one person, Mrs. Walter F. Heineman, refused all co-operation. But, after a thorough investigation, the Association condemned the McCahey-Johnson regime unreservedly and gave such widespread publicity to the situation that matters began slowly to mend. The great thirty-year war in the Chicago schools was, at least momentarily, at an end.[71]

[70] *Chicago Daily News* (March 18, 1938); Benner to Ralph E. Himstead (AAUP), March 22, 1938 (in reply to Himstead to Benner, March 18, 1938). Himstead to Benner, March 31, 1938, suggests that Benner's remarks were circulated by the AAUP. Apparently, the education people at Chicago were actively behind Horner, yet they showed no lack of inclination to fight Johnson and the Machine over the schools. See W. C. Reavis to Benner, March 23, 1938. All in Benner Papers.

[71] See *Certain Personnel Practices*, pp. 45–47, 61. One of the key issues was the summary transfer of (among others) John J. DeBoer, who had directed student

If the College and the University were at least timorous about becoming involved in the Chicago schools, the same could not be said
of their participation in another educational development of great significance during the 1930's and 1940's, the rapid growth of higher
education. Here, perhaps unfortunately, the University's power and
apparent interests coincided, and both the College and its Dean found
reason to support them. We have seen that over the preceding years
the University of Illinois had been forced to develop a concept of its
nature and function and to fashion a compatible policy regarding its
relationship with the other "higher" educational institutions in the
state, both public and private. From the beginning, it had assumed its
theoretical preeminence, but that self-definition had few practical consequences, at least until competition for financial support began to
grow increasingly keen.

In the beginning the University had had to struggle with the legislature for its very existence. It was simultaneously helped and hampered
by federal funds which were capable of inaugurating the experiment
but totally inadequate to maintaining or perfecting it. The "normal
school interests" had a clear and historically prior claim on such state
funds as a none too educationally concerned legislature cared to dis-
pense. By the time the University under Presidents Draper and (particularly) James made a bid to become a modern university in fact
as well as in theory, the normal schools had begun to lose both their
legislative effectiveness and their professional prestige. During the
1920's they had become "teachers' colleges" and thus began slowly to
emerge from their seriously deficient condition.

By the 1930's, however, subtle changes were afoot that turned the
long-standing theoretical problem into an intensely practical one, replete with all sorts of controversial aspects. Two factors were of
particular importance: the enormous growth of the high schools (with
concomitant demands for increasing the secondary teaching force),
and the first real attempts to make a college-level education available
to the general populace at state expense. Secure in its long-held "apex"
or "capstone" theory, the University at first viewed the practical con-

teaching at the Board's teachers' college since 1931. The grounds alleged were his
objections to Johnson's wholesale and authoritarian changes in the curriculum,
particularly the removal of liberal arts requirements. It seems more likely, however, that DeBoer was cashiered for his educational philosophy (decidedly
progressive), and his refusal to acquiesce was an important element in the rebel-
lion of the other teachers. De Boer later joined the Urbana faculty. See pp. 16ff.

sequences of these movements with polite disdain. Soon, however, this disdain turned to active hostility and the once harmless "capstone" theory turned into a practical strategy for rigidly maintaining dominance and control. Since all these developments had a close relationship with the schools, both the College of Education and the Dean personally were ultimately involved.[72]

Dean Benner had recognized at once the need to improve the College's relationships with the state teachers' colleges, if the needs of the schools were to be met. However, when the teachers' colleges moved to expand their programs and incorporate higher levels of study, he was immediately wary of the significance of the move for both the College and the University. And the move toward post–high school course offerings, the genesis of the community or junior college movement, the Dean found extremely "dangerous"—unless, of course, the University assumed leadership and control.[73]

In general, Benner held a view of Illinois higher educational development which was widely shared in the University and (no doubt) elsewhere in the state. There was, on his view, a private sector free to develop as it chose. The University should cooperate as closely as possible with this sector, both in general and (especially) in regard to establishing effective, common standards of teacher preparation. In the public sector, there were three categories of institutions. First and foremost there was to be one university in which all the arts and general sciences would be concentrated, and which would be marked by a decided research emphasis. In addition, there would be certain specialized institutions (such as the medical and other professional colleges) which should be satellites of the principal university—the

[72] According to their annual reports, during the 1936–38 biennium, Illinois State Normal had had thirty-nine "post graduates" regularly enrolled, and 167 in the summer session of 1937. Southern claimed it had grown from "a two-year normal school with a third class rating prior to World War I to a fully accredited four-year teachers college." Its enrollment had jumped from 469 (in 1918) to 1,879 (in 1938), and its faculty from 46 (including one Ph.D.) to 131 (including 32 Ph.D.'s). See 42nd SSPI (1938), pp. 140, 144.

[73] Chase to Benner, March 30, 1932, regarding Benner's immediate concern to establish Illinois leadership. Cf. Benner to Chase, May 27, 1933 (which raises the long-standing "duplication" issue), all in Chase Correspondence. See also College of Education "Annual Report" (1934–35), pp. 1–2, College of Education Papers. For the graduate and junior college issue, see Benner to Willard, December 8, 1936, and Benner to Willard, November 6, 1934, all in Willard Correspondence. The last-cited letter demonstrates clearly that Benner was prepared to act on the issue as early as 1934 but received no support, an interesting fact in light of the later accusations against him in connection with his hearing before the Board.

University's College of Education should eventually be one of these, he thought. Finally, there would be the normal schools or teachers' colleges. Essentially these existed for the provision of elementary teachers, but they might do for the provision of some secondary teachers as well—although this was a grudging admission at best.

Benner's higher educational strategy was not a product of his position at Illinois, and thus merely an attempt to support the University's proclaimed interests. He had been for some time an expert in higher educational theory and planning. The Dean believed quite strongly in a single higher educational system as the best procedure for any state, and he had lent his efforts to developing one in Oregon. He believed in it, he said, because it was more "efficient"—though he carefully distinguished that from "economical." Perhaps less happily, he found that opposition to the concept came only from those whose interests were "narrow." [74]

All the evidence suggests that this general view was shared by most of the University administration and the Trustees. It was also assumed that the University should take any steps necessary to guard its prerogatives, including the most potent step of all, direct attempts at persuading the legislature not to aid its rivals. As the Provost wrote the President early in 1937, "Of this much I am clear. It should be the policy of the University to dominate the educational situation in the State. I believe we are called upon to do that by virtue of our position." He pointed specifically to the growing teachers' colleges which he (like many others, including Benner) thought were becoming derelict in their duty as their fraudulent ambitions rose. They were supposed to produce elementary teachers, and nothing more. "If they will not undertake this responsibility," the Provost suggested provocatively, "I wonder if we could not hit upon some device through which we can bring them to task." Dean Benner had already indicated what device could be utilized when he told the President that the University should investigate the matter and then bring it "to the direct

[74] Benner to Willard, January 8, 1936, College of Education Papers. The Dean's position, while coinciding in certain crucial respects with the administration's, also had one important difference—a difference which cost Benner its support even in this area. The Dean believed that the University could dominate (as he thought it should) only *if* it radically changed its own ways and became a more "liberal" (as he defined it) and more service-oriented institution. The administration, though convinced of the University's right to, and need to, dominate, did not think that dominance hinged upon meeting any such responsibilities—but see next note.

attention of the State Normal School Board and of the Governor." [75]
The issue seemed clear and simple to Benner and others in the administration at Urbana. But the source of this facile resolution of the
problem was a highly dubious historical argument: from the first
the Dean maintained that "the teachers' colleges were established for
the purpose of training teachers for the elementary schools. They have,
in recent years, extended their function to include training for the
high schools as well." If the teachers' colleges persisted in this policy,
he insisted—though their actions were now quite legal, of course—
the University would be "compelled to oppose [them]" and, "in the
long run, be driven to the position of insisting that the function of the
Normal Schools is primarily to prepare teachers for the elementary
schools and the junior high schools on the under-graduate level." As
his clinching argument, Benner accused them of not accomplishing
even that, and he claimed to have the statistics to back the argument
up: in 1936, he stated, only about 13 percent of the graduates of
Illinois State Normal University, for example, had been prepared in
elementary education, in spite of the fact that it was that institution's
"fundamental responsibility." [76]

Benner's argument did not bear careful scrutiny. In the first place,
it was not entirely true that they had all been established to prepare
"elementary" teachers. They had first been established to prepare
teachers for the schools.[77] For all practical purposes, that had *meant*

[75] A. J. Harno to Willard, February 11, 1937, copy (accidentally signed by
Willard) in College of Education Papers. Harno was more open to expanding the
University's provision of the sort of work the teachers' colleges were demanding
than were others in the administration. For Benner's position and the remedy, see
Benner to Willard, February 5, 1935, and Willard to Benner, February 8, 1935,
both in Willard Correspondence.

[76] Benner to Chase, May 27, 1933, Chase Correspondence; and Benner to Willard, February 5, 1935, Willard Correspondence (the source of the second quotation, "compelled to oppose . . .[etc.].") For Benner's figures, see Benner to
Willard, February 1, 1937, copy in College of Education Papers.

[77] According to Section 4 of the 1857 act which established Illinois State
Normal University, its purposes were as follows: "The object of the said normal
universities shall be to qualify teachers for the common schools of the state by
imparting instruction in the art of teaching and all branches of study which
pertain to a common school education, in the elements of the natural sciences,
including agricultural chemistry, animal and vegetable physiology, in the fundamental laws of the United States and of the State of Illinois, in regard to the rights
and duties of citizens, and such other studies as the board of education may from
time to time prescribe." Section 7, which established the county scholarships, required only that the recipients should teach in the "public schools within the
State."

elementary schools, since public secondary education did not yet have any significant role. But Illinois State Normal University had been giving a full bachelor's degree since 1906, and had been preparing high school teachers for decades before that. It was true that many "secondary" teachers—the figures are not easy to arrive at if only because the categories are not always clear—had in fact been prepared at Urbana or the many private colleges. But that was largely an accident, or at least no part of a grand pedagogical design. In any case it was now of merely archaic interest; since the mid-1920's all the "normal schools" had been specifically commissioned to prepare high school teachers. In the second place, Benner himself argued that good secondary teachers needed broad, general education and a deep (although nonspecialized) subject-matter preparation such as only a properly higher educational institution might give. And he had once even argued that the normal schools might very well do this better than the new research-preoccupied universities. Now, when they made their move to do so, both the Dean and the administration found these pretentions dangerous and vexing, although for reasons sufficiently different that they would quarrel over them later. Unfortunately, the real issue was more the University's prestige than the validity of the teachers' colleges' proposals.[78]

The mid-1930's was a critical period for the teachers' colleges, and there was no doubt in the minds of their faculties and administrative officers that the times were ripe for expansion. Indeed, they compelled it. In the eight years before 1934, high school enrollment had

[78] "The Masters Degree Courses in State Colleges," *Illinois Teacher* 23 (December, 1934): 104. See also John W. Cook and James V. McHugh, *A History of the Illinois State Normal University* (Normal, 1892), pp. 56–102; cf. pp. 206, 219, 222; I.S.N.U. [Faculty Committee], *Semi-Centennial History of the Illinois State Normal University, 1859–1907* (n.p. [Normal?], 1907), pp. 82–86, 251–360 (where the alumni catalogue clearly shows how many had taught immediately in high schools). The Normal University's high school had, however, been somewhat more problematical than the elementary school (*Semi-Centennial History*, pp. 48–49). For the attitude of the other "collegiate" institutions, Illinois Wesleyan University at Bloomington appears to be fairly typical. Although at first incorporating elementary preparatory work (even called a "Model School" and utilizing a "normal" instructor very briefly), there is little if any evidence to suggest that Wesleyan was seriously interested in preparing teachers, let alone developing the field of pedagogy. Its eyes were on the *true* "professions," and even when women began to enter, they were trained to be refined companions, not the backbone of the common schools. See Elmo Scott Watson, *The Illinois Wesleyan Story, 1850–1950* (Bloomington, 1950), esp. pp. 81, n. 7 on pp. 212–13, 231, 235, and the founding documents, 250–66.

doubled, and there were now 725 four-year high schools in the state. It was less than candid to suggest that the University and the handful of private colleges which were concerned with the matter were going to supply this rapidly growing educational enterprise with all the teachers it needed. While the teachers' colleges had made some recovery of their lost support and prestige in the 1920's, the Depression had taken its toll with them as well. Their appropriations had been reduced from 10 to 40 percent in recent years, while their "loads" had increased up to 30 percent. The entire system of colleges had managed to secure nothing to expand facilities beyond two new science buildings in 1927. Most important of all, the standards of the teaching profession had made considerable strides since the old "gentleman's agreement" had informally divided the labor of teacher preparation in Illinois. The North Central Association had ruled that all accredited high school principals must have at least a master's degree. By 1929, even the smaller high schools were looking for master's degree–holders, at least for most administrative posts. The University's own Lewis W. Williams, who directed its placement service, had drawn attention to the growing professional standards for all secondary teachers, including the need to furnish the kind of "cultured" teachers which only fuller-scale institutions could educate. At its annual meeting in December, 1934, the Illinois State Teachers' Association had petitioned the Normal School Board to allow the state teachers' colleges to offer a master's degree for both teachers and administrators, since otherwise their graduate simply could not look forward to desirable employment within the state. (The colleges were already planning to do so then, and the permission was not long in coming.) Benner mistakenly cherished the notion that the assembled teachers had merely wished to "give the University a jolt," but there is no reason to believe that their intentions—or at least those of the colleges—were anything but what they suggested prima facie.[79]

[79] *Illinois Teacher* 23 (November, 1934): 84; (December, 1934): 104, 105, 124ff.; Lewis V. Williams, "The Preparation of a High School Teacher," ibid. (January, 1935): 133ff. Also see College of Education "Annual Report" (1933–34), p. 1, College of Education Papers; Benner to Willard, February 5, 1935, Willard Correspondence (the source of the quotation). As Edwin C. Hewett of Normal had remarked many years earlier when the normal schools were also thought to be expendable, it was a "huge joke" to think of doing away with them (or, we might add, limiting their development) in the face of educational demands which outstripped the needs of all the agencies put together. See Cook and McHugh, *History of I.S.N.U.*, p. 216.

Late in 1936, Benner reported to the President that he had uncovered a "most disturbing picture" in respect to the "personal ambitions of President Fairchild of the teachers college at Bloomington [*sic*]." Not only was Fairchild instituting such strange practices as electives and requesting a new library building to prepare for entry into graduate work; he was proposing to create a "pre-medical course," thus signaling his intention to educate nonteachers. The Dean assured the President that neither his fellow presidents nor the Normal school board took this kindly. He claimed that the latter had actually ordered Fairchild to stop "recruiting" students, warned him to "stay out of the territory" of the other colleges, and even ordered him to reduce I.S.N.U.'s enrollment—a series of charges for which there does not appear to be much evidence. But Fairchild posed an extremely dangerous threat, Benner thought, to the University.[80]

Whatever the symbolic value of the proposed premedical course, however, Illinois State Normal chose to make its first real bid for independence in the field of vocational education. The new Smith-Hughes legislation promised funds for development, and President Fairchild suddenly became aware of the "farm" which Illinois State Normal University had long possessed but little used except for revenue purposes. The demand for vocational education teachers, especially in the field of agriculture, was rapidly growing. Students in vocational subjects, though permitted to begin limited studies at some of the normal schools, were (again, by a kind of gentleman's agreement) expected to transfer to the University to complete their work for even the bachelor's. The notion of graduate work in these fields outside Urbana had never been dreamed of.[81] President Willard wrote

[80] Benner to Willard, November 14, 1936, copy in College of Education Papers. Benner believed that the matter was so important it ought to be laid before the University Council. Willard rejected the Dean's advice, suggesting he confer with Deans Carmichael and Mumford (of Agriculture) and the Dean of the Chicago Medical Campus instead. See Willard to Benner, November 24, 1936, College of Education Papers. A few years later, Benner found the new president of Western Illinois State Teachers' College "wholly opportunistic" for the same reason, and both Fairchild and President Pulliam of Southern guilty of "excessive ambitions." Apparently, only Northern and Eastern were regarded as guiltless, but even President Buzzard of Eastern was talking of graduate work within the year. See Benner to Willard, October 18, 1942, College of Education Papers.

[81] "Memorandum Concerning the Statement of President R. W. Fairchild as quoted in the Daily Illini of Wednesday, Nov. 15, 1939" under Benner to Willard, November 22, 1939. Here, however, the Dean admitted that even by his own reckoning I.S.N.U. had been using the farm since 1910 and had been teaching

the U.S. Commisioner of Education to enlist his aid in stopping developments at Normal, and, arguing "duplication," the University
fought the move for several years at the state legislative and executive level.[82]

An attempt to create more cooperation in regard to agricultural
education among all the interested schools, public and private, was
engineered in 1942 at Normal. (In this conference, incidently, President Fairchild seems to have played a constructive and appreciated
role which belies the image of him portrayed by the University.)
M. H. Hamlin, looking back on the whole affair in his 1945–46 annual
report, concisely summarized the issue and the outcome: noting that,
with all the effort expended, "we have made but slight progress in
the past eight years in working out a cooperative arrangement," he
pointed out that both Normal and Carbondale (which latter school
had been cooperative "until the present administration came into
power") were seeking their own fully approved programs. He then
faced the issue squarely. "We have never," he confessed, "been willing
to admit that we cannot provide at the University for an adequate
supply of teachers of vocational agriculture for the State." It was
necessary, he thought, to "recognize that there is no immediate possibility of securing an adequate number of new teachers of vocational
agriculture from the group who enter the University as freshmen. We
must frankly recognize our dependence on about ten other institu-

---

vocational agriculture since 1913. For the demand for agricultural teachers, see
College of Education "Annual Report" (1938–39), pp. 9ff., where Benner admitted
that at least twenty-five *new* agriculture *departments* would be established in
1939–40, and only seventy-five qualified teachers would be graduated. See also
mimeographed report of a statewide conference on the problem, under Benner to
Willard, August 10, 1942. All in College of Education Papers.

[82] Willard to John W. Studebaker (U.S. Commissioner of Education), July 2,
1938, Willard Correspondence. Although the state conference (see previous note)
showed forty-one vacant posts and 415 high school departments requiring constant staffing, Willard had assured the Trustees in late 1939 that "there [was] now
positively no excuse for training greater numbers of Smith-Hughes teachers in
Illinois,'" and urged that in tight times the state should "scrupulously avoid duplication." The Trustees were so impressed they requested Willard to convey the
University's opinion directly to the Governor and the members of the State
Board of Vocational Education. See 40th *Report* (1940), pp. 642–44. Cf. Benner
to Willard, May 21, 1941, College of Education Papers. Note also that the institution's charter was perhaps more favorable to agriculture than Benner realized
—see n. 77 above. The same attitude was present regarding industrial education.
See "Annual Report" (1938–39), p. 4, same location.

tions in the state for transfer students who will qualify." The University was perhaps neither so imperial nor so independent as it had pretended to be.[83]

President Fairchild's "ambitions" had never been very well disguised —if indeed he intended to cloak them at all. Within weeks after the Illinois State Teachers' Association petition for graduate courses, in 1934, Robert Bell Browne, the College of Education's wide-ranging and influential director of extension work, had reported that President Fairchild contemplated replacing retiring faculty with men who had graduate-level credentials and hoped to be teaching at that level by the end of the biennium. The College noted with some alarm that a similar movement was discernible next door in Indiana and that Southern Illinois State Normal was also beginning to take a lead in pressing for more privileges.[84] Benner accused the teachers' college leadership of becoming political and deliberately antagonistic to the University at Urbana—an accusation somewhat gratuitous inasmuch as they were, just as Illinois, dependent upon the politically organized state for their survival. (That survival had been marginal for many years quite precisely because they had not been politically effective.) The Dean informed Willard that, although a state college presidency was about to be filled (the third in the short time since his arrival), neither candidates nor recommendations had been sought from Urbana. From the fact that all the men under consideration had been from the state and yet none were from the University, Benner drew a resounding nonsequitur and thought it an obvious conclusion: "In other words, the Teachers Colleges are falling increasingly into the hands of politics and are becoming in their direction and policies in-

[83] Mimeographed report, under Benner to Willard, August 10, 1922. For Hamlin's remarks, see p. 10 of his report on agricultural education, as prepared for the College's 1945–46 "Annual Report." Both in College of Education Papers.

[84] Benner to A. J. Janata, January 21, 1935, Willard Correspondence. For Browne's report, see Benner to Willard, February 5, 1935; cf. Benner to Willard, February 11, 1935, and Willard to Benner, February 8, 1935 (where the President asked for "confirmatory facts"), all in College of Education Papers. Benner to Willard, June 8, 1935, Willard Correspondence.

President R. W. Fairchild reported by 1940 that Illinois State Normal now had the staff and facilities to meet the "evident" demand for a fifth year of training (43rd SSPI [1940], p. 192). Cf. 44th SSPI (1942), p. 166. From 1936 to 1940, Southern Illinois had grown 78 percent in average enrollment and had added thirty-one faculty positions (43rd SSPI [1940], p. 195). Illinois State, however, decided to remain a strictly professional teacher-preparation institution when the others chose to accept their newly won status as general purpose institutions (45th SSPI [1944], p. 77).

creasingly anti-University." At bottom, however, was doubtless the fact that the colleges had begun to act in concert among themselves and with the professional organizations (as they once had). That could mean, Benner urged, that (unless the University acted) "the resources of the University [would], because of the resulting competition, be reduced for generations to come."[85]

The College's strategy, which the President approved in a general albeit somewhat unenthusiastic way, was principally threefold. First of all, Benner hoped quickly to establish closer relations with the Colleges and shape their intentions more to the Urbana viewpoint. Conferences for this purpose were held in the late 1930's and early 1940's, but they, of course, stemmed the tide only momentarily.[86] The second move, the development of cooperative programs in vocational agriculture, proved equally futile, as we have already noted. (A belated

[85] Benner to Willard, June 8, 1935, Willard Correspondence. The full quotation is as follows: "During the brief time that I have been in Illinois, two Teachers' College presidencies have been filled and a third is to be filled within the next month. In each case, the methods of choice have been largely political. The men considered have been citizens or former citizens of Illinois. No Ph.D. from this institution has been given serious consideration. No recommendations have been sought from this institution. In other words, the Teachers Colleges are falling increasingly into the hand of politics and are becoming in their direction and policies increasingly anti-University." It was, however, all right to fight the colleges' expansionist tendencies politically: Benner had "conversation" with two state senators the next year, and Willard quite obviously approved. See Benner to Willard, March 12, 1936, and reply, March 17, 1936, both in Willard Correspondence.

[86] Benner suggested a conference to aid this as early as 1937, but the University administration thought better of it. See Benner to Harno, March 4, 1937; Benner to Willard, March 11, 1937, College of Education Papers. Cf. Benner to Willard, March 23, 1937, Willard Correspondence. Griffith tried to sound the note of "cooperation" heavily around 1937–38. See File "Conference on Problems of Higher Education," in Record Series 2/9/1, no. 26. See also Griffith's extensive remarks (ten-page) prepared for delivery to the Association of Junior Colleges (February 19, 1938) and the Federation of Illinois Colleges (March 18, 1938), under Griffith to Willard in File "Bureau of Institutional Research," Record Series 2/9/1, no. 25. Private meetings were held to smooth the issues, as with the increasingly active president of Southern Illinois State Normal University, Roscoe Pulliam, in early 1938. See Willard to Harno, Benner, Carmichael, and Griffith, April 7, 1938. The full-scale, continuing conference of all the state institutions was begun in 1940, "not only" because of a concern for the education of teachers but because of the issue of graduate work. Benner frankly admitted it was born in "differences of opinion," especially over the agricultural education issue (College of Education "Annual Report" [1939–40], p. 11). The proposals developed at these conferences led to the "five-year programs" but did not halt the move toward graduate work. See three memoranda presented to the Board of Trustees and appended to the College's "Annual Report" (1940–41), in College of Education Papers.

attempt to provide the teachers' college graduates with graduate scholarships "on the same basis as the [already existing] scholarships for graduates of the recognized four-year colleges of liberal arts in the State of Illinois" did little to increase the flow of students in any of these areas to Urbana.) [87] The third element, which was the most significant (although also unsuccessful in the long run), was the radical increase of extension courses, particularly at the graduate level.

We have already examined this development as an aspect of the College's legitimate desire to reach out and aid the teaching force—a motivation undoubtedly present—but it was also clearly a defensive measure. Benner's 1936 demands for new personnel of graduate faculty quality in curriculum, elementary education, guidance, and rural education, as well as the attempt to provide new graduate work on or off campus in agriculture, commercial education, and philosophy of education, were strongly argued on the basis of "neglect of the field(s)" which was "certain to lead to pressure on the part of the teachers colleges for permission to enter upon graduate work in this area." [88] The hope was to make the campuses of the state colleges the principal extramural graduate centers of the University, thus forestalling their own programs. This plan was put into effect at Carbondale, Normal, and Charleston during the academic year 1936–37; by the following year it was in progress at all five of the other state campuses. The same arguments were used in subsequent years, and by 1940, half the College's graduate thrust was concentrated in such extramural responsibilities.[89]

The area of elementary education posed peculiar problems which provided ostensible justification for both sides to pursue their own interests. Although University students could, of course, enter the elementary schools as teachers on their own, as late as 1926 the College of Education protested loudly that it did not "attempt to prepare teachers for the elementary grades, believing that that work can be more effectively accomplished in the various teachers colleges of the

[87] 39th *Report* (1938), p. 195.
[88] Benner to Willard, December 8, 1936, Willard Correspondence. The Board added two undefined positions.
[89] College of Education "Annual Report" (1936–37), p. 2, College of Education Papers. Cf. 39th *Report* (1938), p. 80. "Annual Report" (1937–38), p. 3; cf. under Willard to Benner, May 18, 1938, and Benner to Willard, June 28, 1938, Willard Correspondence. See also College of Education "Annual Reports" (1938–39), p. 4; (1939–40), p. 2.

state." Benner, however, very soon informed President Chase that the lack of a program at the elementary level placed the University at a great disadvantage, since administrators and supervisory personnel (who had to pursue their graduate work at Urbana, inasmuch as it was not available elsewhere in state institutions) could not get supplementary courses relevant to their specialties. Even though this was causing many to go out of state, the new Dean somewhat cheerlessly admitted that the University's reserve (based on the historic "duplication theory") was at least in earnest that it did not intend to "compete" with the teachers' colleges. By 1936, he found these disadvantages more chafing. The following year, O. F. Weber had produced hard evidence of the University's sagging prestige (based upon its inability to supply elementary-trained administrative personnel). The problem was growing particularly vexing now that Illinois communities were beginning to adopt the "unit" mode of school organization which required administrators competent at all levels from the kindergarten to the high school.[90]

On February 1, 1937, Benner decided the time had come to make a definite bid, whether the colleges liked it or not. He had obtained a copy of a survey by Mabel Carney of Teachers College which showed that Illinois State Normal University (as was also the case with others) placed about one-half its graduates in the high schools, and that those who were going into the elementary level were almost entirely from the two-year course still a part of the institution's program. Only part of the elementary placements had actually prepared for the elementary level. And Miss Carney, who specialized in rural education and had served both in Illinois schools and two of the teachers' colleges, strongly maintained that those who had were prepared very badly. The programs were poor, she thought, and their deficiency ill behooved the Normal University to seek to build its "aspirations towards liberal arts status" instead of bending more effectively to its pedagogical last.[91]

The message was, as usual, very "clear" for the Dean. As he told Willard, "these data convince me, as have conferences with men such as Director Zook, President of the American Council on Education,

<hr />

[90] 36th SSPI (1926), p. 484; Benner to Chase, May 27, 1933, Chase Correspondence; College of Education "Annual Report" (1935–36), pp. 4, 5; (1936–37), p. 1.

[91] Benner to Willard, February 1, 1937, and attached copies of Benner to Mabel Carney, February 1, 1937, and Mabel Carney to Benner, January 21, 1937, Willard Correspondence.

and others, that the College of Education would be wholly justified in entering the field of elementary education at a reasonably early date." He promised that the students admitted to such a new program would be "definitely limited," but the creation of such an undergraduate curriculum was essential to maintaining effectively the graduate program "to which we are already committed." [92] Willard, apparently at least somewhat impressed, sent Benner's proposal off to Dean Carmichael and Provost Harno for their opinions. Carmichael hedged and hesitated, fearing "difficult relations with the Normal schools in the state." The Provost, on the other hand, believed Benner had "touched upon a vital educational problem." He readily agreed that the University ought to offer graduate work relevant to all levels of education, but he was reluctant to "go further and actually train teachers for elementary work," again on the "duplication" theory. The decision was to explore the need further, develop a sound program proposal, and attempt closer cooperation with the state colleges.[93]

When two new faculty posts were authorized as of September, 1937, Benner decided to make a practical move by bringing in, along with the promising curriculum specialist from Florida, B. Othanel Smith, someone who could provide substance to these plans. The College was generally enthusiastic in proposing Edwin Hewett Reeder, who had, ironically, been born at Normal and was the grandson and namesake of one of Illinois State Normal's most noted worthies, Edwin C. Hewett. Reeder's specialty was elementary education, and he had held a post in that area at the Teachers College, Columbia, until 1933. At his summoning, however, he was in exile at the University of Vermont, a philosophically "moderate" refugee (Benner pointed out, perhaps to reassure the President) from a brief progressive-conservative squabble within America's chief pedagogical sanctuary. Upon his arrival, the elementary offerings were increased immediately—an important contribution, Benner thought, to the graduate-level program now "gaining in prestige and influence." [94]

[92] Benner to Willard, February 1, 1937, Willard Correspondence.
[93] A. J. Janata to A. J. Harno and R. D. Carmichael, February 4, 1937; R. D. Carmichael to Willard, February 15, 1937; A. J. Harno to Willard, February 11, 1937, all in Willard Correspondence. For the decision, see Benner to Willard, March 11, 1937, Willard Correspondence.
[94] Benner to Willard, December 8, 1936, and attached (two-page) "Memorandum;" Benner to Janata, March 3, 1937, Willard Correspondence. For details on Reeder's nomination, see Benner to Willard, March 22, 1937, College of Education Papers; 39th *Report* (1938), p. 216; 42nd SSPI (1938), p. 72. College of Education "Annual Report" (1937-38), p. 3, College of Education Papers. Although Reeder

These developments at Urbana did not escape the notice of the College's presumed antagonist at Normal, President Fairchild. Unwittingly, the *Daily Illini* jabbed the old hornet's nest once more when it routinely reported some of Fairchild's remarks in November, 1939. The President, apparently pressed to defend his supposedly expansionist program in vocational agriculture against the still potent shibboleth of "duplication," remarked that the Normal school board had raised no objections when the Urbana institution had begun a "definite program for educating elementary school teachers" some three years previously. That, he suggested, was a duplication far more serious than any created by his agricultural interests.[95]

Benner vehemently denied these nefarious allegations in a six-page memo to Willard a few days later. The Dean defended himself and the honor of the College with an argument reminiscent of those attributed to the presuppression Jesuits in a once popular French saying: "When accused of murdering three men and a dog, the Jesuits always produce the dog alive and prove their enemies liars." The University, Benner insisted, had offered only graduate work, primarily for administrators and teachers already possessing bachelor's degrees. The College had no undergraduate elementary program, he steadfastly maintained, *except* that secondary education students who had been "assured" an elementary school job were sent to do practice teaching at that level, and normal school elementary "graduates"—presumably those who had finished two-year programs—could, if experienced teachers, continue their undergraduate work on Saturday, and during the summer sessions. (He finished the rebuttal with a classic poisoning of the wells, by renewing the attack on the agricultural issue and by reasserting his prior claim that the Normal crowd was failing to help the rural schools —the latter task being, of course, something which no one, in any Illinois college or university, cared to do.) Not long thereafter, the *Catalogue* for 1941–42 announced unmistakable undergraduate courses at the elementary level under the tutelage of another new faculty member, J. Harlan Shores, and the issue passed into oblivion.[96]

---

had been supported by such stalwart "conservatives" at Teachers College as Kandel and Reisner, he had been, according to Benner, released rather than given the headship in elementary education which he merited. The Columbia college wanted someone who better fit its image.

[95] *The Daily Illini,* November 15, 1939.

[96] "Memorandum Concerning the Statement of President R. W. Fairchild as Quoted in the *Daily Illini* of Wednesday, November 15, 1939," in College of Education Papers, esp. pp. 1, 5. *Catalogue* (1941–42), pp. 252ff.

Essentially the same philosophy shaped the role of the University vis-à-vis the development of the junior colleges and the even more ticklish question of a Chicago campus, a movement which arose during this period. In the late summer of 1934, J. F. H. Kaler of Donovan in Iroquois County wrote Professor O. F. Weber of his modest project for starting a community junior college, and the University began to realize that it would have to face the issue of the growing trend toward post–high school education. The Depression had, as we have seen, actually increased high school enrollment. Its otherwise unwelcome provision of "leisure" time, coupled with a renewed popular belief in the efficacy of education, were (according to Mr. Kaler) leading a large number of the better high school graduates to seek further academic work immediately. They were, however, financially unable to do this away from home. The consequence, here as elsewhere, was the junior college project.[97]

Benner had been interested in the movement for some time. He believed that the crucial issue was whether it would be designed to serve a general education rather than a vocational function. In order to assure this, as well as to anticipate the inevitable request to credit work done at these institutions, the Dean strongly encouraged the administration to act quickly. The result, in typically academic fashion, was the somewhat leisurely appointment of a committee under Provost Harno, to study the issue. Benner thought that an immediate network of extension courses would be the quickest and safest way to protect the University, but, as we have seen, the extramural work never approached the necessary level or quantity of offerings.[98]

More than two years later, in December, 1936, there was still no settled University policy on the now rapidly proliferating junior colleges. Comptroller Lloyd Morey proposed that the Bureau of Institu-

[97] F. J. H. Kaler to "Dr. Weber," September 5, 1934, Willard Correspondence. See also copy of the Rev. N. S. Nye to D. E. Lindstrom, January 12, 1935, in College of Education Papers. Nye argued: "I know that this may seem like decentralization of the University but what of it, perhaps this is needful. The University ought to serve all people, not just those who have sufficient means to study away from home." Pointing out that all pay taxes, he asked, "should we not strive to give all a somewhat nearly equal chance?"

[98] Benner to Willard, September 25, October 3, 1934; Willard to Benner, September 27, November 5, 1934, Willard Correspondence. For Benner's philosophy, see his addresses, "The Responsibility of the Modern Junior College" (dated September 20, 1934, and given to students at each of the three new Chicago junior colleges) and "Your Opportunity in the Modern Junior College" (September 21, 1934), where he particularly stressed its liberal arts role as against a one-sided scientific emphasis. All in College of Education Papers.

tional Research be charged to investigate the problem. Benner encouraged this, in order to forestall the "chaotic development" which had characterized secondary school growth in the state. Illinois should, the Dean believed, follow California's lead and establish a state department of education, for this purpose among others. President Willard seconded the proposal to investigate, fearing the junior colleges' frequently "inferior grade" of work and the pressure on higher educational funds they might well create. Acting upon the President's request, the Bureau speedily prepared an exhaustive memorandum giving background information. Griffith and his advisors also favored strict University control and placed considerable emphasis on the threat to the Urbana budget which the potential expansion of the new institutions posed.[99]

By 1938, however, the state legislature had authorized the development of the junior colleges by existing school districts that met necessary criteria for supporting them. The University had had nothing more to offer than a proposal to investigate a special program for freshman and sophomore instruction, and the battle, whether for protection or leadership, was essentially lost. All that the Bureau could counsel was to persuade the superintendent of public instruction and the governor to delay the formation of such colleges until the University came up with better proposals—possibly for two novel, quasi-independent institutions at Champaign-Urbana and Chicago. (Other unspecified sites were also entertained.) [100]

The question of whether to provide a state-controlled institution of higher learning in Chicago had had a considerable history prior to 1938, of course. Although the city was well provided with distinguished private universities and colleges, as well as a number of important specialized institutions, the fact that the nation's second-largest metropolitan area had no full public liberal arts college or university had not escaped notice. The University had held a few classes there from time to time, as we have noticed, but no serious commitment had even been considered. Perhaps as the feeling of turning the corner on the Depression rose, however, higher education proposals swept the city in 1936.

[99] Lloyd Morey to Willard, December 8, 1936; A. J. Janata to Benner, December 11, 1936; Benner to Janata, December 15, 1936; Willard to Harno, December 17, 1936; Griffith to Willard, December 23, 1936 (and accompanying "Memorandum no. 132, Preliminary Data and Comments on Junior Colleges," dated December 21, 1936). All in Willard Correspondence. See also Bureau of Institutional Research "Memoranda" 72 and 81.

[100] Griffith to Willard, April 6, 1938, Willard Correspondence. Note esp. p. 2.

In late spring, Dr. Preston Bradley, a liberal minister with a decidedly (if somewhat harmlessly) social bent, and himself one of Chicago's "institutions," had taken to the air to pump for a municipal university. Aware that if Preston Bradley were for it few would be against it, the proposal of the eminent divine caused a brief flurry of activity at Urbana. Benner feared that such a project would fall into the hands of the Chicago Board of Education, and consequently that President Mc-Cahey and Superintendent Johnson would be in charge. The Dean urged the President and the University to move quickly to establish a fairly extensive extramural "center" in the city to stop the movement. (Extension Director Browne apparently conferred with the two institutions most likely to prove effectively inimical, the University of Chicago and Northwestern, and found them not inclined to oppose such a harmless development.) Unfortunately, Benner's argument for the proposal was less than disinterested, let alone based on the public good—though it should also be recorded that no better plan and no other reasoning was provided by anyone else, apparently. He pointed out to Willard that "nothing more disastrous could occur to us than to have a municipal university develop in Chicago, with the certainty that it would soon make heavy inroads into the support of this University through its demands for state aid." [101]

If the Chicago school board was less antiseptic than the University, it was, however, also a good deal more effective in getting what it wanted. By the fall of 1937, it was proposing to expand its Chicago Normal College into a four-year, degree-granting institution. Although Benner continued to push for some action, the academic leadership (as well as the administration) at Urbana could not make up its mind as to how it might best make its own move. Provost Harno supported the notion of establishing a full college under University auspices, and Benner agreed heartily, but no concrete plans were offered. The Chicago teachers' union, which could have been expected to oppose any scheme of Johnson's, offered to lobby for a University-controlled branch if the men in Urbana would propose it. Still no one acted, including the Dean. In late 1937, the Chicago Board approved a revised plan of Superintendent Johnson's which would bring together the city junior college "system" which it had sponsored in the high

---

[101] Benner to Willard, June 8, 1937, College of Education Papers—the source of the quotation at the end of the paragraph. See also "Report of Actions of University Council of Dec. 3, 1935" (dated December 17, 1935) at same location. Cf. correspondence under Willard to Benner, June 28, 1937, Willard Correspondence.

schools with its normal school. The Dean noted to the President that this brought developments "one step nearer" a city college. For various reasons which lie outside our immediate concern, the proposed city college did not get very far, but neither did the University's project. It was not until after the close of World War II that any concrete move into the city was made by the University, nor did it ever create either centers or campuses elsewhere. Whether by intent or default, any effective, statewide higher educational planning was more than twenty years away.[102]

There is no reason to assume that Dean Benner maliciously discouraged the development of Illinois higher education, whether in Chicago, at the existing colleges, or elsewhere. He did believe, rightly or wrongly, that the University should control if not actually sponsor it. His practical strategy was, however, designed to gain leverage for his own progams by playing on the fear of competition (particularly at the graduate level) which the spectre of higher educational expansion engendered. He hoped the legislature as well as the University would see the financial wisdom of increasing the prestige and effectiveness of the College of Education rather than having to fund a proliferation of less adequate facilities. The University did not respond to his suggestions, nor did the legislature, nor did better and bolder projects gain support. The practical result was, unfortunately, a victory neither for the College nor for the educational needs of the state. The result was a stultifying stand-off which profited no one.[103]

[102] Willard to Benner, October 12, 1937, Willard Correspondence, esp. Willard to Benner, November 29, December 17, 1937. A. J. Harno to Benner, December 1, 1937, Benner to Harno, December 6, 1937, both in College of Education Papers. On Chicago Board approval, see Benner to Willard, November 4, December 16, 1937. There was also a rumor that Southern had been engaging for some years in a "campaign" to convert itself from a "teacher training institution" into a university, either independent or as a branch of the University of Illinois. Willard denied it and wanted the matter investigated. See Willard to the Hon. George M. McKibben (Director of State Department of Finance [which perhaps suggests the location of the problem]), July 3, 1942, College of Education Papers. The cause of the University's inaction is difficult to explain. Perhaps the various departments and admininstrative structures, having developed stable hegemonies, were unwilling to risk new work which might entail their decline in importance.

[103] Benner to Willard, March 1, 1937; College of Education "Annual Report" (1933–34), p. 2; both in College of Education Papers. For Benner's assessment of the response, see "Annual Report" (1940–41), pp. 3ff.; (1944–45), p. 7, same location. The last gave Benner's general review of his entire administration, and he maintained he had proposed a program to prevent expansion and proliferation "without evoking in its behalf any appreciable interest." For the Board's response to such arguments, see, for example, 39th *Report* (1938), p. 129, where the

In the opening years of the 1940's, then, the College of Education found itself in a situation not entirely to its liking. While the College had made obvious gains over its immediate past, it had not come close to fulfilling the vision Benner and the faculty—and especially the newer members—were constructing for it. Many of its essential programs were as yet unaccomplished; some, stillborn in the dry Depression years, had never really begun, others were now frozen by a massive war which was destined to sap the nation's resources for most of a decade. As the Dean saw matters, the College's staffing was entirely inadequate not only for advancing the vital new programs but for maintaining the old ones. And the College's new quarters in the soon-to-be-completed Gregory Hall were at best a far cry from the building dreams which had been entertained since Bagley's early days.[104]

As usual, Benner did not see the difficult straits in which the College lay as dictating a slackening of speed in its attempted progress. Indeed, the Dean believed it was rather a time to act with increased vigor. As the new war approached and suddenly arrived, he feared the same destiny for education due to the war which the Depression had occasioned. Consequently, the crucial matter seemed to be the budget. No real advances over pre-Depression finances were made until the 1940–41 budget, which hit a high for Benner's administration—nearly $216,000. The College hoped to prevent radical cutbacks, on the argument that the war (as any other time of crisis) was not the time to reduce educational efforts. But argument was unavailing, and substantial reductions were made.[105]

Trustees diverted the small income from extramural instruction out of the College and into the University's "General Reserve Fund," and 41st *Report* (1942), pp. 44, 145, 194, where they canceled summer scholarships for teachers and school librarians, in spite of protests from Director Browne, Dean Benner, and even the "Faculty Committee on Fees and Scholarships."

[104] The real change, and any real "progress," had to be measured more by men than either facilities or programs. Of the three guardians of the old pedagogical tripos, only Monroe remained in a significant (if relatively diminished) role. Cameron and Seyboldt, men of undoubted scholarship but of incompatible educational bent, were going or gone. Their replacements, men such as we have mentioned along with others like Kenneth Benne and Archibald Anderson, thought in different terms and weighed themselves and their programs by different criteria. Conflicting criteria issued in conflicting judgments about both the men and their programs, as we have seen.

[105] For budget development, see 36th *Report* (1932), pp. 320–22; 40th *Report* (1940), 418–22, 839–42; 41st *Report* (1942), pp. 495–99. Comparisons are somewhat misleading. For example, athletic coaching was no longer included, of course, but

From the point of view of Benner and the College, the budget raised another and far more explosive issue, the by now enormously influential role of the Bureau of Institutional Research and, more specifically, the para-administrative policy-making of Director Coleman R. Griffith. Under Griffith's disciplined and conscientious direction, the B.I.R. had become a very efficient producer of both internal and external information. But we have already noticed the subtle influence which the construction of "objective" statistics can generate. And, by the late 1930's and early 1940's, the evidence clearly suggests that the influence was no longer subtle. The Bureau rendered opinions which, because they were designed primarily for the ear of the administration, were beyond rebuttal. Indeed, frequently they were, like the ways of God, entirely beyond human ken. The marginalia of the director, quite apart from the formal reports the Bureau rendered through him, came to have potentially as much force as a remonstrance from the Trustees.[106]

The evidence suggests that President Willard thought of himself as a cautious businessman, carefully stewarding the public trust, much the same as Kinley if perhaps with less style. Although he could well have pleaded the times in his defense, the President had never been one to trumpet "bold new programs" in any area—which is not to suggest he made no advances nor cherished any vision—and Education was manifestly among the least of his concerns. The modest budget increases the College negotiated for 1940–41 drew a growingly un-

---

many new responsibilities had been added. Still, the 1931–32 budget level of $196,000 was not even regained until 1939–40.

[106] As one of his first acts, Benner had approved the transfer of Griffith to the College staff, with the proviso that "the arrangement is for one year only and involves no obligation on the part of the College or the University for the future" (Benner to Chase, June 3, 1931, Chase Correspondence).

For an important example of Griffith's role and his conflation of statistics with "confidential" advice, see his response to the College's new professional degree programs in Griffith to Willard, October 14, 1940 (and enclosed draft of a letter for Willard to send to Benner as representing the administration's policy), in Willard Papers. The potential for confusing information-gathering with policy-making had been obvious to some for a long time. For example, Sveinbjorn Johnson, then University Counsel but later Benner's attorney, had pointed it out in 1935. In delivering a legal opinion to the President's office on the implications of some changes in Smith-Hughes programs, Johnson remarked cooly that he supposed "this bit of rather important educational policy will not be finally determined by the Bureau of Educational Research" (Johnson to A. J. Janata, October 10, 1935, in Carmichael Papers, Record Series 7/1/2, no. 4).

sympathetic response from him, as had the almost pathetically small increases requested the year before. (The negotiations both years show that Griffith's personal opinions, as well as the authority of the Bureau, played decisive roles.) [107]

Increasing anxiety over impending budgets was not the only factor capable of heightening the sense of frustration which any relatively aggressive dean might have experienced. There was a general "edginess" in the University community. Possibly the President and the Trustees were convinced that Benner was trying to pressure them into action on the long-delayed building and research programs through its contacts with the educational profession. In any case, as we have noticed, Willard (claiming to act for the Trustees) summoned the Dean to explain his "educational program and public relations policy" before the Board in the late spring of 1941.[108] If his audience proved distracted, or if few results were forthcoming, it may have been because the Trustees were doubtless beginning to nourish anxieties of their own: the University was entering another period of criticism and self-analysis, and one perhaps more abrasive than any it had previously endured. Less than ten months later no less than three "surveys" which involved its destiny were scheduled or underway. Governor Dwight H. Green, heading a new Republican state administration, had appointed Dean George A. Works of the University of Chicago to make a "survey of higher education in Illinois, as represented by the University and the State Normal Schools." The Gov-

---

[107] For example, Benner to Willard, February 16, 1940; Willard to Benner, March 14, 1940; Benner's (seven-page) "Analysis of [B.I.R.] Memorandum No. 223," dated June 3, 1939; all in College of Education Papers. In the "Memorandum," Griffith and/or the Bureau disposed of College plans which the Dean and his faculty had valued highly, and in fact criticized the College faculty's "distinction." Nor was that the first time. Griffith and/or the Bureau—it is always difficult to know which, if there is any distinction, except in the case of Griffith's marginalia and his responses to private queries made by the President—had exercised extremely potent influence as early as 1935: see B.I.R. "Memorandum" no. 67 and several items of correspondence on industrial education under A. J. Janata to Benner, October 3, 1935 (in Record Series 2/9/1, no. 26, under "College of Education"); under H. B. Johnston to Benner, November 5, 1937 (same location), where Griffith attempt to shape policy at University High School; Griffith to Willard, June 21, 1939 (also touching University High School); on practice teaching, under Benner to Willard, March 22, May 19, 1940 (and accompanying letters). Griffith even disputed individual courses, as, for example, Benner to Griffith, July 31, 1940, where the Director questioned the proposal for Ed. 60 ("Child Development and Problems of Education"). All in Willard Correspondence.

[108] See 41st *Report* (1942), p. 283.

ernor was also investigating rates of pay and attempting to correlate them with local costs of living in order to achieve maximum economy. Finally, not to be outdone in zeal for efficiency, the President (at the behest of the Trustees) had engaged the firm of Booz, Fry, Allen and Hamilton to winnow the "business operations of the University." The firm's results proved understandably unacceptable, showing little knowledge of matters academic and even less inclination to inquire into them. The administration, embarrassed by their careless but nonetheless damaging findings, was forced to rebut them at length.[109]

In July, 1942, still another survey, this time by the American Council on Education, was authorized. Although it managed to correct a number of misinterpretations occasioned by the Booz, Fry, Allen and Hamilton report along the way, the occasion for beginning it was a particularly unsavory episode. The state's attorney general, George F. Barrett, had made some inflammatory—and wholly groundless—charges which were widely reported in the press. The University, Mr. Barrett had alleged, had been "on the downgrade since 1934." He succinctly summarized the cause of this retrograde movement by proclaiming that "since 1934 a group of hand-picked political puppets [had] virtually built a political empire in Champaign and Urbana and [had] cloaked their operations and defended their illegal activities behind the shield of education." By "political puppets," the Republican attorney general meant the Board of Trustees, whose members he proclaimed to be the selection of the downstate "democratic machine and the Kelly-Nash machine in Cook County." His inquisition had purportedly been mounted because of "the [Sveinbjorn] Johnson exposure," which he thought warranted an investigation of "the entire

---

[109] Ibid., p. 801. For the rebuttal, see [University of Illinois], *Survey of Business Administration and Organization of the University of Illinois by Booz, Fry, Allen and Hamilton, Combined with Review and Analysis of This Survey, Together with Recommendations by the President of the University of Illinois* (n.p. [Urbana], n.d. [Report rendered August, 1942]).

The College went virtually unscathed. Although the University was castigated for being insufficiently self-critical (see *pink* page 18), Griffith was one of the few praised for "doing an excellent job of planning and establishing objectives and an excellent job of directing and *controlling* their own efforts and those of their *subordinates* so as to achieve the objectives established," and the Bureau was recommended for an increased role (*white* pp. 25, 77; italics ours). If the terms and categories of the report were frequently less than appropriate to a "free" academic community (as above), at times the surveyors were nearly insulting: they found, they said, "among the University's administrators . . . some of the most agile 'fence-sitters' we have ever encountered"—a condemnation Benner at least properly deserved to escape. See *white* p. 27.

administrative branch" of the University. (The charge was that John-son, perhaps not unexpectedly a Democrat, had received a "double salary for two full-time jobs.") Not only did the A.C.E. generally—if not entirely or universally—vindicate the University's reputation; Mr. Barrett's allegations and self-determined punishments against Judge Johnson were overturned by the courts.[110]

The College did not fare badly in any of the surveys. If it was not singled out for special praise, neither was it presented as a glaringly bad example of either scholarly or administrative conditions in the University. The A.C.E. Report, while completely exonerating the University of Barrett's ridiculous charges, was only very mildly favorable toward the University's record of growth during the previous decade—it had grown, but it had not grown as much as it could and perhaps should have. The commission did point specifically to three areas of failure: the faculty's failure to cope adequately with new general education needs; the tendency of other administrative or leadership bodies (and particularly the Bureau of Institutional Research) to assume powers and responsibilities which ought to be the province of the President; and the need for greater participation in the governance of the University.[111] A time in which every aspect of the University's work was subject to scrutiny by friend and foe alike was perhaps not propitious for a strong—and particularly an unpopular —move against its authority structure. Nonetheless, that was the strategy which Dean Benner saw as requisite, as we shall see in the next chapter.

[110] 42nd *Report* (1944), p. 22–24, 1030; Committee of the American Council on Education, *University of Illinois Survey Report* (Washington, 1943), passim.
[111] A.C.E. *Report*, pp. 14, 15–16 (cf. 38–39); p. 17 (cf. 82–84); p. 21 (cf. 71–76, 78–80). The *Report* also suggested a more equitable distribution of graduate student appointments (p. 20; cf. pp. 35–36).

CHAPTER II

❧ *Runnymede*

In the opening days of June, 1944, Dean Thomas E. Benner was summoned by the President's office, to all appearances on a routine matter. When he arrived on the appointed day, June 5, he was ushered into Willard's presence and there began one of the most unusual events in the history of the College—and, indeed, in the history of the University. The President, without explanation or apology, placed in the Dean's hands a signed carbon copy of a letter written two days previously. He was urged to discuss its contents only with the Executive Committee of his College and his closest friends.[1] That letter, in its entirety, read as follows:

Dear President Willard:

We wish to bring to your attention an observation which in time has given rise to a firm conviction that the College of Education lacks effective leadership. A want of confidence in Dean Benner as head of that college has been apparent since an early period in his administration and

[1] President's Office "Schedule Sheet" dated June 3, 1944, from Benner File in Record Series 2/9/1, no. 89. Some details taken from (thirty-nine-page) published pamphlet, *The College of Education of the University of Illinois and Dean Thomas E. Benner—A Factual Record of Educational Leadership, 1931–45*, pp. 1–3, in Benner Papers. According to p. 39 it was published as "the cooperative effort of several staff members of the College of Education. It was edited and

has steadily increased both on and off the campus, especially in recent years. It is our judgment that the College of Education cannot develop satisfactory relations with the secondary schools of the State nor effective programs in teaching and research here at the University under his direction. We believe that he should not be continued as Dean of the College beyond the present term of his appointment.

We are making this statement as members of the University staff each of whom has official obligation with respect to one or more of the important problems now confronting the administration of the College of Education.

Below were the signatures of Robert B. Browne, Director of University Extension; R. D. Carmichael, Dean of the Graduate School; Coleman R. Griffith, Director of the Bureau of Institutional Research; Albert J. Harno, Provost and Dean of the College of Law; M. T. McClure, Dean of the College of Liberal Arts and Sciences; Rexford Newcomb, Dean of the College of Fine and Applied Arts; H. P. Rusk, Dean of the College of Agriculture; H. T. Scovill, Acting Dean of the College of Commerce; and S. C. Staley, Director of the School of Physical Education.[2]

The procedure seems to have taken Benner completely by surprise. No formal attempt (and no known informal one) had been made to ascertain that the President's highly unusual move reflected the wishes of the College which Benner served as Dean. And no evidence was then offered to sustain the questions raised about his competence in the letter. The Executive Committee of the College of Education had been shown the same letter only earlier in the day under substantially similar circumstances, and they appeared to be as surprised as their Dean.[3] The President later stated that the majority of

prepared for publication by a committee [unspecified] of the staff," and was dated June 7, 1945. This pamphlet reproduces the letter of June 3, 1944, and includes various letters of commendation, important statistics, etc., but it was largely based upon Benner's final, summative 1944–45 "Annual Report" to the President. Other evidence suggests that Benner's attorney, Sveinbjorn Johnson, arranged for its publication.

[2] For text of letter, see previous note or copy preserved in Background Presentation File, Benner Papers. This latter copy bears interesting marginalia, apparently by Benner, which suggest the tack of his reply.

[3] *The College of Education . . . and Dean Thomas E. Benner . . .*, pp. 1, 3; Benner to Charles F. Arrowood, July 31, 1944, Benner Papers. The President's Office "Schedule Sheet" shows that the College Executive Committee was originally called for a nine o'clock meeting on June 5. (The letter to Arrowood erroneously puts the date of the meeting on June 3.)

that Committee had at first not only known but agreed with what he "had in mind"—apparently that Benner quietly "retire." The Dean, however, denied that this was so, and there was fairly strong evidence in support of his denial.[4] If anyone in the College knew what was about to transpire, Benner himself was unaware of the impending storm. As he wrote some weeks later to the distinguished historian (and long-time personal friend), Charles F. Arrowood, "This action came without warning of any sort. I had had no previous criticisms, either oral or written, of the work which the college was doing, or of my leadership of that work. For a time I was completely stunned." All in all, Benner could only regard the affair as "the most extraordinary cabal that [he had] ever heard of in the field of higher education."[5]

[4] For Willard's remarks, see "Report of Proceedings before Board of Trustees of the University of Illinois, Union Building, Urbana, Ill. Re: Dean Thomas E. Benner," prepared, signed (and notarized) by T. A. Copple, Court and General Reporters, Chicago, Ill. (hereinafter cited as "Hearing Transcript"), pp. 240 (where the date is also erroneously stated as June 3; for correction, see p. 247), 241, 242. Cf. Benner to C. F. Arrowood, July 31, 1944. Both in the Benner Papers.

[5] Benner to Arrowood, July 31, 1944, Benner Papers. Both Griffith and Browne, who signed, were technically members of the College, of course. However, they do not appear to have involved anyone else in their plans; they certainly did not warn Benner and probably told no one. It would appear that both signers and the administration thought the matter need not, and presumably would not, become public.

The exact chronology of events seems to have been as follows. All the signatories were called for a conference in the President's office at eleven o'clock, June 3, 1944. According to a "Memorandum for Front Office," it was originally scheduled for 10:30 but was changed—the following warning is given: "(N.B. It is important to get them all together at one time.)" The "Memorandum" is located in the Benner File, Record Series 2/9/1, no. 89, Willard Correspondence. Benner believed, and there is evidence to support his belief, that all of them signed at the President's request. See Benner to C. F. Arrowood, July 31, 1944, and "Hearing Transcript," pp. 175ff., Benner Papers. The same day a conference was arranged with W. S. Monroe, E. F. Potthoff, E. H. Reeder, C. W. Sanford, and B. O. Smith. According to the "Schedule Sheet" (see n. 1), Benner was originally to meet with them, but that decision was subsequently changed and the Executive Committee appeared in the morning, Benner later. If anyone told the Dean, he never alluded to it either publicly or in any known private correspondence.

Who wrote the letter? When it became public a few weeks later, the press inferred that the letter had simply come to Willard, more or less without solicitation. Benner at first believed Griffith was behind the whole business, although he did not specifically accuse him of writing the letter. See Benner to Russell D. Gregg, August 1, 1944; Benner to I. Keith Tyler, October 19, 1944 (in which he refers to "those who formulated the letter"); two letters of Benner's to Donald DuShane (of the National Committee for the Defense of Democracy through Education), November 19, 1945 (see esp. p. 5 of the second, which is Benner's resumé of the case and the hearing); all in Benner Papers. Later, during the

We have already examined the remote history of this highly unusual turn of events. The year and one-half which preceded Willard's letter had simply brought to a head issues which had been gradually festering during much of the previous ten years. At the time, in spite of the many difficulties he had encountered, Benner was on the whole optimistic, and perhaps even enthusiastic, about the prospects for the College. As he saw it, in the face of financial disaster and academic conservatism he had made some considerable progress in reviving a moribund College and returning it to its proper sphere of action, the school system of the state. By 1942 he had a plan of action which he believed would provide true professional development and which he believed was based on a sound social and academic philosophy. Although additions had of necessity come very slowly, he now had a fresh faculty nucleus of considerable promise; the thrust of the College was now decidedly more a product of their accomplishments than of the "holdovers," whose reputations (both nationally and locally) had been great but whose productivity in terms of the immediate needs of the state and the College had been slight.

The proximate cause of the move to oust Benner was the Dean's decision to fight the proposed budget cuts for the mid-1940's. As we have seen, he had a clear and very firmly held belief that Education

hearing, Griffith denied that he had written it ("Hearing Transcript," p. 175). A. J. Harno testified that he and R. D. Carmichael actually drew it up, but he alleged that the latter actually prepared the first draft and that it then "passed through other [unspecified] hands." Harno also stated that all nine signers had meetings over the letter and their general strategy before the hearing ("Hearing Transcript," p. 227). Willard in effect admitted later under cross-examination that he had provided the "impetus" for the letter, defending himself as acting "fairly" by dint of his intention to keep the whole affair secret ("Hearing Transcript," pp. 273ff.). Benner wrote both Arrowood and former President Chase that, according to private conversations, at least four of the signatories [unspecified, except as "deans"] denied any real knowledge of the issue involved—they had, Benner thought, merely been told that he had falsified a report, a charge which they later saw was untrue—and soon regretted the fact that they had merely gone along with the President's request. See Benner to Arrowood, July 31, 1944; Benner to H. W. Chase, August 2, 1944 (in both of which letters the Dean at first also mistakenly assumed that the President had written it). See also the second DuShane letter noted above. We shall, of course, examine these matters more carefully in subsequent pages, showing that Benner was probably somewhat mistaken about Griffith's role. However, the fact that the administration built its entire case upon Griffith, Harno, and Carmichael, and that none of the other signers gave, deposed, or submitted any other evidence (although Browne was apparently ready to), lends great weight to the Dean's contention.

was not the proper place for economizing. The effect of this policy, not only on the College but on the schools, had been glaringly demonstrated by the Depression and its aftermath. When war finally came, all parties (except the College and perhaps schoolmen) expected that the University's expenditures would be reduced in the same general way they had always been—"across the board" reductions, no "new" work, and so on.

To the Dean, however, this traditional formula was unsound in theory and unacceptable in practice. In the first place, the College and, along with it, the schools of the state were still not operating at a normal level. They had, on the whole, not yet recovered from the outright losses of the 1930's, let alone expanded to the level indicated by both increasing population and enlarged responsibilities. Second, Benner believed that the College's program could not in any case be reduced in a direct ratio with falling enrollments. If that were done, the College's functions would pass a limit of viability and disintegrate. Furthermore, the program should not, because—and this was a crucial factor in the Dean's assessment of the situation and his strategy—the College's responsibilities to education were not a function of university enrollments or any profit-and-loss calculation based thereon. They were a function of the educational needs of the state. These needs, whatever the enrollments, had not diminished; they had increased. Schools and teachers were even more necessary, and would be more necessary still when the inevitable reconstruction period (which was, after all, already visible by late 1943) finally arrived. As a consequence of this view, Benner elected to press at the very least for a continuation, and if possible an expansion, of his budget, even at a time of general retrenchment. And he determined to fight any battle necessary to hold his ground. Such a posture was bound to appear bellicose and to create a potentially explosive situation within the already volatile University community. For those long since unsympathetic to his sentiments, and unable or unwilling to hear and accept his arguments in the particular case at issue, the Dean's strategy of necessity appeared to be at best a case of muddle-headed thinking and administration. At worst, it was a crashing example of self-serving ambition.[6]

[6] Correspondence under Willard to Lloyd Morey, October 31, 1942 (and esp. Benner to A. J. Janata, October 28, 1942); Benner to Willard, March 15, 1944; and two very important letters, Benner to Willard, January 14, 1943, and (twelve-page) Benner to Willard, April 22, 1943, the latter "sent to Director

Although budget negotiations were the occasion for the battle which was about to break out into the open, they were simply the latest practical manifestations of a fundamental theoretical challenge regarding the proper nature, function, and status of education in the University which Benner had been advancing since his very arrival. True to his style, the Dean did not wage the practical war without attempting strongly to reassert the theoretical convictions which were the groundwork for it. Since he regarded the budget issues of 1943–44 as a crucial nexus in the development of the College, he decided to issue some new theoretical appeals which would match his practical programs in scope and intensity. Thus, between June, 1943, and March, 1944, the Dean, acting for the College, issued three documents which made these beliefs and intentions quite plain. They also infuriated his extra-College colleagues and superiors. The first two documents, one dealing with the relations between the College and the Graduate School and the other arguing that the College was essentially and substantially "understaffed," he termed the College's "little Magna Charta." In respect to the first, he was "hopeful, though not too confident" that the Graduate School would hear the College's arguments "sympathetically." The third report, really a set of documents, dealt with the preparation of teachers of "special subjects." It was perhaps the actual spark which ignited the explosion, although it was not as weighty a challenge as the two which preceded it. To understand the course of events it will be necessary briefly to examine these documents and the exchanges which accompanied them.[7]

On June 17, 1943, Dean Benner sent to Willard and Carmichael a thirteen-page report on "The Status of Education as a Department of the Graduate School" which he had worked up in collaboration with members of his faculty. In the report, the College argued a number of points. It claimed to supply (in prewar years) the largest number of graduate students, while at the same time receiving the least financial aid for research and assistance. Regarding the two doctoral programs the College offered (the Ph.D. and the Ed.D.), it was very critical of the Graduate School's role. The Ed.D. program should, the report argued,

Griffith and Provost Harno for their information and comments" according to a marginal note by "A. J.[anata]." All in Willard Correspondence. See also College of Education "Annual Reports" (1941–42), esp. pp. 9–10, and (1942–43), esp. pp. 4–5, in College of Education Papers.

[7] Benner used the phrase " 'little magna charta' " to the President himself. See his covering letter to the Graduate School document, Benner to Willard, June 17, 1943, Willard Correspondence.

be entirely removed from the jurisdiction of the Graduate School. The reason for this was that it represented a "professional" degree, since the College was in fact a professional school, and therefore its administration and programs should have the same autonomy as, for example, the medical school enjoyed. The College was not, Benner argued, related to any discipline or any pure research style; it was related to the schools and the teachers in them. There was, he said, a prevailing but entirely mistaken belief "that the chief purpose of research and teaching in education is the development and inculcation of teaching methods"—i.e., the traditional content-plus-method approach to the discipline at the University level. While at one time education might properly have been viewed as the traditional disciplines in their bearing on curriculum and method, this was no longer defensible. By not understanding this, the report implied, the Graduate School had limited the College's developing program.[8]

At least outwardly affecting an attitude of Olympian calm, Carmichael, after consulting a few of his most trusted colleagues, issued his rebuttal. On August 26, he sent the President an extensive set of "Comments on Dean Benner's Statement Entitled 'The Status of Education as a Department of the Graduate School' "—without so much as a copy for Benner to see, unless and until the President chose to send one on. He denied the School's inflexibility and insensitivity toward "well-considered" proposals, arguing that the College had presented few of these, and somewhat erratically at that. (He did not state what criteria were required for a "well-considered" proposal, however.) He disagreed that the traditional research doctorate should be regarded in a different light from the "professional" one, insisting that

---

[8] There are several copies of Benner's brief against the Graduate School—indeed, one of his "mistakes" may have been the fact that he circulated it rather too widely. See under Benner to Willard, June 17, 1943, in Record Series 2/9/1, no. 70, Willard Correspondence. This particular copy is esp. important, since it was the one returned by Carmichael to the President and bears the Graduate Dean's extremely hostile marginalia—such as "*so what?*" and "this is pure poppy —etc." See esp. pp. 1, 3, 7, 10. It would appear that criticism was more widespread than in the College of Education alone, however. Griffith sent twenty-five pages of comments on the new "General Division" to "Bill" [Sanford?], February 15, 1943 (with a covering note to A. J. Janata), which are a strong defense of the Graduate School and which therefore suggest that the School may have already been under considerable pressure (in this case from the various surveys) and that Benner's attack (while doubtless more abrasive and pointed) was neither radical nor novel. Griffith's comments, which will be examined more carefully later, can be found in the Bureau of Institutional Research File, Record Series 2/9/1, no. 69.

the same rigorous standards would need to apply if the latter were going "to obtain as high a prestige as possible." He defended the School's judgments about faculty on these same grounds. Furthermore, education was, Carmichael thought, no more professionally oriented than many other fields, for example, physics. He implied that the alleged traditionalism or conservatism of the Graduate School was not a hindrance. It had in fact been a positive element in the admittedly revolutionary growth in physics, chemistry, and biology at the University. It had, he argued, even saved the College of Education from embarrassment on more than one occasion. Finally, Carmichael dismissed the College's lack of assistance, both financial and personal, on the ground that most of its graduate work was "elementary," and that its candidates (since they were teachers) were already employed and therefore didn't need any subsidies.[9]

Benner found Carmichael's comments an "evident misunderstanding" of his position and an evasion of "the fundamental difficulties which trouble us." Consequently, he issued an extensive rejoinder to Carmichael early in the following December: "Comments on the Statement of August 26, 1943, by Dean R. D. Carmichael." [10] In these comments, Benner chose to concentrate heavily on defending his faculty and explaining how he believed Carmichael and the Executive Committee of the Graduate School had prevented their achieving full graduate faculty status in spite of their promise, performance, and wealth of credentials. The test cases were B. Othanel Smith (who, six years after coming, had still been denied full standing), Kenneth Benne (whose thesis Carmichael had disliked, in spite of the candidate's enthusiastic recommendations from such leaders in his field as John

[9] See R. D. Carmichael's "Comments on Dean Benner's Statement Entitled 'The Status of Education as a Department of the Graduate School,'" dated August 26, 1943. Several copies are extant; one can be found in the Graduate School File of the College of Education Papers. Note esp. pp. 2–5, 10–11. See also Carmichael to Benner, August 8, 1943, in Willard Correspondence, which informs Benner he *may* be sent a copy when the President "has had an opportunity to get around to the matter."

The Graduate School's position can be gleaned in part from the Carmichael Papers, Record Series 7/1/2, no. 4, esp. the 1943 File. Unfortunately, much important material has obviously been removed, but there is a first draft of Carmichael's "comments." It is perhaps significant that in no place, here or elsewhere, can there be found any evidence indicating that the School was aware of any inadequacies on its part at any time.

[10] "Comments on the Statement of August 26, 1943, by Dean R. D. Carmichael," under Benner to Willard, December 8, 1943, in Willard Correspondence. (While Benner had sent his original criticism directly to Carmichael, he sent this one through the President, though he provided extra copies.)

Dewey, J. H. Randall, Jr., and William H. Kilpatrick), and Arthur B. Mays (who had been denied status on the curious grounds that the facilities at the University were inadequate for his work).[11] Benner also defended the controversial use of junior faculty on dissertation committees—a practice which Carmichael had called "the method of mediocrity." He pointed out the shortcomings of the University's provision for the physical needs of the College, and he strongly reasserted the necessity of granting the College independent, professional school status, at least for its Ed.D. program.[12] "After an attentive reading of the document," Carmichael told Willard a few weeks later, "I have found no reason to modify anything in my statement of August 26, 1943." [13]

In late June, 1943, ten days after issuing the first criticism of the Graduate School, Benner sent to the President the second document, "The Problem of Understaffing in the College of Education." This fourteen-page analysis was simply an elaborate attempt to show statistically that in comparison with other large and prestigious midwestern institutions, the College of Education of the University of Illinois had advanced very little in quantity of staff. A particular difficulty was alleged to exist at the graduate level. Benner noted that A. W. Nolan and J. A. Clement were soon to retire, and educational psychologist Barker had left, yet the College was being urged to use this as an "opportunity" to phase out their positions. He also drew considerable attention to the lagging building program.[14]

The occasion for this document seems to have been Griffith's prior allegation of "apparent overstaffing" in the College. Together with comptroller Lloyd Morey, the Director of the Bureau of Institutional Research had persuaded Willard to order Benner to cut his financial requests on the basis of student decline. The effect of the "understaffing" document, and the argument it precipitated, will be examined later. In general, however, it served to alarm Griffith and his Bureau just as the "Status" document had alarmed Carmichael and the Graduate School.[15]

[11] "Comments . . . . ," pp. 3–7.
[12] Ibid., esp. pp. 10, 11, 16.
[13] Carmichael to Willard, January 15, 1944, Willard Correspondence.
[14] For "The Problem of Understaffing in the College of Education," see Record Series 2/9/1, no. 81.
[15] Griffith to Willard, January 15, 1943; Griffith to Lloyd Morey, February 3, 1943; and Willard to Benner, February 4, 1943—the last actually written by Morey and Griffith (see Morey to Willard, February 4, 1943). All in Willard Correspondence.

At about the same time, there appeared a quite separate document, not the sole work of the College of Education, dealing with "The Provision at the University of Illinois for Advanced Training of Teachers of Special Subjects." The impetus for this report was the work of William S. Gray of the University of Chicago, who had surveyed the needs of the state in respect to all the "special subjects"—that is, the Smith-Hughes vocational programs, the commercial subjects, art, music, and physical education. Gray had conveyed his findings informally to a committee of the "Six State Supported Institutions of Higher Learning" which were jointly studying teacher preparation. The thrust of their report, based on Gray's findings, was that vocational education was dangerously retarded in Illinois because school administrators did not understand it. They did not understand it because there were insufficient graduate-level programs to create the needed understanding or to prepare the required higher-level personnel to train the teachers in the field.[16]

The "special subjects" document was jointly prepared by Benner, Dean Newcomb of Fine Arts, Dean Rusk of Agriculture, Dean Scovill of Commerce, and Director Staley of Physical Education. In large part it also was critical of the Graduate College for its academic specialist policies which prohibited, or at least discouraged, the development of broad programs suitable for such personnel. For example, M. H. Hamlin had been brought to the campus to teach agricultural education in 1937 but was not allowed full graduate faculty status until 1942, and the advanced programs in the area were blocked by the Graduate School's insistence that they restrict specialization to the field of agriculture alone, whereas by definition they included wider areas. The School's policy, until 1942, had also required a twenty-hour "academic" field even for admission to graduate study, thus ruling out those who had come all the way in a vocational curriculum. It was, in effect, the same argument from a slightly different perspective: the Graduate School, the authors claimed, had a single conception of advanced university work, the preparation of the university scholar-professor, and it rigidly excluded other programs. The graduate administration, the report maintained, did not formulate programs, but it

16 "Report to the President on the Provisions at the University of Illinois for Advanced Training of Teachers of Special Subjects," in File "Education, Graduate Work In," Record Series 2/9/1, no. 81, Willard Correspondence. For connection with "Gray Report," see Benner to Willard, March 17, 1944, Willard Correspondence. Cf. previous treatment of relations with the normal schools, Ch. 10 above.

did "censor" them. "As a result, programs and policies concerning the advanced professional education of teachers and other officers in the public schools are first censored by their committee of very busy men who are, for the most part, primarily interested in other matters." The report closed with the now traditional warning that the University's neglect of this problem constituted an invitation to the other state colleges to begin instruction at the graduate level.[17]

This third report appears to have gathered dust in Willard's office for some time. At the end of June, 1943, it was sent to Robert Browne for his comments, since he had considerable responsibility for extension work and relations with the teachers' colleges. Since the report in effect was a severe criticism of the development of cooperative programs, the responsibility for which was largely Browne's, it is not surprising that he found it an "indictment," although it was well into December before he registered his opinion. He demanded somewhat testily that the writers be asked what they proposed to do, and also asked that Griffith be charged with finding out whether the "understaffing" allegations were true. He also thought the Graduate School ought to be asked whether it was "censoring" programs.[18] Accordingly, some two weeks later, Willard asked the committee to do a revised report, and he informed them about a month later that Carmichael had serious disagreements with the original.[19] Delayed by the slow response of the Bureau, the new "supplementary" report was not issued until March 17, 1944. Again asked to comment, Browne prepared a scathing denunciation of it, blaming Benner for turning what "purports to be a joint enterprise" into an "attack on the budget-making agencies of the university (the President) for alleged failure to provide adequate staff for 'all the programs' of the College of Education." [20]

Browne argued that the College had gotten more than its share of

---

[17] "Special Subjects" Report, passim. The quotation is at p. 18.

[18] Browne to Willard, December 9, 1943, Willard Correspondence.

[19] Willard to Benner, et al., December 22, 1943; Willard to Benner, et al., January 20, 1944, both in Willard Correspondence. Browne, while technically a faculty member in the College, was in practical fact a member of the administration "team." He had little to do with the College and, reportedly, seldom even attended faculty meetings.

[20] Benner to A. J. Janata, February 8, 1944, Willard Correspondence. Browne's remarks are from his (seven-page) holograph "Memo to Pres. A.C.W. in re March 17 report of the Five Deans," with covering note by Griffith, located in Record Series 2/9/1, no. 81. The quotation is at p. 1. See also Benner to Russell D. Gregg, August 1, 1944, Benner Papers, where Benner discusses the issue and reports that Browne's posture came as a "terrible shock" to him.

funds, sharply criticized Monroe and his Bureau for producing "no significant research," accused the industrial education people of merely reinforcing their "reputation for pleasant futility," and suggested that the College's administrative structure had proliferated needlessly. He compared Benner most unfavorably with Chadsey, accusing him of not carrying his load. He also violently attacked the Dean's "committee method" of administration and teaching, agreeing with Carmichael that it was "the method of mediocrity." Browne accused Benner of statistically "rigging" the "understaffing" report, adding that Griffith would prove this "if he had any courage." Finally, among a number of other allegations, Browne blamed Benner for the failure to get the normal schools to work cooperatively in a manner acceptable to the University. In spite of his remark about Griffith, which at least approached being nasty, Browne apparently showed his comments to him. The director of the Bureau, far from being put off, added his own enthusiastic marginalia, commending Browne's attack as making "the essential points." The evidence suggests that this letter was a major turning-point, drawing together all the parties (including the President) since it suggested that the other deans had been so "gullible" that Benner was able to lead them into supporting his private expansionist designs, and since it interpreted the College's budget requests as an intentional attack upon the University's administration.[21]

In addition to attempting to make his case through the medium of the three reports, Dean Benner also continued to exert as much pressure as he could on the building and research programs. The College submitted a new "Supplementary Report" to the University Building Program Committee in March, 1944, emphasizing the new programs (especially in child growth and development) and their all-university features. As he had now been given permission to do, Benner also tried to stir up whatever outside interest in the programs he could, especially among schoolmen and the other colleges. His efforts began to bear fruit in early 1944, resulting in a strong request from the Illinois Education Association that March. By fall, the Trustees were receiving a mounting chorus of requests, most of which pointed out the unfavorable comparison which the Dean claimed existed between the

---

[21] Browne's holograph "Memo," esp. pp. 2, 4, location as above, n. 20. Griffith added comments such as "yes! yes!" and "Instead of thinking himself through his problems, the Dean calls endless Committee Meetings, and then asks that this time be added to teaching load—Consequently, the College is always understaffed."

University and other institutions. The press also took up the cry under leads such as "Educators See Lab School as Growing Issue," particularly after the news of the Dean's attempted ouster leaked out.[22]

If public interest in the building program grew, however, the evidence suggests that the concern of the Board and the administration did not, at least until very much later.[23] In January, 1944, the official building program listed four categories of importance: Class A, those termed "most urgent," contained buildings for animal pathology; the University band; a new generating unit; the reconditioning of Noyes Laboratory, the old agriculture building, etc.; a betatron laboratory; and a chemical storage building. Class B was defined as "urgent," Class C as "desirable," and Class D "proposed for consideration." While ranking within categories was not supposed to be significant, still the College of Education facilities were listed last in Class D. The committee chairman informed Willard that the College's needs were given the lowest priority because they were "proposed chiefly to house a *new program* which is not now in operation." The chairman thought the College might go ahead with some planning, so long as it did not interfere with "more urgent projects," but the President regretted to Benner that no money would be available for architectural studies.[24] If any of the programs were "new"—which was hardly the case—the High School surely was not, and the University architect frankly admitted that "our attitude has been the same as that of everyone else connected with the High School, viz., to do nothing where the school

[22] "Supplementary Report to the University of Illinois Building Program Committee," dated March 27, 1944, Laboratory School File, Record Series 2/9/1, no. 81; Irving F. Pearson (executive secretary of the Illinois Education Association.) to Benner, March 7, 1944, same location. See also Benner to Willard, February 2, 1944, in College of Education Papers (which conveys Eastern Illinois President R. G. Buzzard's warm endorsement), and Benner to Willard, May 29, 1944, Willard Correspondence (which suggests that an overly enthusiastic supporter of the College's plans may have taken Benner's ideas directly to the Trustees). For the Trustee's reaction, see 43rd *Report* (1946), p. 308. Cf. Benner to Willard, February 15, 1945, College of Education Papers; 43rd *Report* (1946), p. 512. For press coverage, see *Urbana Evening Courier* (June 11, 1945).

[23] *Urbana Evening Courier* (June 4, 5, 1945); *Chicago Sun* (June 5, 1945).

[24] See mimeographed list of projects for postwar "Building Program," dated January 4, 1944, on Laboratory School File, Record Series 2/9/1, no. 81, Willard Correspondence; W. C. Huntington (University Building Committee Chairman) to Willard, January 7, 12, 1944, same location. In the latter, Huntington remarked, regarding the "status of the laboratory schools project," that "about all that can be said is that it is still being actively considered by the Building Program Committee." For Willard's refusal of funds, see Willard to Benner, April 14, 1944, same location.

seems to be 'getting along.' " [25] Provost Harno continued to accuse the College of attempting to control a research facility which involved the wider University, even when (as we have seen) it in fact had not done so, and to suggest that its plans were still not "workable." [26] When Governor Dwight Green broadcast the building plans of the University late in 1944, no mention of any Education facilities was made. At that point the Illinois Education Association again objected, but Board President Park Livingston announced that future expansion of facilities would be governed by the timely (and politically expedient) criterion of "Veterans First," a position to which the Board clung tenaciously.[27]

It was in such a confusing and even acrimonious context that Dean Benner submitted not a diminished but an augmented 1944–45 budget on March 22, 1944. He requested some $14,000 in additional funds, including dropping of tuition for the High School, and he based his appeal directly upon the three major reports. Willard had repeatedly warned the Dean that he expected significant budget cuts, including even the outright elimination of existing faculty posts as attrition or military leaves occurred, all on the enrollment-decline argument. The President had in fact just informed Benner that he could make no additions except by comparable reductions, and Benner had protested his ruling very strongly.[28]

[25] E. L. Stouffer (University Architect) to Willard, January 28, 1944, in Laboratory School File, Record Series 2/9/1, no. 81. Note that the University High School problem was the result of a project uncompleted for more than twenty years. Cf. Benner to Willard, January 28, 1944, same location.

[26] A. J. Harno to Willard, April 21, 1944, in Laboratory School File, Record Series 2/9/1, no. 81.

[27] See "Green Discloses Building Program Sought for U of I," *Urbana Sunday Courier* (October 1, 1944); *Urbana Evening Courier* (June 4, 1945). See also 43rd *Report* (1946), p. 382–83, esp. the following: "The President asked the Provost, who is a member of the Building Program Committee, to comment on the matter. The Provost stated that the Laboratory Schools Building had been given more and longer hearings and *more earnest consideration* than any other project before the University Building Program Committee; . . . [the Committee approved its inclusion in the program, but it did not represent as direct a contribution to health, safety, etc., as the others did, and thus] in its present form the project did not conform to our position and programs of research as now drawn, and that such an important matter as this should be given more intensive study than would be possible if construction were to take place during the first biennium . . ." (italics ours). The evidence simply does not support Harno's defense. There was continued mention of the matter, but nothing suggests that discussion was ever taken seriously, and the question of the program's research implications was settled, as we have seen, quite apart from the merits of the case.

[28] Benner to Willard, March 15, 1944, Willard Correspondence. See also

When the College's budget arrived, Comptroller Morey ordered it sent to the Bureau of Institutional Research for examination. Within three days the Bureau reported that both the College and the High School were "quite adequately staffed," and Willard lost no time in informing Benner that he could not "without further study, subscribe to [his] representations of understaffing in the College of Education." The President was, he said, primarily concerned with the health of the University as a whole, and he could not aid some part of it at the expense of the rest. The Dean then tried to soften the tone of his requests, but he still argued that the College had for years been sacrificed for the University, and he pointedly criticized the role of the Bureau in the case, suggesting a conference with its personnel and the comptroller.[29] In mid-April Willard replied in even stronger terms, ruling out any increases for the College or the High School and accusing the Dean of masking "instances of light teaching loads which should be readjusted to reduce teaching costs." He also forbade the High School to drop its tuition charges. Later that month, Benner acknowledged the letter with little comment, but again requested a conference before the President should treat the decision as final. None was held, or apparently even considered. Instead, the investigation was secretly underway during May which would issue in the "no confidence" letter of June 3.[30]

Thus, by the beginning of June, 1944, Benner had sharply and publicly challenged three of the University's most powerful figures— he had in fact alienated their sympathies quite beyond recall. The Dean had now openly opposed Carmichael and the powerful Graduate School. He had heavily pressured Provost Harno in connection with the University's building program and the research developments which hinged upon it. Finally, he had drawn the blood of Robert

---

Willard to Benner, February 2, 1943; Benner to Willard, February 18, 1943; Benner to G. A. McConnell, August 12, 1943; Benner to Willard, March 15, 1943; Willard to Benner, March 29, 1943; Benner to Willard, April 3, 1944. All in College of Education Papers.

[29] Holograph note L[loyd] M[orey] to A. J. Janata, March 22, 1944; A. H. Winakor (of the Bureau of Institutional Research) to Janata, March 28, 1944; Willard Correspondence. Willard to Benner, March 29, 1944 (et. seq., as in n. 28), College of Education Papers.

[30] Willard to Benner, April 17, 1944, College of Education Papers. See also Benner to Willard, April 26, 1944, Willard Correspondence. There is a note, dated May 31, on Willard's folder which contains this letter which reads: "C [oleman] R G[riffith] to report soon on Benner report on status of Col. Ed." Thus matters stood virtually on the eve of the letter of June 3, 1944.

Browne over the issue of the University's provision for vocational education and the delicate question of relations with the teachers' colleges which was implicit in the whole matter. In response, Browne and Carmichael had both proposed enlisting the aid of Griffith in dealing with the College and its bothersome Dean. Griffith had reasons of his own not to be in sympathy with Benner, as we have seen—reasons not diminished by his recent involvement in the halting University Council on Teacher Education where he and the Dean had come to bitter verbal blows. Finally, all three had in turn apparently persuaded the President that the whole move was a distinct threat to his own administration already listing badly under the onslaught of virtually continuous surveys, investigations, and criticisms.[31]

The dispute was, of course, an extremely complex issue, involving mixed questions of fact and philosophy. The factual aspect depended almost exclusively on whether the College was getting its just share of University resources and whether it was in fact "understaffed." These simple questions, however, were (like all questions of "fact," perhaps) hardly free from partially subjective perceptions and necessary judgments of value. If registrations and cost ratios could be conveniently quantified, the justness of appropriations could not. The administration party could argue that many of the courses had light enrollments, for example. On the other hand, the Dean could, and did, insist that that made no difference—he also denied it was wholly true—because the crucial issue was not the immediate situation. The norm had to be, he believed, what a College of Education should in principle be doing, and not the vicissitudes of the moment. The criteria for judgment should be the ideal case and (just as important) the College's sorry financial history, not its immediate state.[32]

[31] Griffith had objected to the Dean's use of facts and statistics from the Bureau of Institutional Research for some time previously. See, for example, Griffith to Benner, June 22, 1943, Willard Correspondence, where the Director warned Benner he might have to "disclaim" the Dean's interpretations of Bureau data. The issues and interrelationships set out in this paragraph provide a summary of the charges and the strategy to come. Their Council battles stemmed from Benner's (and the College's) unwillingness to accept the administrative arrangements of the new all-University body, and their disenchantment with the lack of general education provisions in several of the curricula. This behavior seemed erratic and capricious to Griffith, since the Dean had supposedly backed formation of the Council but then appeared to be resisting it.

[32] There was some tendency to view the whole matter in terms of intra-institutional politics. See, for example, Benner to Russell D. Gregg, August 1, 1944, Benner Papers. The choice of a new president was at hand and doubtless had an effect on matters. Whether Griffith had any ambitions or not, he does

The philosophical issue ran even deeper. With its new faculty nucleus now largely in the ascendancy the College had come to exemplify the broad, general philosophy of education which Benner had articulated from the beginning. Interpreting the practical situation by means of this philosophy, the Dean was convinced, in sum, that the University needed some sort of basic modernization, especially in regard to its general educational function. That meant, for him, a socially defined curriculum which would prepare the student to cope with the demands of modern social, political, and economic life by equipping him with the necessary instruments for dealing with reality. This reality was not to be merely philosophically or scientifically defined; it also had to be consciously understood in a broadly social and cultural sense if the individual was to achieve his desires, especially in the context of a democratic state. Against this, the evidence suggests strongly that the University's academic and administrative leadership (and most of the senior faculty) ranged from the rather mildly (as, for example, Provost Harno) to the quite strongly opposed.[33]

The philosophy of the University was not usually consciously articulated; it did not need to be, since it was historically incarnate in the faculty and administration and their actions and decisions. When matters came to a head, not only in connection with the dispute with the College but in connection with the continuous self-examination which marked the early 1940's, Coleman Griffith did, however, try to make the theoretical issues clear. Since he was a psychologist and actually an "educationist"—although he never failed to stress his heterodoxy both practical and theoretical in respect to prevailing educational doctrines—and when he became, as Provost, a high educa-

---

not seem to have done much to achieve them, even later. He penciled a rough draft of a resignation to Willard in the face of rumors that he was seeking the College deanship in 1945—see File University Administration, 1945. He protested Monroe's being awarded the interim deanship following Benner's removal, on the grounds that Monroe was opposed to the Teacher Education Council and had "left the College in chaos" before—an admission that the Dean might have used well in his own defense. See Griffith to Willard, August 27, 1945. He strongly criticized Willard's administration (noting particularly the low morale and the general lack of faculty confidence) in warning President-elect Stoddard in advance of his arrival—an arrival which Griffith seems genuinely to have welcomed. See Griffith to George D. Stoddard, May 24, 1945. Both in General University Situation File, and all in Griffith Papers.

[33] Benner was still consciously attacking this issue as late as 1943. See under Benner to Willard, March 6, 1943, Willard Correspondence, where the Dean pressed for a basic modernization and a broader and more definite concept of general education.

tional officer, Griffith presumed to speak for the University, and doubtless he did in the main. (The institution did not, of course, speak univocally, but Griffith believed that it should and could, if it shook its often unconscious bemusement with certain modern developments which he thought were actually contradictory to its fundamental beliefs.) [34]

What was this philosophy? At least for Griffith, the need to defend the true liberal arts and sciences had been generated by an antecedent conflict in philosophical and psychological theory. This dispute could be reduced to the inescapable opposition between the psychology of Aristotle and the psychology of Locke, and their correlative conceptions of human nature.[35] To draw the lines simply, Aristotle was right and Locke was disastrously wrong. Aristotle and the orthodox "ancients"—except for Plato and his ilk, of course, whom Griffith found merely a variety of pre-Locke Lockeans, so to speak—believed in reason as a faculty or power to be developed. Locke's contrary psychological theory had emphasized the contents of the mind rather than the process of reasoning. Educational theories based on Locke (with which even proper conservatives had become infected) had grown preoccupied with information rather than the development of intellectual power.[36] The modern university had gone Lockean, tending to see itself in terms of courses rather than as a process of mental maturation. Courses were important, but not when divorced from the process, which should be its concern. Griffith was also rather out of sympathy with the subtle elitism which lurked in Locke, and even in an unscientific Aristotelianism. It had dangerously infected the higher learning and corrupted its social motives. (Here Griffith thought many if not most of his own Urbana colleagues were badly off base.) The University had tended to assume that mental ability existed in fixed

[34] For what follows, see Griffith's twenty-five page manuscript dated February 15, 1943, addressed "Dear Bill." This typescript can be found in the Bureau of Institutional Research File, Record Series 2/9/1, no. 69. An attached longhand note to A. J. Janata suggests that this copy was meant for the President's eyes, and it was in part precipitated by the A.C.E. Survey and its examination of the Division of General Studies. The "Bill" may have been "Will" Sanford.

[35] Ibid., esp. pp. 5, 7–9, 13–14. This was a favorite theme of Griffith's and formed the basis of many of his addresses and manuscripts. See, for example, his "The Human Nature Bases of Conflict in Education," in Record Series 5/1/21, no. 14. He saw Plato as the ultimate source of the difficulty (p. 11).

[36] Griffith's MS, February 15, 1943, pp. 7, 8. Griffith had perhaps more accurately called Locke's theory epistemological than psychological; albeit, for Griffith, there was no such distinction. Psychologists would in any case perfect the work of philosophers (p. 16).

quantity and static form, prior to the higher educational level. The University's task was oversimplified by such a definition: it was merely to present truths. The able students would accept and understand; the feeble would properly be washed out. As a "scientist of human nature" (which he thought all psychologists should be), Griffith believed that his discipline was the key to all educational theorizing and could save higher education from this blunder.[37] His discipline developed the empirically verified descriptions and laws of the process of mental growth by means of which the now undifferentiated mass of students could be "salvaged." (The "professional" emphasis now in vogue was also a disastrous effect of Locke, Griffith thought, since its fundamental strategy was to provide vocational information. Unfortunately, even proper conservatives had fallen for it, not excluding those in the humanities.) [38]

"Progressivism," and particularly the brand currently emanating from Teachers College, was for Griffith (and many of his colleagues) simply the old enemy in his modern organized form. Progressivism was the direct offspring of the illicit cohabitation of Locke and Thorndike on Morningside Heights.[39] This was particularly evident in its then heavy emphasis on curricular reform. Griffith disagreed sharply with "the tremendous vogue of the content notion of education which is urged most consistently by modern educational theorists who can't distinguish between education and propaganda, and by all the curriculum specialists who propose to solve the problems of education by socializing, enriching, redealing, and otherwise manipulating subject matter." [40] And, like many of his colleagues, he also feared the whole matter of increasing governmental "control" of education which they saw as an implicit trend of the times and which doubtless stood in close relation to their attitude toward "progressivism" and its ready acceptance of political activity as a positive good.[41]

[37] Ibid., pp. 3–5, 24. Griffith continued to point this same issue later in "Remarks at Western Illinois State College," dated May 28, 1950. See Record Series 5/1/21, no. 5.

[38] Griffith's MS, Feb. 15, 1943, esp. pp. 9–13. Even "culture" courses were Lockean when content-centered, and should be replaced by more dynamic and maturational studies (p. 20).

[39] Ibid., p. 20. Griffith insisted he was not to be identified with "vulgar educationists, with the new lingo of the intelligence testers, with progressivism . . ." (p. 17).

[40] Ibid., pp. 5–6. Griffith agreed with Browne's criticisms partly on this basis (see n. 20 above), and he later opposed Arthur Bestor on the same ground.

[41] Griffith's very interesting but characteristically elaborate analysis in his (14

The philosophical dispute was quite clearly not limited to pedagogical theory. Political elements and overtones were in direct view. Robert Browne, whose critical reaction was so influential in galvanizing the opposition, was convinced he was being gradually removed from teaching the College's philosophy of education course because he was teaching genuine "philosophy," and not the "questionable New Deal Economics and the new social order gibberish of Teachers' College Columbia." [42] And, from their perspective, many of the Dean's supporters were convinced that there was, at this particular time, a national movement to stop the "liberal" trend exemplified by the New Deal, of which progressivism was popularly seen as the educational instrumentality. Mrs. Walter F. Heineman, the lone liberal independent on the Chicago Board of Education whose record was a striking exception to that of her fellow Board members, wrote Benner of her hope to "live long enough to see the tide turn in this war on education." [43]

Nor were the political aspects seen as merely the manifestations of a vague national temper. The press linked them clearly with the Illinois political situation, which found Democrats now struggling to maintain their position in the face of a new Republican state administration. The Democratic gubernatorial candidate charged that Republicans were

---

pp.) manuscript dated November 23, 1942, prepared for Willard's use before the Trustees in reviewing the Booz, Fry, Allen and Hamilton Survey Report, under Griffith to Willard, November 24, 1942, Willard Correspondence. Griffith feared the Trustees would be sold on the report and accept its (to him) dangerous assumptions. See esp. pp. 4–8.

[42] Robert Browne's holograph "Memo to Pres. A.C.W. . . . ," p. 3, in Record Series 2/9/1, no. 81. Cf. n. 20 above.

[43] Mrs. Walter F. Heineman to Benner, August 2, 1945, Benner Papers. See also "U of I Board Declines to give Dean a Hearing," *Chicago Sun* (June 6, 1945). Some years previously, two College faculty members, William O. Stanley and B. Othanel Smith, had prepared instructional material on inflation and political "pressure groups" which had drawn the wrath of the Farm Bureau and ultimately led to severe friction between Dean H. P. Rusk of the College of Agriculture and Benner (who had refused to "discipline" the faculty members involved). Benner believed that episode was still bothering some of the Trustees. See second letter of Benner to Donald DuShane, November 19, 1945, p. 6, Benner Papers. There is also material from the National Association of Manufacturers (ca. 1943) on the problem of radicals in the schools, in College of Education File, Willard Correspondence, Record Series 2/9/1, no. 70. A much more clearcut (and much more serious) case arose a few years later, in 1949. See Dean Willard B. Spalding (Benner's successor) to K. E. Williamson (Trustee), November 3, 1949, in which a College faculty member, Fred Barnes, was (unjustly) put under an attack which outspokenly linked "Progressive" education and communism.

"meddling" with University affairs.[44] Political analyst John Dreiske tried to link "Parke (Benner must go) Livingston," the president of the Board, with the G.O.P.[45] The new and outspokenly liberal *Chicago Sun*, claiming it had spent four days in intensive investigation, discovered politics at the bottom of Willard's action in the Benner case. Noting that the Dean's attorney, Sveinbjorn Johnson, was "an outstanding liberal" who had publicly charged President Livingston and fellow Trustee Chester Davis (who was vice-president of Chicago Title and Trust) with using their posts for political and business purposes, John McGrath of the *Sun* found Willard's action otherwise hard to explain: "The fact that Benner's resignation was insisted upon by Willard before the latter's own retirement next year, plus the fact that it was bulwarked by the signatures of nine top officials has given rise to a strong suspicion on the campus that the request for the ouster came from powerful sources in Chicago and Springfield whose interest in education sometimes transcends the academic." [46]

It is difficult, however, to view President Willard as consciously at the center of any intricate, politically inspired plot against the College or its Dean, no matter how obvious the swirling eddies of Illinois political currents were throughout the state, including Urbana. Though most University events of 1944–45 were susceptible to a political interpretation, there is little evidence to suggest that they were politically caused. There is, on the other hand, quite sufficient evidence to explain what came to be called "the Benner Case" on both personal and theoretical grounds. The President's role was, however, curious. It reflected a good deal of the vagueness, or perhaps even the ambiguity, of his administration. The two major surveys of the University had come to what appeared to be opposite conclusions: the A.C.E. report finding the administration guilty of an excessive surrender of

[44] Two articles in the *Urbana Sunday Courier* (October 1, 1944). In one, "G.O.P. Rallies Hit New Deal, Judge Johnson," Trustee (and Superintendent of Public Instruction) Vernon Nickell was quoted as charging Sveinbjorn Johnson, Benner's attorney, with being "the snooper for the New Deal on the Republican party in Illinois." In another, "Meddling at U.I. Charged by [Democratic gubernatorial candidate Thomas J.] Courtney," Johnson was praised and a Republican plot discerned. Neither case is very convincing.

[45] *Urbana Evening Courier* (August 14, 1945), where John Dreiske (of the Chicago *Times*) is so quoted in the "About Town" column.

[46] *Chicago Sun* (July 8, 1945), "U of Illinois Head Linked to Dean Benner's Ouster" (datelined July 7). The article made a number of dubious, inadequate statements. McGrath did report that "all signers interviewed"——the article identified none, and left quite ambiguous whether all had been—agreed with the President's action, but none claimed to have "documentary evidence."

leadership, and the Booz, Fry, Allen and Hamilton report finding it too centralized. In a sense, both were right, but the prima facie opposition was only apparent. The University did tend to be monolithic, run from the top down. On the other hand, the President did not himself manage affairs autocratically—quite the reverse. It was, as one observer perceptively put it, something of a "*junta*" which governed instead— though "probably," as the A.C.E. surveyors had said, not at "the conscious intention of the President!" [47] Willard sometimes seemed to claim credit for putting the pressure on Benner, but he also sometimes denied it, and there is no evidence to indicate that he exercised any very strong leadership. Indeed, there were, as we shall see, occasions when he did not appear to know what had happened, let alone initiate what should occur.[48] Griffith himself could be strongly critical of Willard's administration, in private.[49] The President, in short, appears more as a man caught in the middle, the victim of nondirective policies which were suddenly paying unhappily concrete and personal dividends.

What appears to be the case is that Browne, Griffith, Carmichael, and Harno formulated a strategy for dealing with Benner and the College's program, perhaps in counsel with the other signers and with the agreement—rather late in coming—of the President. That strategy was to face the Dean with a written "no confidence" vote from some of his administrative peers in the hope of forcing an immediate resignation. While their theoretical position, their substantive disagreement with Benner's policies and style, was legitimate and even plausible—there were indeed serious questions at issue upon which good men might well differ—their strategy was much less convincing. It appeared to many observers to be ethically dubious, and it was without doubt carelessly conceived, practically speaking. Their attempt was ethically dubious,

[47] The A.C.E. noted that the Provost's office (previously filled by Harno, but before the year 1944-45 was over, in Griffith's hands), the Bureau of Institutional Research, and its Advisory Committee had usurped the "locus of highest educational leadership." See 42nd *Report* (1944), pp. 1033, 1036ff. (the source of the quotations). It also pointed out that the policies of the Graduate School had (as, for example, in chemistry) generally had the effect of making strong departments stronger while others got weaker, and the surveyors criticized the conservatism of the College of Liberal Arts and Sciences (pp. 1098, 1957ff.). Curiously enough, while Education was not condemned, its growth was minimized, yet the administration did not use the report in evidence at the hearing—perhaps because of what it would have introduced about their own position (p. 1083).

[48] Judge Johnson was able to demonstrate this quality in the President later at the hearing, an account of which follows in this chapter.

[49] Griffith to George D. Stoddard, May 24, 1945, Griffith Papers.

if only because it attempted to force a Dean out by applying external pressure, when at least the majority of his collegiate colleagues and those who suffered his governance did not in fact desire it. It was, in addition, an essentially private act, withheld from the public scrutiny which such judgments are expected to undergo in an academic community.[50]

Their strategy was ill conceived if only because it made one dangerous practical assumption: it assumed that Benner would in fact resign quietly. Indeed, it could not work otherwise; it could only raise a host of difficulties of the thorniest sort. Griffith clearly wanted the Dean out by the end of the academic year. If Benner did not resign, however, the question would then be whether or not the President could simply remove him. That possibility was in serious doubt, especially since the Dean was at the middle of his two-year term. But Benner soon clarified the situation. When presented with the letter, he showed not the slightest inclination to resign. He categorically refused to do so. The practical question, then, was whether the President could and should attempt to remove him.[51]

[50] The procedure was not, however, without intriguingly similar institutional precedents which had not escaped publicity. In one puzzling case, H. T. Scovill, Acting Dean of the College of Commerce (and one of the signers) was himself refused permanent appointment by the Board of Trustees three times during the same year, in spite of Willard's apparent recommendation (*Champaign News-Gazette* [October 6, 1944]). Ernest Bernbaum of the English department and Arthur Murphy, the distinguished head of the philosophy department, had both departed under curious circumstances, which at least Bernbaum (a somewhat explosive figure anyway) had not kept entirely quiet. See articles by John McGrath in the *Chicago Sun*, July 8, July 25, 1945. (In the latter, even Robert Zuppke's resignation was alleged to have been forced, and to have "uncovered an impressive amount of bitterness on the campus.") Benner informed Chase that "this technic [expulsion of an administrative officer without consulting his faculty] has been used twice during Willard's administration" (Benner to Chase, August 2, 1944, Benner Papers).

[51] According to an unsigned memorandum dated June 12, 1945 (Benner File, Record Series 2/9/1, no. 89), a conference of all the signers except Staley and Scovill was held at ten o'clock on that date in the President's office. Under an informal, typed note from Janata to Willard, August 9, 1944, there are letters that show the first aim was to secure Benner's *removal* by September 1, 1944. The Provost said that he and Carmichael agreed with Griffith's contention that the non-pro-Benner faculty in the College were in an "intolerable" situation, and that, while the Dean was not "entitled" to a hearing, "he probably should be given one" (Harno to Willard, August 3, 1944). Griffith had urged that "conclusive action be taken immediately" for—again, one of his customarily extensive analyses—nine reasons. They are too long to be reproduced here, but they pointed chiefly to the fact that the *signers* were now under fire, and that Benner might now do further damage to the College and the University. See Griffith to Willard, July

The issue now, however, did not involve the President alone; it put the Trustees squarely in the middle of the dispute, since the power to remove (or appoint) was clearly theirs and not the President's as such. All things being equal, there was no doubt that the Trustees could not be compelled to reappoint at the end of the term, even in a context of repeated appointments or a "good record" on the part of the appointee, nor need they offer grounds for their action. The question was in part whether the general provisions respecting tenure, while clearly not applying beyond an administrator's limited contract, did apply *within* that period.

The University *Statutes* of 1936 stated that a dean was a chief executive officer, responsible to the President, and elected biennially by the Trustees on the President's recommendation. Section 25, which defined tenure, was less clear. Subsection (b) required that cause be shown for discharge and *could* be interpreted to apply to administrative appointees if discharged before the expiration of their appointments. Subsection (c) seemed to suggest more strongly that this was the intended interpretation. Provost Harno, who was a distinguished professor of law, did not believe that interpretation was required. Judge Sveinbjorn Johnson, formerly University Counsel and also a distinguished jurist, disagreed with Harno. First consulted by the administration on its own behalf but later Benner's attorney, Johnson argued that while deans did not enjoy *indefinite* tenure, they could not be removed within the course of their contract except on certain specific grounds. A president's powers, he insisted, excluded those not specified or described, or fairly within explicit powers. There was a legal procedure for removing heads of departments, but none for deans. Hence "the absence of such a provision" implied, he said, "a purpose to exclude the power to remove during the term without cause." In the long run, whatever the merits of either interpretation, those who opposed Benner did not appear (on the face of it) desirous of alleging cause publicly, and they soon decided that the only expedient course was to await the expiration of the Dean's term.[52]

31, 1944. In his note, however, Janata reminded Willard that quick action would require the Board to rescind an existing contract and thus would require a full quorum. He sent all this to Willard, who was on vacation, and proposed to ask (former University Counsel) Sveinbjorn Johnson's opinion.

[52] Pleading the *Statutes* in defense of his action, Willard laid the matter before the Trustees almost immediately, without recommendation, and it was merely "received for the record" (43rd *Report* [1946], p. 15). Since the administration hoped to handle the situation as a routine "administrative" matter, it did not

Had President Willard said nothing more, it is possible that nothing further would have transpired. However, he made one more serious mistake which compounded the mistake already lurking in the letter. A few days after his meeting with the President, Benner wrote to ask if there would be any further "charges" at issue. Willard wrote in return: "In reply to your inquiry of June 9 concerning any other charges than these contained in the statement of June 3rd, I can say none were proposed by those signing that statement." A few weeks later he wrote, "There will be no other charges than those contained in the letter of June 3rd, a copy of which you have." The result of this (possibly innocent) exchange was to give Benner the case he needed: the letter of June 3rd had suggested cause, and Willard had indicated twice that he and the signers were willing to describe their actions as bringing "charges" against him. Benner believed this furnished conclusive evidence that he was being removed, or at least not reappointed, for alleged cause, and to allege cause entitled him to a full hearing.[53]

The Dean formally requested an open hearing before the Board on

---

attempt to make a formal legal case until forced to the next spring. Although he formally recorded his opinion only later, it seems plausible that Harno's interpretation was held from the beginning. He believed that cause *might* have to be shown for discharge *during* an administrative appointment, but that clearly neither cause nor notice in advance would be required (and, hence, no hearing) if an appointment were merely allowed to expire (Harno to Willard, May 16, 1945, Willard Correspondence). His own recommendation (see n. 51 above) shows that at first he was willing to try to discharge Benner immediately. Johnson soon responded with the opposite viewpoint, however: no administrative officer could "divest" another of his position without both cause and hearing, and he later insisted that if nonreappointment were alleged to be for cause, that would also require a hearing. See his "Memorandum," August 4, 1944, Willard Correspondence. The Trustees indicated their position, which paralleled Harno's, in two memoranda of their Secretary (and also an attorney) H. E. Cunningham, "Tenure of Deans" (May 16, 1945) and "Termination of Appointments" (June 1, 1945). All in Willard Correspondence.

Benner himself took a still different view. He argued that the fundamental intent of limited appointment was to protect the faculty over whom any administrator was placed, and that the President was at least morally bound not only not to terminate but in fact to continue an appointment, in the absence of cause, so long as a faculty desired it. (It was to test this interpretation that the College's Executive Committee formally requested the Dean's reappointment shortly after the President made his move.) While this interpretation may have accorded with the traditional spirit of a university, it was not required by the Illinois *Statutes*, it would appear. See "Benner's Analysis of Harno's May 16, 1945, Letter to Willard," in Benner Papers.

[53] Benner to Willard, June 9, 1944; Willard to Benner, June 14, 1944; Willard to Benner, July 10, 1944; all in Willard Correspondence.

July 13, 1944.[54] His belief that he deserved one was further strengthened not only by the description of the action as involving "charges"
but by the fact that the whole affair soon became public. He claimed
that the matter had been bruited about the University community
within days of its occurrence, although Willard and the signers consistently denied that they had broken the allegedly agreed-upon confidence. Whatever the case in regard to private circulation of the details, they were not long in hitting the press.[55] The *Urbana Evening
Courier*, on July 14, reported "Benner's Ouster . . . Asked by Fellow
Deans," suggesting that the Dean was being fired and not simply being declined reappointment. It mentioned a letter and named its signers. The *Champaign News-Gazette* broke the full story two days later,
however, reporting that officers of the Illinois Education Association,
in Pittsburgh to attend the annual meeting of the NEA, were demanding a full explanation. The *Gazette* published the full text of the letter
(with some slight errors), and the whole story was soon given extensive coverage in the Chicago papers. After the United Press had
gotten the report on the wire, Benner explained that he was responsible for releasing the letter and the story, but he claimed he had done
so only after the matter had become public. He claimed he had shown
a copy of the letter to a local reporter, with the understanding that
it was "background" material only and not for publication, but that his
request had been ignored.[56]

[54] Benner to Willard, July 13, 1944, copy in Willard Correspondence. It was
sent confidential, registered, and return receipt requested.

[55] Benner went so far as to insist that the matter had been circulated even before he had received the letter. See *The College of Illinois and Dean Thomas E.
Benner*, pp. 3–4, Benner Papers. That the President's office (and probably the
signers) were alarmed by developments is shown by a curious memorandum,
dated July 17, 1944, and signed by Nancy Blewett, which contains a message
she was charged to deliver by telephone to Browne, Griffith, McClure, Newcomb,
Rusk, and Scovill. The message denied that the letter had been released by the
administration, adding that the copy given to Benner was "the only copy given
out by this Office." There is also a note which says this message had been given
to Carmichael, Harno, and Staley by Willard personally.

[56] *Urbana Evening Courier* (July 14, 19, 1944); *Champaign News-Gazette* (July
16, 1944); *The Daily Illini* (July 15, 19, 1944); *Chicago Tribune* (July 19, 1944);
Chicago Sun (July 19, 1944). See also follow-ups: *Champaign News-Gazette*
(July 23, 27, 1944); *Urbana Evening Courier* (July 30, 1944); *Daily Illini* (July
22, 1944).

That the story broke must have been less than surprising, even to Benner. The
College "Faculty Committee," allegedly without his prompting but hardly without his knowledge, had gone to work spreading the basic contents of the letter
and soliciting support before the end of June. See H. M. Hamlin, et al., to Albert

On July 18, Willard announced to the Trustees that he would not ask for the Dean's reappointment—without proposing to terminate his contract—and also presented Benner's request for a hearing. The Board made no official comment and took no action except to inform Benner of the President's announcement. At first the University authorities took the position that it was a routine administrative matter and consequently a closed case. This attitude was largely fashioned by Provost Harno and the Trustees' Secretary H. E. Cunningham. As a result, the Board did nothing. Neither it nor President Willard made any serious attempt to communicate with the Dean for several months, although Willard and Board President Livingston were quoted on the subject frequently in the press.[57]

As we have already noted, however, Benner took his case to the University's former counsel and a prestigious authority in such matters, Judge Sveinbjorn Johnson. Johnson had insisted that removal was illegal without charges and that charges would then necessitate a hearing. Now, of course, the situation had changed: removal was not contemplated, but publicly known charges had been alleged as the grounds for Benner's nonreappointment. The Judge's interest in the case (which he investigated thoroughly before agreeing to represent the Dean formally) increased considerably as time passed and the Dean was offered no relief. He chided the President when no action had been taken even as late as the following March.[58]

Later that spring, however, the pressure inherent in the situation began to build even more rapidly, and Johnson made up his mind. Benner again requested a hearing in early May. The Trustees discussed the matter more fully this time, but they again decided that it was the President's jurisdiction and so notified the Dean—his first formal reply since the affair had begun almost a year previously.[59] On May 16, visibly tiring of the Trustee's dilatory tactics and convinced that they

Nicholas (president of the Illinois High School Principals' Association), June 29, 1944. A similar leter went to the I.E.A., apparently. The delegates had probably known of it before they left home. All in Benner Papers. For Benner's defense, see *The College of Education of the University of Illinois and Dean Thomas E. Benner*, p. 4.

[57] H. E. Cunningham to Benner, July 19, 1944; Willard to Park Livingston, January 8, July 13, 1945; all in Willard Correspondence. 43rd *Report* (1946), p. 15. See also n. 52 above.

[58] Johnson to Willard, May 16, 1945, Willard Correspondence. Johnson there records that he had discussed the case with Willard on March 31, 1945, before making his decision.

[59] 43rd *Report* (1946), pp. 463, 490.

had a responsibility they could not dodge, Johnson addressed a strong letter to Willard. He emphasized that "on the records of the University there is a statement of 'charges' against Dean Benner signed by nine staff members . . . that he is not fit, therefore, for reappointment." [60] The President replied that the matter was before the Trustees and that Johnson's argument would be considered. Later that month the Trustees again took up the case and, following Harno's opinion, denied there were any "charges" at all and absolved themselves of any jurisdiction once more.[61]

At this action, Johnson lost all patience and he wrote the President a thoroughly indignant protest. He reminded Willard that he had promised to do something, specifically to allow the Dean to face his accusers. Since the Board had "put the whole matter on [his] desk," Johnson requested a formal hearing of all parties before the President. Cutting through the pettifogging which had characterized the case, the Judge insisted the issue was one of fundamental civil rights, since nine presumably responsible men had put their names to a document which threatened the professional reputation of the Dean. It was also now a

<hr />

[60] Johnson to Willard, May 16, 1945, Willard Correspondence. Johnson had pointed out, he said, the potentially bad effect upon all which a public controversy would bring and had suggested a compromise back in March, but he had not heard from the President since. He reminded Willard that there were charges against the Dean on a public record, *by those who had no duty or obligation to make them.* "Unless, therefore—as some of the signers of the statement assert [which suggests Johnson had found out something; he was not given to idle threats]—you prepared this document and in effect directed them to sign it, they are in the position of volunteers, who without any duty in the premises, have become guilty of libel per se against Dean Benner." Furthermore, President Livingston had now asserted publicly that the Dean would have a hearing, yet nothing had been said to Benner. Moreover, a public search for a new Dean was now underway, which suggested a prejudgment of an issue not yet heard. "By refusing to respond frankly and unequivocally to Dean Benner's reiterated request for a hearing, the University has created a new issue which transcends in importance the merits of the Dean's record." It had been, Johnson insisted, a "secret conspiracy." Consequently, "this new issue leaves me no choice but to do my best, not so much for Dean Benner, for he as a person has now become of secondary importance, as for the great and fundamental principle of American justice, which is, in case you and some members of the Board have forgotten, that no man, not the humblest in our midst, not even a confessed murderer, shall be condemned until he has had a chance to be heard upon the charges against him. . . ." Johnson then demanded an answer, reminding the President of a former Board's (more honest) posture in a similar case (in 1941), and threatening a large-scale public disclosure.

[61] See Willard to Johnson, May 19, 1945, Willard Correspondence. 43rd *Report* (1946), pp. 490–92; H. E. Cunningham to Benner, May 28, 1945, Willard Correspondence.

public fact that if the President acted adversely and continued to refuse to recommend reappointment, the force of the "charges" would
be affirmed by inaction. The President had cited these accusations as
the cause of his proposed decision. Should the President continue to
take no action, Johnson thought it would be a "courtesy to point out
what would follow:

> It will be impossible for you or the Board of Trustees or the nine signers
> to avoid an inquiry, publicly and completely, into the allegations in the
> letter of June 3, 1944, the factual basis for them and the circumstances of
> the preparation and signing of this document.

The reason as explanation of the foregoing is this: If you refuse Dean
Benner a hearing, with an opportunity to question the signers and make
a record of their answers if he chooses, he will ask each and all of them
to answer questions concerning the document of June 3, 1944; if they refuse, he will appeal to the Board from your decision and theirs, and ask
for a hearing and an opportunity to examine each of the signers; and if
the Board refuses, Dean Benner *can* file a libel suit against the signers,
and then by subpoena force the signers and any others he has a mind to
call for questioning under oath to respond and submit to examination.
Whether he will take this last step, I do not know, for I have not discussed it with him, but if all other avenues of redress are closed to him, I
would most certainly advise him to do just that. As I pointed out in my
letter of May 16, the document of June 3, 1944 is a libel per se against
Dean Benner.

My letter to you of May 16 sets forth some of the reasons which im-
pel the conclusion that a hearing cannot be denied to Dean Benner
without violating the fundamental concepts not only of academic freedom, but of our entire American system of civil rights. I shall not repeat
these reasons here. Since, however, the decision whether Dean Benner
shall be denied this fundamental right has now become your personal and
official responsibility, I repeat the essence of what I said in the letter mentioned, namely, that in this country it is axiomatic that if a man be accused, he shall be accused publicly and not secretly, and being accused,
shall be heard before he is condemned. I am sure it is not necessary for
me to enlarge upon the proposition that a state university should be the
last place on earth where this principle is either doubted or denied.[62]

On June 11, Willard finally replied: He had received the letter and
would give it "careful consideration," but unfortunately he would be

[62] Johnson to Willard, June 2, 1945, Willard Correspondence.

"very busy" with legislative matters at Springfield for the next three weeks.[63]

Events did not, however, wait for Willard's convenience or more leisurely times. On June 4, the Illinois Education Association had issued a strong public appeal to the Trustees for a hearing, but Livingston again threw it back on Willard's "desk." Other groups followed the IEA's lead.[64] Finally forced to answer publicly, Willard, calling a hearing "unwise," denied that any opportunity would be given Benner, and went on to accuse the Dean of first making the issue public.[65] Tired of being addressed only through the daily papers, on June 24 Benner prepared his own release: since the press appeared to know that the answer was "no," although he had himself not yet been so informed, he would be forced to take his case directly to the public with a full disclosure.[66] Six days later, now some thirteen months since the original letter, the Board of Trustees decided that a closed hearing, with counsel for both sides, was indicated. (President Livingston alluded to the reception of a considerable correspondence on the matter by now, it may be worth noting.) [67] On the morning of July 1, the press gave generous notice to the fact that the Board had "yielded" and even published Johnson's side of the argument over interpretations of the *Statutes*. According to the newspapers, the hearing was set for

[63] Willard to Johnson, June 11, 1945, Willard Correspondence. A similarly casual attitude was evident later, when he pleaded his responsibilities for the University's "legislative program" for failing to answer. See Willard to Johnson, July 5, 1945, Willard Correspondence.

[64] *Chicago Sun* (June 5, 1945), p. 13. The IEA directors called the charges "weak," and castigated the administration's methods on the grounds that they "violate all the principles of good administrative and professional procedure." (Cf. I. F. Pearson to Park Livingston, September 22, 1944.) Other accounts in *Urbana Evening Courier* (June 4, 1945); *Champaign News-Gazette* (June 4, 1945). See also *Chicago Sun* (June 6, 1945), which reported "Appointment up to Willard, Says Head of Trustees." Cf. *Urbana Evening Courier* (June 11, 21, 1945). Under Janata to Livingston, June 6, 1945, there is evidence that the IEA charge on facilities carried the most weight and drew admissions that the College's building programs had been removed from even the distant priorities they had earlier been assigned.

[65] The *Urbana Evening Courier* (June 22, 1945) quoted Willard as calling the hearing "unwise," and carried his accusation that Benner had made the issue public. It also carried the Harno opinion. Cf. *Champaign News-Gazette* (June 22, 1945), which reported Willard had "no intention of granting Dean Thomas E. Benner a hearing . . . ," and *The Daily Illini* (June 22, 1945).

[66] *Urbana Sunday Courier* (June 24, 1945); *Chicago Tribune* (June 24, 1945).

[67] 43rd *Report* (1946), p. 512. Livingston "read several letters . . . received on this matter." The motion was now unanimous.

July 25; Benner had still received no official notice of the Trustees' action on the 15th.[68]

The Dean's prolonged struggle to obtain a hearing had not been the only activity on the campus during the intervening months, of course. Within a matter of days following the letter of June 3, 1944, the entire College faculty was deeply embroiled in the situation. As we have already noted, although Browne and Griffith were technically connected with the College, no regular, full-time college faculty member had signed the letter or, apparently, been consulted in the matter. This fact did not promote the administration's cause. Almost at once an ad hoc faculty committee sprang up, under the leadership of E. H. Reeder, M. H. Hamlin, and B. O. Smith. They determined to focus on the manner in which the affair was handled and to offer a general statement of support. Their tack was that the whole action was contrary to the *Statutes* (which provided for the President to consult the College both about nominations and continued reappointments), since it had been handed them as a fait accompli. In effect, the College's destiny was being determined by those who had no responsibility for it—or at least only a tenuous relationship to it—and they hoped to produce clear evidence that an overwhelming majority of those actually concerned did not support the President's actions. Judge Johnson later bore down heavily on the same theme, pointing out to Willard:

> The statutes of the University give the signers of this attack on Dean Benner and the College no commission to report upon the fitness of their colleagues to serve the University; the minutes of the Board of Trustees contain reference to no action asking or directing them to investigate or report upon the fitness of Dean Benner; you have not claimed that you asked them to investigate or report. In short the action is without prece-

---

[68] *Urbana Sunday Courier* (July 1, 1945), which also cited the effect of outside pressure. Cf. *Chicago Sun* (July 1, 1945); *Champaign News-Gazette* (July 1, 1945). For Benner's lack of notice, see *Urbana Sunday Courier* (July 15, 1945). Willard had informed Johnson, but only very casually; see Willard to Johnson, July 5, 1945, Willard Correspondence. It is interesting to note that, in an extensive article (July 8, 1945), John McGrath of the *Chicago Sun* suggested that Willard had been behind it all, and that the act of the nine signers was not, as *previously believed*, an unsolicited action. This change in strategy may have been the result of Johnson's pointing out that if the signers had not been asked, they could be accused of libel. At least this new tack was taken by the administration during the hearing, although clearly the issue had not been so framed before—as all evidence, including the letter itself, discloses.

dent at Illinois, and, as far as I have been able to ascertain, in the United States.[69]

On July 15, 1944, the "volunteer committee," acting allegedly without Dean Benner's commission or knowledge, issued a statement of "confidence in the professional leadership of Dean Thomas E. Benner." The statement was signed by fourteen of the eighteen full-time, regular members of the College faculty. It was maintained that only two had refused to sign it, and that the others had simply refused to take either a pro or a con position in the matter. In addition, three members on military leave were willing to write their full support. The statement's signers were, as the administration privately noted, long on quantity but short on seniority. They were, by and large, the "Benner faculty," but they were also those who had developed the College's new programs over the previous decade.[70]

The College faculty committee also saw the necessity of countering the latter by demonstrating the support of schoolmen throughout the state, and they directed their attention to their personal contacts and the various professional organizations immediately. As we shall see, their efforts bore considerable fruit. (We have already noticed that the response of the schoolmen was perhaps decisive in getting the hearing set.) In addition, their strategy included formal actions. The College Executive Committee communicated its recommendation for the reappointment of the Dean at the appropriate time. The new Executive Committee was elected with each candidate's stance in re-

[69] *The College of Education of the University of Illinois and Dean Thomas E. Benner,* passim, esp. pp. 1–3. See also Johnson to Willard, May 16, 1945, Willard Correspondence. Cf. nn. 60, 68 above.

[70] See statement by Reeder, et al., to Willard, July 15, 1944, Willard Correspondence. The statement was signed by E. H. Reeder, A. F. Dodge, B. O. Smith, F. H. Finch, A. W. Anderson, C. M. Allen, M. C. Hartley, H. M. Hamlin, C. W. Odell, G. W. Reagan, L. W. Williams, G. M. Blair, W. O. Stanley, and W. E. Harnish. Notably absent were the names of Monroe, Sanford, and Seybolt (who was by now at the end of his career and out of favor with both sides—see under Willard to Carmichael, August 26, 1944; Seybolt to Willard, July 28 and August 11, 1944). See also interview with A. W. Anderson, January, 1962, College of Education Papers; Benner to C. F. Arrowood, July 31, 1944, Benner Papers. For additional letters on Benner's behalf, see under Willard to Reeder, April 20, 1945, Willard Correspondence, esp. those from Kenneth Benne (June 30, 1944), J. Harlan Shores (July 5, 1944), and William Habberton (July 5, 1944). See Willard to Reeder, et al., July 19, 1944, Willard Correspondence (with marginalia calculating the proportion of seniority represented by the signers).

gard to the dispute as the principal factor, and the resulting body petitioned for his retention by a four-to-one margin.[71]

As it became apparent that the Dean would win a hearing before the Board of Trustees, a "case" had to be prepared on the administration's side to supply justification for its actions. Doubtless convinced that its strategy (which assumed that the issue could be treated as a routine administrative decision, and therefore needed no defense in spite of the extended and public controversy) would prevail, virtually nothing had been done. With the authorization of the hearing, the Board also procured the services of Thomas L. Marshall, a senior partner of one of Chicago's most prestigious law firms, Bell, Boyd, and Marshall. Marshall, however, knew little or nothing of the dispute, and perhaps even less about universities and the way they were wont to operate. Therefore, a massive and rapid program not only of case-building but also of education for its counsel had to be assumed by the administration. The hearing was scarcely three weeks away.[72]

The responsibility for building the case largely fell upon Griffith, with some assistance from former Provost Harno. While Carmichael

[71] For example, Irving F. Pearson (executive secretary of IEA) to Willard, July 10, 1944, Willard Correspondence. In this, the first reply from the organization, the point is made that "no single factor, person, nor circumstance can be held responsible" for the College's failures, such as they were. Cf. *The College of Education of the University of Illinois and Dean Thomas E. Benner*, pp. 28–34. For College Executive Committee action, see Reeder to Willard, April 9, 1945, Willard Correspondence. They also suggested deferring the selection of a Dean, if necessary, until a new President had been chosen.

[72] 43rd *Report* (1946), p. 538. Marshall was paid $3,000 for his services, and expense reimbursement of $662.24. Ibid., p. 906. Johnson, in contrast, refused to charge Benner anything for what he called "murdered justice," and he even asked to bear part of the Dean's expense, "pro bono publico," from his own pocket (Johnson to Benner, August 15, 1945). Johnson had spent $209.05 and Benner paid $268.75. See Benner to Johnson, August 20, 1945. Both in Benner Papers. See also H. E. Cunningham to T. L. Marshall, July 5, 1945, Willard Correspondence.

The hearing was only days away and Marshall had not even been furnished the necessary documents. Furthermore, he had a busy schedule—such that material had to be passed to him on the observation platform of the Illinois Central's Panama Limited as it paused at the Champaign depot. He was first briefed at an executive committee meeting of the Board in Chicago, July 3, 1945, and officially appointed on July 5. See Marshall to Willard, July 17, 1945; Willard to Marshall, July 14, 18, 1945; Willard Correspondence. A series of the documents related to the Benner "trial" were returned by Marshall. See under Marshall to Janata, September 6, 1945, in Record Series 2/9/1, no. 100. The material was obviously part of his homework and included the IEA letters, suggesting their key role.

and Willard also later took the stand, and Browne was waiting in the wings to do so if it seemed advisable, the evidence suggests that none of the latter took a very active role in working the issue up. Marshall at least attempted to confer with each of the signers, but none of these conferences appears to have offered substantial evidence. Indeed, as we have already noted, most of the signers demonstrated markedly less enthusiasm for testifying or submitting evidence than they had for affixing their signatures, at least once the dispute had reached such proportions.[73]

Harno, insisting that "the issue is Benner and not the College of Education," largely focused his contribution to the case on the elusive quality of "confidence." This was, he argued, strongly felt to be lacking by his fellow University administrators. He gave little or no genuine evidence, however, that it extended to the Dean's actual colleagues—in fact, he admitted that Benner was on the whole not disliked. His chief difficulties were, according to the former Provost, a certain kind of instability, a tendency toward exaggeration, and the fact that he had been inappropriately argumentative about the budget and the building program. Reflections such as these, while they did in their own way document the "confidence" issue, were obviously not the stuff of which hard cases could be made. As Marshall's strategy at the hearing clearly shows, the meat of the issue had to come from elsewhere.[74]

In his first attempts to work the matter up, Griffith betrayed considerable evidence of the clash in personalities and styles which was involved.[75] He denied explicitly that differences in educational philosophy were significant—though we have seen that there are strong reasons for doubting his claim. He argued much more persuasively that good administration implied not simply good ideas—no one had ever accused the Dean of lacking them, at any rate—but the ability

[73] Marshall to Willard, July 16, 1945, Willard Correspondence. Perhaps they had all envisioned a bloodless coup, but now it had turned into a real battle with a considerable likelihood that any blood spilled might be their own.

[74] Unsigned memorandum, dated July 7, 1945, beginning "My contacts with Dean Benner . . . ," in File College of Education, September, 1945, to February, 1946, Record Series 2/9/1, no. 100. Internal references to the author as "Provost," etc., conclusively prove it was the work of Harno.

[75] For what follows, see signed rough text and final sixty-six-page draft of Griffith's "Statement Regarding the Benner Case." A copy was sent to Marshall, according to C.R.G. to President Willard, July 20, 1945. (Note the late date.) All in Benner Material File, Record Series 5/1/21, no. 5. Quotations will be from the final draft, hereinafter cited as Griffith, "Statement."

to initiate programs, a quite different matter. (The questions of who was to judge such a matter, his faculty colleagues or his administrative peers, and the criteria which delineated grounds for any adverse judgment were not thereby answered, of course.) When he sent a final version of his position to Marshall, however, he opened on, and gave primacy to, the "administrative decision" argument. In this statement, which he apparently intended to use on the stand (although it ran to sixty-six pages), he began as follows: "There is only one question at issue in the so-called Benner case; namely, the right of the chief executive officer of the University of Illinois to arrive at a judgment regarding the administrative capacities of a colleague and to seek verification of his own experience and judgment through a privileged communication from members of the staff. . . . even though they cannot cite chapter and verse from written documents." [76]

Griffith contended, as a consequence, that "the Benner case is not a legal case." The Dean had been accused of no violation; there was simply a mood of "disappointment" over his administrative accomplishments. The belief that Benner had not discharged his responsibilities could not, the Provost admitted, be linked to his performance on any one program, but was rather a "cumulative" judgment based on a host of experiences, many informal. The observations of the administrators who recommended against the Dean's reappointment simply "eventually crystallized." Griffith then attempted in some fifty-eight pages to document what he had already stated was not documentable—perhaps indicating that the "one" issue was not quite so simple after all. Basically, his argument was that the Dean had no real program of his own (which was partly evidenced by his "committee" approach) and that he misused statistical evidence in advancing his proposals for expansion.[77]

Specific instances of Benner's failures had been: (1) the teacher training curricula, which had not been brought into operation efficiently, and the Council on Teacher Education, which Benner had stymied over the administrative issue; (2) inadequate investigation of the junior college "problem," which he had crippled by deemphasizing the Bureau of Educational Research; (3) the failure to develop research programs, which again were alleged to have collapsed due

[76] Griffith, "Statement," p. 1.
[77] Ibid., pp, 1, 2, 6, 10–12. In defending the University, Griffith argued, "it must give preference to plans for expansion where expansion is created by the heaviest student demands" (p. 14).

to restricting the Bureau, denying students access to "the strongest research man" (Robert F. Seybolt) and mishandling the child development project. (Griffith strongly contrasted the qualities of mind necessary for "serious research on fundamental questions" and mere "professional competence.") While Griffith argued that these judgments were not only the conclusions of the nine but those of "large numbers of staff members and administrators," he presented no real evidence either in the document or later in the hearing that such was the case.[78]

Griffith then singled out Benner's handling of the teachers' college issue as "one of the weirdest instances of confusion, lack of leadership, and lack of appreciation of the best interests of the University" that could be "found in the records." Benner had continued to favor the development of special, professionally oriented five-year programs in accordance with the 1941 settlement that had been reached with the state colleges. While he had (like the administration) originally hoped to avert any such expansion, he had become convinced that they represented the best form it could take. The administration and the Graduate School, however, had later quietly agreed to more traditional graduate-level offerings *if* they met the School's customary criteria, on the presumption that these would be easier to control than autonomous professional programs either in the state colleges or at home. They were confused by the Dean's unwillingness to go along with their new policy, a stance which seemed especially odd in that it was a position which really pleased neither side. Benner's apparently erratic behavior was in fact a consistent extension of his long-held belief that traditional graduate-level criteria would be inimical to both the requisite professional orientation and the needed general educational element. Angered, Griffith accused the Dean of having used the situation to advance his own interests, insisting that Benner's continued advocacy of five-year programs now placed "the administration" in the "difficult situation of trying to support a laudable plan for a state-wide system of better facilities for the training of teachers" while at the same time "reserving to itself the right to control education at the graduate level in publicly supported institutions." The University was thus in 1943 (and "without consultation with Dean Benner") forced to "escape from" the "intolerable situation" the Dean had created by pleading the adverse judgment of the

[78] Ibid., pp. 34–35, 37.

Leland Commission, chaired by Dean George A. Works of the University of Chicago.[79]

Finally, the Dean was accused of not using data that "faithfully describe[d] the actual facts" in making his arguments for program and budget, particularly in the case of the "Understaffing" and the "Special Subjects" documents. (It should be noted that the conflict involved exclusively the method of arriving at comparative percentages within the University and in relation to other colleges of education; it did not involve any sort of deliberate falsification or misappropriation.) Characterizing Benner's actions variously as a sort of "statistical carelessness," evidence of "eccentricities," and the "faulty use of statistical data," Griffith's summary judgment was one of "administrative carelessness." Again, "repeated comments," unspecified except as coming from "his own colleagues within the College of Education, from school men throughout the State, and from national leaders in education," were alleged to buttress the adminstration's case.[80]

Perhaps now aware that while they had amassed abundant evidence that the highest administrators at the University—or, at least, a group of them—disliked or disagreed with Benner's ideas or methods, and that the Dean had not adequately carried through some of his responsibilities (such as in the junior and teachers' college question, at least in terms of the administration's criteria) or had given faulty statistical support to his claims, they still had little or no evidence of his disfavor among professional colleagues, Griffith undertook a new and somewhat curious project. On July 6, 1945, just after the decision to

[79] Ibid., pp. 39–41, 42.

[80] Ibid., pp. 48, 58, 60, 65–66. Cf. Griffith to Benner, June 22, 1943, Willard Correspondence. Benner to Willard, August 12, 1944, College of Education Papers (in reply to Harno to Willard, May 31, 1944—note that Harno was also chairman of the Advisory Committee of Griffith's Bureau). See also Benner's "1945–47 Budget of the College of Education, University of Illinois," p. 2 (containing original percentage figures for its growth); Benner to Willard, November 17, 1944; Griffith to Willard, December 7, 1944 (containing the revised percentages; copy sent to Park Livingston). It is extremely important to note that this particular statistical issue was developed only *after* the letter of June 3, and after it became clear that Benner would fight. Griffith was necessarily moderate in his formal accusations. Benner was doubtless careless, perhaps even culpably ignorant of how to develop and use statistics—although he, of course, laid blame for that on the Bureau for not supplying him with better data—but there seems nothing worthy of the kind of campaign that had been mounted against him. The material issue, while there in a sense, seems almost to have been created ex post facto, only after the charge had been made and challenged.

grant a hearing, Griffith wrote some thirty-five deans and directors of other schools of education, it would seem at Willard's instigation. The letters, which were sent special delivery, read as follows:

I need your help on a very difficult problem of judgment. In making its plans for the future, the University of Illinois ought to discover, if it can, what the relative position of its College of Education is when compared with the colleges or schools of education at other universities. Presumably, the bases of judgment might be:

(a) The national reputation and excellence in leadership of the Dean of the College.

(b) The quality of the staff and of their research and other contributions to the cause of professional education.

(c) The level of training and general competence of doctorates from the College.

(d) The services rendered to school systems, and to the formulation of state and national policies, by the College and by its Bureau of Educational Research.

I realize that you may not have sufficient knowledge to formulate a judgment on some of these points, and especially on (c) and (d), but I am wondering if you would be willing to make the following estimate? In so far as your knowledge goes, does the College of Education at the University of Illinois fall in the lower quarter, the middle quarter, or the upper quarter of excellence and distinction in the following group of institutions:

California, Chicago, Columbia, George Peabody, Harvard, Indiana, Iowa, Michigan, Minnesota, New York, Northwestern, North Carolina, Ohio, Purdue, Stanford, Syracuse, Wisconsin, Yale.

If, in addition to your judgment of excellence, you have any comments to offer that would be helpful, I should greatly appreciate them. Your judgment and comments will be held in absolute confidence.

We shall examine certain specific areas of the information gained through the inquiry in connection with the hearing. But when the general results were in, they were not so damning as Willard perhaps thought they would be. Of the thirty replies received, Griffith himself dismissed seven as irrelevant or insufficient; four rated the college in the bottom quarter; seven in the second; seven at about the median; and four either rated the college in the upper quarter or were distinctly "favorable." In comparison to the College's rating at Benner's arrival, examples of which we have already noted, the general impression was decidedly one of progress. There is no evidence that similar inquiries were made within the state or in the College, and at the hearing (except for the signers who testified) not a single letter, resolution, or signed statement from any other faculty member or schoolman anywhere was put into the record as making specific allegations prejudicial to Benner's reputation. Unfortunately for Marshall, the case regarding professional leadership and reputation would be forced to rest largely on hearsay or the most delicate of inferences.[81]

In contrast to Marshall, Judge Johnson had been "on the case" from the start and—a fact of inestimable weight when the hearing finally occurred—he knew universities in general and Illinois in particular inside and out. We have already seen how Benner began at once to defend himself, and his formal case came together smoothly. With his own faculty substantially behind him, the Dean turned to Illinois schoolmen to disprove the charge of no professional confidence within the state.[82] As he took the road to broadcast the College's programs, Benner told his audiences his side of the story, reminding them artfully that "to the allegation of unsatisfactory relations with the schools only the leaders of the schools can reply." [83] Griffith objected to the Dean's strategy, accusing him to Willard of using his staff for "propaganda purposes" and of scheduling conferences

[81] Griffith to Willard, July 28, 1945, Willard Correspondence. There Griffith claimed that the inquiry was made "in response to [Willard's] suggestion." The letter was grossly devious in its intent, although Griffith apparently believed it would not be recognized for what it was—a considerable error, as we shall see. Perhaps he thought the deceptive reference to "future plans" would be accepted as referring merely to the new president's arrival or the rumored search for a new dean. Furthermore, the list against which the College was to be ranked was so select that it would not have even been considered in the same bracket on Benner's arrival. Note also that while a few unfavorable replies were received, they were not used.

[82] This accusation had always puzzled Benner—and, as we shall see further, the administration had little evidence to offer for it. The Dean finally concluded (on grounds perhaps less than sufficient) that an assistant High School Visitor had been responsible (Benner to H. W. Hightower [Effingham], November 15, 1945, Benner Papers). In spite of some of their disagreements, he did not accuse Clevenger, and there is no evidence whatever that the Visitor—who should have known, one would suppose—aided the administration's case.

[83] See several versions of Benner's mimeographed "Some Examples of Developments in the College of Education of the University of Illinois under the Administration of Dean Thomas E. Benner," material from which was used in letters, speeches, etc. It is also recorded (July 25, 1944) that Benner took twenty-six copies of the administration's charges (including the letter?) to a principals' meeting. (The latter is the source of the quotation.) All in Benner's Background Presentation File, Benner Papers.

ostensibly to advance College business when they were in reality to "build up a defense" for himself. (Benner was doubtless unimpressed by such charges, if he heard them, since the administration's case was being constructed on "company time" and, indeed, with considerable expenditure of "company funds.") [84]

Within a short time, the administration's files were beginning to bulge with letters to support the Dean and particularly his proposed building and research programs. Some were from rank-and-file school people, but many came from influential administrators in the most progressive school systems. By early fall, Benner claimed to have heard that the Board had received more than five hundred letters of protest, and he also felt he was being accorded favorable treatment by the press. Although the response was overwhelmingly supportive of Benner, there were occasional exceptions, of course. The principal of Morgan Park High School had "felt for several years that [Benner's] coming was a great mistake," and insisted that he "should have been replaced long ago." Perhaps of more significance, President Franklyn B. Snyder of Northwestern, no doubt in fraternal charity, let Willard know that he had forbidden the Dean of his School of Education to take any part in the dispute. He reassured his brother that "when, if, and as the much publicized hearing is held, and the obstreperous brother appears before your trustees," he hoped the Board would "'mow him down,' in Charlie McCarthy's immortal phrase." [85]

[84] Griffith to Willard, December 7, 1944 (and accompanying correspondence), Willard Correspondence.

[85] Benner to J. Harlan Shores, September 29, 1944, Benner Papers. For examples, see Alden B. Mills (vice-president, Illinois Association of School Boards) to Willard, July 13, 1944; the critical letter is Eston V. Tubbs to Willard, July 19, 1944. All in Willard Correspondence. See also Franklyn B. Snyder to Willard, July 9, 1945, Willard Correspondence. Replying on July 27, after the hearing had been "consummated," Willard thanked Snyder for his "attitude," but he anticipated "more 'fireworks' from the 'educational front.'"

Perhaps one of the more telling personal letters was that of Mrs. Walter F. Heineman to the Trustees' Executive Committee member Chester Davis (a prominent Chicago financier). She strongly protested Benner's proposed dismissal, insisting that the grounds were imprecise, inconclusive, and contrary to her personal experience. After studying the case for several months, she said, her reply was: "Administrative efficiency sounds like a precise term, but it is not. I should like to see a statement of the specific duties in which Dean Benner is less efficient than the other deans at the University, or deans as a professional body." And she added, "To say that the professional standing of the Department of Education among educators of the state is low [she was a member of the Chicago Board of Education], is to make a statement which is belied by the facts as I see them. It needs proof." See copy (sent by her to Willard) of Mrs. W. F. Heineman to Chester Davis, March 26, 1945, Willard Correspondence.

The professional organizations supplied the most telling weight, however. The College's informal "faculty committee" had approached groups such as the Illinois High School Principals' Association with "factual" material and full directions for circulating and registering their protests if they chose to do so.[86] And they did. The Illinois Association of County Superintendents of Schools also returned a strong endorsement, adopted, according to one of their members, without a dissenting vote. In a covering letter to Benner, Superintendent P. S. Conklin (of Rockford) personally assured Benner that, although he had traveled only on a "limited" basis, he had never heard any criticism of the Dean. He suggested that, as schoolmen saw it, the College could do more, but the fault was a need of "increased equipment and personnel," not a new dean. "To my knowledge," he reported, "first hand or from hearsay, there is no basis for any claim that the College of Education is unsatisfactory because of the dean." In fact, he added, "a very enjoyable and wholesome relationship is developing between the county superintendents and the College of Education and I hope it continues to develop." [87]

Trustee Vernon Nickell, formerly of Champaign but now superintendent of public instruction, reported to the Board that he had also received "many letters, resolutions, and telephone calls" in support of the building and research program in particular. He put before the Board a resolution of the Illinois City Superintendents' Association which bore down heavily on the need for "adequate appropriations" and facilities both for Urbana and the other "teacher training institutions" of the state.[88] But it was the Illinois Education Association which applied the most pressure. Almost as soon as the news broke, in July, 1944, the organization's board offered to confer with Willard or "others," in support of the College's needs. That fall they petitioned very strongly for increased research facilities, essentially the proposed laboratory school program. The following May they informed the Board that they found the "purported charges and accusations" to be "weak and unfounded." The board of the Association particularly condemned the methods utilized in the Benner case, arguing that they violated "all principles of good administration and professional

---

[86] H. M. Hamlin et al. to Albert Nicholas (president of Illinois High School Principals' Association), June 29, 1944, Benner Papers.

[87] Illinois Association of County Superintendents of Schools Resolution, dated June 20, 1945; Conklin to Benner, July 6, 1945; Benner Papers.

[88] 43rd *Report* (1946), p. 308.

procedure," and the board insisted that to deny a public hearing in the case would be a "great travesty upon justice." The University found their resolution most difficult to answer, and perhaps no other single act was more responsible for gaining Benner the hearing he sought.[89] By July, like the administration, the Dean and his supporters were ready to make their case, confident that victory and a vindication of the College's program were in the offing.

On a corn-belt hot July 25, 1945, a somewhat reluctant Board of Trustees assembled in the air-conditioned University Union to hear the already famous "Benner Case." Interpreting somewhat advantageously the advice of the AAUP, the Board had stipulated a private hearing—a requirement which Johnson and Benner had finally accepted—and the room was protected from the press and the idly curious by guards.[90] After exchanging the traditional pleasantries and compliments about their respective reputations and intentions, the two attorneys bent to the task. In his opening statement, Marshall, following the administration's long-held contention, insisted that the sole issue was "whether or not that recommendation of President Willard not

[89] Letters of Irving F. Pearson (executive secretary of IEA) to Willard, July 10, 1944; to University of Illinois Board of Trustees (c/o Park Livingston), May 28, 1945; to Park Livingston, September 22, 1944; to Hamlin, Reeder, and Smith, July 10, 1944. Several copies are extant both in Willard Correspondence and in Benner Papers.
The Board found the May 28, 1945, letter very disturbing. At one location of the letter (Benner File, Record Series 2/9/1, no. 89) there is a draft "suggested reply," no author indicated, which first argues that the Association's resolution was improper, since there were "no charges . . . officially levied. . . ." Park Livingston had sent the letter to Janata on May 31, 1945, asking for help in answering it. The reply (Janata to Livingston, June 6, 1945) conveyed a new suggested letter, apparently partly the work of the University's "legal counsel" (H. E. Cunningham?). This response, eventually sent as Livingston to Pearson, June 7, 1945, made no mention of Benner at all, simply stating that no case was before the Board. There is also evidence that copies of Pearson's letter went to all the Board members and also to Griffith.

[90] For official accounts, see 43rd *Report* (1946) pp. 599–602, and supplementary pp. A1–A5 (following p. 615). This source contains the opening statements and a chronology of times and witnesses, along with an allegation that Benner had accepted the hearing as satisfactory. While the Trustees claimed to "impound" the evidence after the hearing itself, p. 600 of the *Report* strongly suggests that a fuller treatment is not accorded the case because it is on view in "the transcript."
See also *Urbana Evening Courier* (July 25, 1945); *Champaign News-Gazette* (July 25, 1945); *Chicago Sun* (July 25, 1945). The decision on form was based on Ralph E. Himstead (of the AAUP) to William E. Britton, June 12, 1945, Willard Correspondence. The AAUP actually only recommended private hearings *in general*, not specifically in this case. See University's request for a ruling in Park Livingston to William E. Britton, May 15, 1945; same location.

to reappoint . . . is arbitrary, without foundation, not in the interests of the University. . . ." The Trustees must, he said, accept or reject the President's proposal on its "merits," and therefore they would need to examine some of the "basic reasons" for his action. But he was careful to add that the "reasons were not charges." As might be expected, Judge Johnson's opening statement took a quite different perspective. There were indeed "charges," although Willard had "steadily tried to ignore, and persuade the public to forget" them and their effect on the Dean. If they were not repudiated, Benner would be branded "forever." He further accused the President of a "startling lack of intellectual candor" for attempting to mask his procedures under the guise of routine administration, and he insisted that a central issue was what would happen to the University if such methods continued to prevail.[91]

Mr. Marshall began his case first, introducing some nineteen exhibits which added little if anything to the problem of settling the factual issue. He then led with his star witness, Provost Coleman R. Griffith.[92] After his authority had been established, Griffith proceeded at once to tear at Benner's ability to plan and execute programs, following as exactly as conditions allowed the statement he had worked up. In extensive testimony, he struck at the Dean's relations with fellow administrators, the issue regarding the use of statistics, and the refusal of the College to carry the programs of the University Council on Teacher Education to completion. (The Provost characterized the last as a "sit-down strike.") Accusing the Dean of "opportunism and some symptoms of erratic and confused leadership," Griffith argued that Benner had attempted "practically to dismantle" the Bureau of Educational Research, and that he had no clear orientation toward genuine university-level research such as might give the College "a name among other colleges of education." The Provost concluded with a lengthy review of the Dean's alleged failure to develop relations with the secondary schools and his mishandling of the developing teachers' college programs—insisting that because of

[91] "Hearing Transcript," pp. 1–21.
[92] Ultimately, Marshall introduced twenty-six items. At first he produced almost exclusively Benner-Willard or Benner-Trustees correspondence, the Trustees' minutes, and some statistics. The administration attorney later entered the two "Special Subjects" documents and Carmichael's reply to Benner's "Graduate School" document (but not the document itself). Curiously, the "Understaffing" report was never introduced by Marshall, even though Griffith's corrective figures were.

his mistakes the University had "played into the hands of the teachers colleges."[93]

After Griffith had completed some two hours of testimony, Johnson took the floor and slowly began to pick away at the allegations. Clearly the judge realized that Griffith and the President represented the issue—Griffith was in fact "the case" so far as "evidence" was concerned, and the President's responsibility was for the procedure. Here Johnson's vast and intimate knowledge of University affairs became of primary significance, as his rapier-sharp questions began to cut larger and larger holes in the administration's contentions. Time and again he forced Griffith to admit that many of the "charges" were simply differing interpretations of situations and the administrative style appropriate to them—matters upon which good men might indeed differ, but hardly grounds for the administration's response. He tried to show that responsibility for "failure" to meet "leadership" obligations seldom rested on any one man in a complex organization— as for example in the question of the teachers' colleges, where the chief signers were all involved and yet had never either done anything themselves or counseled Benner to do so.[94]

With considerable forensic artistry, Johnson saved his strongest attack for the last, the question of Benner's lack of "reputation" outside the campus. He drew from Griffith the admission that he had not a shred of written evidence for this assertion, that it was indeed only an "impression," gained whence he could not remember. It would not be "fair," the Provost suggested, to involve others. Johnson, noting that it was apparently "fair" to use secret information for destructive purposes, then forced Griffith to admit that he had not conveyed these impressions of failure to the Dean for several years, even though when he had done so in the past Benner had always been quite willing to hear of them.[95]

The Judge then sprang his trap: the letters Griffith himself had solicited from other deans of education around the country. Griffith admitted he had received replies to his inquiry, but denied they were

---

[93] "Hearing Transcript," pp. 50–87, but esp. 57, 64, 65, 66, 72ff., 86. It is perhaps significant that on the stand Griffith made no mention of the Dean's relations with his faculty or his reputation nor did he introduce any letters evaluating the College.

[94] Ibid., see, for example, pp. 135–37.

[95] Ibid., pp. 158–62. Pressed for examples of Benner's lack of reputation, Griffith could provide none—except, he finally said, a conversation he had had with some now forgotten school official somewhere "west of Homer."

relevant and said he could not put them in evidence anyway since they were privileged. Johnson then introduced the Provost's own letter into the record, gaining in passing his admission that no such inquiries had ever been made before in attempting to make judgments on an administrator's competence.[96]

Willard's and Griffith's strategy here had been almost unbelievably inept. Perhaps they assumed that the addressees would not recognize the letters for what they were—a curiously naïve assumption given the widespread publicity Benner's situation had already received in the press at large, let alone within the education fraternity. Apparently what happened was that many of those who received the administrator's inquiry not only answered it but sent copies of their letters to Benner, frequently with the express statement that they would be happy to have their judgments made public![97] Others simply wrote in Benner's defense. While many of the responses did not come to light, although they were not introduced by Griffith, they were not left in the administration's files either. Those that did completely demolished Willard's allegations. And those that came to Benner were precisely those which tended to count most heavily against his opponents, since they came from institutions either closest to the University or with great prestige. Though none extant are damning, Johnson put the best in evidence for the Dean.

Dean Arthur J. Klein of Ohio State (who claimed to speak for four other education deans in Ohio), noting the previously sad reputation of the Urbana College, insisted that Benner, especially of late, had made educators believe Illinois could do anything, but he added that "the methods used in the recent attack . . . have destroyed their confidence."[98] Dean Fred B. Knight of Purdue was, if anything, more generous in his praise. He maintained that Benner's "national reputation and general leadership [were] such that it would be very hard to understand why his position would be in jeopardy." He said the Dean had added first-class men, some of whom he would like to lure away, in fact, and he declared that the College's doctorates were so strong that it was one of the first places he would go for an elementary man, and one of the first four or five he would approach for a

---

[96] Ibid., pp. 163–76. Griffith denied writing the letter of June 3 and admitted Benner had not been asked previously about the allegations respecting his professional reputation that it contained. See pp. 175–76.

[97] Ibid., pp. 514ff.

[98] A. J. Klein to Griffith, July 10, 1945. Copies of these letters—the originals presumably were entered in evidence—are all in College of Education Papers.

TEACHERS FOR THE PRAIRIE

secondary man or an administrator. (Only in psychology or testing would he look elsewhere—a fact somewhat damaging to Griffith, of course, since it was his field, and somewhat surprising in view of their friendship.) Knight then tackled the question of the College's general rank:

> In your letter of July 6 you list quite an important group of universities, the list beginning with California and ending with Yale. In my estimation Illinois is at a most conservative appraisal in the middle quarters. There are certain distinguished work at Chicago under Tyler which I do not think is matched by any of the universities which you have mentioned. Ohio has in my estimation been outstanding in many ways and of course Columbia is distinguished not only by its gigantic size but also because of a long list of unusually notable men such as Thorndike, Gates, French, and others.
>
> Hence I would say that it would be very difficult for me to see why the Board of Trustees would have any particular reason to complain about the general status of the College of Education at the University of Illinois. I think it has been embarrassed by lack of quarters which many other universities have provided their colleges of education, and it may be cramped in other ways which I do not know of. . . .[99]

Dean William F. Russell of Teachers College, Columbia, admittedly if controversially prestigious, perhaps bore the most telling witness in a brief and incontrovertibly clear letter. Dean Benner, he said quite bluntly, "has an excellent reputation." The quality of the staff, some of whom were of course the products of his own labors, was also "excellent." "In fact," he said, "I have in mind as soon as possible trying to steal someone from them." The College's doctorates "stand up very well," and while his knowledge of its record of service was small, the one case of which he was aware was "most successful." He closed with a patently complimentary assessment of the College's rank: "I certainly hate to go on record in rating the various schools of education in the country, but I will say this. If I had the opportunity to take over the entire faculty of any one of the institutions you have named, I would choose Illinois ahead of all but five of them. Benner has had real ability in surrounding himself with young men

---

[99] Fred B. Knight (Director, Division of Education and Applied Psychology, Purdue University) to Griffith, July 10, 1945.

of great promise." [100] After a brief exchange over the June 3 letter, Griffith's testimony and Johnson's cross-examination were at an end. The results were hardly as favorable as the administration likely had hoped.[101]

The power of the administration's attack dwindled rapidly after Griffith's testimony. When in mid-afternoon Dean Carmichael took the stand, he offered only brief and (for a mathematician) surprisingly woolly testimony. Arguing it was "not wise, in the interests of the work of the University" to continue Benner as Dean, Carmichael recited his already recorded objections to the Dean's handling of degree requirements—noting that there was indeed a difference in philosophy over the "principles of graduate study" and "the foundations of research." Under considerable prompting by Marshall, he also took issue with Benner's use of facts and faulted his personal lack of research. Marshall supplemented Carmichael's witness by comparing the number of doctorates in education with those in chemistry and then led the mentor of the Graduate School in an evaluation of the research implications of the building program. Johnson devoted little attention to Carmichael. He forced the Dean to admit, surprisingly, that he had meant to imply only that he had usually felt compelled to check Benner's "statements," not his figures; and the Judge demonstrated that most of the general hostility to the Dean to which Carmichael had referred had arisen since the June letter—a considerably

---

[100] William F. Russell to Griffith, July 10, 1945. The *Chicago Sun* had also phoned Russell and on the morning of the hearing had quoted him as saying: "I hope that Benner will be retained. The only charge that can be made against him is that he built up the school rather than himself." See edition of July 25, 1945.

[101] Johnson entered the Klein, Knight, and Russell letters into the record after quoting from them. See "Hearing Transcript," pp. 514–25, cf. 387. He also entered one from Clyde M. Hill which has not been found. He held in addition at least the following letters: H. L. Smith (Indiana) to S. Johnson, July 7, 1945; M. H. Willing (Wisconsin) to S. Johnson, July 9, 1945. William C. Bagley had also telegraphed a very strong pro-Benner statement in advance of the hearing (on the 24th, in response to Johnson's inquiry of the 23rd) which roundly condemned the whole procedure. Smith applauded Benner's "initiative, industry, energy, and courage," and deplored the procedure as "undefensible." Willing's letter, clearly a reply to Griffith's inquiry but addressed to Johnson, also decried the "incredible" charges, insisting that the Dean was a "sane, forceful, liberal and highly intelligent leader in modern education." If he is removed, Willing promised, the University's "sister institutions" would have cause for "alarm and suspicion." Like Klein, Willing specifically stated that his letter was for publication, and none of the respondents gave any restrictions. They appear to have known precisely what they were getting into.

less forceful accusation. Marshall tried to get the Dean's "figures" back in issue, but Carmichael substantially admitted that he only questioned (as a "logician") the implications Benner drew from them.[102]

Dean Harno then took the stand for a relatively brief period, citing the want of confidence in Benner, his passing enthusiasms, and his frequent "superlatives." He also attempted to show that the Dean had misused certain enrollment figures and had (unlike the cheerful co-operation characteristic of other colleges, apparently) mistakenly interpreted budget cuts as prejudice. He criticized the building program on the grounds that the College had no real research underway and because of its large-scale financial implications.[103] Johnson hit back hard, compelling Harno to admit that the College had never argued for exclusive control of the contemplated research facilities, and to grant that enthusiasm was a much-needed quality in getting any program off the ground in a university. Like Griffith and Carmichael, Harno had no evidence that Benner's outside reputation was bad— except for the sorts of "comments" which Harno admitted were constantly drifting about in any college, including his own College of Law. By the end of his testimony he had even conceded that larger than anticipated budget requests were as a rule submitted by most if not all colleges, and he now only hinted that Benner's were not fully substantiated. Furthermore, in spite of Marshall's defensive prompting, Harno virtually admitted that the College had by all reasonable standards been financially neglected in the past.[104]

It was past five o'clock before the President began to recount his side of the issue. After "substantially" agreeing to all the previous testimony, Willard outlined the history of his administrative strategy, maintaining that three of the College's five-man executive committee had agreed with him at first. Claiming he suggested the Dean "retire," the President said that such a procedure was "usual," except that

[102] "Hearing Transcript," pp. 178–90, esp. 181ff. See also pp. 191–96.
[103] Ibid., pp. 203–12, esp. 203, 204ff., 207, 211.
[104] Ibid., 213–15, 218, 222, 230–32. Johnson also pointed out that the University building planners had followed state priorities to the extent of putting a sports building first on the list, although Harno curiously denied knowledge of this! (See p. 215.) When excused, Harno was invited to stay on in the hearing room if he cared to, by Livingston—the proceedings were obviously folksy and friendly for the administration's forces. The Trustees were, in effect, judge and jury; they had a clear stake in one side of the case. Harno was both their legal advisor and one of their principal witnesses. (See p. 232.)

Benner was the first to "resist" it. Willard concluded his surprisingly brief statement by reaffirming that he had "no doubt" of the justification for, and soundness of, his action.[105]

Opening his cross-examination on the issue of the executive committee's support of their Dean, Johnson began what was to be a virtual dismemberment of the President's administration. Under Johnson's withering inquiry, Willard conceded that he had only had the "impression" that a majority of the executive committee had supported his move. Next the President admitted he had only the verbal statements of the signers—which Johnson quickly suggested had not proven very definite during the hearing—to buttress the letter itself. The Judge thereupon characterized these statements as resting only on "anonymous oral statements made to [the signers and not to the President] which they either could not recall or would not disclose," and Willard agreed. In effect, he had admitted that he had acted on pure hearsay, without any attempt to verify the charges or give the Dean an opportunity to counter them. In fact, when pressed, the President could recall no letters of complaint about Benner, though he thougt the files *might* contain some, and he acknowledged that there were such letters regarding other colleges which had not been treated similarly.[106] In quick succession, Johnson forced Willard to confess that he had absolutely no personal knowledge of Benner's reputation among schoolmen and that he had ignored the IEA's offer to talk the problems out. Exploding the claim that Benner had misrepresented the opinions of the other administrators in the controversial "Special Subjects" report, the Judge showed that the President was not even certain of what the report had said in the first place. Finally, Johnson subjected Willard to a blistering examination on the letter of June 3 itself, carefully building the distinction between alleging charges and simply asking for a resignation.[107]

The Judge's strategy with the President was a virtual recapitulation of Benner's defense. It had not been a case of merely not reappointing. The President had chosen to get "evidence," but this "evidence" had come neither from the College, the schools, nor the education profession, but from other administrators. The President had never known

[105] Ibid., p. 233–45. In a marginal comment on his copy of the transcript, Benner denied that Willard had ever suggested he "retire." See p. 242.
[106] Ibid., pp. 247–50. The quotation is at p. 249.
[107] Ibid., pp. 252–74, esp. 267ff., 270–72.

whether the "evidence" was true, and when the signers either could not or would not provide the necessary proof, the administration's defense of its actions simply collapsed into vague hearsay and a welter of personal antagonisms. Visibly shaken, Willard was snatched from further indignities by Board President Livingston's call for a dinner break, since it was now nearly 6:30. The University's carillon rang out with "I Love You Truly" and "The End of a Perfect Day."[108]

Expressing some reluctance, the Trustees agreed to return that evening to hear Benner's side of the dispute, although they took double their allotted dinner hour.[109] About 8:30 the Dean took the stand to present what must have seemed an interminable recounting of what he believed to be evidence in his favor. Interrupted only by the testimony of a representative of some graduate students who had volunteered to speak on his behalf, Benner painstakingly laid out documents and arguments to rebut the administration's attempt to substantiate the signers' allegations.[110] Following the record substantially as we have reconstructed it, he went through the difficulties of the U.C.T.E. (but praised Sanford) and the junior and teachers' college issue. He defended himself in the "facts and figures" matter by alleging that the Bureau of Institutional Research had refused him access to the proper data which Griffith had introduced and that he had consequently been forced to patch together what he could, in good faith. Carmichael's uncooperative attitude, as the Dean saw it, was alleged to have led to the meaningless "quibbles" in which the Graduate School had engaged. He defended his new staff and attempted to rebut the criticisms of his "Understaffing" report. Against Marshall's interrupting cross-examination, Benner tenaciously held to his right to divulge the June 3 letter, since word of the matter had escaped before he had even had the opportunity to make copies for his advisors to see. Finally, at 11:15 P.M., understandably weary and

---

[108] *Champaign News-Gazette* (July 26, 1945).

[109] "Hearing Transcript," pp. 274ff. Well-known Chicago Trustee Dr. Karl Meyer announced that he intended to depart that night (and did), insisting he did not propose "to stay around here all day tomorrow and listen to this. A lot of it is irrelevant." Referring to it as "a trial, so to speak," he protested that the Trustees were "all busy individuals." Johnson pointed out that he had asked for a committee hearing but had been refused, and that Benner had not even begun to make his own case.

[110] In all, Johnson introduced seventy-six documents. For the graduate students, see ibid., pp. 327–40.

describing their allotment of time as "generous," the Board adjourned for the night.[111]

The hearing resumed the following morning at 9:30 A.M. with most of the Board still present. Benner resumed the stand to speak to the laboratory school and research issue, defending himself against the charge that the College desired supreme or even principal control of the child growth facilities. He claimed that Monroe, whose control of research had been absolute, in later years had not cared even to direct research other than his own. Total research, the Dean attempted to show, had increased enormously since his coming. Then, suggesting that he had much more evidence he might offer were it not necessary to spare the Board, Benner surrendered himself to Marshall's offices.[112]

The Trustee's attorney tried to shake the Dean first on his allegedly making the case public. But Benner, on the whole rather effective on the stand, simply refused any blame—if only on the grounds he had not (and could not have) betrayed anything "in advance" of a hearing, since neither the President nor the Board had offered any until less than a month previously. Marshall's next major thrust was to assail the College's general reputation as one which was "falling behind" other universities. To this Benner merely countered that the cause was, as others agreed, not himself but inadequacy of budget and staff. After some further skirmishes, during which Marshall finally lost his temper, it was apparent that the patience of all was growing rather thin. The Dean then made a final attempt to document his leadership capacities and his service to the schools, and, responding positively to Livingston's query about whether he regarded his hearing as a fair one, he stepped down.[113]

It was now approaching midafternoon. Marshall unexpectedly declined to make a closing statement, arguing that although he had been forced to serve as an adversary he would not continue in that role now that the evidence was in. Not so Judge Johnson. Admitting frankly his partisanship, he launched into a ringing summation. Was the President's judgment supported by the evidence? Was it a routine case? Reviewing the evidence at some length, and emphasizing that any administrator must advocate his programs "vigorously," Johnson closed with a replay of his best card: he read extensive quotations

---

[111] Ibid., pp. 283–380, esp. pp. 288–301, 304, 318–27, 340–49, 369–71.
[112] Ibid., pp. 381–402, esp. 381ff., 395–97, 399ff.
[113] Ibid., pp. 422–91, esp. 433, 442ff., 480, 490ff.

from the replies to the letters originally sent by Griffith. At 3:20 P.M., Board President Park Livingston cleared the room and the Trustees went into executive session.[114]

The meeting was reconvened in public session at 5:30 P.M. to announce the Board's decision, presented in the form of an extensive resolution. The first preamble noted that the Trustees had heard more than 100,000 words of testimony and—at least supposedly—examined over 100 exhibits. They next asserted:

> All these conflicting claims seem to the Board to resolve themselves in one single issue;
>
> To wit, is it to the best interests of the University to retain Doctor Benner as Dean of the College of Education and can he hope to function satisfactorily and effectively . . . in view of the intense and fundamental clashes of personalities extending over so long a period of time between Dean Benner and the Deans and Directors necessarily associated with him in joint University-wide undertakings.

The Board then insisted that the evidence suggested unresolvable differences and that "an atmosphere of conflict and dispute . . . [which would] not redound to the interests of the University would be perpetuated. . . ." Furthermore, the Board felt that "the best interests of the University" were "paramount to the interests of one man and that no one man [was] indispensable. . . ." Finally, noting that two-year appointments were the rule and that Benner's was about to expire, and affirming that they were "desirous in all things to uphold the authority and responsibility of the President"—which they had done for fifty years, in respect to appointments—they resolved to accept and confirm the President's recommendation. The battle was over. They then bottled up the evidence, announced their findings to the press and an interested gathering of onlookers, and hurried home.[115]

The press and the onlookers were not all pleased, to say the least. The verdict was greeted by a burst of publicity adverse to the administration. The journalists remembered President Livingston as

[114] Ibid., pp. 492–544, esp. 503ff., 516ff.

[115] Ibid., pp. 545–48. See also 43rd *Report* (1946), pp. 601–2. Willard called the action "unanimous" (see Willard to Franklyn B. Snyder, July 27, 1945), but Meyer, Green, and Luken were in fact absent. Meyer agreed by telephone, apparently finding it unnecessary to consider any more of Benner's case than the part he had heard on the first evening. (He had withdrawn at 10 P.M.)

promising "findings of fact on which our decision is based," but none came forth.[116] The southern lynch party offered the closest parallel to the proceedings, editorialized the *Champaign News-Gazette*, long accustomed to assessing the relative soil of the University's linen in its columns. It was a case of "give him a fair hearing and then hang him," the *Gazette* observed, noting that "the Benner controversy had been fraught with everything but facts so far as the public knows." [117] "Benner Ousted from Deanship," trumpeted the *Daily Illini*. Student outrage, expressed not only in two articles but in an editorial and a columnist's comments, fastened on the air of secrecy and the lack of evidence. But their discontent was merely verbal, in that bygone age, and happily so from the administration's perspective. The Dean's friends were incensed, and they hoped to gain vindication for him in the public domain. A "deep anger" which could be assuaged, she said, by nothing but action moved Cora DeGraff Heineman, the indomitable liberal on the Chicago School Board, to vent her criticism to the *New Republic*.[118]

The education fraternity was, if anything, even more outspoken. "An Unsavory Episode at the University of Illinois," William Chandler Bagley called it. Subjecting the entire procedure to a knowledgeable and penetrating analysis—he had not lost his gift of prose with the declining years—the former dean spoke for many. As others, Bagley lamented the implications of the case, not only for education as a profession but for the university as an institution. Dean Klein of Ohio State found it symptomatic of "a pretty serious fight all over the country." The Secretary of the NEA's National Commission for the Defense of Democracy through Education, purportedly basing his comments on "some inquiry into the case," reached similar con-

[116] *Champaign News-Gazette* (July 26, 1945).

[117] Editorial, *Champaign News-Gazette* (July 29, 1945). Cf. *Urbana Evening Courier* (July 27, 1945), which ran three articles, quoted from pro-Benner letters and singled out Willard, Harno, Griffith, and Carmichael; *Champaign News-Gazette* (July 27, 1945), which also ran three articles, one dealing with the evidence.

[118] *The Daily Illini* (July 27, 1945), which led with "Formal Resolution Passed Rules 'Atmosphere of Conflict, Dispute' Would Continue of [*sic!*] Benner Retained as Dean; Personality Clashes Hinted." The "DI" also quoted H. F. Simonson, Johnson's assistant, that the Board had decided merely on the basis that "there is no indispensable man." See also Cora DeGraff [Mrs. W. F.] Heineman to Benner, July 30, 1945 (with enclosure to the *New Republic*, for Benner's approval) and reply, July 31, 1945, both in Benner Papers.

clusions. It was, he thought, not only a "great injustice" to Benner but "to the cause of education." [119]

Most observers, like Benner himself, had believed that if the case were brought to a hearing it would be settled on its "merits"—i.e., on the truth of the supporting allegations. Of course, nothing of the sort occurred. Whatever meaning the Trustees may have imputed to their action, their concern was at bottom institutional. They were not consciously making a decision about the field of education as a discipline or a profession, nor were they attempting to achieve a posture (pro or con) in respect to liberalism in education. Their problem was clear and wholly (if unfortunately) circumscribed. As the hearing itself suggested, Marshall had said the issue was one thing; Johnson had insisted it was another. Consequently, many of their arguments had passed like trains in the night, rigidly constrained by their separate tracks.

Neither the President's procedures nor the question of justice were really at issue for the Trustees, whatever the arguments of learned counsel. There was a third issue, and it was that which the Board had to decide in order to maintain neither justice, nor higher education in general, but the University of Illinois in particular. That was simply whether a board of trustees ought to back its president. There was just enough evidence to allow them to feel justified in doing so. Needless to say, Benner had not been perfect, and (whether Benner was guilty or not) the letter of the nine had effectively created an intolerable situation whether it had previously existed or not. Moreover, the alternatives were, again from the Trustees' vantage point, disastrous. To have ruled in favor of Benner would have been to assess the President's judgment faulty, of course. With a new president on the way, to cashier the old one mere months before his retirement would not have been encouraging. Thus the only way to handle the affair was to back the President, seal up the evidence, and turn out the "obstreperous brother." While their formal action tended to impugn the Dean—an implication the Board could certainly have done more to avoid, if only by a briefer resolution simply affirming the President's technical right—in practical effect it did not. The Trustees'

[119] For Bagley's article, see *School and Society* 62, no. 16 (August 25. 1945): 118–19; W. C. Bagley to Benner, August 24, 1945, Benner Papers. Bagley's judgment was publicized. See "Benner Has Won His Case, N.Y. Educator [Bagley] Asserts" by John McGrath, *Chicago Sun* (August 1, 1945); *The Daily Illini* (August 29, 1945). See also A. J. Klein to Benner, August 2, 1945; copy of Donald DuShane to H. W. Hightower, August 24, 1945; both in Benner Papers.

silence spoke convincingly on Benner's side, at least in the mouths of interpreters.

Nonetheless, Benner was somewhat stunned. He had been quite convinced he would "win" if he could get a fair hearing. (Believing that what was logically sound or persuasive would in fact prevail was a mistake the Dean had made more than once before, as we have seen.) When the adverse verdict was announced, his first inclination was to leave at once. After reflection and counsel, however, he thought better of it. It was suggested he run for superintendent of public instruction, but the prospect of an office even more vulnerable than a dean's proved understandably unappealing. Instead, that December, he applied for leave without pay to join the Allied Military Government in Austria as a specialist in educational development. After serving with considerable distinction—he was made an honorary member of the University of Vienna in gratitude for his leadership— he returned to his post as professor of education. There, true to his vow not to be a "nuisance" and to resist his "altogether godly leaning toward mayhem" regarding those whom he felt to be responsible, he completed his tenure in exemplary fashion.[120]

Another quiet interregnum under Monroe followed Benner's deanship. During that time most of the former dean's programs and positions (perhaps less abrasively and conspiratorially advanced, and freed from personal disputes) gained acceptance and became policy. The College's budget soared, a belated admission by the administration and Trustees that it had indeed been inadequate.[121] New building promises were made, though even these were late to bear fruit, of course. Most of the members of the new faculty nucleus stayed on, and the intellectual shape which they had provided continued to characterize the College. Under the fresh and decidedly more favorably disposed administration of the new President, George Dinsmore Stoddard—another schoolman—and the energetic leadership of the new permanent Dean, Willard B. Spalding, existing programs deepened and the College grew rapidly in scope and stature. The next period was to be particularly noteworthy for growth in the areas of educational psychology and administration, as well as for extensive de-

[120] Benner to A. W. Anderson, July 30, 1945; Benner to B. O. Smith, July 30, August 8, 1945; Benner to A. J. Klein, August 6, 1945; A. J. Klein to Benner, August 24, 1945; all in Benner Papers. See also 43rd *Report* (1946), p. 936.

[121] The 1945–46 budget came in at over $259,000, including $16,000 for five new full- or part-time staff members; the 1946–47 budget topped $272,000 (43rd *Report* [1946], pp. 750, 1294).

velopment in the field of special education and educational services.[122]

Coleman Griffith opposed many of these moves, and he quarreled with Spalding on occasion almost as bitterly as he had with Benner. At first the Provost's career flourished. In an ironic twist, however, he was himself the victim of a trumped-up "no confidence" proceeding a few years later, one which accompanied the fall of his idol, Stoddard. When news of the ouster of his old enemy reached Benner, he wrote a brief, kind note of sympathy to the deposed Provost which Griffith confessed brought tears to his eyes. Perhaps in their last association, born of equally unjust treatment (whatever the "facts"), these two men whose temperaments were so nearly alike and whose philosophies indeed touched in many places recognized each other. Whether that is so may be a matter of speculation. But, in any case, Thomas Eliot Benner had simultaneously ended an era in the College's development and inaugurated a new one in which, in due time, the College not only met but exceeded the dreams of Charles DeGarmo, Edwin Grant Dexter, and William Chandler Bagley.[123]

Each of the three major eras in the College's history had reflected a peculiar problem. For DeGarmo and his immediate successors, the problem was gaining *entry* into a new academic world, the gaining of some rude presence on the campus. For Tompkins, Dexter, and Bagley, the task had been to demonstrate the *legitimacy* of a new area of inquiry and service which was by then grudgingly accepted on the campus. This, we have seen, was largely a process of attempting to define the new arrival in terms already accepted and of attempting to mask its peculiar interests in the garb of accepted methodologies, a process severely limited by the presumed necessity of utilizing terms and procedures themselves but late arrivals (the social and behavioral sciences). Benner's challenge, made inestimably more difficult by the timidity of Chadsey and the authoritarianism of Kinley, was to press

---

[122] The selection of a new dean was deferred until 1947, at Stoddard's request. Spalding had been superintendent of schools in Portland, Oregon. Stoddard put his weight behind an increased research emphasis in the College (it was its first responsibility, he said) and outspokenly encouraged its moving out into the schools of the state. Spalding strongly agreed. See, for example, minutes of the Council on Teacher Education, s.v. Jan. 21, 1946, College of Education Papers; Spalding's Report, with comments by Stoddard, under Spalding to Stoddard, February 5, 1948, Stoddard Correspondence.

[123] Griffith particularly opposed Spalding's continued importation of "Teachers College" psychologists, and he sometimes nastily questioned the credentials of the College's faculty. For his downfall (July, 1953) and Benner's response, see Griffith to A. S. Adams (president of the A.C.E.), July 29, 1953; Benner to Griffith, July 17, 1953; in Griffith Papers.

the claim for *autonomy*. Less capable of rigorous definition, this phase seems best understood as a campaign to enable education to direct and define its own domain and methods, without the previous almost exclusive recourse to the traditional justifications. Perhaps by nature the most difficult task of all, it had cost the Dean more than any previous advance, and he did not in fact achieve it. The College, however, under enlarged leadership, and in a University which had itself grown more hospitable and less self-conscious and defensive, was substantially granted the right to strive in its own way in its own affairs. With the departure of Benner, it was no longer necessary for the College's deans to look backward.

What, if any, general assessment of "the record" can be made? Such a general judgment depends upon what criteria can be established. Possible criteria rest in turn upon some sort of answer to the question of what "education" as a field is, if indeed it is one. The central concern of educationists, and the field of education, as it generally arose in the American university and at Illinois in particular, was "schooling" as an institutional and cultural process. (That does not, of course, require the study of schooling to be divorced either from professional study in education for practitioners or from the study of educational theories and contributory disciplines.) This definition in terms of the educator's focus appears to offer the possibility of a better criterion for judgment, if only because it is less partial and consequently more able to take account of a complex phenomenon puzzling both to educationists and their colleagues. But it also represents at least a possible description of education as a field of study with defensible boundaries and appropriate procedures and organizing principles.

If the criterion of academic success is that of the individual brilliance of its members, particularly in terms of the traditional disciplines, both the University and the College can be accorded a favorable judgment. There have been distinguished individuals, both as faculty members and as students; important ideas has been offered to the world in this setting; significant bodies of information have been generated. If, however, the criterion for the College's development from 1868 to 1945 is the relationship to schools and schooling, both within the state and in the nation at large, the record is not a good one. The University, as the "apex" of the state's school system, did (and cared to do) little to improve the "base." The schools were on the whole more used than aided, let alone led. While the University pioneered in its own transition to the new-style university, it demanded certain kinds of performance from its "feeders" for which it seldom repaid them. The College shared in this general relationship, rarely successful in demonstrating its commitment to the schools in the face of intra-institutional demands. Where is the stellar school or school system which owes its creation (or even its inspiration) to Urbana, in a degree comparable to those pioneering works whose genesis was Chicago or Columbia? And doubtless the University and the College must accept some blame for the fact that Illinois as a state has obviously lagged both in quantity and quality of public education at all levels, in spite of its quantitatively superior status in wealth and numbers. The same criticism can be made in regard to the nation's second-largest urban school system, sick for most of its years, rarely studied and virtually never helped by College or University. The University, in short, did more for the chemical industry, or the electronics industry, both in terms of theory and technology, than it ever did for the schools of its own state. (The solemnly hung portraits of honored alumni offer eloquent testimony to this fact.) The College, while doubtless often intending otherwise, came to be dominated by the same sort of criteria for success—indeed, it sometimes welcomed them. Thomas Eliot Benner was correct in maintaining that such criteria were inappropriate, and his "little Magna Charta," whatever its pretentions or weaknesses, made the issue clearer than it had ever been before. That title, which he doubtless hoped would be prophetic, wrongly forecast the outcome, however. The Runnymede which ensued was not a triumph but a disaster, since the king and the other barons united against the lone baron who had fomented the plot. Benner was a believing democrat who cherished the notion of the University as the great community in which truth would be dispassionately winnowed from falsehood. But until the University became an intellectual parliament instead of an academic fiefdom, that vision could remain only a hope.

❧ *Pedagogy as a Problem*

Since the last third of the nineteenth century, one of the most vexing problems in American higher education has been the relationship of "pedagogy" or "education" and the closely allied function of teacher preparation to the college or university. Perhaps no other discipline or field of study—and the issue was in part whether pedagogy represented a legitimate discipline or field—suffered a more acrimonious and puzzling entry into the charmed circle of higher studies. Treatments of this historical issue have frequently been marred by serious flaws, principally because most have assumed that both "education" or "pedagogy" and the American "college" or "university" were virtually fixed entities, settled in their nature and operation. The question has consequently been handled in an oversimplified manner, largely ignoring not only the ambiguous, developmental state of the new field of study and the higher institutions to which it sought entry, but also the shifting cultural and social context.

Radical Novelty of the Common School System

The problem posed by pedagogy was and still remains difficult to unravel. The most obvious complicating factor was that pedagogy was a developing field in the most radical sense. It was, in fact, a totally

447

new field, because it arose in relation to a totally new phenomenon, the American public school *system*. Neither "education" nor "teaching" nor "schools" were new, of course. On that account, the members of the prevailing academic structure believed they understood what they were dealing with. They did not recognize that the area of study and inquiry which was knocking feebly at the college gates was in fact a new thing, struggling to find its identity and its way simultaneously. Had the faculty not always been teaching students, and hence been professors of education? asked university presidents, in defense of their slow response to the needs of the common schools. Unfortunately, the new phenomenon could not be defined by traditional educational theorizing. It was not an expanded version of the study of the traditional "art of teaching" as defined ever since the disputes between Plato and the Sophists. The "pedagogy" or "education" which now sought entry was instead the quite concrete effect of the birth of a new *institution*, the American public school. The creation of that new educational instrumentality in the first half of the nineteenth century was an event, an action—not a theoretical revolution. Although the potential implications of that event were still unclear, its logic would prove practically decisive.

Before the early nineteenth century, or perhaps somewhat earlier in certain European nations, the consideration of educational theory and practice had been a widespread but largely amateur preoccupation. It was almost exclusively speculative in development and metaphysical in origin. Frequently it had been based upon some casual advice from a figure whose authority in some other field was transferred to his pronouncements on education, a subject upon which any learned gentleman was supposed to have constructive thought. (Typical examples of such figures would be Locke and Kant.) Failing that, recommendations for educational theory and practice could be extrapolated from authoritative philosophical traditions by logical inference, as indeed they usually were.

By the late eighteenth and early nineteenth centuries, however, a revolutionary change in social and cultural factors required that the problem of educating be approached quite differently. It was necessary to examine pedagogy systematically, critically, and (most important of all) institutionally. The educational implications of democratic political theory and its institutions, and the expanding domain of knowledge, were the crucial factors. Politically and socially, it was implicit that the new society gradually coming into existence had to create itself by means of the participation of all its members. Society could not depend (as it had for Locke, for example) on the wisdom of an elite which, if set right, would prevasively shape the entire body politic. At the same time, the explosive expansion of knowledge made the necessity of universal participation all the more difficult to achieve. Virtually every member was affected by the promising growth of science and the scientific-technological base of the new industrial revolution. Neither the new state nor the new economy could function without a skilled and more fully educated populace, and that required the rapid and widest possible extension of schooling and the wholesale recasting of the traditional content. It required the teaching of new knowledge which no one had previously been taught. It required the deliberate teaching of things which had not needed to be taught except to those already prepared to undertake them—reading and writing, for example. And it required a new, universal institution to take responsibility for this, the common school. In America, the common school was seen as a logical implication of the new knowledge and the new politics and it was created, in most cases virtually overnight, without opportunity to plan or build for its operation. It simply came into existence and had to find both its identity and its way from there.

The crux of the difficulty was that "education" and "teaching" had previously been related almost exclusively to an individual ideal, the growth in private wisdom and piety of the unique person being educated. But educating was now a public institution, a universal social and cultural instrumentality. It now had to be seen as a process of general schooling rather than as an essentially tutorial relationship. A new generation of educational theorists was beginning to see this, though only gradually and somewhat unclearly. Men such as Pestalozzi, Herbart, and Froebel gave educational theory a new and far more methodologically oriented shape. But if these men saw much of the new demand, they were at the same time chronologically antecedent to American school developments, and socially and culturally distant as well. It was not possible merely to transliterate the novel work of German, Swiss or French theorists into American terms. Our national insistence upon a single and entirely locally controlled system, a product of indigenous social and political concepts, had its own educational logic. A further confusion was generated by the fact that the new, educationally revolutionary common school system was introduced alongside a prerevolutionary school system which continued in existence. The private grammar school–academy–college system continued its development throughout the period during which the nation attempted to create a distinctive elementary–secondary–public college and university system. Each system had its own definitions, criteria, and logic, and the resulting failure to communicate (even when purportedly discussing the same matters) was a source of considerable mischief.

Finally, it must be kept in mind that the new educational institution created a new vocation, the "professional" teacher and school administrator. It is perhaps fair to say that the period before the nineteenth century had not known, except for rare periods, any professional teachers. The teaching vocation was not permanent and socially identifiable until at least well into the nineteenth century, and in some sense it has continued to fail to achieve that status, particularly in America. There had always been teachers before, but their teaching had customarily been a function of some other situation or calling—the possession of a peculiar kind or degree of learning, an implication of the clerical vocation, or the resolution of a momentary personal need, to name perhaps the most prevalent. However, the new educators early saw that no merely accidental definition of teaching and schoolkeeping would suffice for the new educational edifice that was being constructed.

Increasing Complexity of Content and Method

The second factor which made difficult the development of professional education and its inclusion within the traditional system was the whole educational enterprise's rapidly increasing complexity. The new knowledge did not merely add to the traditional content given in an education but transformed the definition of the whole enterprise and its method of operation. Science was not merely a new subject; it offered a new way to approach education itself. The trends toward technology, specialization, and the division of labor were not merely peripheral factors; they altered the very concept of pedagogy. Consequently, a host of entirely new questions, responsibilities, and possibilities were set before the would-be educator. Previously, as we have suggested, philosophy and history had been the primary repositories of the knowledge necessary for developing the theory and practice of educating. While there is no doubt that these fields continued to have much to say, there were new considerations which could not be denied. Where before there had been little more than the traditional philosophical theories of *knowledge,* truth, and value, together with an architectonic logic, there were now theories of *learning* and social interaction springing from the new empirical sciences, particularly psychology and sociology. The question of whether education was itself a science or an art, and if so in what sense, became paramount. The relationship between empirical and speculative or deductive procedures became an intense issue. If education was to be principally empirical, what was to be examined? Individual learning processes? The classroom? The teacher? If education was still speculative or deductive, or if there were at least some educational issues which appeared to be capable of settlement only in that fashion, from what principles and by what rules were these speculations and deductions to be made? What authority or consensus regarding truth or value could be presumed in a new nation which consciously eschewed—or at least hoped to eschew—any authoritative principles save certain practical ones? If the school was essentially a social instrumentality, in almost complete contradistinction to its previous largely personal definition, was the locus of educational theory and research as a consequence now more properly in social theory and inquiry? The bewildering array of questions which faced the new educator obviously had a direct and important bearing upon his efforts.

Pedagogical Study and the Preparation of Teachers

The nature of the relationship between the study of education and the preparation of teachers was a third question which complicated the development of the field of education within the American college and university. Which was the business of the university—or were both? As we noted previously, the nature of the study of education itself was by no means clear. The concept of teacher preparation was no clearer. Was the preparation of the teacher primarily the addition of art to content, with perhaps a brief "go" at its practice somewhere along the way? Or was it content plus science, the science of educating? If teaching was an art, was it the natural possession of some few individuals whom we come to recognize? Or was it something which could be transmitted? If it could be transmitted, how? By imitation? By commonsense experience? If educating was a science, and therefore the prospective teacher was to be prepared by being introduced to that science, just what was it? Was the science of educating in some sense sui generis, with its own principles to develop and transmit, or was it merely an amalgam drawn by deduction from other disciplines? Did educationists have something other than a clumsy pastiche to offer their clients? Was administrative authority and responsibility something which properly inhered within the area, or was it delegated from the outside, from the proper disciplinary constituents which were only practically and accidentally united in the case of education? The answer to this question had obvious intra-institutional consequences. Finally, what criteria were to govern the selection, definition, and evaluation of research, increasingly the golden key to true university status?

In short, pedagogy or "education" was in a highly ambiguous state as it entered the American academic scene. If this ambiguity was not by itself sufficient to make education's path of entry into the groves of academe difficult, there were two more factors which made the difficulty inescapable. First of all, higher learning itself was undergoing a profound revolution, for the college and university could remain untouched by the social and intellectual revolution no more than could the common schools.

The Changing Shape of American Higher Education

Prior to the mid-nineteenth century, the American college had been consciously modeled on the English collegiate system, with a consequent emphasis upon a classical literary curriculum, a pronounced theological orientation, a tutorial-recitation method, and a close communal residential structure. Its intent had been concentrated on a personal, moral, and educative end in the traditional sense—i.e., as an opportunity for individual growth in knowledge and virtue, or wisdom. Insofar as the nation had developed "universities," they were again largely English in their orientation, consisting of aggregations of colleges along with traditional vocational-professional schools in their midst. There is no doubt that these colleges and universities had distinctively American features, and that the whole apparatus was under increasing criticism from at least the beginning of the nineteenth century onward. Jefferson's designs for William and Mary and his later accomplishments at Virginia, or the caustic objections of Barnard and Wayland, illustrate this fact sufficiently; they were by no means alone. But, on the whole, the American collegiate and university ideal remained little changed in practice until past the middle of the century.

By the mid-nineteenth century, however, the environing social and cultural changes had reached a point where their implications for higher learning could no longer be denied. And by this time new models were at hand, most obviously the newly resuscitated German universities (especially Berlin), and the first break in the English tradition, the University of London. The pursuit of knowledge for its own sake, the research ideal as opposed to a principally educative function, increasingly served as the model for prestige. Scholarly productivity rather than the perfection of personal character became the criterion for evaluation of the enterprise. There was also an increasing practical concern which befitted the American temper. And this practical concern, when wedded to the growingly pervasive belief in science as the ground of hope for resolving virtually all problems, helped to father the distinctively American form of the new university, the land grant institution. This institution, devoted to a science clearly defined by the needs of an increasingly technological and industrial society, and dedicated to a concept of service designed to raise immediately the lot of the general populace, consciously attempted to eschew much of the academic past.

Had the new university (in either its "German" or its indigenous land grant form) simply replaced the existing higher educational structure, matters might have been clearer. But it did not. There continued to be not simply two but really three models for American higher institutions: the traditional college, the new pure research university, and the still newer land grant ideal. This fact contributed to considerable ambiguity within the higher learning itself. The concept of curriculum and the criteria for the evaluation of the enterprise were extremely difficult to establish under the circumstances. A faculty of necessity drawn from various and often wholly traditional backgrounds found the problem of defining a proper course of study (and an administrative scheme relevant to it) very puzzling indeed. Was the university to be devoted principally to the education of individual students? To the pursuit of specialized knowledge? Or to the resolution of immediate problems and the answering of social demands? Criteria appropriate to one of the models were frequently utilized to determine the value of procedures generated by one of the others. If the pursuit of a unified and transcendent truth and value served as the central point upon which all proper university intellectual activity turned, and furnished the principle of personal identity which gave

focus to its educational intent, what then of the increasing but un-
deniably productive differentiation of knowledge in the particular
disciplines, especially in the proliferating sciences?

Institutes, High Schools, and Normal Schools

Still another factor complicated the entry and acceptance of education on the American university scene. We have suggested that
education, as a novel field of inquiry and a new professional responsibility, arose within a society whose existing educational structure,
particularly at the higher levels, had been dictated by a "prerevolutionary" society and culture. The structure antedated the revolutionary
American political and social experiment, and the triumph of science and
technology. As a consequence, the new "discipline"—if such it was—
had to enter the academic establishment through the back door. There
was no room for it in the early nineteenth-century American college,
and little more for it in the narrow list of professional studies admitted
to struggling American universities of the traditional type. It is of inestimable importance that the common school system was created *just
before* the cultural and academic revolution began to affect the American college and university to any serious degree. When the need for
provision of both a body of thought and a body of practitioners for
the vast new school system suddenly became a reality, only the old
college and university, and their related system of lower schools, were
present. These institutions were simply unable to see, let alone to
remedy the problem that the common schools posed. It slipped from
view if only because, at the beginning, the common school system was
almost exclusively elementary, and therefore its content bore at that
time no apparent relation to "higher" work. The "art" of teaching, on
the other hand, was not a traditional realm of thought or inquiry;
therefore it was no part of a college or university's responsibility, save
in the sense that it was assumed that teaching occurred there and could
be appropriated from mere imitation or observation.

The traditional college and university held its ground relatively
effectively until well past the middle of the century, and in many cases
long afterward. By the 1850's and 1860's, however, the need for an
enormous body of new teachers was obvious. Since the traditional
doors remained effectively closed, yet some institutionalized process
for meeting the need was clearly required, the only alternative was to
create such an agency outside the academic establishment. At first the

preparation of teachers had to occur on a largely informal basis through study groups and institutes, taught not by distinguished scholars who gave exclusive attention to such matters but by the school administrators who had been created by the enabling legislation and who were charged with the responsibility for making it work. It was principally the state and county superintendents, together with a growing body of administrators in larger systems, who developed the regimen for preparing teachers.

It soon became obvious that such an informal, ad hoc arrangement was both insufficient and inadequate. By that time, two alternatives were available. The first was the common school system's own creation, the American high school—the new "college of the people," as it was frequently styled. The second was the importation and development of the normal school, an academic structure entirely devoted to the professional preparation of teachers. As a consequence, in the early years, the great bulk of common school teachers were drawn from the high school (sometimes via its attached "normal department," usually under the supervision of local or county school administrators) or from casually prepared academy- or college-attenders who received informal training for their vocation in the form of study groups and institutes. The development of educational thought, and the preparation of the cadre of educational leaders, rapidly fell to the normal schools, since they alone had any well-defined interest in the matter. The consequence of this development was that, when the new American university began to accord entry to the field of education and accept responsibility for conscious teacher preparation, there was already an indigenous agency in existence. The question of the relationship of the new work in the universities to the customary agencies then became inescapable.

As long as all the elements in the problem (the schools, the educational "profession," and the existing college and university structure) were in flux, attempting a definition of their nature and proper mode of operation de novo and in the face of puzzling new demands, and as long as they were enmeshed in profound social and cultural changes, any settlement of the place of education in the university was bound to be tenuous and fragile. As might be expected, the settlement was frequently more a product of individuals and momentary adjustments than of fixed and ordered principles. And the essentially conservative tendency of all schools, at whatever level, resulted in a further general characteristic: the whole educational apparatus tended to *reflect* rather than shape the rapid changes surrounding it. The locus of these changes was outside the educational enterprise. Consequently, the changes within the schools were usually compelled rather than constructed, a response to events and developments whose sources lay elsewhere.

Illinois as a Case in Point

The state of Illinois and the University of Illinois offer concrete opportunities for exploring many of the difficulties we have examined. The University, in passage from the traditional college and university model, mirrored the conflict between the old and the new, together with the peculiar difficulties of the land grant movement. The state's schools, and its teacher preparation–normal school apparatus, also embodied both the problems and the hard-won achievements of the new school system. The state itself contained all the conflicting educational, political, and social elements against which the development of an alliance between the schools and the new higher learning had to take place.

The University of Illinois could not "make up its mind" how to view the preparation of teachers, or the relation of that function to the correlative question of the study of education, for two principal reasons: first, the University itself was understandably not clear as to its own nature and mission; second, "education" and "educationist" likewise did not clearly specify what "education" was, what it should do, and how it should accomplish its work. There was, however, an existing institution and a task: the new common school and its quite concrete requirements. The question was how to translate and interpret that institution and those tasks.

The ambiguity which afflicted the University was in large measure the ambiguity which lay in the land grant ideal and its own historical situation. It seems clear that the land grant university thirsted for the classical prestige of the traditional American college and university. Its curriculum and regimen, for all their attempts at novelty, demonstrate that fairly obviously. Latin orations never gained a foothold, but diplomas and caps and gowns (roundly rejected by Arnold Tompkins in the 1890's as a foreign importation) did. By its centennial, the University featured an expensively bemedaled President and colorfully caparisoned marshalls in its processions, even as students were beginning to wear the common stuff of "the people." But, even where the decision was for a forthright departure, it was not easy to achieve, if only because some concept of the new ideal had to be formulated. And, as with the common schools and the colleges of education, this conceptualization had largely to take place after the fact. Perhaps one matter posed a particular difficulty: while the land grant institution could shuck the rhetoric and trappings of the traditional college and university, it could not so easily shuck the *educational function* which the college supplied. It would have been relatively easy to create a new technical institute. However, once the new university chose to enroll and to promise to *educate* undergraduates (even while it trained them in the socially necessary skills) the problem became much more complex. A new conception of an educational institution was a good deal more difficult to come by than a new trade school.

The new "university" was by political definition aimed at the *direct* engagement of "agriculture" and the "mechanic arts." Yet the curious fact seems to be that it never fulfilled that intention—nor perhaps should it have. The university ran through three phases of its own, phases which corresponded somewhat loosely to those which characterized the field of education. These phases may be defined in terms of the three sorts of "graduates" which the new institution was to generate: *practitioners, technologists,* and *theorists.*

Agriculture was to be the new institution's most obvious preoccupation. Nonetheless, agriculture was for a considerable period its *least* effective area of endeavor. Even as late as the 1890's, it was proposed to drop the field entirely. In that curious fact, there is a good deal to be learned. The purported mission to practical agriculture mirrored the populist context of the new university and the height of scientific fervor within the environing culture. Every man required elevation, and he was to be raised by the direct application to his life of the power of science. Now, while "science" offered an attractive general ideal, particular applications of its power were not nearly so easy to formulate or grasp. In the case of agriculture, this was particularly true: the genuine practical agriculturist, the "plain farmer," could not see its practical use. He was right: his sons could learn to plow—if that was what "agriculture" was—better at home. And the designers of the new institution had largely failed to see, in their enthusiasm, that the scientific study of agriculture had to precede, by some years, the preparation of scientific practitioners of agriculture.

Something comparable occurred in the case of the mechanic arts. The aim was, again, the direct elevation of the "industrial classes." But they did not soon come; and when they did, they did not come to learn mechanics. To make matters worse, they did not come to learn theoretical science either (at least for some time), let alone the prestigious arts of the literary culture from which they had long before been separated. If the new university could have no immediate success in either objective, however, there was a third possibility: the technology which lay between the unmerchandisable practice and that pure, theoretical science for which the new university was not yet ready itself.

In a sense, the land grant university never served its original purpose in either area. It rapidly abandoned its primitive platform of direct aid to the masses—the forerunner of Frank Laubach's "each one teach one"—and entered the field of technology, devoting its resources to the increasingly important *middle* man. In a newly technologized society, that was in the long run a much more important—indeed, crucially necessary—function anyway. Thence, under the onslaught of the scathing criticisms of the Germanophiles, the Veblens, the Flexners, and the Hutchinses, it moved (by the 1930's and 1940's) into a commanding position in the pursuit of "pure" inquiry—in addition to, rather than abandoning, its popular and profitable technology.

The Quest for Autonomy

We may now connect the corresponding phases in the university and the field of education. Education did not need the university, nor did the university perceive any relationship to that field, during the first blush of the populist, practitioner phase. In the institute–normal school apparatus, the schools had the required engine for the direct preparation of practitioners. Preceding, as we have noticed, the land grant institutions, this apparatus was already deeply imbued with all the evangelical fervor which called forth the new universities even when it could not really support them. Within education, we may point to a concrete parallel: the model- and practice-school preoccupation in teacher preparation was the phenomenon comparable to the new institution's fields and shops.

In the second period, in which technology was ascendant, education and the university had a much clearer relationship. The same era marked the normal school's attempt to become a broader, more technical and professional "teachers' college." The kind of "service" the university could and did render, and the kind of assistance the schools and the teacher-preparation agencies needed, were at this point much closer together. And again, within the field, the age of the *demon-*

stration school was paramount. It was here that education effected a stable presence on the campus and began the struggle to achieve its legitimacy.

While education was beginning to persuade the new academic community of its legitimacy, however, the university also began to move toward pure science and art and to emphasize the theorist both in its student body and its faculty. With the advent of this pure-science phase, or the immediate prelude to it, the field of education suffered its most severe crisis. During the 1920's and 1930's, the University of Illinois was coming to choose pure science and art, and the University was less able than ever to see education as a legitimate component. However, education itself made no clear claim and pursued no more consistent strategy during those crucial years. The new "discipline" was divided, and conditions did not favor the resolution of that division. Consequently pedagogy was forced to make its own way haltingly, remaining largely in the technological stage. Its movement to the pure theoretical stage, a necessary step if it was to gain genuine autonomy in the changing university, was hampered by the difficulty of defining precisely what an educational theorist was. Here again, the final attempt to redefine the "Academy" at Illinois, this time as a genuine laboratory school—a laboratory for educationists, that is, as opposed to a testing ground for other disciplines—was illustrative of the tension and difficulty.

Another theme which is of more than routine interest is the at least purported attempt of pedagogy to move from a deductive approach to education and teacher preparation to an inductive or empirical one. Here it appears that the change was more apparent than real. In an important sense, education did not abandon the deductive approach; it merely substituted one source of the deduction for another.

As we have already suggested, early nineteenth-century educational theory—insofar as there was much of a body of theory—was largely generated directly from a philosophical base, usually a Kantian or post-Kantian epistemology. Its psychological doctrines were obtained, on the whole, in the same manner. Pedagogy's claim to "scientific" status meant that a body of universal and indubitable principles had been deduced, whence practical maxims could be generated and thus shape and evaluate practice. Correspondingly, educational disputes were to be settled by the canons of deductive logic much more than at the bar of practice.

Illinois's shift to Herbartian approaches to pedagogy, as elsewhere, was significant if ultimately unsatisfactory. The advantage of Herbartianism was that it considered the process of learning dynamically, and not merely as a deduction from a theory of knowledge. Its difficulty, among others, was that it joined a logically derived theory of subject matter to a speculatively derived psychology. This psychology was nonexperimental, as well. The Herbartians did believe in *testing* their theories, of course, and therefore they were greatly concerned with establishing practice and demonstration schools; but they did not generate their hypotheses from such experience, on the whole. And Herbartianism was essentially nonenvironmental. It tended to view the learner as the principal (if not the whole) source of educational activity. While this was an important advance, it was a far less radical departure from the past than was necessary for a more thorough revolution.

With the rise of new laboratory psychologies, Herbartianism was almost immediately eclipsed. These new psychologies were not only dynamic but developmental, in the mold of the new Darwinian science from which they were sprung. They viewed all *knowing* as a *learning process,* a process which was concrete, experimentally defined, and essentially environmental. Since learning was a reciprocal process of interaction between the organism and its environment, the whole relationship had to be considered—not merely some particular part, as John Dewey pointed out. While that was the general thrust of the new psychologies, in practice the particular effects came out differently, especially in education. In the first place, educational theorists leapt to their deductive habits once again. If learning was the most fundamental aspect of an education, the argument implicitly ran, and if psychology was the science of learning, then both educational generalizations and pedagogical specifics could be deduced from the psychological theories and the data they generated. Given the pre-eminence of a still crude Darwinism and its emphasis on the continuity of nature, these deductions could just as well be made from evidence extrapolated from the animal laboratory as any other place. If the rats or the chickens altered their behavior in response to a particular pattern of stimuli, a mandate for changing the elementary school program had clearly emerged.

The new psychological recipe for educational perfection begged or ignored a number of questions, many of which had to wait a considerable period of time to be asked. Again we need not attribute that oversight—baleful as its influence perhaps was—either to ignorance or malice. One of the unexamined assumptions was that *any* act of learning was sufficiently like what went on in the schools to justify deducing educational principles of tactics from it. In particular, that meant that *educational* theory and *school* practice could be deduced, *mutatis mutandis*, from laboratory situations. (The number of changes thought necessary were minimal.) The difficulty at issue here was not merely the result of philosophical wrongheadedness; it was in fact curiously bad science. The assumption really failed to take account of the full import of the environmentalism which purportedly shaped the new theories. The school and the laboratory were *not* equivalent environments, and there was really no reason to assume—even if all the other hasty and disputable assumptions implicit in the theories were granted —that the interactive process was really the same. Or, to put it positively, the general shapes of the new psychological approaches ought to have militated (as they did, for example, in the case of Colonel Francis Parker) toward the scientific observation of the *classroom of the school*, not (at least exclusively) the psychologists' darkened laboratories, as the source for educational paradigms. Furthermore, the school was not only a physical environment but a social and cultural environment as well, and that inescapably involved the formulation of educational principles in the murky realms of value definition. While the scientific method might, as at least the pragmatists believed, eventually take into account social and cultural realms of meaning (including even their inescapable value structures), that was, on anyone's inspection, still far from an accomplished fact. Even if it might be possible to look to science as a whole for definitions of education as a whole—though that did not perhaps need to be granted—it was at least naïvely premature to deduce virtually the whole of education from one relatively narrow aspect of one science.

Within the general University community there was, of course, considerable opposition to the attempt to recast education in this new mold. Unfortunately, however, most of this opposition was little, if any, more clear-headed. On the whole, the established academic interests either had no psychology (on various grounds) or had only a speculative philosophical psychology drawn from one of the traditional epistemological theories. Consequently, their view of the problem was effectively restricted and the force of their objections essentially negative. Some were bitterly opposed to the disintegration of knowledge which they (quite rightly, we think) saw as the result of the new psychological theories and the pedagogy these theories fathered. But their opposition was categorical, narrowly philosophical, and negative, and it led to no constructive dialogue. Since the issue as they formulated it was not resolvable in terms of the intellectual encounter proper to a university, their only alternative was to restrict these new fields, and particularly education, by the invocation of institutional power.

Ideological Conflict and Institutional Warfare

By the 1930's, leading educationists were coming to see that their interests, both as touching the preparation of teachers and as touching the field of education as such, lay principally within the schools. Furthermore, as befit these convictions, they were also persuaded that educational theory required a much broader base (and hence a much broader field of inquiry) than had characterized it previously. The impossibility of creating such a reconstruction in the field of education without the requisite autonomy for its practitioners brought about an almost inevitable confrontation. The administration, and even many educationists, were the products of a previous intellectual age, and they were not willing to settle the question other than in terms of institutional power. But it is the ideological conflict which tied together the resulting disputes over research, service, the nature and function of laboratory schools, and the new programs for the preparation of teachers and educational specialists.

In view of the new educational theorists who were coming to Illinois as well as to other states and institutions, education was practically and dynamically related to the society which environed it. It was, they agreed, principally determined by its role as an institution functioning within a specific society at a specific point in history and in a particular context. Educational theorists had always, from the time of Plato himself, seen that educational theories were logically related to social *theories.* The crucial difference in the "new" education was that education was seen as functionally related to existing social and cultural *dynamics.* As a consequence, its proper focus lay not in theories of education but in practical and institutional realities. Theoretical considerations were important not as the source of educational doctrines by themselves, but as illuminating the approach to the schools as institutions within a social and cultural context and as providing critical criteria and shaping inquiry. It was, finally, this special focus which defined the peculiar "subject matter" of education, a subject matter neither reducible to, nor merely an aggregate of, the traditional disciplines and inquiries.

The analogy with medicine, long popular with educators, might have helped clarify matters, but it was susceptible to at least one serious misinterpretation. On that analogy, it could be suggested that doctors did study chemistry, but that they did not *teach* it. They study and *practice* medicine. It can be (and frequently was) argued that teachers study chemistry, for example, and that that is also what they teach. Consequently, teachers could be seen as more directly dependent upon the constituent disciplines than were physicians. The misinterpretation of the analogy arises from a failure to apply it entirely. The new educators, including men such as Dewey, were arguing that teachers did *not* teach the chemistry they learned in the disciplines. As teachers in the common schools their aim was larger—something roughly akin to the achievement of social and cultural "health." They were not primarily concerned with preparing initiates for the disciplines and to so regard them was seriously to obscure their real function (and consequently to misdefine education). The practical question was whether the larger aspect, directly related to the society and the culture as a whole, had a unique character which merited an autonomous and professional institutionalization within the university. And a further corollary was that, if education were to have work at the graduate level, it must be shaped by this peculiar educational matter and not be restricted to programs in the "basic disciplines" of which it was erroneously conceived to be the directly derived function.

The "disciplinary" issue, while undoubtedly posing a theoretical question of importance, may also be seen in another light—as a continuation of old squabbles within higher education itsself. One of the most notorious events after 1945 was the eruption of the debate with historian Arthur Bestor—a debate which achieved national prominence and gained the sympathies of many both within and outside the University of Illinois. Consciously styled by Bestor and the group of disciplinary advocates who rapidly formed around him as a defense of the schools and the nation's youth—and perhaps of the nation itself— one might argue instead that the whole movement was rather a defense of traditional university interests. One would be hard put to admire, let alone hold above criticism, the "life adjustment" education against which they crusaded. It was little more than the crudely psychologized form of a moribund progressivism. But the "soft" pedagogy was at best a foil for more immediate concerns. If the concepts of learning and schooling which were being hammered out in the public educational enterprise were victorious (which by the 1950's appeared might well be the case), they not only carried implications for the preparation of teachers that directly touched the University and its programs, but they also threatened the traditional definition of higher learning. Could even the University any longer remain merely the haven of discrete and disinterested disciplinary inquiry? Pointing with alarm to such developments as a plot against the good of the nation's children and their schools was perhaps the best defense of the graduate school bloc, which had for years enjoyed its own interlocking directorate with undergraduate and secondary education in spite of repeated criticisms by men who could hardly be considered educationists.

Finally, confusion over the disciplinary issue was of central importance in the failure to find common ground with the normal school apparatus. The normal schools were constitutionally committed to the concept of education as a definable study in itself and to the necessity of professional autonomy. In practice, however, they tended to study and teach teaching without studying education. The University, on the other hand, attempted to study education—still defined largely in terms of its aggregate disciplines—without reference to teaching. That neither approach was satisfactory might have been obvious, but the difficulty was compounded by the tendency of the University, and even some of its own educationists, to judge the normal school in the light of discrete disciplinary criteria appropriate to the traditional university graduate school. As a consequence, the normal schools in Illinois as elsewhere were always judged to be second rate, in a sense which they could escape only by denying their central commitment.

The Problem Restated

Pedagogy, we have then argued, posed a novel challenge to American higher educational development due to the radical novelty to the institution from which it sprang, the new common school system. Pedagogy was the concrete image of a new social responsibility rather than a logically defined field, and it sought admission to a higher education apparatus which was itself undergoing radical change and therefore torn by unclear and sometimes conflicting notions of its own nature and goals. The consequence was an enormous potential for generating institutional ambiguities which made it virtually impossible to see any way to relate pedagogy to higher learning either logically or operationally. The resulting stand-off required the new "profession" —which, it must be noted, was a profession in hope rather than fact, and perhaps still is—to develop its own instruments for meeting the challenge, in all too many cases tragically cut off from the rest of American higher education.

The University of Illinois and the common school system of the state clearly exemplified both these inherent ambiguities and practical difficulties. As a new land grant institution, itself the most novel and ambiguous form of the new American university, Illinois traversed three stages in its development: the attempt to directly apply the benefits of science to the problems of the practitioner; the attempt to supply a new body of scientific middlemen, the technologists, for an expanding industrial empire; and the provision of "pure" scientists and theoreticians to a society finally convinced of their utility—at least when understood in terms of its own interests. Pedagogy, on the other hand, had already developed its own apparatus for the direct provision of practitioners, and at the beginning its personnel had little obvious need of higher learning since the common schools were essentially elementary institutions. Educationists tried, with conspicuous lack of success, to relate their growing interests and developing methods to the latter stages. As professionals, they could be viewed as technologists; but their technology seemed less than legitimate when viewed apart from some theoretical roots, and the proper definition and location of its theoretical roots within the university posed puzzling institutional problems. As "pure" educational theorists, professors of pedagogy encountered severe difficulties because it was not clear precisely what phenomenon they were theorizing about. In fact, for most members of the academy, pedagogy was at best an aggregate of phenomena and theories already undergoing legitimate scrutiny in the community. Finally, an already murky situation was further muddled by the fact that developments within the university and (even more so) in the surrounding society and culture at large ran ahead of changes within the "field" of education. In the resulting flux, any commonly accepted identity was extremely difficult to define and justify; consequently, any stable operational autonomy was almost impossible to achieve.

Lacking sufficient grounds for conceptual agreement, then, the gaining of personal power and the negotiating of temporary institutional settlements above appeared strategically possible. The consequence was institutional conflict and a growing lack of communication between university-oriented educationists and the developing professional fraternity, including the normal school cadre who had been carrying the burden of practical school reform. Consequently, university-based educationists were frequently less productive of leadership or significant practical reform within the schools and the "profession" than might have been anticipated, or at least hoped.

When Charles DeGarmo brought Herbartianism to the world and to the campus at Illinois, and when Colonel Francis Parker revitalized the Cook County Normal School, they had not seen themselves as the advocates of improved philosophical systems but as educational revolutionaries. They were not interested merely in subtle deductions or corrigible educational propositions, nor were they concerned with achieving scholarly legitimacy by an academic masquerade. They began in the schools and they ended in the schools, whereas far too many of their successors began in the university and ended in it. DeGarmo, like many of his cohorts, decried the naïve "empiricism"—a crude commonsense observation and trial-and-error methodology—which had characterized the struggling new field. Philosophy and psychology offered more subtle discriminations and more productive models for viewing the schools, but they were not substitutes for them. Educational theorizing was not merely a study but was inescapably linked to an activity that took place in schools rather than in laboratories or verbal paradigms. The university, resting on its Olympian heights, might provide a peculiar and fruitful vantage point for viewing the events "below," but one dared not remain too long in its rarified atmosphere and idealized converse. The hope for a productive relationship between schoolmen and academicians in the long run lay in the fact that, as Abraham Flexner noted, the American university was making its way down from the mountain to take up its abode among men. The schools lay on the plain, and they still do. Nor is the long and difficult descent yet complete.

BIBLIOGRAPHY

PRIMARY SOURCES

General University Records, Special Collections, and Personal Papers

NOTE: Unless otherwise indicated, all locations and Record Series numbers for unpublished primary sources refer to the Archives of the University of Illinois.

Allen, Ralph. Papers. Box 2 in Allen Family Papers, 1774–1967. Record Series 41/20/21.

Alumni Class Files. Record Series 26/4/5.

Alumni Morgue. Record Series 26/4/1.

American Council on Education. *University of Illinois Survey Report.* [Washington, D.C.,] 1943.

Burrill, Thomas J. Correspondence, 1892, 1894, in T. J. Burrill Papers. Record Series 2/3/0.

———. Papers, 1863–64, 1875, 1877–78. Record Series 15/4/20. See also Record Series 2/3/0/2, 15/4/19.

Carmichael, Robert D. Papers. Record Series 7/1/2, no. 4.

College of Literature and Arts. College and Departmental Letterbooks and Correspondence. Record Series 15/1/2, 4, 10.

———. "Literature and Arts Minute Books," 1878–1909. Record Series 15/1/7.

"College of Natural Science Minute Books," 1878–1912. Record Series 15/1/6.

Department of Psychology. History. Record Series 15/19/5.

Draper, Andrew S. Faculty Correspondence, 1894–1904. Record Series 2/4/2.

———. General Correspondence, 1894–1904. Record Series 2/4/3.

———. Letterbooks, 1894–1904. Record Series 2/4/3.

———. Personal Letters, 1892–1913. Record Series 2/4/5.

Examination Papers, 1875–76. Record Series 41/30/20, no. 3.

Graduate College Administrative Correspondence. Record Series 7/1/2.

Gregory, John M. Papers, 1838–98. Record Series 2/1/1.

———. Scrapbook. Record Series 2/1/11.

Griffith, Coleman R. Papers. Record Series 5/1/21.

Hatch, Richard A., comp. *Some Founding Papers of the University of Illinois.* Urbana, 1967.

The Illini. (Later, *The Daily Illini.*) University of Illinois student newspaper.

James, Edmund J. Faculty Correspondence, 1904–15. Record Series 2/5/6.

———. General Correspondence, 1904–19. Record Series 2/5/3.

———. General Letterbooks, 1904–6. Record Series 2/5/4.

———. General and Subject Scrapbooks. Record Series 2/5/10, 11.

———. Speeches. Record Series 2/5/6.

Kelley, James H., ed. *Alumni Record.* Urbana, 1913.

Kinley, David. General Correspondence, 1919–30. Record Series 2/6/1.

———. "The President's Report." (Issued in the series of "University of Illinois Bulletins" from 1922–23 through 1929–30.)

Peabody, Selim H. Papers. Record Series 2/2/1.

———. Speeches and Sermons, 1881–91, 1894. Record Series 2/2/1, no. 1.

"Publications Scrapbook, 1868–90." Record Series 2/1/11.

"Regents' Letterbook, 1879–94." Record Series 2/1/6.

Scott, Franklin W., ed. *The Alumni Record of the University of Illinois.* Urbana, 1906.

Shamel, Charles H. Papers, 1874–1949. Record Series 26/20/3.

———. "Autobiography." Charles H. Shamel Papers, Record Series 26/20/3.

———. "Diary." Charles H. Shamel Papers, Record Series 26/20/3.

Stephens, Carl. Papers, 1912–15. Record Series 26/1/20.

The Student. (Predecessor to *The Illini.*)

Talbot, Arthur N. Papers, 1877–1942. Record Series 11/5/21.

University of Illinois. *The Alumni Quarterly.*

———. Bulletins. A number of series were issued under this general title, with varying numbers and descriptions.

———. *Circular and Catalogue of the Officers and Students of the Illinois*

Industrial University [and subsequent varying titles], 1869—. Record Series 25/3/0/1.

———. "Faculty Record," 1868-1901. Record Series 4/1/1.

———. *Inaugural of Edmund Janes James, Ph.D., LL.D., as President of the University of Illinois.* Urbana, 1906.

———. Board of Trustees published *Reports*, 1867-1946. Record Series 1/0/2. These *Reports*, issued biennially except during some early years, may be supplemented by the *Trustees' Transactions*. In most cases they contain the same material, and they have been consulted only where some variance, or addition, might have been significant.

———. *Statutes.*

———. *Survey of Business Administration and Organization of the University of Illinois by Booz, Fry, Allen and Hamilton, Combined with Review and Analysis of This Survey, Together with Recommendations by the President of the University of Illinois.* N.p., n.d. (This mimeographed report was presented August 1, 1942.)

———, and Superintendent of Public Instruction. *Conditions for the Recognition and Accrediting of Illinois Secondary Schools.* N.p., n.d. (Issued at various dates during the late 1920's until the end of the University's visitation program. Previously the University and the superintendent of public instruction issued their publications separately.)

Willard, Arthur Cutts. General Correspondence, 1934-46. Record Series 2/9/1.

Federal, State, and City Documents

Chicago Board of Education, Department of Child Study and Pedagogical Investigation. *Child Study Report.* 3 vols. Chicago, 1899-1901.

Chicago Board of Education. *Proceedings.* 1872—.

City of Chicago, Department of Public Instruction. *Annual Reports of the Board of Education,* 1854—.

Congressional Globe, 35 Congress, 1 Session.

State of Illinois. *Report of Committee on Courses of Study and Faculty for the Illinois Industrial University.* Springfield, 1867.

———. *Biennial Reports of the Superintendent of Public Instruction.* Springfield. (Title number and years of reports vary according to volumes.)

———. Board of Education of the State of Illinois. *Proceedings.* 1857-1912.

U.S. Bureau of Education (and various titles). Bulletins and circulars.

U.S. Commissioner of Education. *Reports of the Commissioner of Education.*

[United States Office of Education.] *National Survey of the Education of Teachers.* Bulletin 1933, vol. 6, no. 10.

College of Education Papers, Records, and
Collections of Personal Papers

Benner, Thomas E. Papers, 1930–1962, 1967, 1969. Record Series 10/1/21.
College of Education, Bureau of Educational Research. Bulletins.
———. College of Education History Papers. Record Series 10/1/11.
———. College Policy and Plans Reports, 1915, 1943–52. Record Series 10/1/0/2.
———. University High School Academy Publications, 1905–10. Record Series 10/12/0/16.
DeBoer, John J. Papers, 1936, 1940, 1945–55. Record Series 10/7/20.
Education Scrapbooks, 1942–49. Record Series 10/1/30.
Johnston, Charles H. Papers, 1902–3, 1907–17. Record Series 10/1/20.
Monroe, Walter S. Papers, 1912–13, 1917–26, 1930–40, 1949–50, 1956. Record Series 10/10/20.
"Report of Proceedings before Board of Trustees of the University of Illinois, Union Building, Urbana, Illinois. Re: Dean Thomas E. Benner." (Prepared by T. A. Copple, Court and General Reporters, Chicago.)
Tompkins, Arnold. Papers. Illinois State University Archives.
University of Illinois. *Bulletins;* [special issues] *Proceedings of the High School Conferences, 1905–41.* (While these were, strictly speaking, University rather than College functions, they were primarily the work of the High School Visitor and the Education faculty.)

Writings by or about Education Faculty Members

Bagley, William C. *A Century of the Universal School.* New York, 1937.
———. "The Distinction between Academic and Professional Subjects," *NEA Proceedings,* 1918, pp. 229–34.
———. "Dr. Coffman's Study of the Teaching Population," *School and Home Education* 31, no. 3 (November, 1911): 91–92.
———. *The Educative Process.* New York, 1905.
———. "Experience and Teaching Efficiency," *School and Home Education* 30, no. 2 (October, 1910): 45.
———. "A Further Advantage of Paying Salaries to Normal School Cadets," *School and Home Education* 31, no. 3 (November, 1911): 93–94.
———. "History of the Department and School of Education [of the University of Illinois]." (Prepared in 1916.) Copy in Record Series 10/1/10.
———. "Ideals Versus Generalized Habits," *School and Home Education* 24, no, 3 (November, 1904): 102–6.
———. "The Injustice of Low Standards," *School and Home Education* 31, no. 3 (November, 1911): 921.

————. "Qualities of Merit in High School Teachers," *School and Home Education* 31, no. 8 (April, 1912): 319–20.

————. "The Qualities of Merit in Teachers," *School and Home Education* 30, no. 2 (October, 1910): 44–45.

————. "The Remedy: Normal School Training at Public Expense," *School and Home Education* 31, no. 3 (November, 1911): 93.

————. "Some Implications of the Ruediger-Strayer Investigation," *School and Home Education* 30, no. 2 (October, 1910): 45–46.

————. "Some Objections Considered," *School and Home Education* 31, no. 3 (November, 1911): 94.

————. "Some Possible Functions of a School of Education," *School and Home Education* 30, no. 4 (December, 1910): 136–41.

————. "A Summary of Arguments for a School of Education," *School and Home Education* 30, no. 5 (January, 1911): 177–78.

————, Learned, William J., et al. *The Professional Preparation of Teachers for American Public Schools.* (Carnegie Foundation Bulletin no. 14.) New York, 1920.

————, and Rugg, H. O. "The Content of American History as Taught in the Seventh and Eighth Grades," *University of Illinois Bulletin,* vol. 13, no. 51, *School of Education Bulletin* no. 16. Urbana: University of Illinois, 1916. 59 pp.

Bode, Boyd H. *Conflicting Psychologies of Learning.* Boston, 1929.

————. *Fundamentals of Education.* New York, 1921.

————. *How We Learn.* Boston, 1940.

————. *Modern Educational Theories.* New York, 1927.

Bonser, Frederick Gordon. "A Statistical Study of Illinois High Schools," *The University Studies,* n.s., vol. 1, no. 3 (May, 1902).

Brown, George A. "An Election of Eminent Educators," *School and Home Education* 32, no. 1 (September, 1912): 4–5.

Chadsey, Charles E. *The Status of the Superintendent.* (First Yearbook of the Department of Superintendence of the NEA.) Washington, D.C., 1923.

————. *The Summary of the Show Cause Proceedings, People of Illinois vs. Peter A. Mortenson and Charles E. Chadsey, in the Matter of People of Illinois vs. Albert H. Severinghaus, et al.,* no. B-53, 706 (n.p., n.d.). Privately printed pamphlet.

The College of Education of the University of Illinois and Dean Thomas E. Benner—A Factual Record of Educational Leadership, 1931–45. (This privately printed pamphlet was "the cooperative effort of several staff members of the College of Education" and was dated June 7, 1945.)

Colvin, Stephen S. *An Introduction to High School Teaching.* New York, 1917.

————. *The Learning Process.* New York, 1911, 1931.

————, ed. *Studies from the Psychological Laboratory of the University of Illinois* (special series of *Psychological Monographs* 11, no. 1 [whole no. 44]). November, 1909.

————, and Bagley, William C. *Human Behavior, a First Book in Psychology for Teachers.* 2nd rev. ed. New York, 1929.

DeGarmo, Charles. *Aesthetic Education.* Syracuse, 1913.

————. *The Essentials of Method.* Boston, 1889.

————. *Herbart and the Herbartians.* New York, 1896.

————. *Interest and Education, the Doctrine of Interest and Its Concrete Application.* New York, 1902.

————. *Principles of Secondary Education.* New York, 1907–10.

————. "Scope and Character of Pedagogical Work in Universities," *NEA Proceedings* (1892), pp. 772–80.

————, et al. "Relative Advantages and Limitations of Universities and Schools in Preparing Secondary Teachers," *The Education and Training of Secondary Teachers* (4th Yearbook of the National Society for the Scientific Study of Education, Part I), pp. 89–92. Chicago, 1905.

Dexter, Edwin Grant. *A History of Education in the United States,* New York, 1904.

————. "The Present Status and Personnel of the Secondary Teaching Force in the United States," *The Education and Training of Secondary Teachers,* pp. 49–62.

————. "Review of the Educative Process," *The School Review* 14, no. 6 (June, 1906): 464–65.

"Dr. E. G. Dexter, Superintendent at Puerto Rico," *School and Home Education* 27, no. 1 (September, 1907): 36.

Eckoff, William J., trans. *Herbart's ABC of Sense-Perception, and Minor Pedagogical Works.* New York, 1896.

Griffith, Coleman R. Papers. Record Series 5/1/21. (These papers contain manuscripts of several of Griffith's psychological and educational writings.)

Hollister, H. A. "Present Status of the High School in Illinois," *School and Home Education* 25, no. 7 (March, 1906).

Johnston, Charles Hughes. "The Junior High School," *Educational Administration and Supervision* 2 (1916): 413–25.

————. "The Junior High School," *Journal of Education* 84, no. 4 (whole no. 2090) (July 27, 1916): 91.

McMurry, Charles A. *Elements of General Method, Based on the Principles of Herbart.* New York, 1892, 1903.

————. *Handbook of Practice for Teachers.* New York, 1914.

————, and McMurry, Frank M. *The Method of Recitation.* New York, 1903.

————. "Discussion of the Training of Secondary Teachers, *The Place of*

Vocational Subjects in the High-School Curriculum (4th Yearbook of the National Society for the Scientific Study of Education, Part II), pp. 53–55. Bloomington, 1905.

McMurry, Frank M. *How to Study and Teaching How to Study*. Boston, 1909.

———. "Death of Louis H. Galbreath," *School and Home Education* 19 (September, 1889): 45–46.

———. "The Relation of Theory to Practice in the Education of Teachers," *3rd Yearbook of the National Society for the Scientific Study of Education*, pp. 9–64. Chicago, 1904.

Monroe, Walter S., ed. *Encyclopedia of Educational Research*. New York, 1941. (Rev. ed., New York, 1950.)

———. *Teaching-Learning Theory and Teacher Education, 1890–1950*. Urbana, 1952.

———. *Ten Years of Educational Research, 1918–27*. (University of Illinois, Bureau of Educational Research, Bulletin no. 42.) Urbana, 1928.

———; DeVoss, James C.; and Kelly, Frederick J. *Educational Tests and Measurements*. Boston, 1917.

———; DeVoss, James C.; and Reagan, George W. *Educational Psychology*. Garden City, 1930.

———, and Engelhart, Max D. *The Scientific Study of Educational Problems*. New York, 1936.

Straight, Wood C. "An Election of Eminent Educators, VII—Bagley," *Brooklyn Daily Eagle*, June 3, 1912.

Tompkins, Arnold. *The Philosophy of School Management*. Boston, 1898.

———. *The Philosophy of Teaching*. Boston, 1894.

———. *The Science of Discourse*. Greencastle, Ind., 1889.

———. "The Normal School Problem," *Illinois School Journal* 36 (January, 1891): 15–24.

Whipple, Guy M. "Review of Classroom Management," *Educational Review* 35 (May, 1908): 516–20.

Professional Educational Journals, Records, and Special Collections

American Journal of Education. Hartford, 1855–82.

American Normal School Association. *Addresses and Journal of Proceedings, 1866, 1870*. In 1866, the organization, which had been founded in 1858, affiliated with the NEA, merging completely in 1870.

Chicago Teachers' Federation. *Bulletins*. 1901–8.

Education. Boston, 1880—.

Educational Review. New York, etc., 1891–1928. (Merged with *School and Society*.)

Illinois School Journal (1881–89) and *Public School Journal* (1889–98). Predecessors to *School and Home Education*.

Illinois Schoolmaster. Chicago and Normal, 1868–76.

Illinois Teacher. Peoria, 1855–73.

Illinois Teacher. Mt. Morris, etc., 1913–40. (Journal of the Illinois State Teachers' Association, which became the Illinois Education Association in 1936. After 1940, the journal was called *Illinois Education*.)

Journal of Educational Psychology. Baltimore, 1910—.

Journal of Educational Research. Bloomington, 1920—.

Margaret Haley's Bulletin (and slightly varying titles). Chicago. 1915–31 (suspended, 1916–25).

National Normal Exponent. Cincinnati, 1868–92(?).

National Normal Reunion (?).

School and Home Education. Normal and Bloomington, 1898–1922.

School and Society. New York, etc., 1915—.

Transactions of the Illinois State Horticultural Society for 1871, Being the Sixteenth Annual Meeting Held at Jacksonville, December 12, 13, 14, and 15. . . . N.s., vol. 5. Chicago, 1872.

Bateman, Newton. Papers. Illinois State University Archives.

———. Bateman Manuscripts, Archives of the State of Illinois, Springfield.

Cook, John W. Papers. Illinois State University Archives.

Edwards, Richard. Papers. Illinois State University Archives.

Fairchild, Raymond W. Papers. Illinois State University Archives.

Felmley, David. Papers. Illinois State University Archives.

Hewitt, Edwin C. Papers. Illinois State University Archives.

Hovey, Charles E. Papers. Illinois State University Archives.

Tompkins, Arnold. Papers. Illinois State University Archives.

Turner, Jonathan Baldwin. Turner Manuscripts. Archives of the State of Illinois, Springfield.

University of Illinois, School of Education Papers. Illinois State University Archives.

*Contemporary Published Works and Articles Dealing with
University Reform, the Normal Schools, and
the Development of Professional Education*

Adams, Charles Kendall. "The Teaching of Pedagogy in Colleges and Universities," *Academy* 3 (1888): 469–81.

Bachman, Frank P. *Training and Certification of High School Teachers*. ([George Peabody College] Field Studies, no. 2.) Nashville, 1930.

Barnard, Henry. *Normal Schools and Other Institutions, Agencies, and Means Designed for the Professional Education of Teachers*. 2 vols.

Bateman, Newton, and Selby, Paul. *An Historical Encyclopedia of Illinois.* 2 vols. Chicago, 1905.

Brown, George P. "Pedagogy in the State University," *School and Home Education* 18 (April, 1899): 431–33.

———. "The Place of the Normal Schools," *School and Home Education* 17 (September, 1907): 12–14.

Chicago Bureau of Public Efficiency [not an official agency]. *Chicago School Finances, 1915–25. General Summary and Conclusions.* (Report no. 63.) Chicago, 1927.

[Chicago] Citizens' Schools Committee. *Chicago's Schools.*

Cook, John W. *Educational History of Illinois.* Chicago, 1912.

———, and McHugh, James V. *A History of the Illinois State Normal University.* Normal, 1882.

Dewey, John. "Education as a University Study," *Columbia University Quarterly* 9 (June, 1907): 284–90.

———. "Pedagogy as a University Discipline," *University [of Chicago] Record* 1 (September 18, 25, 1896): 353.

Eliot, Charles W. *Educational Reform.* New York, 1909.

———. "The New Education: Its Organization," *Atlantic Monthly* 23 (February, 1869): 203–20; (March, 1869): 358–67.

Farrington, F. E. "Practice Work in University Departments of Education," *Observation and Practice Teaching: Yearbook of the National Society of College Teachers of Education, 1909.*

Fowle, William B. *The Teachers Institute; or, Familiar Hints to Young Teachers.* New York, 1875.

Gordy, J. P. *Rise and Growth of the Normal School Idea in the United States.* (U.S. Bureau of Education, Circular of Information, no. 8.) Washington, D.C., 1891.

Gray, William S., ed. *The Academic and Professional Preparation of Secondary Teachers.* (Vol. 7, "Proceedings of the Institute for Administrative Officers of Higher Institutions, 1935.") Chicago, 1935.

———, ed. *General Education, Its Nature, Scope, and Essential Elements.* (Vol. 6, "Proceedings of the Institute for Administrative Officers of Higher Institutions, 1934.") Chicago, 1934.

———, ed. *The Training of College Teachers.* (Vol. 2, "Proceedings of the Institute for Administrative Officers of Higher Institutions, 1930.") Chicago, 1930.

Guerin, John; Wiley, M. Mills; and Sonsteby, John J., et al. *Suppressed Records of the Board of Education of the City of Chicago.* Chicago, 1909.

Hall, Samuel R. *Lectures on School-Keeping.* Boston, 1829.

Harper, Charles A. *A Century of Public Teacher Education, the Story of*

the State Teachers Colleges as They Evolved from the Normal Schools.
Washington, D.C., 1939.

————. *Development of the Teachers College in the United States, with Special Reference to the Illinois State Normal University.* Bloomington, 1935.

Haven, Joseph. *Mental Philosophy: Including the Intellect, Sensibilities, and Will.* Boston, 1864.

Henderson, Joseph L. *Admission to College by Certificate.* New York, 1912.

The Herbart Society for the Scientific Study of Teaching. *Yearbooks* (1895–1900).

Hill, Clyde M. *A Decade of Progress in Teacher Training.* (Teachers College, Columbia University, Contributions to Education, no, 223.) New York, 1927.

Hinsdale, B. A. "Pedagogical Chairs in Colleges and Universities," *NEA Proceedings* (1889): 559–68.

Illinois State University [Faculty Committee]. *Semi-Centennial History of the Illinois State Normal University, 1857–1907.* [Normal], 1907.

James, William. *Principles of Psychology.* 2 vols. New York, 1890.

————. *Psychology: Briefer Course.* New York, 1915. (Orig. ed., 1892.)

————. *Talks to Teachers on Psychology.* New ed. New York, 1939.

Johnston, Shepherd, ed. *Historical Sketches of the Public School System of the City of Chicago, to the Close of the School Year 1878–79.* Chicago, 1880.

Jordan, David Starr. *The Trend of the American University.* Stanford, 1929.

Luckey, G. W. A. *The Professional Training of Secondary Teachers in the United States.* New York, 1903.

McManis, John T. *Ella Flagg Young and a Half-Century of the Chicago Public Schools.* Chicago, 1916.

Manchester, O. L. *The Normal School Crisis.* Springfield, 1921. (Pamphlet published by the state superintendent of public instruction.)

Monroe, Paul, ed. *Cyclopedia of Education.* 5 vols. New York, 1911–13.

Munsterberg, Hugh. "The Danger from Experimental Psychology," *Atlantic Monthly* 81 (February, 1898): 159–67.

————. *Psychology and the Teacher.* New York, 1909.

National Commission for the Defense of Democracy through Education of the NEA of the U.S. *Certain Personnel Practices in the Chicago Public Schools.* Washington, 1945.

National Conference on Secondary Education and Its Problems, Held at Northwestern University October 30 and 31, 1903. Evanston, 1904.

National Education Association. *Addresses and Proceedings.* (Published in various locations.)

The National Society for the Scientific Study of Education. *Yearbooks.* (Successor to the Herbart Society.)

National Society for the Study of Education. *Yearbooks.* (Successor to the National Society for the Scientific Study of Education.)

Page, David P. *Theory and Practice of Teaching,* ed. S. Y. Gillan. Milwaukee, 1901.

Peik, Wesley Ernest. *The Professional Education of High School Teachers, an Analysis and Evaluation of the Prescribed Courses in Education for Prospective High School Teachers at the University of Minnesota.* Minneapolis, 1930.

Pillsbury, William L. "Historical Sketches of the State Normal Universities and the University of Illinois," [State of Illinois], *17th Biennial Report of the Superintendent of Public Instruction.* Springfield, 1888.

Rosenkranz, Karl. *Pedagogics as a System,* trans. Anna C. Brackett. St. Louis, 1872. (This edition, reprinted from the *Journal of Speculative Philosophy,* has bound with it: Brackett, Anna C. *The Science of Education, a Paraphrase of Rosenkranz.* St. Louis, 1878.)

Royce, Josiah. "Is There a Science of Education?" *Educational Review* 1 (January, 1891): 15–25; (February, 1891): 121–32.

Russell, James Earl. "The Spirit of Teachers College," *Columbia University Quarterly* 9 (June, 1907): 278–84.

Seeley, Levi. "Pedagogical Training in Colleges Where There Is No Chair of Pedagogy," *Proceedings and Addresses of the National Educational Association, 1890,* p. 673.

Sewall, J. B. "College Instruction in Pedagogy," *Academy* 4 (1889): 449–54.

Snedden, David S. *Educational Sociology for Beginners.* New York, 1928.

———. *Sociological Determination of Objectives in Education.* Philadelphia, 1921.

Snow, Louis Franklin. *The College Curriculum in the United States.* New York, 1907.

Suzzallo, Henry. "The Status of Education in American Universities," *Columbia University Quarterly* 9 (June, 1907): 290–300.

Thorndike, Edward Lee. *Animal Intelligence.* New York, 1911.

———. "The Contribution of Psychology to Education," *Journal of Educational Psychology* 1 (January, 1910): 5–12.

———. *Educational Psychology.* 3 vols. New York, 1913.

———. *Educational Psychology: Briefer Course.* New York, 1914.

———. *Human Learning.* New York, 1931.

———. *Psychology and the Science of Education,* ed. Geraldine M. Joncich. (Teachers College, Columbia University, Classics in Education, No. 12.) New York, 1962.

Writings by the General University Faculty

Draper, Andrew S. "The Ethics of Getting Teachers and of Getting Positions," *Educational Review* 20 (June, 1900): 30–43.
Gregory, John Milton. "The Christian Elements of Character." Record Series 2/1/1. No. 3.
———. *The Seven Laws of Teaching*. Boston, 1886.
James, Edmund J. "The Function of the State University," *Science*, n.s., 22, no. 568 (November 17, 1905): 609–28.
———. "The Higher Education of Teachers at the University of Jena," *Journal of Education* 18 (Dec. 6, 13, 1883).
[———, ed.] *Sixteen Years at the University of Illinois*. Urbana, 1920.
Kinley, David. *The Autobiography of David Kinley*. Urbana, 1949.
Potthoff, E. F. *The Combinations of Subjects of Specialization for High School Teachers of Foreign Languages*. (Office of the Provost, Studies in Higher Education, no. 3.) Urbana, 1942.
———. "Some Factors Which Should Guide the University of Illinois in the Education for Illinois High Schools." (Mimeographed version of the Potthoff Report.) Record Series 2/9/1, no. 18.
Powell, Burt E. Papers. Record Series 39/1/20.
———. Semi-Centennial History of the University of Illinois. Vol. I. *The Movement for Industrial Education and the Establishment of the University, 1840–70*. Urbana, 1918.
Stephens, Carl. MS history, Stephens Papers. Record Series 26/1/21.

General Newspapers and Periodicals

NOTE: Titles may vary slightly—e.g., in distinguishing between Sunday and weekday editions—but not so that identification will be difficult.

Atlantic Monthly.
Bloomington Pantagraph.
Champaign Gazette.
Chicago's American.
Chicago Daily News.
Chicago Daily Times.
Chicago Herald and Examiner.
Chicago Sun.
Chicago Tribune.
Forum. New York, 1886–1930.
Urbana Evening Courier.

SECONDARY SOURCES

Manuscripts and Dissertations

Hubbell, Leigh G. "The Development of University Departments of Education in Six States of the Middle West with Special Reference to Their Contributions to Secondary School Progress." Ph.D. dissertation, Catholic University of America, 1924.

Johanningmeier, E. V. "A Study of William Chandler Bagley's Educational Doctrines and His Program for Teacher Preparation, 1895–1918." Ph.D. dissertation, University of Illinois, 1967.

Johnson, Henry C., Jr. "The Preparation of Teachers as a University Function: The Case of the University of Illinois." Ph.D. dissertation, University of Illinois, 1970.

Johnson, Ronald M. "Captain of Education: An Intellectual Biography of Andrew S. Draper, 1848–1913." Ph.D. dissertation, University of Illinois, 1970.

Kersey, Harry A. "John Milton Gregory as a Midwestern Educator, 1852–1880." Ph.D. dissertation, University of Illinois, 1965.

Krolikowski, Walter P. "Arnold Tompkins: Midwest Philosopher and Educator." Ph.D. dissertation, University of Illinois, 1965.

Pulliam, John D. "A History of the Struggle for a Free Common School System in Illinois from 1818 to the Civil War." Ph.D. dissertation, University of Illinois, 1965.

Rhodes, Dent M. "Professional Models for the American Teacher, 1815–1915." Ph.D. dissertation, Ohio State University, 1965.

Robarts James Richard. "The Rise of Educational Science in America." Ph.D. dissertation, University of Illinois, 1963.

Rutkowski, Edward. *A Study of Various Viewpoints [Regarding] Schools of Education . . . 1890–1905.* Michigan State University, 1963. Privately printed.

Spiegle, Edward F. "Historical Study of the Formation and Early Growth of Western Montana College of Education." Master's thesis, Western Montana College of Education, 1952.

Swanson, Richard Allen. "Edmund J. James, 1855–1925: A 'Conservative Progressive' in American Higher Education." Ph.D. dissertation, University of Illinois, 1966.

Books

[American Council on Education.] Commission on Teacher Education. *The Improvement of Teacher Education: A Final Report by the Commission on Teacher Education.* Washington, D.C., 1946.

Belting, Paul E. *The Development of the Free Public High School in Illinois to 1860.* Springfield, 1919.

Bishop, Morris. *A History of Cornell.* Ithaca, 1962.

Boring, Edwin G. *History of Experimental Psychology.* 2nd ed. New York, 1950.

Borrowman, Merle L. *The Liberal and Technical in Teacher Education.* New York, 1956.

————, ed. *Teacher Education in America: A Documentary History.* (Teachers College, Columbia University, Classics Education, no. 24.) New York, 1965.

Brubacher, John S., and Rudy, S. Willis. *Higher Education in Transition.* New York, 1958.

Butts, R. Freeman. *The College Charts Its Course: Historical Conceptions and Current Proposals.* New York, 1939.

Callahan, Raymond E. *Education and the Cult of Efficiency.* Chicago, 1962.

Clark, Hannah B. *The Public Schools of Chicago, a Sociological Study.* Chicago, 1897.

Cole, Arthur C. *The Era of the Civil War, 1848–70.* (Vol. 3 in 6 vol. Centennial History of Illinois.) Chicago, 1922.

Counts, George S. *School and Society in Chicago.* New York, 1928.

Cremin, Lawrence. *The Transformation of the School, Progressivism in American Education, 1876–1957.* New York, 1961.

————; Shannon, David A.; and Townsend, Mary Evelyn. *A History of Teachers College, Columbia University.* New York, 1954.

Curti, Merle. *The Growth of American Thought.* New York, 1951.

————. *The Social Ideas of American Educators.* Patterson, N.J., 1959.

————, and Carstensen, Vernon. *The University of Wisconsin, a History.* Madison, 1949.

Davis, Calvin Olin. *A History of the North Central Association of Colleges and Secondary Schools, 1895–1945.* Ann Arbor, 1945.

Dunkle, Harold Baker. *Herbart and Education.* New York, 1969.

Eddy, Edward D., Jr. *Colleges for Our Land and Time: The Land-Grant Idea in American Education.* New York, 1956.

Edwards, Newton, and Richey, Herman G. *The School in the American Social Order.* 2nd ed. Boston, 1963.

Elliott, Edward C., and Chambers, M. M., comps. *Charters and Basic Laws of Selected American Universities and Colleges.* New York, 1934.

Elsbree, Willard S. *The American Teacher.* New York, 1939.

Fox, Dixon Ryan. *Dr. Eliphalet Nott, 1773–1866, and the American Spirit.* Princeton, 1944.

Girling, Katharine Peabody. *Selim Hobart Peabody, a Biography.* Urbana, 1923.

Gregory, Allene. *John Milton Gregory: A Biography.* Chicago, 1923.

Hawkins, Hugh. *Pioneer: A History of the Johns Hopkins University, 1874–89.* Ithaca, 1960.

Hofstadter, Richard, and Hardy, C. DeWitt. *The Development and Scope of Higher Education in the United States.* New York, 1956.

——, and Metzger, Walter P. *The Development of Academic Freedom in the United States,* New York, 1955.

Horner, Harlan Hoyt. *The Life and Work of Andrew Sloan Draper.* Urbana, 1934.

Hug, Elsie. *Seventy-five Years in Education: The Role of the School of Education, New York University, 1890–1965.* New York, 1965.

Kandell, I. L. *William Chandler Bagley: Stalwart Educator.* New York, 1961.

Kersey, Harry A. *John Milton Gregory and the University of Illinois.* Urbana, 1968.

Krug, Edward A. *The Shaping of the American High School.* New York, 1964.

Kuhn, Madison. *Michigan State, the First Hundred Years.* Lansing, 1955.

Lentz, Eli G. *Seventy-five Years in Retrospect, from Normal School to Teachers College to University, Southern Illinois University, 1874–1949.* Carbondale, Illinois, 1955.

Mangun, Vernon L. *The American Normal School: Its Rise and Development in Massachusetts.* Baltimore, 1928. (Introduction by William C. Bagley.)

Marshall, Helen E. *Grandest of Enterprises, Illinois State Normal University, 1857–1957.* Normal, 1956.

Merriam, Charles E. *Chicago, a More Intimate View of Urban Politics.* New York, 1929.

Nevins, Allan. *Illinois.* New York, 1917.

Pangburn, Jesse M. *The Evolution of the American Teachers College* (Teachers College, Columbia University, Contributions to Education, no. 500.) New York, 1932.

Pierce, Bessie Louise. *History of Chicago.* 3 vols. Chicago, 1937, 1940, 1957.

Plochman, George Kimball. *The Ordeal of Southern Illinois University.* Carbondale, Illinois, n.d. [1957?]

Rammelkamp, Charles Henry. *Illinois College, a Centennial History, 1829–1929.* New Haven, 1928.

Raymond, Andrew V. *Union University: Its History, Influence, Characteristics and Equipment.* 3 vols. New York, 1907.

Ross, Earle D. *Democracy's College: The Land Grant Movement in the Formative Stage.* Ames, Iowa, 1942.

Rudolph, Frederick. *The American College and University: A History.* New York, 1962.

Schmidt, George P. *The Liberal Arts College.* New Brunswick, 1957.

————. *The Old Time College President.* New York, 1930.

Solberg, Winton U. *The University of Illinois, 1867–94: An Intellectual and Cultural History.* Urbana, 1968.

Storr, Richard J. *The Beginning of Graduate Education in America.* Chicago, 1953.

————. *Harper's University, the Beginnings: A History of the University of Chicago.* Chicago, 1966.

Tewksbury, Donald G. *The Founding of American Colleges and Universities before the Civil War.* New York, 1932.

Van Santvoord, C., and Lewis, Taylor. *Memoirs of Eliphalet Nott, D.D., LL.D.* New York, 1876.

Veysey, Laurence R. *The Emergence of the American University.* Chicago, 1965.

Viles, Jonas. *The University of Missouri: A Centennial History, 1839–1939.* Columbia, Mo., 1939.

Wagenknecht, Edward. *Chicago.* Norman, Okla., 1964.

Ward, Estelle Frances. *The Story of Northwestern University.* New York, 1924.

Watson, Elmo Scott. *The Illinois Wesleyan Story, 1850–1950.* Bloomington, 1950.

Webster, Martha Farnham. *Seventy-five Significant Years—The Story of Knox College.* Galesburg, Ill., 1912.

Welter, Rush. *Popular Education and Democratic Thought in America.* New York, 1962.

Wilde, Arthur Herbert, ed. *Northwestern University 1855–1905, a History.* 4 vols. New York, 1905.

Articles

Andrews, Benjamin R. "The Schools of Teachers College," *Columbia University Quarterly* 9 (June, 1907): 335–41.

Baker, Franklin T. "A Sketch of the History of Teachers College," *Columbia University Quarterly* 9 (June, 1907): 315–20.

Boring, Edwin G. "Edward Bradford Titchener," *American Journal of Psychology* 38, no. 4 (October, 1927): 489–506.

Canfield, James H. "New York City as a Center for Educational Study," *Columbia University Quarterly* 9 (June, 1907): 310–15.

Geyer, D. L. "Century of Educational Progress in Chicago, 1833–1933," *Chicago School Journal* 15 (January, 1933): 54–83.

Johanningmeier, E. V. "William Chandler Bagley's Changing Views on the Relationship Between Psychology and Education," *History of Education Quarterly* 9, no. 1 (Spring, 1969): 3–27.

————, and Johnson, Henry C. "Charles DeGarmo, Where Are You—

Now That We Need You?" *Philosophy of Education 1969: Proceedings of the Twenty-fifth Annual Meeting of the Philosophy of Education Society . . . 1969*, pp. 190–99. Carbondale, 1969.

Katz, Michael B. "From Theory to Survey in Graduate Schools of Education," *Journal of Higher Education* 37, no. 6 (June, 1966): 325–34.

Monroe, Paul. "Professional Distribution of the Graduates of Columbia University and of Teachers College," *Columbia University Quarterly* 9 (June, 1907): 301–10.

INDEX

Abbot, Lyman, 155, 190
Academy, University of Illinois: as practice school, 148, 164-65, 167-68, 202; and Frank Hamsher, 151; Dexter on, 164; and Carnegie Foundation, 164-65; C. W. McConn on, 164-70, 183; function of, 165-71, 183; as preparatory school, 166; curriculum of, 167-68; requested by High School Conference, 168; as an experimental school, 169-70; S. S. Colvin on, 170; as a typical high school, 170-71; faculty of, 171; as a model school, 171-72; expenditures of, 173; closing of, 174-75, 179; effects of closing, 187; mentioned, 150. *See also* Preparatory department; University High School; Laboratory school
Accreditation of schools. *See* Visitation and accreditation; High School Visitor; Clevenger, A. W.; Hollister, H. A.
Adams, Charles Kendall: and pedagogy in the university, 62n
Adams, John Quincy, Jr.: and the new education, 69n
Adams, Roger, 279n

Addams, Jane, 155
Agricultural education: and Smith-Hughes programs, 240; mentioned, 234, 457. *See also* Smith-Hughes programs; Vocational education
Alabama Polytechnic Institute: and T. E. Benner, 284
Alabama, State Department of Education of: and T. E. Benner, 284
Alumni Quarterly, University of Illinois: on High School Conference, 213
American Association for the Advancement of Science, 129
American Association of University Professors: and Chicago public schools, 364-65; and Benner hearing, 430
American Association of University Women: and child growth and development program, 331
American Council on Education: and College of Education, 286; and survey of the University, 387-88, 406n, 409-10
American Geographical Association, 129
American Geographic Society, 129

Anderson, Archibald W., 384n
Anderson, H. H.: and Committee on Child Development, 333
Anderson, Lewis F.: and history of education, 196
Andrews, E. B.: and University of Nebraska, 132
Angell, James R., 91, 155
Appointments Committee, 284. *See also* Placement Service
Aristotle: in philosophy course, 35n; C. R. Griffith on, 406-7
Armstrong, J. E. (Trustee): and A. S. Draper, 79; mentioned, 120
Aron, Henry: library purchased, 196
Aron Library: and L. F. Anderson, 196
Arrowood, C. F.: lectures by, 299; and Benner case, 391; mentioned, 392n
Articulation, University–high school: H. A. Hollister on, 212-13; and visitation-accreditation, 351-52
Association of Junior Colleges: and C. R. Griffith, 375n
Athletic Association, University of Illinois: and athletic coaching program, 254-55
Athletic coaching program: and College of Education, 252-57; growth and treatment of faculty, 253-55; enrollments in, 254; and faculty salaries, 254-55; and University High School, 255; divorced from College of Education, 276; budgets compared, 330; mentioned, 234
Athletics: and high school teachers' conferences, 74

Babcock, Kendrick C.; and methods courses, 304; mentioned, 215
Bagley, William C. (Director): on laboratory school as practice school, 154, 156, 171; state and national activities of, 155, 188, 206, 207, 210-11; on "The Qualities of Merit in Teachers," 156-57; and federal education programs, 156, 160; as author and editor, 156n, 195-96, 206, 207; on teacher preparation, 156, 157, 158, 190-92, 223; and L. D. Coffman's study of teaching force, 158-59, 190; biography, 160-63; and University of Chicago, 161; and University of Michigan, 161; and Cornell University, 161, 162; and Montana State Normal College, 162; on psychology and education, 162, 190, 194-95; as school principal, 163; and campaign for laboratory school, 164, 175; and Teachers College, Columbia University, 164, 188-89; on status and function of School of Education, 177-85; on practice teaching, 178-80; on special education, 180; on graduate work in education, 180-81; on educational research, 182-83, 184, 198-99; departure from University, 186, 188-89; and normal schools, 189; appointed director of School of Education, 192; on Thorndike-Woodworth experiments, 194-95; and Education faculty, 196-99; courses taught by, 202, 209; and B. H. Bode, 200, 206; on extension work, 207-8; and summer sessions, 209, 210; educational philosophy of, 220; and Bureau of Educational Research, 247-48; and Education deanship, 283; and Kappa Delta Pi, 346; and University High School buildings, 348; and Benner case, 435n, 441; and College of Education, 444; mentioned, 77, 145, 153, 219, 220, 233, 298, Chs. 6 and 7 passim
Bain, Alexander: and *Education as a Science*, 67
Baker, Ira O., 95
Balliet, Superintendent: lectures for E. G. Dexter, 130
Bane, Lita: and Committee on Child Development, 333
Barker, Roger G., 397
Barnard, Henry: and pedagogy in the university, 62; mentioned, 452
Barnes, Fred: and "communism," 408n
Barrett, George F. (Attorney General): and University of Illinois, 387-88
Basedow, Johann Bernard, 196
Bateman, Newton D. (State Superintendent): and improvement of teacher education, 32n; on high school organization, 48
Battersea Normal School, 130
Bayliss, Alfred J. (State Superintendent), 110n, 112, 120, 151, 176
Beard, Charles A.: and W. C. Bagley, 207

Belting, Paul E.: and secondary education, 236

Bentley, Isaac M.: and psychology, 161, 199, 256n

Benne, Kenneth: and Benner case, 396-97; mentioned, 384n

Benner, Thomas E. (Dean): and Education deanship, 282, 284; biography, 284-85; on educational needs in Depression, 288; philosophy of teacher preparation of, 289-90, 294-97; and progressive education, 289-90; philosophy of education of, 290-94, 405; and Abraham Flexner, 291; and relation of social philosophy and education, 291-93; and Walter Lippmann, 292; and federal education programs, 293; on high schools, 294; and College of Liberal Arts and Sciences, 294, 304-5; new policies proposed by, 297-98; faculty cleavage due to appointments by, 300; and professionalization, 307; and teachers' colleges, 309, 367-79; and David Kinley, 324; growing hostility of, 325; accomplishments of, 325-26; and elementary laboratory school, 332-36; and C. R. Griffith, 335; and University High School, 338-48 passim; and appointed superintendency, 350; and Illinois Educational Commission, 350; proposes state "Board of Education," 350; and Galesburg survey, 353; and Chicago public schools, 362-65; and A. W. Clevenger, 364n; on higher education planning, 367-68; and College of Education as a professional school, 368; and elementary work, 377-79; and junior colleges, 380-81; and Chicago campus, 382-83; and extramural work, 384n; summoned by Trustees, 386; and Allied Military Government, 443; and University of Vienna, 443; mentioned, Chs. 9, 10, 11 passim. *See also* Benner case; Benner hearing; Benner letter

Benner case: and Galesburg survey, 353n; and teachers' colleges, 367n, 400-402; Benner summoned by Willard, 389; initiation of, 391n; and College of Education budget, 392-93, 402-3, 404; theoretical and philosophical issues in, 392-407; and K. Benne,

396-97; and R. D. Carmichael, 396-97, 403, 438; and "Special Subjects" document, 398; and R. B. Browne, 399n, 400, 403-4; and building program, 400-402; and Graduate School, 403; and A. J. Harno, 403; and statistics, 404n, 425, 438; and Benner's philosophy of education, 405; political factors in, 408-9; and Benner's resignation, 410-11; legal issues in, 411-20; Benner's interpretation of, 413n; and alleged "charges," 413-14, 416; requests for hearing on, 413-19, 421; and H. E. Cunningham, 415; and Benner's legal strategy, 415-20; administration argument on, 421-27; and "administrative decision" argument, 423; and C. R. Griffith, 423-25; and comparison with other universities, 426; Benner's defense in, 427-30; and criticism of Benner, 428; and "understaffing" document, 438; mentioned, Ch. 11 passim. *See also* Benner, Thomas E.; Benner hearing; Benner letter

Benner hearing: and Board of Trustees, 430; hearing described, 430-40; administration case at, 431-38; R. D. Carmichael testimony at, 436-38; T. E. Benner testimony at, 438-39; and T. L. Marshall, 439; S. Johnson's summation at, 439-40; Trustees' verdict at, 440; response to verdict at, 440-43; and National Commission for the Defense of Democracy through Education, 441-42. *See also* Benner, Thomas E.; Benner case; Benner letter

Benner letter: and Benner case, 389-90; authorship of, 391n; and T. E. Benner, 391n; investigation behind, 403; and S. Johnson, 416-17; alleged libelous, 417-18, 419n; and C. R. Griffith, 433n; and A. C. Willard testimony, 437. *See also* Benner, Thomas E.; Benner case; Benner hearing

Berlin, University of: and C. R. Griffith, 277

Bernbaum, Ernest: departure of, 411n

Bestor, Arthur: and progressivism, 463-64; and C. R. Griffith, 407n

Blaine, Mrs. Emmons, 143

Blair, Francis G. (State Superintendent):

Blair, Francis G. (*continued*)
and Illinois School Survey, 210; and increased responsibilities facing schools and teachers, 235-36; on normal school conditions, 245-46; and visitation-accreditation program, 259
Blair, Glenn M.: and changes in educational psychology, 312
Blewett, Nancy: and Benner case, 414n
Bloomington Philosophical Club: and Charles DeGarmo, 68
Board of Regents, New York, 89
Board of Trustees, University of Illinois: and request for pedagogical chair, 59; and demonstration school, 76; and School of Education, 138, 148-49, 185; closes Academy, 174-75; and College of Education, 187-90, 203, 401, and Bureau of Educational Research, 200; and William C. Bagley, 206-7; refuses teachers' scrip, 288; summons Benner, 336; and visitation-accreditation, 351; and teachers' college development, 368; and George F. Barrett, 387-88; and Benner case, 408n, 412, 415-18, 440, 442
Bode, Boyd H.: and W. C. Bagley, 200, 206; and phillosophy of education, 200, 237; and David Kinley, 229n; and Education deanship, 281; and College of Education reforms, 298, 298n; mentioned, 146
Bogan, William J. (Superintendent): and Chicago public schools, 361-62
Bogart, E. L., 275n
Bolton, T. L., 125
Boone, Richard Gause, 97
Booz, Fry, Allen and Hamilton: survey by, 387, 408n, 410
Boring, Edwin G., 162, 199
Bradley, Preston: and Chicago campus, 382
Branch, Francis Burke, 90
Brooklyn Daily Eagle: on W. C. Bagley, 154
Brooks, Rev. Charles: founded normal school, 39
Brooks, Stratton D.: on drop-out problem, 127; on summer session, 131; and courses on science and administration, 132, 133; resignation of, 211; mentioned, 112, 120, 142

Brown, Elmer Ellsworth, 40n, 136
Brown, George P.: and Bloomington Philosophical Club, 68; on pedagogy at the University of Illinois, 107; mentioned, 40n, 91
Brown, Stanley J., 120
Browne, Robert B.: on curriculum courses, 298; and philosophy of education, 314; and Chicago campus, 382; and extramural work, 384n; and Benner letter, 390, 391n, 392n, and "Special Subjects" document, 399-400; and C. R. Griffith, 404; and political issues in Benner case, 408; and Benner case, 410, 414n, 419, 422
Brown University, 113, 129, 170, 198
Bryan, William L., 91-92
Buckingham, Burdett R.: and Bureau of Educational Research, 248-49, 252
Building program, College of Education, 397. *See also* Building program, University of Illinois; University High School; Educational research
Building program, University of Illinois: E. J. James and, 174-75, 177; and Benner case, 400-402. *See also* Building program, College of Education; University High School; Educational research
Bullard, Samuel A. (Trustee), 108
Bureau of Correspondence, University of Illinois, 182, 208-9
Bureau of Educational Research, University of Illinois: and University of Michigan, 200; development of, 200, 247-52; and W. C. Bagley, 224; and testing movement, 243; early program of, 248-49; new role of, 259-60; C. E. Chadsey on, 260; limited by T. E. Benner, 330; and research policy, 330-31; criticized by R. B. Browne, 400; and Benner case, 424, 431; mentioned, 265n. *See also* Testing movement; Bureau of Educational Service
Bureau of Educational Service, University of Illinois, 200. *See also* Bureau of Educational Research
Bureau of Institutional Research, University of Illinois: created, 276; and child development laboratory, 332-35; policy-making by, 335, 336n, 410n; and visitation-accreditation, 363; and

junior colleges, 380-81; and College of Education development, 385; and American Council on Education survey, 388, 410n; and College of Education budget, 403; and T. E. Benner, 425n, 438. *See also* Griffith, Coleman R.

Bureau of Salesmanship Research in the Carnegie Institute of Technology: and G. M. Whipple, 200

Burrill, Thomas J. (Regent): biography 71; and laboratory school, 76-77; and C. A. McMurry, 79; on accreditation, 96; appointed acting president, 110; on Arnold Tompkins's replacement, 111, 113; on study of pedagogy, 121; on assistance for high schools, 211-12; mentioned, 3, 40n, 67, 87, 106

Butler, Nicholas Murray: and pedagogy in the university, 62, 99-100; mentioned, 89, 111, 130, 155

Buzzard, R. G.: and teachers' college development, 377n; and College of Education development, 401n

California, State of: and junior colleges, 381

California, University of: practice school at, 167, 173

Cameron, Edward H.: and educational psychology, 236; and philosophy of education, 237; and Committee of Nine, 275; and Education deanship, 280-81, 283; and educational theory, 299; and College of Education development, 384n

"Cardinal principles," 207

Carmichael, Robert D. (Dean): and Education deanship, 280n; and professional degree program, 313, 320-23; and T. E. Benner, 320, 395-96; and child development laboratory, 333; and Kurt Lewin, 334; and teachers' college development, 372n; and elementary education, 378; and Benner letter 390, 392n; and "Special Subjects" document, 399; and C. R. Griffith, 404, 411n; and Benner case, 410, 414n, 421-22, 435-36; and *Urbana Evening Courier*, 441n

Carnegie Foundation: on University Academy, 164-65; and Missouri teachers' survey, 188

Carnegie Institute of Technology, Bureau of Salesmanship Research, 200

Carney, Mabel: and Illinois State Normal University, 377

Carter, James G.: and Lexington, Massachusetts, Normal School, 39

Cattell, James McKeen: on E. G. Dexter, 114

Century (magazine), 99

Cermak, Anton J. (Mayor), 361

Certification of teachers: early examination for, 6-7; and scientific subjects, 53, 56; and University of Illinois, 139-41, 150, 234; requirements for, 235, 260, 271; for secondary level, 300n; and North Central Association, 300n; mentioned, 7, 10, 15

Chadsey, Charles E. (Dean): and Education deanship, 224; biography, 225-26; and teacher preparation curricula, 236-37; and University High School, 242-44; and David Kinley, 244-45; death of, 262; and Chicago public schools, 225-26, 358; compared with Benner, 400; and College of Education, 444; mentioned, 214, Ch. 8 passim

Champaign News Gazette: on Benner hearing verdict, 441

Charters, Werrett Wallace: appointment of, 214; and E. J. James, 224; and Education deanship, 281; and College of Education reforms, 298n; mentioned, 233

Chase, Harry W. (President): biography, 274; administrative policy of, 274-75; contrasted with David Kinley, 274-75; attitude toward College of Education, 274, 303; and University reform, 277; personal style of, 278; resigns, 279; and Education deanship, 282-84; mentioned, 327, 392n

Chicago campus, University of Illinois, 380-83

Chicago Center for Smith-Hughes programs, 238-39, 318

Chicago Daily News: and Chicago public schools, 364

Chicago, University of: and graduate study in education, 181; and College of Education, 212, 446; and Illinois schools, 142-43, 262, 328; and Wil-

Chicago, University of (*continued*)
liam S. Gray, 310; and Chicago public schools, 360-61, 362; and Chicago campus, 382; mentioned, 102, 161, 195

Chicago Board of Education: and Chicago public schools, 355-65; and Chicago campus, 382

Chicago Federation of Teachers: and Margaret Haley, 357-58; and Chicago public schools, 365; and Chicago campus, 382

Chicago Manual Training School, 143

Chicago Normal College: and Chicago public schools, 365; and Chicago campus, 382. *See also* Cook County Normal School

Chicago public schools: and C. E. Chadsey, 225-26; growth of, 354-55; and University of Illinois, 354-66; statistics on, 355; history of, 355-63, 365; organization of, 358

Chicago Schools Committee: and T. E. Benner, 363

Chicago Tribune: and Chicago public schools, 364; mentioned, 137

Child-centered education, 55-56

Child growth and development: and educational research, 331-35; programs at other universities, 332

Child Study, Illinois Society for: and W. O. Krohn, 74

Child study movement, 74, 129

Clark, Thomas Arkle, 139

Clark University: and W. O. Krohn, 73; and H. W. Chase, 274

Classical studies: S. H. Peabody on, 66

Classroom Management: and W. C. Bagley, 164, 190

Clement, J. A.: and secondary education, 236; and Galesburg school survey, 353; mentioned, 397

Cleveland (Ohio) Normal School, 108

Clevenger, A. W.: and visitation-accreditation, 351, 357n; and Education deanship, 280n; and Chicago public schools, 364n; and Benner case, 427n

Coble, A. H.: and professional degrees, 323; mentioned, 279n

Coffman, Lotus Delta: and study of teaching force, 158, 190; appointed, 197; departure for Minnesota, 197; and educational sociology, 209; directs Illinois School Survey, 197, 210-

11; and *The Illinois Teacher*, 211; and Illinois State Teachers' Association, 211; and David Kinley, 231n; and Education deanship, 281-82; influence on schools, 328; mentioned, 195, 214

Colorado State Normal School, 113

Columbia College: and Teachers College, Columbia University, 89

Colvin, Stephen S.: biography, 125-26; appointed acting director, 153; and practice teaching, 170; mentioned, 129, 154

Comenius, Johann Amos, 55, 196

Commercial education: and University High School, 244; added to College of Education, 312-13

Commission on Emergency and Readjustment of the National Education Association: and W. C. Bagley, 207

Commission on the Mental Examination of Recruits of the National Research Council, 207

Committee of Nine (University of Illinois): and university reform, 275-77; membership of, 275n; and College of Education, 276; and physical education, 276

Committee of Seventeen: on practice teaching, 173

Committee of Ten (NEA), 171, 207

Committee on a Program of Training and Research in Child Development (Graduate School): and laboratory school, 333

Committee on Psychological and Pedagogical Aspects of Military Discipline: and W. C. Bagley, 207

Compayré, Gabriel: and *History of Education*, 67

Conference of the Six State-Supported Institutions of Higher Education in Illinois, 310n

Conklin, P. S.: and Benner case, 429

Cook, John W.: on professional literature, 33n; and *Illinois Schoolmaster*, 54n; on chair of pedagogy at the University of Illinois, 67-68; and F. M. McMurry, 78; and C. A. McMurry, 79; mentioned, 107, 110n, 136

Cook County Normal School: and F. W. Parker, 107; and progressivism, 466; mentioned, 39, 143

Cooley, Edwin G. (Superintendent): and Chicago public schools, 120, 359

Cooper, Thomas: influence on science and education, 52

Cornell University: and Charles De-Garmo, 70; and practice school, 167; mentioned, 158, 161, 192

Counts, George S: and Education deanship, 281; on Chicago public schools, 360, 361n

Courtney, Thomas J., 409n

Crane Junior College case: and Chicago public schools, 362

Curriculum development: and College of Education, 289; and T. E. Benner, 298

Cunningham, H. E.: and Committee of Nine, 275n; and Benner case, 415

Daily Illini: on School of Education, 151, 184, 186; and Benner hearing verdict, 441

Daniels, Arthur H. (President): on W. C. Bagley, 193-94; and College of Education, 237; appointed interim president, 279; and Education deanship, 280

Darrow, Clarence: and Chicago public schools, 362n

Dartmouth College: and H. W. Chase, 274; mentioned, 197

Darwinism: and educational theory, 460

Davenport, Eugene (Dean): and Bureau of Educational Research tests, 251

Davis, Chester (Trustee): and charges by S. Johnson, 409; and Cora DeGraff Heineman, 428n

DeBoer, John J.: and Chicago public schools, 365n

DeGarmo, Charles: and professionalization of teaching, 40n; appointed, 67; biography, 68; and courses at University of Illinois, 69; work at University, 69-70; departure of, 70-73; educational philosophy of, 71-73; and Herbartianism, 71-73, 466; and *Herbart and the Herbartians*, 72; and laboratory school, 72-73; and E. J. James, 136-37; and Cornell University, 161, 192; and W. C. Bagley, 192; and College of Education, 444; mentioned, 111, 136, 162, 189, 191

Demonstration school: and child growth and development research, 332; and home economics education, 332-35. *See also* Educational research; Laboratory school

DePauw University, 6, 92

Depression (1929): and the schools, 265-67, 270-73; effect on University, 273; effect on students, 287-88; and Smith-Hughes programs, 317; and normal schools, 371; and junior colleges, 380; and Chicago campus, 381; and College of Education, 384, 393

Descartes, René, 35n

Dever, William E. (Mayor): and Chicago public schools, 359-61

Dewey, John: *Psychology* of, 68; and University of Chicago, 143, 183; and graduate study in education, 181; on science and educational theory, 201; and College of Education, 237; and Smith-Hughes programs, 238; and methodological curriculum, 270; and T. E. Benner, 297n; and Margaret Haley, 357; and Kenneth Benne, 397; mentioned, 91, 102, 111, 155, 162, 188

Dexter, Edwin G. (Director): and courses of study at Illinois, 117-20, 130-31, 132-33; on training high school teachers, 123; on teacher market, 123; on establishing School of Education, 123-24; duties of, 124; and psychology, 125; on S. S. Colvin, 125-26; and school men, 128; professional activity of, 128-29; on state of education department, 141-48; on normal school training, 143; on practice work, 148; appointed director of School of Education, 150-51; resignation, 152; on Academy or practice school, 164; on science of education, 189; and College of Education, 444; mentioned, 192, 219, Ch. 5 passim

Dibelka, James R., 185

Dodge, Arthur F.: and Graduate School, 321

Dolch, E. W.: and educational psychology, 312

Draper, Andrew Sloan (President): on replacement for F. M. McMurry, 79; and W. J. Eckoff, 82; and University growth, 83; on high school visitation, 89-90, 93-94, 96-97; and New York

Draper, Andrew Sloan (*continued*)
state, 89, 134; on A. Tompkins, 90-91; and role of pedagogy, 90, 93-94; on practice school, 94, 181n; on psychology and education, 111, 113; and E. G. Dexter, 114; on psychology, 126; and drop-out problem, 127; and normal schools, 366; mentioned, 40n, 87, 88, 92-93, 104-15 passim, 120
Dreiske, John: on Benner case, 409
Dunlap, Mathias L.: and regency, 24n
Duplication theory: and teachers' college development, 373, 379; and elementary education, 377, 378
DuShane, Donald: and Benner verdict, 441-42
Dutton, Samuel P., 130
Dwight, Timothy: on his education, 34n

Eastern Illinois State Teachers' College: and P. E. Belting, 236; and extramural programs, 349n; mentioned, 98, 197
Eastern Illinois Teachers' Association: on School of Education building, 175-76
Eckoff, William Julius: appointed, 79; biography, 79; and Herbartianism, 79-82; and David Kinley, 81-82; resignation of, 82; and courses of study at university, 117; mentioned, 90
Education, College of: organization of, 187, 203; Trustees and, 187, 190, 203, 401; reputation of, 219, 285-86; enrollment in, 259, 287, 311, 325n; relations with Illinois schools, 261-62; deanship of, 280-84; conditions in, 286; salaries, 286-87; budget, 286, 384-86, 402-3; effect of Depression on, 287-88; and friction with University administration, 310; as a professional school, 315n; staffing of, 300, 325n, 384, 400; and academic imperialism, 326; and relations with other University colleges, 327; faculty distinction of, 335, 396; situation of in 1940's, 384-88; and University surveys, 387-88; assessment of, 445-56. *See also* School of Education; Building program, College of Education; University High School
Education, courses of study in: and early curriculum, 30-36, 67, 82; and early science education, 33, 67; and methods courses, 37-39, 131, 298, 301; first graduate level, 66, 206; S. H. Peabody proposes chair for, 67-68; and W. O. Krohn, 73-74; and psychology, 74-75; and F. M. McMurry, 75-77; and W. J. Eckoff, 80-82, 117; and history of education, 96, 132-33; and Arnold Tompkins, 117-18; and E. G. Dexter, 117-20, 131, 132-33; general scope of, 117-21, 201-2, 204, 298-99, 311-12; and Herbartianism, 118-19; and Senate, 139-40; and aesthetic education, 195; and administration courses, 236, 299, 377; and psychological emphasis, 298-99; and social philosophy, 299; and curriculum development courses, 301; and vocational education, 301; and school law, 311; and teachers' college development, 376-79; and rural education, 379. *See also* Teacher preparation programs; and under specific subjects
Education, Department of: E. G. Dexter on state of, 141-48
Education, School of: Arnold Tompkins on, 104, 105, 106; E. G. Dexter on, 123-24; David Felmley on, 138, 139n; Trustees on, 138, 148-49, 185-86; authorized, 149; entrance requirements of, 150; E. G. Dexter appointed director of, 150-51; *Daily Illini* on, 151, 184, 186; E. J. James compares, 152-53; building for, 175-76, 185; Bagley on status and function of, 177-85; funds appropriated for, 185-86; W. C. Bagley appointed director of, 192; enrollment in, 209
Education Doctor (Ed.D.). *See* Professional degree programs
Education faculty: publications of, 128
Educational Newsgleaner, 136
Educational psychology: and E. G. Dexter, 125; and W. C. Bagley, 209; and E. H. Cameron, 236; practical orientation of, 312; and G. M. Blair, 312. *See also* Education, courses of study in; Education and psychology
Education and psychology: early relation of, 41, 75; and W. O. Krohn, 73; A. S. Draper on, 111, 113; general relationship of, 125, 133, 162, 194-95, 459-62; at University of Chicago, 143;

and transfer of training, 146-47, 162, 194; and Thorndike-Woodworth experiments, 146-47, 194-95; W. C. Bagley on, 162, 189, 190, 191-95; E. L. Thorndike on, 195n; and David Kinley, 228-30; A. J. Harno on, 324-25; and University High School program, 342; C. R. Griffith on, 406-7. *See also* Educational psychology; Science of education; Education, courses of study in

Education as a university study: and J. M. Gregory, 27, 29; and theory of knowledge, 35n; concept of, 20, 37-43, 220-23, 445; and University of Iowa, 61; and University of Michigan, 61-62; S. H. Peabody on, 61-66; C. W. Eliot on, 62; growth of in American universities, 62-63; A. S. Draper on, 90, 93-94; Arnold Tompkins on, 94; George P. Brown on, 107; T. J. Burrill on, 121; and status of teacher-training programs, 121-22; and David Kinley, 124, 144-48, 196; and the traditional disciplines, 191-92, 220-23

Educative Process: and W. C. Bagley, 164, 189, 204

Edwards, Richard (State Superintendent): on school curriculum, 50

Eight-year study: and the Progressive Education Association, 273

Eliot, Charles W: and pedagogy in universities, 62; mentioned, 155

Encyclopedia of Educational Research: and W. S. Monroe, 330

Englewood (Illinois) High School, 49

Equalitarianism: and high schools, 48

Essentials of Method: and Charles De-Garmo, 119

Evenden, Edward S: and Education deanship, 281-82

Executive Committee, College of Education: and Benner case, 420-21; and A. C. Willard, 436

Extension courses. *See* Extramural programs

Extramural programs: established, 70; and David Kinley, 196; and L. D. Coffman, 207, 209; and W. C. Bagley, 207-8, 209; and in-service training, 208; and testing movement, 248; development of, 348-50; and teachers' college development, 376; and Chi-

cago campus, 382; and Benner case, 390-91; mentioned, 182, 207

Faculty committee, College of Education: and Benner case, 414n, 419-21

Fairchild, R. W.: and teachers' college development, 372-74, 379n

Federal education programs: and E. J. James, 137, 156; W. C. Bagley on, 156, 160; and F. G. Blair, 232; and C. E. Chadsey, 232; and David Kinley, 232; C. R. Griffith on, 407; mentioned, 137, 156, 160. *See also* Smith-Hughes program

Federation of Illinois Colleges: and C. R. Griffith, 375n

Felmley, David: on normal school philosophy, 41n; and Herbartianism, 69n; and School of Education at Urbana, 138, 139n, 176-77; and conditions in normal schools, 245; mentioned, 9

Filene, Edward A.: on commercial interests and the schools, 292

Fitzpatrick, John H.: and Chicago public schools, 362

Five-year programs: development of, 308-11; and state teachers' colleges, 309; lack of success of, 310; and Illinois State Normal University, 374n; and Benner case, 424

Fletcher, H. F., 275n

Flexner, Abraham E.: on American higher education, 466; mentioned, 458

Flower, Lucy (Trustee): and education at the University of Illinois, 110 111n, 112n, 113n

Forbes, Stephen: on courses for science teachers, 122; mentioned, 61, 105, 106, 139

Ford, Guy S.: and David Kinley, 231n

Francke, Augustus Herman, 196

Franklin, Benjamin: influence of on science and education, 52; mentioned, 55

Froebel, Frederick: and educational theory, 38, 196, 449

Galbreath, Louis H., 110

Galesburg school survey: and College of Education, 353-54

Gastman, E. A.: on science teaching, 54

General education: decline of, 305; and five-year programs, 309; and vocational education, 319

George-Deen Act: and vocational education, 317

German influence on American education: and S. H. Peabody, 47; and Charles DeGarmo, 67n, 68; and F. M. McMurry, 75; and W. J. Eckoff, 79-81; and C. R. Griffith, 277; T. E. Benner on, 291, 296; mentioned, 62, 196, 453, 458

Gladden, Washington: and the University of Illinois, 71n

Goethe, Johann Wolfgang von, 55

Gordy, J. P.: appointed to faculty, 70n

Graduate School, University of Illinois: and David Kinley, 227; and College of Education, 237, 322; and University Council on Teacher Education, 303; and professional degrees of the College of Education, 316, 319-23; and vocational education, 321; and control of research, 335; and Benner case, 394, 424; and "Special Subjects" document, 398; policies of, 398, 410n

Graduate work in education. See Teacher education programs

Gray, William S.: and study on preparation of secondary school teachers, 268n, 269; and teachers of special subjects, 310; and "Special Subjects" document, 398

Green, Dwight H. (Governor): and University of Illinois, 386, 402

Greene, Evarts B., 154, 192-93

Gregory, John M. (Regent): elected, 24; biography, 24-25; social views of, 25; on religion and education, 25, 27; as common school leader, 26; and education as a university study, 26, 27; and first curriculum, 29; and NEA, 30; address of to Illinois State Horticultural Society, 31-32; courses taught by, 34-36; on education as a science, 41; and growth of University of Illinois, 59-60; mentioned, 19, 44, 83

Gregory Hall, 347-48

Griffith, Coleman R.: and Bureau of Institutional Research, 276; biography, 277; on T. E. Benner and Teachers College, 297n; attitude toward education, 305-6, 323, 385-86;

and professional degrees, 315n; and Chicago Cubs, 321; T. E. Benner's view of, 325; and progressivism, 326; and Committee on Child Development, 333; and junior colleges, 381; and Benner letter, 390, 391n, 392n; and Graduate School, 395n; and overstaffing, 397; and R. B. Browne, 399, 400, 400n, 407n; and W. S. Monroe, 405n; and G. D. Stoddard, 405n; and A. C. Willard, 405n; educational philosophy of, 405-7; and Benner case, 410, 411n, 414n, 419, 421, 422-27, 427-28, 431-35; and Benner's resignation, 411; and letter on College of Education, 325-27, 432-35; and Urbana Evening Courier, 441n; ouster of, 444; and W. B. Spalding, 444; mentioned, 256n, Ch. 11 passim. See also Bureau of Institutional Research

Haley, Margaret: and Chicago public schools, 357-58

Hall, G. Stanley: and study of pedagogy, 62, 77n; and W. O. Krohn, 74; mentioned, 41, 111, 111, 115

Hall, Mary E., 213

Hall, Rev. Samuel R.: and first normal school, 39; on science of education, 40; mentioned, 190

Halle, University of: and Charles DeGarmo, 71; and F. M. McMurry, 75; mentioned, 136

Hall-Quest, Alfred: and Education deanship, 281

Hamilton, Sir William: and early philosophy courses, 31n, 35n

Hamlin, H. M.: and agricultural education, 318; on teachers' college development, 373-74; and faculty committee in Benner case, 419

Hamsher, Frank: and University Academy, 151-52

Hanus, Paul: and T. E. Benner, 285; mentioned, 129, 130

Harno, A. J.: and Committee of Nine, 275; and University Council on Teacher Education, 303n; on professional education, 323-25; and College of Education, 369n; and elementary education, 378; and junior colleges, 380; and Chicago campus, 382; and

Benner letter, 390, 392n; and College of Education research policy, 402; and Benner's philosophy of education, 405; and Benner case, 410, 411n, 412, 414n, 418n, 421-22, 436; and Trustees, 415; and Bureau of Institutional Research, 425n; and *Urbana Evening Courier,* 441n

Harper, William Rainey: and pedagogy in universities, 62; and Chicago public schools, 356, 358

Harper Commission: and Chicago public schools, 358

Harris, William T., 91, 111

Harrison, Carter H. (Mayor): and Chicago public schools, 356

Harvard University: and T. E. Benner, 284; and professional degrees, 321; and University High School, 344; mentioned, 129, 136, 152

Hays, Will: and educational films, 262

Hecker, Julius, 196

Hegelianism: and Herbartianism, 68

Heineman, Mrs. W. F. (Cora DeGraff): and Chicago public schools, 365; and progressivism, 408; and Benner case, 428n, 441

Henry, Nelson B.: and Chicago public schools, 362

Herbart, Johann Friedrich: and educational theory, 38, 71, 196, 449

Herbartianism: and educational reform, 68-69; and Illinois State Normal University, 69; and Charles DeGarmo, 71-73; and F. M. McMurry, 75, 76; and W. J. Eckoff, 79-82; and courses of study, 118-19, 161, 208, 459-60, 466

Herriot, M. E.: and David Kinley, 244n

Hewett, Edwin C.: and *Illinois Schoolmaster,* 54n; on importance of normal schools, 371; and E. H. Reeder, 378

Higher education: in early America, 20-21; and the state university, 134-35; and the fragmentation of knowledge, 295-97

High School Conferences: and practice teaching, 168; recommended by H. A. Hollister, 211; origin of, 211-12; initiated, 212; and University of Chicago, 212; *Alumni Quarterly* on, 213; on High School Visitor, 258; mentioned, 208, 213. *See also* High School Visitor

High School Education: and C. H. Johnston, 197

High School Visitor: A. S. Draper on, 89-90, 93-94; as public relations officer, 147; moved to president's office, 203; criticizes University High School, 340; and Chicago public schools, 361, 363-64; mentioned, 112, 142, 147, 211. *See also* High School Conference; Visitation and accreditation; Hollister, H. A.; Clevenger, A. W.

Hill, Clyde M.: and Benner hearing, 435n

Hinsdale, B. A.: and pedagogy in universities, 62n; and Charles DeGarmo, 72; mentioned, 130

History of Education in the United States: and E. G. Dexter, 113

Hoit, O. W (Trustee), 185

Hollister, H. A.: appointed High School Visitor, 211; and organization of North Central Association, 211; and High School Conferences, 212-13; and visitation and accreditation, 257-59, 351; mentioned, 142, 214, 219. *See also* High School Visitor; High School Conference; Visitation and accreditation

Holly, Charles Elmer: dissertation of, 195

Home economics education: and Smith-Hughes programs, 240; withdrawal from College of Education, 301, 312; and demonstration school, 332-35; mentioned, 234

Horner, Henry (Governor): and College of Education building program, 345; and University of Illinois, 365

Huff, George: and athletic coaching program, 252-57; as lobbyist, 274

Hunter, Thomas, 89

Huntington, W. C.: and laboratory school, 401n

Hutchins, Robert: and Chicago public schools, 362; mentioned, 458

Illinois, State of: early history of, 11-12; and land grant movement, 21-23; and commitment to popular education, 261n; and junior college legislation, 381

Illinois, University of: early course of

Illinois, University of (*continued*)
study in, 3, 29; attitude toward education, 19-20, 31, 121-22, 124, 144-48, 193-94; early history of, 24; and opposition to academic tradition, 24; classical studies at, 29; student life at, 36; early graduates of entering teaching, 36, 64; and need to be distinguished from high school, 43; and chair in pedagogy, 58, 64; and normal schools, 138n, 329, 368; financial policy of toward University High School, 243-44; and royalties for faculty, 250-52; and faculty salaries, 255, 273; and the Depression, 273; enrollment at, 273, 287; and university reform movements, 274-77; and institutional surveys, 386-88
Illinois Association of County Superintendents: and Benner case, 429
Illinois City Superintendents Association: and Benner case, 429
Illinois College: and Charles Shamel, 6
Illinois Education Association: and College of Education building needs, 402; and Benner case, 414, 421n, 429-30; and Board of Trustees, 418; and A. C. Willard, 437. *See also* Illinois State Teachers' Association
Illinois Educational Commission: and teachers' salaries, 271n; and study of school problems, 350
Illinois Farm Bureau: and Benner case, 408n
Illinois Federation of Women's Clubs: and child growth and development movement, 331
Illinois High School Principals' Association: and Benner case 429
Illinois Industrial University, 4n, 19, 20. *See also* Illinois, University of
Illinois Press Association: and journalism building, 345
Illinois School Journal, 136
Illinois Schoolmaster: and University of Illinois, 59n
Illinois Schoolmaster's Club, 128
Illinois School Survey, 197, 210
Illinois State Normal University: founding of, 22, 39; and Stephen Forbes, 61; and Charles DeGarmo, 67, 68; Faculty Club at, 68; and C. A. McMurry, 77; graduate work at,

310n; and extramural programs, 349n; and secondary teachers, 369-71; and teachers' college development, 369-79; high school at, 370n; and premedical courses, 372; mentioned, 57, 98, 107, 109, 135. *See also* Fairchild, R. W.; Felmley, David; Normal school movement
Illinois State Teachers' Association: meetings of, 8-9, 36; and J. M. Gregory, 30; and L. D. Coffman, 41; on high school–college articulation, 46-48; proposes pedagogical chair at Urbana, 58; and S. H. Peabody's address, 64; and University of Illinois, 70; requests practice school, 164; and W. C. Bagley, 210; and Depression, 273; and Normal school board, 371; and teachers' college development, 374; mentioned, 128, 137
Illinois Wesleyan University: and Charles Samuel, 6; and teacher preparation, 370n
Imperialism, academic: and E. J. James, 134-35; David Felmley on, 138-39, 176-77; and visitation-accreditation, 351; and the University of Illinois, 329, 366-67, 383; and the teachers' colleges, 368-79, 379-83; and College of Education, 445-46
Indiana, State of: and teachers' college development, 374
Indiana State Normal School, 92
Indiana University: normal department at, 39; mentioned, 92, 435n
Industrial education: criticized by R. B. Browne, 400; mentioned, 234, 457-58. *See also* Extramural programs; Smith-Hughes programs; Vocational education
Institutes, teachers': meetings of, 6, 131, 272
Internationalen Societie für Schulhygiene, 129
Internship programs, 349
Iowa, State University of: normal department at, 39; and special education, 180; and Kurt Lewin, 334-35
Itinerant teacher training: and extramural programs, 348

Jacobs, Walter B.: on practice teaching at Brown University, 170

James, Edmund Janes: and professionalization of teaching, 40n; replaces A. S. Draper, 134; on role of the state university, 134-35; on graduate study, 135; philosophy of education of, 135; on School or College of Education, 135, 137, 138n, 139n, 152-53; biography, 136; and Charles DeGarmo, 136-37; on federal education programs, 137, 156, 238; on a national university, 156; and campaign for a laboratory school, 175, 177; and teacher preparation, 220; decline and resignation of, 224; and University High School, 224; and normal schools, 366; mentioned, 87, 154, 192, 210, 219

James, George F., 110n

James, William: and education courses, 73; mentioned, 162

Janata, A. J.: and Benner case, 395n; mentioned, Ch. 11 passim

Jastrow, Joseph, 161

Jefferson, Thomas: influence on science and education, 52; mentioned, 452

Jena, University of: and American Herbartian educators, 71; and F. M. McMurry, 75; mentioned, 196

Johns Hopkins University: and David Kinley, 227

Johnson, Sveinbjorn: "exposure" of, 387-88; and University administrative policy, 385n; and Benner letter, 390n; and Benner case, 409, 412, 421n, 427, 442; legal strategy of, 415-20; on University *Statutes*, 419-20; and C. R. Griffith, 432-35; and A. C. Willard, 437-38; and Benner hearing, 438n

Johnson, William H. (Superintendent): and T. E. Benner, 354; and Chicago public schools, 362-65; and teacher transfers, 365; and textbook royalties, 365; and Chicago campus, 382

Johnston, Charles Hughes: appointment of, 197; biography, 197; accidental death of, 197; and Illinois School Survey, 211; and junior high school movement, 245

Johnston, Nell (Mrs. Charles H.): and comparative education, 236; and entrance examinations, 352

Jones, Lewis E., 91

Jones, W. A., 100

Jordan, David Starr, 155

Journal of Educational Psychology, 155

Journalism department: and building program, 345

Judd, Charles H.: on science of education, 169, 201; on experimental school, 169; and expansion of high school subjects, 270n; and Chicago public schools, 362n; mentioned, 204

Junior colleges: and University of Illinois, 380-81

Junior high school movement: and University High School, 245; and laboratory school plans, 344; and Chicago public schools, 359. *See also* Johnston, Charles Hughes

Kalamazoo case, 26

Kalamazoo College: J. M. Gregory at, 19, 26-27

Kaler, J. F. H.: and junior colleges, 380

Kandel, I. L.: on W. C. Bagley, 161; and E. H. Reeder, 379n

Kansas, University of, 129, 197

Kant, Immanuel, 448

Kantianism: and J. M. Gregory, 27; and education courses, 73

Kappa Delta Pi: Trustees commemorate founding of, 346

Katz, Michael: on University of Chicago science of education, 201; mentioned, 200

Kelly, F. J.: and Education deanship, 282-84

Kelly-Nash "machine": and Chicago public schools, 361-65; and George F. Barrett, 387

Kilpatrick, William H.: and Kenneth Benne, 397

Kinley, David (President): and W. J. Eckoff, 81-82; and W. O. Krohn, 81-82; on graduate study, 88-89; on E. G. Dexter, 124; attitude toward education, 124, 220, 226, 229-33, 247; on pedagogy and School of Education, 144-48; on psychology, 145, 146; on University High School, 148, 186-87; on L. F. Anderson, 196; on education "fieldwork" and scholarship, 196; and Bureau of Educational Research, 200, 250-52; elected president, 219, 224; on role of general education, 223-24; philosophy of education of, 226, 227-30; biography, 227; conser-

Kinley, David (*continued*)
vatism of, 228n, 250; attitude toward agriculture, 229; attitude toward social sciences, 229-30; administrative policies of, 247, 327; on psychology and education, 250; and athletics, 256-57; retirement of, 262; and H. W. Chase, 265; and university reform, 277; and Education deanship, 280, 281-82; and College of Education building, 286; and A. C. Willard, 385; and College of Education, 444; mentioned, 87, 103, 115, 141, 264, Ch. 8 passim
Kirk, James, 90
Klein, Arthur J.: on College of Education, 285; and Benner case, 433, 441
Knight, Fred B.: and Benner case, 433-34
Knights of Columbus: and Smith-Hughes programs, 239n
Kratz, H. E., 90
Krohn, William O.: appointed, 73; biography, 73; resignation of, 82; mentioned, 120n
Krolikowski, Walter P.: on Arnold Tompkins, 88n, 91, 95n, 96n, 97n, 98n, 99n, 101, 107n, 109
Kyte, George C.: and Education deanship, 282-83

Laboratory school: and teacher preparation, 58n, 458-59; and DeGarmo at Illinois State Normal University, 67n; and Herbartianism, 72; and University of Illinois, 72; and F. M. McMurry, 76, 77; and W. J. Eckoff, 81; Arnold Tompkins on, 94; as practice school, 94, 164; A. S. Draper on, 94, 181n; at University of Chicago, 143; W. C. Bagley on, 154, 156, 171, 175; and request of Illinois State Teachers' Association, 164; and Cornell University, 167; and University of California, 167; and University of Mississippi, 167; and University of Wisconsin, 167; and National Society of College Teachers of Education, 167, 173; and C. H. Judd, 169; and academies as preparatory schools, 172-73; and John Dewey, 183; and University High School, 242-44; and

child growth and development programs, 332-35; and College of Education, 336-44; concept of, 336-38, 341-44; and junior high school work, 344; and Benner case, 401-2, 439
Land Grant Act: and further funds for, 67
Land grant movement: and State of Illinois, 21-23; and agricultural interests in Illinois, 22; and classical studies, 22-23; utilitarian emphasis in, 31; J. M. Gregory's interpretation of, 31, 60; concept of, 456-57
Laubach, Frank, 458
Learned, William S.: directs Carnegie survey, 188
Leibnitz, Gottfried Wilhelm von, 196
Lewin, Kurt: and child development laboratory, 334-35
Library and museum, pedagogical: at University of Illinois, 124
Liberal Arts and Sciences, College of: and methods courses, 244, 304; and T. E. Benner, 294; and teacher preparation according to T. E. Benner, 296; and education courses, 299, 303n; and American Council on Education Survey, 410n. *See also* Literature and Arts, College of; Literature and Science, College of
Literature and Arts, College of: and David Kinley, 227. *See also* Liberal Arts and Sciences, College of; Literature and Science, College of
Literature and Science, College of: and preparation of teachers, 59. *See also* Liberal Arts and Sciences, College of; Literature and Arts, College of
Lincoln, Abraham: signs Morrill Act, 20
Literary societies: and Charles Shamel, 5; mentioned, 3
"Little Magna Charta": and Benner case, 394, 446
Livingston, Park: and University building program, 402; and S. Johnson, 409; and Benner case, 415, 416n; and Illinois Education Association, 430n; and Benner hearing, 436n, 438; and Benner hearing verdict, 440-41
Locke, John: and University of Illinois philosophy courses, 35n; C. R. Grif-

fith on influence of, 406-7; mentioned, 448

Loeb, Jacob: and Chicago public schools, 358

Loeb, Jacques, 161

Loyola University: and William H. Johnson, 363

Lundgren, C. L.: and athletic coaching program, 253n

Luther, Martin, 196

McAndrew, William (Superintendent): and Chicago public schools, 359-61

McCahey, James B.: and Chicago public schools, 361-65; and Chicago campus, 382

McClure, M. T.: and Committee of Nine, 275n; and Benner letter, 390; and Benner case, 414n

McCollum v. *Champaign Board of Education,* 338n

McConn, Charles M.: appointed to Academy, 152; and Carnegie Foundation on Academy, 164-65; on function of Academy, 165-70, 183; mentioned, 251

McGilvery, John E., 97, 102, 108

McGrath, John: on Benner case, 401

McHarry, L. J.: and David Kinley, 244n

McKay, F. M., 79

McKinley, W. B. (Senator): and economics chair at University of Illinois, 229

McMurry, Charles A.: and Illinois State Normal University, 77, 79; mentioned, 109

McMurry, Frank M.: appointed, 75; biography, 75; and Illinois State Normal University, 75; and Charles DeGarmo, 75, 78; and laboratory school, 77; and first summer session, 77; and Franklin School (Buffalo, New York), 78; resignation of, 78; and practice teaching, 202; mentioned, 109, 110

Major, Elliot W., 188

Mann, Horace: and early normal schools, 39

Marshall, Thomas L.: and Benner case, 421, 430-31, 439, 442; and C. R. Griffith, 423

Martin, John, 155

Masters in Education (M.Ed.). *See* Professional degree programs

Mattheisen, Mr. (LaSalle, Illinois, Board of Education), 112n

Maxwell, Superintendent, 130

Mays, Arthur B.: and industrial education, 236; and Smith-Hughes programs, 239, 317; and Graduate School, 397

Mead, George Herbert, 91

Meger, S. A., 105

Melancthon, Philip, 196

Melby, Ernest O.: and Chicago public schools, 364n

Mental discipline, 146-47

Merriam, Charles E.: and Chicago schools, 360, 362n

Method of the Recitation: and Charles and Frank McMurry, 119

Meumann, Professor: and G. M. Whipple, 199

Meyer, Karl (Trustee): and Benner hearing, 438n, 440n

Michigan, University of: and Charles Shamel, 6; and first chair in pedagogy, 26; J. M. Gregory on pedagogy at, 29; Bureau of Educational Reference and Research, 200; Bureau of Tests and Measurements, 200; and A. W. Clevenger, 351; mentioned, 89, 197

Michigan Agricultural College, 160

Michigan State Teachers' Association: and J. M. Gregory, 26

Military Tract Teachers' Association, 176

Mill, John Stuart: in early University of Illinois philosophy courses, 31n

Minnesota, University of: and training school, 173; mentioned, 197

Mississippi, University of: and practice school, 167

Missouri, University of: and practice school, 167; mentioned, 198

Model school. *See* Laboratory school

Modern High School: and C. H. Johnston, 197

Monroe, Walter Scott: and educational research, 236, 312; and royalties, 252; appointed acting dean, 264-65; and Education deanship, 280-81, 283; and University Council on Teacher Edu-

Monroe, Walter Scott (*continued*) cation, 303; and Bureau of Educational Research, 330-31; and College of Education development, 384n; and Benner case, 391, 439; criticized by R. B. Browne, 400; and interim deanship, 443; mentioned, 122

Montana State Normal College, 163

Moore, A. W., 91

Moore, H. F.: and Committee of Nine, 275n

Moral training and education: J. M. Gregory on, 28

Morehouse, Francis, 202

Morey, Lloyd: and College of Education budget, 289, 403; and junior colleges, 380-81; and overstaffing, 397

Morrill Act: signed, 20; early history of, 22. *See also* Turner, Jonathan B.

Morrison, John Cayce: and Education deanship, 282

Morrison Hotel case: and Chicago public schools, 364n

Mortenson, Peter A.: and C. E. Chadsey, 225

Moulton, E. J.: and teachers' college development, 310n

Muckrakers, 155

Mumford, Herbert W.: and A. C. Willard, 279n; and vocational education programs, 317; and teachers' college development, 372n

Munsterberg, Hugo: on psychology and education, 41n; mentioned, 162

Murphy, Arthur: departure of, 411n

Music, School of: and methods courses, 244

Music education, 234

Musselman, T. E.: and W. C. Bagley's classes, 203

National Association of High School Inspectors and Supervisors: and T. E. Benner, 272n

National Association of State Universities: on practice teaching, 173

National Commission for the Defense of Democracy through Education: and Benner verdict, 441-42

National Commission on the Reorganization of Secondary Education: and C. H. Johnston, 207

National Education Association: and J. M. Gregory, 30; Committee of Ten and Illinois certification, 56; and Charles DeGarmo, 72; and W. C. Bagley, 207; and C. E. Chadsey, 225; and Chicago public schools, 365; and Benner verdict, 441-42; mentioned, 129, 414

National Research Council Commission on the Mental Examination of Recruits: and G. M. Whipple, 207

National Society for the Scientific Study of Education, 129

National Society of College Teachers of Education: on practice teaching, 167, 173; mentioned, 129

Natural Science, College of: and pedagogy, 66

Nebraska, University of: high school at, 174; mentioned, 115, 125

Newcomb, Rexford: and Benner letter, 390; and "Special Subjects" document, 398; and Benner case, 414n

New Deal: and progressivism, 408

New Education: rise of, 55-56; and child-centered concept, 55-56; and F. W. Parker, 69n; and John Quincy Adams, Jr., 69n

New England Journal of Education, 98

New Republic: and Benner verdict, 441

New York College for the Training of Teachers: and Columbia University, 99

New York University: and chair of educational philosophy, 38

Nickell, Vernon (Trustee): and Benner case, 429

Nightingale, A. F., 177

Nolan, A. W.: and secondary education, 236; and Smith-Hughes program, 239n; mentioned, 397

Normal School Board, Illinois State: and T. E. Benner, 369; and teachers' college development, 372; and elementary education at Illinois, 379

Normal school movement: origin and development of, 38-41, 454-55; and high school normal departments, 49, 272

Normal schools: private foundations in Illinois, 39; curriculum in, 40; expansion proposed, 57; and University of Illinois, 138n, 223, 245-46, 366; E. G.

Dexter on, 143; graduates of, in teaching, 235, 328; conditions in, 245-46; and teachers' colleges, 272, 458; distinguished from colleges of education, 294; and popular education, 366

North Carolina, University of: and H. W. Chase, 265, 274

North Central Association of Colleges and Secondary Schools: organization of, 211; and teacher education curricula, 234; and visitation-accreditation, 258, 351; and E. F. Potthoff study, 269; and school administration programs, 371

Northwestern University: and Charles Shamel, 6; influence of on schools, 328; and Chicago public schools, 362, 364n; and Chicago campus, 382; and F. B. Snyder, 428

Norton, Edwin L., 152, 153

Nott, Eliphalet: and J. M. Gregory, 25; philosophy of, 33

Nye, N. S.: on junior colleges, 380n

Odell, C. W.: and educational research, 236

Oglesby, Richard J. (Governor): and land grant university, 24

Ohio State University: practice school at, 167; and education college reforms, 298n; mentioned, 196

Ohio Wesleyan University, 195

Olander, M. M.: and athletic coaching program, 256n

Oldfather, W. A.: and Committee of Nine, 275n

O'Shea, Michael Vincent, 110, 129, 130, 161, 162, 204

Otis law: and Chicago public schools, 358

Page, Walter, 155, 190

Parent education. *See* Child growth and development

Parker, Francis W.: and New Education, 69n; and Cook County Normal School, 78, 460; and Margaret Haley, 357; mentioned, 39, 98, 107, 355n

Parkhurst, C. H.: on public schools, 48

Parochial schools: fear of, 47; and practice teaching, 338n; and Chicago public schools, 360-61

Peabody, Selim H. (President): on expansion of public education, 46-48; attitude toward education, 59, 61-66; named regent, 60-61; biography, 60-61; and NEA Committee on Higher Education, 61; and elective system, 61; and Illinois State Normal University, 61; on normal schools, 61; educational philosophy of, 61-62, 64-65; defense of University teacher education program, 63-66; and classical studies, 65; and Charles DeGarmo, 70, 72; resignation, 71

Pedagogical library and museum, 124, 126, 132

Pennsylvania, University of, 137

Pestalozzi, Johann Heinrich: and educational theory, 449; mentioned, 38, 196

Pestalozzianism: and J. M. Gregory, 27; and Herbartianism, 69

Philadelphia Centennial Exposition (1876): University exhibits at, 35

Philanthropy, educational: S. H. Peabody on, 65n

Philosophy department: and B. H. Bode, 237

Philosophy of education: in early Illinois curriculum, 31; and B. H. Bode, 200; and educational theory, 298

Philosophy of School Management: and Arnold Tompkins, 92

Philosophy of Teaching: and Arnold Tompkins, 92, 100

Physical education: curriculum in, 260-61; separated from College of Education, 276, mentioned, 234

Pickard, J. L.: and regency, 24n

Pinckney, Daniel J.: and regency, 24n

Placement service, 121, 350n

Plato: C. R. Griffith on, 406; and educational theory, 448; mentioned, 55

Platoon system: and Chicago public schools, 359

Post, Wiley, 361

Potthoff, E. F.: and Benner case, 391n

Potthoff study on teacher education: origin, 266n, 268-70; and academic courses, 302; and University Council on Teacher Education, 303n; and five-year programs, 309

Practice teaching: and early education curriculum, 76; and W. J. Eckoff, 81; E. G. Dexter on, 148; and Frank

Practice teaching (*continued*)
Hamsher, 151-52; W. C. Bagley on, 154, 156, 178-80, 202; Senate on, 164; and National Society of College Teachers of Education, 167, 173; S. S. Colvin on, 170; Committee of Seventeen on, 173; National Association of State Universities on, 173; and F. M. McMurry, 202; enrollment in, 338; and Smith-Hughes programs, 240; and University High School, 244, 336-37, 341; expansion to local schools, 337-38; and supervisors of, 337; and parochial schools, 338n; mentioned, 141, 150, 202, 234
Preparatory department: function of, 44; and University High School, 339. *See also* Academy; Laboratory school; University High School
Princeton (Illinois) High School: as first township high school, 50
Principals examination case: and Chicago public schools, 363
Professional degree program: proposed and approved, 314-16; distinguished from Ph.D., 314n; and dispute over research policy, 321-22; and Benner case, 394-95, 424; mentioned, 309, 313, 397. *See also* Teacher preparation programs, graduate
Professionalization: early development of, 18; and chair of pedagogy at Michigan, 26; and normal school movement, 40; and S. H. Peabody, 66; as response to Depression, 270-73; and College of Education, 299n, 368; encouraged by T. E. Benner, 306-8; and Margaret Haley, 357-58; and teachers' unions, 357-58; and "Loeb Rule," 358; and Benner case, 395; C. R. Griffith on, 407; mentioned, 15, 450
Progressive Education Association: and Depression schools, 273; and T. E. Benner, 293
Progressivism and education: and David Kinley, 233; and F. G. Blair, 261n; and the schools, 270-71; and teacher preparation courses, 314; and school and society courses, 315; C. R. Griffith on, 326, 407-8; and College of Education, 300, 462-64

Psycho-educational Clinic: and Glenn M. Blair, 332; and E. W. Dolch, 332
Psychology department: created, 74-75, 126; and educational research, 333
Psychology, field of: and S. S. Colvin, 126; empirical emphasis and E. G. Dexter, 126; A. S. Draper on, 126; David Kinley on, 145; and philosophy, 162; and H. W. Chase, 274; mentioned, 161
Psychology and education. *See* Education and psychology
Psychological Review, 125
Public School Journal, 91
Public School Publishing Company: and educational tests, 251-52
Pulliam, Roscoe: and teachers' college development, 372n, 375n
Putnam County Farmers Convention (Granville, 1851), 22

Quintilian, 80

Raab, Henry: on township high schools, 50n; on practical education, 54-55; on the New Education, 55-56; on scientific study for teachers, 57-58
Randall, John H.: and Kenneth Benne, 397
Ratke, Wolfgang, 196
Reavis, W. C.: and Education deanship, 281, 282
Reeder, Edwin H.: and professionalization, 308; and elementary education work, 313, 378; and committee on child development, 333; and Galesburg survey, 353; and Benner case, 391n; and Faculty Committee, 419
Rein, Wilhelm, 71
Religion and education: in early higher education, 20; and ecumenism, 25; and study of the Bible, 28; and science, 54
Research, educational: early studies at Illinois, 126-27; and W. C. Bagley, 182-83, 184; courses dropped, 312; and graduate assistantships, 329; and College of Education, 329-36; and child growth and development, 331-35; outside pressure for, 336; and R. D. Carmichael, 435; mentioned, 234
Robinson, James Harvey, 136

Roosevelt, Franklin Delano (President): and George-Deen Act, 317

Roosevelt, Theodore (President), 116

Roosevelt, Theodore, Jr.: and T. E. Benner, 285

Rosenkranz, Karl: and philosophy of education, 67

Rousseau, J. J., 38

Ruediger, William Carl: on "qualities of merit in teachers," 156

Rugg, Harold O.: dissertation on transfer of training, 195; and W. C. Bagley, 195-96; and social studies, 195-96; and testing movement, 248n; mentioned, 102, 213-14

Rusk, H. P.: and Committee of Nine, 275n; and Benner letter, 390; and "Special Subjects" document, 398; and Benner case, 408n, 414n

Russell, James Earl: on E. G. Dexter, 113-14; at Illinois, 130, 132; and W. C. Bagley, 188; mentioned, 110, 112

Russell, William F.: and Benner hearing, 434-35

Rutgers University: and T. E. Benner, 285

Ryley, Buchanan, 130, 132

Sanford, Charles Wilson: and University Council on Teacher Education, 303n; and professionalization, 308; and professional degrees, 320; and laboratory school, 339-44; and internship program, 350n; and Benner case, 391n; and T. E. Benner, 438

Schlesinger, Arthur: and Chicago public schools, 360

School and Home Education: on E. G. Dexter, 116; mentioned, 107, 155

School of Education. *See* Education, School of; Education, College of

Schools, common and elementary: enrollment and attendance at, 5, 13, 16, 265-66, 272n; early curriculum, 6, 14, 27; early teachers in, 8-9; organization of, 11, 12, 13, 14, 377; growth of, 13; facilities and equipment in, 14, 16, 266, 272n; criticisms of, 17-18; conditions at Depression, 265-66; influence of universities outside Illinois on, 328

Schools, rural: early characteristics of, 8-9; and College of Education curriculum, 261; facilities in, 261; conditions in, 266; waning interest in, 301

Schools, secondary: curriculum in, 6, 50, 269-70; normal departments in, 9-10; early growth of in Illinois, 37, 48-52, 260; 265, 272n; national growth of, 46-47, 455; facilities and equipment in, 49, 272n; township organization of, 50; enrollment in, 51, 235, 260, 265, 272n, 370-71; conditions in, 234-35, 265-66; and T. E. Benner, 294; influence of universities outside Illinois on, 328; and the normal schools, 366; and unit districts, 377

School surveys: and Galesburg case, 353-54

Science: as a cultural ideal, 21, 27, 52-53, 449, 457; J. M. Gregory on, 27; in early Illinois curriculum, 29; and T. E. Benner, 290-99; pure *v.* applied, 329; mentioned, 4

Science and education: in early curriculum, 7; and Herbert Spencer, 52-53; increasing relationship between, 52-56; and evaluation, 54; and religion, 54; and new behavioral sciences, 56; in relation to teacher education, 57-58; and Charles DeGarmo, 69; John Dewey on, 201; influence of, 329, 450-51, 459-62. *See also* Bureau of Educational Research; Science of education

Science education programs: and Stephen Forbes, 122; and Stratton Brooks, 132-33

Science of Discourse: and Arnold Tompkins, 92

Science of education: J. M. Gregory on, 28; S. R. Hall on, 40; and growth of psychology, 41; and normal schools, 58; at University of Michigan, 62; development in American universities, 62; C. H. Judd on, 169, 201; John Dewey on, 181; and W. C. Bagley, 189; E. G. Dexter on, 189; at University of Chicago, 200; Michael Katz on, 200-201; development of, 221-22; and David Kinley, 228-30; mentioned, 30n, 31n, 201. *See also*

Science of education (*continued*)
Science and education; Bureau of Educational Research
Scovill, H. T.: and College building program, 346; and Benner case, 390, 411n, 414n; appointment denied, 411n
Scott, Walter Dill: and Chicago public schools, 362
Scottish realism: and early Illinois philosophy courses, 31n
Senate, University of Illinois: and requirements for teacher preparation curricula, 139-40; on School of Education, 149-50; on practice teaching, 164; and University Academy, 174; and College of Education, 187, 203; and H. W. Chase, 275; and professional degrees, 314; and visitation-accreditation, 351
Sewall, J. B.: and pedagogy in American universities, 62n
Seybolt, R. F.: and educational history, 236, 299; and Education deanship, 281, 283; and College of Education development, 384; and Benner case, 424
Shamel, Charles H.: and University of Illinois, 3; biography, 3-10; gains certificate, 4; at teachers' institutes, 6; and teaching position, 7; mentioned, 52, 159, 160, 161
Shawhan, George P.: on preparation of science teachers, 122
Shores, J. Harlan: and elementary education, 379
Simonson, H. F.: and Benner verdict, 441n
Sisson, Edward O., 151-52
"Six State Supported Institutions of Higher Learning": and William S. Gray, 398
Small, Albion W.: and education courses, 74
Smith, B. Othanel: and curriculum study, 301; and professionalization, 308; appointment, 378; and Benner case, 391n, 396, 408n, 419; and Faculty Committee, 419
Smith, H. L.: and Benner hearing, 435n
Smith, T. V.: lectures in philosophy of education, 301n; and Chicago public schools, 362
Smith-Hughes Act: and David Kinley,

239; and George-Deen Act, 317; mentioned, 214
Smith-Hughes programs: developed, 238-40; and T. E. Benner, 293; and teachers' college development, 372-74, 379; and George-Deen Act, 317; expansion of, 317-19; mentioned, 234, 385n
Snyder, Franklin B.: and Benner case, 428
Snyder, Z. X.: at Illinois, 113, 132
Social Composition of the Teaching Population: and L. D. Coffman, 158
Société Jean-Jacques Rousseau, 129
Sociology and education: early relationship of, 42; extramural work in, 209; regular course instituted, 314
Soldan, Frank, 130
"Some Factors Which Should Guide the University of Illinois in the Education of Teachers for Illinois High Schools." *See* Potthoff study
Southern Illinois Normal School. *See* Southern Illinois University
Southern Illinois University: founding of, 39; and the New Education, 56n; and extramural programs, 349n; and teachers' college development, 373-74, 383n; mentioned, 57, 98
South Side Academy (Chicago, Illinois), 143
Spalding, Willard B.: and educational psychology, 312; deanship of, 443-44
Special education: W. C. Bagley on, 180; and University of Iowa, 180; and E. H. Cameron, 236
"Special Subjects" document: and Benner case, 398-400; and Benner hearing, 431n, 437
Spencer, Herbert: and influence on science and education, 52-53; and education courses, 73
Spiegel, M. J.: and Illinois Educational Commission, 271n
Spiegle, Edward F., 163
Staley, S. C.: and Benner letter, 390; and "Special Subjects" document, 398; and Benner case, 411n, 414n
Stanley, William O.: and philosophy of education, 314; and Benner case, 408n
State Teachers' Association. *See* under various states

Statistical methods, 205-6

"Status of Education" document: and Benner case, 394-97, 431n

Statutes, University of Illinois: A. J. Harno on, 412, 413n; and Benner case, 412, 413n, 418; and H. E. Cunningham, 415; and College of Education faculty, 419; S. Johnson on, 419-20

Stearns, John William, 161, 192

Stoddard, George D. (President): and academic change, 327; presidency of, 443-44

Stormzand, M. J., 204

Stouffer, E. L.: and College of Education building program, 401-2

Stowe, Calvin E., 39

Stoy, Karl Volkmar: and J. F. Herbart, 71

Straight, Wood C.: on W. C. Bagley, 154-55

Strayer, George Drayton: on "the qualities of merit in teachers," 156; on experimental schools, 169-70; and Chicago public schools, 362n

Studebaker, John W.: and teachers' college development, 373

Summer sessions: first held, 77; and W. J. Eckoff, 81; and Arnold Tompkins, 103-4; E. G. Dexter's courses for, 130-31; and S. D. Brooks, 131; attendance at, 133; at University of Chicago and Wisconsin, 209; and W. C. Bagley, 209, 210; faculty attitude toward, 209-10; mentioned, 103-4, 207, 209

Survey of courses and curricula of the University of Illinois at Champaign Urbana: on teacher education, 303n

Swanson, Richard A., 134n, 135, 136n, 137n

Swarthmore College: and Charles De-Garmo, 70

Taylorville, Illinois: and Charles Shamel, 6

Teacher education: J. M. Gregory on, 28-36; and general education, 29, 295-96; and university-level subject matter, 37-43; and child-centered education, 55-56; and distinction between elementary and secondary schools, 56; and scientific training, 57-58; Arnold

Tompkins on, 98-107 passim; N. M. Butler on, 99-100; E. G. Dexter on, 123; W C. Bagley on, 156, 157, 158, 190-92; and problem of specialization, 179-80, 270n, 323-25; T. E. Benner on, 294-97; as all-university function, 297, 302-3; shift in emphasis in, 301; concept of, 445, 451-52, 463-64. *See also* Education, courses of study in; Education as a university study; Teacher education programs; Education and science; Science of education; University Council on Teacher Education

Teacher education literature, 8, 15n, 32-33, 42n, 53, 57n, 67, 68, 73, 80

Teacher preparation programs, graduate: and other universities, 38-39, 63, 181, 323n; NEA on, 63; and David Kinley, 83, 88-89; Arnold Tompkins on, 98-107; and E. J. James, 135; W. C. Bagley on, 180-81, 224; first doctoral student at Urbana, 195; curriculum for, 206, 237-38, 308-13; and extramural locations, 208, 273, 288; and Saturday classes, 273; and College of Education, 288; and Benner case, 394-95, 435. *See also* Professional degree programs; Education, courses of study in; Education as a university study

Teacher preparation programs, undergraduate: early provision for, 6, 7, 21, 29; curriculum and course requirements, 69, 139-40, 234, 260-61, 298-301, 308, 310n, 312; and University of Illinois, 88, 139; and "two-track" system, 234, 299n, 305-6; admission and retention of candidates in, 307, 352; elementary education programs initiated, 313, 377. *See also* Education, courses of study in; Education as a university study

Teachers associations. *See* under various states

Teachers' bureau, 121

Teachers College, Columbia University: and W. C. Bagley, 164, 188-89; and normal school department, 189; influence on schools, 262, 328; T. E. Benner at, 284; and Mabel Carney, 377; and E. H. Reeder, 378; and C. R. Griffith, 407; and R. B. Browne, 408;

Teachers College (*continued*)
and College of Education, 444n, 446;
mentioned, 164

Teachers' colleges: and graduate work, 272, 367n; response to teachers' demands, 273; and five-year programs, 309; opposition of E. J. Moulton, 310n; and educational research, 329; and University of Illinois, 367-79; and T. E. Benner, 369-70; conditions in, 370-71; and Benner case, 424, 431-32. *See also* Imperialism, academic; Normal schools

Teaching force: and teaching as a social access route, 4; salaries of, 7, 12, 16, 49, 272; educational level of, 14, 17, 18, 51-52, 158-59, 190, 235, 260, 267-69, 272n; supply and demand, 51-52, 102, 141, 158; effectiveness of, 156-57; L. D. Coffman on, 158, 190; and problem of specialization, 235-36; and Depression, 270-71, 288; and "communism," 271. *See also* Professionalization

Testing movement: and National Research Council Commission on the Mental Examination of Recruits, 207; and other universities, 248; and B. R. Buckingham, 248-52; and standardized tests, 249-52; mentioned, 199. *See also* Bureau of Educational Research

Thompson, William Hale ("Big Bill"): and Chicago public schools, 358-61

Thorndike, Edward Lee: on psychology and education, 195n; and W. C. Bagley, 223; and progressivism, 407; mentioned, 162, 199

Thorndike-Woodworth experiments, 146-47, 194-95

Thwing, Charles F.: and pedagogical courses at Illinois, 74

Titchener, Edward Bradford, 41, 161-62, 198, 200, 205

Tompkins, Arnold: on practice school, 94; on study of pedagogy, 94, 98-107; on visitation-accreditation, 95-96; speaking engagements of, 97-98; on teacher preparation, 98-107; on summer session, 103-4; on school of pedagogy, 104-6; resignation of, 108, 152, 188; subsequent career of, 109-11; course of study developed by, 117-18; and College of Education, 444; mentioned, 114-15, 145, 189, 192, Ch. 4 passim

Topological psychology: and Kurt Lewin, 334

Townsend, E. J.: and University High School, 242

Transfer of training, 146-47, 162, 194

Tribune property case: and Chicago public schools, 356

Trustees, University of Illinois Board of. *See* Board of Trustees

Turner, Jonathan Baldwin: and Morrill Act, 21-23; on practicality in education, 31; opposition of to joining university and normal school, 43. *See also* Morrill Act

Tubbs, Eston V.: and Benner case, 428

Two-track school system: and Chicago public schools, 359

"Understaffing" document: and Benner case, 394, 397, 431n

Union College: and J. M. Gregory, 33; mentioned, 24

Unit school districts: and elementary education study at Illinois, 377

Unitarian Fellowship for Social Justice: and Chicago public schools, 364n

United Press: and Benner case, 414

University Council on Teacher Education, 302-3, 404, 431, 438

University High School: and David Kinley, 148, 186-87, 240-44, 246, 338; and E. J. James, 175; proposed to name for E. J. James, 224n; and W. W. Charters, 240; early development of, 240-44; and H. W. Chase, 278; nature and function of, 336-48; appropriations for, 339; enrollment in, 339-40; facilities in, 339-40; faculty growth in, 339-40; summer session, 340; and problems in the schools, 341-42; C. W. Sanford on objectives of, 341-43; as a preparatory school, 343-44; building program for, 343, 345-48; and rating by Harvard University, 344; and Board of Trustees, 345-46; mentioned, 148, 171. *See also* Academy; Laboratory school; Preparatory department

University of Illinois Contributions to Education, 127

University of Illinois School of Education Bulletins, 128
University reform movements: national scope of, 277
Urban education, 120
Urbana Evening Courier: and Benner verdict, 441n
Urbanization: and the schools, 11

Van Sickel, James H., 130, 132
Veblen, Thorstein: and David Kinley, 233; mentioned, 458
Vermont, University of: and E. H. Reeder, 378
Visitation and accreditation: origin at University of Illinois, 44; and F. M. McMurry, 78; and A. S. Draper, 78, 83, 90-97; Arnold Tompkins on, 95-96; T. J. Burrill on, 96; H. A. Hollister on, 212-13; problems of, 257-59, 351-54, 361-65; and T. E. Benner, 352; and school surveys, 352-53; and Chicago public schools, 363; mentioned, 95-96, 120, 208. *See also* High School Visitor; Hollister, H. A.; Clevenger, A. W.
Vocational education: and George-Deen Act, 317; leadership from other universities, 318; diminishes general education, 319; and Graduate School, 321-22; and Chicago public schools, 359; mentioned, 205, 301. *See also* Education, courses of study in; Extramural programs; Smith-Hughes programs; and under specific courses

Ward, Lester Frank: on public schools, 34n
Washburne, Carleton W.: and Bureau of Educational Research, 250
Washington, Booker T., 155
Washington, University of, 152
Wayland, Francis: and normal department at Brown University, 38; mentioned, 452
Weather Influences: An Empirical Study of the Mental Effects of Definite Meteorological Conditions: and E. G. Dexter, 113
Weber, Oscar F.: and philosophy of education, 314n; and Illinois Educa-tional Commission, 350; and Galesburg survey, 353; and elementary education, 377; and junior colleges, 380
Wendell Phillips High School case: and Chicago public schools, 358
Wesley Methodist Church: and University High School, 243n
Western Reserve University, 115
Wharton School of Finance and Economy, University of Pennsylvania, 137
Wheeler, Benjamin Ide, 173
Whipple, Guy Montrose: on Bagley's *Classroom Management,* 190; biography, 198; W. C. Bagley on, 198-99; appointed, 199; resignation, 200; leave of absence for, 214; and Bureau of Educational Research, 247-48; mentioned, 205
White, Andrew D.: on the American university, 34n
White, J. M., 185
Whitney, Allen S.: and high school visitation at University of Michigan, 211; and North Central Association, 211
Wilder, Henry W., 88
Willard, Arthur Cutts (President): appointed, 279; biography, 279; and the schools, 279; administrative policy of, 279-80, 385, 410, 436-37; and educational reform, 295; and University Council on Teacher Education, 303; and practice teaching, 337; and extramural programs, 348n; and Galesburg survey, 353; and Chicago public schools, 363-64; and teachers' college development, 372n; and elementary education, 378; and junior colleges, 381; and T. E. Benner, 386; and Benner case, 390-92, 404, 409-10, 414n, 415, 417-18, 422, 433, 436-38; and Benner letter, 391n, 392n, 417-18, 419n; and College of Education budget, 397, 402, 403; and "Special Subjects" document, 399; and Illinois Education Association, 429; and Griffith letter, 433; and Benner hearing, 436-38
Williams, Lewis W.: and University High School, 241, 338; salary of, 286; and secondary teachers, 371
William and Mary, College of: and science, 52; mentioned, 452

Willing, M. H.: and Benner case, 325n
Wilson, Kenneth ("Tug"): and Chicago public schools, 362n
Winakor, A. H.: and Bureau of Institutional Research, 276
Winsor, P. L.: and Committee of Nine, 275n
Wisconsin, University of: normal department at, 39; practice school attempted, 167; and David Kinley, 227; and R. F. Seybolt, 236; and fragmentation of knowledge, 296; mentioned, 129, 152, 161, 192, 204
Wood, Norman N.: and regency, 24n
Wood, Robert: and Illinois Educational Commission, 271n
Woodrow, Herbert: and Education deanship, 280n; and Committee on Child Development, 333
Woodworth, Robert S.: and W. C. Bagley, 223; mentioned, 162
Woody, Thomas: lectures by, 299
Worcester Academy, 113

Works, George A.: and Education deanship, 281; and Illinois higher education survey, 386
World War II: effect on vocational education, 318; and College of Education budget, 384
Wundt, Wilhelm, 41
Wye, Theodora E., 213

Yale University: and science, 52; and W. O. Krohn, 73; and E. H. Cameron, 247n
Young, Ella Flagg: and L. D. Coffman, 210-11; and Chicago public schools, 357; mentioned, 197

Zeublin, Charles, 155
Zook, George F.: and Education deanship, 281-82; and American Council on Education, 377
Zuppke, Robert Carl: and athletic coaching program, 253-57; resignation, 411n